Borderline

BORDERLINE

Reflections on War, Sex, and Church

∽

STAN GOFF

Foreword by Amy Laura Hall

CASCADE Books • Eugene, Oregon

BORDERLINE
Reflections on War, Sex, and Church

Copyright © 2015 Stan Goff. All rights reserved. Except for brief quotations in critical publications or reviews, no part of this book may be reproduced in any manner without prior written permission from the publisher. Write: Permissions. Wipf and Stock Publishers, 199 W. 8th Ave., Suite 3, Eugene, OR 97401.

Cascade Books
An Imprint of Wipf and Stock Publishers
199 W. 8th Ave., Suite 3
Eugene, OR 97401

www.wipfandstock.com

ISBN 13: 978-1-62564-485-5

Cataloguing-in-Publication Data

Goff, Stanley.

    Borderline : reflections on war, sex, and church / Stan Goff ; foreword by Amy Laura Hall.

    xxvi + 446 p. ; 23 cm. Includes bibliographical references and index(es).

    ISBN 13: 978-1-62564-485-5

    1. Masculinity. 2. Masculinity—Religious aspects—Christianity. 3. Feminism. 4. Sex—Political aspects—United States—History—20th century. 5. Masculinity—Political aspects. 6. United States—Military policy. 7. United States—Armed forces. I. Hall, Amy Laura. II. Title.

HQ1090 .G653 2015

Manufactured in the U.S.A.   02/09/2015

To Sherry

Turning toward the woman, Jesus said to Simon, "Do you see this woman?"

—Luke 7:43a

They will beat their swords into plowshares
    and their spears into pruning hooks.
Nation will not take up sword against nation,
    nor will they train for war anymore.

—Isaiah 2:4

Contents

Foreword by Amy Laura Hall | vii
Preface | vii
Acknowledgments | vii

1 Introduction | 1

2 My Acquaintance with a Christian Soldier and Serial Rapist | 8

3 Forest Troop | 28

4 Body Counts | 32

5 Ontology of the Witch Hunt | 42

6 Ecologies of Power | 47

7 The Rise of the Lawyers | 54

8 Misbegotten Man | 63

9 Eros and War | 71

10 Practice Makes Perfect | 77

11 The Masculine Fortress | 86

12 Torture and Redemption | 92

13 The Pope's Army | 100

14 Sleepwalking | 111

15 Genealogy | 119

16 Bodies and Objects | 126

17 Contagious Prefix | 139

18 Just, Civil, and Total War—Sanctification of State | 150

19 A Bodyguard of Lies: Girl Story and Boy Story | 176

20 Origin Myths | 205

21 Paradox of Domination | 230

22 Disgust, Transgression, and Sex | 251

23 Respectability | 261

24 Progress and Fear of the Feminine | 271

25 Shell Shock | 289

26 Nation, Race, and Hygiene | 299

27 The Art of Depression | 313

28 Homos and Harlots | 328

29 Second World War | 340

30 Bombs, Babies, and 'Burbs | 356

31 The Herd | 376

32 Taboo | 386

33 Consent | 390

34 Clarifications | 398

Bibliography | 417
Index of Names | 437
Index of Biblical References | 445

Foreword

"Veterans won't confide in civilians about war."

A military chaplain said this to me. I have been dealing with war for a long time, and I disagree. I've been granted chances to pray with, lament, and hear about resurrection joy, with war veterans. I listened as a veteran used distancing pronouns to tell us "one has to" and "one was trained to," explaining how shooting animals for food allowed him to focus his aim and kill for D-day, when other men around him subconsciously aimed askew. A living witness to Patton's infamous speech told our class "war is hell, and it doesn't solve anything." My father, a civilian pastor, helped veterans of the Cold War recover from their visceral reaction to a Cambodian family our congregation sponsored for immigration. A Gulf War veteran explained why he and his wife avoid church on two Sundays—Veteran's Sunday and Mother's Day. Their loss was discordant with the celebratory aspect of both. A soldier on leave from Afghanistan told me that parenting was the hardest work on return, because you can't tell a resentful teenager to do push-ups.

Veterans will trust some civilians, given grace and opportunity. But trust requires being up close and uncomfortable, with neither the awe of "heroism" nor the fear that trauma is contagious. The book you are holding is just such a trusting gift.

I teach at a university where, for more than three decades, students have heard from Stanley Hauerwas about why they should take the national flag out of the Christian church's sanctuary. Stan Goff's *Borderline* digs radically (at the roots) into this matter. Why are veterans in the U.S. treated as uniquely heroic? Why does the American flag compete with the Lord's Supper as a symbolic aperture of truth—the icon through which we can see the narrative of ultimate sacrifice?

Stan Goff has helped me see that, for much of Western culture, *war* separates boys from men. As the dividing line between merely potential manliness and actualized manliness, participation in war also divides men from women. *Borderline* shows how the division of man from woman is vital in order for the imaginative power of war to conquer the Christian hope for love.

Years ago, Stan named something called "the ick factor" as an aspect of the warrior mentality. Women are gross, because we represent the lowest, downward point, a ladder up which boys must climb in order to become men. Because women bleed unheroically during menstruation, weep more readily, secrete fluids that can't be measured for their potency, run less swiftly, ski downhill or race our bobsled in a less virile way, women are the "ick" that is, paradoxically, sexually desirable. *Borderline* unpacks this paradox.

The warrior mentality is *gynophobic*—a concept that Stan elucidates often in this book. Some young women I know also use the term *femmephobia*, a useful notion for understanding the "decoy" aspect of the modern "female warrior" figure. Women can serve as warriors too, as long as we resemble men in the warrior role. We can join the *brotherhood* as contingently "honorary males." The female warrior is a *decoy* suggesting war is no longer patriarchal.

These same women, however, must maintain the sexual order in all other ways. I am thinking now of the strange television warrior, the 2011 *Homeland*'s fragile Carrie Mathison. A woman can participate in warrior culture as long as she weeps copiously on screen, screams with apparent irrationality, falls in love with and has sex with a man who could and just might kill her, and variously makes clear that she can be flamboyantly feminine. She is decidedly not the usual male warrior. Stan's writing has helped me to see that *Homeland* is a dangerously sophisticated *decoy* narrative.

I confess I am tempted to call Stan one of my heroes. I know. I am a Christian. Jesus should be my only hero. I am a feminist. I should eschew the entire concept of heroism. Perhaps there is a better term. But here's the thing. When I write a note to Stan or when I write about his writing, I don't flinch. I write as a feminist, without flinching. I can't think of another Christian man writing today, at least not one who is older than thirty and not openly gay, about whom I can say that. I composed the paragraph above this one without flinching—without worrying that Stan will say I'm being cruel to men or trying to declare the end of men or being rhetorically prone to overgeneralization about the rules that govern "masculinity." Let me put it even more plainly. Stan Goff is a man, a Christian, and a feminist. Full stop. Praise God, this is no small matter. This gives me hope for greater trust in real time, face-to-face conversations with men and women about the toll war takes on men and women.

There are several ways that this book is a major contribution, even a reset button, for Christians eager to talk about and write about pacifism, but also about war and sex. Stan offers a gracefully truthful word to Christians who defend the canonical, Western tradition, especially Christians who admire Alasdair MacIntyre. Stan Goff is an admirer of MacIntyre, and so his correction to contemporary MacIntyreans is subtle, but significant. *Borderline* shows how chivalry turns on an axis of weakness versus strength with sex as the motor. If Christianity is cast as a pristine jewel, or a virginal hymen, to be protected with one's pen as a sword, then Christian scholarship becomes an honorable war. If chivalry provides the rule book for Christian scholarship, then women who are strong or sexually potent, or men who are obviously vulnerable or gay, are a threat to chivalry.[1] (Virginal, submissive women, or powerful, asexual men, can serve as useful ballasts for, rather than threats to, chivalry.) Writing as a Christian is not a matter of honor and dishonor. I need to live and pray and write in a different imaginative world than that.

Christianity cannot be primarily about protecting God's Word from those who would soil or steal it. Gosh, Jesus somehow appears all over the confounded globe at the Mass, in little pieces, with bits of him here and there, willy-nilly, neither ordered nor counted nor carefully distributed. Who can protect that?

Borderline offers a stalwart, brotherly word to Christian men who have come under academic fire as less than manly. This book invites unrepentant pacifists to shrug off their detractors as schoolyard bullies. I am thinking here of James Hunter's gussied up but still pugilistic taunt at Stanley Hauerwas, that Hauerwas is either insufficiently honest about his desire "To Change the World" or insufficiently courageous to take up a holy charge "To Change the World." It is hard not to respond to that sort of charge without getting into what my dad would call a "pissing contest with a skunk." Here at Duke, an apocryphal story circulates each year that both MacIntyre and Hauerwas have told audiences that they argue against violence because without a commitment to nonviolence, they might beat the living shit out of those with whom they disagree. As a woman, I have never found that terribly helpful, because it still trades on hyper-masculinity, stirred with a dash of stoicism. Not only could these two men kick your ass, so the story suggests, but they have the extraordinary self-discipline not to do so. Of course, that is neither of them at his best, right? It isn't representative of their scholarship or their better instincts. But, in a theological brawl, muscular Christianity is an alluring temptation. I myself have been known to compare myself to Madame Lafarge from *A Tale of Two Cities*, saying that, if I believed in the death

---

1. Chivalry is derived from the word for cavalry, a mounted soldier, the dominant form of soldiery in medieval war. *Chevalerie* means "of the horse," a horseman. The term is rooted in war.

penalty, I wouldn't know just where to stop. It is the same temptation. *Mea culpa*. If Christian writing is a battle of potency versus impotency, then it's difficult to resist the temptation to defend oneself as potent.

Borderline is also an antidote to a version of what Kara Slade has called an "add Eucharist and stir" recipe for theological ethics. This theological error goes something like this: diagnose problem X; prescribe more blood/wine and body/bread; bake at 350 for two years, and the problem will cook into a new cake. Sometimes writers toss in the brilliance of Mozart, or, alternatively, a Quaker form of slow, patient, democratic consensus; but the gist is the same. I've been guilty of it myself, especially when I am worn out from marriage or divorce, or from being a divorced mother of two daughters. At times, I am tired and have no better answer to my young, intensely inquisitive seminary students than "go to church, and consume yourself some Jesus with extra Jesus!" Sometimes it's right. Sometimes it's theological marijuana.

Sometimes, when I found myself giving blurry, exhausted, sincerely pious answers to the misery of war waged by the U.S. around the world, I would knock on Stanley Hauerwas's office door, invariably interrupting a phone conversation with one of his many friends, and ask him what he thought. He wouldn't give me a word about "abundance," or ask us to "pray together," or tell me I needed to "just trust in the power of reconciliation." He was never obnoxious that way. He would give me a stern and grouchy history lesson about who sold weapons to whom and where the bullets came from. He'd hand me a book I should have already read, about the many little ways that war is sold to people who are just trying to make ends meet. He'd sometimes seem a bit annoyed that he was having to teach a political science major with supposedly leftist tendencies and a Yale PhD about the basics of power and capitalism and war.

But mixing religion and politics is hard work, particularly as a teacher and an attentively present mother to two little girls. Mixing true prayer, unsentimental piety, and micro-politics is even harder, especially when writing right here in the belly of the New South. *Borderline* combines many of those aspects in one place.

Borderline is a gift to civilians, veterans, students, pastors, and writers who try to write about our being holy together. Stan Goff has written a love letter of hope for those of us who are trying to hold fast to Christian feminism, or Christian pacifism, or . . . just plain Christianity. I say this as someone who has been shamed by the very Jesus who was supposed to be the source of our freedom.

I recommend a movie in case you are slightly overwhelmed by the historical detail in *Borderline*. It's a movie written about how to read Holy Scripture. This little 2009 movie is named *The Secret of Kells*. In this intricately illustrated film, a little boy who is being trained to build an impenetrable fortress against the enemy learns instead a love for the beautiful, complex detail in the *Book of Kells*. And the battle for which this young artist is supposed to be training is not a pretty one. War in this movie is brutal, not sentimental. The scenes where the Vikings attack Ireland are so graphically horrible that my daughters still haven't forgiven me to this day for suggesting we all watch this on "movie night" five years ago.

War is a powerful aphrodisiac, Stan Goff writes, because it helps men feel like real men and some women feel like real women protected by real men. But that is not what Christianity is about. Warrior myths are not true, nor war beautiful.

The microcosmic Christian work of living faithfully in the U.S., of living in the shadow of American dominance and militarism, draws on the best we have to give. Living faithfully draws on my ability to hear the details of what Dwight D. Eisenhower called "the military industrial complex" as it lives and thrives and makes its beastly being. And it draws on my ability to hear and see and taste that, in spite of all that, the Lord is Good. God is Good. Indeed. Love without war is very hard work. And joy comes in the morning.

Amy Laura Hall

Preface

> I do have the modest ambition to make every Christian in America aware that as a Christian they have a problem with war.
>
> —Stanley Hauerwas[1]

Philosophy and theory are great. I like them both a lot. But the stories are the thing. Schema and paradigm are really nice, but the story is where the skin is in the game. I want to tell you some stories, but I will need a little theory, a little philosophy, a few schemas and paradigms, and a little cultural criticism to make the stories tell you the stories within the stories. Narrative theologians say that Christians are a "story-formed community," so if stories are formative, then we have to attend to all the stories that form us, especially those stories that might be forming us prior to the story of Christ and that might hold us back from fuller participation in the story of Christ.

This book is about what it means to be manly, in particular what our stories about manliness are in relation to women, war, and faith. Some readers might think that what manliness is in relation to women is a different story than the story of being manly about war. I think I can convince you that these are not two stories, but the same story from different angles. I am a Christian man, and I write this book for Christians (anyone can read it, though). The problem is that this story, regardless of the angle from which you tell it, is a different story than the one told by the Gospels. That's a problem, because many of us men, to one degree or another, are trying to live into both stories at the same time.

War and the male contempt for and oppression of women coexist across time. That contempt and oppression change form to fit other changes, but the facts of war, of male contempt for women, and male oppression

1. Hauerwas, "Going On," para. 16.

of women are stubbornly transhistorical. They have common roots in hard-heartedness, conquest, and domination that penetrate deeply into the minds of men, all the way down to our infancies. Constructions of masculinity, over time, and influenced by war, have led men to hate (and fear!) something they call effeminacy. Effeminacy is not a curse *on* a man unless it is also a curse *against* women. War leads men to fear vulnerability, which we see as effeminate. And yet, as Christians, we might compare this mode of thought to "the way of the cross," which is vulnerability even unto death.

War is about domination, and "manly" men extend that domination to women. As men, we learn to want women and fear them all at once. We want to love women, but love means allowing someone inside our boundaries, and this implies a kind of vulnerability. Love means recognizing and being recognized, being yours and still mine; but when fear of vulnerability sets aside mutuality between men and women, even sex comes to be associated with domination, the "sexual object" becoming an object of aggression and hostility, just as a military enemy is an object of aggression and hostility. War is about meeting "threats," real or imagined, and women have long been described as threats to men, even by the church fathers—sexual threats, to be sure, but this is too similar to a soldier in his fortress or bunker, defending against an enemy, to ignore. War and stories of war provide the conceptual coordinates for men's relations to others, especially to women.

Christian men, like Christian women, are called to live into a particular story that is dramatically different from the rest of "the world." The story of a man conquering his enemies or conquering women—that is, the manstory that counts vulnerability as a vice—is not the story of Christ.

I am in a special position to tell these two incompatible stories, and some of the theorists, theologians, and philosophers I will cite are in unique positions to open up the stories within the stories. Together, we might explain why masculinity constructed as domination, in war and in relation to women, is really just one story . . . of manliness. I intend to make a case that *this very construction* has steered the church away from the story in the Gospels. I think I can show why we cannot separate war and the contempt for and subjugation of women, *why* this is the same story. Stick with me, and when you reach the end, you be the judge.

I was born in 1951. That was the year that the United States Army conducted its first infantry exercise for a nuclear war. I slept with a teddy bear. When I was three, my mother had me take tap lessons. I was a sensitive kid (my mother and father called it "tender-hearted"), and I cried when we had to take the Christmas tree down. I was also raised on television and film that depicted men proving themselves *as men* by shooting people with guns and blowing things up with explosives. In so doing, they always redeemed a piece of the world. I dressed up as best I could like TV representations of the Lone Ranger, Swamp Fox, and the Gray Ghost and imagined I was a guerrilla soldier. My family was a hunting family, and I was allowed to use actual firearms by the time I was six. Some of my school curriculum had been designed by the John Birch Society, and my father kept a copy of a book by J. Edgar Hoover titled *Masters of Deceit: The Story of Communism in America and How to Fight It*.

To fight communism, I became a parachute infantryman in the United States Army. On my nineteenth birthday, I boarded an airplane that took me to what was then called the Republic of Vietnam.

Time passed. Things happened.

On my forty-third birthday, I was in my eighth active conflict area, Haiti. By then, I was, in the army's taxonomy, an 18-Zulu-5-Victor-Whiskey-8, which meant a Ranger-qualified Special Forces Operations and Intelligence Sergeant and a military freefall parachutist. I had taught at the Jungle Operations Training Center in Panama and at the United States Military Academy at West Point. I had performed missions under official cover in Latin America and participated in direct combat operations in East Asia, the Caribbean, and Africa. I had been a member of what was once called Delta Force. I had served in three Airborne Ranger units and two Special Forces Groups. I had "advised" foreign national military and security personnel who moonlighted as kidnappers and death squads. I had terrorized and brutalized people who were weak and poor. I had burned houses, killed poor farmers' livestock, and lied on command to family, journalists, and the public in whose name I "did my job." I had maimed people. I had exploited prostituted women, who exist on the periphery of every military activity. I had pursued women instrumentally for sex, and I had devalued women to the same extent that I worked to become the opposite of those expectations I held for women. I became for a time a divorced alcoholic who left a damage trail that included the suffering of my own daughter, a very young witness to this insanity.

I had taken human life.

For all this, I was held in the highest esteem by my fellow citizens of the United States, especially by other men. What I did in the military is still called "service," and people still thank me for it even though they have no clue what I actually did or what I was actually like.

"Amazing grace," goes the familiar hymn, "how sweet the sound, that saved a wretch like me." A fitting word to be etched under my name on a grave marker: *Wretch*.

And yet on Easter Day in 2008, at the age of fifty-six, I was baptized. I've been thinking about this book ever since, so if anyone asks me how long it took to write this book, one true answer is "around six years, the first five of them going over these issues again and again in my mind." An even truer answer would be "since around 2001." And the truest of all is "sixty-three years."

In a very real way my engagement with feminism led me into the church, and war led me to feminism. There are probably few people who narrate their conversion to Christianity that way. It's been a pretty peculiar life, from teddy bears and tap lessons to kicking the shit out of poor people in other countries.[2] It was feminist thought that gave me some real insight into how that happened. Feminists confronted me with the subject of power and privilege, specifically how power is gendered, and how privilege attaches to gender. Feminists taught me that my power as a male provides me the privilege to pretend that I have no power as a male.

In the wake of the September 11 attacks and the national frenzy to go to war, I was obliged as an opponent of that war to articulate my opposition in the framework of a criticism of militarism—on which I was seen as an "expert" because of the length and diversity of my military experience. I found, on reflection, that no account of militarism or my own engagement with it was possible without an account of my own lifetime struggle to prove my masculinity. Yet I found that people who were antiwar seldom addressed the topic of gender. In fact, they often used the same gendered conceits as the prowar people. I remember the criticism leveled at President Bush and Vice President Cheney for being "chickenhawks," a term used to describe men who promoted war without having actually been soldiers. My "antiwar" comrades were saying that these men lacked the "masculine" chops to promote war, because they hadn't earned the right through combat. The only people I found who were critical of this were those who were studying war as a *gendered* phenomenon. So if I wanted to get to the bottom of

---

2. Don't let my "bad language" be a stumbling block. I will use words in this book that are not usually associated with Christian writing but that are part of our culture's vernacular speech. Honestly, they are part of my vernacular speech, too. I grew up among profane people and was in the army for a long time. I am not sure how to connect what I have to say about culture and Christianity by tiptoeing around language. We are constituted in so many ways by language. What I describe about war will be far more obscene than a few "bad words."

militarism, I had to study gender as a division of power; and that led me into the arms of feminism.

Studying feminism is not easy for men because all our unexamined privilege is exposed in the process. Our little hideaways are exposed. Our blind spots are revealed. Not only did feminism disabuse me of some of my blind spots when I was professing secular leftism after the army—a response to my shame and rage about the military—but feminism exposed me to (what for me were) fresh philosophical insights. I was confronted with challenges to some of my foundational beliefs, like "objectivity" and the fallacy that truth can be ascertained apart from one's standpoint and apart from power. When these ideas were no longer tenable, thanks to feminists who were convincing in their criticism, my own prejudice against faith—based on *objectivism*[3]—was undermined, and I became open to hearing what "religious" people had to say.

I decided to look into Christianity for a while, thinking it was something I ought to know more about. At some point while I was gazing into the Jordan River, a Jew from ancient Nazareth with rough hands and a loving heart reached up and pulled me in. For the first time in my life, death did not have the last word. That's a pretty big deal for anyone. For me, it meant everything I'd thought I'd known about being a man had changed, because as a man my life had always been determined by death; I had always operated on the assumption that death had the last word. Had I not been prepared by feminism and its insights into my life (and sins) as a man—had feminism not prepared me to relinquish the control that I'd needed to be "a man"—might have rejected the vulnerability that Jesus demands before I ever got to the good parts. God does indeed work in mysterious ways.

The man that I was when I was kicking the shit out of poor people abroad was not about vulnerability, about loving anyone, much less an enemy. I was never quite arrogant enough to call myself an atheist, but I was an agnostic without any special questions. Manhood, martial manhood, a death cult, I've come to see, was my religion.

Stanley Hauerwas bought my lunch for me one day at Duke University in 2008, having never seen me before in his life, and he said, "You need to write your memoirs." He was writing his at the time, and he's very interested in repentant soldiers, so it was a reasonable thing for him to say to me. But I

---

3. The philosophical conviction that "reality" exists independent of the mind and can be ascertained as such—not to be confused with capitalized Objectivism, the crackpot philosophy of the Ayn Rand cult.

haven't written a memoir; I've written this book. I hope that, if he reads it at some point, I will have come close enough with this sometimes autobiographical book to make him smile.

I also hope that this book—which will say harsh, discomfiting things about sex, war, and manhood—will open a door for other Christian men to take, as the twelve-steppers say, a "fearless moral inventory" of themselves in light of those things that we can learn when we see them from other standpoints. The suffering of women that our feminist sisters have brought to our attention can, in this way, be understood as a gift, and not as a threat, as the suffering of the beaten Jew on the road to Jericho was a gift to the Samaritan who was given the opportunity to love by *choosing* the beaten man as his neighbor (Luke 10:25–37). The gift that feminism gives is the opportunity to love by *choosing* our sisters, in themselves and in their suffering, and in so doing to prolong the Incarnation. After all, the story of the Samaritan and his choice was told by the One who emptied himself of divine prerogative and suffered the ultimate humiliation of the cross (Phil 2:5–8). The least we can do, as men, is renounce our male prerogative.

In a story from the seventh chapter of Luke's Gospel (7:36–50), Jesus is a dinner guest at the home of Simon the Pharisee. A woman, who has fallen out of social favor in the eyes of the Pharisee and his male cohort, enters the house and begins what must have been a very discomfiting display of affection. Simon has not extended the usual courtesy of washing the dust from Jesus' feet before the meal, and this unnamed woman performs the service by crying tears upon Jesus' feet and wiping them away with her hair. She washes his feet with her own body. In the usual telling of the story, we hear Jesus rebuke Simon for his failure of courtesy, and we pass over Jesus' opening question as if it were merely an attention-getter: "Do you see this woman?"

Hit the pause button. This is a real question. Do you *see* this woman? This is the question I will be asking readers throughout the book.

When I was in El Salvador in the 1980s, I watched a beggar with no legs making his way through Zona Rosa—a well-to-do commercial district in San Salvador lined with chic shops and restaurants that the vast majority of Salvadorans could never afford. The well-dressed young *ricos* walked right past the legless beggar with not even a tic in their conversations. I suddenly realized that, for all practical purposes, this man was invisible. He was *there*, flesh and blood advancing down the sidewalk on wooden blocks held in his hands, past the abjections of spat-out gum, wind-blown trash, cigarette butts, and dog shit; and this striking image was abracadabra-ed into nonexistence by a cultural sleight of mind that cloaked their *rico* power in the same move that made him invisible.

In the film *Dirty Pretty Things*, undocumented foreigners are living underground in London. Unexpectedly entangled in the trade in human transplant organs, a Nigerian fugitive named Okway is asked during the third act by a wealthy English organ purchaser, who *were* he and his two women companions (one an English prostitute and another a sexually exploited Turkish hotel cleaner). Okway replies sardonically, "We are the people you don't see. We drive your cabs, and clean your rooms, and suck your cocks." It is a film about social invisibility in a society driven by the opposite of Christ's compassion.

Regarding compassion, Walter Brueggemann has written that "compassion constitutes a radical form of criticism, for it announces that the hurt is to be taken seriously, that the hurt is not to be accepted as normal and natural but is an abnormal and unacceptable condition for humanness."[4] People who are unseen in war are hurt, by war itself *and* by not being seen. Women are being *hurt* by not being seen. These are moral bottom lines no matter how many layers of derivative rationalization are used to conceal them. The hurt is to be taken seriously.

When I imagine Simon and his other guests before the embarrassing display of tearful foot-washing, I see them avert their faces as they attempt to rebuke Jesus for the company he is keeping. Until the woman entered this house, she was invisible, and they want her to be invisible again. Yet Jesus responds first not with his own rebuke for their failure of courtesy, but with a simple and profoundly damning question: Do you *see* this woman?

This is a remarkable, yet too often unremarked, thing about almost two millennia of history and scholarship within and without the church. Women, as subjects, as persons in their own right, are mainly invisible. I will argue that, for Christians, feminism confronts us not with an ideology but with the more tangible and urgent issue of standpoint. The gift that feminism has given us is not a new set of rules but an enhanced capacity for men to know what it is like to stand in a woman's place, to know more about what it is like to be a woman, to *see* women. Feminism pulls our recalcitrant hands away from our eyes and insists that we *see* women—real, enfleshed, breathing, hungering, thinking, feeling, loving women who are imprisoned

---

4. Brueggemann, *Prophetic Imagination*, 88.

within the structures of male power, structures both visible and invisible. Feminism calls on us to *recognize* real women beyond our concupiscent imaginations and outside the vast symbolic universe of that male power. As a body of work by and for women, feminism has taken the first step by standing where *women* stand to look at a world that men command; and the view is astonishingly different.

If I am unconvincing in my other arguments here, I would ask readers, especially men, henceforth to do at least one thing, and that is to take into account the standpoints of women-as-women, and to look at the question of sex-and-power as a part of every form of discernment. I don't believe, based on my own journey through the heart of a very aggressive and highly esteemed form of masculinity, that we can do this without first removing some beams from our own eyes. The first step has to be asking ourselves, before we ask any other question, how does this or that situation or this or that question relate to my ideas about being a man? These ideas exert a powerful influence over every other question, over every area of our lives; and yet, what we often consider to be normal, gender-free, turns out upon close and honest examination to be determined by our standpoints as men, as the people who have a collective power in the world at the expense of other people who are women.

Nothing is gender-neutral. If our intuition is that something is gender-neutral, I'll wager that this "neutrality" is based on making what is "male" the normative sun around which everything else must turn. In an especially terrible way, that "maleness" that poses as neutrality has been shaped by man's great obscenity, war, which Mussolini called the male equivalent of childbirth.

Acknowledgments

Since this book has taken almost sixty-three years to write, as fractured and as meager as it may be, it is impossible to acknowledge everyone who has contributed to it; and that applies well beyond the brilliant minds and careers that are cited within these pages. The first acknowledgment has to be God, for obvious and not so obvious reasons. I know that the hand of God has been in my life even when it went unacknowledged, even denied; and I know that God's hand has been visible in the people I have encountered along the way—even and perhaps especially those whose names I have never known and those whose names I once knew and have forgotten. I thought for quite a while that seeming to be always out of sync with my own time was some kind of curse; but I've come to reconsider that now. Thank you everyone who has contributed to my being strange, or I'd have never been able to embrace the strangeness of this adventure that has been called the kingdom of God. It is not being strange that is responsible for everything I've gotten wrong here, but being a broken human in a broken world . . . maybe that's strange enough on its own account.

The first personal acknowledgment has to go to Sherry, the woman who has shared a home with me for the last two and a half decades, through enough crazy changes to fill a bookshelf, and still stayed. During the writing of this book, she has tolerated my being gone-while-present a lot of the time, worked her ass off at home and by doing thankless wage labor, tramped through Central America with me for a year, and a whole bunch of other life stuff that I can't even begin to list here. Ten days after we were married, I was shipped off to Colombia for three months, and within two years, I had been deployed to three conflict areas. It takes a resilient person to stick with anyone through that, then twelve years of intense political activism, lost jobs, teenagers, multiple moves, grandkids, family deaths, family fishing trips, shitty bosses, graduations, kids joining the military and going to war, hiking through state parks, illnesses and injuries, watching the same goofy movies dozens of times, family fights, family reunions, bottle rocket fights, swimming in the ocean, weddings, barbecues, long-distance separations, divorces, court appearances, busted pipes and busted cars, conversion to Christianity, bird-watching, and every so often periods of blissful, quiet, and restful solitude. That is Sherry and me. God put us together. Thank you, God.

Then there is the rest of my family, my fractured and stitched together *mestizo* family, my beloved (writing) daughter Élan Kesilman; my beloved step-children, Jesse Hobbs, Jayme Travers, and Jeremy Hobbs; my beloved grandchildren, Jayden Hobbs, Jaycen Jones Hobbs, Alyssia Hobbs, Janae Travers, Jayla Travers, and most recently born, Adriana Hobbs; my mother, Jean Goff, who gave me life, kept me alive, and taught me to read; my late father, Stewart Goff, who told me, "Always root for the underdog"; my sister and brother, Celia Wildroot and Glen Goff, who shared my turbulent childhood and early adulthood, and who are both so generous of heart it makes me want to weep sometimes. I am no more and no less than what I am to all these people—my kin—who together constitute my existence.

Like so many people who are part of modernity's Diaspora, I have "friends" through the Internet. Among them are a few people with whom I correspond to a greater degree than others and for whom I feel real affection and gratitude. There *can* be such a thing as virtual friendship like the epistolary friendships of old. A few of these friends had a real hand in this book.

Charlie Collier is my editor, and I met him on Facebook before I ever proposed a book for Cascade. He is patient, intelligent, and knows how to cut compassionately—ideal virtues for an editor. This book would not have happened without him. God bless him.

I was also blessed on this project by a lot of brilliant Christian women scholars with whom I correspond. I met Amy Laura Hall one time in person, and spoke with her for only a few minutes, but that was after a presentation to my church in Raleigh several years ago against progressive utilitarianism. That talk has colored my view of things ever since. She has been generous, insightful, and encouraging, even after Sherry and I decamped from the Triangle to Central America and landed in southeast Michigan—a long way from Amy Laura's digs at Duke Divinity School in Durham. Amy Laura consented to write the foreword to *Borderline*, and in exchange for that generosity and the overwhelming generosity of the foreword itself, I will withhold my rebuke for her using the word *hero*.

Another virtual friend from Duke Divinity School, now an Episcopalian priest, is Kara Slade. Kara is one of those people some call "scary smart," with a genuine and infectious passion for theology. She charitably took the time out of her perpetual-motion life to look over this manuscript with a

Acknowledgments

mind to preventing my worst theological errors (and those that remain are the product of my own stubbornness and ignorance).

Likewise, Jodie Boyer Hatlem—my border-hopping, Foucault-quoting, Mennonite virtual friend—consented to read the rough draft. She was the first to do so, and her suggestions were the catalyst for almost all of the initial revisions, because they were *all* good suggestions.

I would be remiss if I didn't also acknowledge De Clarke, my editor for *Sex & War*, an earlier (pre-conversion) attempt to come to terms with gender and militarism. De has corresponded with me since 2005. She tutored me in feminism, and she introduced me to Ivan Illich, that mad Croatian Catholic priest and social critic from whom I first learned to appreciate what a staggeringly mysterious and gracious thing the Incarnation really is.

Davin Heckman deserves a hat tip, too. Not only did he offer friendship as a co-parishioner before he ran away from home, he gave me a copy of his excellent book *A Small World*, which figured into the latter chapters of this one; and he let me raid the Siena Heights University library when they were about to throw away a mountain of books.

I also need to acknowledge my friend Barbara Zelter, who led me into the faith with her example and her friendship. Barbara also introduced me to Reverend Greg Moore, who befriended me, came after me on a motorcycle, and finally baptized me in 2008, *then* introduced me to both Stanley Hauerwas and Amy Laura Hall. Stanley Hauerwas is specially acknowledged throughout the book for his influence and provocation. As to Amy Laura Hall, not only does she figure prominently in the book, she has been throughout the process of writing it a source of enormous inspiration and support.

A special thanks to the Adrian Dominican Sisters, whose lives are a testament to why women should be fully included in the life of the church, with special thanks to Sr. Carol Coston, my gardening friend, Sr. Molly Giller, who led me through RCIA, and Prioress Sr. Attracta Kelly, who practiced immigration law in Raleigh when I was there, only to migrate here to Michigan to apply her considerable skills in the service of her sisters.

Thanks to my friend Father Bob Schramm, who handed me over to a community garden and presided over my Catholic confirmation in 2012.

It was only near the end of the publication process that I became virtually acquainted with Jacob Martin, the copy editor for *Borderline*. I have told him, and I will say it again here: copyediting is holy work. The book is immeasurably better for his tactful, sensitive, and attentive interventions.

1

Introduction

War is implicated in masculinity. Masculinity is implicated in war. Masculinity is implicated in the contempt for and domination of women. Together, these are implicated in the greatest sins of the church.

Borderline is about two questions. First, why have Christians been so warlike? Second, why do Christian men still caricature, dominate, misrepresent, condescend to, and dismiss women? I am convinced that these two questions must be answered together. In the various reflections that make up this book I hope to make a case for the following claims. Masculinity is very often constructed as domination and violence—direct violence or sublimated and vicarious violence. War is one of the most powerful formative practices in the development of masculinity understood as domination and violence; and recursively, masculinity established as domination and violence reproduces the practice of war. In societies that celebrate war, domination-masculinity is likewise celebrated and becomes a norm to which men, speaking here of *males*, aspire; and war becomes a defining metaphor for male agency. When this kind of aggression is valued, its opposite is devalued. When "male" aggression is valued, "female" lack of aggression is devalued, meaning that women themselves, associated with this "womanly" trait, come to be identified as a negative. Being a good man has come to mean being *not* like a woman. In this way, war contributes significantly to the hatred of women, and reciprocally, contempt for women contributes to the reproduction of war.

I will advance the claim, and attempt to support it, that the practice of war *inevitably* produces and reproduces the hatred of and contempt for women, even when that hatred and contempt is papered over by sentimentalized pseudo-affection for "our women" or "good women" whom war must "protect." This relation between war and misogyny exists even when it is unacknowledged in contexts where war is spoken of apart from the devaluation of women, and when the devaluation of women takes place apart from any explicit discussion of war. I will further advance the claim that unexamined notions of masculinity act as a cherished intuition operating prior to the "rational" defense of war as a practice, even the defense of "just war."

I will also suggest that the life and teachings of Jesus undermine both those pre-rational and pseudo-rational justifications for mistreating and marginalizing women, because those justifications are entailments of masculinity constructed as violent power and not humble servanthood.

In critiquing both militarism and gendered violence, I will try to unpack how militarism and gender operate in our own milieu, and so I will also make an argument that liberal modernity, contrary to the clam that it does away with "religious" violence and replaces it with a "secular," rational and peaceful order, reproduces the problem of violent power in a uniquely modern imperial form.

None of these arguments about gender, implicit or explicit, are premised on biological determinism or the notion that masculinity and femininity are *synonymous* with being biologically male and female, even though the examination of these cultural phenomena will show that most people in most times *do* in fact conflate biological sex with masculinity and femininity. Anyone seeking some "resolution" to the false dichotomy of nature versus nurture will be frustrated by this book. I do not believe they can be separated, so I won't try.

The reason that feminist scholarship, emerging within a liberal milieu, is important is not on account of its variable relationship with liberalism, but on account of the ways that these works, often highly critical of liberalism, have described and affirmed the *standpoints* of women, as women. I use the plural to avoid the idea that there is a single woman's standpoint. The standpoint of a peasant woman in Oaxaca and the standpoint of a well-to-do, professional white woman in Chicago are necessarily and decidedly different.

In every encounter in gendered society, and all known societies are gendered, the standpoint of the woman or women in each encounter is different from that of a man or men because of gendered (not merely biological) difference, and too often because of the domination and subjection that are attached to that difference. Men and women experience life differently, and to exclude the standpoint(s) of women is to render women invisible in order to treat the standpoint(s) of the men in those encounters as normative.

Introduction

If feminism has taught us anything, it has shown us that what was once considered modern universalism was in fact male universalism, and what was once considered modern objectivity was in fact male objectivity. I will be bringing a number of key feminists into conversation with Christianity throughout the book, even though many of them are not Christians, because some Christians and several feminists share a good deal of common ground.

In discussions of contemporary attitudes about sex and aggression, I will show a number of ways in which sex and violence, sex and domination, are understood as the same thing—and how, in a glaring contradiction, contemporary liberal culture denies this common association with ideas about sex existing apart from the reality of social power.

This book will provide a rough genealogy of church-and-war alongside church-and-sex in which the reader can discern how often, and often terribly, the church has allowed itself to be pulled away from the example and the teachings of Jesus of Nazareth by the fallen world, by power through control and domination, instead of what Kathryn Tanner has called the profligacy of Christ's grace. Rather than one consistent approach to questions about sex and/or war, what the record shows is that the church has consistently *adapted its practices and pronouncements to worldly power* with an eye to preserving the church's political influence and church men's prerogative. In a way, telling this story about the church's allowing itself to be diverted by power is the central goal of this book, even if a special emphasis is placed on war and sex. Whether we are looking at the Constantinian compromise or the Crusades or the witch trials or the Reformation or the wars of modernity, we will see again and again how the church has been pulled away from the Gospels by the material and cultural potency of the principalities and powers. This is not a new story; I just want to reveal how it looks when we examine it through the twin lenses of war and gender, and through the eyes of a former soldier, once sex and war have been de-naturalized.

The theological debates that animate some of these epochs are important but are secondary to my focus. The main question is, Why has the church been so consistently pulled away from the teachings and example of Christ by the world (a world constituted by male power and by war)? My tentative and partial answer is that men, males, bear a special responsibility for these failures, and that our attachment to something called "manhood," especially as that relates to sex and war, has significantly reproduced these failures. In many cases, maybe most cases, we, like those uniformed men who stood below the cross of Christ, know not what we do. We do not understand gendered power even as we wield it; and we wield it not knowing we have it. So *Borderline* will talk about this power with the modest hope of increasing that understanding just a little.

This book is aimed at how masculinity informs the way Christian men view war, and how war informs our view of what it means to be men. It contends that how we view women underwrites our notions of masculinity, and that how we view men in relation to women informs how we think about war.

I will touch on the origins of liberal philosophy, the evolution of modernity, the development of the modern nation-state, and modern war. There is no credible account of the associations between war and masculinity without an account of the most consistent and identifiable agent of war today, which is the state. The evolution of war, and the evolution of masculinity inflected by the practice of war, will be incomprehensible without it.

There are several premises that this book challenges, directly or by inference, about war and the state. Modern war, as will become abundantly clear, cannot be conformed to *any* just-war rationale without first reinterpreting just-war principles through multiple layers of conceptual derivation and prevarication. The descriptions of the state that generally background the pacifism–just war debate assume a lot more than they explain. They not only assume the state as some constant in human society, when the state is actually a latecomer, but they also assume that the state is some static quality that serves to protect order, control violence, deliver justice, and so on. History does not support either idea, the stasis of form or the idealized functionalist account, without being disingenuously revised to fit a predetermined agenda. Representatives from both sides of this debate have claimed on occasion that the state is "necessary," when a more accurate term might be "contingently unavoidable." Legalized political authority, in its many forms, has over a few millennia insinuated itself into human affairs with a force that ensured societies would become self-organized around and through that authority, even though human beings lived without such authority for tens of thousands of years.[1] The state is not *necessary* in the way, for example, that oxygen is *necessary* for human life. It is necessary, that is, *contingently unavoidable*, in the same way that a car is *necessary* to find a job in some places in the United States or that money is *necessary* to survive in a commodified society. The claim that the state is *necessary* in the former sense is ideological, not descriptive. All "theories" of war that begin with the "necessity of the state" as a premise are not theories in the sense of scientific

---

1. By the state, here, I mean a political authority backed by a legalized monopoly on force. The nation-state, which is the subject of several chapters in the book, is a unique form of this political authority that is distinctly modern.

theory, the summary of conclusions that are so far confirmed by the body of evidence, but ideological presumptions disguised as theories.

As a Christian, I am not trying in this book to "make the case" for pacifism. I don't need an account of the state, war, or masculinity to underwrite my commitment to nonviolence, because that commitment is based on my belief that war has been abolished in the kingdom of God, even as we live now between Pentecost and Parousia. I know that war is still a feature of the world and promises to remain so for the foreseeable future. Any number of Christian pacifists can and have explicated peace through Christology and eschatology better than I can. There's no reason for me to conduct a detailed reiteration of their arguments.[2]

Christian pacifists dislike that war is brought into the sanctuary. "Hear, hear!" I say, agreeing with others who have already said it better. My point is that we are *also* bringing war into the sanctuary with our masculinity, and that by prioritizing an uncritical devotion to a particular kind of manhood, we continue to naturalize not just that version of manhood but war itself.

In what follows, I will challenge the usual moral accounts of war, wherein people obsessively tease out questions of good and evil based on the unpredictable outcomes and alleged motivations for war. My own experience as an insider and my own insights as an (admittedly very) amateur historian have revealed that historical outcomes are always mixed, often morally incomprehensible, and *never* final. In the real world, the justifications for going to war are, frankly, nearly always a pack of lies with a few convenient half-truths papering over the authentic and deeply sinful motivations that precede the bombs and bullets.

In the course of this book, I will provide examples of what men do to make war, to practice for war, to mentally prepare for war, and to learn to love war. It is nothing like the sterile and/or idealized accounts in war "theories" or war stories promulgated by various propaganda and entertainment media. (I confess to having difficulty making this distinction nowadays.)

There was a time when I myself advocated various justifications for violence, in writing and on the record. That was before I began to understand the relationship between my "sexual identity" and my experience of war—real, symbolic, and imaginary.

The organization of the chapters is aimed ultimately at an autobiographical account. While it may be counterintuitive to chronicle Pope Urban II's war machinations in the eleventh century to explain Stan Goff's military career in the twentieth century, and then to use that to explain the

---

2. Stanley Hauerwas, quoted above, is among the most prominent living theologians to articulate this peace theology, in which he was strongly influenced by the writings of John Howard Yoder and Karl Barth. Dorothy Day was also an eschatological pacifist.

relation between war, sex, and church, that is exactly what I'm trying to do. Think of it as flying towards a destination, reading about it on the way, then descending through the clouds. First, you see the curvature of the horizon, then the fields and roads and rivers. Then there is a distant landing strip getting closer and closer. You cross over highway overpasses, grass, runway lights. The tarmac appears out the window and reaches up for the landing gear.

In the first chapter, I will tell a story of which I was a part. This is your travel brochure for the flight. In the second chapter, I'll situate the first story in a bit of interesting primatology. Takeoff. In the third, I will go back four thousand years to get a handle on martial masculinity. Now we're cruising above the clouds. We will fly forward through time, pausing to illuminate history in a conversation with contemporary scholarship, especially feminist scholarship. We will pass through the history of the church, the Crusades, the Reformation, and into early modernity. This is the macro-history that I share with most readers in one way or another; and so it is a *group* autobiography. Then we will narrow the focus from the eighteenth century to the twentieth, flying in smaller circles over the Atlantic, then over the United States. As we approach the early twentieth century, I will begin to descend, describing—again, with occasional scholarly interventions and editorial asides—the formation of the specific culture into which I was born. In this respect, this will still be a group autobiography, albeit for a smaller pool of people, especially Western white men. As we approach the last few chapters, we will establish an historical context for the household into which I was born, then take a few snapshots of a childhood that began just a few years after World War II. My accounts will become increasingly personal until—after hundreds of pages of historical reorientation—you will rejoin me, this actual person, after having left me in the 1980s in the first chapter. Then you will take a few trips with me to places like Vietnam and Somalia and Haiti, where we can talk again as contemporaries; and I can explain after all why this is important to me—and, I believe, to you—as a Christian.

I will ask you to prepare for some turbulence along the way. The association of sex with domination, aggression, and hostility is simultaneously real and concealed by spiritual-talk about how sex is sacred, liberal-talk about how sex is harmless fun, or medical-talk about how sex is "healthy." So when I describe the ways in which sex is not spiritual, not harmless, not "healthy" (God forbid it is therapeutic!), descriptions that will go against the grain of right and left in the dreary modern debates about sex, I will provide a lot of examples of the ways in which sex is so often about hostility, cruelty, and humiliation. The accumulated weight of these descriptions, as I can attest after having intentionally sat with them for over a decade now, may well leave readers in a state of dislocation and doubt about their own lives as sexual beings. This may be necessary; but it is also necessary for me to remind myself and readers at the outset that, while the revelation that sex and power cannot be separated is essential and fraught with responsibility, we are not destined to live out the worst of our potentialities. At the risk of employing a cliché, love can indeed redeem sex from power.

There are men who are not living into the worst of this cultural fusion of sex and domination; and there are men of good will who want to do better. Moreover, sex can, under the right conditions, be simultaneously moral, mutual, and enjoyable without being exploitative or objectifying—and yes, even fun. How could a former soldier who comes into the church with the gift of the renunciation of violence not believe in everyday redemptions?

There will be places in the book where I will leave certain questions, and the reader, hanging. This is probably an indication that I haven't yet worked it all out myself; but it is also an invitation to readers to fill in the blanks for themselves. Having a lot of questions doesn't mean I have all the answers.

There is a good deal of political talk in this book, and there are some critiques of politics and economics that are commonly associated with political programs that claim to hold the keys to correction. This book does not endorse anything that looks, smells, walks, or talks like a political party or a political program. I am actually very pessimistic about the prospects of worldly politics changing the terrifying trajectory on which modern hubris has launched us. My hope for the future is not in politics, and certainly not in the politics I advocated in my pre-Christian past, but in the risen Christ.

Borderline is intended for discernment, not politics, unless you count the church as its own politics. Then and only then—yes!—let's get political. Let's live out the politics of vulnerability for all to see. Gramsci wrote about "pessimism of the intellect, optimism of the will." I believe in "pessimism of the intellect, optimism of faith." It is about good news for all of us, but especially for men. I write this book as a witness to the power of death in the service of domination, of domination in the service of death, and as one who has been liberated by the knowledge that I never again have to raise my hand against another human being, that I never again have to dominate, humiliate, or retaliate against anyone. For men, this is very good news indeed. It means the door can be opened to God's greatest gift—love.

He who was most vulnerable; He who *saw* women through the veil of cultural invisibility (and told us to follow); He, having shed no other's blood, went to the cross.

He is risen.

Jesus is Lord.

2

My Acquaintance with a Christian Soldier and Serial Rapist

> Men's interest in patriarchy is condensed in hegemonic masculinity and is defended by all the cultural machinery that exalts hegemonic masculinity. It is institutionalized in the state; enforced by violence, intimidation and ridicule in the lives of straight men . . . and enforced by violence against women and gay men.
>
> —R. W. Connell[1]

> Once children have been indoctrinated into the expectations of a dominator society, they may never outgrow the need to locate all evil outside themselves. Even as adults they tend to scapegoat others for all that is wrong in the world. They continue to depend on group identification and the upholding of social norms for a sense of well-being.
>
> —Walter Wink[2]

---

1. Connell, *Masculinities*, 241.
2. Wink, "Myth of Redemptive Violence," para. 18.

TESTING, TESTING

In the spring of 1981, at the age of twenty-nine, I volunteered for the Selection and Assessment Course for 1st Special Forces Operational Detachment-Delta, a.k.a. "Delta Force." I was working as an interim platoon sergeant at 2nd Ranger Battalion in Ft. Lewis, Washington, outside Tacoma. Onto an already demanding physical training program conducted each morning and augmented by the nature of Rangering, I had added evening three-mile runs with a fifty-pound rucksack on my back and two five-pound ankle weights over my boots.[3]

When I arrived in Camp Dawson, West Virginia, in March, separated completely there from the world of women, there was spring snow on the ground. Heavy-bodied whitetail deer grazed on the airfield at dusk. The surface of the Cheat River crawled kaleidoscopically between the blue-gray mountains of a leafless Appalachia. There was no shouting by the cadre, who were in civilian clothes with relaxed grooming standards, nothing like the shorn, shaved, starched, and shouting cadre of most military schools. In fact, there was a quiet, icy distance about them. Verbal instructions were monosyllabic and studiously without affect. Instructions and a schedule were silently posted each morning on an easel-mounted chalkboard inside the double front doors of the brick barracks. The whole environment was designed to break with all markers of familiarity we might know from our regular army units and our lives. We spent hours idle in the billets for the first three days, left to wonder whether we were already being observed, and what exactly the cadre might be "assessing" in each of us. The unit was highly secretive, as were the performance standards for selection and assessment, and therefore steeped in a mystique that grew fat on hints and rumors. The only standard we had for performance, in a course we all knew would select only around 20 percent of those who came, was to "do the best you can." Save nothing. Do not pace yourself. Give everything and see what happens. Man stuff.

One day, we took an eight-hour battery of standardized psychological tests. We were exhausted by penciling in the bubbles, answering (*a*) strongly agree, (*b*) agree, (*c*) don't know, (*d*) disagree, or (*e*) strongly disagree, in response to statements like "I have black, tarry stools," "I like tall women," "It disgusts me to put a worm on a hook," and "For the most part, people understand me."

After supper, we returned to the barracks, where we were instructed to report to formation with forty-five-pound rucksacks at eight that same

---

3. The military then was only beginning to understand cumulative trauma disorders, so I was unaware that I was paying installments on some future debilities.

evening. With perfect precision, at exactly eight o'clock, as we stood in formation exhaling vapor into the night chill, the selection cadre rolled up with eight covered military pickups and parked them exactly the same distance apart; a driver climbed out of each and stood in front of the formation. In turn, each driver called out the roster numbers of his passengers and we mounted up. They zipped the covers closed around us without another word, blinding us to our surroundings, and the convoy pulled out of Camp Dawson. The only sensation left inside the canvas enclosures was that of switching direction and climbing, then descending, then climbing again for around forty-five minutes. Then we stopped. The zippers were opened, and we dismounted into more snow on a high gravel road in a thick hardwood forest. Our names were called again. We each replied, "Here."

Sergeant Major Cheney, looking like a lost hunter in the dark with his down vest and cowboy hat, directed each of us to tie an activated plastic chemical light ("chemlite") to our rucksacks, and told us not to use flashlights except in a medical emergency. He instructed us to follow the markers and signs on the gravel road, and to go until we were told to stop. Understood? Yes, we said in unison. Then go!

We all burst down the road like top-heavy marathoners. Within moments, we could hear the first grunts as men careened onto the patches of ice and crashed. Everyone fell, a lot. No one knew how far we would go, but the rumor was almost twenty miles. Chemlites marked the route. The chemlites would partially blind us, making the dark darker between them. Within minutes, I was bathed in sweat. The downslope became the upslope, then down again, as we tore like half-blind sasquatches through the West Virginia mountains.

I had always been a moderate starter, warming up and gradually pouring on speed to burn through the end of runs and ruck marches. I don't know exactly when I started to notice that I was gradually passing exhausted men. First there was one, then another, then a pair here and there. I would hear their feet scuffing in front of me and my own feet scuffing up behind them. I had emptied both one-quart canteens within an hour and could already feel the effects of dehydration. But I kept reeling in the next man. At some point I calculated that I must be among the front-runners. Passing was merciless. We were instructed from the beginning to conduct the course as a "singleton." Unless someone was in immediate danger of losing life or limb, we were not to assist or encourage . . . or even speak.

I had learned well from the army, especially in Vietnam and in the Rangers, how to be both in my body and out of it, over it, above it, commanding it like an abusive father commands a cowed and obedient son. My boots were soaked from the snow patches, my socks wet, my feet macerated

Acquaintance with a Christian Soldier and Serial Rapist

and swelling in the boots. My shoulders screamed at the sharpening pinch of the ruck straps. My leg muscles quivered. My throat burned with panting in the icy air. And I passed more men.

At the end of the event, I stumbled into Camp Dawson, still half-running and on the verge of exhaustion, eighteen miles total, and reported in to two cadre members who recorded my arrival on a clipboard and instructed me to go to the barracks. When I went into the barracks, there were only two men, and it was obvious they'd arrived not long before. I was third out of almost sixty men, and I felt triumphant.

I sipped water and let the exhaustion overtake me. I showered in my wet clothes to wash them, threw them into a dryer, treated two blisters, and enjoyed watching more men arrive through the night. Our first physical test had passed. I was among the chosen. One candidate—that's what we were called, candidates—staggered in, having remembered me pass him in a moment of supreme exhaustion, and said good-naturedly, "Goff, you're a fucking animal." I waved it away, secretly satisfied. In the military, nothing matters so much as recognition and reputation. Securing them can be a career in itself.

At around three that morning, however, I had unfamiliar sensations in my thighs. When I tried to get up and walk to the bathroom, it was blindingly apparent that I had gone beyond pushing myself and had transgressed the real boundaries of my own quadriceps. I was not strained, I was injured. I went out the following day for collective training to prepare us for the rest of the course. We ended up walking almost seven more miles, and the pain in my quads, just above my knees, was so severe by the end of the day that climbing stairs made my face sweat.

Rather than make a big production of it, I quietly packed my gear in the dark barracks that night and painfully dragged it over to the cadre Charge of Quarters in the headquarters building. He moved me into a holding barracks out of sight of the rest of the candidates, had me eat in the mess hall after they were gone, and put me on a plane back to Tacoma two days later. I was on physically restricted duty for more than six weeks afterward with two torn quadriceps.

Outwardly, I was fatalistic. Inwardly, I felt like a failure. Somehow, I had not adequately prepared myself.

Later that year, I reenlisted with a promise to be reassigned to the Jungle Operations Training Center in Fort Sherman, Panama. My marriage was psychotic—and our daughter, Élan, was our hostage. Panama would be the geographic cure. (Yeah, right.) It didn't work, of course. In fact, things got a lot worse. My career was going very well, however, because I volunteered for twice the time that any other school cadre did to endure the harsh conditions of the jungle with the training battalions. In my professional life, the recognition and reputation were nothing but up. I was almost an icon at work. But at home there was an atmosphere of toxic history and recrimination that none of us knew how to escape. When the Delta recruiters came back in 1982, I had already made up my mind. I wanted to attend the next Selection and Assessment Course. I wanted to do it again.

My preparation this time became maniacal. I carried twice what anyone else did to the field, and I stayed in the field, sleeping in the jungle, four days a week. I reeked so badly when I came in that I had to undress on the porch so I wouldn't foul the house. On days I was in from the field, I would catch a ride to Gatun Locks on the canal, eight miles from home, and run back... not jog, *run*. Six-and-a-half-minute miles, my lungs trying to burst out of my chest as I sprinted the last half mile. I swam with the barracudas in laps around the lagoon. I pushed and jerked the weights in the un-air-conditioned gym, gulping down four and five gallons of water a day.

My fellow Jungle School cadre looked at me like I was an alien. The more insane my household became—where Élan ("Laney"), then just six, was forced to witness our madness—the more obsessed I became with outdoing everyone in everything. Not only did I run faster and farther, carry more weight, and stay longer in the field, but my classes were more animated and effective, my preparations more detailed, my evaluations more precise, my command of the doctrine and my tactical acumen more studiously developed than anyone else's. It looked like courage or will or endurance or commitment, but at bottom it was fear and obsession.

When I showed up at Camp Dawson again in March 1982, I had never been so single-mindedly committed to anything. All choices had been foreclosed, my mind made up. Regardless of the outcomes, I would not quit. If the quadriceps failed, if the back failed, if the feet failed, then they would fail. If I was carried off in an ambulance or fished out of a strip mine, so be it; but there would be no quitting. My mind would overcome my body. There was far more at stake than episodic escape from my marriage. This was Delta Force! The highest priority unit in the army, the masculine pinnacle from which you could look down at the other elites, down on the Ranger tabs and green berets, this was where you would be exposed to the darkest skills of power projection. This was the secret world into which one could disappear and reemerge with recognition and reputation that was carried on whispers and hints. And inside the man, there was a little boy who was scaling the treacherous wall of his own self-doubt.

For a month, the course progressed. The actual selection phase lasted for around two weeks, during which each person, alone, would navigate overland with map and compass from point to designated point, using no roads, never knowing how far he would go each day, or when he was at his last rendezvous point (RV). Some days we would go merely seven or eight miles, other days as many as twenty-five miles. Each night, we would be directed to a camp near our last RV; the following morning we would begin anew. Each day, there were fewer of us. Men fell behind the (unknown) time standards, or they became injured, or they quit. At night in the camps, the cadre forbade us to talk about the course, but we would quietly try to compare who'd been seen, who had disappeared, or, as we said, who had been "carried away by the Black Chinook."

We had all heard the rumor about the final movement: a forty-mile trek that finalized the physical portion of the course. One night, we were all collected together at one camp. There were only about twenty-five of us left of the original sixty. The cadre handed out new flashlight batteries, and checked our HF emergency transponders. Be prepared to move out at midnight, they said. Everyone pretended to sleep.

At five-minute intervals, beginning at midnight, we were given our RV coordinates, released, and told this time we could use the roads. I was released at around 1:30 a.m., with a rucksack that weighed fifty-five pounds before I added the water, all according to instruction. We were also hand-carrying simulated M-16s made of metal rods and hard rubber that weighed around eight pounds apiece.

At each RV, the rucksack was weighed. I had passed four RVs and covered about thirteen miles when I pulled into an RV not far from Bear Mountain. The scale showed my rucksack weighing fifty-four pounds—one pound light. I assured the cadre member that it had weighed out correctly, and at fifty-six to fifty-seven pounds at each previous RV. One of the two cadre instructed me to open the rucksack, then placed a large flat rock in it.

"Don't lose this," he said. It took my rucksack weight to sixty-four pounds. I was still angry miles later—not about the weight, but at believing I was the victim of bad scales, and about the delay—when I failed to compass check a turn in Bear Mountain Trail and followed a sign instead. Forty-five minutes later, I realized I had been ascending when I should have been descending. I checked my map. I had gone three miles the wrong way up Bear Mountain Trail.

Damn, damn, damn, damn, *damn*! Three miles out, three miles back, a six-mile detour that would lose me at least seventy-eight minutes! I jogged back down Bear Mountain Trail until I passed the point where I'd made the wrong turn, telling myself the whole time that I had just failed selection on a stupid rookie error after all this shit. But the prime directive kicked in. Don't rest. Don't think. Don't quit.

I continued downhill alongside a turbulent mountain stream that had drowned a candidate one year earlier, and I noticed that my feet began to ache—not the usual ruck march ache, but something that felt like the bones were trying to push through the flesh. Don't quit.

I hit an RV at a swinging bridge where I blathered manically about a wrong turn to the taciturn faces of the two cadre who looked ominously at their watches. I crossed a highway near Parsons, West Virginia, then tried to take a shortcut off-road through a mountain laurel thicket that chewed me up and spit me out onto an RV at the top of a mountain. Two cadre were listening to the radio, and Alberto Salazar had just finished the Boston Marathon in under two hours and nine minutes. While my rucksack was being weighed, I remarked on Salazar's time, and heard the first humor from anyone in the Delta Selection cadre.

Don Feeney, a cadre member, said, "He just did in two hours what it took you all day to do." Ha, ha. If that was the twenty-six-mile point, I had gone thirty-two because of my little six-mile detour on Bear Mountain. He had just told me, without realizing it, that I had fourteen miles to go.

At the top of a large flat mountain nearby, there was a huge shallow swamp sitting in the miles-wide dish, perhaps an ancient volcanic crater. Through the middle of that swamp, a swamp that was not designated a swamp on the maps we used, is a soggy path called Plantation Trail. To this day I don't know how long that trail is, but I remember that it soaked my feet with every step and transformed the sensation of the bones trying to stick through the flesh into a bright-hot pain that made every step like a hammer slamming into an anvil that vibrated from my feet all the way into my childhood memories.

In a kind of delirium, I slogged across Plantation Trail with an Emmylou Harris song in my head. It was about a millworker, and the lyrics went, "Me and my machine, for the rest of the morning, for the rest of the afternoon, for the rest of my life." In my head, the song became, "Me and my RV, for the rest of the morning, for the rest of the afternoon, for the rest of my life." By the time I stepped onto dry ground from Plantation Trail, I was singing my new song aloud to drown out the messages from my feet and back. "Don't quit" was no longer a brave self-challenge; it was just a monotonous noise like a cardiac monitor in an ICU.

Staggering down some gravel road at dusk, the pain in my feet had merged with the pain in my shoulders and back. I had *become* pain. My only purpose in life had become to chip-chip one silently screaming foot in front of the other. I almost walked through the next RV with my head down.

Captain James Knight and Sergeant Major Don Cheney stopped me and said I would be allowed to use my flashlight for the rest of the course,

Acquaintance with a Christian Soldier and Serial Rapist

and that they wanted to check the batteries. No, I told them. My flashlight was fine; but if I removed my rucksack long enough to get out the flashlight, I was afraid my muscles would freeze up and I wouldn't be able to shoulder it again. Cheney glowered angrily and ordered me to give up the rucksack. I was arguing with him when Knight smiled and shook my hand. I was then sure that I was having a mental breakdown. What was this stupid smile about?

"Congratulations," said Knight. "You just completed the endurance march." I had walked forty-six miles.

"Will you let me have that rucksack now?" asked Cheney. I hit the quick release and let the ruck drop to the ground. My shoulders surged with relief.

"Sergeant Goff," said Knight, "would you like a beer?"

"Sir," I said, "I'd suck your dick for a beer."

MY MENTOR

Fourteen of us made it. Terry Gilden, an old associate from 2nd Ranger Battalion, had finished with stress fractures in both shins. He *wanted* it. He would be killed in Beirut in two years.

Nancy Hartsock has said that the desire to overcome the body is closely related to a loathing of the body.[4] The ability to ignore feelings, to not feel, is closely associated with what Mab Segrest calls "the anesthesia of power."[5] What does this say, then, when we attend to a central truth of the Christian faith, that God became flesh, and in so doing sanctified flesh? Christian psychologist Richard Beck, in his book *Unclean*, says that the fleshy body reminds us of death.[6] We are humiliated by our flesh.

Hartsock:

> In pornography, feeling is conquered by projecting emotions onto the victim who is humiliated by bodily appetites, by reducing the women to the status of a feeling body, and in "snuff" films to a literal corpse.... Thus, sensuality and bodily concerns, [an] aspect of eros, take representative form. They become entangled with and point toward death . . . the death of feeling as

---

4. Hartsock, *Money, Sex, and Power*, 188.
5. Segrest, *Born to Belonging*, 162.
6. Beck, *Unclean*, 143–53.

well as the death of the body.... The denial of the body is in part due to the fact that it is a reminder of mortality and therefore of death.... Knowledge of the body is knowledge of death.[7]

Eros develops as the fusion of emotion and symbol that overwrites our activity in the world. That connection is sexualized early and deeply; and the sexuality of it is constructed as "unequal *complementarity*," in Jessica Benjamin's use—a unity of opposites at the expense of mutuality.[8] In a society where military practice becomes central to the stability of that society's hierarchies, that demutualized complementarity is armed and dangerous. *Bodies* matter.

At Delta, I finished what was called the Operator's Training Course (OTC) and was assigned to B Squadron, now well known to military aficionados who have read Eric Haney's book *Inside Delta Force: The Story of America's Elite Counterterrorist Unit.* Haney was eventually my team leader there. My first assignment was to Tommy Corbett's team of assaulters—people who specialized in close-quarter battle inside buildings, aircraft, trains, and buses. One member of the team was a man named Marshall Brown.

Marshall adopted me. He was small and wiry like me, and like me he had a great deal of nervous energy. We were very compatible that way. Marshall was one of the most dedicated—one might even say obsessive—"operators" in Delta. He received a lot of recognition, had a good reputation. A very fast medium-distance runner, he practiced his every skill religiously and was one of the finest pistol marksmen and "practical" shooters in the unit.[9] A former Golden Knight freefall parachutist, he had participated in the failed raid in Iran in 1979.

Marshall would take me to the McKellars Lodge pistol range at Ft. Bragg on the weekends with ammunition from the unit, where he would drill me mercilessly and coach me on the fine points of pistol shooting on the match-quality .45 caliber Colts that were standard issue in the unit. Between shooting on the job and Marshall's weekend sessions, it was not unusual for me to fire 2,500 rounds of pistol ammunition a week. Marshall was showing me his peculiar intensity, an intensity that was highly valued in the unit.

---

7. Hartsock, *Money, Sex, and Power*, 188.
8. Benjamin, *Bonds of Love*, 220.
9. Practical shooting is a sport now, organized around "reactive" targets and simulated combat scenarios.

Marshall was single and lived in a trailer. He had his own personal pistols at home. Marshall went to International Practical Shooting Confederation (IPSC) competitions every chance he got, and he practiced dry firing, quick draw, magazine change, and position changes when he was at home. He also practiced his lock-picking, his climbing, and his various surreptitious entry techniques. He read his OTC manual constantly to stay abreast of his tradecraft and explosives.

When I first came to the team, he took me aside and told me, "This unit is at war. Never forget that."

Marshall was a Texan. I didn't know it at the time, but he was raised by an emotionally abusive father who set standards for his behavior to which he could never measure up. His mother was also subject to the despotism of the father, and by some accounts she never intervened (in what, I've never learned). This is partly speculation, but it seems like the army was a place where Marshall could work hard to earn the accolades he'd never received from his father, a place where the rules were clearly spelled out and if you really understood them and didn't violate them, you wouldn't get into trouble. Those who know little about the military do not understand the value of this kind of bureaucratic consistency for anyone who has suffered from capricious domestic power—and that includes women who have suffered from capricious domestic power.

Marshall enjoyed a good practical joke, and would often place Vaseline under doorknobs, turn windshield washer nozzles to squirt people riding on the passenger side of his car, and reach into the shower when your eyes were closed against the cascading shampoo and switch off the hot water. He was playful despite his weird intensity. Practical jokes are often little displays of cruelty, but that's not what we saw. We all had a cruel streak. It's a man thing, substitution for and inoculation against direct affection.

Marshall was always seeking new training opportunities. One time he and I had asked to design a field-training exercise and were riding dirt bikes to look over our training area. We were buzzing over a fire trail, and I had fallen behind him, so I rolled back the accelerator to catch up. When I rounded a turn, Marshall was straddling the bike perpendicular to a deep erosion ditch. For me, it was too late. My bike dove into the ditch and the front wheel fell short of the far side, launching me over the handlebars to land face-first on the other side. The next thing I remember is looking up at an alarmed Marshall calling my name over and over again. My mouth was full of clay. My neck was throbbing. While I sat up and scooped the clay off my lower teeth, Marshall told me that I landed directly on my face, while the rest of me traveled over my head. He though my neck was broken and was sure I had been killed. When he had calmed down, he remarked that it was a good thing we did our strength training and that it had probably saved my life.

I have had problems ever since with periodic spasms in my neck.

When we were finished with the day or deployed, Delta would drink. Delta drank a lot. Our punishment for poor marksmanship or other training errors was to buy the squadron a case of beer. The other favored pastime was marital infidelity, most operators being married men with mortgages. Marshall was not married, didn't womanize (as far as anyone knew), and when he drank with us, it would be an hour or so at a time, nursing maybe half a beer, after which he would quietly retire and leave us to our debaucheries.

There were exceptions to this whoopee-tendency, of course: a couple of very religious men, including William "Jerry" Boykin, a retired general now who gained infamy with his very public 2003 pronouncement that Muslims don't worship a "real God."[10] Jerry unsuccessfully pressured most of the rest of us to attend right-wing prayer breakfasts. A few gave in.

Marshall was most concerned with his physical edge, and seemed frankly to be rather shy on the subject of sex. Sex was everywhere at Delta, though. And Delta Force in those days had the biggest collections of pornographic videos I have ever seen, hundreds of them.

One of the most odious tasks in the military is Charge of Quarters, or staff duty. That's a rotating duty where you stay awake all night by a telephone. At Delta it was no different, and every three or four weeks or so one could expect to be put on staff duty for twenty-four slow-moving hours of wakefulness. In Delta, however, because it was closed to the public, behind gates with surveillance cameras and buzzers, the men could keep themselves awake by watching these pornographic videos, one after another, all night long. The joke around the unit was that the wives were asking why their husbands were always so horny when they finished staff duty.

The wives, of course, had no idea that they were themselves then being used as masturbation aids while we thought about the films. I watched them, too, whacking off like a monkey in the privacy of the army's top-secret unit headquarters. I have no idea if Marshall watched the pornographic videos. Marshall was squeamish about the subject of sex in conversation.

At any rate, our teams were reorganized, and my contact with Marshall became less constant. Marshall had fallen under the thrall of a slightly loony Delta physician who was experimenting on us with performance-enhancing diets and quack cures. Marshall would show up at your table at lunch and point to the sugar jar, saying, "That's white poison."

---

10. Cooper, "General Casts War in Religious Terms," para. 4.

At some point in 1985, Marshall joined a church, one that promoted a kind of macho Christianity. He'd been hanging out more and more with Lance Fennick, an ex-Ranger who was a church member and who attended Boykin's killers-for-Christ prayer breakfasts. One day, Marshall and I got into an argument when I said, in whatever context it was, that it's better to tell your daughter about birth control than not. He launched into a tirade about how that was giving her permission to sin.

I *was* an irresponsible parent, but it had nothing to do with Marshall's outburst.

In 1987, Marshall got married and left the unit.

"I HAVE TO DO THIS"

We were psychologically tested during Selection. We were administered the aforementioned battery of diagnostic assistance tests, with names like Thematic Apperception Test, Minnesota Multiphasic Personality Inventory, and the like. The day after the "forty(-six) miler," we were queued up to have a conversation with the unit psychologist who had reviewed our answers as to whether we had black tarry stools, liked tall women, minded putting worms on hooks, or felt that people understood us. As we understood it, Delta did not want to train a member to become a proficient sniper, then learn one day that one of its members was sitting in a public tower picking off random "targets," as the ex-Marine Charles Whitman had on the campus of the University of Texas at Austin in 1966. At that point, I wasn't questioning what kind of psychologist works for a unit like Delta, or what might be wrong with him. We had a pleasant interview during which I intrigued him with my knowledge of Sartre and Camus; I manipulated him. He gave me a pass. This psychologist was eventually fired during his own sex scandal, as was a subsequent commander of Delta.

The psychological evaluation didn't screen out crooks, because almost the entire unit became embroiled in the fraud scheme that threw us into the crisis that contributed to my expulsion in December 1986. We were dummying up rent receipts all over the world, after the State Department paid our rent, and collecting the reimbursements from the army when we came home. It worked great until one guy had a crisis of conscience and exposed the whole unit. The officers probably knew, but didn't want to acknowledge that they knew.

Apparently, these psychological evaluations didn't screen out rapists either.

In 1988, an investigation began when two women were attacked in Raleigh, apparently by the same man, a stranger. He climbed in through their second-story windows, hooded and dressed in black. He ordered them to silence with a knife held at their throats, covered their faces, then raped them. During the rapes, he apologized, telling them that he didn't want to hurt them and that "I have to do this."[11]

On June 11, 1989, in Cranston, Rhode Island, Marshall Brown was taken into custody and charged with the rapes of two Rhode Island women. The rapist had used the same *modus operandi* as in the North Carolina attack. While in custody, Marshall was deferential to the police, calling them by their ranks and observing a scrupulous courtesy. Police described him as soft-spoken. He even spoke approvingly of the professionalism of the arrests and complimented one officer on his handcuffing technique. He had been arrested for prowling in Fayetteville, North Carolina, earlier that May, whereupon he had forfeited his bond for a dismissal of the charge.

Marshall went to work in jail, studying the patterns of the Federal Marshals who transported him to and from court, and making friends with an impressionable twenty-year-old inmate named Frederick Heon. Marshall stayed in shape in jail, using his exercise periods to run. On July 30, he was cuffed to another prisoner in the back of a Federal Marshal van and driven to Providence to attend his hearing. When the back door opened, Marshall, who had picked open his handcuffs, walked with the escorting marshal and his fellow inmate for a few steps, then sprang past the startled Federal Marshals and ran like an Olympic athlete up the street and out of sight. None of the Marshals was fit enough to pursue Marshall, and he got clean away. "Simplicity" is a Principle of War.

Heon was out on bail and had rented a car, per Marshall's instructions. He was waiting at an appointed rendezvous point and drove Marshall to the Connecticut state line. Heon then went to a church where he was told he'd find money, which wasn't there. Three days later, Marshall was caught in a stolen car and rearrested. Marshall told the police about Heon's assistance, and Heon was taken back to jail for a parole violation. Marshall had burglarized a house fifteen miles outside of Providence for food and credit cards, and was camping in a pine grove nearby. He stole the car in the same neighborhood. Now back in custody, he admitted to nine rapes in Rhode Island, Texas, Arizona, and North Carolina.

---

11. Information on what happened with Marshall Brown was gleaned from newspaper articles, in addition to my own interviews with members of Marshall's family, who consented to talk about his case on the condition that they remain unnamed. I also corroborated aspects of the case in conversations with former members of the unit.

Acquaintance with a Christian Soldier and Serial Rapist

Marshall had been attending the Navy version of a sergeants-major academy in Norfolk when he was caught the first time. His wife, Michelle, who was taking care of their young son, was stunned.

I can't pretend to understand Marshall Brown, even after spending many hours with him and going on one combat operation with him. I have heard the statement that rape is not sex, it is an exercise of power, but I don't buy it. Rape is violent power, but it is *sexual*. Rape is sex, *violent* sex. Sex is routinely practiced, portrayed, and understood as a form of aggression and power. This is recognized in our everyday speech, even while it is denied by many policy-makers and by liberal academics; and it is denied in the ridiculous statement that "rape is not about sex, but power."

One of Marshall's in-laws spoke with me many years later and said that Marshall told him that he felt he had to use his skills somehow or he'd begin to lose them. Marshall saw the rapes as a training opportunity, at some level, and therefore the women as training aids.

Marshall, even as he was violating these thoroughly terrified women with a knife held to their throats, and arousing himself to an orgasm in the process, was apologizing and explaining to them: "I have to do this." Marshall had jumped out of airplanes a thousand times, was a proficient technical climber, and had been in combat. It wasn't some generic rush he needed, but transgression.

Hartsock has said that "without the boundary to violate, the thrill of transgression would disappear."[12]

Marshall's criminality was not in spite of his religious conversion, his squeamishness about sex, or his uptight WASP upbringing in East Texas. It was an outcome of all those things, but also of a masculinity defined by a *culture* of rape, and a man who had made a career of *pursuing* that masculinity. The transgressions of his career—invasions of other countries, for example, or killing—were legally sanctioned. Why should it surprise anyone that he crossed the fuzzy line between legal and social sanction? He lived on that line. I lived on that line.

"We live in a culture that condones and celebrates rape," says bell hooks.[13] Catharine MacKinnon says that "male and female are created through the eroticization of dominance and submission. The man/woman difference and the dominance/submission dynamic define each other. This is the social

---

12. Hartsock, *Money, Sex, and Power*, 172.
13. hooks, "Seduced," 235.

meaning of sex and the distinctly feminist account of gender inequality."[14] Robert Jensen says, "Rape is illegal, but the sexual ethic that underlies rape is woven into the fabric of the culture."[15] A culture that defines the male as a sexual aggressor, the do-er, the taker, the subject, and the female as the done-to, the taken-from, and the object, is a culture that has defined the parameters of *rape* and normalized them. The only rape that is illegal is the kind that Marshall committed. The definition is narrow, and the bar of legal proof is very, very high. Rape has to be understood simultaneously as both social and personal, because social control is exercised through individuals, and with individual bodies.

"The defense of injustice in gender relations constantly appeals to difference," says R. W. Connell, "to a masculine/feminine opposition defining one place for female bodies and another place for male. But this is never 'difference' in a purely logical sense."[16] Difference is felt in the body. We have all been trained in what we find erotically arousing, for example, and that training is embedded in a culture where gender does not merely constitute difference. That difference is used to justify hierarchy, domination, and conquest. Eros is culturally trained. Masculinity as institution and ideology posits a subject-object duality between Man and the Other (be that other woman, lesser man, colony, or nature), and defines masculine practice as

---

14. MacKinnon, *Feminist Theory of State*, 113. A point of both concurrence and disagreement occurs here between the theses of this book and radical feminism as represented by MacKinnon and others. Radical feminists have opposed their constructivist sisters on the latter's claim that "sex" is totally constructed. Biological differences between men and women are stipulated by the radical feminists, sometimes almost to the point of a flirtation with biological determinism. This author's account provisionally agrees with the radicals—there very much is such a thing as biological sex, and radically constructivist suggestions to the contrary can be almost perverse in their denial that *Homo sapiens* are mammals that reproduce sexually—requiring two sexes. Moreover, radical feminists will often stipulate that these biological differences translate—albeit through cultural filters—into actual differences in propensities for behavior. The argument of radical feminists is that domination and dependency ascribed to difference is not inevitable (a point on which I agree), which leads radical feminists to see being a woman as a political category. Again, I don't disagree; but I do disagree with the tendency in this feminist tradition to make women as political subjects a totalizing category. Finally, as we will cover in subsequent chapters, I find talk about "rights" and "equality" to be too problematic and contradictory to use them the way the radicals do, i.e., "women's equality." The answer to violence and domination are not found in liberal philosophy's rights-talk and equality-talk, even though I am opposed to the violence and domination that this kind of talk aims ineffectively to undo. I agree with MacKinnon that "sex," in the social sense she is using the term, is constructed around the eroticization of male domination and female degradation.

15. Jensen, "Rape Is Normal," para. 11.

16. Connell, *Masculinities*, 231.

conquest, often even of one's own body—like my own experience with Delta selection and a host of other military "pain-schools."

In the military, the exercise of professional sadomasochism in preparation for the violence of warfare is often sexualized in our vernacular and disguised as humor. Allusions to pseudo-Victorian naughtiness are common. When I told a captain I would fellate him for a beer, I was playing at being a whore—a transgression that was allowed and understood as *just play* because I had already, by virtue of my membership in the fraternity of blood called special operations, and by walking forty-six miles, displayed my masculine *bona fides*. Without the imaginary female whore or the imaginary homosexual, *and my proof of masculinity*, my humorous assent to a beer would not have been properly understood.

"There is a surprising degree of consensus that hostility and domination, as opposed to intimacy and physical pleasure, are central to sexual excitement," writes Nancy Hartsock.[17]

Most pornography conventions that are marketed to males involve fetishization of body parts or types, one form of objectification, and the humiliation and degradation of the objectified female by her own purported (and performed) insatiability, her enslavement to desire (simulated for male audiences). Hostility, expressed as the desire to see the female-other degraded and humiliated, is eroticized. It is about *power*, yes, but it is also emphatically about *sex*.

Those who dealt with Marshall from the time he was arrested remarked how polite he was throughout the whole process, how observant and supportive of social conventions. Implicit in these remarks was the idea that rape—and in this case, serial rape—is *aberrant* in this society. But rape is not seen as fundamentally aberrant in this society, it is seen as *excess*, as crossing a line, and at times as *provoked* excess (as in warfare). Hidden within the open public discourse about rape are exclusively male assumptions, and in this space rape is routinely portrayed as understandable and even at times desirable. Many people see prison rape, for example, as an appropriate and just form of extrajudicial punishment ("He had it coming").

Socially, rape serves as an extrajudicial instrument of social control. bell hooks says that "rape of women by men is a ritual that daily perpetuates and maintains sexist oppression and exploitation."[18] And in the same way, the exercise of male prerogative in rape and the exercise of military prerogative in killing carries with it a transgressive thrill that is socially sanctioned (against designated enemies, against Abu Ghraib prisoners, against "fallen"

---

17. Hartsock, *Money, Sex, and Power*, 172.
18. hooks, *Outlaw Culture*, 109.

women, against convicts who "have it coming"). This is the fusion of the subjective experience of desire and violence with the socially instrumental and eroticized violence of rape.

Inga Muscio, in describing the traumatic and illuminating discovery that her mother was raped at the age of nine, concludes that "rape . . . viewed merely as a crime . . . is the fundamental, primal, most destructive way to seize and maintain control in a patriarchal society"[19]—little realizing as she wrote, I'd wager, that a military principle of strategy against an enemy uses the same language: "Seize and maintain the initiative." A friend of mine wrote me once,

> The language reveals this at every turn. Men—in the "man talk" they speak in all male environments and increasingly in general discourse, even when women or children are present—often use metaphors of rape (male-male rape, for example) to indicate aggression, anger, submission, domination. Just bend over . . . we really took it in the shorts that time . . . check out the Web site today, Juan Cole just ripped Goldstein a new ass . . . I've got a hard-on for that SOB . . . he just rolled over for it . . . he thinks I'm his bitch . . . did you hear him reaming that guy out . . . and of course, the routine uses of "to fuck" as in "fuck you," "we are so fucked," "that's fucked," plus the pejoratives applied to the "submissive/receptive" role, as in . . . he's such a scumbag (recipient for sperm) . . . that sucks . . . what a cocksucker . . . and so on. The very texture of the vernacular expresses everything any sociologist could want to know about the association of sex and aggression, sex and ranking, etc.—and then every mawkish pop song rambles on about (hetero)sex being exactly equal to and definitive of Love, tra la la. It's a wonder we don't drop in our tracks from terminal cognitive dissonance.[20]

Marshall did not appear to be abnormal because he was not *ab*-normal. He was, if anything, *hyper*-normal, as a male, going above and beyond the call of duty (expected of commandos) to preserve social stability. MacKinnon says that the implication that rape is psychopathological serves as a smokescreen by validating the notion that rape is not about sex—because if it is about sex, then "sexuality" itself comes under review as a construction of power.[21] This is exactly why both MacKinnon and her late colleague, Andrea Dworkin, were vilified by both the right and the left. People don't want to go there. "Rape becomes something a *rapist* does, as if he were a separate

19. Muscio, *Cunt*, 146.
20. E-mail message from De Clarke, my editor for *Sex & War*.
21. MacKinnon, *Toward a Feminist Theory of the State*.

species. But no personality disorder distinguishes most rapists from *normal* men," says MacKinnon.²²

Marshall Brown served in a profession with a constant subtext of coercion, and in a field within that profession (Delta Force/Special Operations) where we were expected to work outside the rules, behind the scenes, in the shadows, employing a host of very specialized skills, to "preserve a [white male hetero-normative] way of life." The expectation of us was that we would go "above and beyond the call of duty," or we wouldn't have suffered the kind of extreme physical trials we accepted in selection just to qualify for a chance to be in the unit. And for that, we were, in the traditional military mind, *entitled*.

His outrage at my suggestion that my daughter might be given information about birth control, his affinity for a killer-Christian Americanism, his commitment to take profound risks on behalf of maintaining a social order, are all perfectly consistent with the manner in which he carried out these rapes. With the same *sangfroid* that accompanied his acceptance of the collateral damage that would have resulted had the 1979 Iranian rescue mission succeeded,²³ Marshall Brown accepted the psychological wreckage that he left scattered around each of his rape victims.

"Rape," writes Muscio, "makes you wonder if there's a safe place."²⁴ And that's the point, isn't it? If you don't want to be raped by a man, you need the protection of a man. It's the psychosexual protection racket—and Marshall was an enforcer.

Maria Mies writes about feminist anti-rape campaigns in Bombay and Delhi, where activists were astonished to discover that as women came to the cities from the countryside, where feminist activists assumed rape was a backward feudal vestige, like dowry murders, the frequency of rape exploded. The fastest-growing group of perpetrators was the police. These feminists were slow to associate the increasing number of rapes with the increasing independence and political agency of women.²⁵ Rape punishes women who get out of their places. This is often displayed as a "playful" theme in pornography.

Rape has been massively expanded in modernity with its gender destabilizations. Ivan Illich, repeating Mies's assertion that modern rape has a particular character that responds to gender destabilizations, writes, "American women now fear . . . rape as the supreme physical expression of

---

22. Ibid., 145.

23. Planners conceded that hundreds and perhaps thousands of Iranian civilians would have been killed had the rescue mission reached Tehran.

24. Muscio, *Cunt*, 142.

25. Mies, *Patriarchy and Accumulation*, 153.

modern sexism."[26] This phenomenon need not be a conscious strategy by the actual perpetrators. It *fits* within our social imaginary.

When Marshall Brown became a serial rapist in 1988 (we think), the institution with which he identified absolutely, the military, was undergoing a series of significant transformations with regard to women. In 1973, when I was taking my first break in service, women constituted 1.6 percent of the United States armed forces. When Marshall and I participated in the invasion of Grenada in 1983, the ensuing occupation included 170 Army women. In 1987, a woman graduated first in her class from the Naval Academy. By 1989, when Marshall was first arrested—and three years after Lissa Young graduated from West Point as the first female Deputy Commander of the Corps of Cadets—the percentage of women in the armed forces had leapt to 10.8 percent. Marshall, with his East Texas upbringing, could hardly have missed this, or the fact that 30 percent of these women were African American. By the time Marshall was arrested, 59 percent of the army's occupational *specialties* were open to women (that's not the same as 59 percent of the individual positions in the armed forces). Women were being rated as test pilots. Lissa Young, whom I knew from my time as a teacher at West Point, was flying Chinook helicopters—a radical incursion into the male domain.

With this new influx of military women came another dynamic: fraternization, as the military calls it. Men and women in the military were interacting socially, dating, having sex, and getting married. The male-male and female-female liaisons remained as much as possible under the official radar. But among these "heterosexual" pairings, there were significantly higher numbers of interracial relationships than in the civilian sector. The most frequent "new" combination among those *in uniform* was black male/white female. Marshall was sure to notice that, too. In fact, it was a constant subject of conversation among white male troops, many of whom expressed outrage at this black male infiltration and white female "betrayal." Resentment was directed at the black men, but with lynching not an option, that same fierce, sullen rage was redirected at the white women, who were referred to as "zebra-women" and "mudsharks."

When Kimberle Crenshaw wrote "Demarginalizing the Intersection of Race and Sex,"[27] she noted that a "singular focus on rape as a manifestation of male power over female sexuality tends to eclipse the use of rape as a weapon of racial terror," pointing to black women's virtually "unprotected" status. In the same essay describing the mixture of white and male social

---

26. Illich, *Gender*, 31.
27. Crenshaw, "Demarginalizing," 158–59.

power, she shows how *white men* attempt "to regulate the sexuality of white women."²⁸

White-nationalist masculinity is profoundly threatened by a perceived inability to control the "sexuality" of white women, creating what Connell calls "sexual vertigo."²⁹ This recombinant mixture of sexual and racial construction that obliges white men to both "control" and "protect white womanhood" is ignited as violence against both women and black men. The bogeyman of the potent black satyr *raping* the white woman has accompanied virtually every call in the United States for anti-black pogroms. It is hardly coincidental that assertions of black social agency have been met with expanded outbreaks of racial terror, or that rape was projected onto black men by white men; and it is likewise not a coincidence that police rapes increased in Bombay when women began organizing politically.

Connell says that "violence is part of a system of domination, but is at the same time a measure of its imperfection. A thoroughly legitimate hierarchy would have less need to intimidate. The scale of contemporary violence points to crisis tendencies in the modern gender order."³⁰

When Marshall Brown began his career as a serial rapist, there were myriad influences on his "target selection." Marshall went through Special Forces training at Camp Mackall, where a sign read, "Rule #1: There are no rules. Rule #2: Obey the first rule." Marshall was the commando—root word *command*—who follows orders without question within established hierarchies. He was committed in his role as the colonizer's paladin, with its admixture of violent conquest and "civilization" to be imposed outside those disciplinary restraints. He policed boundaries, and he also, using his status as one who belonged *inside* the defensive male perimeter, transgressed them.

I knew Marshall Brown. He could not be reduced to some other species called *rapist* and slid into the appropriate drawer. Among other things, he was an exceptional soldier.

---

28. Ibid., 160.
29. Connell, *Masculinities*, 84.
30. Ibid.

3

Forest Troop

Do you not realize that Eve is you? The curse God pronounced on your sex weighs still on the world. Guilty, you must bear its hardships. You are the devil's gateway, you desecrated that fatal tree, you first betrayed the law of God, you who softened up with your cajoling words the man against whom the devil could not prevail by force. The image of God, the man Adam, you broke him, it was child's play to you. You deserved death, and it was the son of God who had to die!

—Tertullian (160–225)[1]

If I speak in the tongues of men and of angels, but have not love, I am only a resounding gong or a clanging cymbal. If I have the gift of prophecy and can fathom all mysteries and all knowledge, and if I have a faith that can move mountains but have not love, I am nothing.

—1 Corinthians 13:1–2

In 2004, the peer-reviewed journal *PLOS Biology* published an article titled "Emergence of Peaceful Culture in Baboons," documenting the fieldwork of neurologist Robert Sapolsky and neuropsychologist Lisa Share. Sapolsky

---

1. Quoted in Tarico, "Christian Leaders," para. 4.

remarked that while he studied baboons as a young researcher in Kenya—in his case, using baboons to study the physiological effects of stress—he found the animals to be highly disagreeable. The dominant males in "Forest Troop," Sapolsky's study group, brutalized smaller males and females alike, taking the best of everything and impulsively and unpredictably attacking or harassing other members of the troop. It was an ideal environment to research stress responses, because the big baboons passed the abuse they suffered from bigger baboons down to smaller baboons. The entire troop was in a chronically bad mood from recycled male abuse.

But then a catastrophe befell Forest Troop and ended Sapolsky and Share's stress research. The baboons were scavenging food from a tourist facility that was infected with bovine tuberculosis, and the disease wiped out most of the males in the troop. Males died because Forest Troop was run by dominant males. A feeding order was established in which females and juveniles were not permitted to feed until the adult males had had their fill. The contaminated food was meat, coveted by baboons, and so the adult males, dominant males first, appropriated all the meat for themselves and unintentionally saved many of their female and juvenile counterparts.

The troop had a culture of bullying. Weaker baboons were bullied by the more dominant ones, and they in turn dished it out to those baboons who were weaker than they. In a sense, this was *mimetic* violence, violence learned by emulation.

In 1993, Sapolsky and Share returned to Kenya and rejoined Forest Troop. What they found was that, while the ratio of female to male was more than two to one respectively just after the dominant-male die-off, the ratio had returned to approximately half and half. That was no particular surprise. Pubescent male baboons migrate into new troops. The surprise was how pacific the troop remained, long after the loss of the former dominant males. The troop was highly cooperative and generally nonaggressive, more so than another troop they observed during this period, a kind of control group that hadn't undergone the mass death of males. Sapolsky's characterization of baboons as unpleasant creatures was premature. It wasn't baboons *per se*. The Forest Troop had a *culture* that through violence and emulation of violence reproduced a kind of culture-wide hatefulness.

The implications of this research for those who still dichotomize nature and nurture is perhaps the first issue that comes to mind with this story. Our genetic cousins in Kenya seem to have shown us that even other primates share two characteristics with human beings: their individual formation was strongly influenced by culture, and there had been a strong correspondence between violence and the category *male*.

We can name this in a scientific study of baboons without much controversy. However, we don't seem to notice it when we talk about human beings in human societies. When there is a saturation news story about a mass shooting, for example, we obsessively go over racial statistics and access to guns and speculate whether or not the shooter was a loner or an outcast, whether music or video games drove him mad. We seldom take much note of the fact that mass shooters are overwhelmingly male. I suspect that if there were suddenly a rash of mass shootings by women, then gender would become *the* story. We have come to accept the correspondence between violence and maleness as normative and therefore unremarkable. Female mass shooters would be non-normative, therefore remarkable.

Forest Troop's is a redemptive tale because it shows that with changes in the culture, the members of a society can more readily and peacefully flourish. We humans are, as baboons are to a far lesser degree, biologically determined *not to be biologically determined*.[2] Our biological selves cannot be understood apart from culture. We *can* change; but change also has to happen in the culture that incorporates and forms us. Hopefully, it doesn't always happen with the kind of rough justice that was visited on the Forest Troop males.

What does this story of baboons say to Christians?

I submit that the Gospels say the same thing—that we can be redeemed from violence, in a sense more appropriate to human beings, with our vastly greater creative capacity for good or ill. The human analog of Forest Troop's violent male authoritarianism was what Jesus of Nazareth set himself against in word and deed. Jesus heralded new life, but he cast off domination . . . even unto death on a cross.

It may be that Forest Troop, over time, reverted to its authoritarian bullying. Human beings seem to revert from relatively pacific associations to hardness of heart. In two centuries, leaders in the Christian church went from Jesus's directive to love without ceasing and Paul's warning to the Corinthians about love (quoted above) to Tertullian's venomous attack on womankind (likewise quoted above).

2. This paradoxical-sounding statement is not really a paradox. Human anatomy and physiology are obviously biological; but human beings are "built" in such a way that most of their behavior is learned. We are "built" to learn. What we learn varies based on differences in our environments. Biological determinism is most commonly associated with schools of thought that claim our *actions* are programmed by biology in the way instinctual behavior is in other animals. The diversity of human behaviors as well as research on human learning has proven that environmental factors are far more determinative of human decisions and actions than biology. See chapter 10, on "mimesis."

Instead of reversion from peace to violence, and from love to hate, Christ showed us that we can be redeemed. We live in a redeemed world. Christ did not say, "It will eventually be accomplished." He said, "It is accomplished." What is left to us is acceptance of that redemption. We need not be Forest Troop. We can be that community that calls itself "the body of Christ," witnesses to the redemption that was accomplished in cross and resurrection.

4

Body Counts

The Almighty exists and acts and speaks here in the form of One who is weak and impotent, the eternal as One who is temporal and perishing, the Most High in the deepest humility. The Holy One stands in the place and under the accusation of a sinner with other sinners. The glorious One is covered with shame. The One who lives forever has fallen prey to death. The Creator is subjected to and overcome by the onslaught of that which is not. In short, the Lord is a servant, a slave. And it is not accidental. It could not be otherwise.

—Karl Barth, *Church Dogmatics* IV.1.59

Fierce is the dragon and cunning the asp; but women have the malice of both.

—St. Gregory of Nazianzus (329–89)[1]

Lately we see the rise, not for the first time, of a tendency I call the macho-church—churches led and peopled by men who are frantic about what they consider a "crisis of masculinity" in Christianity. In the macho-church, the character of King David is given a special place; then Jesus is grafted onto David the warrior in order to preserve a masculinity that is rightly associated with David and mistakenly associated with Jesus. This is nothing new.

---

1. Quoted in Bufe, *Heretic's Handbook*, 125.

Jesus's own disciples mistakenly expected him to become a Davidic warrior figure; and that was why the cross was such a scandal.

The term *masculinity* (and *masculinities*) is going to reoccur in this book. Before we continue, then, we need a shared understanding of the term, and why I use the singular and the plural. I am appropriating the term, along with its complement, *femininity* (and *femininities*), from the academic field of "gender studies." Understandings of masculinity and femininity differ from time to time and place to place.

If I say, "He is very masculine," you and I know who *he* is and we share some notion of what "masculine" means. It is a concrete statement about an actual person. When we add the "-ity" suffix to make "masculinity," we abstract a *general* idea about the meaning of masculine from its concrete instantiations. We emancipate the phenomenon from actual space-time. There is an advantage to this, and a danger.

The advantage is that we can criticize the idea apart from its specific context. The danger is confusing these abstractions with embodied reality. "Poverty," for example, is a useful notion in discourse about economic conditions, but superimposed on an actual person who is poor in a particular way, it can become a distortion that leads us to treat actual persons as categories like "clients" or "problems" or "resources."

The objective of studying masculinity and femininity for our purposes is to de-naturalize them. "Naturalization" treats the existing order of things as if it were decreed by nature. We are familiar with the conventional wisdom that "men are *naturally* more aggressive than women." This appeal to "the natural" attempts to place relations of power beyond critical analysis. "It's just nature, so there's nothing we can do about it" implies something akin to natural *law*.

The point of cataloguing various types of masculinity is to make it possible to pull specific kinds of masculinity and specific aspects of various masculinities into critical range. A *natural law*—the Second Law of Thermodynamics, for example—does *not* operate differently in either time or place. However, what is masculine in twenty-first-century Houston is different from what was masculine in, say, third-century rural Persia. "Nature" cannot explain this difference.

Masculinity implies *gender*. The binary of masculine-feminine is constitutive of gender, which is more than *biological* sexual differentiations. Gender, as we will use it here, is a *social* system that divides social activities between the two biologically normative sexes.[2] Social gender, with which we are concerned here, and which exists in all known societies without exception, marks the complementary difference between the tools, clothing, practices, spaces, preoccupations, and even language that are typically associated with men and women. Certain medieval European women had a different kind of scythe than their men, for example, with which to do different forms of work, but this *difference* did not automatically confer *hierarchy* or relative value, even though it did function complementarily as a division of labor. Both men and women were doing work essential to their community's subsistence, for which both received recognition and esteem. Gender in the social sense, however, most often *does* combine hierarchy with complementarity, which is where this book will place a special emphasis, because men are overwhelmingly on the top of that hierarchy and women on the bottom. Men use that power, often violently, to maintain the hierarchy across generations.

The tools, clothing, practices, spaces, preoccupations, and language of *men* constitute a *masculine sphere* in a given society. *Masculinity* is where the social and psychological are merged as an *episteme*—a way of knowing that is shared within a culture.[3] A masculinity is both an archetype and an attitude.[4] Men adopt what they feel is the appropriate attitude to live into an archetype. Not every man can live into the prevailing masculine archetypes, so he sometimes does so vicariously and symbolically. Think here

---

2. This does not mean that there are not exceptions to being a reproductively functional biological male or female—for example, a person who is hermaphroditic, or a male or female who is incapable, for one reason or another, of biological reproduction. It means that the majority of people fall into one biological category, male or female, and that these categories are *recognized* as not just reproductively normative but as the basis for a binary social system that differentiates men and women socially. Sexual dysphoria, which is sometimes called transexuality, on the other hand, is a psychological diagnosis for people who might be otherwise reproductively "normal." This is a subject that combines medical diagnostic categories and social (gender) norms. These issues are important and complicated, but outside the scope of this particular discussion.

3. This is a term we will use with some frequency throughout the rest of the book. Its meaning is borrowed from French philosopher Michel Foucault. It does not mean knowledge as a direct reflection of reality—for example, "There is a tree outside my window and I *know* that tree is there"—but a set of shared cultural assumptions that are so frankly accepted that their bases are largely unquestioned, giving them the appearance of the kind of direct knowledge evident in the example of the tree. When we say an *episteme* is a "way of knowing," we are not validating that way of knowing as either unchanging or universal.

4. We will also use the term *archetype* frequently in this book. This is not the archetype associated with Jungian psychology, but with literature and other forms of storytelling. An archetype, for our purposes, is a recognizable kind of character in recurring story contexts.

about modern American football. Not every American male can be an NFL player, but a man can participate in the *ideal* as a fan, thereby valorizing the archetype. That football culture then leads many men to use football as an analogy for work, life, relationships, politics, war, etc.

Masculine ideals differ among different peoples in different times, and so one particular masculine ideal cannot tell us everything about actual men in every time and place. It does, however, give us an insight into the dominant men in that very particular culture and time. The works of Homer, for example, give us some insight into how an ideal masculinity was constructed for men of the dominant class in Greece in the eighth century BC.

Our set of *socially shared certainties*, or *epistemes*—like those of every epoch and place—structure the world to make it apprehensible. Ways of knowing give us a sense of order and security. Notions like masculinity are enmeshed within a larger worldview, and any disruption of one notion—like masculinity—has the potential to disrupt the entire *episteme*, because the various facets of any *episteme* are interlocking or mutually defined. Disruption of one facet contributes to a sense of insecurity, which can lead to fear, which can lead to anger and reaction or, conversely, to a revised *episteme*, a revision in the set of socially shared certainties.

If disruptions in masculinity can disrupt the rest of an *episteme*, then likewise, any disruption elsewhere in the *episteme* might create a crisis of masculinity. Revolutions are disruptions of the status quo, and they are always characterized to some degree by an *epistemic crisis*—a crisis of *doubt* about socially shared certainties, therefore a crisis characterized by uncertainty and fear. The theological conviction undergirding this entire book is that the life, death, and resurrection of Jesus of Nazareth is the decisive revolution of all time—God's revolution—which inaugurated a political life of a new sort called the kingdom of heaven. This revolution engendered the *epistemic crisis* that we are still living through, because it puts the *episteme* of "the world" in doubt.

In focusing on the relationship between church, war, masculinity, and the status of women in the church, we have to look at what this new life means for masculinity, particularly as it is inflected by the practice of war, and then at how these constructions of masculinity are inflected (and inflicted) on women. Our understanding of men's actions taken *against* women will be limited to the extent that our understanding of masculinity is limited.

I have just denied that masculinities are transhistorical, changeless across time. At the risk of sounding contradictory, I must insist that there *is* one transhistorical phenomenon that is exclusively associated with masculinity, with men, and that is war. Not all war is alike, and it can be shown that differences in the practice of war result in differences in masculinity influenced by war. Yet there are transhistorical constants in the practice of war: violence, hierarchy, compartmentalization, dehumanization, and boundary enforcement. These then translate into transhistorical aspects of masculinity in societies that practice war.

I turn now to the lives of two Jews who are central figures in our biblical narrative: David and Jesus. How is masculinity constructed for David by his biographers, and how different are Jesus's teachings and example from that same construction? The point of this comparison is to understand the implications of Jesus's teachings and life for how members of the church think and conduct ourselves with regard to war and gender. Here I have no choice but to take a basic theological position that is likely to be controversial.

Here is my position.

Jesus's teachings and example were meant for real people, for us, and they were not meant to be foreclosed by pragmatism. Jesus's ethic of self-giving, neighbor-love, enemy-love, and sacrificial service are not anachronisms that apply only to first-century Palestine. Nothing in Jesus's teachings or example suggests that Christians must take up the "responsibilities" of political power, compromise self-giving, turn neighbor-love into clientelism, set aside enemy-love in defense of nation, or eschew sacrificial service in the name of political pragmatism.

Jesus's teachings and example do have *actual* social significance for us, now, and cannot be launched into an extraterrestrial orbit and deferred until we are all conveniently dead.

The Gospels provide us with a way of being that transcends time and place understood as "the way of the cross."

Works and faith are inseparable.

The world is redeemed in Christ, and not by progress, technology, democracy, political revolution, money, education, or any other idol.

These assertions form the basis of my own conviction, as a layman, that the good news of the Gospels is that we have moved beyond violence. Violence and domination characterize a world in rebellion. Yet we can embody the kingdom of heaven as the body of Christ—the peaceable kingdom—here and now, as testimony to the redemptive lordship of Christ to a broken world.

That is where I start. So now let's look at David.

If masculinity changes with circumstances, then why does David's masculinity have anything to do with Jesus's person, though centuries separate them, and what does David have to do with us today? My answer is, again, that there are elements of masculinity that are transhistorical because there are elements of war that are transhistorical.

Old Testament scholar David J. A. Clines, in chapter 10 of his *Interested Parties: The Ideology of Writers and Readers of the Hebrew Bible*, provides an outline of Davidic masculinity.[5] Clines's examination of Davidic masculinity will not appear particularly strange to us, because much of what he describes to us about Davidic masculinity is still recognizable today. We live in a warlike society, just as David did, and we also shower military leaders with accolades for their military virtues, real or imagined.

Clines begins with five basic rules for being masculine *in the modern West.*[6]

First, *do not be like a woman.* Second, *be successful.* While the meaning of success has changed, over time, from accomplishments of various kinds to the making of money, it relates in every case to "winning." Be a winner. Third, *be aggressive.* This can be conflated with, and even overlap with, courage, but it also and primarily has something to do with demeanor. Get in some faces. Don't back down. Fourth, *be sexual.* By that Clines means displaying a constant interest in sex that suggests you are always "up" and ready for it. It also generally suggests the objectification of women, understood as a primal male drive. Finally, *be self-reliant.* Real men don't *need* other people.

With these points of reference, we can readily see them in ourselves. Clines establishes the coordinates for understanding what he calls a "hegemonic masculinity." The noun *hegemony* and the modifier *hegemonic* were used by the Italian social theorist Antonio Gramsci in the 1930s. It means the way power is exercised in stable societies prior to violence or the threat of violence. It refers to the general population's precritical acceptance of norms established by the dominant class in society, a class that also controls the signifiers and meanings that constitute knowledge and culture. When most people have accepted the point of view of the dominant class—in

---

5. Clines, *Interested Parties*, 212–43.
6. Ibid.

Gramsci's case, he was referring to the business class—then they have accepted a version of reality that creates conformity without force. *Hegemonic masculinity*, then, is a widely accepted version of masculinity that conforms to the beliefs or the needs of a dominant fraction within a society and that is supportive of the structures of that society.[7]

The story of David was not written simply as an historical chronicle, says Clines, but as the presentation of a hegemonic masculine archetype—an idealized version of how masculinity was actually constructed during, and for some time after, David's life.

The key characteristic of David was that he was a fighter, a military leader. David is described as "a mighty man of valor" (1 Sam 16:14). He fights wars, a lot of wars; David fights Philistines, Amalekites, Moabites, Arameans, Syrians, and Edomites, totaling up a body count of around 140,000 people, killing fourteen by his own hand.[8]

A second character trait of the Davidic man is persuasive speech. He is described as a man who is skillful at direct persuasion, "intelligent of speech" (1 Sam 16:18). David uses words skillfully as instruments of control.

David is frequently called beautiful. Physical beauty, in David's case, and in the case of several other Hebrew luminaries, was not understood as a lucky accident, but as a sign of God's favor, and therefore worthy of praise.

David bonds with men. David does not have women friends. He has wives and concubines who are essentially invisible, except when they figure into particular episodes in which he has moral failures—like rape and conspiracy to murder (2 Sam 11). Some of his friendships are genuinely affective and some are coldly instrumental, but when it comes to the kind of mutual recognition we today assume between friends or colleagues, David did not get friendly or collegial with women.

Reading about David and Jonathan today, we might be tempted to call the descriptions of their love homoerotic, but it was unlikely that this is what the author(s) meant in their own time. Real men loved real men, and they *had sex* with women. When David describes his friendship with Jonathan, he says it is better than anything a man can experience with a woman.[9] Clines describes David as "a womanless man." Obviously, David *had* women, in the sense of owning them.

---

7. Tosh, "Hegemonic Masculinity," 41–59.
8. Clines, *Interested Parties*, 215.
9. Ibid., 223.

"But," writes Clines, "it is a striking feature of the David story that the males are so casual about women, and that women are so marginal to the lives of the protagonists."[10]

David, in fact, is proud to have kept himself "clean" of women, meaning presumably from the context that he is not influenced in his decisions by them. He has lapses due to his lust for Bathsheba. By today's standards, he certainly would be accused of raping Bathsheba, even if his male contemporaries would have understood the act as one of royal prerogative. And he is rebuked by Nathan, the prophetic challenger to David's exercise of power, when David sends Bathsheba's husband, Uriah, to his certain death in order to have Bathsheba for his own.

The reason neither David nor his male contemporaries ever felt compelled to define their masculinity *against* women, as Clines does in his account of modern masculinity, and the reason there would be no modern squeamishness about calling a man beautiful, was precisely that men's and women's gendered realms were so thoroughly separate. Men's absolute domination of and separation from women was unquestioned. Women were not subjects in the sense of having any real agency, unless they were "up to no good" as social disruptors, and so there was no threat of a man being confused with a woman. Men's sphere did not overlap with women's, and men and women were certainly not structurally competitive with one another, as they are today, in an economy of monetized scarcity.[11]

Conflict was restricted to the sphere of men. When Amnon rapes Tamar, it is Absalom, her brother, who is the offended one. After Tamar leaves the stage in shame, we never hear from her again, and conflict between David and Absalom carries the story forward when Absolom gets his vengeance by killing Amnon (2 Sam 13:23–29).

Clines follows his comparison of modern and Davidic masculinities with an interesting account of modern male scholarship on the subject of David. There has been a good deal of censorship and misrepresentation of aspects of Davidic masculinity that runs counter to modern sensibilities. A David who is beautiful is rewritten as having superior moral quality, and the leader of the people who would produce the Prince of Peace has his

---

10. Ibid., 225.

11. Monetized scarcity will be a recurrent point in the book. Briefly, this term refers to the transformation of society from subsistence (very local production and consumption) and partial subsistence—in which people had little to no need for money—to monetization, with production and consumption being separated by more space and greater specialization. The latter creates an ever more general dependence on money for survival, whereupon the finite amount of money, combined with greater accumulation by some against others, sets up competition between people for disbursements of this scarce medium (money).

embarrassing body count summarized as "being a bold leader."[12] It is as if modern male scholars (and modern males) want to find ways to approve of David to underwrite their own versions of masculinity. In the hands of many modern male scholars, Clines shows, the complex and sanguinary story of David as understood by early Hebrews has been sanitized and reworked.[13]

This reworking was on the agenda of a movement called "muscular Christianity" that deployed the sanitized David as its central icon.[14] Muscular Christianity was conceived in the mid-nineteenth century by Charles Kingsley and Thomas Hughes, who had become alarmed, during a period of gender destabilization, that the Church of England was threatened with "effeminacy."[15] The image of Jesus was too gentle, and the overrepresentation of women in the sanctuaries was having a "feminizing effect" on the clergy and the music, thus "endangering" the men.[16]

But when we look at Jesus in the Gospels, he radically supplants the form of David's kingship. He refuses to fight and tells his followers to "turn the other cheek" when they are assaulted. He never kills anyone. In his greatest vexation he turns over tables and stampedes livestock. His speeches are

---

12. Clines, *Interested Parties*, 231–33.

13. Clines summarizes his conclusions about why this sanitization takes place: "What I should like to suggest is that what male scholars (most who have written on the David story are males, not surprisingly) are responding to in the character of David is his masculinity, of which they themselves approve or to which they themselves are attracted. They view his masculinity through the lens of their own, of course, but there is enough commonality for them to identify themselves and their own desire with David. This is a gender-based hero-worship. They can, and must, excuse his faults and crimes because he is at bottom a man after their own heart—which is to say, their own image of masculinity" (ibid., 236).

14. Putney, "Muscular Christianity."

15. Kingsley was also a proponent of social Darwinist racial theories, which he merged with his biblical interpretation into an amalgam he called "natural theology": "Physical science is proving more and more the immense importance of Race; the importance of hereditary powers, hereditary organs, hereditary habits, in all organised beings, from the lowest plant to the highest animal. She is proving more and more the omnipresent action of the differences between races; how the more favoured race (she cannot avoid using the epithet) exterminates the less favoured, or at least expels it, and forces it, under penalty of death, to adapt itself to new circumstances; and, in a word, that competition between every race and every individual of that race, and reward according to deserts, is (as far as we can see) an universal law of living things. And she says—for the facts of history prove it—that as it is among the races of plants and animals, so it has been unto this day among the races of men" ("The Natural Theology of the Future," paper read at Sion College, 1871).

16. One young man in the thrall of this movement's present-day manifestation wrote me via email recently that "Jesus was a thirty-something male who was ripped from hard work." "Ripped," of course, is a body-building term, used in the context of our discussion to portray Jesus as the opposite of "effeminate."

few, short, and counterintuitive, addressed not to the important men of the world but to the lowest of the low; and when he converses with influential men, he speaks to them obliquely using parables and verbal traps. He makes multiple and meaningful contacts with women, befriending them, violating table protocol and purity codes with them, protecting them from legal punishment, making them messengers of new life, and, of course, asking that question at Simon the Pharisee's table: "Do you see this woman?" Jesus does not have sexual congress with anyone, and he says scandalous things about divorce as well as subversive things about the traditional patriarchal family (Matt 19:1-12; Matt 10:35-39). He teaches love, care, and forgiveness, to the chagrin of his disciples; and he lives as a beggar when he conducts his mission. He washes Peter's feet, rebukes the use of the sword, and submits to his own execution. He does not appear to "win" until God intervenes after his death, not to wreak vengeance on his killers but to resurrect him.

All constructions of masculinity forged in war, yesterday and today, require an enemy. To be a *real man* one must be measured *against* an enemy, whether that enemy is another tribe, "race," or nation, a persecutor, or the "opposite" sex. David gained esteem by fighting and killing more and more enemies. Jesus neutralized the category with the command to forgive and forgive again.

"But I tell you, love your enemies and pray for those who persecute you" (Matt 5:44).

The fact that his own disciples continually expect him to unleash a Davidic form of power (Luke 9:46-48), a nationalistic revival (John 6:15; Acts 1:6), and the fact that this form of power was central to Jesus's own temptations by the evil one (Mark 1:12-13; Matt 4:1-11; Luke 4:1-13), only serve to highlight how Jesus, in following David, supplants David, and how this rejection of Davidic power—along with David's martial masculinity—is absolutely central to the Gospel stories. David figures heavily into the expectations that accompany Jesus, expectations that serve to make Jesus's actual example all the more startling.

It is unsurprising that men, even men in the church, have continually tried to overthrow Jesus the peacemaker and friend of women. It is also unsurprising that the vehicle for that attempted overthrow has so frequently been war. During one episode of war, the church marked women as "collateral damage" in a particularly shocking and shameful way: witch killing.

5

Ontology of the Witch Hunt

Remember that God took the rib out of Adam's body, not a part of his soul, to make her. She was not made in the image of God, like man.

—St. Ambrose (339–97)[1]

There is neither Jew nor Greek, slave nor free, male nor female, for you are all one in Christ Jesus.

—Galatians 3:28

A dominant impression in popular Western culture is that witch hunts were a medieval artifact of Western Christianity. Most of us have the idea that witch hunts were the products of superstition, which was swept aside by the Enlightenment certainties of natural science. In fact, the subject of witch persecutions is far more complex, and a little surprising. Alan Kors and Edward Peters's book *Witchcraft in Europe, 1100–1700* begins with what strikes us as paradoxical:

> It seems to us [in]comprehensible that *after* our alleged period of primitive experience in the West, after our "Dark Ages," during the centuries of dynamic intellectual experimentation, the

---

1. Quoted in Phelips, *Churches and Modern Thought*, 291.

Renaissance, the Reformation, and, more perplexing still, during that seventeenth century which we continue to consider "the Age of Reason" and "the Age of Scientific Revolution," Europeans engaged in a systematic and furious assault upon men and women believed to be witches.[2]

Studies show that belief in witchcraft, as a malevolent and *efficacious* practice, existed in early China, Babylonia, and Egypt. Laws against it were promulgated in these various societies, as well as in pre-Christian Europe and imperial Rome.[3] Hebrew law forbade all forms of sorcery and divination, though in the context of Hebrew monotheism, these practices were understood less as dangerously efficacious than as idolatrous alienation of affection from the true God. The word translated as "witch" in an infamous translation of a verse from Exodus—"a witch shall not be suffered to live" (Exod 22:18)—is the Hebrew *kashaph*, which appears in Strong's Concordance[4] and has multiple meanings in its use in the Bible, including "poisoner" and "fortune teller." Though it is primarily associated with women, the term is used six times in masculine form in the Hebrew Scriptures.[5]

Romans were compulsive record keepers, and one of the earliest indicators of the popular association of witchcraft with *women* is an account from 331 BCE, in which 170 women were executed for witchcraft.[6] The designated witches were convicted of causing an epidemic. Epidemic was again the catalyst from 182–80 BCE,[7] during which time various Roman authorities put approximately five thousand of these "witches" to death. By the sixth century, somewhat mythologized accounts were written of pagan Vistula River Goth anti-witch campaigns. In the Gothic accounts, witches were exclusively women.[8] There were pre-Christian associations of females with dangerous sorcery in both Germanic and Roman society.

For the first four centuries of Christianity, Christians themselves were emphatically opposed to executing witches. That opposition continued into the time of Charlemagne.[9] The Lombard Code stated, "Let nobody presume to kill a foreign serving maid or female servant as a witch, for it is not possible, nor ought to be believed by Christian minds." The Roman practice

---

2. Kors and Peters, *Witchcraft in Europe*, 3–4.
3. Orr, "Witch; Witchcraft."
4. Strong, *Strong's Concordance*, 1518.
5. Geauvreau, "A Brief Word Study on 'Witch/Witchcraft/Witchcrafts.'"
6. McCafferty, "Strega and Witchcraft," lines 29–30.
7. Ibid., lines 30–31.
8. Jordanes, *Origins and Deeds of Goths*, chapter 24.
9. McKittterick, *Early Middle Ages*, 140.

of killing women as witches was actually curtailed by increasing Christian influence in Roman society after the Constantinian conversion. Between 300 and 700 CE, the church implemented laws against "devil worshipping" and sorcery, but *as heresies*, and the punishments were generally mild. St. Augustine called witchcraft "illusion, not a crime." And the First Synod of St. Patrick reads,

> A Christian who *believes* that there is a vampire in the world, that is to say, a witch, is to be anathematized; whoever *lays that reputation* upon a living being shall not be received into the Church until he revokes with his own voice the crime that he has committed.[10]

In 906, the Vatican declared the belief in witchcraft (in its *efficacy*) to be heretical. Gratian, writing in the *Canon Episcopi* in 1140, expressed the belief that Satan was the source of witchcraft and that he had among the people his servants who subscribed to it; but in this case, again, it was *the belief* in witchcraft that was the work of Satan, which was not to say the "craft" was efficacious. Gratian did, however, lay at women's feet the "weakness of mind" that opened the door to the heresy, with the claim that women were more likely *to believe in* witchcraft.[11]

> Those are held captive by the Devil who, leaving their creator, seek the aid of the Devil. And so the Holy Church must be cleansed of this pest. It is also not to be omitted that some wicked women, perverted by the Devil, seduced by illusions and phantasms of demons, believe and profess themselves, in the hours of the night, to ride upon certain beasts with Diana, the goddess of pagans, and an innumerable multitude of women, and in the silence of the dead of night to traverse great spaces of the earth.... For an innumerable multitude, deceived by this false opinion, believe this to be true, and so believing, wander from the right faith.[12]

Heresy is a terrible sin for Gratian, to be sure, but he is still clearly calling witchcraft a "false opinion" and denying that these women actually zip through the night skies astride gravity-defying quadrupeds. The bishop of Worms wrote a long treatise circa 1020, in which he discounted the supposed efficacy of sorcery, witchcraft, and other purported forms of magic.[13]

---

10. First Synod of St. Patrick, my italics; cited in Bulliet et al., *Earth and Its Peoples*, 266.

11. Kors and Peters, *Witchcraft in Europe*, 29.

12. Gratian, *Decretum*, cited in ibid.

13. Jolly et al., *Witchcraft and Magic in Europe*, 205.

Ontology of the Witch Hunt

Sixty years later, Pope Gregory VII beseeched the king of Denmark to end witch burnings, which were becoming an occasional response to events like crop failure.[14]

Kors and Peters, themselves astonished when their research located witch hunts within the Enlightenment, argue that the outbreak of "witch" persecution actually corresponds to the late development of a formal Scholastic ontology—or beliefs about the nature of being—regarding the devil, which laid down the juridical basis for witch trials.[15]

> Before the work of the scholastic philosophers and systematic theologians in the twelfth and thirteenth centuries . . . the role of the demons in the affairs of man was part of a variegated folklore, and their activities ranged from the horrific and utterly diabolical to a mere impishness and mischievousness, often betraying a whimsical humor. In Aquinas and his contemporaries this folklore became complex and rigorous Church doctrine. The demons . . . were a hierarchically organized army in the service of Satan . . . [who] could tempt human beings into their service . . . the visible agents of diabolical power. Once the witch had come to be understood in this new context, the logic of the witch hunt and execution became manifest and compelling.[16]

In Kors and Peters's account, the systematic thinking of Scholasticism was a precondition for the juridical mindset of the pre-Enlightenment and Enlightenment, but there is no account of war or misogyny as additional causative factors. While the formal ontology was a late arrival that did become an important antecedent to the beginning of the "witch" terrorism of the fifteenth through the seventeenth centuries, this *ontology* was neither the first nor the sole cause of those terrors, even though it served as witch-killing's legal justification.

The church had denounced sorcery and witchcraft centuries prior to the Enlightenment, using the same basic argument that we use today in response to claims of magic and sorcery—that it is illusory. So how did the church, western Europe, and even the American Colonies, from the fifteenth to the seventeenth centuries, devolve into the orgy of witch persecution that targeted four women for every man?

---

14 Thurston "Witchcraft," lines 77–80.

15. Scholasticism was the method of thought in late medieval universities, in which truths were "proven" in formalized disputations.

16. Kors and Peters, *Witchcraft in Europe*, 8–9.

The majority of witch persecutions were under civil, not ecclesial, authority. And contrary to many modern impressions, accusations, trials, and witnesses were highly localized. Witch trials were not characteristic of all Europe or even most of Europe. Around twenty-six thousand witches would be put to death in what is now Germany. Only four witch burnings seem to have ever taken place in Ireland.[17] The areas that are now Germany and France excelled in the killings. The diversity of the Middle Ages is only infrequently remarked, but Europe was a highly complicated patchwork of communities, customs, and languages at the time. Witch trials and executions were sporadic, local, and frequently caused by mass panics in conjunction with the scapegoating of people (mostly women) who were already unpopular in the community. Personal and interfamilial vendettas as well as naked self-interest played a role in many accusations.

Women comprised nearly half of all accusers and hostile witnesses in documented cases.[18] Women, like their male contemporaries, and formed by the same customs and narratives, internalized the belief system developed in support of the witch hunts. Structural male power can and does exist without translating into exclusively male initiative and agency. Social control entails the consent of the governed through shared ideas. And some women who made the accusations likely felt their own accusations inoculated them from becoming targets. The participation of women in these outbreaks has multiple explanations, not the least of which is accommodation in various forms to male power.

Three developments contributed to the perversion of the Gospels and led to church participation in "witch" killing, First, the church became the captive of politics and war. Second, the church adopted the surrounding cultures' mistrust of and contempt for women. Finally, the church went down the path of what Ivan Illich called the institutional "criminalization of sin."[19]

17. Monter, *Witchcraft and Magic in Europe*, 12.

18. Jones, "European Witch-Hunts," sec. 2, lines 5–8; sec. 5, lines 22–31.

19. Illich, *Rivers North of the Future*, 80–94. "The Christian is called to be faithful not to the gods, or to the city's rules, but to a face, a person; and, consequently, the darkness he allows to enter him by breaking faith acquires a completely new taste. This is the experience of sinfulness. It is an experience of confusion in front of the infinitely good, but it always holds the possibility of sweet tears, which express sorrow and trust in forgiveness. This dimension of the very personal, very intimate failure is changed through criminalization, and through the way in which forgiveness becomes a matter of legal remission of crime, his sorrow and his hope in God's mercy becomes a secondary issue. His legalization of love opens the individual to new fears. Darkness takes new shapes: the fear of demons, the fear of witches, the fear of magic. And the depth of these fears is also expressed in the new hope in science as the way of banishing this darkness" (ibid., 93–94).

6

Ecologies of Power

The whole of her body is nothing less than phlegm, blood, bile, rheum and the fluid of digested food. . . . If you consider what is stored up behind those lovely eyes, the angle of the nose, the mouth and the cheeks you will agree that the well-proportioned body is only a whitened sepulchre.

—St. John Chrysostom (347–407)[1]

For our struggle is not against flesh and blood, but against the rulers, against the authorities, against the powers of this dark world and against the spiritual forces of evil in the heavenly realms.

—Ephesians 6:12

The fourteenth century brought bubonic plague to Europe. International trade (which facilitated the movement of rats) and urbanization (greater concentration of human populations) acted as the accelerants for the disease. Popular superstitions were inflamed by the experience, and the Romano-Germanic fear of witches was fanned from dying ember to consuming flame in the face of mass death against which there seemed no defense.

The plague dramatically shifted the demographics of Europe, increasing the value of labor and empowering peasants to the point that they began

---

1. Quoted in Aquilina, "Chrysostom and Marriage," para. 16.

to rebel throughout Europe.[2] The general state of unrest led to accusations and counter-accusations among church officials and political authorities, at a time when corruption had become endemic in the Roman Catholic Church. Nothing was so unpopular among the masses of Europe as the selling of indulgences, coerced bribes given to clergy in exchange for clerical "intervention" to pray dead loved ones out of a twelfth-century Roman Catholic invention: purgatory. Pope Sixtus IV implemented the indulgence system through a network of collection agents as a new papal revenue stream to pay off Crusade ransoms.[3]

In 1492, the same year in which Isabella and Ferdinand of Spain expelled Muslims and Jews from the Iberian Peninsula and financed Cristobal Colon's western expedition, Rodrigo de Borgia, a member of the notorious Borgia political clan, took office as Pope Alexander VI. He scandalized Europe with his elaborate political machinations, his accumulation of wealth, his infamous sexual appetites, and his bald-faced nepotism.[4] Alexander rigged the Sacred College of Cardinals by appointing twelve of his own at once, one being his own son. Borgia and his family had great influence on the Vatican by virtue of their enormous wealth. The fast track was prepared for Borgia well before he ascended to the papacy. Trained initially as a Doctor of Law, within three years of his ordination as a priest, this ex-lawyer became a bishop. The long-standing arrangements of church and political authority, sometimes fractious, had shifted into a direct church-political merger in the person of Alexander/Borgia. Popular dissatisfaction had increased to a boiling point when the pope's political maneuvering inadvertently sparked a minor war between Franks and Neapolitans. This set off another shockwave of political realignment that in turn resulted in greater social dislocation and popular discontent.[5]

The breakdown of the Reformation and the crises of modernity were and are in many respects based on *structural* inconsistencies that preceded the Reformation. The breakdown of Christendom (Christianity in power) was based substantially on the failure of Christians, especially powerful Christian men, to practice what they preached. And that failure can be attributed to the practices necessary for retaining political power.

Brad Gregory writes that "judged on [its] own terms and with respect to the objectives of [its] own leading protagonists, medieval Christendom failed."[6] In 1517, when Luther published his Ninety-Five Theses, criticisms

2. Dyer, *Making a Living*, 271–72.
3. Swanson, *Indulgences in Late Medieval England*, 78.
4. Walton, "The Scandalous Reputation of Pope Alexander VI."
5. Loughlin, "Pope Alexander VI."
6. Gregory, *Unintended Reformation*, 365.

of the Roman Catholic hierarchy were hungrily received by masses of people who had been thrown into chronic uncertainty by the tectonic political shifts then taking place in Europe. In 1525, Huldrych Zwingli introduced a new liturgy as an alternative to Mass in Zurich. In 1530, Jean Calvin broke with the church and founded yet another theological tradition that would oppose itself to the Roman Catholic Church. The Protestant Reformation had begun.[7]

Small wars erupted, and by 1618 there would be the very big, very complex, and very destructive Thirty Years' War. Between the Reformation and the Thirty Years' War, Protestant fought Catholic, Protestant fought Protestant, and even Catholic fought Catholic.[8] These conflicts created an increasingly hateful rhetoric on all sides and the equation of enemies with evil—a kind of vulgar dualism that mapped easily onto the psychic terrain of a Romano-Germanic Europe now in upheaval.[9] This rhetoric increasingly included accusations of devil-alliance and witchcraft. Suspicions of one another, as members of the "legitimate church" or not, transmogrified into accusations of witchcraft; and as in all societies that are placed on a martial footing, suspicion of one's own people accompanied obsession about the supposed (and sometimes actual) plots of enemy spies. Suspicion is a way of life in wartime; accusations followed.

The church had been aligned with political authority since Constantine joined the church and Theodosius established it as the "official church of the Roman Empire." While monasticism resisted "the world," the church hierarchy, *modeling itself* on political hierarchies, adapted its practices and doctrine to accommodate the exercise of official male power.

The example of Jesus—a gentle and pacific Savior, preaching redemption by love—was eclipsed in the beginning of the second century by a growing reaction against the spiritual equality of women in the early Christian view.[10] The emerging church, reflecting the surrounding society, was dominated by men—who appear to have suffered the perennial and world-bound temptation to embrace a masculinity *constructed* as domination.

Whether through exposure to warlike secular rulers before its establishment or through operating within the halls of power after its establishment,

---

7. Ibid., 74–128.
8. Holy Roman Emperor Charles V actually invaded the Vatican in 1527.
9. Horn, "Protestant Reformation."
10. King, "Women in Ancient Christianity"; Kroeger, "Neglected History."

the church forgot its early gender subversions and its generally nonviolent character. The gender subversion and nonviolence were forgotten together, because the preparation for and practice of war is and has throughout recorded history nearly always been constitutive of male power, the practice of which is still understood as a high masculine virtue.

Two centuries after the church's establishment, Emperor Justinian I, a leader who pursued a policy of constant war, appointed its principle bishops.[11] Justinian, in his military attempts to restore the old Roman Empire from his capital in Constantinople, was trying to pick up the pieces of empire that had been chipped away by "barbarian" incursions and political intrigue. Justinian believed that his empire ought to have one, and only one religion; and so the faith was employed instrumentally for political purpose.[12]

Justinian, given his soldier's mindset, sought to "protect the purity of the church" by executing heretics.[13] The Christian church, which just four centuries earlier had been the victim of persecution by the Roman authorities, now set about the persecution of the "other." That this departure was initiated by a leader immersed in the business of war is not coincidental. Heresy was punishable by death. What the church now had to lose was power. It was Stanley Hauerwas who said, "Never think that you need to protect God. Because anytime you think you need to protect God, you can be sure that you are worshiping an idol."[14] Yet the leaders of the church did not opt, as Christ had, to take the way of the cross. On the contrary, the church adapted to the successor regime of those who had executed Jesus.

There were complex circumstances leading to this phase shift. The church had not first sought power, but rather had fallen into it. For a critical period in history, the church had become the institution with literate people who had administrative experience and the public moral standing to legitimize power. Power had changed hands so many times that "the oldest institution in Western Europe by the eleventh century, self-consciously tracing an uninterrupted history back a thousand years, was the papacy."[15] The church, in its alliance with power since Theodosius, now found itself the most stable political force in Europe, where political borders and rulers were changing with the seasons. The church, in other words, had trapped itself into a kind of political responsibility that was never anticipated by

---

11. Haldon, *Byzantium*, 169–79.
12. Wyeth, "Justinian I."
13. Ibid.
14. Quoted in Cavanaugh, "Faith Fires Back."
15. Tyerman, *God's War*, 4.

the early church, and one that now forced the militarily powerless church to align itself with shifting politico-military leaderships, choosing in many cases what appeared to be the lesser of several evils. In this way, the church used its own accumulation of power to paradoxically become the servant not of "the least of them," but of political authorities that themselves proved to be transient.

As authorities shifted and multiplied, the church found itself subject to intrigue, having established itself with bases later divided. By the eleventh century, the Great Schism had separated the Eastern and Western churches, the Western church aligning with the bishop of Rome against the bishop of Constantinople,[16] a schism that was temporarily resolved by an adventure that armed the church itself: the Crusades.

By the twelfth century, the horse collar and horseshoe came into broad use in central Europe, allowing heavy ploughs to work the moist soil. Larger fields were planted farther from home, and agrarians began to concentrate in small villages.[17] These towns became parishes, where local merchants began the process of monetary accumulation that would eventually allow them to usurp the power of the feudal lords. The first steps were taken toward urbanization. This nascent business class would also be drawn into the Reformation as partisans of Protestantism, which would come to preach, against the church doctrines of the past, that the accumulation of wealth is virtuous and that giving alms to the poor encourages sloth.[18]

From 1378 to 1417, there was a schism *within* the Roman Catholic Church, wherein two different popes were recognized by two competing factions.[19] These destabilizations coincided with various social disruptions. The church had lashed itself to an unstable political ecology, in which the temptation to pragmatism became increasingly irresistible. When witch persecution began in parts of Europe, the church was already accommodating so many practices that are antithetical to the Gospels that embracing the notion of witchcraft, especially as a way of demonizing enemies or terrorizing subjects, was as easy as spelling B-O-R-G-I-A. Just add the hatred of women, and stir.

---

16. Fortescue, "The Eastern Schism."
17. Illich, *Rivers North of the Future*, 83–84.
18. Gregory, *Unintended Reformation*, 249–62.
19. Ibid., 142–43.

It was during this period of dissolution within the church and of early urbanization that the church established the Inquisition, a loose confederation of church officials who tried people for heresy. Begun in the eleventh century, alongside the First Crusade, the Inquisition or *inquisitio haereticae pravitatis* (inquiry into heretical perversity) was a network of tribunals that rarely practiced torture, acquitted a goodly number of people, and only infrequently used the death penalty (administered not under ecclesial but secular authority).[20] After Justinian, the church had stopped putting people to death for heresy, resuming capital punishment in 1022, six centuries later.[21] This moderation was abandoned in response to the threat of Protestantism, and by the fifteenth century capital punishment had also become a weapon against Jews and Muslims, especially in Spain.[22]

The Inquisition was not synonymous with witch persecutions, though approximately five hundred executions were the result of the Inquisition during the period of the witch hunts. Many of these, however, were convictions based on *heresy*, witchcraft still being seen as a superstition. Even during the witch-craze between 1576 and 1640, more than half of those tried only as witches by Inquisition clerics were acquitted.[23] In 1258, Pope Alexander IV had explicitly forbidden the trial of witches by inquisitors.[24] "The Inquisitors deputed to investigate heresy," he wrote, "must not intrude into investigations of divination or sorcery without knowledge of manifest heresy involved."[25]

Pope John XXII reversed the church's position on witches in 1326,[26] after two attempts on his life, one with poison (associated in the medieval mind with witches). The fear of witches was becoming more widespread throughout Europe and many priests were infected with it, leading them to petition the more cautious pope for an expansion of the inquisitorial charter to include prosecution of witches. The church participated in witch-pogroms, in part, because the church had become the captive of politics. It found itself competing for the loyalty of Christians in the wake of war, schism, plague, and reformation, demanding loyalty by force on the one hand and pandering where necessary to popular prejudices and illusions that it had previously rejected. The church's incoherence in both this prac-

20. Saraiva, *Marrano Factory*, xxx.
21. Gregory, *Salvation at Stake*, 31.
22. Kamen, *Spanish Inquisition*, 17.
23. Gibbons, "Recent Developments."
24. Kors and Peters, *Witchcraft in Europe*, 79.
25. Cited in ibid., 190–91.
26. Ibid., 82.

tice of persecuting "witches" and attempting to salvage political power was a reflection of this unstable political ecology.

The Crusades (1096–1291) were undertaken in part to unify European Christendom in a time of great political turmoil, and had inured the church to war—including the violent extermination of those accused of heresy. With war comes the logic of war, including "collateral damage" and tactical massacre; and when Christians massacred other Christians who were the cohabitants of Muslim communities, or Catholics who lived among "heretics," it was seen as tactical necessity. In this period, Christians were already routinely killing Christians, even though in 1054 the Council of Narbonne declared that "no Christian shall kill another Christian, for whoever kills a Christian undoubtedly sheds the blood of Christ."[27] By the time the church was attacking renegade Christians in the Albigensian Crusade (1209–29), in what is now southern France, the church was *endorsing massacres* of heretics. During the massacre of men, women, and children at Beziers in 1209, troops appealed to the abbot with the dilemma that some Catholics lived among the residents, to which the abbot replied, "Kill them all, and God will know his own."[28]

The hard-heartedness of the practice of war became part of the church's political language. That this hard-heartedness could so easily be turned against "witches" should be no surprise. By the sixteenth century, Christians were killing Christians throughout Europe in mutually organized warfare. Christians had fully embraced the world's death-dealing man-sport of war. Those accused of witchcraft were caught in the cultural crossfire.

A major development in the political ecology of the witch-hunt was the development of the juridical mindset.[29]

27. Cited in Wallace-Murphy and Hopkins, *Custodians of Truth*, 168.

28. Oldenbourg, *Massacre at Montségur*, 109.

29. This juridical mindset was an aspect of what Kors and Peters referred to as the "ontology of the witch hunts."

7

The Rise of the Lawyers

Wherefore if forgers of money and other evil-doers are forthwith condemned to death by the secular authority, much more reason is there for heretics, as soon as they are convicted of heresy, to be not only excommunicated but even put to death.

—St. Thomas Aquinas[1]

With the New Testament, some very new forms of perception—not only of conception but also of perception—came into the world. I believe that these forms have had a definitive influence on our Western manner of living, shaping our way of thinking about what is good and desirable. I also believe that this influence has been mediated by the Christian Church, which bases its authority on its claim to speak for the New Testament. The Church... attempted to safeguard the newness of the Gospel by institutionalizing it, and in this way the newness got corrupted.

—Ivan Illich[2]

---

1. Aquinas, *Summa Theologica* II-II.11.3.
2. Illich, *Rivers North of the Future*, 106.

The Rise of the Lawyers

In the second quote above, the priest and scholar Ivan Illich, in an interview just prior to his death, was reflecting on what he termed "the criminalization of sin," the first step down the road to organized violence by Christians.

The church's later vulnerability to the siren calls of modernity corresponded to the multiplication of hypocrisies by a warlike church. There is little doubt that people themselves were sick to death of wars, and these wars' association with the church was clear and well understood. This loss of general credibility began with people's *willingness* to disbelieve, which had nothing to do with the superiority of a science that was not yet developed, and everything to do with the dissonance between church preaching and practice. The church's institutionalization under conditions of establishment made this inevitable. The church's claim to infallibility included the complex development of a comprehensive, self-justifying worldview. Once aspects of that integrated worldview were disproven in part (consider Galileo), the institution reacted defensively. It sought to impose the old "truths" as doctrine, by force if necessary, long after the church's erroneous claims with regard to "natural science" were publicly viable. This reaction to the church's epistemological crisis undermined and *is still undermining* the church's credibility. This struggle between church and the Enlightenment cannot be grasped through some evidentiary debate that sees the sides as antithetical. The Enlightenment grew *directly out of the church*. Illich has made a compelling case that modernity is not the opposite of Christianity, but its deep and demonic perversion.[3]

Rodrigo de Borgia, a.k.a. Pope Alexander VI, was a lawyer. To understand the co-emergence of the Enlightenment, the warring nation-state, and witch persecutions, one must also understand the influence of lawyers in a European ruling mindset that was increasingly juridical. Criminalizing sin required the interpretation of law, and this is where Kors and Peters's assertion that the solidifying ontology of Scholasticism underwrote the witch hunts has merit. It helps explain the rise of the lawyers.

Witch-killing coevolved with the Enlightenment and shared many of the beliefs and assumptions of the so-called fathers of the Enlightenment. First case in point is Jean Bodin. A Catholic, Bodin is remembered principally as a lawyer and political philosopher. His political philosophy revolved around social order, which was perceived to be in short supply during his life (1530–96). He specifically called for the establishment of powerful central states. He called for dialogue between the various Abrahamic religions, and he placed minimal emphasis on the church as a political actor. He is rightly

---

3. Illich, *Rivers North of the Future*, 59–63.

seen as one of the fathers of the Enlightenment, and yet his life will always be notorious for his enthusiasm for killing women as witches. Mies writes,

> The persecution of the witches was a manifestation of the rising modern society and not, as is usually believed, a remnant of the irrational "dark" Middle Ages. This is most clearly shown by Jean Bodin, the French theoretician of the new mercantilist economic doctrine. Jean Bodin was the founder of the quantitative theory of money, of the modern concept of sovereignty and of mercantilist populationism. He was a staunch defender of modern rationalism, and was at the same time one of the most vocal proponents of state ordained massacres and tortures of the witches.[4]

Bodin believed, prefiguring Hobbes and Hegel, in an absolutist state, whose principle responsibilities included supplying human beings for the labor force. He believed that witches and midwives were enemies of the state because, according to Bodin, they caused infertility and performed abortions. He further believed that "witches" taught women birth control, a practice he equated with murder. Bodin wrote a pamphlet against purported witches that was remarkable above all for the cruelty of its recommended punishments for witchcraft. Witches should be prosecuted, according to Jean Bodin, based on the idea that women practicing witchcraft outnumbered men by a ratio of fifty to one.[5]

Bodin sketched out a post-aristocratic society that would be ruled by his own up-and-coming urban mercantile class. Note how the role of women has changed in Bodin's rationale. Whatever degrading beliefs about women preceded this era, Bodin has introduced a new and utilitarian instrumentality to the proper role of women, that is, as breeders. They are required to produce workers to power the new future being mapped out by Bodin and his contemporaries. These origins of the technocratic nation-state marked the beginning of the rule of lawyers. Bodin himself practiced law, but in previous periods, the interpretation of law was neither needed nor greatly emphasized in the day-to-day life of most people, whose relations were not juridical. Mies writes that "there is a direct connection between the witch pogroms and the emergence of the professionalization of law."[6] With the emerging nation-state, Roman law was being adopted to replace Germanic law, and universities were opening law schools to train *juris doctors* who

---

4. Mies, *Patriarchy and Accumulation*, 83–84.
5. Ibid., 84.
6. Ibid.

could effectively manipulate and interpret the complexities of ever more technical law.[7]

Many people were chagrined by the sudden growth in the number of lawyers, complaining that they were generally lazy, parasitic young men who twisted reason in order to allow the rich to gain at the expense of the poor. There was actually a good deal of truth in this assessment. One cannot help remembering Jesus's encounters with the scribes, the lawyers of his day, and his rebuke that they had let the letter of the law trump its spirit (Mark 2:27).

One sixteenth-century chronicle stated, "In our times, jurisprudencia smiles at everybody, so that everyone wants to become a doctor in law. Most are attracted to this field of studies out of greed for money and ambition."[8] Witch trials were big business. Each one employed a host of judges and lawyers, who competed in verbal puffery with one another to extend and thereby raise the costs (and payouts) of the trial, which even included bills for the alcohol consumed by the soldiers who pursued and captured the suspects.[9]

Witch-trial funds were used to partially finance the Thirty Years' War.[10]

I cannot avoid a discussion of the *Malleus Maleficarum*. This was the notorious witch-hunting guide penned in 1486 by the German priest Heinrich Kramer, a.k.a. Institorius. Jacob Springer is listed as a coauthor, but scholars believe his name was added to lend the book credibility.[11] It is hard to say whether this book was one of the motors of violent misogyny in the emerging Enlightenment, or whether Kramer was a cultural expression of existing popular misogynistic notions and practices. In either case, we can see it now as a tract that actively promotes the idea of witches against the more skeptical voices of the church that had in the past denounced these ideas as popular superstitions. It is not accidental, in my view, that Protestants and Catholics reciprocally demonized one another, and in so doing resuscitated these superstitions; nor does it surprise me that Protestants actually exceeded Catholics in their enthusiasm for killing accused "witches."

Kramer was a crackpot who stumbled into a niche. Prior to his glory days as an authority on witchcraft, he had been run out of the province of

---

7. Gregory, *Unintended Reformation*, 324–25.
8. Cited in Mies, *Patriarchy and Accumulation*, 84.
9. Ibid., 85.
10. Ibid.
11. Broedel, *Malleus Maleficarum*, 16.

Tyrol for his near-crazed indictments of several women there as witches. The local bishop called Kramer "a senile old man."[12] But a papal bull had been issued two years prior to the publication of *Malleus Maleficarum*. *Summis desiderantes affectibus*, issued by Pope Innocent VIII (1432–92), gave official church recognition to the existence of witches and called on the Inquisition (already established) to intervene. When the church assented to the witch-burning craze, Kramer's book was adopted as the authoritative text on witchcraft. A new invention called a printing press ensured its wide distribution. Between 1487 and 1669, thirty-six editions were published.[13] The "senile old man" became famous on the burnt bodies of women. The title of the book means "the hammer of the witches." (The word *witches* translates the Latin *maleficarum*, which is the feminine form of the noun.) The reason women are more likely to be witches, explains Kramer, is related to the multiple deficiencies inhering in every woman: lust, inability to reason, weakness . . . but mostly lust.

The purported insatiability of women was nothing new. Men had and have been projecting their own desires onto women for millennia. What was new in this case was the rise of the lawyers.

The growth of towns gave rise to the parish church, which became the organizing center of life in these new villages. New religious practices and rituals flourished in these towns, such as local relic veneration, special saints' days, festivals, and local rules that governed in the name of the church's idea of hospitality and neighborliness. These practices fit well together in these villages, where most people knew most other people very well and were probably related to them at least by marriage. The greater density of settlement also led to the need for greater administrative control within the population to ensure the peaceful settlement of public concerns and disputes. To accommodate the greater scale of administration, a new juridical idea crept into the thinking of administrators: contract.

Contractarianism, which would come into full flower with Hobbes four centuries hence, germinated in twelfth-century Europe. Seven centuries earlier, the *Codex Theodosianus* was published (438 AD) by its namesake, Theodosius, the emperor of Rome. In this comprehensive legal code, for the first time oaths were taken to be legal instruments. Early Christians did not take oaths as a matter of spiritual discipline; they are prohibited in

---

12. MacCulloch, *Reformation*, 563–68.
13. Russell and Cohn, *Malleus Maleficarum*, 234.

Matt 5:33–37.[14] The Codex did not merely overturn the Christian antipathy for oath-swearing; it made the oath a secular legal instrument, a legal obligation. Most Christians went for centuries afterward never taking an oath of any kind. It was not necessary in the locally self-sufficient ways that peasants managed their lives. But the contract was legally established.[15] So the oath lay in waiting. The newly necessary administrators of the new medieval villages picked it back up. They made it part of a new notion called contract.

Contract disembodies an agreement from its other social contexts and validates it only before the officers of law. The distinction between contract (a modern notion) and covenant (a notion reaching back to the origins of the Hebrews) is that a contract is predicated on suspicion. It places limits on the obligations spelled out, whereas a covenant is based on love or family, and it implies obligations without limit.

The first way the church adopted this legal notion of contract was with regard to marriage, already seen as a covenant in Christian thought.[16] Heretofore, there had been various customs within Christendom for making marriages. Some were parentally arranged, others were assisted by matchmakers, and so forth. The norms varied, but no one had ever conceived of the idea that the man and the woman making the union would select each other as equals before the law. It was the Roman Catholic Church that introduced this idea of a woman consenting as an equal with her own future partner. The first known reference to this legal consent to marriage is in a twelfth-century letter from Heloise to Abelard, when she left her religious life to pursue him.[17] A woman was free until she had undertaken the contract, whereupon the conditions of said contract obliged her to obey her husband, and required him to protect and provide for her. The contractual agreement, as Carole Pateman describes it,[18] was for female obedience in exchange for male protection. A grown woman (twelve years old for females; the age of marital consent for males was fourteen) was an agent legally free to submit to this subordinate status with whomever she chose. And as Pateman also points out, husbands had a "sex right" within that contractual relation. It has only been in the last decade or so that we have acknowledged such a thing as marital rape precisely because that "sex right" has been integral, if unnamed, to male-dominant cultural beliefs about relations within marriage,

---

14. Illich, *Rivers North of the Future*, 85–86.
15. Ibid., 86.
16. Ibid., 86–87.
17. Ibid., 88.
18. Pateman, *Sexual Contract*.

just as that same "sex right" has influenced the modern male idea of an entitlement to sex.[19]

By 1215, when the Fourth Lateran Council was convened by the church, the marriage contract was recognized throughout the church, and women were further confirmed in this newfound portion of legal equality when the same council mandated yearly, private confession "for men and women." In most places, prior to this practice, confessions had been in public, not exclusively in a private session with the priest.[20]

The contract migrated into the parish system, giving rise to a changed, and far more juridical, outlook on the practices of the church.[21] In this new procedure, God is necessary, but now *as a witness*. With time, the citizens of the ever larger and more concentrated cities of Europe increasingly relied on contract. Consequently, the educated urban class came to see society as contractual, prefiguring the idea of a social contract that would accompany the emergence of modernity and the nation-state.

The major sin within marriage was adultery; and as the church had adopted the juridical role of law enforcer in making this new thing—*legal marriage*—the idea of sin became conflated with the idea of lawbreaking, of crime. Sin had now become crime, placing its resolution not in Christ, and not even before an organic community, but before the administrative authorities. Contract and another new notion, conscience, emerged in relation to one another.[22] Prefiguring Bentham by more than four hundred years, the church used the notion of conscience (an internal forum) as a way of extending its rule-making into the psychic interior of its members, a kind of late-medieval panopticon. Conscience would also become a kind of precondition for the development of the nation-state and its "citizen."[23]

> If we want to understand the idea of *patria* of the seventeenth, eighteenth, and nineteenth centuries, the idea of fatherland, the

---

19. Ibid., 1.

20. Illich, *Rivers North of the Future*, 89.

21. Ibid., 86. "This re-introduction of oaths reaches an epochal point in the twelfth century at the height of feudalism, which was based on *conjuratio*, or oath-taking. It was then that the relation of love in its supreme form, the commitment of a man and a woman to each other forever, on the model of the Gospel, became defined as a juridical act, through which an entity called marriage comes into existence."

22. Ibid., 186–93.

23. Illich, *Gender*, 158. "[Conscience] could be used by the historian to describe an enterprise that was decisively shaped by the Church through the institutionalization of the sacrament of Penance in the twelfth century, an enterprise that since has been followed by other techniques. I would call conscientization all professionally planned and administered rituals that have as their purpose the internalization of a religious or secular ideology."

The Rise of the Lawyers

idea of mother tongue, to which I owe sacred loyalty, the idea of *pro patria mori*, that I can die for my fatherland, the idea of citizenship as something to which my conscience obligates me, then we have to understand the appearance of the internal forum [conscience] in the Middle Ages.[24]

The Reformation broke over the church with Luther's theses in 1517. The church was shattered into pieces. The Roman Church found itself in competition for the loyalty of princes and peasants. Between the multiple confessions, the public square had been converted into a competitive marketplace, wherein each faction was branding itself and pitting that brand against another. In this kind of sectarian devolution, each faction finds it necessary to differentiate itself from the others, and those areas of former agreement are swallowed up in the escalation of both sectarian hostility and opportunistic salesmanship.

In response to this emergency, the Council of Trent was convened between 1545 and 1563. In it, the Roman church referred to itself as a *societas perfecta*, a perfect society, *based in law*.[25] The church now prefigures Hobbes's "contractual" state in *Leviathan*. Illich says of the council's self-description that it was "a self-understanding . . . reflected in the legal and philosophical thinking of the time, which had begun to portray the state in the same terms, that is, as a perfect society whose citizens internalize the laws and constitution of the state as demands of conscience."[26]

Basing his gospel exegesis on the Parable of the Good Samaritan in Luke 10:25–37, Illich interprets the story to be one where the old boundaries are erased in the new life, where one can see the divine in the face of the other whom one chooses, as the Samaritan chose a wounded and despised foreigner as a friend.[27] In Luke, says Illich, the oaths of the Old Testament are combined with a covenant. In the new life, the covenant remains, but the oath as social glue is *replaced* by the Holy Spirit (*not* by law).

The rise of the juridical mindset ushered in the power of the lawyers, whom we see in Mies's account as leaders in systemizing the torture and killing of "witches." It starts with the *Codex Theodosianus*, in which oath-taking

---

24. Illich, *Rivers North of the Future*, 93.
25. Ibid., 92–93.
26. Ibid., 92.
27. Ibid., 177.

becomes a legal instrument.[28] With the *Codex*, the primitive Christian way of enacting its own community—with communion and a shared kiss (the *conspiratio*, the exchange of the Holy Spirit through the exchange of breath, a kiss on the mouth)—had been overturned. With it went the primacy of highly personal, covenantal relations maintained by scrupulous honesty, which constituted a people whose virtue transcends mere law, a *beloved* community: "You are not under the law" (Gal 5:18).

Codified law became the new basis of community conformity.

What was formerly categorized as sin was transformed into crime. Church as community was further trumped by church as governor. Church merged with empire, then with states, then was broken into pieces by the Reformation to compete for state sponsors and popular bases. The state *assumed* the law, *mastered* the churches, and reestablished them as *dependencies*. This, and not "Dark Ages" superstition, was the backdrop for the systematic attack on women accused of being witches.

---

28. Ibid., 86.

8

Misbegotten Man

I don't see what sort of help woman was created to provide man with, if one excludes procreation. If woman is not given to man for help in bearing children, for what help could she be? To till the earth together? If help were needed for that, man would have been a better help for man. The same goes for comfort in solitude. How much more pleasure is it for life and conversation when two friends live together than when a man and a woman cohabitate?[1]

—St. Augustine (354–450 AD)

He told them still another parable: "The kingdom of heaven is like yeast that a woman took and mixed into about sixty pounds of flour until it worked all through the dough."

—Matthew 13:33

The witch hunts of Europe ended by the dawn of the nineteenth century. The Roman Catholic Church has *never* renounced its late-medieval position that witchcraft is real—even though its former position that witchcraft is an inefficacious superstition flies in the face of the Thomist realism that supposedly animates the church's current relationship to science, notwithstanding

---

1. Augustine, *De genesi ad litteram* 9.5–9.

Thomas's own claim—based on the ontology of his day—that witches ought to be killed. But neither power dislocations nor the church's transition from witch-skeptical to witch-believing can explain how women came to be burned, by Catholic and Protestant alike, as witches, at a ratio of four to one compared with men. Prior to these contingent circumstances, males had already seized a monopoly on social power at the expense of women (and their children).

This reign of men over women cannot be accurately dated, because this reality was already manifest when humans began recording their activities for posterity. As seems to be the case in all relations of dominion-subjugation, the dominator needs to belittle the one who is subjugated; he needs to strip her of full membership in the *ethnos*. Nowadays, we see women's devaluation in a specific and modern form, and therefore we might say a woman is stripped of her full *personhood*. In wars, the enemy always earns an epithet (the first I heard was "gook" for Vietnamese), as a signifier of his or her status as "less-than." Without this devaluation, it is extremely difficult to subjugate a people or kill a person one doesn't even know. One needs to revile in order to subjugate. That may explain why many of the so-called church fathers went on record so unabashedly about their feelings of revulsion and contempt for women-as-women. The rule of men-as-men, if history is any indicator, will always tend toward the denigration of women-as-women.

Church misogyny by powerful men, and cultural contempt for women among men generally, combined to become a central factor leading the church into its participation in the witch hunts—and, I will contend, into the wars that opened the door to the witch hunts. Misogyny, war; war, misogyny. Which came first? Chicken or egg?

Steven Katz writes,

> The medieval conception of women shares much with the corresponding medieval conception of Jews. In both cases, a perennial attribution of secret, bountiful, malicious "power" is made. Women are anathematized and cast as witches because of the enduring grotesque fears they generate in respect of their putative abilities to control men and thereby coerce, for their own ends, male-dominated Christian society. Whatever the social and psychological determinants operative in this abiding obsession, there can be no denying the consequential reality of such anxiety in medieval Christendom. Linked to theological traditions of Eve and Lilith, women are perceived as embodiments of inexhaustible negativity. Though not quite quasi-literal incarnations of the Devil as were Jews, women are, rather, their

ontological "first cousins" who, like the Jews, emerge from the "left" or sinister side of being.[2]

In fact, a study of the church of the first and second centuries shows that Christianity in its origins was more egalitarian and gender subversive than surrounding cultures.[3] The original trajectory of the Gospels aims toward spiritual fusion with the other; and the reassertion of first male domination, then male-dominant political power, corresponding with the practice of war, after the second century was a centuries-long and male reactionary response against the most gender-revolutionary implications of "the way of the cross."

Jesus refused every male prerogative of power. He was not a husband. He was not a father. He was not a political leader. He was not a soldier. He was not a religious official. These were the typical male power roles of his day. He was, in fact, a *tekton*, a low-paid craftsman from a peasant village of fewer than five hundred people.[4]

Jesus's life and teachings ran *against* the practices of violence that were seen then and now as the province of males; yet nothing, aside from perhaps money, has been more consistently subversive of the Gospels than dominator masculinity. The most transhistorically consistent and formative practice that underwrites dominator masculinity is war, acting in every society as an incubator for violence that penetrates society in every fissure. Does war-masculinity always require for its existence a subjected femininity? Or does the subjugation of women provide men with a model for the subjugation of others? In either case, we know that a subjected femininity must be despised.

By the time Origen and Tertullian penned their own works of theology in the second and third centuries, they projected their own desires onto women, casting women as lustful, disorderly creatures. Some of the period's "observations" regarding women were simply fallacious naturalization uninformed by modern categories of analysis. Many prominent Christian men, however, used language that was venomous. Bishop Clement of Alexandria said of women that "the consciousness of their own nature must evoke feelings of shame."[5] St. Jerome called women "the root of all evil."[6] Shortly after the church had been co-opted into the political craft by the murderous Constantine, Augustine of Hippo would establish himself as the preemi-

---

2. Katz, *Holocaust*, 435.
3. Kroeger, "Neglected History."
4. Jenks, "The Quest for the Historical Nazareth."
5. Clement of Alexandria, *Paedagogus III*.
6. Knight, *Honest to Man*, 120.

nent theologian of the church. His contempt for women was so powerful that he, born of a woman, asked aloud why God had "created them at all."[7] The exegetical justification of this contempt for women was taken from the story of Adam and Eve.[8] Eve succumbed to temptation and beguiled Adam into sharing her sin. This idea fit with prevailing attitudes about women that treated the lust of the male as a kind of bewitchment authored by the female, as if she had chloroformed him. Male lust was projected as female will—carnal creature that she was, and lacking any capacity to understand or control herself except through obedience to father, husband, or brother.

The tautological claim made by the church was that women are tainted with Eve's weakness because Eve was a woman. In later teachings on sex and the church, the church changes its story, from the Eve-woman tautology to the woman is an "imperfect man" argument. Later still, we have naturalized gender stereotypes to describe "complementarity," and the precedential *non sequitur* of "apostolic succession."

I am not arguing against any idea of gender complementarity here. By definition, gender is a complementary phenomenon that is, according to all available historical and anthropological evidence, present in all stable societies.[9] My disagreement with male church officials is that they are opportunistic in the way they deploy the term to sustain the same male privilege that attained before *complementarity* replaced women with being *misbegotten*, which replaced the woman-Eve tautology. Even though these stories underwriting women's subjection to men in the church and exclusion from church practices *change* radically over time, only the facts of women's exclusion from priesthood and subordination to men *remain constant*. I speak here as a Catholic who prays for our repentance.

Disgust with and the active contempt for women had crept into the language of the church fathers by the second century. The church systematically reversed the progressive inclusion exemplified in the Gospels, and began with women to reinstate a form of systematic exclusion. Read the thirteenth-century account of women penned by St. Albertus Magnus (1200–1280), and it is little wonder that the church would participate in the persecution of women as "witches." It is surprising the churchmen didn't go after women sooner:

---

7. Phelips, *Churches and Modern Thought*, 203.

8. Beginning with 1 Timothy, written at the beginning of the second century.

9. This is a controversial claim, even as the historical record shows consistent and transhistorical complementarity. The controversy surrounds the idea that this is inevitable, because in so many cases, this complementariness is also associated with a male-over-female hierarchy. While complementariness does not automatically confer hierarchy, the frequency of this association has raised a high index of suspicion, especially among feminists.

> Woman is less qualified [than man] for moral behavior. For the woman contains more liquid than man, and it is a property of liquid to take things up easily and to hold unto them poorly. Liquids are easily moved, hence women are inconstant and curious. When a woman has relations with a man, she would like, as much as possible, to be lying with another man at the same time. Woman knows nothing about fidelity. Believe me, if you give her your trust, you will be disappointed. Trust an experienced teacher. For this reason prudent men share their plans and actions least of all with their wives. Woman is a misbegotten man and has a faulty and defective nature in comparison to his. Therefore she is unsure in herself. What she cannot get, she seeks to obtain through lying and diabolical deceptions. And so, to put it briefly, one must be on one's guard with every woman, as if she were a poisonous snake and the horned devil. If I could say what I know about women, the world would be astonished. . . . Woman is strictly speaking not cleverer but slyer (more cunning) than man. Cleverness sounds like something good, slyness sounds like something evil. Thus in evil and perverse doings woman is cleverer, that is, slyer, than man. Her feelings drive woman toward every evil, just as reason impels man toward all good.[10]

Woman is a "misbegotten man." It is a birth defect common to all women. All of them must be approached like devils and venomous snakes. These claims about the nature of women prefigured, in stark language, the identification in advance of women as criminal suspects in the practice of efficacious witchcraft. And *war* rehearsed the violence of Christian men who moved against women identified as witches.

Thomas Aquinas, writing his *Summa Theologica* in the thirteenth century, holds to the assumption of women's physical inferiorities (understood through what is now a completely archaic notion of physiology), but rebukes anyone who exercises contempt for women, to whom he ascribes spiritual equality. And so we see the reorientation of churchmen's claims about women.

> It was right for the woman to be made from a rib of man. First, to signify the social union of man and woman, for the woman should neither use authority over man, and so she was not made

---

10. *Quaestiones super de animalibus* XV q. 11, cited in Phelips, *Churches and Modern Thought*, 203.

from his head; nor was it right for her to be subject to man's contempt as his slave, and so she was not made from his feet.[11]

In 1988, Pope John Paul II, speaking to women religious in Turin, said,

> In proclaiming the truth about the human person, it makes its specific contribution in confirming the perfect equality of man and woman as the image of God and his interlocutors. Man and woman, in that they are the image of God, make visible in the universe the unity of God who lives not in solitude but in communion: the One and Triune God. In establishing the Kingdom of God Jesus goes back to this original communion so that a there is neither Jew nor Greek, there is neither slave nor free person, there is not male and female; for you are all one in Christ Jesus.

This statement is in fact used in a way consistent with his *refusal* to consider ending women's exclusion from the priesthood; but the language has been purged of the misogynistic bile that was freely spoken by earlier churchmen as the received (male) wisdom of the time, stated with confidence by the church's most revered male intellectuals.

The exclusion of women was originally based on descriptions of women that were physically inaccurate, on a literal interpretation of Genesis, and fundamentally on an overt and earnest *contempt* for women in general that predated Christianity. As each of these justifications for the exclusion of women fell, the Roman Church *reinscribed* the exclusion of women in *new narratives*, the current narrative being that the original apostles were all men (a *non sequitur*, and probably even not true). My church's exclusion of women from full participation in the church, then, has only one consistent thread throughout: male power. It is this consistency within inconsistency that raises the suspicion of plain bad faith. When my church today speaks of feminism, it speaks only to liberal feminism, as if that were the only kind of feminism there is. This is surely disingenuous, given the scholastic aptitudes of the Roman Catholic Church's bishops, cardinals, and pope. I will let other confessions speak for themselves. Cursory research exposes this fallacy that feminism and liberalism are necessarily synonymous. Liberal feminism is but one feminist strain among several. If I were being suspicious, I might believe that the church, which has a sound and defensible critique of liberalism, is selecting only the weakest tradition in terms of its philosophical defensibility, and avoiding those feminist voices that address the issue of oppressive power (and male violence) more directly and defensibly. Antiliberal

---

11. *Summa Theologica* I q. 92, a. 3.

Misbegotten Man

feminists[12] have consistently articulated the standpoints of women from a perspective that does not, as liberals tend to do, try to dissociate sex from power. They have named the co-identification of violence with masculinity and the association of masculinity with violence as a transhistorical phenomenon. This correspondence between masculinity and violence has shape-shifted more than once, but the basic pairing persists. There is one consistent, predominantly male activity that can at least to some degree account for this persistence by its transhistorical character, and that is war.

This does not mean that I endorse "radical" and other nonliberal feminisms in every regard. But Christians who seek to understand the failure of the Christian male to show compassion for women will discover the footprints of these feminists all along their path. They have something to teach us about where women stand and about why we should *see* the women who are standing there. If Christians can incorporate the insights of Aristotle, or anthropology, or Baudrillard, or molecular biology, we can certainly incorporate the valid insights of feminist thinkers.

Maria Mies, a feminist whose research is included in this account of witch hunts, has an interpretive framework not far from that of Catholic Ivan Illich.[13] Her work has shown clearly that the history of witch burning points a finger at proto-liberalism, the emerging state, and the fathers of the Enlightenment. This brief history serves as a window on the early *development* of male dominance *as it exists today*, which is certainly distinct from the imaginations, symbols, and realities of male supremacy in the past. The church's most recent philosophical pronouncements, especially my own Roman Catholic confession's, have been the *least* defensible in rigorous debate about women (and by extension, about sex). The church's strength in rigorous debate is its critique of post-Enlightenment modernity, specifically liberalism, by postliberal theologians and philosophers from several confessions, including Hans Frei, George Lindbeck, Alasdair MacIntyre, Amy

---

12. These include radical feminists, eco-feminists, Marxist-feminists, third-world feminists, black feminists, womanists, and Christian feminists, among others.

13. The "subsistence perspective," shared by Illich and Mies, is critical of the modern political right *and* left for their shared commitment to "radical technological optimism" and the modern division of labor with its powerful bureaucratic superstructure. The subsistence perspective advocates for relocalization of power and practices that close the distance between production and consumption. "Subsistence" means both production of one's livelihood at or near home combined with voluntary simplicity as a way of shifting away from dependence on money, industrial production, and complex, unsustainable technical infrastructure. This perspective is closely related to the movement for "community resilience" and Christian initiatives for a "new agrarianism," represented by, among others, Wendell Berry and Norman Wirzba.

Laura Hall, William Cavanaugh, Catherine Pickstock, Stanley Hauerwas, Kathryn Tanner, and many more.

The Western churches can all trace their lineage prior to the Reformation to the Roman Catholic Church; and as the witch trials show, the arguments in support of church doctrine and practice have been inconsistent. What has been consistent is the tendency of the church (and post-Reformation, the churches) to align itself with political power and accommodate itself to popular culture against the grain of the Gospels. Those confessions that did not align themselves with politico-military sponsors, like the Anabaptists, were violently persecuted and marginalized.

Four topics require greater explication before we can proceed in our argument. These topics inflect on one another throughout that argument. One of those topics is, obviously, liberalism. Another is feminism, or at least specific insights from the body of feminist thought. A third is war as a practice, and how it is constitutive of certain forms of masculinity. Finally, we need to study the history of the church in its relation to the three preceding topics, as a means of synthesizing conclusions. For now, we look at war.

9

Eros and War

War alone brings up to its highest tension all human energy and puts the stamp of nobility upon a people who have the courage to meet it. War is to man what maternity is to woman. I do not believe in peace, but I find it depressing and a negation of all human virtues of man.

—Benito Mussolini[1]

If there were no erotic or sentimental investment in the state, if our identities as modern sexually defined subjects did not take the state to be the primary object and therefore the partner on whom our identity depends, what could explain our passion for "la patria"?

—Doris Sommer[2]

War is among the most formative practices underwriting masculinity constructed as violence. This is a simple claim, but it is buried in rationalization and silence. The rationalizations we will get to; but the silence is our refusal to acknowledge that certain *men*, not homologous "human beings," have exercised a monopoly on organized violence since prehistory. The history of

---

1. Quoted in Johari, *Contemporary Political Theory*, 706.
2. Sommer, *Foundational Fictions*, 41.

the Ardennes is a history of men and women; but the history of the Battle of the Bulge is a boy-story.

War is organized armed violence, intended to destroy social infrastructure and human life, and it is directed by one collective against another collective. The list of the "types" of war is still growing because individual wars are adaptive from all preceding wars. Facing new circumstances with each instantiation, war gives rise to new technologies, new tactics, and new doctrines. So we hear about total war, general war, guerrilla war, air-land war, asymmetrical war, wars of liberation . . . There seems to be no end to the creativity of violence.

In the twentieth century, more than two hundred million human beings had their lives cut short by warfare.[3] That was the approximate world population of humans during the birth of Jesus. During the An Lushan Rebellion of AD 755–63, the death toll, though inexact, was certainly in the millions. Thirteenth-century Mongol armies slaughtered several millions. The fourteenth and fifteenth centuries saw more than ten million dispatched, according to some sources, by the Turkic Muslim leader Tamarlane;[4] while the American Civil War was raging, the Taiping Rebellion in China may have claimed as many as twenty million lives,[5] overlapping with the Dungan Revolt (also in what is modern China), which claimed around ten million more.

World War II tops all wars, with seventy-three million dead, including approximately forty-five million civilians. The United States suffered the loss of approximately 418,500 people, or .32 percent of its total population, with the Soviet Union losing the highest number, more than twenty-three million, or nearly 14 percent of its total population. Germany lost nearly 10 percent of its population, with around seven million dead, in addition to the 180,000 or so German Jews who were shot, starved, or gassed.[6] Japan lost over three million out of just over seventy-one million people—about 4 percent.[7]

More recently, counting deaths from secondary causes, like disease outbreaks among soldiers and refugees, it is estimated that 380,000 people a

---

3. Leitenberg, "Deaths in Wars and Conflicts."

4. Saunders, *Mongol Conquests*, 174.

5. Leung, "Taiping Rebellion."

6. More than 5.8 million European Jews were killed by the Nazis, along with Slavs, Roma, Christian Poles, homosexuals, disabled people, and political dissidents, totaling approximately 11 million in all.

7. O'Brien, "World War II Casualties."

year, on average, died in wars during the period 1985–94, a period in which I was very active in the army.[8] In addition to deaths, there are even higher numbers of people wounded, many suffering permanent disability; and an untold number of combatants and noncombatants are psychologically scarred by warfare. The scale might be news to some, but the reality of war's destruction ought not to be, nor should men's continued participation in war (now joined by a few women).

Men *love* war.

William Broyles Jr., writing for *Esquire* in 1984, in an article titled "Why Men Love War," said, "I'm talking about why thoughtful, loving men can love war even while knowing and hating it. Like any love, the love of war is built on a complex of often contradictory reasons. Some of them are fairly painless to discuss; others go almost too deep, stir the caldron too much."[9]

War is both attractive and addictive because of its intensity. War offers up a smorgasbord of "Holy shit! Did you fucking see that?" experiences. The stuff boys learn to like early in their lives, the stuff of "male bonding." War offers up *transgression* with all its thrills. I can burn a house. I can blow up a vehicle or a bridge. I can kill. I can slip away to an exotic whorehouse and smoke opium, drop a grenade into a well. I can mutilate corpses. Broyles writes that "war, since it steals our youth, offers a sanction to play boys' games."[10] War offers friend-and-foe clarity and allows you to outsource moral decision-making. It also allows otherwise mediocre people to shine. Ulysses Grant sold firewood before he was a general. Himmler was a chicken farmer. These are the more benign reasons men love war, according to Broyles, reminiscing about his time in Vietnam. There are others, too.

> The love of war stems from the union, deep in the core of our being, between sex and destruction, beauty and horror, love and death. War may be the only way in which most men touch the mythic domains in our soul. It is, for men, at some terrible level, the closest thing to what childbirth is for women: the initiation into the power of life and death.[11]

Stating it plainly, many men who actually participate in combat (actual combat, or unresisted offensive operations) learn to love killing people. It

8. Scaruffi, "Wars and Casualties."
9. Broyles, "Why Men Love War," para. 13.
10. Ibid., para. 15.
11. Ibid., para. 13.

makes them godlike; and it makes them alive, as seen by the contrast with the nonliving bodies at their feet.

Despite the brutal honesty on display in the essay by Broyles, war culture is a culture of lies; the most important lie is that men who make war hate war. That is actually the exception. They might hate the discomforts and inconveniences of field life (though now, American soldiers can return to air-conditioned barracks after a combat operation), but they are jacked up by adrenaline and death. I hated authority, which might sound strange coming from a former career soldier. But I can't begin to describe to anyone who hasn't done it what it feels like to step off for an operation. It is an altered state.

In modern U.S. media, things like murdering civilians and desecrating bodies are attributed to "bad apples." These actions are not, we are told, representative of most of our "heroes." The simplest rebuttal is that these things happen in units. "Individual soldier" is an oxymoron. Soldiers operate in groups, and these kinds of actions are group actions. Wartime atrocities are "male bonding" in action. As Broyles's article suggests, for many men, violence becomes eroticized:

> Most men who have been to war, and most women who have been around it, remember that never in their lives did they have so heightened a sexuality. War is, in short, a turn-on. War cloaks men in a coat that conceals the limits and inadequacies of their separate natures. It gives them all aura, a collective power, an almost animal force.[12]

War has been around for a very long time. The first recorded war, waged between the Sumerians and the Elamites, occurred in approximately 3000 BCE.[13] Archeological evidence suggests that as early as the late Paleolithic era, war was fought using primarily bows, clubs, and slings. It seems safe to assume that population densities were lower, and that these weapons did not inflict anything like modern numbers of casualties.

With population concentration, war changed; it was no longer the relatively low-intensity, short-duration affair that it had been when people mostly hunted and gathered. Agriculture slowed migration and established fixed communities. It created accumulations of wealth that served as

---

12. Ibid., para. 49.
13. Mark, "War."

temptations to plunder. Agriculture was also labor-intensive, which served as a temptation to enforced slavery.

A reasonable historical speculation is that once war was established by a raiding military force against an agricultural community, the community itself was incited to strengthen its defense, so, over time, there occurred the adoption of specifically offensive and defensive tactics, techniques, and technology. Each innovation was met with a counter-innovation; and this set up the dynamic of the arms race. We can track this developmental dynamic throughout history.

At the organizational level, ineffectual leadership is eventually weeded out by defeat (though sometimes replaced by new *forms* of ineffectual leadership), and leadership itself becomes devoted, above all other considerations, to material efficacy. This does not happen immediately, as the history of military blunders attests, but over time and at great cost. To be effective in warfare, as Clausewitz says in his schema, there must be something called "unity of command," or the centralization of decision-making in one person: a commander. When entire societies, then, are placed on a war footing, the entire society necessarily reflects the strict hierarchy of military organization, as well as its cultural authoritarianism. Given that war has always been a predominantly male-directed enterprise, militaristic societies tend to strengthen the power of males and validate the bellicosity of males. In addition to war technology, then, the key ingredients in warfare are hierarchical social organization and the various incentives for war. Hierarchies can facilitate war. War certainly facilitates hierarchies. These hierarchies are created by and commanded by men, so societies at war are male-ruled societies, even when the head of a modern state happens to be female.

In most premodern societies, adult women spent a good deal of time nursing and nurturing children, which reduced their mobility. Gravid women nurse children; and nursing moms are unlikely to seek opportunities for armed combat. That is not to say that women cannot fight in war; they have, some with the same skill, endurance, and determination as anyone else. That does not change the male character of war. These women, like some women leaders today, were willing to behave like the men who preceded them and to refrain from undermining the essential male character of their enterprise. They became honorary men.

In a bizarre scene from the execrable film *G.I. Jane*, Demi Moore's character comes into her own as a woman undergoing SEAL training when she beats up her instructor, then bellows over her vanquished foe, "Suck my dick!"

The masculine *character* of the military institution is represented through the *association* of probative masculinity with sexual humiliation of the other. The female officer had become an honorary man, as indicated in subsequent scenes where she is finally accepted among the other SEAL trainees. In her "passing over" into honorary masculinity, she combines violence with a symbolic demand for sexual subjugation, for sexual tribute from a vanquished foe. This is recognizable to us, because we have heard this expression ourselves used in exactly this way, as the eroticization of violence and the feminization of submission (being receptive). Her vanquished counterpart is humiliated, that is, feminized.

In the end, G.I. Jane shows her stuff by killing Arabs, and becoming an equal female in the imperial order. This is liberal feminism, or "equality."

10

Practice Makes Perfect

Being and becoming similar are factors which are essential for children's development, and gradually establish their relationship to the world, to themselves, and to language.

—Christoph Wulf[1]

Would the military welcome pilots who worried if dropping bombs might incur civilian casualties?

—Stanley Hauerwas[2]

Men who are soldiers practice techniques and tactics designed to kill *the* enemy. (Trainers always say "the enemy," never "an enemy.") In any society that maintains a standing military, the permanence of the state of war is assumed, even if it is not active at the moment. Even when they are not in combat, soldiers practice for combat against the enemy. Without the enemy, the soldier has no reason for being.

If you practice playing cards every day, you will think about cards a good deal of the time. I pulled guard duty for a solid week once in a tent in

---

1. Wulf, "Mimetic Learning," para. 12.
2. Hauerwas, "Christian Soldiers," para. 6.

the snow. There were four of us. We sat around the stove and played spades every day, all day. At night, I began to dream about cards. Likewise, if you practice killing every day, you'll think a lot about killing. You'll dream about killing. You'll construct hypothetical situations in your mind for killing, and for not being killed. You *become* killing.

If you are rewarded with high esteem for being a soldier, and higher esteem still for success in war, the "good" becomes killing, because that is the practical task of the combat soldier.[3] People seek out the good; they seek out opportunities for goods. So the combat soldier seeks—out of self-defense, out of peer pressure, out of the desire for greater esteem in the eyes of his fellows, and out of a desire to achieve a certain type of masculinity—to be a better killer, as well as a proficient apologist for his actions and the actions of his comrades. The highest virtue in the Heroic and Classical Ages was achieved in combat. One could argue that in the militaristic nation in which I live today, the United States, this is again true. Our veneration of soldiers borders on idolatry.

The practice of war changes men. It forms them. In any standing military, there is a shocking and abrupt period of basic training, an intense formative process that transforms the civilian into a soldier. If there were no need for a particular kind of formation for military service, there would be no need for the shock treatment of basic training, or "boot camp." Theologian Stanley Hauerwas notes, with some regret, that mainstream churches in the United States are so subordinate to state and secular culture that church is reduced to a footnote—the church cannot compare with the Marine Corps in the formation of its membership.

When I was preparing to go through basic training forty-five years ago, I lost count of the men who told me that time in the army would make me "a man." Given that I had already reached the age of majority with the requisite physiology, it seems obvious that they were talking about something more than being an adult male. Merriam-Webster defines *masculine* as "having *qualities appropriate to or usually associated with* a man." So, how do certain qualities and behaviors come to be associated with men? This is the difference between gender—embedded social expectations and practices that differ between men and women—and the more empirical category of biological sex.

If the archetypical practice of men is war, then those characteristics associated with war-fighting men come to be seen as characteristic of masculinity. When men's practice is domination and conquest, then the best

---

3. Not all soldiers in modern bureaucratic militaries, though the public often thinks of all soldiers as combat soldiers.

male is understood to be the one who most effectively dominates and conquers. In militaristic societies, these characteristics come to be understood as *male* virtues. Courage and strength, yes, even endurance, but also careless cruelty, or in a more biblical idiom, hard-heartedness. Warriors must have the ability to see others as mere objects and to do what psychologists call compartmentalizing. Commanders of Nazi death camps could still be good family men.[4]

The formative process for masculinity in every society begins at birth. At the age of nine months, an average human infant is already exercising a more advanced form of mimetic learning than any other primate, including our Forest Troop baboons. Yet the cultural impact on the troop of their mimetic disruption with the mass death of males was profound. I believe this speaks to the relationship between mimetic learning in the individual and the cultural determination of identity. Speaking here of mimesis, we mean more than mere imitation. It is the establishment of a person's relationship to the world around her or him. It is embodied, and mimetic learning is "constitutive of social, artistic, and practical action."[5] When we watch the formation of small children, we see in them an apparently innate mimetic capacity. They emulate our voices, our facial expressions, our particular choreographies of body language; and in their doing so, we also see the transformation of mimesis, to habit, to discovery of context, to understanding, as the child matures. As Aristotle might say, the child "actualizes" his or her potential.

We learn how to behave socially by mimesis. Mimesis is intersubjective. We relate to others and acquire not only their habits but also their feelings and desires. "To be able to act 'correctly,' under given circumstances," says anthropologist Christoph Wulf, "people need practical knowledge gained in sensual and corporeal mimetic processes of learning which take place in the corresponding fields of action. The characteristics of social action in a given culture, too, can only be grasped by approaching them mimetically. Practical knowledge and social action are to a large extent the result of cultural and historical conditions."[6]

Non-mimetic actions like mental reflection, analysis, even the development of daily routines, are built fundamentally on a mimetic foundation. Prior to the capacity for conceptual practices and the development of routines, mimesis makes one progressively more similar to familiar

---

4. See Hall, "'Kindly' Auschwitz Commander."
5. Wulf, "Mimetic Learning," para. 1.
6. Ibid., para. 16.

others; and thereby, mimesis is also the basis for making one less and less similar to certain nonfamiliar others, that is, people of different societies or cultures. Most of us have observed this direct transmission of culture and identity, even and especially in its current state of flux. Consider for a moment any familiar, white middle-class culture in any place in the United States. Consider at the same time a working-class African American family somewhere nearby. Children in each setting grow up imitating the speech, gestures, emotional cues, and customs of their families of origin. And there are observable distinctions between each. Now, consider that the children of these two cultures attend the same school. To a significant degree, each group of children is likely to practice self-segregation, especially those who have had the least contact in the past with the "other" group. The similarities that characterize each group constitute an identity that is learned mimetically, and consolidated with powerful emotional resonance. Each culture is, likewise, established in the mind of a child. In forming one type of similarity with members of one's own culture, one accentuates another type of difference from members of a different culture.

Consider also, especially since legal segregation was abolished, that many of the same kids today, through cultural transmission and especially through electronic media, may begin to imitate one another across cultural lines, and thereby take on some of the cultural characteristics of the other. For better or for worse, the most common sites for this transmission are still consumer spaces, but intercultural families are also now becoming a little more common. Oddly enough, interracial marriages are more common in the U.S. Army than any other sector I know; but one factor that makes this possible is the cultural distinction of the military and military communities, and the common experience of formation that all military members undergo—which makes them different in certain ways from surrounding civilian cultures.

Mimetic learning, according to Wulf, is simultaneously the "appropriation of the world and the constitution of the subject."[7] There is no functional separation between self and surrounding world. The subject is constituted directly through that appropriation, and that appropriation is aimed at belonging. Belonging is a particular and crucial kind of *recognition*. Linda Kintz says that each of these formative experiences, mimetic and supra-mimetic, is associated with the belongingness of the home and the affirmation and nurturing that took place there from infancy. In this, the formative behaviors and attitudes of any subject are accompanied by a deep emotional or, as Kintz calls it, *affective* resonance.[8] As people grow into

---

7. Ibid., para. 18.
8. Kintz, *Between Jesus and the Market*.

legally recognized adults, the practices and attitudes they learned prior to their conceptual development remain, powerfully influencing and in many ways defending a subject's identity. This affective resonance is primary.

"The intensity of mattering," writes Kintz, "while ideologically constructed, is nevertheless 'always beyond ideological challenge because it is *called into existence* affectively."[9] Philosopher and cultural critic Slavoj Žižek describes the intersubjectivity of this resonance in formation:

> The desire staged in fantasy is not the subject's own, but the other's desire, the desire of those around me with whom I interact: fantasy is an answer to "You're saying this, but what is it that you effectively want by saying it?" The original question of desire is not directly "What do I want?," but "What do others want from me? What do they see in me? What am I for the others?"[10]

Children are at the center of a web of relations that serves as "a kind of catalyst and battlefield for the desires of those around" them.[11] The child absorbs various social games, including "language games" with all their meanings, from this interplay and even from conflict. In failing to fully understand them, the child[12] will substitute fantasy for explanation. *Original fantasies are formed with the desire to be desired.* It is in this emotional sojourn of early childhood formation that sexual desire is competitively mentored, as is the apprehension of those norms that will constitute a gendered identity. With few exceptions, nothing in a child's development is more relentlessly policed from an early age than his or her gendered identity.

Wulf emphasizes the moral ambivalence of mimetic learning. Mimesis can advance and extend the person into the world around him, or it can lead to vulgar imitation. Mimesis itself is nonviolent, involving not *conflict* but *encounter*. That characteristic nonviolence is undermined by *desire*, as René Girard describes it. Mimetic desire begins as the imitation of desire, but upon learning to desire the same objects as those from whom one learned, the role model and the mimetic-learner come into conflict.[13] One artistic formulation of this is Oedipus; but the object is not always sexual. It can relate to any desire that is learned by mimesis. This dynamic of conflict over shared desires gives rise to social fractures, which Gerard believes led to the custom of scapegoating, first with an actual goat, but eventually with

---

9. Ibid., 61.
10. Žižek, "Connections of the Freudian Field," para. 9.
11. Ibid., para. 10.
12. See chapter 22 on "magical thinking."
13. Andrade, "René Girard."

sacrificed human beings. For Girard, a Catholic, the revelation of Christ undermines this form of "mediation."[14]

Mimesis is a form of learning that is deeply embodied, because it is practical. We *do* mimesis with our bodies. "Sexual desire is awakened and developed in mimetic processes. There, sexual difference is experienced, and sexual identity is learned and acquired."[15]

With the ascendance of social learning theory, metropolitan society learned and popularized a new term: *role model*. Since then, there has been a lot of attention paid to the function of role models in "social learning." Virtue ethicists assert the importance of models in character development, which is a kind of *apprenticeship*, or the internalization of certain virtues related to certain practices.

Every parent I know, myself included, has seen mimesis in action—imitation, habituation, and, finally, understanding. At two, a child will imitate a parent sweeping the floor. At ten, she has incorporated this into her routine chores. At fifteen, she knows when a floor needs sweeping and has an appreciation for the value of the before-and-after difference. In Haiti, where I have spent a good deal of time, children in the countryside begin performing adult tasks as soon as they are big enough because the performance of these tasks—carrying water, washing clothes, gathering wood, repairing structures, animal husbandry, hoeing and harvesting, etc.—qualifies them as fuller members of their society. They begin imitating adults early; and they learn very quickly, because they are not put into age-segregated schools for "formal," abstract learning.

Self-help schemas, especially for communities that are experiencing certain social crises affecting the young, emphasize the importance of role models, whether women modeling for girls, men for boys, or adults of one ethnicity or another for children of that same group. In particular, we hear a great deal about boys needing better male role models. What we don't hear is the underlying rationale for why a particular kind of role model might be good but another not good. The presumption is that men who conform most closely to the expectations of respectable society are those who are most worthy of emulation; and the call for better role models is deployed as a defense against both social deviance and various "feminizations" of men.

Boys growing up on farms more or less consistently learned at the hands of a father how to be a farmer. More often than not in the U.S., that meant a nationalistic farmer, a Protestant farmer, and a white farmer. In 1910, African American farmers were not seen by the dominant culture as

14. Ibid.
15. Wulf, "Mimetic Learning," para. 26.

normative; and with the able assistance of a racist USDA, the number of actual black farmers plummeted (another story).[16] Migration to the more pluralist city presented boys with a lot more potential role models, many of them perceived to be dangerous to the optimization of young men, in a period when optimization of human beings was the modern project, to the point where the ideas of eugenics became wildly popular among the "progressive" U.S. intelligentsia.

Men are direct models for boys, as well as for other men. Men featured in local narratives are indirect models for boys and men. Men featured in cultural narratives are indirect models for boys and men. Men invented and portrayed in modern mass cultural production are indirect, but often hegemonic, models for boys and men.

"War is a counter-church. It is the most determinative moral experience many people have," writes Stanley Hauerwas.[17] It is actually the most determinative moral experience that many (and mostly) *men* have.

"Models" alone do not account for the type of person one becomes. Once the imitation of the mentor has progressed to mastery, the specific practices of a person exert a more distinct formative effect on his personality and character. If this is controversial, it is because noxious actions in a community might emerge from practices the community deems essential. If the public hires an executioner, for example, people should be unsurprised that the actual person performing executions exhibits otherwise antisocial behavior. People know he is formed to some degree by his practice; yet they do not want to make the association lest it cast doubt on the practice of executions, which they desire out of fear of social chaos or the lust for revenge.

When I was in the army, even when I was out of uniform, and even when my grooming standards were relaxed for specific occasions, I was still recognizable as a soldier by other people in the GI town of Fayetteville, North Carolina, where about thirty-five thousand soldiers roamed through the streets. My attitudes, my comportment, my speech, etc., were those of a soldier. When I was reclassified as a Special Forces medic, I was sent to a yearlong indoctrination and training course as an SF medic, then placed on a team. Within a year on the team, I was different than I had been in the infantry. I thought like a medic, practiced as a medic, and began to see the world more biologically than I had before. A new part of my job was

---

16. Grant et al., "Black Farmers United."
17. Hauerwas, "Just War Theory?"

nurturing, though in the army we'd have been loath to call it that. And I became more attentive to the needs of others than I had been in the infantry.

People are formed by practices, and the practices themselves, when they conform to the standards of a community of practitioners, are *praxis*—practices consistent with some theory or set of norms. People are not inevitably determined by praxis, or else there would be no possibility of redemption for anyone formed by malevolent practices; but praxis is powerfully influential.

Alasdair MacIntyre has drawn out the relationship between community, practice, and institution. Each practice has certain rules and values that facilitate certain goods. For example, if one is a chess player, a practitioner of chess, one uses the framework of rules and values that make chess what it is, and the good for the practitioner is the satisfaction of mastery of the many aspects of the game. In MacIntyre's account, as in Aristotle's and Aquinas's, this kind of satisfaction—the satisfaction of mastery within the practice—is what is called an *internal good*. Increasing mastery aims toward excellence, and in each practice there are numerous forms of excellence. A basketball player might become highly proficient at three-point shots, so much so that she is recognized at the top of her sport. Other basketball players who have not achieved that accuracy and consistency nonetheless practice more frequently to improve it with an eye to excellence. Excellence is the aiming-point of repetitious practice.

The connection between the practitioners, the preservation of the practice's rules, values, and traditions, and the development of many practices seems to require some institutional framework. At certain scales, all human organizations articulate structures that administer, manage, and express the values of a practice. The pickup basketball shooter at the city park may not have any direct affiliation with basketball institutions, but he relates to his sport through them and the most excellent players, whom those various basketball institutions support.

But there is a contradiction in the kinds of goods available through practices of any kind. The chess player who took pleasure in her mastery of the game received an *internal good*. If that same chess player began to play in the park and win money, she might still enjoy her mastery of the game, but the additional good, money, is an *external good*. She can get money through other means than playing chess, and money works as money independent of chess. Internality and externality here describe two different moral dimensions. There is a general recognition that sometimes external goods can become corruptive of internal goods. A government official who accepts a bribe (an external good to his practice) is therein compromised in his ability to correctly and diligently execute his office on behalf of the public (which ought to be the decisive internal good—excellence in public service).

Institutions themselves are *oriented* to external goods. In administrative, managerial, and entrepreneurial enterprises, material support for the institutions themselves is required, and so the acquisition of money becomes a very compelling external good. The people who staff the institutions confront situations where the good of the practice and the good of the institution, in particular as it relates to the self-interests of institutional staff and executives, can come into conflict. This tendency is built into institutions and is constitutive of them. Institutions are inherently corruptible (*not* inherently corrupt) because the goods of control and acquisition that benefit management might come into conflict with the goods of the practice. The administrative tail begins to wag the practical dog. The wrong good is emphasized. Jesus pointed this out to some of his critics when he said the Sabbath is made for people, not people for the Sabbath (Mark 2:27).

Finally, there is the question of the practice itself. One might have been a proficient overseer on a slave plantation in the pre-Civil War American South. Where is the referent to which we might turn to establish the good or evil of practices, regardless of the coherence and institutional stability of the practice?

War as a practice tends toward the ethic of pure consequentialism, of the end justifying the means. Might literally makes right. Whatever the internal goods might be for the practitioner, there is still a moral question unanswered *by* a practice about the practice itself.

11

~

The Masculine Fortress

And he took bread, gave thanks and broke it, and gave it to them, saying, "This is my body given for you; do this in remembrance of me." In the same way, after the supper he took the cup, saying, "This cup is the new covenant in my blood, which is poured out for you."

—Luke 22:19–20

I call a strategy a calculation (or manipulation) of power relationships that becomes possible as soon as a subject with will and power (a business, an army, a city, a scientific institution) can be isolated. It postulates a place that can be delimited as its own and serve as the base from which relations with an exteriority composed of targets or threats (customers or competitors, enemies, the country surrounding the city, objectives and objects of research, etc.) can be managed.... Every "strategic" rationalization seeks first of all its "own" place, that is, the place of its own power and will, from an "environment." A Cartesian attitude, if you wish: it is an effort to delimit one's own place in a world bewitched by the powers of the Other. It is also the typical attitude of modern science, politics, and military strategy.

—Michel de Certeau[1]

1. Certeau, *Practice of Everyday Life*, 35–36.

In chapter 2 I wrote, of serial rapist Marshall Brown, that "Marshall was the commando—root word *command*—who follows orders without question within established hierarchies. He was committed in his role as the colonizer's paladin, with its admixture of violent conquest and 'civilization' to be imposed outside those disciplinary restraints. He policed boundaries, and he also, using his status as one who belonged *inside* the defensive male perimeter, transgressed them." In this chapter, we will explain how this reference to a "defensive male perimeter" is more than merely metaphorical, but constitutive of many masculinities.

Mark's Gospel was a war gospel, written circa AD 68, perhaps just months before the Romans burned the temple in Jerusalem. Hebrew rebels had made some significant advances against the Romans, and young Hebrew men were under tremendous pressure—not least from their own pride in Hebrew military successes against Roman soldiers—to join the rebellion. Mark's Gospel was likely written, in part, as an effort to dissuade the new and ideally nonviolent followers of Jesus from joining the armed struggle.[2] What Mark, as a follower of Jesus during a time and in a place of constant warfare, may have recognized is that the practice of war is inherently corrupt and corruptive, which was certainly lost on subsequent men leading the church. The ethos of Christ consistently dismantled social boundaries, including the kind of boundary that served as a "defensive male perimeter" for Marshall Brown and the kind of boundary dangerously intuited by Mark's male contemporaries as constitutive of their own masculinity.

In *The Practice of Everyday Life*, French Jesuit intellectual Michel de Certeau (1925–86) describes a difference between strategy and tactics. He alters the military meaning of tactics—which is a subset of operations/which is a subset of strategy. De Certeau uses the term *tactics* to describe something *opposed to* strategy.[3] This requires a bit of explanation, so I beg the reader's patience.

In military parlance, tactics are a *subset* of strategy, not its *opposite*. In de Certeau, they are opposites.

Strategy for the military relates to national or overarching objectives. Strategy is executed through various campaigns—the subset of strategy. Campaigns are further broken down into specific combat engagements, or battles. The techniques employed in the battlespace are called *tactics*, and

---

2. Myers, *Binding the Strong Man*, 39–84.
3. De Certeau, *Practice of Everyday Life*, 29–41.

the tactical level is a subset of the campaign. This can be represented visually as Strategy > Campaign > Tactics.

A small unit—a modern light infantry platoon, for example—might be part of a counterinsurgency campaign in a certain region, which is part of a national strategy. Imagine this exemplary platoon on a long-range, dismounted patrol. They establish a patrol base to rest and plan, this platoon will establish a *perimeter*, a single, continuous boundary with an inside and an outside. A perimeter is formed when the members of the platoon face outward, establishing interlocking fields of fire. What that means is the sectors, observed by individual platoon members, overlap one another to create a kind of ring of death. If anyone enters into any member's field of fire, that person is subject to be shot; and because every sector overlaps, that person will be fired upon from two locations. Everyone aims *outward*; no one aims *inward*. In the center of this perimeter, the command element establishes a little position in which to supervise, communicate, and plan. In military parlance, the security perimeter is a *tactic*, a technique employed at a specific place in the battlespace.

However, in de Certeau's terms, this perimeter is a highly *strategic* action. Here is the crucial difference between the military's use of the terms *strategy* and *tactics* and de Certeau's; and *we are going to adopt de Certeau's use of the terms.*

Strategy, for de Certeau, means a self-isolating calculus.[4] That is to say, strategy begins with an enemy (even if that enemy is seen as a "target population" or, in business, a competitor or client) who is the *object* of your intentions, and upon whom you desire to impose your will. A strategist requires a place—some segregated dwelling for the strategy's executors. Strategy requires a base of operations, some place that is on the inside—central to the execution of the strategy, and separated from the surrounding environment, everywhere that is *not* committed to the strategy but influences the strategy's object, and therefore yet another part of the strategic calculus. *Isolation* is a strategic necessity.[5]

Look at our notional light infantry platoon. Look at the actual headquarters for Monsanto, Lockheed-Martin, Yale University, the Vatican, or, sometimes, the suburban family. There is a barrier separating *us*, the insiders, from *them*, the outsiders. There is planning to impose our will on someone outside—a "target."

Institutions embody strategic logic.

We have built an entire edifice of business, teaching, medicine, transportation, food production, and politics based on the isolationist logic of

4. Ibid.
5. Ibid.

strategy. *Homo economicus* is a strategic isolate. He is alone, competing with others for scarce resources, and he is suspicious.

There is a presumption of existing power that is available to the strategist, at least enough to preserve the barrier between us and them. If that presumption is absent, a person will necessarily become *tactical*, in the way de Certeau describes *tactics*, which is another word for "making do." De Certeau sees tactics as resistance to "the rituals and representations that institutions seek to impose upon them."[6] Tactics, for de Certeau, violate or ignore boundaries.

The de Certeauan *tactic* is the way persons take things given by institutions and culture, and then make them their own by creatively re-employing them or by going around them. These tactics, which de Certeau collectively calls *bricolage*, are actually subversive of institutions because they undermine the meanings attached to institutional imperatives. *Bricolage* is not a strategy for de Certeau, but an anthropology—the real way of the world of human beings that stands as a contradiction to strategy, which always seeks not only to bend people to a purpose not their own, but to control the emergent unpredictability of space-time. *Bricolage* is itemized resistance or adaptation against the norm.

One member of our platoon might want to heat his rations, but have nothing with which to make a smokeless fire. He might crack open his claymore mine and dig out a little ball of the C-4 explosive, which will ignite without exploding (explosion requires heat *and* shock simultaneously); and he might light the C-4, which burns hotly and without smoke, and cook his rations. An instrument produced to kill is transformed into cooking fuel. This has actually been done by soldiers who carried claymore mines. De Certeau would call this a *tactic*, a making-do, an example of *bricolage*.

De Certeau's characterization of strategy is not the military's use-definition related to overarching objectives. While I am dispensing with the military's doctrinal definition, the de Certeau–derived "strategy" is central to both the organization and the practice of the military, as well as to most enterprises in modern metropolitan society, where the strategic orientation has been assured by the dominance of the competitive market in structuring social relations (which is modeled on war). The prime directive is *control the boundary*.

The "us-them" strategic separation, that is, the organizational logic of strategy, is a military concept that has colonized both male and modern thought. In practice, it is exemplified in the military as a hierarchical structure, in which each level of the hierarchy is insulated from levels below it in order to control them. It is a series of strategic redoubts, like fortresses. The

6. Ibid.

division commander controls the boundary between him and his staff, and between his staff and that of the brigade commander, who in turn controls the boundary between him and his staff, and his staff and that of his battalion commanders, who in turn control the boundary between battalion headquarters and the subordinate companies. These circles of control are *strategic*. They self-isolate for the purpose of exerting control from the inside over the outside.

If all this looks familiar, it is because this strategic orientation has been adopted across society, by institutions, which have emulated the military. In modern metropolitan culture, where the market and its competitive logic have been allowed to predominate, enterprises model their activities on war. Strategic logic, then, is manifest at every level that requires bureaucratic management, as applicable to IBM or the Social Security Administration or the National Football League as it is to the army, navy, air force, marines, or coast guard. The antagonistic logic of the battlefield easily overlays the antagonistic logic of competitive markets and bureaucratic control; and both overlay the antagonistic logic of conquest-masculinity. The difference is that this logic is applied to the accumulation of economic power in the case of markets or the administration of large-scale programs, and to the imposition of direct violence in the case of military operations.

Because this paradigm is common to men who have been formed in a warlike culture, any actual description of it from outside the paradigmatic logic is incomprehensible to the same men. This is reputed to be the way of the world. It is naturalized, even though it has its concrete historical antecedents in war.

Yet *bricolage*, the tactics of "everyday life," not only keeps the social order afloat in unacknowledged and unstudied ways (from cheating on taxes, to working under the table, to carpooling, to growing food in a garden, etc.), it is indicative of a kind of deep and nonresistant resistance that outlives social orders, which I take as a hopeful glimpse of some genuinely essential human nature. Maintenance of boundaries requires control. That control is exercised along the boundaries. *Bricolage*, which is sometimes seen as the way of women, renders established boundaries permeable.

One of the psychological manifestations of this preoccupation with boundaries growing out of war-thought among men is male fear of *fusion*.[7] Women constitute a danger to men, and that is the danger of *fusion*, the permeation of boundaries implied by mutual emotional surrender. The presumed weakness and irrationality of women is actually understood as a *contaminant* to men; and men police the boundary of this fear with control

---

7. I have borrowed this term from Nancy C. M. Hartsock.

over women. Men may cross the boundary, in the same way a solider leaves his firebase to conduct an operation, but no one from the outside is allowed inside the perimeter. Intimacy is a form of danger—the danger that one might be found out, but also the danger of becoming *vulnerable*. Vulnerability is what war-making and war-making metaphors aim to minimize; and the coincidence of male fear of vulnerability and this imperative of war is one we can ill afford to overlook. Christians are called, precisely, to *be* vulnerable (Matt 10:16).

The antidote to fusion is control, and we see this in ideas about sex. Women are seen as conquests or dangers, never to be allowed inside the perimeter of either the male ego or of "men's space." The term for a man who allows a woman to have too great a decision-making role in a relationship is "pussy-whipped," an accusation that was directed at me once (by a male leftist!) on account of my affinity for feminist scholars' work in my own writing. This is seen as a form of *surrender* (a military metaphor).

One of the thrills of sex for many men is the idea of entering a woman to degrade and humiliate (anal sex is a very popular porn genre, for example, as are so-called gang bangs), the act of sex from the male standpoint being compared to shooting or stabbing or raiding; and the thrill is that of the transgression and simultaneous maintenance of a boundary—a strategic redoubt—to run back into. In any *strategic* encounter, sallying forth from a redoubt for an attack or a conquest, figurative or literal, is transgression as a function of power and privilege, the privilege of deciding who is and is not allowed to cross the boundary. During a military patrol, the patrolling unit has a special plan for exiting and re-entering the "friendly" lines that ensures no enemy can infiltrate during the crossing. Pornography, with its growing popularity on the Internet, lets men have all the control and none of the vulnerability of intimacy, thereby evading the danger of *fusion*, while indulging fantasies that convert women into objects.

During the buildup to the 2003 invasion of Iraq, Karich & Associates filed for a patent on "Shock and Awe" condoms, marketed as "a great way to say you are USA." Written on the package was "With new Bunker Buster technology," and "You'll get a real BANG out of these"—as direct a reference as anyone could cite of the weaponized phallus that mirrors, in actual war, the phallicized weapon.

For a real look at military lore and the association of violence with both sex and redemption, however, we can explore the "modern social imaginary"[8] through art. The following chapter turns, then, to a popular film.

---

8. Taylor, *Modern Social Imaginaries*, 23.

12

Torture and Redemption

Christians worship a God who was tortured to death by the empire; it is this God who saves by saying no to violence on the cross. Our penance, then, would take the form of resisting the idolatry of nation and state and its attendant violence.

—WILLIAM CAVANAUGH[1]

The myth of redemptive violence is the simplest, laziest, most exciting, uncomplicated, irrational, and primitive depiction of evil the world has ever known. Furthermore, its orientation toward evil is one into which virtually all modern children (boys especially) are socialized in the process of maturation.

—WALTER WINK[2]

Charles Taylor describes a "social imaginary" as "broader and deeper than the intellectual schemes people may entertain when they think about social reality in a disengaged mode."[3] This has to do with not only notions

---

1. Cavanaugh, *Migrations of the Holy*, 113.
2. Wink, "Redemptive Violence," para. 17.
3. Taylor, *Modern Social Imaginaries*, 23.

Torture and Redemption

of sociability beyond immediate experience, but also with how things "fit together" in both a normative and moral sense.

On September 24, 2004, CNN reported that charges had been brought against three U.S. Navy SEALs in the death of an Iraqi detainee,[4] part of a much larger damage control investigation in the wake of the Abu Ghraib photo scandal, an investigation that quietly expanded to 222 abuse cases, fifty-four of which had resulted in detainee deaths.[5] This particular set of charges managed to push the story back into the media because of the involvement of SEALs, who, like all Special Operations troops, are masculine national icons.

In that same month, my eighteen-year-old son brought home a rented DVD of the Denzel Washington hit *Man on Fire*. I generally avoid watching films that feature guns and fireballs on the promotional posters, but on this particular day, there were three hours to kill, and it was an opportunity to do *something* with my son that *he* wanted to do, even if it was just catching a movie.

Man on Fire is well written, expertly acted, skillfully directed, and edgily edited, with plenty of whip pans and jump-cuts for the MTV generation. Denzel Washington's character, a Special Operations veteran struggling with anesthetic alcoholism and the grim memories of his imperial adventures, is drawn into a complex Mexican kidnapping scheme as the bodyguard for a terminally intelligent and charming little girl, an American expat child named Pita living in dark and dangerous Mexico City with her extremely attractive parents, an Americanized Mexican father and an American mother.

Man on Fire begins with that favored escapist film convention in the United States, the salt 'n' peppa buddy-team—always reassuring to America in its stubborn denial of our still-racialized reality. Washington is a black actor who has consistently strong crossover appeal with white audiences. In an early reveal scene, Washington's character, Creasy, appears with his white former special-ops colleague, Rayburn (Christopher Walken), a dissipated but likeable expatriate himself. Rayburn is portrayed as sympathetic even though he is backgrounded by bikini-clad, nubile young women somewhere in *Latinoamérica*—the expat with some money taking advantage of the favorable exchange rates. Creasy asks Rayburn, "Do you think God will ever forgive us for what we've done?"

Rayburn replies, simply, "No."

As this exchange suggests, a pseudo-Christianity is integrated into the theme and the plot throughout the film, including a story of redemption. However, *Man on Fire* is really a sly male revenge fantasy. The question

4. Phillips, "Rush Transcript."
5. Haynes, "Footage Exposes Abuse."

about God's forgiveness and the fact that Creasy carries, reads, and commits to memory portions of his Bible (which the cosmopolitan Creasy quotes in Spanish to a Mexican nun, before telling her he is a "lost sheep") are combined with a hypnotic and elegiac background score that clearly makes Hollywood-God the film's main invisible character. There is an almost easygoing character development in the first half of the film that draws the audience emotionally into Creasy's guilt and pain. God intervenes with an epiphany for Creasy when he attempts suicide with his pistol and the bullet fails to fire. Drunk and crying in the pouring night rain with his favorite song, Linda Rondstadt's "Blue Bayou," wailing away (I told you this film is blatantly manipulative), Creasy calls his friend, Rayburn, and asks what it means when a bullet fails to fire—not letting on that he has attempted to blow his own head off.

Rayburn knows intuitively, of course, and he shares some Hollywood-concocted special-ops lore that "a bullet never lies." This is Creasy's Damascene moment, his conversion, after which he gives up the booze and becomes fair Pita's surrogate father, even as her own treacherous (Mexican) father plots to have her kidnapped for the insurance (he will die by the same truthful bullet later in the film).

In Act II, Creasy and the child fall into filial love, whereupon Pita is kidnapped. Creasy is gravely wounded in a heroic attempt to foil the kidnapping, the plan goes sour, and Pita is killed. This is the cue for Creasy to become the instrument of God's justice, of course, and even before he is mended from his ever more Christlike and manly wounds, he begins to hunt down, systematically (and even sexually) torture, then exterminate every participant in the kidnapping and ostensible murder of fair Pita. The audience is carried along via its well-massaged emotions, and we are invited to wallow in the vengeful cruelty of Creasy cutting off a crooked Mexican cop's fingers with pruning shears as part of an interrogation, and other graphic cruelties.

In the film's key revenge scene, Creasy captures and renders unconscious one of the evil Mexican co-conspirators. When the bad guy awakens, Creasy tells him that his rectum is packed with explosives for which Creasy holds the remote detonator. In other words, Creasy has penetrated his victim, anally raped him, topped him, feminized him by making him his "bitch."

Comparisons to the frequent celebration of prison rape as an instrument of revenge are irresistible here. Creasy shows an utter lack of empathy, while the captured and violated bad guy shudders and weeps ("cries like a little bitch") in his terror. The audience is invited to share in Creasy's sadistic *enjoyment* of the captive's suffering. In the climactic end to this scene (pun totally intended), as Creasy walks away, leaving the captive cuffed to a car in the background, the explosive detonates behind our hero—a fiery and sexually symbolic shock and awe, a blazing, gasoline-powered "money shot."

In a fine imperial flourish, the honest but ineffectual Mexican police stand aside while the American warrior Creasy delivers God's justice in a lethal wave of violent masculine revenge-energy, until the denouement when Creasy, now Christlike, walks willingly to his death in exchange for Pita (who, it turns out, is alive after all), telling her he is going "home to Blue Bayou." Creasy, who believed he could not be forgiven by God, instead serves as God's instrument of war and is redeemed.

The male revenge fantasy, with its redemption through violence, is the constant retelling of a cultural myth. As Rosemary Hennessey writes,

> As one of the most pervasive forms of cultural narrative in industrialized societies, commercial film serves as an extremely powerful vehicle of myth. The mythic status of Hollywood films is of course enabled and buttressed by corporate endorsement and financial backing for distribution and promotion. To some extent the scripts that do get picked up manage to be supported because they already articulate a culture's social imaginary—the prevailing images a society needs to project about itself in order to maintain certain features of its organization.[6]

Film participates in meaning-making, and the audience participates in the film. Linda Kintz renames the social imaginary the "national popular ... based not on content but effects."[7] We recognize and embrace the formula for male revenge fantasy, one of the most popular film genres, the theme of which *is* redemption through violence. Creasy redeems himself and the situation, and earns God's forgiveness, in a bloodbath. But it is more. Go back to that scene, that anal rape by explosives, and see again that sex and violence are understood to have interchangeable meanings. See, again, the meaning of sexually receptive (woman) as conquered.

In 1999 I stumbled onto an episode of *This American Life* titled "Lockup." It was about prison. The third act was called "Who's Your Daddy?"[8] It was a reading from ex-con Stephen Donaldson's pamphlet telling new convicts how to survive in prison through protective sexual pairing. Here's the description of the segment:

6. Hennessy, *Profit and Pleasure*, 144.
7. Kintz, *Between Jesus and the Market*, 60.
8. Donaldson, "Who's Your Daddy?"

> A reading of a pamphlet written by ex-con Stephen Donaldson for heterosexual men who are about to enter prison, about how to "hook up" with a stronger man—a "daddy" or "jocker"—who'll provide protection in return for sex. He explains the rules and mores that govern this part of American prison culture. There's no graphic language and there are no graphic images in this story, but it does acknowledge the existence of sexual acts. Read by Larry DiStasi.[9]

Donaldson's pamphlet contained matter-of-fact, step-by-step instructions on how the new convict should shop for a strong man (a jocker, a "top") and how to manage the relationship with him (as the "catcher," or bottom)—the men's prison version of how to get the right husband. A very animated on-line discussion followed.

One comment: "Memo to myself: don't go to prison."

Another comment: "Disturbing article. I'm not into constantly losing fights only to get raped at the end. And no way would I catch for someone. I would either become a jocker, or stay in solitary. Unbelievable—what a different world."

More: "Oh. My. God. It's one thing to joke about 'Federal Pound-Me-in-the-Ass Prison,' but this article's matter-of-fact presentation exposes the horror. Can't prison authorities do something about this? Like maybe investigate and prosecute all rapes?"

And this: "Wow. The section at the end on Adaptation was really interesting. It must be completely world-altering to start out a jail sentence straight and then slowly have your identity punk'd. Reading stuff like this reminds me of the kind of horrific practices that happened in previous centuries of human history and in animal tribes. Not much has changed, in some ways."

Finally (this one caused some to get angry): "Ah yes, there's nothing to get red-blooded men fired up about rape than a good ol' drop-the-soap story. By the way, it happens to a woman about once every 2 minutes, according to the DOJ."

This is how gender is constructed specifically as a *sexual* hierarchy, with women as the punks, and punks as the women. In this case, the instruction booklet is not talking about "rape," as we define it around the legal category of consent, but how to avoid "rape" by consenting to receptive sex with one powerful man. Legally speaking, the prisoner who accepts one jocker for protection is engaged in "consensual" sex. This is one way that men might understand what it is like to be women, how rape as a constant

---

9. Ibid.

threat for modern women serves as one form of pressure for women to accept the perennial sexual-contract: protection in exchange for obedience. It is not new. Article 213 of the Napoleonic Code (1804) stated, "The man owes the wife protection, she owes him obedience."[10] But imagining prison rape (and prison "consent") might make it real for men. Men who have been raped do not have to imagine it. For those who haven't, maybe this example will help them "*see* this woman."

In the online comments section, men tried to find *anything* to make this different from what happens to women: "women are not locked up by the state," "rape doesn't generally happen in the ass," and so forth. The avoidance is visceral, desperate. I *can't* be a "catcher"! We have to stop *prison* rape . . . oh yeah, and all other rape, too (as an afterthought). This is a kind of microcosm of women's condition, and for the so-called instant of "consent," because it is *not* metaphorical; it is real, and it is happening to *men*, and *that* makes it suddenly an urgent issue.

How do we now parlay that outrage into an understanding that this is what some feminists are saying about "sex"? They are not talking about equal pay or equal access to the levers of power, but about the sexual subjugation of women-as-women by men-as-men. This is how rape and battering and the renting of Indian women's wombs as surrogate mothers and international sex-trafficking and the explosion of misogynistic Internet pornography are related. They don't happen to women because women are the same as men. They happen to women *because they are women*.

If we want to get to the root of homophobia, then we have to understand that it is underwritten by the devaluation of women. The policing of what Adrienne Rich called "compulsory heterosexuality" is the enforcement of a gender regime that is defined by the devaluation of women.[11] And while there are biblical references to same-sex unions (for example, in Lev 18:21–22), the idea of "heterosexual" versus "homosexual" is distinctly modern, an artifact of the modern propensity, during successive destabilizations of gender, to define masculinity as *not-woman*. Neither term, *heterosexuality* or *homosexuality*, even appears in the language until 1890.[12]

What does it tell us that men's most terrified reaction to the idea of prison is the fear that women experience all the time? What does it tell us that the worst punishment is to be made *like a woman*, a "catcher"?

"*Do you see this woman?*"

10. Mosse, *Image of Man*, 28.
11. Rich, "Compulsory Heterosexuality."
12. Illich, *Gender*, 148.

Women's choices cannot be reduced to the fear of rape (though men can never know how this possibility haunts the thoughts of women, except perhaps when men face prison); but that power and comparative powerlessness (the lack of desirable choices) makes the world of women and the world of men different. We *know* it is different because we can participate happily in Creasy's symbolic rape of the "bad guy," where violence is redemptive *as well as sexual*; and if we were to be shown a similar scene, this time with a woman as the victim of Creasy's vengeance, it would take on a wholly different meaning. Part of the bad guy's punishment was to be made receptive, to be made *like a woman*.

Creasy was the man, the conquerer, the jocker.

In the bloodstained prison cells of Abu Ghraib, the prisoners were "softened up" by feminizing them, by placing panties over their heads, by forcing their faces into one another's crotches, by having them placed on a leash in the hands of an honorary-male woman who was herself sexually partnered with a dominant and sadistic prison guard. As with the Forest Troop baboons, cruelty was passed down through the hierarchy.

You can tune into *Law and Order* reruns and hear your favorite protagonist tell the so-called perps (there is that dehumanization prior to control!), "I'm gonna make you my bitch," or smiling as they warn the bad guy that he is about to go to prison, where he will become someone's "bitch."

In 2004, when I watched *Man on Fire* with my son and when Navy SEALs were investigated for torture, rape, and murder, the United States was still freshly traumatized by September 11, 2001, and being fed militarism in large doses, including and especially our national pastime of soldier-worship.

"A bullet never lies" is the emotionally resonant wisdom of a divinely sanctioned male death cult, which is not feeding the culture but interacting with it as it acquiesces to, nay, feeds into and relishes male violence. In a sense, then, *Man on Fire* was the cultural recoding of precisely the rationale deployed within the American culture as the troops were deployed to Afghanistan and Iraq: a mission, sanctioned by God to deliver his retributive justice, that rationalizes the suspension of ineffectual law in favor of raw masculine violence against the caricatures of Evil, and that might require that we commit torture and even murder to serve a higher call for justice and order.

Creasy, disguised as a black man to divert us from the fascistic content of this film, is the strong, violent father: a constant in the emotional cosmos of Mussolini, of Franco, of Hitler. So we should not have been shocked to hear that SEALs were committing torture and even murder. Nor should we have been taken aback when we discovered that by the end of 2004 there were dozens of these cases that were no longer worthy of publishing even on page 10 of the paper. The same cultural interaction that combines producer and viewer as participants in the meaning-making of male revenge fantasy films signals to "journalists," via our shared social imaginary, what is and is not appropriate. If the story cannot be mapped onto the symbolic and emotional terrain of providential America, then it is not done at all. It is disappeared or spun as an aberration from our God-given destiny as bearers of the light to the deviant brown people of the world. That Denzel Washington is himself brown not only does not change this message, it gives it an Americo-mythic "melting pot" cover. Washington's character is a color *decoy*. His targets were the *other* brown savages, people on the other side of the defensive perimeter. We can shift this symbolism to accommodate new contingencies. It was a rabbi in North Carolina who told me once, "Arabs have become the West's new Jews."

In reality, Special Operations units have fewer African Americans than any other units in the military, but we need all the myths in a worldview basket, and Hollywood accommodates: imperial myths, melting pot myths, and hegemonic military masculinity myths, to "articulate a culture's social imaginary—the prevailing images a society needs to project about itself in order to maintain certain features of its organization."

The reality, in those places where the real military is obliged to do the real "wet work,"[13] in the prisons and torture rooms, is that they are needed to terrify the inconvenient population into submission, a reality not suitable for Hollywood. Without the myths, without Denzel's tragic pose and truthful bullets, his willingness to saw the fingers off of Mexicans to get the information needed to protect the innocent from Evil, how are we to cosign for Abu Ghraib, for "rendition," for "enhanced interrogation techniques"?

We aren't even seeing the real victims any longer—the corpses on ice, with one young GI leering over a lifeless face; the naked bodies piled on one another; the hooded men hung by their handcuffs. Thousands of horrific new photographs were repressed, and instead we get *Man on Fire*, redeeming himself before God with unspeakable violence. Mike Davis calls this intentional denial "ostrich-consensus."[14]

In the next chapter, we will study a centuries-long historical instance of Christianity being reinterpreted into redemptive violence: the Crusades.

---

13. An old KGB term for missions that required killing.
14. Davis, "The Perfect Fire."

13

The Pope's Army

The reality of the Crusades becomes more shabby the more one knows about it.

—Diarmaid MacCulloch[1]

Again, the devil took him to a very high mountain and showed him all the kingdoms of the world and their splendor. "All this I will give you," he said, "if you will bow down and worship me."

Jesus said to him, "Away from me, Satan! For it is written: 'Worship the Lord your God, and serve him only.'"

—Matthew 4:8–10

Modernity has an unexpected genealogy. It was midwifed by Christianity—not by the faith itself, but through faith in political power (Christendom) and its adoption of the practice of war.[2] Some people have called Christianity in power a heresy, others a temptation, that is, the "Constantinian" heresy or temptation. What that means is not directly related to Constantine, the murderous Roman emperor who famously converted, though his name serves as a kind of historical and semiotic marker. What it marks is

---

1. MacCulloch, "Holy Beach-Towel Hypothesis," para. 4.
2. Gregory, *Unintended Reformation*, 1–2.

the temptation of the church to *impose* Christianity, punish heresies, and criminalize sin, using the organs of armed political authority. As some theologians point out, the Constantinian temptation is any temptation for the church to try to rule society.[3] This temptation is still around, on the "right" and the "left" within Christianity.

The ultimate political power is the power to legally kill. Once we started killing heretics, the next step into war was difficult to avoid. We had already substituted killing for love as our way of being with others. Many early Christians first accepted the Roman Empire, frightened as they were of some of the people outside of the Roman Empire. Then Christians began cooperating with the empire. Then they found themselves holding political power. Finally, they began using it.[4] Before long, Christians came to apologize for, define the parameters of, and participate in organized warfare, though on a small scale. But the door to war had been opened, and it just took martial leadership and the right circumstances for the church to go to war on its own, which is exactly what the Western Church did during the Crusades. Christopher Tyerman takes us back to a scene in Europe a little more than a thousand years ago:

> On 12 April 1096, a young castellan, Achard of Monmerle, pledged property to the great Burgundian monastery of Cluny in return for 2,000 Lyons shillings and four mules so that he could accomplish his intention to join "the journey to Jerusalem to fight for God against pagans and Saracens." In a similar deal with the abbey of St. Victor at Marseilles four months later the brothers Geoffrey and Guy were reported as wishing to seek Jerusalem "both for the grace of pilgrimage and under the protection of God, to exterminate the wickedness and unrestrained rage of the pagans by which innumerable Christians have already been oppressed, made captive and killed." The experience of that campaign, which cost Achard his life near Jaffa in 1099, convinced his companions that they were the army of God "fighting for Christ," their casualties martyrs, their cause supported in battle by the saints of heaven themselves, George, Demetrius and Blaise, "knights of Christ," their success assured because "God fights for us." They were no more than pursuing the task given them by [Pope] Urban II on his preaching tour of 1095–6, who, in his own words to the Flemish in December 1095, hearing that the Turks had "in their frenzy invaded and ravaged the churches of God in the east" and "seized the Holy

---

3. Cavanaugh, "Stan the Man," in Berkman and Cartwright, *Hauerwas Reader*, 29–30.

4. Tyerman, *God's War*, 1–24.

City," had at Clermont "imposed on them the obligation to undertake such a military enterprise for the remission of all their sins."[5]

That's right: the Vicar of Christ told members of the Roman Catholic Church that if they fought, they would receive a free pass to heaven. So begins Christopher Tyerman's 1,024-page account of the Crusades, *God's War*. Church historian Diarmaid MacCulloch calls the Crusades "the bizarre centuries-long episode in which Western Christianity willfully ignored its Master's principles of love and forgiveness."[6] The Crusades were that, but they were also the church being swallowed whole by the politics of secular power, and by the logic of power being seen through the lens of war. In this logic, the enemy is never loved, but destroyed.

Stanley Hauerwas is a committed Christian pacifist who has had an immeasurable influence on me. He is also very good about giving soldiers the benefit of the doubt. Influenced by Alasdair MacIntyre, who sees vestiges of a virtue-ethic in soldiery—for example, the emphasis on honor—Hauerwas likewise, and charitably, abstains from demonizing soldiers. Neither will I demonize soldiers, having been one for quite some time; but I do want to look at soldiery in a way that also challenges these most charitable views. In MacIntyre's account of goods and practices, he notes that there is a moral difference between being a good farmer and a good burglar;[7] and I am going to suggest that soldiery is closer to the latter than the former in terms of what it contributes to the common good. My experience of war is that war, as a practice, does not inculcate honor as often as hatred, hostility, cruelty, and the fragmentation of the soldier's personality. Bad soldiers do not make war a bad thing. War invariably makes soldiers do bad things, and we become what we do.

Moral degradation is *inherent* in the practice of war. Once the determination is made that some will have to be killed, those targeted have had the value of their existence erased in the minds of soldiers. This objectification of the enemy is not the end of it. Soldiers learn how to demonstrate their solidarity with one another through acts of escalating cruelty against the enemy. Nothing in "just war" theory or doctrine accounts for this inevitability, this transformation of the person of the soldier into a brute, or the transformation of a society that has accepted the logics of war into a brutalized and

---

5. Ibid., 27.
6. Ibid., from a blurb on the dust jacket.
7. MacIntyre, *After Virtue*, 187–94.

brutalizing society. The nearer a society is drawn toward totalizing power, the greater the potential for totalizing degradation. The more totalizing the military is in any society, the more likely that society will generally manifest the kinds of degradation associated with war; and war as a transhistorical phenomenon has been transhistorically male, which leads me to conclude that men are those who are most *degraded* by war—not victimized, *degraded*. Many more people than soldiers are victimized by war. "Degradation" here means degeneration into a lower moral condition.

In 1098, Christian soldiers en route to Jerusalem forced the capitulation of the Muslim town of Ma'arra. When the residents surrendered, the Christians massacred all eight thousand or so of them. It was getting cold, and food was in short supply. Christian soldiers began eating the massacre victims. Journals describe men carving hams from the buttocks of murdered adults and cooking murdered infants on spits.[8] This was facilitated by Pope Urban II, a brilliant politician who designed the First Crusade and who finalized the corresponding church doctrine leading to actions like the massacre at Ma'arra. He accomplished the latter by taking the church's apology for war embodied in "just war" doctrine and reinterpreting that doctrine into a new one called "holy war."

The story begins with a church crisis.

"The oldest institution in western Europe in the eleventh century, self-consciously tracing an uninterrupted history back a thousand years, was the papacy," writes Tyerman.[9] The reason, of course, is that political institutions were emerging and disappearing throughout most of Europe, which was in a state of near-constant, low-level warfare. A cauldron of ethnic displacement driven by war had destabilized one regime after another, and the church, given its Constantinian charter to play at power, was caught in the middle more than once. This was sometimes advantageous to the church and other times not. Prior to the Reformation, there was only one church in western Europe, and that was the Roman Catholic Church, putting the church in a position of power by default, even as instability continued to be the norm. And all was not well *within* the institutional church. A series of forty-one "antipopes" had been seated against the will of the church since 235 CE, by factions of political leaders and bishops. Some controversies were doctrinal;

---

8. Peters, *First Crusade*, 84.
9. Tyerman, *God's War*, 4.

and many were plain political calculation. The church had managed to hang onto its primacy, but at the cost of its autonomy.[10]

In 800 CE, Pope Leo III crowned Charlemagne, king of the Franks. This created the Holy Roman Empire, which would persist until 1806. The power to appoint popes shifted from the bishops to the emperors, who selected several outrageously inappropriate people for the job, who in turn sanctified the crown for political purposes. In one example, in 955, Otto I was crowned in Rome by twenty-five-year-old Pope John XII. The young pope himself was a mediocre intellect, and his completely debauched lifestyle led to his death at age twenty-seven, apparently from a stroke suffered while coupling with a married woman.[11] Such was the corrupted, symbiotic state of political and papal authority. In response, a powerful reform movement developed in the church that advocated for papal autonomy (and clerical celibacy). The straw that broke the camel's back was Holy Roman Emperor King Henry IV, a.k.a. King of the Germans. Kings had appropriated the power to appoint popes when Henry IV was crowned at the ripe old age of fifteen. The very idea that an adolescent might appoint the Vicar of Christ was anathema. And so the Investiture Controversy was on.[12]

Henry grew up. He learned the art of warfare and used it liberally. At the age of twenty-six, King Henry IV was told, and none too gently, by Pope Gregory VII that popes had the God-given authority to appoint or depose kings. The struggle between young King Henry IV and Pope Gregory VII led the king to appoint sycophant bishops and publicly contest church decrees. In 1075, Gregory VII began excommunicating bishops, letting Henry know he was on the short list himself. Gregory was kidnapped in Rome, then freed by Roman supporters. Gregory claimed (quite possibly accurately) that Henry was behind the kidnapping. In 1076, the pope made good on his threat, excommunicating Henry. Henry then convened the Synod of Worms, deposing Gregory from the papacy. Gregory defied Henry, remaining in Rome at the head of the church. In 1080, Henry launched an expedition that took four years to invade Rome, whereupon he installed the "antipope" Guibert of Ravenna, who in turn crowned Henry as the emperor. Antipope Guibert (Clement III) remained in place for a decade, supported by German military power. The reform movement had facilitated its opposite. The church was in exile.[13]

Desiderius succeeded Gregory VII in 1080. Renamed Pope Victor III, this reformer died in 1087, and the cardinal bishop of Ostia, Oto de Lagery,

10. Ibid., 991–92.
11. Mann, *Lives of the Popes*, 891–999.
12. Chisholm, "Gregory VII."
13. Ibid.

became Pope Urban II. When he inherited the throne of Peter, Urban II inherited a western Europe in a state of near political collapse due to constant warring between unstable principalities.[14]

Feudalism was a system based on preparation for war. Lords were military men who served their commanders in exchange for land. The leader of any fiefdom was above all a soldier. More precisely, *soldier* meant heavy cavalry—a man on a horse, who could stick sword-bearing opponents with a long lance extending well past the head of his mount, thus keeping him out of harm's way.

By the time Pope Urban II took office, Europe was crawling with landed cavalrymen, many of whom were continually seeking war as economic opportunity and exercising unspeakable cruelty to enforce their wills. These soldier-lords *were* by and large Christian as Christians had come to understand themselves within the Constantinian church. Their predominant interpretation of their own faith was that once having become a member of the church, they could sin rather boldly so long as they did adequate penance to ensure admission into heaven.[15] So while they did engage in terrible cruelty, it would be inaccurate to suggest they did so with impunity of conscience. They accepted the existence of heaven and hell, these rough believers, living in a time when death was more ubiquitously in evidence, and were constantly looking over their spiritual shoulders at eternity. There are accounts of men who had killed in war living in a state of near panic until they could find absolution, a process they firmly believed to be mechanically efficacious.[16]

Urban II looked at Europe in this situation—saturated with competing military powers, the church bent before the political authorities—and seven years into his tenure he struck out on a course to consolidate the power of the church in Europe, via Jerusalem. Beseeched by Christian Byzantine Emperor Alexios I Komnenos for assistance against invading Turks in what is now Istanbul, Urban II devised a plan to create an Army of the Church. That army would transcend European polities; it would be the Army of Christendom, directed by the pope himself. Augustine's careful writings on war in his "just war" explications were replaced by something that, at the time, sounded to the medieval ear like a prelude to the *eschaton*, the apocalyptic fulfillment of the Scriptures: *the holy war*.[17]

---

14. Tyerman, *God's War*, 45.
15. Glaber, *Historarium*, 61.
16. Ibid.
17. Tyerman, *God's War*, 45–50.

Holy war, first conceptualized by Gregory VII, was something qualitatively different from anything in history. Gregory VII had used the idea to limited effect in his investiture struggle with Henry IV, with an army he called the Militia of St. Peter. Gregory VII actually tried to organize a venture against the Seljuk Turks in 1074, selling the Crusade as a means for the reconciliation of the East-West schism; but his project never gained traction.[18] Pope Urban II, however, was a brilliant administrator, a charismatic communicator, and a skilled public relations strategist. His campaign in support of a Christian army that would march to the Holy Land to assist Christian brothers and sisters in peril at Constantinople caught fire.

The Byzantine emperor who had requested assistance had no idea how enormous (and enormously unpredictable) this force would eventually be. Urban II himself was shocked at the success of his mobilizations for war. Urban explicitly promised the "pilgrims in arms" that they would be shriven of all sin from now until death. Participation in war would be counted as *penance for all sins*. The Crusades were actually publicized as *penitential war*.[19] Urban made war commensurate with religious devotion, with prayer, guaranteeing absolution in advance for *anything any Crusader did* while on mission. This turned out to be the historical equivalent of striking flint in a mine full of gas. He had cynically deployed an idea that, for the medieval European noble and his retinue, proved irresistible—eternal bliss in exchange for combat.

During the campaign to recruit and mobilize Crusaders, Urban's public relations machine worked overtime to sell the war. The propaganda described Turkish and Muslim atrocities against fellow Christians from Constantinople to Jerusalem. Most of these stories were complete fabrications, prefiguring much modern war propaganda[20] (such as the false stories in 1990 of Iraqi soldiers dumping Kuwaiti babies out of incubators to die).[21]

One demagogic preacher called Peter the Hermit took up the call and assembled a rabble army that beat the main forces to the gates of Constantinople. Peter's troops arrived with a bloodlust that had been heightened by conducting pogroms and massacres against Jewish villages along their route of march. They plundered as they went and arrived in Constantinople with "a lean, hungry look"; Emperor Alexios locked them out of the city with justifiable anxiety.[22] This ominous beginning set the tone for a series of

18. Ibid., 49–51.
19. Ibid., 49–50.
20. Ibid., 67–68.
21. Stauber and Rampton, "How PR Sold the War."
22. Tyerman, *God's War*, 78–81.

wars—Crusades and Reformation wars—that would span nearly five hundred years.[23]

Historian of the Crusades Steven Runciman concludes, "Holy War itself was nothing more than a long act of intolerance in the name of God, which is the sin against the Holy Ghost."[24] According to Tyerman, it was necessary to find ways around the Sermon on the Mount: "Being extravagantly well versed in the highest traditions of classical learning, the Church Fathers did this rather well."[25]

During these holy wars, chains of command broke down, objectives were changed and opportunities exploited, alliances shifted and atrocities occurred. Constant, savage atrocities, gratuitous in their cruelty, were visited upon not only Muslim combatants but also civilians, including Christian civilians, and en route on Jewish communities.[26] The propaganda took no account that most of the Muslim communities had Christians living peacefully among them, or that Catholics were living alongside "heretics." Christians were killed along with Muslims during massacres in Muslim communities; and in 1209, when anti-heretic Crusaders appealed to their chaplain, Abbot Arnaud Aimery, for guidance on distinguishing Catholic from Cathar (Christian!) heretics at Beziers, the abbot is reported to have told them to kill the entire population. He was afraid some would claim to be Catholic in order to escape the sword. "Kill them all," he said. "The Lord knows who are his own." An estimated twenty thousand were killed in an orgy of violence. "The legates laconically recorded 'our men spared no one, irrespective of rank, sex, or age.'"[27]

During the seven-month siege of Antioch in 1097–98, when things were looking grim for the pope's army, the leaders decided to make some gesture to mollify God in their hour of doubt. That gesture was to gather all the females who had followed the Crusader camps, everyone from wives, to washerwomen, to servants, and expel them to a distant bivouac. The perception was that women were somehow an impurity, casting a bad mojo on the camps.[28]

The stories after this First Crusade were just as unsavory when subsequent Crusades broke out over the next two centuries. Europe, the church, and the headmen of the period were being formed by and were perpetuating

23. Ibid., 78–81.
24. Runciman, *History of the Crusades*, 3:480.
25. Tyerman, *God's War*, 29.
26. Ibid., 58–122.
27. Ibid., 590–91.
28. Ibid., 138.

a constant state of warfare. All war conducted by Christian leaders came to be euphemized as "crusade," no matter how cynical or corrupt the actual motivations. In 1095, Pope Urban II issued his summons to Jerusalem; by the beginning of the fourteenth century, crusades were taken up routinely against Christian neighbors in Europe. It had become a way of life and a vehicle for social mobility. The militarism of men had become the organizing principle within the church itself.

The great "Wars of Religion" that plagued Europe from 1524 to 1697 were but a continuation of crusading, which had begun and ended with political maps that were changed with the frequency of undershirts. But war itself, the developmental dynamic of war, led to a new, uniquely war-based form of polity, namely, the nation-state.

Wars required recruitment propaganda, administration, funding, and logistics. As certain emerging states proved, centralization of power grew alongside the ability to conflate secular adventures with holy war.

> The French were following the Maccabees in seeking God's assistance, confident that those who died "for the justice of king and realm will receive the crown of martyrdom from God." The argument embraced central elements of repeated attempts in the later Middle Ages to elevate national secular conflicts into holy wars, analogous or, occasionally, synonymous with crusading: monarchical holiness; the identification of king and nation; the providential destiny of a specially favored *patria*; the consequent perfidy and evil of that nation's enemies; the translation of crusade and holy war privileges to lay warfare; the promise of salvation; and the testing of unrelated political contests against the requirements of the recovery of the Holy Land. The success of such efforts profoundly affected western political culture and marked one of the most significant of the crusade's legacies to succeeding generations.[29]

The rising cost of warfare required greater centralization of taxation, which gave the winnowed remainder of regional rulers increased authority within ever more geographically specific and stable boundaries. The church, now having gone through dozens of popes and dozens more political alliances and breakups, was left on the sidelines. The church had been a co-pioneer in the processes of mustering for perpetual war; but lay rulers were

---

29. Ibid., 906.

poised to best take advantage of these methods. The princes made war, and their monopoly on its practice, with its inhering centralization of secular authority, would eventually usurp the church. William Cavanaugh writes, "The eventual elimination of the church from the public sphere was prepared by the dominance of the princes over the Church in the sixteenth century."[30]

Propaganda convinced people that their own nations were the elect. Military hierarchies elevated war leaders to the status of quasi-deities identified with a particular people. Military necessity consolidated and centralized power and legitimated these secular authorities. The *patria*, or fatherland, came to be consecrated as holy and its defense a religious obligation. This was the genesis of the modern nation-state, and for it to work, *war itself* became sanctified in order to associate national interests with some universal good.

Christians had acquired a centuries-long habit of making war, an easy norm of war, a ready resort to war; and that was shaped principally and directly by crusading. War has its own instrumental logics, not amenable to characterizations of virtue outside of war. The object of war that is common to all war, regardless of other justifying rationales, is victory—which is synonymous with the defeat, conquest, or destruction of the enemy. Those who pursue the most pragmatic, not the most "moral," solutions to the problems encountered on the way to victory are more likely to win. The decisive moral move in elevating pragmatism above morality is to set aside the moral rationale for war—for example, to end an injustice or defend a people or protect a way of life—as the final word on the morality of the enterprise. When the victory is declared "the higher good," then moral questions about the actual *conduct* of war are subsumed; and with that, the illusion of "just war" is effectively and *inevitably* undermined.

Because success in war requires unity of command as well as secrecy, those at the top of military hierarchies—even if there is, as in the United States, a civil authority above actual military commanders—become the *custodians of the higher good*, and the soldier becomes an instrument, a means, who no longer carries the burden of moral decisions. Morality is outsourced, and the soldier, traditionally a man, is allowed and encouraged to direct his focus on "his job," which is to destroy lives and property. Given that character is formed by habituation, it becomes almost inevitable, barring some epistemological crisis for the soldier himself, that he will come to associate virtue with his ability to kill people and destroy property.

---

30. Cavanaugh, "Fire Strong Enough to Consume," para. 16.

Psychologically, this requires compartmentalization, the dehumanization of enemies,[31] contempt for occupied peoples, and inoculating oneself against the danger of fusion. It requires learning hard-heartedness. Empathy, nurturing, and relationality are understood by the soldier and by his male apologists, in any culture where war interacts with a sexual division of labor and sexual hierarchy, as "womanly" and as a threat to the efficacy of soldiers. No soldier today, even the few female soldiers, wants a reputation as "a pussy."

So what is learned in the formation of the soldier is contempt for what is "womanly," which translates in his mind to contempt for women—so much the easier when that contempt for women is in place prior to the initiation of hostilities.

---

31. Beck, *Unclean*, calls this *infrahumanization*.

14

Sleepwalking

Before he commenced whipping Aunt Hester, he took her into the kitchen, and stripped her from neck to waist, leaving her neck, shoulders, and back entirely naked. Then he told her to cross her hands.... "Now, you damned bitch, I'll learn you how to disobey my orders!"... The louder she screamed, the harder he whipped; and where the blood ran fastest, there he whipped the longest. He would whip her to make her scream, and whip her to make her hush; and not until overcome by fatigue, would he cease to swing the blood-clotted cowskin.[1]

—Frederick Douglass

When he saw Jesus from a distance, he ran and fell on his knees in front of him. He shouted at the top of his voice, "What do you want with me, Jesus, Son of the Most High God? In God's name don't torture me!" For Jesus had said to him, "Come out of this man, you impure spirit!"

　Then Jesus asked him, "What is your name?"

　"My name is Legion," he replied, "for we are many."

—Mark 5:6–9

---

1. Douglass, *Narrative*, 22.

Nancy Hartsock writes that "the highest good for the warrior-hero is not . . . a quiet conscience, but enjoyment of public esteem, and through this esteem, immortality."[2]

> Just as the warrior-hero faced the conflicts between community and nature in extreme form on the battlefield, so he faces this dualism in extreme form within his own being. He fights to win reputation, as well as to preserve the community. It is perhaps the importance of public reputation that leads to the externalization of emotions. If to "lose face" is unbearable because it is to lose moral identity, how then can one explain actions one would be ashamed to acknowledge as one's own?[3]

This heroic age construct is still cultivated in service academies like West Point, where I once taught military science. It tells us little about actual military practice, so it has become a kind of anachronism when measured against another dogma at West Point—that to be a commissioned officer is to become a "manager of violence."

The majority of those in the modern American military never see combat, even in wartime, and so these ideas of honor, integrity, and duty, associated with fighting, are now signs painted on buildings around military installations. The public has learned to bless everyone who wears a uniform for "contributing to the effort." The reputation soldiers enjoy in a militaristic society they may not enjoy within the military, where there is a powerful prestige hierarchy between combat specialties and the many who are truck drivers, finance clerks, cooks, medical technicians, dental hygienists, personnel administrators, or mechanics. The public mystique serves everyone—the institution, the troops with their increased standing in general society, and the nation-state for whom they have become representative. For the actual modern military, the internal hierarchy of prestige remains a kind of family secret.

There is another family secret, too. Combat is seldom heroic. Success in combat is predicated on caution and planning. Much combat is outrageously one-sided and therefore akin to plain murder, especially when preparatory attacks are being made, as they are by the American military, with highly technical, highly lethal, standoff weapons like fighter-bombers and armed, unmanned aerial drones. The majority of casualties in most combat are not combatants but civilians, killed or wounded not only directly by soldiers, who today kill more civilians then they do combatants,[4] but also

---

2. Hartsock, *Money, Sex, and Power*, 188.

3. Ibid., 188–89.

4. BBC, "Ethical War," para. 2. Seventy-five percent of war casualties are now civilians.

by bombs, missiles, and aerial chain guns. Most ground troops who shoot seldom see what they are shooting or know whether they are personally responsible for any of the bodies they pile up after combat engagements.

The "mythic immortality" that Hartsock describes, fantasized by men socialized for martial masculinity, is quietly understood by those in the military to be semi-fraudulent. The power of the modern imperial military is more akin to construction crews destroying wildlife habitat by building strip malls . . . or to systematically planned serial rapes. Modern war's systematic instrumentality far outweighs "heroism." The fraudulence of the military myth does not neutralize the cultural power of the myth. It is used to discipline those within the military if they display any reluctance to "perform," and it is used to discipline the public in a liturgy of arms, genuflecting before the military as an inviolable cultural altar. Imagine if someone were to display a yard sign or bumper sticker that declared, "I do not support the troops."

Masculinities destabilize.

American masculinity faces a dual challenge. Military failure has challenged the myth of American military supremacy; and consumerism constantly destabilizes hegemonic masculinity.[5] American consumption is central to a global accumulation regime; and militarism is central to American power. In response to this dual crisis, we get the dissemination of masculine myth via the male revenge fantasy.

The defeat of Western forces in both Iraq and Afghanistan—and these *are* defeats when measured as political outcomes—have, like Vietnam before them, demonstrated that Western, in particular *American*, military supremacy is only a technical reality; and at the same time these conflicts have proven that technical superiority is not synonymous with strategic superiority. On the contrary, asymmetric warfare can transform technical superiority into a strategic disadvantage. This is a blow not only to martial masculinity but also to the instrumental and technical masculinity that can be traced back to the Baconian revolution.

The process of ever-expanding commodification that is necessary for economic "growth" to continue and that depends on the increasingly aggressive production of demand—convincing people that they *must have* the newest things—is now teaching men what it used to teach only women: you must market yourself as a sexual commodity. Men are targeted by the

---

5. The modern "metrosexual" is, above all, a consumer.

demand-production experts—advertisers—by fashion, cosmetics, fad diets, and exercise programs that begin, as they do when targeting women, by planting the seeds of chronic sexual insecurity (am I sexually desirable enough?) in order to drive them to the checkout counters. In the same way that fashion must constantly reinvent itself to create fresh demand, the goalposts for what is desirable are moved back again and again, creating serial destabilizations of masculinities now more and more defined, apart from conflict, as sexual desirability.

Hervé Juvin described this destabilization of masculinity as part of the destabilization of the body by liberal modernity. In his book *The Coming of the Body*, he describes the paradox of disembodiment from time, place, suffering, and God, which has led to the fantasy of technological immortality, the obsession with longevity, and the worship of "youth." The messianic delusion of communism, says Juvin, the reinvention of the human being, has been perversely accomplished by capitalism,[6] which is selling us renewable bodies through fad diets, plastic surgery, quack supplements, and even the eugenics-colored notion of procreation without sex.[7]

Scott Stephens describes this dream of risk-free hedonism:

> In this light, the most conspicuous fixtures of Western culture—cosmetics, cosmetic surgery, antiperspirants, perfumes, hair removal, hairstyling, body sculpting, body building, body piercing, body art, transsexualism, androgyny, anorexia, abortion—can be seen for what they are: so many manifestations of the same *religion of the body*. They each signal the desire to overcome the givenness and imperfections of nature, the assertion of the will over the pliant stuff of the flesh.
>
> But, as is the case with every false god, the supposed freedom *over* the body soon reveals itself to be a form of submission *to* the body. For it is not simply that the body has been liberated to pursue its own enjoyment. Rather, the unrelenting demand to be beautiful, to be sexually available, enslaves the body within what Sarah Coakley has called "*sweaty* Pelagianism"[8]—a self-

---

6. My use of the term *capitalism* throughout the book is in every case qualified. Any number of historians and theorists have established a sound historical case for the claim that "capitalism" is a reification, that the term did not come into use until the eighteenth century, that by any of its various definitions it is difficult to fix its "origins," and that it is—except as a familiar linguistic marker as it is used here—an essentially ideological category, whether used by "pro-capitalists" or "anti-capitalists."

7. Juvin, *The Coming of the Body*.

8. Coakley, *Powers and Submissions*, 155: "Devoid now of religious meaning or of the capacity for any fluidity into the divine, shorn of any expectation of new life beyond the grave, [the body] has shrunk to the limits of individual fleshliness; hence our only

righteous and utterly oppressive asceticism dedicated to the achievement and maintenance of sterile, unblemished, aseptic bodies.[9]

Paradoxically, as we will see in chapters 16 and 17, this process is an aspect of what we will call modern *disembodiment*.

Male supremacy, in history, is challenged by the destabilization of various masculinities, but this challenge is never met with abandonment, only reframing. The response to any destabilization of one masculine archetype is to reseat male power in a new archetype, in much the same way the church over the centuries has recast its rationale for the exclusion of women.

It is no accident that films like *Dirty Harry* (1971) and *Death Wish* (1974) came on the scene—nihilistic splatter-flicks featuring a lone male avenger and set *inside* the United States—just as the U.S. was seeing the inevitability of its defeat in Vietnam. It is no accident that *Man on Fire* corresponded in its moral rationalization, the "tempo task,"[10] to the governmental rationalization for the employment of "enhanced interrogation techniques," that is, torture, when the myth of American military invincibility was being dismantled again in Southwest Asia. The destabilization of masculinity is followed by a reactionary reassertion of it.

There were two images that predominated on the airwaves on September 11, 2001. One of them was the hypnotically controlled and uniform repetition of the film clips of aircraft crashing into the buildings and the billowing erasure of the Manhattan skyline. The other was the authoritative father. He was everywhere, in every guise, embodied not only in George W. Bush but also in a surfeit of self-anointed "terrorism experts," and in the ubiquitous big-dick posturing by male politicians and reporters. The whole nation was being carried along on a narrative straight out of the male revenge fantasy. The state of emergency obliged the women and children to figuratively

---

hope seems to reside in keeping it alive, youthful, consuming, sexually active, and jogging on (literally), for as long as possible.... [This is what] from a Christian standpoint we may deem a sweaty Pelagianism.... For in the late-twentieth-century affluent West, the 'body,' to be sure, is sexually affirmed, but also puritanically punished in matters of diet and exercise."

Pelagianism was a fourth-century heresy that claimed perfection can be attained in this life through will and without divine grace.

9. Stephens, "'This Is My Body.'"

10. Eisenstein, "Film Form": the "tempo task" is a film convention in which the protagonist is forced by impending peril to forego the rules to get the job done and save lives.

cringe in the background, while the martial warrior-father prepared to unleash his pure, supra-rational masculine energy on the evildoers. The nation became the family, and its preservation depended upon the restoration of absolute authority to the tough white father.

Ann Kibbey, writing about the political climate in the U.S. at the time, pointed out how effectively the Bush handlers had used the mythic American signifier of the Western film in the run-up to the 2003 invasion of Iraq.[11]

> Liberals . . . have had difficulty in believing that a much-discredited American film genre, the Western, could suddenly be structuring and mandating U.S. political rhetoric. It is—from Bush's "Wanted Dead or Alive" Bin Laden poster, to Colin Powell's insistence that "time is running out" as we cut to the chase, to the numerous U.S. television and print media that report daily on the "Showdown" or "Standoff" with Iraq.[12]

Kibbey borrows the term "tempo task" (used above) from Sergei Eisenstein to describe the sense of urgency that was injected into public discourse as preparation for war. The "tempo task" allows the protagonist to forget the rules to get the job done and save lives. Typically, this is when the women and children are pushed back into the house, while the man goes out into the street for the showdown, or when the bomb is ticking and the bad guy has the information beaten out of him just in time. The "tempo task" has become the modern default for war-making propaganda, but also for the reclamation of martial male prerogative. Yet for all its bright-eyed energy, this reclamation of power also requires a peculiar form of somnambulance. In Jacqui Alexander's words,

> To this process of fragmentation of mind, body, and spirit we gave the name colonization—a set of exploitative practices usually understood in political, ideological, and aesthetic terms. We saw its minute operation in dualistic and hierarchical thinking—divisions among mind, body, spirit; between sacred and secular; male and female; heterosexual and homosexual; rich and poor; the erotic and the Divine. It is a thinking always in negation, often translated into singular explanations for oppression, such as racism versus sexism, with less attention to how these systems work together.
>
> Internal colonization leaves us dealing with alienation from the body, from the self—the "other" is in the self. It is the othering of ourselves. So we exist for them, not for ourselves. For

---

11. Kibbey, "Gender and the American Ideology of War."
12. Ibid., para. 1.

some kind of them. It produces a love/hate relationship with our oppressors. We want to be sovereign, but don't let us be too sovereign. Instead of taking out the pain and examining it, we act out of negation. It's the lateral violence we visit on each other.[13]

The masculinity of Marshall Brown—my former friend, the Delta Force commando and serial rapist—and indeed many men in the military did not hover in the air as history passed through them in some parallel dimension. His was one form of masculinity among many, all in a state of profound disequilibrium that co-responds with concrete social processes. It was Western masculinity. It was military masculinity. It was Southern masculinity. It was one form of "Christian" masculinity. But in every case, it *required*, was defined against, and was only possible with the enemy-other, with "woman" as its hated antithesis.

Fanon, himself a proponent of a form of anticolonial, masculine violence, said that violence breaks the colonial mirror, because the colonizer sees in his victim his own degraded self.[14]

Violent masculinity is somnambulant, dreaming away inside the cold, lightless spaces of a stony, male ego-fortress. If there is a way out, it will require first a wakefulness. Maybe a touch of that wakefulness was what kept me (and many others) from going into that room where Marshall Brown went and placed a knife to a woman's throat in her own bed, invading her shocked and adrenaline-drenched body with his own and making her wonder for the rest of her days if there was a safe place. The invasion of the penis, the invasion of the lash, the invasion of the bullet. The mirrors are broken to prevent our waking, but these mirrors are in fact the living bodies of human beings. *Perfect* masculinity is, in the medicalized jargon of our age, sociopathic—perfected only when purged of empathy of any kind. Wakefulness is the precondition of our recovery.

Mab Segrest says, "It is only in the present moment that transformative reconfigurations of self can occur."[15] She calls the somnambulance of male power, embodied in militarism, *anesthesia*: "the anesthesia of power."[16] In what she terms the "metaphysic of genocide," people "don't need to respond to what they can pretend they do not know, and they don't know what they can't feel."[17] Somewhere, between this *danse du mort* of colonizer-colonized and the disengagement that begins the process of undoing, is a dangerous

13. Quoted in Segrest, *Born to Belonging*, 202.
14. Fanon, *Black Skin, White Masks*, 216–22.
15. Segrest, *Born to Belonging*, 36.
16. Ibid.
17. Ibid.

terrain, an abject terrain, where in the casting aside of old norms in the absence of new ones, there are no limits. If total depravity corresponds to total control, chaos corresponds to the deconstruction of that control and that depravity. This, at least, is the intuition of sexual vertigo.

With the slow death of an imperial-frontier masculinity that defined much of Marshall Brown's nationalistic machismo, under assault by gay Boy Scouts and even by consumer culture, a newer, far less stable masculinity is becoming hegemonic, inside and outside the military: the addictive narcissism of American consumer capitalism that, rather than liberating women from internalized oppression, has dangerously consigned men to that self-exploiting space with them. Sometimes, this is a space with no rules. Men are now developing eating disorders and being lashed through the malls by fashion. This state of constant and inescapable disequilibrium dissolves old masculinities and femininities and reformulates new ones, and with it throws the relations between men and women into confusion and disarray. The faster the social change, the more deeply is this destabilization felt on the skins, in the bellies, and in the very psyches of individuals. It is this disequilibrium—global, financial, social, and sexual—that has given rise to strategies that have shifted the discourse from the public to the private, from the social to the individual, and which has allowed those with the most material power to redefine themselves, in the resultant confusion, as victims. Just as the rich have redefined themselves as the victims of the poor, men shift premises to construct themselves as the victims of masculinized women.

In reaction, we get *Man on Fire* as a new myth and Marshall Brown as a new reality.

As Jesus told his somnabulent disciples at Gethsemane, "Stay awake!" (Mark 13:37).

15

Genealogy

It is as easy to disentangle these remote causations as to tell at a river's mouth which waters come from which glaciers and from which tributaries.

—Jacques Maritain[1]

Not surprisingly, given the traditional prominence of warfare for masculine prestige, an updated and idealized version of the soldier provided one form of masculine claim on the nation, and vice versa.[2]

—John Horne

Ti tig se tig, say the Haitians: "The child of the tiger is a tiger." The child of war is war.

If crusading is the grandfather of modernity, then the Reformation is the father. I use male pronouns because the principle actors in this drama of war and political economy were overwhelmingly men. War is still integral to the development of both capitalist modernity (as well as its Promethean mirror, socialism) and its philosophy, liberalism. But let it be said, wrong as liberalism may be (and I think it is), it may yet be the traumatic event that

---

1. Quoted in Gregory, *Unintended Reformation*, 361.
2. Horne, "Age of Nation-States," 26.

brings the church to full repentance for its participation in and co-optation by violent masculinity.

In postmodernity (which isn't *post* anything), the shine's come off of the idol of progress, the invisible hand of the market has shown that it is not benign, and liberalism's moral incoherence can be almost mathematically demonstrated. But when the church and its members decry acquisitive individualism, we have to make our confessions. *Nostra culpa*. It was our embrace of *war* that gave liberalism its birth, and our embrace of martial masculinity that fertilized the roots of war.

After the Crusades, doctrinal dispute accompanied social revolution, and more than one confession came to state power in the West. More war was the result—a natural progression, given the church's embrace of male violence in the centuries preceding the Reformation. Modernity emerged not as an alternative to Christianity but as a false alternative to chronic warfare.

That a system predicated on acquisitiveness—even eventually calling acquisitiveness a virtue—would form in the belly of the church would have been seen by earlier Christians as perverse. But that is what happened. This unintended reformation began in what is now called the Netherlands.[3] Surrounded by sanguinary religious wars throughout Europe, the Dutch, led by local merchants and traders, found they could make more money if they set aside religious differences and traded freely between the various confessions. Weapons makers were doing a lively business thanks to the wars, but for everyone else who was in the business of making money—a minority in Europe, but an up-and-coming one—the grindingly incessant wars, including both the Thirty Years' War (1618–48) and the English Civil War (1642–51), represented terrible losses. The rationalizations for war, ever more transparently false, had eroded confidence in the churches' moral authority, downright delegitimating them in some cases. Many city-dwelling merchants, beginning with the Dutch, decided to focus their lives on a more pacific and rewarding enterprise than mass slaughter—the accumulation of money:

> In this way, early modern Christian rulers and their subjects paradoxically became the agents of their colonization by capitalism and consumption. By their actions, they essentially turned

---

3. Gregory, *Unintended Reformation*, 276–97.

their backs on biblical teachings about material things, teachings that had largely been shared across confessional lines.[4]

Gregory shows how the Dutch experiment in mercantile tolerance inaugurated the peculiar formative history of the modern nation-state. One of the characteristics of previous political-military adventures was that they were ruler-centric. Boundaries were malleable. Fighting for control and resources was driven by perceived economic necessity or for military strategic advantage, and motivated by personal ambition (or even malice and revenge). War, with all its universalizing pretensions, had become the intensely personal business of specific rulers.

The nation-state would be more formal, fixed as much as possible *within* a geographic boundary that defined domain as primary and the ruler as a replaceable part. This afforded a military advantage, because technical and tactical attention could be focused on the security of a fixed boundary over time. Within that boundary, rulers could secure a measure of stability sufficient to engage in social engineering. So even though the nation-state developed in part as a reaction against a form of warfare that seemed to know few boundaries, the state was itself fundamentally predicated on the preparation for war.

In an area more or less corresponding to present-day Luxembourg, Belgium, and the Netherlands, the Holy Roman Empire held sway until the sixteenth century, and the region was divided between dukes for political control and bishops for religious control. Emperor Charles V unified seventeen provinces in 1549 for administrative control, and his son Philip II continued this administrative centralization. Then a dispute between Philip and William of Orange ignited a war that would rage for eighty long years.[5] There were multiple Christian confessions in the seventeen provinces, and more than one had gained access to administrative apparatuses in the region, because of which the people and the local administrators found a common complaint about being under Hapsburg rule at all. The Holy Roman Empire was taxing them heavily to make its wars, and during the course of this Eighty Years' War the idea of independence gained considerable ground. To make a long story short, a new entity emerged on the political map of Europe—the Dutch Republic. A republic was governed by representatives from the various components of a political *federation*.[6] Initially united *militarily* to defend its territory from the Spanish army, the Dutch Republic had created a nascent modern nation-state. Territory became primary;

4. Ibid., 278.
5. Offen, "Eighty Years War."
6. Butler, "Rise of the Dutch Republic."

and defense of fixed territory gave them unexpected and fortuitous tactical advantages that allowed the new state to endure. Moreover, it required a cross-confessional tolerance to sustain. The unexpected and likewise fortuitous advantage of that tolerance was that traders and merchants from around Europe found a place where they could seek financial advantage with a wider array of other merchants and financiers than they could in religiously homogeneous zones; and the Dutch Republic found itself getting very rich. The first stock market was opened there through the Dutch East India Company in 1602.[7]

Rather than fight interminable wars near home, the merchant state discovered the financial military expedition—distant expeditions targeting profitable resources to fuel the local economy. The locus of military violence shifted from proximate neighbor to colony. This colonization was consciously tied to the expansion of the national economy, in the search for material feedstocks and foreign slaves, as opposed to the mere plunder of rulers that marked early European expeditions to the Americas.

The Dutch Republic took a step beyond the confessional states that had subordinated church to state, as in Catholic Spain or Lutheran Sweden. Putatively governed by Protestants, the Dutch Republic effectively relegated religion to a "private" sector that could be ignored altogether in the "public" sphere.[8] While this was politically expedient, it prefigured the eventual theological transformation of Jesus himself from social exemplar to a kind of personal, spiritual elixir—itself prefigured by the instrumental magic of the sacraments taught in the thirteenth century and by "penitential war," wherein the wave of a hand could preemptively pardon.

The successes of the Dutch Republic were closely watched. They produced new ideas in philosophy that likewise deviated from past Christian doctrine, even though some of them—Descartes most notably (see the following chapter)—were developed by observant Christians. Most notable among political philosophers was Thomas Hobbes (1558-1679), whose philosophy explicitly substituted the state for God. Men's *violence* was not called into question, but how that violence was to be directed to amplify rather than inhibit the prosperity of the increasingly powerful urban merchants and bankers.

> The "wars of religion" prompted dramatic innovations in political thought that, beginning most clearly with Hobbes, rejected the idea that had been at the heart of politics for well over a millennium—that a ruler's principle obligation was to protect

---

7. Gregory, *Unintended Reformation*, 274-79
8. Ibid., 275.

and promote God's truth as the foundation that made possible shared Christian life in fidelity to Jesus' commands.[9]

That is not to say that rulers met these expectations. Religious claims were in many cases a cynical veneer for tawdry political machinations, giving rise to a loss of confidence in those claims.[10] The church hierarchy brought the anti-Christian practices and secular philosophy of modernity on itself with war and politics. Hobbes gave the new philosophy its most enduring political-philosophical basis, shifting the emphasis from Prince to State: "Whereas Machiavelli had been cynical and pragmatic in *The Prince*, Hobbes was principled and systematic in *The Leviathan*."[11]

Hobbes was terrified by the implications of the beheading of King Charles I of England by fanatical Protestants in 1649.[12] *The Leviathan* was published only two years later (1651). Hobbes described the nation-state; Machiavelli described the actions of princes—the distinction clear between earlier leader-centric politics and a sovereign *polity* within an administered geographic boundary. The role of the state as sovereign, said Hobbes, was to safeguard the power of the state, and that included safeguarding that power *against* religion. This idea of separating church and state would find its greatest actualization in the United States Constitution a century and a half later. The notion of a public versus private realm, elucidated in Hobbes and practiced in the Dutch Republic, would become a cornerstone of liberal philosophy as well as the epistemological basis for transforming Christian faith from a community affair into a personal one.

In Hobbes's philosophizing and in the emerging modern actuality, this meant that male violence in the form of social control and warfare would become the exclusive purview of the geographically bounded nation-state, practiced in the *public* sphere, and women—who had been coworkers, albeit in a gendered society, in a society based on household production—were relegated by men who entered this new public realm to the *private* domain.

As the Dutch example spread, driven by increasing profits, so did the power of the money-men. Money speeded access to the kinds of materials

---

9. Ibid., 162.

10. Paradoxically, this still serves as the premise of the notion that "religion" is the greatest source of violence in the world, because those who make these claims ignore the more secular motivations of the war leaders just as effectively as those leaders themselves did. In effect, this simplistic critique of "religion" (a modern *anthropological* category) is based on the lie, told by war leaders themselves to justify their wars, that faith motivated those armed conflicts which were, in fact, motivated by secular political considerations.

11. Gregory, *Unintended Reformation*, 162.

12. Ibid.

that were necessary for both investments and emerging military technical developments that were put at the service of the nation-state for the exploitation of foreign peripheries.

Gregory's thesis challenges Weber's earlier one that Protestantism formed the foundation of capitalism, saying that Weber got it backwards.

When the Reformation happened, the overwhelming majority of European Christians still lived as subsistence agriculturists, for whom money was a useful addendum to home and village production, but nothing like the universal necessity (and thereby dependency) that it is for us now. Until the peasantry was separated from its capacity for subsistence, the money-men would not hold decisive political power. Moreover, regardless of the various doctrinal disputes between Protestant and Roman Catholic, and between several Protestant confessions, all Christians at the time would have found the ideas of later liberals—that selfishness or greed could be seen as a virtue, or that acquisitive individualism should be the organizing principle of a society—to be scandalous.

Over time, faith was foregrounded by the state. The state needed money, and the new money-men had money. The state became dependent on the money-men, and the church had become dependent on and subservient to the state. The temptations of acquisitive individualism became a cultural powerhouse; and as merchants and bankers rose to new dominance, philosophical apologies for their values emerged along with them. Churches, dependent on the dominant class for money and subordinate to the new nation-state's power, came to adjust their teachings accordingly.[13]

---

13. See Illich, "Educational Enterprise," paras. 29–33: "Churches also have their problems with a Jesus whose only economics are jokes. A savior undermines the foundations of any social doctrine of the Church. But that is what He does, whenever He is faced with money matters. According to Mark 12:13 there was a group of Herodians who wanted to catch Him in His own words. They ask 'Must we pay tribute to Caesar?' You know His answer: 'Give me a coin—tell me whose profile is on it!' Of course they answer 'Caesar's.'

The drachma is a weight of silver marked with Caesar's effigy.

A Roman coin was no impersonal silver dollar; there was none of that 'trust in God' or adornment with a presidential portrait. A denarius was a piece of precious metal branded, as it were, like a heifer, with the sign of the personal owner. Not the Treasury, but Caesar coins and owns the currency. Only if this characteristic of Roman currency is understood, one grasps the analogy between the answer to the devil who tempted Him with power and to the Herodians who tempt Him with money. His response is clear: abandon all that which has been branded by Caesar; but then, enjoy the knowledge that everything, everything else is God's, and therefore is to be used by you.

The message is so simple: Jesus jokes about Caesar. He shrugs off his control. And not only at that one instance . . . Remember the occasion at the Lake of Capharnaum, when Peter is asked to pay a twopenny tax. Jesus sends him to throw a line into the lake and pick the coin he needs from the mouth of the first fish that bites. Oriental stories up

Weber looked at *later* Calvinism's doctrinal justifications for acquisitive individualism and at capitalism more fully formed, saw the correspondence, and ascribed the opposite relation of cause and effect. For Weber, Protestantism formed capitalism. For Gregory, capitalism *re-*formed Protestantism. Gregory does not dispute all of Weber's connections. Gregory concedes that once the Protestant doctrine of "justification by faith alone" entrenched itself, it caused believers to infer that success in business was material evidence that they were God's predestined elect. But over time, the virtue of *thrift* that remained important as an expression of humility and responsibility within Calvinism was jettisoned. Dependence upon faith was transmuted by modernity—specifically, capitalist modernity—into the active "virtue" of self-centered consumption.

Masculinity and war were also *re-formed* in this new epoch. As we shall see in the next chapter on the "fortified self," modern liberalism, for all its objectively neutral pretensions, was a decidedly and self-consciously masculine and warlike philosophical orientation.

Modernity, as we know it, was until the seventeenth century considered largely incompatible with Christian belief in *caritas*, or neighbor-love. War discredited Christendom, and the baby got thrown out with the bathwater. The churches had subordinated themselves to states, built up by the money-men, conquest, and colonial extraction—the very bases of capital expansion. Catholics involved themselves in this plunder as vigorously as Protestants in the beginning, though by the nineteenth and twentieth centuries power was concentrated in predominantly Protestant Britain, then in the predominantly Protestant United States. Those Christian confessions that did not align themselves with a state were marginalized and persecuted by the magisterial confessions; and they would find refuge in those very states where religious tolerance, provided a religious body did not dissent from the state, was the norm.

The Reformation tied the Crusades to the emergence of modernity. Men's wars, though changing form, were a constant. A peculiar philosophical development accompanied this period of *re-*formation: "the flight to objectivity."

---

to the time of *Thousand Nights and One Night* are full of beggars who catch the fish that has swallowed a piece of gold. His gesture is that of a clown; it shows that this miracle is not meant to prove him omnipotent but indifferent to matters of money. Who wants power [like Caesar] submits to the Devil and who wants denarri submits to the Caesar."

16

Bodies and Objects

The notion that the world of objects and the world of subjects are separable, in any other than an analytical sense, has been an illusion from the start.

—Alf Hornborg[1]

Americans do not have to believe in God, because they believe that it is a good thing simply to believe: all they need is a general belief in belief. That is why we have never been able to produce interesting atheists in the U.S. The god most Americans say they believe in is not interesting enough to deny.

—Stanley Hauerwas[2]

Incarnation has the Latin word *carnis* as its root: meat, or flesh. Incarnation, then, means enfleshment, being as a physical body that occupies a specific space and time.

> God didn't become man, he became flesh. I believe . . . in a God who is enfleshed, and who has given the Samaritan, as a being drowned in carnality, the possibility of creating a relationship by which an unknown, chance encounter becomes for him the

---

1. Hornborg, "Knowledge of Persons," para. 4.
2. Hauerwas, "How Real Is America's Faith?," para. 3.

reason for his existence, as he becomes the reason for the other's survival—not just in a physical sense, but a deeper sense, as a human being. This is not a spiritual relationship. This is not a fantasy. This is not merely the ritual act which generates a myth. This is an act which prolongs the Incarnation.[3]

Illich's focus on *embodiment*, and consequently on the histories of physical perception, is animated by his concern that modernity and postmodernity have led to the trivialization of the Gospels and the trivialization of the significance of the Incarnation. Illich believed that our epoch is not "secular"—as in the opposite of that other anthropological category, "religious"—but a profound perversion of the Christian Gospels' "good news." This disembodiment and a consequent trivialization of Christian belief (see Hauerwas quote above) has some key historical and philosophical turning points. One of them is the work of René Descartes (1596–1650).

In 1987, Susan Bordo wrote *The Flight to Objectivity: Essays on Cartesianism and Culture*,[4] identifying a key moment in the philosophical development of modernity and modern male supremacy. Her secular views on the "flight to objectivity" merge with the Christian convictions of Ivan Illich. Bordo is a feminist who has paid particular attention to René Descartes's philosophy and influence, and I'll rely on her in this chapter to unpack the gender at the heart of a supposedly genderless "objectivity" for which Descartes is largely responsible in modern culture.

Descartes is associated with something that in philosophical shorthand is called simply "Cartesian dualism." Descartes was a Roman Catholic as well as a mathematician who, interestingly enough, lived in the Dutch Republic. His "dualism" is generally cited in works addressed to the philosophically initiated. In this study of gender, war, and the church, we need to briefly explain Descartes's "dualism" to those who may not be immersed in philosophy, because his ideas led to many of our current philosophical, cultural, and even psychological impasses. Descartes is often cited as a "father of science," and our own time is dominated by a presumption that science holds a universal key to truth.

> Descartes led the way in the seventeenth century, establishing an ideal that would endure for centuries: that of the autonomous, self-sufficient, individual philosopher who demonstrates the truth based on reason alone, without relying on anyone else.[5]

---

3. Illich, *Rivers North of the Future*, 207.
4. Bordo, *Flight to Objectivity*.
5. Gregory, *Unintended Reformation*, 114.

A pertinent observation, this nonetheless does not help the less philosophically initiated get at the core of what Descartes did in a way that illuminates his role in something we will call modern disembodiment. *Flight to Objectivity* is a meditation on Descartes's *Meditations on First Philosophy*, with an eye to that aspect of Descartes and his legacy that is largely ignored—gender, which in turn cannot be dissociated from war. War, "religious war," gave rise in a very direct way to the works of Descartes and of those who followed him into the modern era.[6]

Bordo's book begins with a discussion of Cartesian anxiety, or Cartesian *doubt*. Descartes's philosophical ideas did not appear in an historical vacuum. Descartes's *Meditations* were not based on *unfounded* anxiety. Anxiety based on political instability, as we saw with Hobbes, was characteristic of the age. Seventeenth-century Europe, in addition to reeling from a brutal series of wars, was also a period when medieval cosmological certainties were overturned by Copernicus and Galileo. The very way of knowing that had prevailed in medieval Christendom was undermined by the astronomical calculations of mathematicians like Descartes and by technologies like the telescope, making this period one of deep epistemological crisis against a background of apparent political chaos.

Using precepts from anthropologist Mary Douglas,[7] Bordo studies how epistemological boundaries were first disestablished then reestablished, beginning with Descartes's origin myth—a nightmare about a cosmic evil genius. This malevolent specter is the original character in the *Meditations*, which outlines a kind of radical skepticism. Unmoored by new knowledges, the *senses* are just that evil genius, because they make it impossible for a human being to know for sure whether he (Descartes, like all his contemporaries, spoke of *men* as normative humans) is awake or dreaming, perceiving or hallucinating. Our senses tell us that the sun revolves around the earth, that the earth is bigger than the sun. The senses (read: bodies) are liars, deceivers, the very carriers of madness.

> For the *whole* of my existence—sleeping, wakefulness, internal certitudes, prejudices, beliefs about the external world, feelings, the sense of embodiment—may be the result of a grand demonic deception which we cannot get *beyond* to determine the true state of things. At each step of the first *Meditation*, the possible boundaries of illusion widen: at first it is only "certain persons"—the mad—who are victims; then it is every person, but only some of the time; and finally, it is everyone, all of the

---

6. Bordo, *Flight to Objectivity*.
7. Douglas, *Purity and Danger*.

time, who may be the subjects of a deception so encompassing that there is no *conceivable* perspective from which to judge its correspondence with reality. The sane may have distance on the mad and the wakeful may, in retrospect, have distance on the dream, but the specter of the Evil Genius allows no distance at all. It is a specter of complete entrapment.[8]

I remember when I was a child entertaining the fantasy from time to time that I was in a great dream-machine that produced my every perception—that nothing I knew was real, and that I was in the grip of a grand illusion. I doubt I am alone in having daydreamed about such a thing. Descartes used this fantasy—again, against the backdrop of Europe's most dislocative epistemological crisis—as the *foundation* of a new form of knowledge.

Descartes, being a practicing Catholic, retracted from pure, unanchored solipsism by locating a ground in God. God is a guarantor of truth for Descartes, though later philosophers—taking Descartes's own starting points—will show that God can be sidelined by Descartes's ideas and eventually set aside altogether. God, for Descartes, is pulled inside the mind where he can do battle with the demon of infinite skepticism. Prior to Descartes, there was no mind—as the *opposite* of a body—to be pulled inside. There was reason as a faculty, but not a mind-body split. This split is the basis of Descartes's "dualism," or two-ness. For Descartes, there was one faculty that could—with proper and godly discipline—hold in check the chaotic deceptions of the body/senses: the *dis-embodied* mind.

Descartes's simple formulation *Cogito, ergo sum* ("I think, therefore I am") is the basic and definitive statement of his claim. What is radical about this is not obvious to us today, because modern Westerners have grown up absorbing the premise that mind and the body exist apart in two realms—interior and exterior.

Prior to Descartes, people assumed a profound connectedness between everything in creation. The cosmos, the soil, children, politics—these were all in some mutually constituting relation to each other. Things *fit*.[9] If you have an old copy of *The Riverside Shakespeare*, in the middle of the combined works of the Renaissance bard is a collection of pictures, reproductions of medieval and Renaissance art. These are not perspectival art, which begins showing up in Europe during the revival of Euclidean geometry in the fifteenth century. These pictures show *ideas*—concentric rings of celestial being, great chains that connect the parts of the body to the parts of the political leadership to the parts of the universe, humors, blindfolded

---

8. Bordo, *Flight to Objectivity*, 21.
9. Illich, *Rivers North of the Future*, 132.

women standing on balls before a moon, alongside open-eyed men standing on blocks before the sun, and so forth. These images reflected that infinite complementarity that Ivan Illich describes as "a certainty that there is a correspondence between what is here and what is beyond."[10]

Bordo points to the emergence of perspectival art, the displacement of meaning by representation, in conjunction with the emergence of Descartes's ideas. Prior to this era, reason was the counterpoint to corruptible desire, but the idea of a mind-body split was inconceivable in a universe where proportionality, fit, correspondence mutually constituted all things as a reflection of God's singular hand in creation. Male and female were understood this way, even if in a hierarchical manner. Heaven and earth were mutually constitutive, with earth being a mother and heaven a father. There was *no decisive borderline* between complementary realms. Yet, Descartes separates mind from body in just such a decisive way. He calls the two realms *res cogitans*, the mind, and *res externa*, the external. In his time, this is a shattering discontinuity.

For the first time, the self—that is, *the mind*—is seen as something separate from the world, even one's own body. For the first time, we are conceived of as living in a permanent state of voyeurism—peering through a window at what is going on outside. We are watchers instead of participants. This is a radical boundary-metaphysic, the mind becoming one person's lonely bunker. The mind is the subject. All else is *object*. We are ghosts in a machine. Descartes writes in *Meditation V*,

> For although I am of such a nature that as long as I understand anything very clearly and distinctly, I am naturally impelled to believe it to be true, yet because I am also of such a nature that I cannot have my mind constantly fixed on the same object in order to perceive it clearly, and as I often recollect having formed a past judgment without at the same time properly recollecting the reasons that led me to make it, it may happen meanwhile that other reasons present themselves to me, which would easily cause me to change my opinion, if I were ignorant of the facts of the existence of God, and thus I should have no true and certain knowledge, but only vague and vacillating opinion.[11]

This state of anxiety, of doubt, is so powerful that objects require our laserlike focus and constant attention. Now you see it; now you don't. Bordo calls this "epistemological instability."[12] Descartes was reflecting the

---

10. Ibid.
11. Descartes, *Meditations*, 68.
12. Bordo, *Flight to Objectivity*, 30.

social instability caused by the wars of his post-Reformation epoch, and the *epistemological* crisis caused by Galileo and company.

> When [the] world had itself been transformed by Galileo and his colleagues, what had seemed so simple and natural took on the aspect of a mystery. In the new world their renderings of knowledge appeared no longer as statements of a fact, but as posing of a problem. Fresh knowledge made knowledge itself seem impossible in the world it purported to describe.[13]

Perceptions were always understood to have the capacity for fallibility, even among the ancient Greeks. But this was something new. A no-man's-land had been established between sense and reality where before there had been intercourse. The self had been driven into a kind of fortification, with all things outside understood as suspicious. This martial episteme had entered decisively into the very heart of metaphysics.

Mary Douglas describes various cultural norms associated with purity and taboos, and she concludes that all societies have psychic demarcations—in fact, no society can be effectively constituted without some notion of outside and inside, of where there is order and what might threaten chaos. We must avoid a purely psychological critique of Descartes, because while anxiety is understood in the (post)modern mind as primarily a therapeutic issue, something that happens in an already Cartesianized self, epistemological crisis is social. This seventeenth-century epistemological crisis was characterized by the terrifying shifts of these boundaries; and Descartes was reinscribing a new internal-external, purity-pollution paradigm to recapture order from chaos. Descartes felt that he needed to re-ground conviction, but to do so he had to invent "the mind" as something that is "inner." Bordo describes this invention in a chapter titled "The Emergence of Inwardness." The fact that we now find this idea of the inward mind so unremarkable is a testament to the broad acceptance of Descartes's episteme.

In his schema, the problem became "subjectivity." *Subjectivity* is a beguiler, a tempter, something for which we ought to be on the lookout, a valid source of anxiety. The mind must be protected from its tendency toward self-deception. Yet, from within this fog of interiority emerges a new kind of vertigo: locatedness.[14] Prior to these developments people understood where they belonged, perceiving in all things proportionality, a fittedness. Personhood was belonging. Practices, narrative orders, and community traditions, as well as intra-community relations and kinship, were determinative of who one was and how one understood oneself. One's actual, spatial location

13. Randall, *Career of Philosophy*, quoted in ibid., 33.
14. Bordo, *Flight to Objectivity*, 58–59.

was a shifting reality secured within this state of belonging. One knew who one was. Blaise Pascal eloquently describes this new location-vertigo:

> When I consider the brief span of my life absorbed into an eternity which comes before and after . . . the small space I occupy and which I see swallowed up in the infinite immensity of spaces of which I know nothing and which know nothing of me, I take fright and am amazed to see myself here rather than there: there is no reason for me to be here rather than there, now rather than then.[15]

The telescope and Copernicus's assertion that the earth was no longer the center of this vastly expanded universe (now conceived of as the "gaping jaws of infinity") had decentered human beings and made their actual, physical *location* at any given time a source of consummate dread. This new existential boundary (inside one's own head) and this dread-in-location suggested a new kind of fear, one that still haunts us as the loss of meaning. God was no longer the author of a fitted world, but a life preserver in a limitless sea of doubt.

As we shall see, with the reassertion of a new form of masculinity, post-Descartes, even *this* need for God begins to fade into the background. This new scandal of particularity corresponded to the emergence of perspectival space in art. Art now assumes an imaginary (and *located*) viewer, an interiorized and terrifyingly lonely voyeur gazing out at representations stripped of any meaning. How to resolve such terrible anxiety? Not altogether surprisingly, as a mathematician, Descartes resolved his own doubt with mathematics.

Descartes entertained the idea of some totalizing philosophy, some grand universal theory, that could overcome this doubt, and so he fell upon the idea of something called "pure thought" underwritten by "pure perception," which we might recognize today as the totalizing truth claims put forward by some on behalf of physical science. Bordo observes,

> Such perception, far from embracing the whole, demands the disentangling of the various objects of knowledge *from* the whole of things, and beaming a light on the essential separateness of each—its own pure and discrete nature, revealed as *it* is, free of the "distortions" of subjectivity. Arithmetic and geometry are natural models for the science that will result.[16]

---

15. *Pensées*, quoted in ibid., 60.
16. Bordo, *Flight to Objectivity*, 76.

This attention to discrete and exteriorized *objects*—exteriorized from the *strategic redoubt*, the policed boundary, the military standpoint, mediated (policed) by the purity of numbers—will become the new basis of "knowledge" understood now as "objective." The ground is now prepared for the totalizing truth claim at the center of a new episteme—empiricism—as the purifier of understanding. It becomes clear why Bordo titles her book *The Flight to Objectivity* (emphasis on "to"). Objectivity was a refuge for the lonesome, anxious, and decentered self. And here is where Descartes unwittingly opened the door to the now "uninteresting" atheism of the modern world.

> What we are enabled to see ... is a historical movement away from a transcendent God as the only legitimate object of worship to the establishing of the *human intellect* as godly, and as appropriately to be revered and submitted to—once "purified" of all that stands in the way of its godliness. Shortly, for modern science, God will indeed become downright superfluous. ... The godly intellect is on the way to becoming the true deity of the modern era.[17]

Descartes opened the door to modernity; but it was others who walked through. His was a conceptual revolution, not yet a methodology. When that methodology was conceptualized, it would be conceptualized as masculine by Francis Bacon and others. Bacon's "scientist" was explicitly a man (and nature was explicitly female), and empiricism brought a new masculinity to the fore: that of the *dispassionate* fact collector.

> "Fact" is in modern culture a folk-concept with an aristocratic ancestry. When Lord Chancellor Bacon as part of the propaganda for his astonishing and idiosyncratic amalgam of past Platonism and future empiricism enjoined his followers to abjure speculation and collect facts, he was immediately understood ... to have identified facts as collector's items, to be gathered in with the same kind of enthusiasm that at other times has informed the collection of Spode china or the numbers of railway engines. ... that the scientist is a kind of magpie; it was also to suppose that the observer can confront a fact face to face without any theoretical interpretation imposing itself.[18]

Bordo's last chapter is called "The Cartesian Masculinization." The history of the Cartesian pivot is a step-change in the way masculinity is

---

17. Ibid., 81.
18. MacIntyre, *After Virtue*, 79.

constructed, even though male social dominance is a constant before, during, and after this transition into modernity. The basis of that dominance undergoes a dramatic transformation, one that was also mapped by Carolyn Merchant[19] as "the death of nature" and by Maria Mies[20] as nature's co-colonization with women and economic peripheries. Prior to Cartesianism, male and female were undoubtedly understood hierarchically, but they were understood complementarily. The masculine and feminine were understood, as all things were, to be proportionalities, mutually constitutive, fitted, in a world that had not yet been externalized by the fortified self and then atomized into "facts." Masculinity was conceived as an active agent, and femininity as a passive agent, with female passivity understood as a kind of essential and fertile receptivity. God was understood as masculine, and the world—the earth—as feminine. The earth was understood as a maternal presence, as a great mother of all things, living and not, and as such was given reverence. This was true of all premodern cultures, including Western Christendom.[21]

Merchant points out that ancient mining was considered a kind of midwifing of minerals, which required great spiritual preparation as well as great care in execution.[22]

> Minerals and metals ripened in the uterus of the Earth Mother, mines were compared to her vagina, and metallurgy was the human hastening of the living metal in the artificial womb of the furnace.... Miners offered propitiation to the deities of the soil, performed ceremonial sacrifices, and observed strict cleanliness, sexual abstinence, fasting, before violating the sacredness of the living earth by sinking a mine.[23]

Even in the complex cosmology of medieval Christendom, every particle in the universe was seen as animated by God, pregnant with potentiality. Objectivity changed all that.

Karl Stern, a late Jewish convert to Catholicism under the influence of Dorothy Day, born in Germany and naturalized as a Canadian citizen after the Nazi takeover, was a psychiatrist and a neurologist as well as an author. In his book *The Flight from Woman*,[24] the title of which Bordo intentionally

---

19. Merchant, *Death of Nature*.
20. Mies, *Patriarchy and Accumulation*.
21. Merchant, *Death of Nature*, 3–13.
22. Ibid., 4.
23. Ibid.
24. Stern, *Flight from Woman*.

echoes, Stern noted how modernity's "flight to objectivity" was an attempt to *escape* the feminine altogether.

> If a kind of Cartesian ideal were ever fulfilled, i.e., if the whole of nature were only what can be explained in terms of mathematical relationships—then we would look at the world with a fearful sense of alienation, with that utter loss of reality with which a future schizophrenic child looks at his mother. A machine cannot give birth.[25]

The machine became the metaphor for the objectified universe after the scientific revolution. The natural world was understood figuratively as feminine, as is apparent from the writings of Bacon and the other "fathers" of modernity; but female "nature" was not merely subdued. As Merchant notes, it was killed. The pure *res extensa* came to be understood as a machine, a clock, a collection of matter and energy that was essentially inert. The feminine principle or force was understood prior to Descartes as that of sympathy, relationality, nurturing, a yielding affection. With Descartes, the universe was placed under the control of *definition* and stripped of its divinity. Purity for Descartes was discrete mathematics that disaggregated the parts of the universe to hold them under scrutiny, the kind of anatomical study that required collections of fact, or a corpse. What had to be *purged* from the mind to achieve this purity—what was *dangerous*, as Mary Douglas would say—was sympathy, relationality, an attitude of care or yielding affection. If Cartesian anxiety was a "crisis of parturition," then the Cartesian revolution was matricide. "For the mechanists," writes Bordo, "the female world-soul did not die; rather the world *is* dead. There is nothing to mourn, nothing to lament.... The 'otherness' of nature is now what allows it to be known."[26] Bordo calls this de-animation of nature a "reaction-formation." A component of this reaction-formation, or the "flight from woman," was the *fear of fusion* described by Hartsock, *the effacement of boundaries* between two subjects. Richard Beck, in *Unclean*, notes that love and disgust exist reciprocally in relation to boundaries, which serve as a kind of policed military perimeter: "As the self gets symbolically extended so does ... the primal psychology that monitors the boundary of the body.... The boundary of the body is extended to include the other."[27]

The erasure of boundaries, seen as a feminine characteristic (women make new people inside their own bodies, after all), is perceived as a threat by the Cartesian subject, the masculine mind purified by mathematics. This

25. Stern, "Descartes and Gender," 31.
26. Bordo, *Flight to Objectivity*, 108.
27. Beck, *Unclean*, 86.

reaction-formation is *objectification*, a term that has grown so familiar in discussions of sex that it is not routinely associated with its philosophical antecedents in philosophy, that is, subject-*object* dualism and the notion of *object*-ivity as antagonistic to a perilous subjectivity.

Objectification, in a sexual sense, is *reducing* another person to a sexual *object*. In war, objectification *reduces* the other to a dead body. In Descartes, the *pure* mind is only possible after anatomical dissection, *reducing* the attentive focus to the discrete parts. Cartesianism is—above all—*reductive objectification*.

Men in premodern, male-dominant societies believed that women were inherently dangerous. They were bearers of chaos. This corresponds to descriptions of female-nature as capricious or hostile. The Greek deity Chaos, initially genderless, was later portrayed as female. She was goddess of a "formless void," a kind of pre-existence similar to that described in Genesis. When these ancient ideas were merged with early European Christianity, "fickle" women were portrayed as requiring the headship of men, who ostensibly had the rational faculties required to control women's dangerous and potentially destabilizing impulses.

When the depredations and dislocations of the sixteenth and seventeenth centuries threw the world as it was perceived by dominant men into apparent chaos, women and effeminacy became the cultural scapegoats, as we saw in the accounts of the witch trials that peaked precisely then. Bordo calls the century between 1550 and 1650 "a particularly gynophobic century."[28] We saw in an earlier chapter how women, accused as witches, were engaging in child murder (through abortion and contraception), causing crops to fail, bewitching men, and so forth.

> Such fantasies were not limited to a fanatic fringe. Among the scientific set, we find the image of the witch, the willful, wanton virago, projected onto generative nature, whose scientific exploration, as Merchant points out, is metaphorically linked to a witch trial. The "secrets" of nature are imagined as deliberately and slyly "concealed" from the scientist.[29]

Francis Bacon referred to matter as "a common harlot ... [with] an appetite and inclination to dissolve the world and fall back into the old chaos." Bacon referred to the scientific enterprise in terms that sounded uncannily like

---

28. Bordo, *Flight to Objectivity*, 108.
29. Ibid., 109.

torturing confessions out of witches, of "tearing nature open to reveal her secrets": "I am come in very truth leading to you Nature with all her children to bind her to your service and make her your slave."[30] Bacon, an English Christian, reinterpreted Genesis to support his approach. He claimed that the fall described in Genesis involved the loss of man's dominion over nature. He believed that these losses could be recuperated though intellectual effort. As Allen Verhey writes, "To repair the loss of dominion, to reestablish Adam's dominion, was made one of the objectives of the Royal Society."[31]

Submission for Bacon and Descartes was still a masculine virtue, but only submission to (masculinized) *objectivity*, which serves in their cosmos almost like a military superior, giving them guidance in their war against subjectivity (the body) and nature (and women). Bacon's language is not far removed from that of Columbus, who in 1492, writing about his first encounter with indigenous Tainos in the "new" world, said that "with fifty men they can all be subjugated and made to do what is required of them."[32] The scientific revolution, the witch trials, the extreme gynophobia of the fifteenth and sixteenth centuries, the rise of the nation-state (prefiguring the liberal nation-state), and colonialism were all aspects of the same period and place. This correspondence was analyzed by Maria Mies, who noted the metaphorical similarities between women, nature, and colonies—all marked for domination by the ascendant, scientific, and moneyed European male.[33] Women were compared to a turbulent and dangerous nature, nature compared to voracious women, and colonies described as effeminate and requiring white, male headship—the danger of the absence of male headship being social chaos.[34]

Objectivity, control, domination, the suppression of sympathy, and the conquest of the female body (actual or metaphorical) are even today seen as aspects of masculinity, though we treat the Cartesian separations that still dominate our own ideas as if they were *un*-gendered, when gender was always embedded in gender-neutral language. The essential masculinity of *objectivity* was assumed. The story of objectivity's origins in modern male normativity, and the corresponding invisibility of women, is then concealed from later generations by gender-neutral language.

The significance of Bordo's book for this writer, as I work through the association between war, masculinity, modernity, and Christianity, is her

30. Bacon, "Masculine Birth of Time," cited in Bordo, *Flight to Objectivity*, 36.
31. Verhey, *Nature and Altering It*, 56.
32. From Columbus's journal of the first voyage, in Bourne, *Voyages of Columbus*, 114.
33. Mies, *Patriarchy and Accumulation*, 109.
34. Or "barbarism."

focus on Descartes's actual work, and the genealogy she constructs with it. Cartesian dualism is still saddling the world with consequences. In a world that has been declared dead and therefore infinitely exploitable, once "beneficial" technologies have begun to show their malevolent undersides. Alf Hornborg summarizes thus:

> In Cartesian modernity... the inclination to distinguish the self from its material surroundings is conducive to the inclination to treat even people as objects devoid of deeper significance.[35]

---

35. Hornborg, *Power of the Machine*, 137.

17

Contagious Prefix

So what did these prophets have to say to the Church . . . ? I think they had to announce a mystery, which was that the final evil that would bring the world to an end was already present. This evil was called the Anti-Christ, and the Church was identified as the milieu in which it would nest. The Church had gone pregnant with an evil which could have found no nesting place in the Old Testament. Paul in the second chapter of his second letter to the Thessalonians calls this new reality the *mysterium iniquitatis*, the mystery of evil. . . . The more I try to examine the present as an historical entity, the more it seems confusing, unbelievable, and incomprehensible. It forces me to accept a set of axioms for which I find no parallels in past societies and displays a puzzling kind of horror, cruelty, and degradation with no precedent in other historical epochs.[1]

—Ivan Illich

A crucial condition for [exclusive humanism] was a new sense of the self and its place in the cosmos: not open and porous and vulnerable to a world of spirits and powers, but what I want to call buffered.[2]

—Charles Taylor

1. Illich, *Rivers North of the Future*, 59–60.
2. Taylor, *Secular Age*, 27.

"To hell with the future," Monsignor Ivan Illich says. "It is a man-eating idol."[3]

"Modernity and decadent Christianity are enemies in one sense, but in another sense, they are deeply connected to one another and mirror one another," writes Father Robert Barron.[4]

What do two priests have against modernity, against progress, against "the future"? To begin to answer that question, we will begin with *dis-*, a Latin prefix that means "away from," or the opposite of whatever it modifies. In our case, we will examine the terms *disembedding, disembodiment, disenchantment,* and *disaggregation* for their meaning and mutual association.

"In many pre-modern, traditional societies," Alasdair MacIntyre explains in *After Virtue*, "it is through his or her membership in a variety of social groups that the individual identifies himself or herself and is identified by others. I am brother, cousin and grandson, member of this household, that village, this tribe. These were not characteristics that belonged to human beings accidentally, to be stripped away in order to discover 'the real me.'"[5]

Persons were *embedded* in these social relations, which for them defined obligations and expectations. Their physical selves inhabited actual locations in actual periods of time. They understood their bodies, their embodiment, as part of a collective *history*. Absent these connections and the kinds of recognition from others that go with them, the embedded, concrete, premodern individual would have been bereft, experiencing herself or himself as nothing, as socially dead. That is not saying this person was static or unchanging, but that this individual saw both *self* and *life* as integrated within a community's journey. Not only were our premodern ancestors on a journey, but that common journey had a destination. They had a direction, and in many senses they had customs and norms that functioned not unlike a compass to keep them aimed at that destination, which for each person meant completing one's life on the correct path. MacIntyre explains "philosophical happiness" in this context by quoting a Greek proverb: "Call no man happy until he is dead."[6] This sense of journey and direction once provided the criteria for day-to-day actions and for the various projects and duties that comprised a human life.

---

3. Illich, *Rivers North of the Future*, xix.
4. Barron, *Priority of Christ*, 16.
5. MacIntyre, *After Virtue*, 33.
6. Ibid., 34.

With the emergence of modernity, this embeddedness is lost. The *individual* is reconceptualized as a being without specificity, without relations, and without roots in a community or history. "Individual" becomes a cipher, in the hands of both philosophy and law, for someone who is simultaneously everywhere and nowhere. Tradition-based orientations for action disappear, and the person becomes *dis*embedded. This disembedding "passes to some degree unnoticed, for it is celebrated historically for the most part not as a loss, but as a self-congratulatory gain, as the emergence of the individual freed on the one hand from the social bonds of those constraining hierarchies which the modern world rejected at its birth and on the other hand from what modernity has taken to be the superstitions of teleology."[7]

By removing persons (who shall henceforth be "individuals"—history-free, genderless, ageless, and without a place) from the actual kinships, friendships, customs, and commitments that constitute one's embodied social existence, modernity has asserted a form of "equality" that requires us to *ignore* these roots of personhood. History, family, customs, and community are philosophically and *legally* irrelevant. And with them, the fleshy body disappears. "The individual," an abstraction in law and philosophy, *dis*embodies us. When the basis of our social existence is denied, we are also living "outside our own skins" in the Gnostic universe of the modern, separated in body and spirit.

Barbara Duden, in her history of the perception of the pregnant female body,[8] describes a corresponding uprootedness through the professional mediation of embodied experience. Modern technology that looks directly into the expectant mother's womb has changed women's experience of themselves during pregnancy. The direct bodily ("haptic") experience (*proprioception*) of the past is now mediated by an optical technology (e.g., ultrasound) which makes the pregnant woman a kind of outside observer of her own insides. A pregnant woman now attends first to the image in the ultrasound, and only secondarily to how she feels (which is now itself a decentered evaluation of one's own body in the search for symptoms and dangers). Her experience has become professionally mediated and optic, instead of direct and haptic. She is outside herself, literally looking in. Duden calls this a "skinning" of the woman by medical technology.

In the case of both social existence and personal perception, modern disembodying practices and outlooks are placed under the stewardship of "experts," be they social scientists, medical doctors, teachers, therapists, bureaucrats, or entertainers. This is Ivan Illich's nightmare, the institutional corruption of the fleshly embodied Gospel exemplified in the Parable of the

7. Ibid., 34.
8. Duden, *Disembodying Women*.

Good Samaritan. This direct and bodily relation has morphed into the technological service-society, where depersonalized humans spend their lives in a state of dependency on a grid of ideas and materials that are produced and managed by the "radical monopolies" of experts.

The *disembodiment* described by Duden and Illich corresponds to a scientific *disenchantment* with nature, the *disembedding* of the economy from local control and production, and the *dissolution* of stable communities that heretofore anchored one's personhood.

Karl Polanyi described disembedding as the ready relocation of people away from a network of nonmarket relationships and direct participation in the community into un-*familiar* (sharing a word root with *family*) surroundings. The person is resituated in an impersonalized milieu determined by money, market abstractions, and industrial monoculture.[9] Polanyi said we are re-embedded in that more impersonal milieu, where the market rules as the only form of economy, and where we are now captive to that market—which leaves us metaphysically *dis*embedded in the sense used by MacIntyre. Instead of being embedded in community, kinship, and tradition, we become "resources," which can be bought and sold on the market. We live in a society where nearly everything has been converted into a commodity, including ourselves. Want, even hunger, now impels us from place to place like interchangeable parts.[10]

Disembodiment corresponds not only to MacIntyre's description of an "individual" who is nowhere and everywhere but also to the way that modern ideas, modern language, and impersonal institutions treat *the body itself* as an alienable object[11] and create the idea in the minds of actual persons that they must experience the body, as Duden describes, through the many mediations of institutions that thrive in a disenchanted and disembedding world. We know our bodies now as *instruments*, which are organized into systems, which are intelligible only through science, medicine, and therapy—mediating, impersonal, and ever more monopolistic *institutions*, instead of place, practices, kinship, friendship, and narrative community.

Max Weber's study of bureaucracy describes the institutional disembodiment created by modern bureaucracy alongside a metaphysical *disenchantment*—the world losing its sense of mystical wonder, of places losing

9. Polanyi, *Great Transformation*, 171–86.
10. Ibid.
11. The implications of an "alienable body"—of a body one can even rent or sell, while a legal "self" remains legally separate—are covered in chapter 20, "Origin Myths."

their sacred status. "The fate of our times," said Weber, "is characterized by rationalization and intellectualization and, above all, by the *disenchantment of the world*."[12] Weber describes this process ambivalently; but Carolyn Merchant's book, cited in the preceding chapter, traces the genealogy of that de-sacralization of nature by the "fathers" of the Enlightenment, calling it "the death of nature."[13] The objectification of nature, the reduction of nature to mere matter and energy without meaning that was accompanied by the elevation of natural science to a totalizing truth claim, was prerequisite for wholesale environmental exploitation.[14]

Merchant maps the history of attitudes toward nature. She shows how the idea of nature as *alive* was jettisoned in the period between the Reformation and the Industrial Revolution.[15] This is dramatically different than the dominion over the earth narrated in the Bible, which begins with an anti-urban tract and ends with an anti-imperial one. In Scripture, there is no doubt that human beings are granted the power to selectively subdue other elements and creatures, but there is also little doubt that this implies a form of humble stewardship for something—creation—which the Bible reminds us belongs to God, as we do, and as such is sacred (Ps 50:9–12; Hag 2:8).

Every society, Christian or not, before this critical period from the sixteenth to the nineteenth centuries, had in common some belief that nature is both animate and aware. Natural philosophy "killed" (a feminized) nature. Certain male human beings came to be understood as subjects, and the sum of all that is not human came to be understood as objects—as things to be acted upon, but with no vitality or awareness or naturally occurring relationship we are obliged to respect. The formerly living world was reduced to a corpse on the anatomy table of modern science that would be dissected to identify and catalog its disaggregated forms and functions as "facts."

Merchant describes the de-animation of nature through the fifteenth- and sixteenth-century alchemist Agrippa, who wanted to elevate man alongside God in his dominion over nature (echoes of Genesis), yet who himself still bitterly opposed mining and other rapacious extractions from nature. Merchant says that Bacon "stood Agrippa on his head," by agreeing with the apotheosis of man over nature, but insisting that the material world be aggressively *conquered* and *subdued*[16]—all in those gendered terms

---

12. Weber, "Science as a Vocation."
13. Merchant, *Death of Nature*.
14. General purpose money—sponsored by the nation-state—has been the indispensible extraction-and-exchange accelerator for this ecologic destruction.
15. This modern Western idea of a dead nature—of nature's de-sacralization and the masculine trope of "conquering" nature—has now become globally hegemonic.
16. Merchant, *Death of Nature*, 184–85.

that compared the quest for knowledge to the interrogation and torture of witches.[17]

> Francis Bacon's use of metaphors to characterize his nascent concept of experimentation must be interpreted within the historical context of his time. His approach to experimentation is one in which nature is constrained by the "violence of impediments" and is made new by "art and the hand of man." His language about nature should be placed in the context of the history of the contained, controlled experiment, a concept that emerges from juridical practice, from the idea of nature in bonds, and from the tradition of the secrets of nature in settings such as the courtroom, the anatomy theater, and the laboratory.[18]

The lawyer joins the anatomist. The lawyer interrogates the "witch," as the scientist interrogates nature, demanding *her* secrets, which, if necessary, will be tortured from her. Mechanical devices, the "tools of science," will be used to subdue chaotic nature and impose order. Bacon cited the Bible and claimed he was reclaiming the "dominion" over nature that the Scriptures mandated, but there was a qualitative difference between his endeavors and his language and that of the Scriptures that warned first and foremost against pride.

The anatomist, like the one who claims the bodies of executed "witches" for his experiments, disaggregated nature, atomized it, reduced it to parts—the very opposite of what Illich described as a "fitted" cosmos.

> Look at the change in the meaning of nature between classical and modern times, as the historian Carolyn Merchant has done. . . . One thing was certain in antiquity: nature was alive. There were different and conflicting philosophical interpretations of what nature was; but to all of them was common the certainty that *natura nacitura dicitur*, that nature is a concept, an idea, an experience derived from birth-giving.[19]

Philosophy, in particular "natural philosophy," with its highly efficacious means for the manipulation of nature ("violent impediments") and using the power of that efficacy, established itself as the new king of philosophy. This came to be reflected in popular culture. It is reflected in our culture today, in ways so terrifying that we have now become disenchanted with

---

17. Bacon was an enthusiastic supporter of witch hunts. He was, in fact, attorney general to King James I while James was trying and killing "witches."

18. Merchant, "Violence of Impediments," 731.

19. Illich, *Rivers North of the Future*, 69.

disenchantment—the postmodern paradox. It is in response to disenchantment and its terrible sense of loss that we have seen the proliferation of a whole menu of "spiritual" fads.

With Descartes, each thing in nature became something *in-itself*, separate from the whole, and with this mechanized world, God's ever constant will was replaced by a cosmic clockmaker who winds up the universe according to natural laws, which can now run while God takes a nap. This does not immediately supplant God, but it creates the conditions wherein God can be dispensed with at a later date. And so the ground was prepared for secular modernity to emerge. That lack of a "second thought" that Weber referred to as "disenchantment" was set up by Descartes and advanced by Bacon. Nature is an *object*, purely for our *use*. A dead and dissected objectivity is, at last, the cure for our dangerous subjectivity.

Disaggregation, the separation of reality into dissociated taxonomies, the pretense that reality can be separated into various parts which can then be studied and evaluated independent of one another, begins with Descartes's "thing in-itself." It can be seen most clearly today in the organization of the modern university. MacIntyre outlined three developments in the modern research university that could be traced to the displacement of Aristotle's universalism by Cartesian atomism.[20] First, the university made extraordinary discoveries in various fields, especially the sciences. These discoveries, however, required funding, and so the direction of research efforts was determined in large part by who funded the research and to what purpose. Second, the new universities provided an increasing pool of specialized experts to support the expansion of an industrial capitalist society. Undergraduate studies are now largely an initiation into graduate specialties that are determined by professional job markets. Increasing specialization is an aspect of de-skilling.[21] In the academy, this has led to a proliferation of disciplines, subdisciplines, and sub-subdisciplines, in which the gradu-

---

20. MacIntyre, *God, Philosophy, Universities*, 173–75.

21. De-skilling is the economic process wherein greater specialization leads to the ability to employ people with fewer trained skills. For example, one very skilled generalist might be able to build a car. But a person with fewer skills can be used to build carburetors; and a person with hardly any skills at all can run a machine that stamps out a single part for a carburetor. Modern economies are all characterized by progressive specialization and its consequent de-skilling. This places increasing control over productive processes in the hands of professional managers, whose "skill" is not technical but managerial; and it creates greater general dependency on money for survival. The first institutions to practice systematic specialization and de-skilling were armies.

ate student and eventual professional or expert neither comprehends nor needs to know the larger social, moral, political, or economic context of the work that he or she does. Third, as research dedicated to both economic expansion and greater specialization goes deeper into ever more specialized fields of inquiry, universities become increasingly expensive and come to resemble for-profit corporations producing commodities.

MacIntyre differentiates these universities from the first late medieval universities, which sought not to advance economic interests but to increase one's understanding of the world as a whole and of the relationships between the aspects of the world. That is, the universe-ity sought to advance a shared understanding of the universe. MacIntyre cribs Clark Kerr in saying that modern universities might better be called "multiversities."[22]

This book is attempting to provide a less specialized and more general context to our understanding of war, church, and gender. For that reason, we are covering each in the evolving contexts of the Middle Ages, of modernity and "capitalism,"[23] and of the historical development of the United States, which is now the dominant nation-state in a global world order.

Liberalism formed as a reaction against the wars of Reformation throughout Europe. The central power of the nation-state concentrated in conjunction with the epistemological crisis that midwifed modernity. That crisis was manifest in an inability to articulate a coherent moral vision consistent with newly emerging political categories. So the hyper-plural society we see today is a direct outcome of the breakup of the church in western Europe, though not in the way people commonly believe.

For good and ill, by the immediate pre-Reformation period, the Roman Catholic Church, speaking here not only of the Magisterium but of a very diverse and widely scattered popular church, was central to social organization and culture all over the region. There was not one cosmos for

---

22. MacIntyre, *God, Philosophy, Universities*, 174.

23. The term "capitalism" is used advisedly here, ergo the scare quotes. What are understood today as capitalist relations of finance, production, and consumption were not by any means new when the nation-state emerged from the earlier inter-city-state system. Many theorists date such relations to as early as 1204 and the sack of Constantinople during the Fourth Crusade, which resulted in a flood of looted silver and gold to northern Italy and the Low Countries (becoming the basis for banking and finance), followed by a century of colonial extraction from Byzantium to Europe—establishing a core-periphery dynamic upon which European accumulation could build. The material impetus for the emergence of the nation-state was, in large part, the need for larger stable polities to accommodate expanded capital accumulation.

day-to-day life and another for theology on Sundays. Religious beliefs and beliefs about the way the world worked were completely integrated into a singular worldview that could not have recognized today's practice of compartmentalizing the various areas of our lives.

When the Reformation began, the expectation of reformers was that returning directly to Scripture for guidance, as opposed to reliance on the church hierarchy's interpretation of Scripture, would place Christianity on a stable and institutionally uncorrupted foundation. This idea of *sola scriptura*, however, failed to anticipate how quickly and deeply various readers of the same scriptures would interpret the scriptures' meanings differently.

The first schism and the Lutheran breakaway rapidly devolved into a cacophony of sectarian division. As alliances formed between emerging "churches" (now plural) and emerging nation-states, the wars that followed took on the aspect of religious sectarianism while retaining their essential character as political wars between nation-states.

Nation-states that had diverse Christian sects within national boundaries recognized the potential of religious disputes to destabilize the body politic, and to deny access to profits for the rising merchant class, so the idea of religious freedom arose in response to the threat of sectarian instability and the depredations of chronic warfare.

Cultures within states that adopted religious tolerance generally remained religiously homogeneous, at least in specific locations, and the vast majority of western Europeans were, in one form or another, still *Christians*.

So when liberalization began, the kinds of social stability that relied on shared moral axioms within any community actually remained, though it was carried by Christian culture *apart from the law*. Some new laws, taking their cue from the Dutch, forbade religious persecution; but the law had little power to prescribe moral action. People continued to act based on shared *Christian* moral assumptions. The state was largely not responsible for moral formation or guidance, and churches sustained this essential social function, which benefited the state with social stability.

States depending upon moral cohesion maintained by churches learned soon enough that some people would leave Christian teachings behind, along with the church, and not be subject to church (as prescribed by state) on the very moral questions that the state, by law, had abandoned. Soon enough, too, the increasing pluralism of society left the law with no recourse but the propagation of volumes of detailed law, and the state became the referee for a rapidly multiplying collection of social conflicts. The only final authority then was the law; and the highest social virtue became *obedience* to state law. In this way, we can have a person today who has never been trained in the virtues of prudence, courage, justice, etc., but because he or she does not break any laws, this person is called *virtuous*.

Brad Gregory writes that "the threat of subversion and fears of heterodoxy in the conflicts between confessionalizing Catholic and magisterial Protestant rulers made *obedience* the central virtue of early modern Europe."[24]

What Gregory does not say here, though he gives readers plenty of evidence for it in his descriptions of the "religious" wars that engendered the Reformation, is that blind obedience is also the highest day-to-day virtue in the armed forces. When wars and rumors of wars are generally manifest, states inevitably strengthen central power; and military practice comes to subordinate all other practices of governance to itself. Even as I write, executive prerogative and the surveillance state are being expanded in our time to prosecute a shadowy "war" on an abstract noun.[25] Gregory cites the "threat of subversion," which is the constant preoccupation of military leaders who depend on schemes and secrets in their contest with the enemy. In all these respects, we can see how the state is fundamentally military.

When I was a recruit in Basic Combat Training for the army, we were taught our doctrine and tactics around a shape-shifter called The Enemy. No specific enemy was ever named, though we knew in the case of counter-guerilla operations, The Enemy seemed very Vietnamese; and in the case of The Conventional Enemy, he seemed very Russian. In doctrinal statements, as has been the case in militaries since the general acceptance of Clausewitz as a theoretician of war, The Enemy is an abstract constant; fill in the blank when the time comes for an actual blood-and-bombs war.

Something happens to men's thinking when they study war. They become antagonistic beings. Warfare creates its own logic, in which The Enemy and his destruction become the lodestar of a whole culture's enterprise. In this way, the identification of and neutralization of a supply of enemies becomes a central and intrinsic feature of the nation-state, as well as the individual soldier.

This is a problem for Christians, because Matthew 5 commands us to love our enemies and even to pray for those who persecute us. No directive from Jesus has been subjected to more lawyering by men to find a loophole, with the possible exception of our legal squirming with regard to what Jesus

---

24. Gregory, *Unintended Reformation*, 232.
25. "Terrorism."

said about being rich (Matt 19:24). Jesus confronts this tendency to displace the spirit of the law using the letter of the law by the scribes and Pharisees (Mark 2:27). He confronts those key logics of war—the impermeable boundary (Luke 10:25–37), the will to power (Matt 4:8–9), and the reliance on violence to achieve justice. One is not called to return injury for injury or even to exercise the "right" of self-defense; rather, Jesus says, forgive without limit (Matt 18:22), turn the other cheek (Matt 5:39), answer hatred with love (Luke 6:27). War inevitably forms its practitioners in the opposite logic, else they could not practice war.

War changed; the enemy changed; and war technology made war lethal and destructive on a scale beyond what anyone could have imagined before the twentieth century. That lethality, that scale of destruction, is one of the inevitable features in the evolution of modernity. War formed the nation-states of Europe and is their central capacity. The *raison d'etre* of the governments of nation-states remains to this day to conduct warfare, whether defensive or offensive. International borders are universally militarized, guarded by men in uniforms with weapons.

Even during the misnamed "hundred years' peace" (1815–1914) in Europe, when European armies left one another more or less alone, they were extending and consolidating their colonial peripheries with shoulder-guns, bayonets, and cannons.

During this same period of the great European standoff, the United States attacked Mexico, warred against indigenous people, and attacked the Spanish almost unceasingly.[26] In the middle of these other wars, the United States split and went to war with itself in what many call the first *modern* war.

---

26. Polanyi, *Great Transformation*, 3–19.

18

Just, Civil, and Total War— Sanctification of State

In exploring the Civil War through moral lenses, one sees just how unprepared Americans were for such a cataclysm in the moral sense no less than the military or political. And unlike politics and military arsenals, which geared up to meet the challenge, the ability to fix a moral stance never progressed. Rather, it regressed. On all sides—clerical, political, journalistic, military, artistic, and intellectual—the historian searches in vain for moral criticism directed at one's own cause. Talk of war certainly bristled from the pages of the secular press and civic assemblies, and statesmen, clergy, and intellectuals raged against the unjust conduct of the enemy.[1]

—Harry S. Stout

The evaluation of these conditions for moral legitimacy belongs to the prudential judgment of those who have responsibility for the common good.

—Catechism of the Roman Catholic Church, Paragraph 2309

---

1. Stout, *Upon the Altar*, xvii.

Just, Civil, and Total War—Sanctification of State

Karl Polanyi, writing of Europe, called the period from 1815 to 1914 "the hundred years' peace."[2] In that period, the great European nation-states, now consolidated as Russia, England, France, Austria, Italy, and Prussia, had only two brief flare-ups of war between them: the Crimean War and the Franco-Prussian War. This was not a peace based on goodwill but on calculating pragmatism as Europe fattened on an accumulation regime pioneered in the Dutch Republic and expanded through European colonial acquisition. That regime was based on capital investment in a partnership between banks and merchants, and enforced through serial enclosures of commons that attacked subsistence economy. This de-ruralization forced peasants out of the countryside and into wage labor in the cities' manufactories, and established their dependence on money for survival in the new urban slums.[3]

The "hundred years' peace" was based on a balance of power. The buildup of military capacity among several states was accompanied by mutual suspicion, such that when one state threatened the capacity for belligerence against another, shared fear from bordering states compelled the latter into strategic alliance.

In the interstices of this pragmatic peace, the money-men flourished. One investment that exploded was in combustion machinery, giving birth to an unprecedented scale of mass production. The scientific revolution successfully substituted combustible energy for slaves.

This new system—the term *capitalism* was not invented until midway through the "hundred years' peace"—had several requirements. It required a general purpose currency. It required enough wage workers to man the machinery. It required banks to make loans for initial investments. It required the externalization of costs (e.g., rivers in which to dump industrial effluvia, or free access to minerals) sufficient to guarantee a profit so the investor could both pay off his loans and flourish financially. And it required markets sufficient to soak up expanding production. The state was the guarantor for these requirements; but there was one other feature of this system that became a driver. After a certain period, the market would become saturated, and the rate of profit—profit being the motive for production—would inevitably fall. This new accumulation regime had to expand or die; and for this it needed to do two things: to conquer new exploitable peripheries and to create demand for new commodities. Today, this imperative to expand has an economic euphemism—growth.

While Europe probed farther and farther into Africa, Asia, and the Americas, a new polity had taken root in North America, where it was

2. Polanyi, *Great Transformation*, 5.
3. Ibid., 108–16.

rapidly becoming an economic contender with Europe: the United States. Some of the United States' leaders began to use the language of divine providence to describe expansion not as accumulation, but as a mission. The missionary language was crystallized in the notion of Manifest Destiny.[4] The actual goal of this idea's boosters was the forcible appropriation of large tracts of land west of the newly formed United States. Encoded in the language of Manifest Destiny was the idea of *redemption* of the world through the spread of divinely sanctioned American values.[5]

There was one major constraint on this ambition, however. The new nation was divided into two, contingently complementary economic systems with distinct dominant class cultures—one based on mercantilism and industrial manufacture in the North, and the other on mass agricultural production using commodified African slaves as labor in the South. The cotton produced in the South was up-valued into textiles in the North, but this *economic* complementariness had *political* contradictions. Each system favored its own rules of governance, and so the United States, powerful as it already was, limped along with these contradictory rules of governance in its first few decades.

When the question of expansion into new territories was raised, there was an inhering conflict between those who wanted to use slave labor and those who wanted to use "free labor," meaning wage laborers. Each system had its own advantages for its stewards, and also its own rules; and each system, if co-located, would be in direct competition with the other.

In the early nineteenth century, the newly independent Mexico wanted to establish population outposts in the northeast, and it unwisely invited all comers, who would be Anglo-Americans, to take over land in a region called Mexican Texas. Slave owners took advantage of this proposal, East Texas being cotton country; but in 1824, Mexico set upon a plan for gradual emancipation and an end to slavery, so the slave-owning Texas immigrants revolted. Led by Sam Houston, a veteran of the War of 1812, the Texans defeated the Mexican armed forces and established the Republic of Texas. In 1845, the United States annexed Texas, justifying this move with Manifest Destiny. The Mexican government still claimed Texas as its own, and war broke out between Mexico and the United States. The manifest destinists saw this war as an expansion opportunity, with their covetous eyes cast as far as California, and the war was aimed at the conquest of land.

The war was not universally popular, and some of the political fault lines that developed around it would persist and grow into a conflagration within a decade and a half. Abolitionists and Whigs, among the latter a

---

4. O'Sullivan, "Nation of Futurity," 426–30.
5. Miller, *Native America*, 120.

politician named Abraham Lincoln, opposed the war as the expansion of the slave economy; and Southern Democrats became the war's cheerleaders.[6]

The war against the inferior military forces of Mexico was prosecuted with utter brutality. When it concluded with the Treaty of Guadalupe Hidalgo in 1848, it had also blooded a fresh crop of American military officers that included Jefferson Davis, Ulysses Grant, Robert E. Lee, George McClellan, William Sherman, "Stonewall" Jackson, Ambrose Burnside, and Braxton Bragg.[7]

The Civil War was fought during a period of rapid industrialization. The railroad, the telegraph, aerial reconnaissance balloons, submarines, ironclad ships, rifling of firearms and artillery, and manufactured goods like clothing and equipment—all were introduced together in the American Civil War in a particular way that marks it as the first "modern war." The Civil War was also our first "total" war, or a war wherein the whole resources of a society are marshaled and the differentiation between civilian and combatant breaks down (civilians had been killed in the past, but the differentiation was still recognized).

At certain thresholds in any enterprise, a change in quantity is transformed into a change in quality. Qualitative changes of this kind are seldom predictable. Machine factories and rail lines provided the conditions for fielding unheard of numbers of combatants. New technology tied these vast armies to these new lines of communication and supply, changing every strategic calculus from the past. The companies that supplied the materiel, the telegraphs, and the rail lines became fabulously rich and accrued a new kind of political power. To finance the output of war materiel, industrialists needed credit, and so *haute finance* was centrally positioned in the new war economy and would grow into a powerful and permanent feature of society. The great size of military units, training in a now obsolete Napoleonic doctrine, and the unanticipated effects of rifled barrels at close range transformed Civil War engagements into rivers of blood. Modernity met war in a staggering symbiosis.

Harry Stout's account shows how the modern governing apparatus, with its partnership between nation-state and "civil society," was already taking shape during the Civil War as something recognizable to us today.[8] The specific kinds of relations and interdependencies that characterize the

---

6. Stout, *Upon the Altar*, xviii.
7. Waugh, "Mexican War."
8. Stout, *Upon the Altar*.

modern politics of war can be seen even in Stout's brief description of the Civil War. We need only think back to the buildup for the past several U.S. military adventures to see the war-makers' echo chamber, which includes "the secular press and civic assemblies, the statesmen, clergy, and intellectuals" of the United States.

Stout calls West Point the first seminary of American nationalism's civil religion,[9] which produced the aforementioned generals—baptized in blood during the conquest of Mexican territory—who would lead the slaughter between North and South. I once taught "military science" at the United States Military Academy at West Point. First-year military science included the freshman's obligation to commit to memory the principles of war developed by Clausewitz. One of those principles is called unity of command, that is, centralization of power.

The primacy of war for the state is discernible in law. Using the United States as an example, the one office that cannot be left unfilled for even a day is that of the presidency. The reason is that the absence of one commander-in-chief of the armed forces creates an unacceptable risk of the loss of "unity of command." This is the reason that executive power is continually expanded and grudgingly surrendered, and the reason that the most substantial expansions of executive power are during periods of armed conflict and conquest. War and centralization of power feed off of one another. Centralization of authority is integral to war, a precondition of war; and it spawns the temptation to war. The American Civil War was fought for centralization of power, and its outcome was a vastly increased executive authority.

The struggle for centralization of power was also a struggle over the construction of masculinity.

> Masculine roles were changing in the nineteenth century; the Southern ideal of manhood was beginning to become obsolete in the face of the new Self-Made Man of the Market Revolution. In order to protect their homes and preserve their manliness, Southern men embarked on the bloody affair known as the American Civil War.[10]

American flags are placed in the front of almost every Christian church sanctuary in the United States. Prior to the Civil War, the only national flags most United States citizens would see were on ships. The stars and stripes were neither icon nor idol. With the quasi-religious calls on either side of the Civil War to defend their respective civil religions, their nationalisms,

---

9. Ibid., xix.
10. Carroll, "Confederate Masculinity," abstract, para. 2.

the status of the flag took on the religious significance of both. Stout describes the apotheosis of the nation symbolized by the flag:

> [After 1861], the clearest and most literal emblem of patriotism and resolve was the national flag. Churches, storefronts, homes, and government buildings all waved flags as a sign of loyalty and support. A nation festooned with flags is a nation at war.[11]

This description could well have been used of the U.S. immediately after the attacks on the World Trade Center in 2001. I knew people who, for a time, displayed flags out of fear that they would be held in suspicion if they failed to display them. My own children feared our house might come under attack because I refused to hang a flag. Where Jesus had once said that "whoever is not against us is for us" (Mark 9:40), the president flipped the script and ominously told Congress on September 20, 2001, "Either you're with us, or you are with the terrorists."

The Civil War incorporated mass media into the public-private war partnership. Steam presses that printed penny papers sprouted like mushrooms, especially in the North. What had been micro-enterprises with limited demand, thanks to "wars and rumors of war," started selling out on the streets. For big papers like the *New York Herald* and the *New York Tribune*, war was very big business. The more strident (and manly) the papers' voices in support of war, the more copy they sold.

On April 19, 1861, the *New York Tribune* wrote,

> The defection of Virginia shows that little can be hoped for from the loyalty of the dominant party in the Border slave states, and the Government should prepare for a great war. At least 200,000 men should be called out in addition to the regular army.[12]

Modern mainstream media has evolved since the Civil War, with the suggestive power of television and the hot-sheet information flow of the Internet. Media is concentrated into transnational for-profit corporations. The manipulative science of Edward Bernays's "public relations" has been perfected.[13] This indirect, media-to-military, service-for-pay support of war,

---

11. Stout, *Upon the Altar*, 28.

12. Ibid., 31.

13. Bernays (1891–1995), Sigmund Frued's nephew, is seen by many as the father of modern public relations, which uses psychological research to more effectively manipulate the public. More will be said about him in chapter 26, "Nation, Race, and Hygiene."

however, germinated during the Civil War. The media translated the war to the public as titillation, jingo patriotism, fantasy projection, entertainment, and of course . . . manhood. The stage was set for the Age of Simulation, an age into which we ourselves were all born. Propaganda has long been integral to war, but the vastly expanding scale of modern enterprise gave rise to a vastly more effective propaganda for the mass-homogenization of public attitudes.

The profit-making character of media, then and now, demanded an escalation of salaciousness and spectacle to continually whet the appetite of a consuming public. French philosopher Jean Baudrillard would later call this volatile dynamic "hyper-reality"—proxy or "virtual" reality.[14]

In April 1861, the *Charleston Mercury* would write,

> The matter is now plain. State after State in the South sees the deadly development, and are moving to take their part in the grand effort to redeem their liberties. It is not a contest for righteous taxation. It is not a contest for the security of slave property. It is a contest for freedom and free government, in which everything dear to man is involved.[15]

High-flown moral and religious language were placed in the service of the war by North and South alike. Propaganda systematically "subordinated to war, honor, and *manliness*"[16] the citizens of each side. One Southern editor wrote,

> The South fights . . . for honor, character, standing, and reputation. She must not only wipe off the stigma of *effeminacy* with which Abolition has branded her, but she must prove that she possesses the high-toned chivalry, that enduring and indomitable courage that is peculiar to a privileged caste.[17]

The construction of the Southern male, based on honor, was defined against blacks, who Southern white men defined as lacking the innate capacity for honor. Any attack on slavery was a direct affront to Southern manhood. As Jacob Friefeld writes,

> To take away that against which honor was defined was to take away the Southern man's honor and therefore his *manhood*. Furthermore, characterizing slavery in a negative light . . . was a manipulation of the Southern man's world of appearances.

14. Kellner, "Jean Baudrillard."
15. Quoted in Stout, *Upon the Altar*, 33.
16. Ibid., 33.
17. Ibid., 91, my italics.

> The man of honor portrayed slavery as a positive institution; to characterize it in any other way was a form of giving a Southern man a lie, a situation that called for a duel.[18]

And so the duel was on, and it would become a monumental bloodbath—the most costly war in history as counted in loss of U.S. life. While the buildup to the war seized the consciousness of men North and South, the clergy of the large churches fanned the flames of war from the pulpit. Both the North and the South claimed that Christ was on their side. The church had become the captive of war culture and martial masculinity, again.

Northern masculinity was modeled to a degree in the image of Victorian manhood from commercial cities. Southern masculinity was more Continental, archaic, and honor-based.[19] The Revolutionary War had left the stamp of *republican* manhood on both, birthed by the American and French Revolutions and nurtured by the success of the expansionist war against Mexico. The Mexican War, in which most of the generals on both sides of the Civil War had made their prior reputations, was underwritten by a nascent *imperial* masculinity that narrated westward expansion as a providential mark of *progress*.[20] This expansionism privileged a *frontier* masculinity based on a probative contest between civilized men at arms and a wild, chaotic nature, which also included the less than fully human inhabitants of coveted land.[21]

The West Point–trained generals of the Civil War who fought the Mexicans were indoctrinated with the national religion—the Revolutionary narrative of "independence," by a blood sacrifice. The urbane Northerner and the aristocratic Southerner each had a distinct cultural identity, but both shared a masculine lineage that passed through Jefferson and Jackson, with their republican ideals of masculine citizenship. Moreover, generals on both sides measured themselves, as men, against two general groups of people: nonwhites (which included some European immigrants) and women. In war, they would be defined against one another to see who were the *superior* males.

18. Friefeld, "Oh the Confusion of It All," para. 8.

19. Note the reference above to *chivalry*—and that the Ku Klux Klan calls itself the *Knights* of the KKK.

20. See chapter 24, "Progress and Fear of the Feminine."

21. Frontier masculinity is still a powerful cultural trope in the United States, as evidenced by our undying attraction to the genre of the Western. Nearly every American white man my age played Cowboys and Indians; the Indians, like the wilderness, the bears and wolves, the harsh weather, and the women, were mere backdrops and props in the articulation of this masculine ideal. See chapters 27, "The Art of Depression," and chapter 30, "Bombs, Babies, and 'Burbs."

Instead of seeing each other as men from different regions, Northern and Southern men looked upon each other as being of one nation, based on their common independence, their superiority to darker people, and their common differences from women. When the crisis of secession began, Northerners and Southerners did not see each other as two cultures attacking an opposite worldview; instead they looked at each other as having perverse views within a shared value system, and the two sides communicated as such. When the two regions collided in sectional conflict, they used arguments that assumed a shared masculinity while the meanings of their arguments were transformed through two cultural (mis)interpretations. Such misinterpretations often made Northern rhetoric more inflammatory to Southern men of honor while diminishing the ferocity of Southern rhetoric in Northern eyes.[22]

Noted above, the honor-masculinity of the South wanted a duel, and secession was the ritual slap in the face that would inaugurate a duel. Friefeld calls Northern insensitivity to Southern honor codes their "illiteracy in the language of honor."[23] Many of the mercantile Northerners were calculators, the embodiment of post-Enlightenment disenchantment. They could not understand why Southerners were insulted by Northern offers of monetary advantage in exchange for keeping the union. In many cases, the Northern argument against slavery had no hint of moral content. It was seen as inefficient compared to a system of "free labor," which could be controlled not "paternally," but by the pangs of hunger and the all-too-human enslavement to desire and avarice. The reactionary South, according to the free-labor advocates, had become the last drag on the emergence of the new American nation-state.

> Several Southern states had seceded, thereby upholding their Southern honor and preserving their manhood through a duel. Meanwhile, the North, controlled by Republicans, refused to surrender forts or ports to the Southern gentlemen based on their own ideas of an indivisible Union and economic stability. More states would eventually secede, but both sides, operating within separate frameworks of manhood, had already started their journey on the confused road to war.[24]

In this confusion, a revised Southern masculinity appeared, inflamed by Southern clergy, based on a fear of reversal, the fear of "black rule." The honorable Southern white man was about to be *victimized* by Northern

---

22. Friefeld, "Oh the Confusion of It All," para. 12.
23. Ibid.
24. Ibid., para. 13.

Just, Civil, and Total War — Sanctification of State 159

aggression (and by extension, by "Negroes"). The North was provocatively portrayed as treating the South as its black slave. This comparison inflamed the Southern masculine imagination. When the war would be lost, this sense of victimization and its attendant fear of black political power would shape the murderous masculinity of the Ku Klux Klan, openly valorized as heroes in the United States well into the twentieth century.[25] The threat of this role reversal was also understood as a threat of feminization, which could only be met by arms. From an editorial in the Richmond *Daily Dispatch*, 1862:

> War, then, has within it the seeds of good, seeds which must be fertilized by blood to bring forth a harvest of blessings. And if ever there was a war that demanded at once the energies of the patriot and the benediction of the Christian, it is a war in defense of homes and altars, of civil liberty, of social virtue, of life itself, and of all that makes life worth living.[26]

The Civil War was not a duel; it was a charnel house — the merger of mass production, machinofacture, and warfare. Human bodies paid a shocking price. The West Point graduates were schooled in the frontal assault, effective in the Mexican War, which always ended with a bayonet charge. Every officer wanted a successful bayonet charge, at least in his masculine imagination. Digging in for the defense was seen as "effeminate."[27] Even after a series of frontal assaults against entrenched defenses piled up corpses by the tens of thousands, the generals continued with their bloody anachronism, only to be *celebrated* on the home front based on the number of lives lost in battles. The greater the numbers, the greater the battle, the greater the glory in the service "of all that makes life worth living."

A horrified General Evander Law at Cold Harbor, Virginia, immune to the press accolades, witnessed the reality of this new form of war as the casualty rate exceeded 116 men a minute. "This was not war," he wrote, "but murder." The battle he had witnessed had accomplished little for either side.[28] General Law was seeing firsthand and naming the exterminist face of

---

25. President Woodrow Wilson, leader in the Progressive Movement, was sworn in by Chief Justice of the United States Edward D. White, a former Klan member who had done "night patrols in New Orleans" when he was young. Wilson had a special White House screening in 1915 of the D. W. Griffiths film *Birth of a Nation*, in which the Klan was portrayed as a national savior. Public officials, with the notable exception of a few Southerners, began to distance themselves from the Klan in the 1930s as their association with lynching campaigns became more scandalous.

26. Cowardin and Hammersley, "War and Peace," para. 9.

27. Collins, *Sport in Capitalist Society*, 41.

28. Stout, *Upon the Altar*, xiv.

modern war, and the way the boundary between murder and combat was being effaced with increasing industrial efficiency.

The first modern general of the war was Thomas "Stonewall" Jackson, the hero of the Battle of Bull Run and terror of the Shenandoah. With the legend of Jackson came the anointing of the *modern* general associating masculinity with single-minded ruthlessness. His subordinate commander, General Alexander Lawton, described him thus:

> He had no sympathy with human infirmity. He was a one-idea'd man. He looked upon broken down men and stragglers as the same thing. He classed all who were weak and weary, who fainted by the wayside, as men wanting in patriotism. If a man's face was white as cotton and his pulse so low that you could not feel it, he merely looked upon him impatiently as an inefficient soldier and rode off, out of patience. He was the true type of all great soldiers. The successful warrior of the world, he did not value human life where he had an object to accomplish. He could order men to their death as a matter of course.[29]

It would be difficult to find a more direct passage from a practitioner of war that highlights the contrast between men of war and Jesus, who tells us to love both neighbor and enemy. By the time of the Civil War, Christ had been successfully separated from the world and relegated to a cosmic realm separate from human experience. War allowed us one liturgy for the kingship of the risen Christ and another for the nation. In the tension between the liturgy that ends with "my peace I give you" and the liturgy of the nation, the nation's liturgy of war swallowed whole the peace of Christ.

Jackson ordered his men before battle: no prisoners. The massacre mentality of the Crusades had returned, but now American Christians were killing other American Christians.

The proportionality and discrimination that had been criteria for "just war" evaporated.[30] General William Tecumseh Sherman's name would be

---

29. Cited in Woodward, *Mary Chestnut's Civil War*, 499–500.

30. Mattox, "Augustine," 3c. St. Augustine said that war can only be just if it meets two criteria: *jus ad bellum* and *jus in bello*, that is, just in the *decision* to war and just in its *conduct*. *Jus ad bellum* means there is *just authority, just cause, right intention*, and *last resort*—no off-the-books soldiers, no overreactions, no motive of revenge or gain, and no other option. *Jus in bello* entails *proportionality, discrimination*, and *responsibility*. *Proportionality* means only enough force is used as is necessary to meet the criteria of just cause and just intention; *discrimination* means discriminating between combatants and noncombatants, and *not targeting civilians*; and *responsibility* means that a country is not responsible for unexpected side effects of its military activity as long as the following three conditions are met: the action must carry the intention to produce good consequences, the bad effects are *not intended*, and the good of the war must outweigh the damage done by it.

associated in history with ruthlessness, both in the Civil War, during which he intentionally took the war to Southern civilians, and after the war as a proponent of Indian extermination. Sherman's great campaign of arson through the Southern hinterland was morally established by Jackson, and by the patriotism-inflamed approval of this new form of war on both sides of the struggle. Blood "fertilized" blessings, so a lot of blood fertilized a lot of blessings. The church was captured within two competing nationalisms, an objective demonstration of how nation—any nation—could come to trump Christ. After setbacks, national fast days were announced on both sides to get back into the good graces of the Lord; but in another sense, these national days of fasting were consecrating the nation, the *civil* religion, which was being forged with a blood sacrifice. The great traditions of the church were echoed in the national rhetoric of both sides to cast an aura of sanctification. We were reaping what we had sown.

Lincoln was among the most bloodthirsty, praising Grant even after great casualties as a general. "He fights," said Lincoln.[31] The famous reticence of McClellan has been attributed to cowardice and to ambition, though McClellan comported himself well on the battlefield. His primary reason for resisting Lincoln's orders was that he believed in *just war* as articulated by the Christian philosopher Thomas Aquinas; and he saw clearly that the battles of this war were being conducted in a way that was not "proportional." The treatment of the enemy was out of proportion to the wrong, and he rejected the acceptance of civilian casualties as the price of war.[32] McClellan wrote,

> [War] should be conducted upon the highest principles known to Christian civilization. It should not be a war looking to the subjugation of the people of any State in any event. It should not be at all a war upon population, but against armed forces and political organization. Neither confiscation of property, political executions of persons, territorial organization of States, or forcible abolition of slavery should be contemplated for a moment. In prosecuting the war all private property and unarmed persons should be strictly protected, subject only to the necessity of military operation.[33]

His refusal to see the issue of slavery as decisive for war was shared by most Northerners, even as slavery was the structural contradiction that had given rise to the war. Northern Democrats were already arguing for white supremacy and postwar apartheid, even if slavery was to be abolished. McClellan's

---

31. "Ulysses S. Grant," para. 6.
32. Stout, *Upon the Altar*, 137.
33. Sears, *Papers of George B. McClellan*, 344–45.

reluctance to embrace modern war, with its inhering lack of proportionality, was decisive in losing his job as commander of the Army of the Potomac.

When Lincoln did replace McClellan, he sent in General John Pope, a veteran of battles in the west, where his cruelty and punishment of civilians was as legendary as his tactical acumen was mediocre.[34] He gave the impression of being fierce and was known as a braggart. At the Second Battle of Bull Run, with Pope in command of Union forces, little was accomplished for either side. It was a warm September, and war diaries describe the bodies bloating beyond recognition within hours.[35] Lincoln would learn, when Pope was defeated during this battle with the loss of 16,054 men, that total war would not be accomplished by a fierce demeanor, but by calculating *sangfroid*. Cold instrumentalism would be the new master of war, and war was the new master of modern society. As Lincoln said when questioned about his prosecution of the war,

> What would you have me do in my position? Would you drop the war where it is? Or would you prosecute it in future with elder stalk squirts charged with rosewater? Would you deal lighter blows rather than heavy ones? Would you give up the contest, leaving any available means unapplied? I am in no boastful mood. I shall not do more than I can, and I shall do all that I can, to save the government, which is my sworn duty as well as my personal inclination. I shall do nothing in malice.[36]

"What would you have me do in my position?" The office and *his oath* were his map and compass, as is true of any good bureaucrat. We mustn't forget that Lincoln was—like Jean Bodin, like Borgia, and like the scribes of the New Testament—a lawyer. He said "nothing in malice." This is a far cry from the spirit of the bayonet that thrilled the graduates of West Point. Off the record, there is no talk of God's providence in the war, but instead an instrumentalism that is summed up thus: I will deal as many heavy blows as I have to in order to maximize my efficacy (Lincoln says "all that I can, and no more than I can") in pursuit of victory.

> Faced with his own embarrassing defeats and unimaginable losses at First Bull Run, Shiloh, and the Seven Days', Lincoln and his Northern commanders came to the shared and *accurate* understanding that limited war would not work.[37]

---

34. Stout, *Upon the Altar*, 141–44.
35. Ibid.
36. Letter to Cuthbert Bullitt, July 28, 1862, in Basler, *Abraham Lincoln*, 650.
37. Stout, *Upon the Altar*, 140.

Proportionality, one of the pillars of just war doctrine, now confronted with the face of modern war, crumbled. The war had not taken on the character of insurrection/counter-insurrection, but the character of a war between two separate nation-states, and one in which victory would require attacks against the whole of an enemy society. Total war meant that civilians would suffer, and this suffering had to be accepted. If society must be changed through rifle, cannon, torch, and gallows, then war could be waged against the society entire. The Emancipation Proclamation was part of this very decision and was conceived of as an instrument of war, as an *economic* attack against the South. No part of what went before the Emancipation Proclamation can effectively negate the fact that manumission was a good thing; likewise, the goodness of manumission in no way excuses any of the cruelties or violence that contributed to the milieu in which manumission happened. The point is that modernity and "total" war were conjoined twins. This fact was now formative of American culture, American power, American masculinity, and American church.

Even before the signature appointments of Grant and Sherman—the latter, a former banker, would embody strategic instrumentality and total war perhaps more than any other figure—Lincoln gave his approval to "foraging." That is, army units could pillage and steal from local populations.[38] Pope's troops terrorized their way south to the final defeat at Second Bull Run; and the war took a new turn. There was no longer any such thing as a noncombatant. The arson of homes was added to the tactical repertoire, as was the summary execution of suspected guerrillas. This foreshadows my own experience as a nineteen-year-old in Vietnam, where we were the serial arsonists leaving trails of ashes and tears.

Once these tactics were inaugurated, both sides engaged in unspeakable cruelty. A distinctly modern and instrumental military leadership was combined with pillaging soldiers. This state of lawlessness—of arson, pillage, murder, and rape, perpetrated against "enemy civilians"—was used as an early "weapon of mass destruction." The psyche of the enemy had to be destroyed as surely as a tactically significant bridge or an armory. When General Sherman, still on the western front in Memphis, suffered guerrilla attacks on Union gunboats, he destroyed the town of Randolph, Tennessee. When a subsequent attack came, he retaliated by destroying all the buildings and crops along fifteen miles of the Mississippi.[39] Lincoln's modern war paladin, Sherman, was being perfected in Memphis. He cared not for the alleged moral purpose of the war—Sherman hated Jews, blacks, Mexicans,

---

38. Carnahan, *Lincoln on Trial*, 41.
39. Ibid., 155.

and Indians equally. His goal in everything, this consequentialist banker turned general, was to achieve a given result. The means? Honor no longer mattered, the old rules concerning civilians no longer mattered; only the mission. After the war, Sherman called for Indian extermination as "the final solution to the Indian problem."[40]

I once ran the Consolidated Sniper Training Program for 2nd Battalion, 7th Special Forces. The popular idea of a sniper is someone who shoots at people from a hidden position. In military parlance, it means a marksman who can fire at long distances with extreme accuracy. In fact, modern snipers and their earlier counterparts use a second person in their position, a "spotter," who can look downrange with field glasses or a telescope and observe the strike of the bullet (the recoil disrupts the sight-picture for the shooter). The spotter calls adjustments—for example, "You hit high and left, and he's hiding behind the water barrel." Then the shooter can "hold off" low and right from center-of-mass on the water barrel. Ideally, snipers' positions are never identified by their "targets." In a properly prepared position, a sniper might fire a single shot at enemy troops half a mile away. If he fires only one shot and has taken care to prevent dust from giving away his position, his enemy cannot identify the shooter's position. On the receiving end of a supersonic shot, one first hears a loud "snap," which is the round passing overhead; only afterwards does one hear the much quieter "thump" made by the refilling vacuum in the barrel of the gun. The combined sound is called a "crack-thump." The direction of the thump is what tells the "targets" who survive where the shot came from, but only in a very general direction. So it is difficult, if not impossible, to "suppress" a sniper by firing near his position to "get his head down." Snipers shoot people who are too far away to effectively shoot back. That's the idea.

Prior to the Civil War, there was a belief held by many that this tactic was not honorable. It was more akin to murder than combat. Snipers, under ideal conditions, want each shot to be an uncomplicated, uncontested murder. Align the sights, squeeze the trigger, ride the recoil. Someone dies. Your spotter will confirm. Find another target. Repeat.

"The most successful sniper is the one who commits cold-blooded murder." This was drilled into me during my own training as a sniper.

40. Dilorenzo, "Indian Genocide," para. 25. Hitler, another modern commander-in-chief, would borrow Sherman's language for his own special program—and used the U.S. destruction of indigenous American societies as the model for a Europe without Jews (a mission prepared by a warlike and anti-Semitic church).

Just, Civil, and Total War—Sanctification of State 165

In 1864, General John Sedgwick was directing artillery emplacements at Spotsylvania, shouting abuse at the Confederate lines eight hundred yards away, when a .45 caliber British Wentworth in the hands of a Confederate sharpshooter fired the bullet that passed through the general's head and ended his command.[41] *One shot* shuffled the entire chain of command. That's efficacy—a real cost-benefit bargain.

When I was a member of the army's counterterrorist organization in the mid-eighties, I was first an assaulter, then a sniper. An assaulter has to break into a crisis site and engage his opponents at close range. The tactics for this are called close-quarter battle (CQB). The appropriate weapons, if there are hostages, are nine-millimeter submachine guns and semiautomatic pistols. As a sniper, a good deal of my job was going to the range, firing high-powered rifles from various distances, with various ammunition, in various conditions, and recording this data in books, one book for each of my three sniper guns (like different golf clubs for different shots). If a sniper fires during a mission, that single shot is the result of countless hours of practice, record-keeping, and calculation. One of my colleagues called it "Dial-a-Kill."

There is another difference for the sniper, inasmuch as the sniper doesn't see his handiwork up close, like an assaulter. It's more of a technical specialty. When I was a sniper, we ribbed the assaulters by calling them "knuckle-draggers." Modern warfare has generated a new kind of sniper, even less the "knuckle-dragger," but the questions about morality that are raised by sniping remain. This new kind of sniper is not a trained marksman but a video-gamer who pilots remote, armed aerial drones into position to rain explosives down on top of people halfway around the world. Snipers shoot people who are too far away to effectively shoot back. Drone warfare has perfected the sniper. Drones launch guided missiles with explosives. If the sniper is dishonorable according to a genteel masculinity, or sinful to a peace-seeking Christian, when he kills an identified enemy who poses no threat to the sniper, at least the sniper still adheres to the just-war notion of proportionality. He can actually, in most cases, ensure that he does not shoot bystanders, and he knows what is going on in his sector. He won't mistake a wedding party for a band of guerrillas. Such is not the case with "unmanned aerial drones."[42] Theologian Stanley Hauerwas writes,

---

41. Rhea, *Battles for Spotsylvania*, 96.

42. The unmanned aerial drone cannot discriminate between targets like a rifle sniper. Explosives cannot discriminate inside the bursting radius of the explosives. Drones have killed a lot of civilians, who are then routinely declared combatants after the strike.

> Most Americans don't seem to be too bothered by the realities of the current wars. It is as if they have become but another video game. In truth, the wars themselves are increasingly shaped by technologies that make them seem gamelike. Young men and women can kill people around the world while sitting in comfortable chairs in underground bunkers in Colorado. At the end of the work day, they can go home and watch Little League baseball. I find it hard to imagine what it means to live this way.[43]

If the ethos of the sniper evolves into the unmanned drone, the ethos of Sherman, pillaging his way to the sea to rip up the material basis of a society, prefigures "strategic bombing." The Civil War let out a genie that won't go back in. Modern war, at the end of the day, is about one thing and one thing only: efficacy. Just war theory, then, has to be adjusted in support of efficacy.

> Just-war reasoning becomes a tool of statecraft, most commonly used by the state to justify war, rather than a moral discipline for the church to grapple with questions of violence.[44]

Paragraph 2309 of today's Catholic Catechism states, "The evaluation of [the conditions for legitimate use of military force] *belongs to the prudential judgment of those who have responsibility for the common good*"—that is, the government. There is no longer any reason for the church to articulate a moral position on war. In this very statement, the moral decision has been outsourced to the state (because, we say elsewhere, without a shred of historical evidence to support it, that the state is "organized for the common good"). We can skip all the previous guidelines and just lockstep into our tanks and bombers.

Photojournalism was another innovation of the American Civil War, and from the Civil War we have the first widely circulated photo images of actual war dead. There is nothing like a photo of a wide ditch filled with mangled corpses to take the shine off of war back on the home front. The starkest of war photography brings the most profane of realities back from the battlefield and into a civil society that had been intoxicated by the rhetorical sacralization of war. The power of these images was quickly recognized, and in short order, censors selected and edited photographs for propaganda purposes, the photojournalists themselves complying with their respective

---

43. Hauerwas, *War and the American Difference*, 1.
44. Cavanaugh, *Migrations of the Holy*, 44–45.

governments. Heroically posed photographs of generals, too, were circulated. Military leaders became the saints of the state.

> By 1864 both North and South had acknowledged that generals stood as a breed apart, as "brilliant" in the business of killing as philosophers with ideas or painters on canvas. They stood as the warrior priests of America's dawning civil religion, entrusted with making the sacrificial blood offerings that would incarnate the national faith.[45]

Abolitionist William R. Williams, writing in 1863 for *The Liberator*, composed what can be seen now as an apology for total war, shifting the rationale for "just war" from a consideration of legitimate need (e.g., self-defense) and proportionality (e.g., minimum necessary force) to a utilitarian calculus that justified the means by the nobility of the *cause* for which the war was fought. As the blood sacrifices of the war mounted inconceivably, ending slavery became that redemptive rationale. Williams wrote,

> Since the object of a just war is to suppress injustice and compel justice, we have a right to put in practice against our enemy every measure that will tend to weaken or disable him from maintaining his injustice. To this end, we are at liberty to choose any and *all such methods as we may deem most efficacious*.[46]

Once the Emancipation Proclamation was issued, pragmatic as its strategic motivations were, a new "higher good" was articulated for the North's mission, and neither side would "look back to restrained codes or charity."[47] Total war—war on whole societies in which there was a moral justification for targeting civilian as well as combatant—was here and here to stay. Lincoln's legal advisor, a lawyer named Francis Lieber, wrote the new foreign policy document that made this explicit.[48]

"Lieber's Code" legally dispensed with two just-war principles in one fell swoop: proportionality and discrimination. A key statement in that code read, "*Military necessity*, as understood by modern civilized nations, consists in the necessity of those measures which are indispensable for securing the ends of the war."[49] *Necessity* would subsume other categories. The ends justify the means. Ostensibly written to place limits on unjust combat practices, many already common, this equivocation in the first formal code

---

45. Stout, *Upon the Altar*, 321.
46. Ibid., 174, my italics.
47. Ibid., 187.
48. Ibid., 188.
49. General Orders No. 100:14, 1863.

of warfare, one that prefigures today's Geneva and Hague Conventions, formalized a contradiction. It tacitly acknowledges that modern war *cannot* simultaneously be "just," in the Augustinian or Thomist sense, and effective. Rather than say, as Augustine and Aquinas had, that only as much force as necessary for the immediate objective ought to be used and that civilians were off limits, Lieber wrote, "The principle has been more and more acknowledged that the unarmed citizen is to be spared in person, property, and honor *as much as the exigencies of war will admit.*"[50] This elastic clause would become the loophole through which Sherman would ravage Southern farms in 1864, and through which twenty-two thousand Dresden civilians would be firebombed to death in 1944, and through which fell two atomic bombs on Japanese cities. David Bosco puts the point on it: "Lieber had crafted a protean document that could bless the most restrained campaign or the most brutal."[51]

Prisoner neglect became prisoner abuse during the Civil War. Men were starving to death and dying of disease by the thousands in prison camps in the North and South. When the South refused to return black Union troops for prisoner exchanges, the exchanges ended, and the camps filled to many times over capacity. A cold hatred was settling on troops from both sides, from the horrors of the battlefield, and the thirst for vengeance was slaked on prisoners as well as civilians. Newspapers whipped up these emotions, and troops on both sides began to pillage against civilians, even when commanders like Lee had issued explicit orders to the contrary. Lieber was mindful of these acts and sought through his code to ameliorate these abuses, but he opened the door to making civilian targeting a doctrine based on "military necessity."

In March 1864, Lincoln appointed Grant the overall commander of Union forces, and gave him a free hand to plan the South's defeat. Grant chose Sherman and Sheridan as his adjacent troop commanders, attaching himself to Meade along the Potomac. Grant's plan was for himself and Meade to engage Lee directly in northern Virginia, while Sheridan swept through the Shenandoah Valley and Sherman marched to Atlanta. Grant's instructions to Sheridan and Sherman were blunt and brutal. Take the war to the civilians, and destroy where necessary the Southern armies' means of subsistence, even when that was also the means of subsistence for the whole people.[52] Southern "partisans," led by the likes of Nathan Bedford Forrest, later the first Grand Wizard of the Ku Klux Klan, committed mas-

---

50. Bosco, "Moral Principle," para. 16, my italics.
51. Ibid.
52. Stout, *Upon the Altar*, 395–424.

sacres. Sheridan rampaged through the Shenandoah, arresting every male under the age of fifty and putting farms to the torch. Sherman left a trail of ashes across the South, sending even civilian women to prison camps, and culminated his drive by leveling Atlanta with artillery.[53]

Modern war was fully born, and a modern kind of military leader with it, a man unafraid to use the most lethal technologies in history to make hell on earth, to unleash cruelty without limit. These men became the new icons of masculinity. From the pulpits of the North and South came paeans to the war's masculinity.

> At the beginning of the war, Southern pulpits and the secular press had been engaged in a common enterprise: banging the drum for a "Christian" and "*manly*" war effort.[54]

Chamberlain, the hero general of the Battle for Little Round Top at Gettysburg, wrote this religious acclamation to the new national masculinity:

> All around, strange mingled roar—shouts of defiance, rally, and desperation; and underneath, murmured entreaty and stifled moans' gasping prayers, snatches of Sabbath song, whispers of loved names; everywhere men torn and broken, staggering, creeping, quivering on the earth, and dead faces with strangely fixed eyes staring into the sky. Things which cannot be told—nor dreamed. How men held on, each one knows—not I. But *manhood* commands admiration.[55]

Manliness was consecrated with a blood sacrifice, and the blood sacrifice of the nation came to supersede the blood sacrifice of Jesus. The *nation* became the new deity. At Gettysburg, Lincoln consolidated the civil religion with the nation's most well-remembered homily. Stout calls the Gettysburg address "America's greatest sermon."[56] That sermon became part of the American liturgy, sacred words that infused the war with a spiritual significance that perseveres into the present, wherein all our soldiers are heroes and martyrs, redeeming the "government of the people, by the people, for the people," however true or not that might have been, with tidal waves of violence. War, as Stout suggests in his title, would be the manly nation's altar. American Congregational minister Horace Bushnell wrote, in 1863, in an essay titled "The Doctrine of Loyalty":

---

53. Ibid.
54. Ibid., 210.
55. Trulock, *In the Hands of Providence*, 145, my italics.
56. Stout, *Upon the Altar*, 241.

> How far the loyal sentiment reaches and how much it carries with it, or after it, must also be noted. It yields up willingly husbands, fathers, brothers, and sons, consenting to the fearful chance of a home always desolate. It offers body, and blood, and life, on the altar of its devotion. It is a fact, a political worship, offering to seal itself by a martyrdom in the field. Wonderful, grandly honorable fact, that human nature can be lifted by an inspiration so high, even in the fallen state of wrong and evil.[57]

Not only does this validate Lincoln's dream of a civil religion, it reiterates war, in its redemptive guise, as the province and *glory* of males, of "husbands, fathers, brothers, and sons." A *Richmond Daily Whig* editorial proclaimed in *pagan* terms the connection between masculinity and war in nationalist discourse, as well as the separation now possible between manhood and Christianity, with the nation as the new religion:

> The glory of Athens and Sparta were acquired by making every man a soldier, and considering non-combatants as drones in the national hive. . . . No simpler principle, no dearer homes, no fairer land were ever fought for, bled for, died for than hang upon the issue of this conflict. Natal rights and native land, hereditary titles to property, the immunities of free citizenship, the sanctities of the hearthstone, the appealing voice of innocent and helpless womanhood—all can touch the heart or nerve the arm, cry trumpet-tongued all the brave and true men to fight this fight out to victory or death.[58]

"We must be ready to give up our sons, brothers, friends," declared a pastor at a funeral for Union soldiers James T. Stebbins and Myron E. Stowell, "if we cannot go ourselves—to hardships, sufferings, dangers and death if need be, for the preservation of our government and the Freedom of the nation. We should lay them, willing sacrifices, upon the altar."[59]

Like Abraham and Isaac—obedience to nation is now comparable to obedience to God.

In Lincoln's second inaugural address, he proclaims, "With malice toward none; with charity for all; with firmness in the right, as God gives us to see the right, let us strive on to finish the work we are in; to bind up the nation's wounds; to care for him who shall have borne the battle, and for his widow and orphan—to do all which may achieve and cherish a just, and a

---

57. Bushnell, "Doctrine of Loyalty," 573.

58. *Richmond Daily Whig*, July 10, 1863, quoted in Stout and Grasso, "Civil War, Religion, and Communications," 338.

59. Stout, *Upon the Altar*, 341.

Just, Civil, and Total War—Sanctification of State 171

lasting peace, among ourselves, and with all nations."[60] When Chamberlain eulogizes the assassinated Lincoln in April 1865, he declares grandly that

> Henceforth that flag is the legend which we bequeath to future generations, of that severe and solemn struggle for the nation's life. . . . Henceforth the red on it is deeper, for the crimson with which the blood of countless martyrs has colored it; the white on it is purer, for the pure sacrifice and self-surrender of those who went to their graves upbearing it; the blue on it is heavenlier, for the great constancy of those dead heroes, whose memory becomes henceforth as the immutable upper skies that canopy our land, gleaming with stars wherein we read their glory and duty. . . . Yea, now behold a deeper crimson, a purer white, a heavenlier blue. A President's blood is on it, who died because he dared to hold it in the forefront of the nation. The life of the President, who died in the nation's Capitol, becomes, henceforth, an integral part of the life of the Republic. In Him the accidents of the visible flesh are changed to the permanence of an invisible and heroic spirit.[61]

In 1863, N. H. Schenk, a Baltimore pastor who was one of the few to break publicly with the calls to blood-soaked patriotism, said presciently, "The ranks thinned to-day are filled to-morrow and the mournful dead march is directly changed into the gleeful quickstep. And as we grow indifferent to the value of life, we become proportionally indifferent to those great moral interests attached to life. . . . We have suddenly become not only a military, but a warlike people."[62] His was a lonely Christocentric voice in a bloodthirsty masculine wilderness.

"In an era of Western ascendancy," write Carolyn Marvin and David Ingle, "the triumph of Christianity clearly meant the triumph of the states of Christianity, among them the most powerful of modern states, the United States."[63] They continue:

> Though religions have survived and flourished in persecution and powerlessness, supplicants nevertheless take manifestations of power as blessed evidence of the truth of faith. Still, in the religiously plural society of the United States, sectarian faith is optional for citizens, as everyone knows. Americans have rarely

---

60. Lincoln, "Second Inaugural Address," para. 4.
61. Chamberlain, "Assassination of Lincoln," para. 9, capitalization of "Him" in the original.
62. Stout, *Upon the Altar*, 273–74.
63. Marvin and Ingle, *Blood Sacrifice*, 9.

bled, sacrificed, or died for Christianity or any other sectarian faith. Americans have often bled, sacrificed, and died for their country. This fact is an important clue to its religious power. Though denominations are permitted to exist in the United States, they are not permitted to kill, for their beliefs are not officially true. What is really true in any society is what is worth killing for, and what citizens might be compelled to sacrifice their lives for.[64]

In 2003, when the officials of the Roman Catholic Church stood solidly against the U.S. invasion and occupation of Iraq, Professor William T. Cavanaugh asked fellow Catholics whether this official denunciation of the war should compel Catholics to oppose the war more vigorously,[65] even to refuse participation. Cavanaugh argues that if our allegiance to the Gospels and our allegiance to the state are contradictory, allegiance to the Gospels (and the church as the body of Christ) ought to take precedence. Cavanaugh's piece is directed at, among others, fellow Catholics who had embraced neoconservatism, and who stood against the pope when he denounced the war. Writes Cavanaugh,

> It is one thing to argue, on just-war grounds, against the overwhelming judgment of the pope and worldwide bishops, that the recent campaign in Iraq was morally justifiable. It is another thing to argue that the pope and bishops are not qualified to make such judgments. Neoconservative Catholic commentators and others have been trying to mitigate their embarrassment over being at odds with the pope on this issue by claiming that it is not really the church's call to make. Decisions about if and when we Catholics should kill should be left to the president. I believe this line of thinking is dangerously wrong.[66]

Of course, this is exactly what the current Catechism teaches American Catholics, as we saw in the second epigraph to this chapter. The decision about the morality of any war is effectively outsourced by the church to the state, which is the "providential" guardian of the "common good." One of the neoconservative Catholics cited by Cavanaugh was Archbishop to the Department of Defense Edwin O'Brien, who reassured Catholic soldiers

---

64. Ibid.
65. Cavanaugh, "At Odds with the Pope," para. 2.
66. Ibid.

Just, Civil, and Total War—Sanctification of State 173

who had questions about a split allegiance to church and state that they could in good conscience accept the orders of the president without being responsible for determining for themselves the justness of the war. *Te absolvo.* In a backhanded way, we have returned to the rationale of penitential war that Urban II used to muster troops for his Crusade—absolution in advance.

The crux of Cavanaugh's opposition to this notion is the use of "just war" theory: theory that attempts to apply some standard of justice to the conduct of war. Cavanaugh coyly avoids saying whether or not he accepts "just war" theory. His point is that Pope Benedict and his American neoconservative detractors were using "just war" theory in very different ways. The pope used the standards of just-war theory to argue for greater critical attention to the background of the war—its motives, its methods, and its outcomes—and thereby to hold off the option of war as long as humanly possible. The neoconservative Catholics, like the warring nation-state itself, used just-war standards to rationalize exactly what the state intended to do from the start: to go to war. The neoconservatives, as part of their argument, insisted that *the state takes precedence over the church* in certain matters (war being the key one); and moreover that church members themselves are obliged, once the decision to go to war is made, to "support the troops," a public relations euphemism for "accepting the war."

"Right-wing commentators have hastened to assert the right of the individual Catholic to dissent from the judgment of the pope and bishops on contingent matters of prudential judgment, such as the application of the just-war theory in a particular case," writes Cavanaugh.[67] Cavanaugh's complaint is that while dissent from the Vatican can be legitimate, that the hierarchy can make mistakes, none of these commentators asserted a right to likewise dissent from the state once it resolved to make war. I agree. I wish our Catechism didn't tell us otherwise.

Many contradictions inside the church generate crises of conscience, and the church itself gives individual conscience a high priority; however, the conscience, such as it is, ought to be formed in deliberative discernment and not be blindly obedient to the diktat of the secular state. That formation and discernment happens in communion with the church and should be governed by the Holy Spirit. When the entire church hierarchy declares a war unjust, as it did in the case of Iraq (with the exception of a few American bishops), Cavanaugh says that Catholics ought to take it very seriously.

"Pope John Paul II's opinion should count more than Donald Rumsfeld's or Bill O'Reilly's," writes Cavanaugh, even though that is not what our Catechism currently teaches.

67. Ibid., para. 10.

Pacifist Catholics and non-pacifist Catholics (and Christians more generally) ought to be able to find common ground in this discussion, out of plain goodwill first, but also because Christian pacifism of the sort some of us profess does not deny that force can be efficacious, even efficacious to achieve, in some cases, certain good outcomes. Our objection—I am speaking now as an unabashed pacifist—is to Christian participation in violence, and our commitment is the positive obligation to seek reconciliation and make peace. When wars can be shown to be venal, stupid, and reckless, we can certainly voice our objection to those aspects of a war without being forced to make a ritual denunciation of war in general. Venality, stupidity, and recklessness are real things. They can and do often make already bad situations far worse. Naming them as venality, stupidity, and recklessness is truth-telling. I want us to factor masculinity into that process of discernment.

Certain frameworks of masculinity predispose us to discern in particular ways, and furthermore, many women have learned from their own dominant male culture to discern through those same lenses, through the twin guises of "necessity" and identification with a masculinized (and imperial) nationalism. Just-war doctrine began after the Constantinian compromise, when the church already identified itself with the governing authorities and set itself up in the manner of a shadow government. The doctrine has been adapted, but in doing so, the convictions of the church, and not the convictions of political rulers, have been the only thing to shift enough to make this adaptation possible.

Even by Augustinian standards, "just war" is now incompatible with *all* modern war. The American Civil War completed the modern process of subordinating church to state and of *sacralizing the modern state*. What makes modern war incompatible with Augustinian just-war doctrine is that modern war is *total* war, and also that it is war for which the moral determination is outsourced to the state. This is exactly how churchmen came to follow Hitler.

Actual wars arise from very material social forces. I mentioned that in the beginning of this chapter, and I mention it again now, because those forces—wealth accumulation and expansion, which have become the self-organized drivers of social evolution—are difficult to fit into moral narratives. This is true of wars past and present; and equally true is that when the public focuses more closely on the material sources of war, it begins to measure the costs of war differently. It is not easy to "sell" a war to the public because we need to make more money, conquer more colonies, or have access to cheaper food or more oil to maintain economic expansion. Discernment of the material causes of war is crucial, and it can be seditious. In the next chapter, we will look at one way we are distracted from this kind of discernment—a method that redirects our attention from the political and material bases of power to the identification with compelling individual characters: "the war story."

19

A Bodyguard of Lies: Girl Story and Boy Story

> Do your best to present yourself to God as one approved, a worker who has no need to be ashamed, rightly handling the word of truth.
>
> —2 Timothy 2:15

GIRL STORY[1]

> [Jessica] Lynch, a 19-year-old supply clerk, continued firing at the Iraqis even after she sustained multiple gunshot wounds and watched several other soldiers in her unit die around her. . . . "She was fighting to the death," the official said. "She did not want to be taken alive."[2]

Susan Jeffords, in her essay "Telling the War Story," says, "This trend away from the war itself to the people who fought in it shifts the war from a national to a personal experience, making it possible for viewers to forget the specific historical and political forces that caused the war."[3] This shift is

---

1. Portions of this section reproduce earlier reporting I did on the Jessica Lynch incident. See Goff, "Jessica Lynch, Plural." Used by permission.
2. Schmidt and Loeb, "She Was Fighting to the Death," paras. 2–3.
3. Jeffords, "Telling the War Story," 225.

consonant with "support the troops" appeals that oblige the public to drop all critique of leadership or interrogation of geopolitical motives to ensure we do not disempower, and thereby endanger, our loved ones in uniform. We are allowed to have differing individual opinions about a war, provided they are motivated by patriotism (the civil religion), but we are expected to rally round our team once the war is on.

Jeffords focused her studies on war films as an ideological transmission belt for war, but I want to focus on how the actual military now tries to tell war stories in ways that are consistent with familiar war-film conventions. It is a peculiarity of our time that the spectator society, infinitely reflexive, not only creates art, whereupon life imitates art, but that the two are becoming less and less distinguishable. Embedded "reporters" carry cameras as they accompany troops, and we can all pretend that the cameras themselves are immune to Heisenberg: that in the very act of observing, the observer changes the character of that which is observed. Troops, like everyone else, behave differently in front of cameras. Hervé Juvin writes that "self-reflexivity makes every individual his own producer/director, his own eavesdropping audience, generalizing telereality with everyone his own star on his own screen."[4] Speaking now as an American, with the able assistance of the press, the public can be treated to an irresistible series of lurid and titillating feature attractions that continually reproduce a national mythology.

Sometimes the mythology breaks down.

> Therefore, having put away falsehood, let each one of you speak the truth with his neighbor, for we are members one of another.
> (Eph 4:25)

I don't know a great deal about the actual Jessica Lynch, and neither do most people. For those who may not remember, Jessica Lynch was a solider wounded in Iraq who became a kind of national Rorschach test when the military concocted a story about her wounding, her capture, and her "rescue" in 2003.

Jessica Lynch was raised just south of the Ohio River Valley in Palestine, West Virginia. The Little Kanawha River and Hughes River run nearby. Extractive industries, in particular coal and timber, have long colonized Appalachia. As these industries have become ever more mechanized, coal colonies like Palestine have suffered high rates of unemployment. The mountaintop-removal/valley-fill method of coal mining has reduced the

---

4. Juvin, *Coming of the Body*, 84–85.

mining labor force to 10 percent of its former levels, even as it irrevocably reconfigures the landscapes and livelihoods of the people who live there.[5] The only region in the United States with an overwhelming white majority where the poverty figures are county by county consistently above 15 percent reaches from Scott and Fentress counties in the mountains of northeastern Tennessee, across eastern Kentucky, and includes all of West Virginia. There is only one county in West Virginia with poverty rates below 20 percent: Putnam. Wirt County, West Virginia has only five small towns: Munday, Elizabeth, Creston, Brohard, and Palestine. Wirt County and neighboring Ritchie County are more fortunate than some of their adjacent counties. Wirt and Ritchie have poverty rates—using the federal government's grossly understated criteria—only around 29 percent. Nearby Calhoun and Gilmer counties have poverty rates above 35 percent.

Whether you are a Marsh Arab from Iraq or an early twentieth-century West Virginia subsistence farmer, sometimes the worst luck in the world is to live on top of a large deposit of fossil hydrocarbons. When the fossil fuel age began, the carbon energy, trapped for millions of years underground beneath the blue haze and the lush green forests, was monetized. The mechanical cotton gins of the South and the Northern industrial manufactories that were being born out of slave cotton became insatiable in their appetite for coal. The aspiring coal barons arrived with their gun thugs and the full backing of the United States government, and the whole region of Appalachia was subjugated to King Coal, the cousin of King Cotton.[6]

When mountaintop removal replaced shaft-mining in the latter twentieth century, the majority of those who worked in the mines became not just landless but economically redundant.

Like their counterparts in other poor regions, young people look at their situation and select from the menu of options that are available. Some nurture tragic dreams of celebrity. Some deal drugs and then sink into addiction themselves. A few compete for the handful of public-sector jobs that are available in a shrinking economy. And some get a free ticket out of town, the offer of some training and money for an education, and a regular paycheck, by joining the military.

This is the real story of Jessica Lynch. She wanted to teach school. She needed money to get her education.[7] She signed on the dotted line and entered the contradictory world that is the United States Army. There could have been worse things. Pornographers troll for women like Jessica Lynch:

---

5. McQuaid, "Mining the Mountains."
6. Corbin, *Life, Work, and Rebellion*.
7. Gibbs, "At Home."

slender, blonde, with an air of girl-next-door innocence, the humiliation of which titillates the main (male) consumers of pornography. Perhaps she would have escaped Palestine to be featured in the porn collection used to entertain the staff duty NCO at Delta Force. Wealthy men are also quick to colonize young women like Jessica Lynch as models, mistresses, and trophy wives. Just add a little dental work and silicone.

By contrast, even in the masculinist culture of the modern American military, she might find an element of juridical equality and access to some new competencies. This belief leads many young women to choose the military. A supply clerk is a supply clerk, ungendered; the military provides an opportunity for women to enjoy the kind of instrumentality that is the historical prerogative of masculinity. A degree of independence is accessible within the military's institutional framework, along with job training, a written guarantee of some money for college, and a way out of places like Palestine. Jessica could pay for school with her GI Bill and get a certificate for a public-sector job teaching kindergarten.

As she was undergoing her initial training as a supply clerk, and during her initial assignment to the 507th Maintenance Company in Ft. Bliss, Texas, plans were being drafted and redrafted for the military conquest and occupation of Iraq.[8] Jessica Lynch was nineteen when she was deployed to Kuwait to support the impending invasion of Iraq. Like so many young people for whom the military is a sector-selection economic strategy, she was unschooled in geopolitics. They were simply "doing their job" by participating in the upcoming invasion.

The invasion was delayed by international resistance in the form of a massive antiwar movement, and that resistance included the loss of the Turkish and Saudi offensive fronts. The overwhelming and militant opposition to the war around the world forced many politicians in other countries to resist U.S. demands for international cooperation. France, Germany, Russia, and China resisted in the United Nations, while Saudi Arabia and, even more surprisingly, Turkey denied the U.S. access to their countries to launch American or British ground offensives. Consequently, almost the entire United States ground force was forced to drive north into Iraq along a single axis out of Kuwait that would bifurcate into two columns along the Tigris and Euphrates Rivers. The invasion was launched during sandstorm season.

On March 21, an inconceivable mass of military vehicles crawled northwest along the main axis of advance, with units blending and weaving among each other in the open terrain—a small unit commander's

---

8. Rosenberg, "Real Story of Jessica Lynch's Convoy." The following account of Lynch's story is based largely on Rosenberg's reporting.

accountability nightmare. Jessica Lynch was driving a five-ton truck with an equipment trailer attached. The sandstorms that had plagued the invasion task force left a heavy residue of dust in every moving part of every machine and weapon, in the corners of eyes and the folds of skin, and between clothing and body. The frantic movement schedules and the sand undermined mechanical maintenance, troop comfort, and attentiveness.

Lynch's unit was supporting the 3rd Mechanized Infantry Division, the main combat force aimed ultimately at Baghdad. The 507th was not a combat unit, and they never anticipated combat. The intelligence summaries issued by Central Command (CENTCOM) still reflected the triumphalist delusions of Donald Rumsfeld. The optimistic predictions of Rumsfeld's slick Iraqi advisor, Ahmad Chalabi, were that Iraqi soldiers would surrender on sight.

The convoy went nonstop for a grueling forty-eight hours, using blackout-drive infrared headlights and night vision goggles during periods of darkness. They were gritty-eyed, nodding off, and exhausted. Lynch's truck, like many others—casualties of the sandstorms and the schedules—died and was hitched to a giant recovery vehicle. She was put aboard her company First Sergeant's Humvee, where she could nod off fitfully while the bleary-eyed driver, another young woman named Lori Pietsewa, fought sleep behind the wheel. As the horizon-to-horizon convoy approached the outskirts of Nasiriyah on March 23, units were channeled along narrower roads, and the convoy routes were branched. The sun was not yet up when the First Sergeant's Humvee, leading the 507th convoy, encountered a U.S. traffic control checkpoint at the intersection of Highway 1, their main avenue of advance, and Highway 7, which went due north toward the center of Nasiriyah. No one has established exactly which military policeman was working at that checkpoint, or what his or her directions were, or how exhausted the MP might have been. It was dark. People were stupefied with fatigue. The First Sergeant and the 507th Company Commander, Captain Troy King, had GPS navigation systems. They claim they had no maps to consult when these hi-tech gadgets lied or failed. The truth is that no one in the 507th expected that there would be any need to actually navigate. They were part of a growling, miles-long river of northbound steel and diesel, and these checkpoints were there to direct them as passively compliant traffic. Pietsewa and the First Sergeant, Robert Dowdy, looked at some nameless military policeman, who raised a hand toward Highway 7, and so directed Jessica Lynch into a future of terror, pain, dislocation, lies, and fame.

The sun rose over the 507th as it was creeping steadily along Highway 7, its addled leadership now making excuses to itself for discrepancies in the GPS systems. No military leader likes to admit that a mistake has been made, especially when he is still unsure whether it's been made or not. He is like the proud father at the wheel of the family car not yet prepared to admit that he is lost. Surely, that day, as the 507th passed through Marine units instead of Army units, the doubt went deeper. But they were traveling generally north, so they drove on. They hadn't crossed the Euphrates, which was there like a great geographical backstop. The commander bit back his self-doubt while he tried to puzzle out the contradictions between his GPS readings and an operations order that was jumbled in his sleep-deprived brain . . . and still they drove on. In the emerging morning light, they found themselves driving into Nasiriyah with thirty-three sleep-starved support troops and sixteen vehicles. Rising up around them were buildings where most people were apparently still abed.

A bridge suddenly appeared in front of them. They crossed over it, but after a couple of miles—perhaps after an anxious discussion—the leaders realized that they had crossed the Euphrates River. Iraqis began to appear on the streets. Captain King then ordered them to turn the convoy around. They were definitely, oh so very definitely, in the wrong place.

Vehicle traffic began to clutter the streets as the convoy went through the clumsy business of turning sixteen massive military vehicles about in the tight thoroughfares of downtown Nasiriyah.

There were Iraqis carrying Kalashnikovs. Lynch's unit spotted actual manned Iraqi tanks.

They looked at the Iraqi soldiers, and the Iraqi soldiers looked back. But the CENTCOM intelligence summary had said the Iraqis would either be friendly or they would surrender, and the 507th was not a combat unit. Right?

Their greatest desire now was to be back in the company of a real combat unit. The adrenaline began to make headway against their deep muscular fatigue. At just after 7 a.m. they could hear a fierce firefight in the distance. The Marines they had passed earlier were in contact. Some began to wonder, if they will fire on the Marine infantry and armor, won't they fire on this collection of mechanics and clerks?

Hearts slamming, the convoy made several false turns in Nasiriyah, becoming ever more confused about their location. Their disorganization became evident to the Iraqis. When they attempted to reorganize themselves, now split over two narrow streets and trying to turn around, an Iraqi pickup truck turned around to make a slow second pass of the convoy, two men inside now frankly and ominously assessing the disorganized American unit. In a few minutes, a second pickup with a mounted machine gun wheeled past them and around a corner.

One portion of the convoy was still out of sight from the other. Their hands shaking and their mouths dry, they began to sense that they had strayed outside of everything they knew and everything they had ever trained for. They were prey.

A few bullets suddenly snapped past them from buildings on both sides of the street. Orders were shouted and radioed.

"Get out!"

Then the sprinkle of gunfire became a storm.

Bullets cracked lethally, on full automatic now, smacking into the vehicles, then RPGs hit with full-throated explosions. As the detachment frantically tried to maneuver their vehicles, Iraqis threw tires into the street to block escape routes. Down another street, a bus was being pulled forward to block that avenue of escape.

Dowdy jumped off the Humvee and attempted to direct the other vehicles back into a semblance of order to escape the intensifying ambush. Moments later he wilted from bullet wounds, dead. Two soldiers whose vehicle had been disabled leapt aboard Pietsewa's vehicle. Pietsewa, the two who'd jumped aboard, and Lynch careened wildly over the street as if trying to actually dodge the bullets, finding every avenue blocked and now covered by Iraqi fighters, then Pietsewa lost control. Lynch was gripping whatever she could find inside the careening vehicle. The Humvee smashed to a halt under the trailer hitch of one of the convoy's destroyed semi-trucks. Jessica Lynch saw Pietsewa and the others vaguely, unable to assess their conditions or her own. She managed to drag herself out of the Humvee with a broken femur. She began praying as she crumbled onto the street. For Jessica Lynch, the day was over. The concussion from a gaping head wound sustained during the crash caused her to lose consciousness.

There is a contradiction here yet unresolved, a story that her rifle jammed, which would mean she attempted to put it into action—but in this series of presumptions, I am presuming from the severity of her injuries that she was in shock and it was unlikely she attempted to operate an assault rifle. It happens in the movies, but this was no movie. Her ankle was dislocated. Her femur was fractured and releasing blood into the muscle of her thigh. Her arm was broken (it takes two hands to put an assault rifle into action), and she had a large, copiously bleeding laceration on her head. Pietsewa, her best friend (and a woman of the Hopi Nation), was already in deep shock. Part of the convoy, with Marine assistance that finally arrived, escaped.

Once the attack was over, the Iraqi troops took Lynch and Pietsewa to the Nasiriyah military hospital. Had they not, she would have bled to death. Pietsewa expired en route from her injuries.

Dr. Jamal Kadhim Shwail and Dr. Harith al-Houssona examined Lynch. She was in shock with precariously low blood pressure. Not knowing the extent of Lynch's musculoskeletal injuries or whether there was spinal damage, they could not afford to jostle her to remove the layers of combat gear, uniform, body armor, and web gear. They had to use bandage scissors to cut away the equipment and clothing, which was still fully secured to her body. She was infused with fluids, including three units of whole blood—two donated on the spot by Iraqi hospital staff—catheterized, splinted, her head sutured, and transported to Saddam Hospital, also in Nasiriyah, for surgery on her dangerously fractured femur.[9]

Dr. Mahdi Khafazi performed the surgery.[10]

During Lynch's convalescence, Dr. Harith Houssona, a twenty-four-year-old physician, and several nurses befriended Lynch. Iraqi military commanders considered her a prisoner of war but, given the severity of her injuries, gave the hospital staff wide latitude and little oversight.[11] Seven days into the ordeal, most of the Iraqi military left as part of a general tactical retreat to the north, and Houssona ordered Jessica Lynch to be returned to the American military.

One Iraqi officer and an ambulance driver named Sabah Khazaal tried to transport Lynch back to the Americans. The reasoning was that an ambulance is protected under the Geneva Conventions and wouldn't be fired upon. It didn't work. When the ambulance came within three hundred meters of the army checkpoint, U.S. soldiers opened fire on it, nearly killing Lynch after she was well on her way to a successful convalescence and repatriation to the United States.[12]

It is probably coincidental that a detachment of SEALs and Rangers were deployed for a "special" mission on April Fools' Day. One of the Ranger privates on security for this "mission" was Pat Tillman, a former player for the NFL's Arizona Cardinals who had given up a multimillion dollar contract to join the military after September 11.

Several things were "special" about this "mission." First, special teams like this are generally employed on sensitive missions, for which the tactics and techniques are highly classified. Second, special teams like this, given the classified techniques and tactics they use, would not take along a civilian

9. Potter, "The Real 'Saving Private Lynch.'"
10. Ibid.
11. Ibid.
12. Kampfner, "The Truth about Jessica."

cameraman who could record classified techniques unnecessarily and possibly become an impediment to the operation's success. Third, there was no threat to warrant the use of these classified tactics and techniques.[13]

It was well known to American military intelligence, by the time the so-called rescue of Jessica Lynch was planned, that the Iraqi military was abandoning Nasiriyah as tactically untenable. Civilians were moving freely between Nasiriyah and American positions on the outskirts of the city. Wily opportunists were among them, one in particular a lawyer named Mohammed al-Rehaief. The official story is that al-Rehaief reported Lynch's "captivity" to the Americans, and CENTCOM then organized a special ops rescue mission. Given what we know now, including that al-Rehaief has become rich and lives in the United States, it seems likely that al-Rehaief, whose wife worked in the hospital, told him about Lynch. He went to the Americans, who then began debriefing him.[14] The war was going very badly for American forces at that point. Doubt was emerging in the anesthetized consciousness of America, and to keep the patient asleep, the War Department needed a publicity boost. Al-Rehaief was offered a free trip to America for him and his family, where he would be given a book deal and a lobbying job.[15]

He was sent back to the hospital to gather specific information on floor plans and door locations, while the "special" unit began planning the "rescue" of PFC Lynch. The public affairs officer of CENTCOM was put on high alert, and the whole Department of Defense "Wag-the-Dog Bureau" went into action, including the Rendon Group.

The Rendon Group had been around through both the Clinton and Bush II administrations. It was not the only public relations outfit feeding at the public trough, but Rendon was emblematic. Rendon stage-managed much of the run-up to the 2003 quagmire in Iraq; it was largely responsible for the organization of a new Iraqi quisling regime—dubbed *by Rendon* the "Iraqi National Congress," complete with the new regime head and convicted embezzler Ahmad Chalabi. Said one unnamed State Department official in a moment of candor, "Were it not for Rendon, the Chalabi group wouldn't even be on the map." Neither would Jessica Lynch's "rescue," because a rescue is not what happened.[16] It was a staged military operation—staged for the entertainment media with the purpose of injecting some war optimism into the American mass consciousness, a made-for-television movie short.[17]

13. Ibid.
14. Goff, "Jessica Lynch, Plural."
15. Piore, "Why I Risked My Life."
16. Bamford, "Man Who Sold the War."
17. Kampfner, "The Truth about Jessica."

Rendon had picked up where Hill & Knowlton, the Gulf War I perception managers, left off. (Hill & Knowlton, on contract with the U.S. government, hatched the story of Kuwaiti babies being thrown from their incubators by Iraqi soldiers that mobilized a press frenzy and massive public support for the Bush I invasion. The story turned out to be a complete fabrication.) John Rendon, former Democratic Party consultant and Rendon Group's founder, boasted once to the National Security Council, "If any of you either participated in the liberation of Kuwait City... or if you watched it on television, you would have seen hundreds of Kuwaitis waving small American flags. Did you ever stop to wonder how the people of Kuwait City, after being held hostage for seven long and painful months, were able to get handheld American flags? And for that matter, the flags of other coalition countries? Well, you now know the answer. That was one of my jobs."[18]

The shifting fictional account of "What happened to Jessica Lynch?" likely originated in the White House's Office of Global Communications—an office essentially run by Rendon people.[19] They generated "news stories" to be released through CENTCOM and elsewhere faster than the press could keep up in order to push deadlines and competition and thereby inhibit fact-checking. The stories came apart, but the fabrications were allowed to "linger" without comment, even when they proved inaccurate—and remained uncorrected—a few days later.

"Linger" was an industry term of art employed by military psychological operations (PSYOPS) when I was in Special Forces. This tactic is combined with message control—explaining why masculine bluster like "Americans are not the running kind" showed up in two separate speeches given on the same day by different members of the administration—redefining all opposition to U.S. actions as terrorists, and building false associations through repetition: "echoing," another industry word. How many times did we hear "September 11," "terrorists," and "Saddam Hussein" in the same breath? This is a PSYOPS technique, a method to "construct memory," and the "target audience" is not the enemy. It is the citizenry of the United States.

If caught, they reconfigured stories with elliptical language, then let it linger some more. Weapons of mass destruction became a "weapons program," a "seeking" of WMD. George Tenet's CIA "had questions" about the British forgery... er, "dossier." By the time this book is published, who will remember the Jessica Lynch fable, or care?

Some of these constructed tales were so lurid they should have defied imagination. But the American press, always a stronghold of healthy

18. Rossi, *What Every American Should Know*, 232.
19. Armistead, *Information Operations*, 134–36.

skepticism, lapped up the Jessica Lynch fiction like Basset hounds around a broken jug of milk. The press pool at CENTCOM headquarters in Qatar dutifully echoed a sham-saga to the entire world.

Concept.

The pretty, plucky, white American female soldier fights off the degenerate, cowardly, less than fully human Iraqis, emptying her magazine into several of the evildoers until, even though she is multiply shot and stabbed, she is overwhelmed and taken prisoner. CENTCOM solemnly left the question of sexual assault open and let the public imagination run with it. Wicked Fedayeen interrogators reportedly cuffed her around in the hospital.

Then, the epitome of moral American manhood, Special Operations, comes on the set to rescue our heroine, fallen beneath the assaults of the unmanly Arabs. The true Manly Men rescue the Captive Plucky Princess, reaffirming the roles of male and female, in a damsel-in-distress narrative, and the national imaginary is reconstituted in all its proper hierarchies. To paraphrase Susan Jeffords, at a time when American military invincibility is being called into question by Iraqi resistance, a display of heroic, militarized male power can provide a "compensatory national identity."[20]

Susan Schmidt and Vernon Leob of the *Washington Post* were positively fawning on April 10 when they regurgitated the "leaked" story of Jessica Lynch's fight to the death with the deviant Iraqis and her subsequent rescue, complete with subtitles like, "Fighting to the Death," "Talk about Spunk," and "Classic Special Ops."[21] The latter refers to that "daring special operations raid" that "rescued" Lynch. The story "echoed" breathily across the airwaves and the pages of ostensibly respectable magazines and newspapers. The public memory was "constructed" through repetition. As questions were raised, the story was allowed to "linger."

On May 15th, John Kampfner wrote, "Her rescue will go down as one of the most stunning pieces of news management yet conceived. It provides a remarkable insight into the real influence of Hollywood producers on the Pentagon's media managers, and has produced a template from which America hopes to present its future wars."[22] Americans don't read the *Guardian*, where Kampfner's investigative piece appeared. Most still believe the rescue fiction. The Special Operations "raid" was conducted with zero resistance, exactly as they expected. They knew in advance that the Iraqi combatants had already withdrawn. But to give the filmed event the feel of authenticity, they cut the power to the hospital (putting every patient there in danger), explosively breached doors that hospital staff would have will-

20. Jeffords, "Telling the War Story," 230.
21. Schmidt and Loeb, "She Was Fighting to the Death."
22. Kampfner, "Truth about Jessica," para. 2.

ingly opened for them, and gratuitously flex-cuffed two hospital employees, taking one prisoner for several days, as well as two patients, one with an intravenous infusion.[23]

That was edited out of the film version.

Then came doubts as the Lynch fight-to-the-death story collapsed, and then the ellipsis. Lynch's actual experiences were "still being sorted out," said CENTCOM. They were obscured by "the fog of war," a fog generated from the White House Office of Global Communications. Lynch herself, the real person, was held incommunicado. The spinmeisters, taking their cue from Hollywood, mobilized an ersatz feminism and constructed their tale of the spunky woman soldier, kind of a *GI Jane* meets *Courage Under Fire*.

In a plural society like the United States, male social power does not assign women one monolithic "script." Zillah Eisenstein has said that modern society restlessly "renegotiates" masculinity and femininity, often using what she calls "gender decoys"—individual women in power and individual women as spokespersons for enterprises that are still dominated by males and for males.[24] Lynch had been grotesquely exploited by the Army Office of Public Affairs, but now she was going to undergo multiple transformations. Like women in all situations, she was one female body who would now be defined against a diversity of agendas. Her subordination as a woman, her *femininity*, was not abolished. It was diversified, like a product line that is losing market share.

As quickly as the fiction of the fight to the death was released, liberal feminists came forward to seize this proof of women's fitness for combat. She *was* GI Jane. This version ran headlong into a red-meat, reactionary backlash. Anti-feminists seized on the phony reports to attack supporters of women in combat. As the battle-to-the-death story unraveled, the liberals were silenced by the conservatives arguing *against* women's "fitness" for combat. Another faction argued against women valorizing military violence. Compassionate conservatives decried women's "better natures" being at risk. As my friend De Clarke put it, "No one could resist the piñata of political symbolism that was Jessica during her fifteen minutes of fame."

Jessica Lynch, *the person*, was invisible, while her definitions were played like instruments in competing orchestras. Why didn't the press cover the *men* who died fighting? Why did Jessica Lynch receive a Bronze Star? Why didn't anyone point out that Pietsewa, a woman, allegedly "lost control" under fire? Lynch's defenders then portrayed her as a poor, picked-on girl. Jessica Lynch was chosen because she was a *white* woman soldier,

---

23. Ibid., para. 10.
24. Eisenstein, "Disciplining Female Bodies," 20.

another can of worms. The father of one male soldier—who had reportedly fought fiercely before being killed—excoriated Lynch when her book deal was signed. So did a host of others. Now she would become a gold digger (another female stereotype), a woman ruthlessly exploiting the deaths of brave male soldiers to make money.

So went the perception managers' attempt to mobilize patriotism and "feminist" sentiment for the war. A big box office, but bad reviews.

BOY STORY

> Through the firing, Tillman's voice was heard issuing fire commands to take the fight to the enemy on the dominating high ground. Only after his team engaged the well-armed enemy did it appear their fires diminished.
>
> —From the citation awarding the Silver Star to Corporal Pat Tillman, 2004

As the squabble over the meanings of Jessica Lynch faded, the war in Iraq became more difficult for the American commanders, military and civilian. In early 2004, a Shia rebellion around Najaf,[25] combined with a stunning tactical defeat of U.S. forces in Fallujah, put U.S. forces on their heels.[26] In April, Seymour Hersh advised the government that he was about to release an explosive report on detainee abuse at the U.S. detention facility in Abu Ghraib, complete with lurid photographs of U.S. military police holding detainees on leashes, letting attack dogs at them, torturing them, and forcing them to simulate homosexual acts while nude.[27] The war was steadily losing public support.[28]

While the dust-up over Jessica Lynch died down, Company A, 2nd Ranger Battalion, 75th Ranger Regiment was assigned to a base of operations in Paktia Province, Afghanistan. Pat Tillman, former Arizona Cardinals safety, was a Specialist-4 in that unit, as was his brother Kevin; the brothers had joined the army together in May 2002. Pat was the most famous enlisted man in the United States military.

25. Arraff et al.,"Seven U.S. Troops Die."
26. Mansur and Mushtaq, "Al Jazeera Reporters."
27. Hersh, "Torture at Abu Ghraib." A whole chapter could be written on the association of sex and hostility, as well as "feminization" of the enemy, based on Abu Ghraib.
28. Pew Research Center, "Public Attitudes Toward the War in Iraq."

Tillman was raised by his parents with his two brothers, Kevin and Richard, near San Jose, California. His mother taught school, and his father—who lived nearby after a divorce—was an attorney. The boys lived near a large state park, and they were rambunctious, outdoorsy types. Pat was the eldest. He showed athletic prowess early on. He was also intellectually curious, somewhat self-deprecating, and had a lisp. He married the same girl he'd been dating since early high school just before he enlisted.

The Tillman boys were raised with a very conventional sense of ethics, but they adhered to those ethics, and all of them believed in basic honesty. They were patriotic without being overly demonstrative. After the September 11 attacks, when war began to seem inevitable, Pat and Kevin quietly talked about it, and Pat decided that if other people had to go, then his contract to play professional ball had to take a back seat to his sense of duty. It was a civil religion, to be sure, but at least Pat Tillman could say he wasn't conflicted about it, because he never professed any sort of "religious" faith. Shortly after the September 11 attacks, in a rare moment of self-revelation about his decision to enlist, Pat explained, "I was dumbfounded by everything that was going on. In times like this, you stop and think how good we have it. . . . A lot of my family has gone and fought in wars, and I haven't really done a damn thing as far as laying myself on the line like that."[29] Unlike Jessica Lynch, who saw the military as an economic strategy, a way to get some money for college and a few new skills, Tillman was motivated by the commonly held beliefs that life in the United States was essentially good, that it was good because it was based on principles like freedom, law, and sacrifice, and that men have a responsibility to the *polis* in times of danger to "lay themselves on the line." Privilege, like that which he was enjoying because of his athletic talent and his comfortable middle-class upbringing, should not serve as an excuse to let others shoulder that responsibility. While the underlying beliefs are certainly subject to the critique in this book—beliefs about civil religion, about war, and about masculinity—it is also important to point out that, given the episteme that Pat Tillman had, he was making an ethical, a virtuous, and a selfless decision. His attitude about the war, however, would change.

The brothers went to Iraq, and, as indicated above, they played a peripheral role in the faked Jessica Lynch rescue. Moreover, Pat's firsthand observations of the brutal conduct of the war in Iraq disillusioned him, leaving him to remark to a buddy once, "This war is so fucking illegal." His brother said that when the decision was taken to invade Iraq, Pat, who understood

---

29. Smith, "Heart of a Cardinal."

that Iraq had nothing to do with 9/11, was taken aback, even though he considered it his duty to fulfill his contract with the military.

The following year, when Pat and Kevin were in Afghanistan, their platoon—2nd Platoon, also called "The Blacksheep"—was given a reconnaissance-in-force mission, meaning they were to cautiously approach a series of locations, assess the activity there, fight if they made enemy contact or, if not, report on what they observed and did.

Some background is needed before we tell the rest of the story.

Donald Rumsfeld engineered a substantial change in organization and doctrine for the military, placing great emphasis on special operations because of their secrecy, and emphasizing "metrics." A former pharmaceutical company president and medical biotech CEO, he believed that numbers not only tell the story, but that by increasing the right numbers and decreasing the wrong ones, one succeeds. This is inflected on the system for officer advancement, called the Officer Personnel Management System (OPMS). OPMS gives enormous power to any officer's "rater," who happens to be the officer's immediate supervisor. Platoon leaders are "rated" by their company commanders, company commanders by battalion commanders, battalion commanders by brigade commanders, and so on. The unofficial rule is that *any officer who is rated below the maximum* after his or her first Officer Evaluation Report (OER) will be "passed over" for promotion when he or she becomes eligible. Given that there are always fewer "slots" for officers as they climb the ladder, this establishes a ruthless Spencerian logic. Any officer who is "passed over" needs to polish that résumé and begin looking for a job outside the armed forces. Raters, in other words, have the power of professional life and death over subordinate officers. This is a system in which tactical acumen and operational soundness are secondary to pleasing one's rater. This system normalizes a particular kind of officer—one who can perform well enough to make his or her commander look good, but also one who is willing to fit himself or herself to the idiosyncrasies of the rater, a politically alert "yes-man." Certain competencies are retained, but a certain kind of mediocrity is as well. Any officer who is so competent that he or she causes a less competent rater to feel threatened, for example, will not long survive without concealing his or her superior competence and/or shifting credit for accomplishments to the rater. This system ensures that—as we said in the army—"the shit always rolls downhill." Not only the shit, but the mindset.

If the secretary of defense is a micromanager—as Rumsfeld was known to be—then the things he likes will quickly become the things that his generals and all their subordinate officers like, and the things he doesn't like will soon find disfavor in the ranks, too. Rumsfeld was a metrics-man.

In short order, every officer in the military was talking "metrics" and seeking ways to accentuate the right metrics and eliminate the wrong metrics. A similar thing had happened under Westmoreland in Vietnam, when "body counts" became the metric, whereupon we either killed more people and called them enemy troops, or we added three chickens and a pig to the four people killed in contact, and doubled our metric.

Rumsfeld was sitting in his office waiting for his metrics, and his generals were in their offices waiting for their metrics, and the colonels waited for the majors and the majors waited for the captains, and the captains pushed the platoon leaders . . . for good metrics. Good metrics meant a good rating, and mediocre metrics might mean a point below the maximum on one's next OER, which means *hasta luego*, hope your résumé is in order, don't let the door hit you in the ass on the way out.

The Tactical Operations Center (TOC) in Khoust, Afghanistan, on April 21, 2004, housed 2nd Ranger Battalion—in all, around six hundred men at the time. The TOC was commanded by Major David Hodne, who worked for the Special Operations Command (SOCOM), and the Rangers were under his operational control. Major Hodne had an operations center where the various Ranger units in 2nd Battalion could be tracked on their assigned missions. If he had three platoons out, for example, and each of them was given three reconnaissance targets for the next three days, that would mean nine reconnaissance targets. This is hypothetical at this point, because SOCOM missions are highly classified. But completing nine targets would be, in this case, the desired *metric*. When Major Hodne reported to his supervisor, he told him that he had nine targets in the next three days; and at the end of those three days, if every target was occupied and observed by the designated platoon, Major Hodne would report that nine reconnaissance missions were completed within his sector in the last three days, and he could accompany the report with nine reconnaissance debriefings. Major Hodne remained in the operations center during these missions, and he maintained contact with his subordinate commanders by radio. His focus was on his tracking board where every checkmark for a completed mission improved his metrics, and therefore his career prospects.

The Blacksheep Platoon, 2nd Platoon, Alpha Company—Pat and Kevin Tillman's platoon—was on a non-hypothetical reconnaissance mission on April 22. Their target was a village called Manah. The platoon leader was First Lieutenant David Uthlaut.[30] Late in the morning, near a village

---

30. The rest of this story is the result of this author's review of more than two thousand pages of military documents, and interviews with several of the soldiers involved, including extensive conversations with Kevin Tillman. I worked directly with the Tillman family for almost a year on their investigation of these events, and I have read

called Magarah, one of the platoon's vehicles, a Humvee, broke down. This presented Uthlaut with a dilemma. The terrain was very inhospitable to vehicles, the roads little more than rocky wadis, and his own vehicles did not have the towing capacity to drag the deadlined vehicle with them. Various attempts to revive or tow the vehicle failed, and after several hours, the platoon began to worry about being stranded on low ground in mountainous terrain in a region that was unfriendly to foreign troops. It was broad daylight, and any Afghani who left the village could easily inform others that there were stranded American troops over near Magarah. The target, Manah, was still several kilometers away, and through the bottom of a long, steep canyon.

Uthlaut called his predicament in, requesting assistance to tow the vehicle or permission to destroy the vehicle. The TOC informed him that towing was not an option given the distance and security concerns, and that destroying the vehicle would give enemy troops a photo opportunity to claim they took out a vehicle. Uthlaut then found an Afghani driver with a "jinga truck" who said he would tow the broken humvee for a fee. Hodne became personally involved at this point, telling Uthlaut that he could bring the downed vehicle in, but only if Uthlaut split the platoon in half—half accompanying the dead hummer, and half proceeding to Manah, where Hodne ordered Uthlaut to "have boots on the ground by dusk."

Metrics were involved.

Uthlaut took a professional risk at this point and argued with Hodne, protesting that the rugged terrain would likely interrupt inter-platoon communications and that splitting the platoon would dangerously degrade the unit's ability to defend itself if attacked. Hodne overruled Uthlaut, and reiterated his "boots on the ground" directive. It was mid-afternoon, and Uthlaut was forced to reorganize and replan in just over an hour. The platoon was broken into two "serials," or half-platoons—one to accompany the jinga truck and dead hummer north through Tit, toward the main highway, and the other to continue west through the canyon toward Manah.

---

every statement taken by every troop in the platoon, as well as the summaries of three consecutive military investigations. I sat in with the family when they questioned representatives of the Special Operations Command, and questioned those representatives myself. The conclusions here were published in a three-part series for *Counterpunch* in 2006 and were the basis of a documentary film by Amir Bar-Lev titled *The Tillman Story*. This investigation resulted in the firing of a two-star general and a congressional investigation. No assertion made herein has ever been challenged publicly or privately by those named, nor were the same assertions ever challenged in Mary "Dannie" Tillman's book about her son's death and her investigation, *Boots on the Ground by Dusk*.

A Bodyguard of Lies: Girl Story and Boy Story

Meanwhile, the word had gotten out on the stranded platoon, and a group of two or three Afghani (possibly Taliban) fighters were watching from the top of the canyon, almost eight hundred meters away.

Serial 1 was Pat Tillman's, and they were headed directly to Manah. Serial 2 had Kevin Tillman and the "albatross" vehicle. When the platoon headed away from Magarah, they were traveling about five miles an hour to negotiate the rocky roads. The sun was getting low.

When they reached the intersection to turn north through Tit, Serial 2 broke away and headed up the steep wadi that joined the main highway several miles away. Serial 1 headed into the sunless canyon. The two or three Afghani fighters followed along above them from the southern ridge, observing down at a range of more than eight hundred meters and more than five hundred feet of elevation. Within minutes after splitting, the two serials lost communication with each other. Serial 2 found the northern road impassable for the jinga truck pulling the "albatross," so they decided to return to the intersection, head into the canyon, and rejoin Serial 1. When the Afghani fighters saw the second serial return, they let Serial 1 continue unmolested.

At this juncture in our story, we need to pause for a little more background.

Rangers are shock infantry who have special missions like airfield seizure or outer-ring security for outfits like Delta or SEAL Team 6. Like all Special Operations elements, they are the beneficiaries of an officially sanctioned mystique that serves as good public relations and as an ostensible deterrent. So the Department of Defense as well as the National Command Authority above them have a stake in the preservation and propagation of that mystique, which reinforces patriotism and American militarism with a kind of collective pride in these "elite" units. By keeping their missions secret—which certainly has some value in terms of actual operational security—the state can selectively report on their operations in ways that enhance that mystique.

Ranger units are subject to strict discipline and rigorous physical training. They practice certain key missions so often that these predictable missions—like airfield seizure, for example—are inscribed in the units' collective memory. Reconnaissance-in-force is *not* a predictable mission; it is akin to what we called "search and destroy" in Vietnam: looking for a fight, then figuring out the tactics once the unit is in contact. Rangers are generally young. An eighteen-year-old can sign up, and if he can hack the various schools and orientation programs, he's in. There are senior noncommissioned officers in the Rangers who are less than thirty years old; and the average first lieutenant—like Uthlaut—who commands a platoon is around twenty-four years old. Rangers are required to test slightly above average on the army's version of an IQ, but they are not generally college educated.[31] These young men are very aggressive. They are selected for aggression, and then they are groomed for greater aggression. When the army sends Rangers somewhere, it has to be someplace where the army accepts that a lot of people may be killed and a lot of things might be destroyed. A new Ranger in Pat Tillman's platoon, in one of the post-incident statements, said frankly, "I wanted to be in a firefight." Having been in a firefight is a coveted rite of passage; the more the better, as far as most Rangers are concerned. That is why some people refer to them as *shock* infantry.

Modern Ranger platoons—when mounted as they were between Magarah and Manah that day—carry a staggering amount of firepower: hundreds of thousands of rounds of ammunition for automatic assault rifles and machine guns; thousands of rounds of 40mm grenades that can be fired on full automatic, each with a five-meter bursting radius; dozens of shoulder-fired antitank rockets; hand grenades with high explosive; white phosphorus (an incendiary for burning equipment and people) and signal smoke. All this in the hands of about forty men who *want* to use it.

The rules for using this firepower are threefold: (*a*) Law of Land Warfare (LLW), (*b*) the unit's standing operating procedures (SOP), and (*c*) the theater's rules of engagement (ROE).

The LLW is part of the Geneva Conventions and forbids certain practices, such as intentionally killing civilians or firing into habitations when no fire has been received from them. All soldiers in the world are subject to this law, whether they routinely violate it or not; and the other two standards—SOP and ROE—are *subordinate* to this law. SOP and ROE can impose greater restrictions on the use of firepower, but they cannot legally loosen the Geneva standard.

In Afghanistan, the theater command's ROE stated that no "target" was to be "engaged" (meaning no person was to be shot or blown up) unless the shooter had established a "positive identification" that distinguished that person as friend, foe, or noncombatant.

In the Ranger regiment, the SOP stated that fires initiated by team leaders and squad leaders would serve as a signal to subordinate troops to fire on the same targets. If your nineteen-year-old team leader began firing into a

---

31. Another little-known fact, outside of the Special Operations community, is that Ranger units have per capita the fewest black people of any units in the army, with the exception of Delta. That is an important story, but it is another story.

house, you were then obliged to fire into the same house—even though this SOP might cause a solider to contravene the standards established by Geneva (targeting nonhostile civilians) *and* the ROE (positive identification).

The Ranger SOP is the only one that "makes sense" to experienced infantrymen, for a number of reasons, which demonstrates again what we saw with the Civil War about modern war contradicting just-war standards. This contradiction would have consequences for the Blacksheep Platoon.

Serial 1 exited the canyon onto a rocky, rolling hillside with several houses whose inhabitants, when they saw the convoy, went inside, leaving their goats to graze. The convoy halted. The sun was dropping over the horizon, but there was good light. Uthlaut and his radio operator, Jade Lane, walked up alongside one of the houses, trying to get on higher ground and reestablish radio contact with Serial 2, which Uthlaut still believed was heading north toward the highway. The rest of Serial 1 dismounted and formed a hasty security perimeter around the houses. Pat Tillman was with Staff Sergeant Matthew Weeks, one of Pat's team members named Bryan O'Neal, and one Afghan Militia Force (AMF) solider named Thani.

Inside the darkening canyon, meanwhile, Serial 2 crawled along, bounding over the stony wadi floor, when there was an explosion on the canyon wall above them that rained down debris. One of the Afghan fighters had fired an old Soviet rocket-propelled grenade (RPG) into the canyon from the ridge above. The shot came from almost eight hundred meters away, which meant there was little chance that this two-hundred-meter weapon would hit anything at which it was aimed. This was a fairly typical guerrilla tactic—a harassment ambush—designed to slow people down, confuse leaders, and cause them to burn up ammunition. It worked.

One Ranger believed he might have seen two silhouettes on the ridgeline, and the serial opened up on the ridge—just as ineffectively as the Afghan fighters' fire had been. Canyons echo and amplify sound, and within seconds, the entire serial unleashed a deafening volume of fire—assault rifles, machine guns, and 40mm—at the now empty ridge. In a situation like this, everyone assumes that someone else knows what they are firing at, so they join in.

Uthlaut's serial heard this roar of gunfire and explosions, as Uthlaut desperately and unsuccessfully tried to make radio contact.

Serial 2 eventually ceased fire and began to crawl through the canyon again, the troops now in a highly restless state.

Pat Tillman, Bryan O'Neal, Thani, and SSG Weeks were in a position about forty meters north of the road, observing the mouth of the canyon and the distant, stony southern ridge across the road.

Then the Afghan fighters sprayed a short burst of Kalashnikov fire into the canyon and ran southwest away from the action, provoking another apocalyptic and canyon-amplified volume of fire from Serial 2.

Pat observed distant movement on the southern ridge that may have been the Afghan fighters, and requested permission from Weeks to pursue with his team. Weeks told Pat, sensibly, to stay put and wait for Serial 2. Pat, O'Bryan, and Thani then squatted together behind a big boulder to watch the canyon mouth.

The lead vehicle in Serial 2 was commanded by SSG Greg Baker, with seven people aboard—one driving, and the others armed with a pintle-mounted .50 caliber machine gun, two squad automatic weapons (light machine guns), one portable crew-served machine gun, and two assault rifles, one with a grenade launcher. As Baker's vehicle reached the mouth of the canyon, coming into view of the houses, the .50 caliber opened up on the houses (and on Uthlaut and Lane, who were there trying to communicate with them), violating both Geneva and the ROE. The rest of the vehicle came into view of Pat's position, when someone on the vehicle called out, "Target, three-o'clock!" The vehicular team stopped and opened up on Tillman, O'Neal, and Thani. Thani was killed outright. Tillman and O'Neal took cover behind the rock as it was peppered with fire. Tillman shouted for a cease fire, even calling out his name: "It's Tillman. I'm Pat fucking Tillman!" Baker's crew did not hear, so Pat threw a red smoke grenade out from the position in the hope it would signal a cease fire and let them know they were shooting their own people.

The firing stopped. Tillman and O'Bryan stood and waved at the vehicle, which had begun moving again. Then the vehicle stopped once more. Members of Baker's crew dismounted, opening fire again. Pat was killed instantly when a three-round burst hit him in the face. O'Neal dropped back behind the rock, between two dead men, as the fire continued. Moments later, when Serial 2 realized what they had done, Uthlaut consolidated the platoon and kept Kevin away from Pat's body. Uthlaut called in the situation.

Once he contacted the TOC, the situation was taken out of his hands. He was told to say nothing, direct the platoon to say nothing, and to prepare for extraction. Kevin was told his brother had been killed, but not that it was by fratricide. Kevin had been near the rear of Serial 2, which was still in the canyon when the friendly fire had happened. Within thirty minutes, a helicopter took Kevin away and another retrieved the bodies of Pat and Thani. Uthlaut and Lane had been wounded, though not gravely. The platoon flew back to the TOC, with strict instructions to speak to no one about what had happened, not even each other.

The most famous enlisted man in the United States Armed Forces had just been killed by his own men in what the military referred to as a "clusterfuck."

There is one thing no officer or NCO ever wants to do: withhold bad news and risk letting one's superiors be ambushed by it. Every member of the chain of command wants to know something bad as soon as possible so the damage control can begin as soon as possible. Screw-ups, as we said in the army, are not wine—they don't improve with age. In this case, Uthlaut's immediate supervisor was Major Hodne, who had himself, only hours before, given the order, against Uthlaut's advice as commander on the ground, to split the platoon. As Tillman's body cooled in the morgue, where orders were given to secure his clothing and equipment,[32] Hodne confronted the fact that his order has resulted in two "friendly" deaths, as Baker was facing the fact that he had opened up on a nonhostile village (violation of Geneva) and on his own troops (violation of the ROE).

Hodne was reporting the fratricide to his chain of command, which traced up to General Stanley McChrystal—then commander of the Joint Special Operations Command (JSOC)—and to General John Abizaid, commander of CENTCOM. Given the gravity of this situation at a time when the military was facing the serial embarrassments of Najaf/Fallujah and Abu Ghraib, this bad news was certainly passed along to the army chief of staff and Secretary of Defense Donald Rumsfeld. Rumsfeld did not tell President Bush . . . yet.

Within hours, the media were given an intentionally false account of Tillman's death. Pat Tillman, according to the news release, was killed during intense combat with the enemy, in which he saved many lives; and he was to be awarded the Silver Star for his heroism.[33]

Within days of this ploy to transform's Pat's body into a recruiting poster and deflect attention from Abu Ghraib, hundreds of Rangers in Paktia Province knew that their government was involved in a massive public deception. The spin doctors were telling a story of martial masculinity in sacrificial service to the American civil religion.

---

32. Subsequently burned along with his personal journal.

33. He was also laterally and posthumously promoted to corporal, to make him an NCO in support of the story that he was directing troops in combat.

NBC News ran a story with the headline "Ex-NFL Star Tillman Makes 'Ultimate Sacrifice.'"

> Pat Tillman, who gave up the glamorous life of a professional football star to join the Army Rangers, was remembered as a role model of courage and patriotism Friday after military officials said he had been killed in action in Afghanistan.
>
> "Pat Tillman was an inspiration on and off the football field, as with all who have made the ultimate sacrifice in the war on terror. His family is in the thoughts and prayers of President and Mrs. Bush," Taylor Gross, a spokesman for the White House, said in a statement.
>
> Sen. John McCain, R-Ariz., the author of a recent book about courage, said he was "heartbroken" and raised the prospect that "the tragic loss of this extraordinary young man" could be a "heavy blow to our nation's morale, as it is surely a grievous injury to his loved ones."
>
> Tillman, 27, was a member of the 2nd Battalion, 75th Ranger Regiment, based at Fort Lewis, Wash. The battalion was involved in Operation Mountain Storm in southeastern Afghanistan, part of the U.S. campaign against fighters of the al-Qaida terror network and the former Taliban government along the Afghanistan-Pakistan border, military officials told NBC News.
>
> U.S. military spokesman Lt. Col. Matthew Beevers said Saturday that Tillman was killed Thursday night in a firefight at about 7 p.m. on a road near Sperah, about 25 miles southwest of a U.S. base at Khost.
>
> After coming under fire, Tillman's patrol got out of their vehicles and gave chase, moving toward the spot of the ambush. Beevers said the fighting was "sustained" and lasted 15–20 minutes.
>
> Beevers said Tillman was killed by enemy fire, but he had no information about what type of weapons were involved in the assault, or whether he died instantly.
>
> An Afghan militiaman fighting alongside Tillman also was killed, and two other U.S. soldiers were wounded.
>
> A local Afghan commander, Gen. Khial Bas, told The Associated Press that nine enemy fighters were killed in the confrontation.
>
> Bas said six other enemy fighters were believed to have escaped. Beevers said he had no information about any enemy fighters killed.[34]

---

34. "Ex-NFL Star Tillman Makes 'Ultimate Sacrifice.'"

A Bodyguard of Lies: Girl Story and Boy Story

Neither NBC editors nor the public noted some familiar phrases in the story, which was almost verbatim from a military press release. This story was dated April 29, yet the Associated Press, on April 16, almost a week before Pat Tillman was killed, had run a story titled "General Meyers visits Afghanistan," in which the following text appeared:

> Taliban insurgents attacked Afghan soldiers in eastern Khost province, along the border with Pakistan, killing two soldiers and injuring two others, Gen. Khial Bas, the local Afghan military commander, told The Associated Press on Friday. He said nine militants were killed in the exchange of rocket and machine-gun fire on Wednesday . . .

Someone had simply transposed the old story into the new fiction.

The problem was the paper trail. The Silver Star made good copy and supported the fictional version—but a Silver Star is an award that requires three things: a narrative account of what happened, statements from witnesses that support the account, and the signature of a general. Writing false statements and directing others to write false statements are illegal in the military, as are fraudulent awards.

Hodne and Baker—the former subject to having his operational judgment called into question and the latter subject to being prosecuted for Geneva and ROE violations—could breathe easy, because the higher-ups had seen fit to make the actual details of the incident disappear. "We must, indeed, all hang together," Ben Franklin famously said, "or, most assuredly, we shall all hang separately." A blanket of silence fell over the chain of command. But in the rush to both cover up and take advantage, a simple fact was incomprehensibly overlooked: hundreds of men knew. Rangers talk with one another. And these hundreds of men would be returning home in five weeks, where they would share experiences with family and drink in bars, and where the total control of the TOC would be replaced by the wide open spaces of Tacoma.

On April 29, 2004, just one week after Tillman was killed, President Bush was preparing a speech in which he intended to cite the heroism of Pat Tillman. General Stanley McChrystal sent the president a secret memorandum in which he said, essentially, Tillman was killed by his own men. Don't repeat the official story, Mr. President, because *if* this comes out (the "if" was emphasized) we will all be embarrassed. Now, even the president was in the loop.

At the end of May, 2nd Ranger Battalion was on its way home. By mid-May, the chain of command had come to realize the fact that their secret was going to surface. On May 29, after protesting that he did not want to do it,

General Philip R. Kensinger Jr., commanding general of the United States Army Special Operations Command (USASOC), gave a press conference in which he cryptically announced that there was an investigation underway that might suggest that Tillman was a victim of battlefield fratricide.

The whole story came out slowly, after more than two years of intense investigation by Pat's mother, "Dannie" Tillman. It resulted in a congressional hearing—which softballed the chain of command (thanking them for their service) and let them off without so much as a slap on the wrist. Kensinger was made the sacrificial goat and fired (with his pension intact).

There had been two additional investigations, each of which was conducted with direction from above that influenced its conclusions, and each of which was heavily redacted by the time Dannie Tillman received it. It was too dark to see, they concluded. But a check of the light conditions at the actual time the shooting occurred showed that this was a lie. Tillman, O'Bryan, and Thani were at a position 250 meters away, said the reports. This, too, was a fabrication: the distance was about 35 to 40 meters. The shooters' vehicle was still moving when they opened fire. Witnesses, after they'd left the battalion, including O'Bryan, said the vehicle stopped twice to concentrate its fire. The troops were keyed up from heavy contact with an enemy force of a dozen Afghan fighters armed with mortars. But no witness ever observed more than one or two persons; a mortar would not have impacted the way the RPG did; and there was not a scratch on a single member of Serial 2 or on any of their vehicles. All the conclusions of the "investigations" were spun to create "a fog of war" to justify the shootings.

Why so many lies? Why so many retrenchments of lies? Because it appeared to be a win-win-win situation. The mystique could be protected. The violations of law and policy would go unanswered. The errors in judgment by the TOC commander would be overlooked. The chaotic nature of the actual war and the recklessness of U.S. forces could be concealed. And the chain of command all the way to Washington, DC, could be shielded from accountability for the original lies: "We didn't have all the information. It was just a mistake."

Had it not been for the dogged persistence of Tillman's mother, who learned quickly that officialdom does not make statements to represent reality but to support its agendas, the cover-up would never have been exposed.

Just as was the case with Jessica Lynch—who appeared at the congressional hearing with the Tillman family—Pat Tillman's story became public property, appropriated for every conceivable notion and agenda. Prowar people set out to prove that Pat was "still a hero." Antiwar people seized on the cover-up. Conspiracy theorists claimed Pat was assassinated because he'd read some Chomsky. The real person of Pat Tillman, just like the real person of Jessica Lynch, was simultaneously cast as a character in a war story that concealed the political realities of the war, then recast by competing agendas when the lies were revealed.

But two other realities were concealed in both the propaganda fictions and the agenda-driven accounts. The actual nature of modern war, as it concretely was in Nasiriyah and Magarah, turns the principles of proportionality and discrimination into an obscene joke. And as the bloodthirsty Churchill observed, "In wartime, truth is so precious that *she* should *always* be attended by a *bodyguard of lies*."

In relating these four stories, two unvarnished approximations of what happened and two official fictions that were subsequently exposed, I have said nothing about being Christian. Now I will raise the question, how do Christians relate to these stories? What do we learn from them? What does it mean to us that this is the face of actual war—that deception is inherent in war, not only for "operational security," which is predictably cited to justify deception, but also for concealing wrongdoing, incompetence, and even the true motivations of leaders? Perhaps more to the point of this book, how do Christians interrogate accounts of gender? How do Christians interrogate accounts of war? What will make us reliable witnesses? Can American Christians continue to accept the premises of American exceptionalism? Do most American Christians even know what American exceptionalism is? How does American exceptionalism inflect militarism, and vice versa? When it does, and we represent America, is "America" a conquering white male?

A few years after the selectively secret Special Operations commanders had colluded in the film production of the Jessica Lynch rescue, Delta Force and the Rangers allowed a Hollywood director and his staff unprecedented access to facilities, personnel, and even some tactics of these secretive units for the purpose of producing *Black Hawk Down*, Ridley Scott's account of the Bakara firefight in Mogadishu, in which eighteen U.S. troops were killed and dozens wounded. Access was given precisely because, as Jeffords said, the film took attention "away from the war itself to the people who fought in it, shift[ing] the war from a national to a personal experience, making it possible for viewers to forget the specific historical and political forces that caused the war."

The film accurately reproduced certain key events, inaccurately reproduced others, and omitted several aspects of this protracted street battle. It did not represent the reality of Task Force Ranger in Mogadishu, nor could it have.[35]

In 2012, director Katherine Bigelow received Department of Defense cooperation for her (and the government's) fictionalized account[36] of the killing of Osama bin Laden, *Zero Dark Thirty*, a film that—like *Man on Fire*—used the "tempo task" to justify torture—even when the story line about the torture was itself a fabrication.[37]

Perhaps the most egregious cover-up, and one that has stimulated neither public outrage nor official investigation, is that of LaVena Johnson, who was murdered and declared a suicide.

Dr. John and Linda Johnson lived in Florissant, Missouri, about ten miles from where I graduated from high school in 1969. Their daughter LaVena was five feet one inch tall and a high school honor student who joined the army in 2005. She was nineteen when she was deployed to Iraq as a Private First Class. LaVena Johnson was black with a "funny black name," and she wasn't killed in "the fog of war" or an ambush, but by American men, so her case has received little public attention.

Camp Anaconda, outside of Balad, Iraq, was as big as a town. People could actually wander off and get lost in it. On July 19th, her fellow soldiers saw her leave her tent after dark with a reflective belt for safety, and she went to the Post Exchange (PX, a military convenience store). Her debit card statement showed that she made it to the PX.

Her family and the public were told she committed suicide that night. Johnson is still listed as a suicide by the military, which has refused for reasons unknown to conduct an investigation into her death. She was found dead in the tent of Kellogg, Brown & Root contractors.[38] She was shot with a rifle through the left temple (you have to imagine someone doing this with an M-16, left arm outstretched, holding the handgrip and trigger housing backwards to shoot herself sideways), beaten, her hands burned, and her vagina scorched out with lye. Little else is known, because her family, after looking at the autopsy, asked the government to investigate—but the government ignored them in favor of the suicide thesis. No one ever suggested that she was suicidal, or why someone contemplating suicide would stop off

---

35. The author was assigned to Task Force Ranger in Mogadishu as the senior medic with the Ranger component prior to the Bakara firefight.

36. Olson, "Not ONE Word."

37. McDermott, "Zero Dark Thirty."

38. Jordan, "Who Killed LaVena L. Johnson?"

to buy a snack before killing herself in a distant tent. Her nose was broken. She had a black eye. Several teeth were loose and her lip was torn and swollen. Even though her family has been relentless in pursuit of the truth, the army has not cooperated; neither has it ordered an independent investigation. Consequently, little is known about what actually happened to her.[39]

LaVena Johnson's story does not make a good "war story."

Rape by fellow soldiers, in fact, was a greater danger for female soldiers in Iraq and Afghanistan than enemy action; and it was routinely covered up by local chains of command with little to no intervention from above.[40] These contractors, moreover, are not consultants in suits but armed mercenaries who have been guilty of destruction of property, rape, murder, torture, drug trafficking, and sex trafficking in several theaters.[41]

It is hard to ignore how, in each of the fictions propagated by the government and the press about Lynch and Tillman, the false stories were close approximations of film conventions, mapped onto a pre-existing social imaginary—a narrative about American providential favor, about a hegemonic white masculinity, about "civilization" and the role of the soldier (as well as the militarized police) to police this boundary between Us and Them. The military's inhering misogyny, its rape culture, its outposts of white supremacy in the "elite" units, do not fit into that narrative. Neither do these inconvenient stories, like Abu Ghraib or the death of LaVena Johnson, fit into a liberal feminist narrative where the only problem with the armed forces is that it hasn't opened up to enough women.

In a society in which "consumers" have been habituated to being constantly entertained, and a culture where life imitates art imitates life in a kind of infinite and ever more self-conscious reflexivity, where the camera has made of us all both actor and spectator, where war is now reproduced as (boys') games and (boys') games are used to train for war, we cannot apprehend the relation between gender and war, between gender and church, between church and war, without some account of the audiovisual motion picture, this voyeuristic probe, this tempter to narcissism, this accountability cutout, this powerful and penetrative tool that can tell terrible truths and frighteningly effective lies.

The war story, as Jeffords says, transfers our attention from social conditions to individuals, to the characters in the story. Triumph or tragedy, our focus is on that person—not on culture, political structures, or history. Context is effaced. The background is naturalized and thereby placed beyond

39. Ibid.
40. Broadbent, "Rape in the US Military."
41. Amnesty International, "Private Military and Security Companies."

the grasp of critical intervention. Moreover, the bodyguard of lies that accompany war are a form of mass manipulation; and these "war stories" are tools of manipulation. As Christians, this ought to present us with an ethical dilemma. We are called to be truth-tellers, forthright in our relations with others. In this respect, not only war, but our whole epoch, must come under review, because we know that culture forms us personally. What happens to the idea and experience of self in a world where one is *obliged by custom and accepted practice* to objectify others and manipulate them? That's something the next chapter aims to answer.

20

Origin Myths

In such condition there is no place for industry, because the fruit thereof is uncertain, and consequently, no culture of the earth, no navigation, nor the use of commodities that may be imported by sea, no commodious building, no instruments of moving and removing such things as require much force, no knowledge of the face of the earth, no account of time, no arts, no letters, no society, and which is worst of all, continual fear and danger of violent death, and the life of man, solitary, poor, nasty, brutish, and short.

—Thomas Hobbes, *Leviathan*, XXI.9

Though the earth, and all inferior creatures, be common to all men, yet every man has a property in his own person: this nobody has any right to but himself. The labour of his body, and the work of his hands, we may say, are properly his. Whatsoever then he removes out of the state that nature hath provided, and left it in, he hath mixed his labour with, and joined to it something that is his own, and thereby makes it his property.

—John Locke, *Two Treatises of Government and A Letter Concerning Toleration*, 2.25

What happens to the idea and experience of self in a world where one is *obliged by custom and accepted practice* to objectify others and manipulate them? To answer that question, we need to take a kind of philosophical detour, because war and sex are both imbricated in our modern and highly manipulative culture. That culture has changed the experience of the self in ways that are problematic for the church as the body of Christ. In particular, we will need to get to the bottom of what we mean when we speak of *liberalism*.

One of the central confusions created by the use of the words *liberal* and *liberalism* is that their historical and popular definitions are different. In the United States and other Anglophone nations, liberal is now understood as the opposite of "conservative." Liberal is identified with toleration of social difference, including in sexual matters, and with the advocacy of some degree of economic redistribution from the prevailing regime of accumulation. Conservative is identified with cultural conformity around dominant cultural norms, including older norms of sexual behavior, and with the advocacy of self-reliance and resistance to economic redistribution from those with greater means to those of lesser means.

Historically, the terms *liberal* and *liberalism* are identified with the political philosophy that accompanied the rise to power of the business class and with *republican* government, that is, an indirect form of representative government.[1] Historical liberalism, sometimes called *classical* liberalism, includes both tendencies that are identified as "liberal" and "conservative" in modern political discourse. Beneath the conflicts between these two liberal tendencies—liberal liberalism and conservative liberalism—there is a shared philosophical consensus that can be traced back to Descartes. It is a consensus with *masculine* philosophical roots.

Alasdair MacIntyre described this shared consensus, using two key twentieth-century philosophers as representatives of liberal-liberalism and conservative-liberalism—John Rawls (1921–2002) and Robert Nozick (1938–2002), who represent the "liberal" and "conservative" aspects, respectively. MacIntyre's explanation is found in his book *After Virtue*,[2] and

---

1. Elections determine not laws and administrative policies, generally speaking, but "representatives" who will determine, interpret, and execute laws and administrative policies. In practice, this form of government has passed a limited degree of power to the grassroots of society, while retaining an overwhelming degree of control for those with the greatest resources, i.e., money, in framing what will and will not be subject to public debate as well as who can afford to run for office.

2. MacIntyre, *After Virtue*, 244–52.

it begins with two hypothetical people, whom MacIntyre imaginatively named *A* and *B*.

A works as a construction worker (liberal archetypes are male), has bought a modest house, sent his two kids to college, and pays for his ailing mother's medical care. He has not saved a great deal, but he manages to do those things he considers important. There is a threat to raise his taxes, and he considers this an injustice. He earned what he has by his own hard work. He is fairly entitled to it; and taking any of it away with higher taxes is wrong. He will vote for political candidates who refuse to raise his taxes.

B is an associate professor with some savings and investments tucked away. He studies social inequality and finds it cannot be explained purely on the basis of merit. He sees an element of injustice in the disparity between rich and poor. He acknowledges that "economic growth is necessary" but believes we need some redistributive mechanism that ensures certain necessities and prevents great suffering. He believes great suffering can lead to social instability. He will vote for political candidates who are willing to employ redistributive taxation to ameliorate that suffering.

A and *B* are both preoccupied with something called "justice," but they define justice in different and incompatible ways. During the 1990s when money was circulating freely from financial bubbles that hadn't yet broken, *A* was getting all kinds of work, and *B* found his favorite nonprofits flush with grant money from brimming foundation portofolios. Neither of them was as acutely aware of injustice then, and they might even have voted for some of the same candidates. After the 2007–8 Wall Street debacle and the subsequent period of high unemployment and increased poverty—greater scarcity of money, that is—the incompatibility of their conceptions of justice became more sharply apparent, their politics more polarized.

The conservative-liberal (*A*) believes redistribution is *unjust* because acquisition was *just*. Inequality is something we must accept in the name of this version of justice. The liberal-liberal (*B*) believes a degree of redistribution qualifies as justice (and stability) and that limits on acquisition exercised through redistribution are required to facilitate justice. This imposition *against* some acquisition defines justice. There is no common philosophical ground.

The *A* position is that of Robert Nozick, and the *B* position that of John Rawls.

So what unites them as classical liberals?

First of all, scarcity is assumed by both, because money-dependence in a growth economy is a structural condition of scarcity. Second, each treats the "individual" as an abstraction. Both Rawls and Nozick are "social contractarians." One says that "rights" mean possessive entitlement and the other says that individuals bear certain "rights" to the satisfaction of needs, but both treat the concepts of "individual" and "rights" as foundational, universal.

> It is, from both standpoints, as though we had been shipwrecked on an uninhabited island with a group of other individuals, each of whom is a stranger to me and to all of the others. What have to be worked out are rules which will safeguard each one of us maximally in such a situation. Nozick's premise concerning rights introduces a strong set of constraints; we do know that certain types of interference with each other are absolutely prohibited. But there is a limit to the bonds between us, a limit set by our private and competing interests.[3]

This sounds logical to us, because in our own modern experience most people really are strangers, with little connection to us or each other. We operate to an increasing degree within a network of legal contracts, defining obligations in an impersonal way. It is very difficult for us to agree about questions of justice or virtue apart from contractual conditions.

What do we mean by contract, and more specifically, what is this idea within historical liberalism called "social contract"?

British historian Carole Pateman, author of *The Sexual Contract*, says, "Telling stories of all kinds is the major way that human beings have endeavoured to make sense of themselves and their social world."[4] Pateman describes stories that underwrite the idea of social contract, which, she shows, is itself an outgrowth of something she calls the "sexual contract." There are several stories that are used to describe social contract, and when we look at Rawls and Nozick closely, we find that there are origin myths of liberal philosophy.

Rawls has a myth called "The Original Position," about a group of people who get together to decide what rules they will need to live together. In Rawls's story, all of the people in the group are afflicted with a form of amnesia, which Rawls calls "the veil of ignorance."[5] None of the people engaged in this very important deliberation together knows himself. He has no social status, no ethnic tradition, no beliefs, no history, no relationships, nothing. He is, however, grown with children and the "head of a household," which for Rawls meant a man. His characters are so abstract that they can't even have bodies, which might betray one of the realities that must remain

---

3. Ibid., 251.
4. Pateman, *Sexual Contract*, 1.
5. Freeman, "Original Position."

Origin Myths

concealed behind the veil. Together, they are a music played with only one note on no particular instrument.

Robert Nozick has a different story. His is named "The Original Act of Acquisition."[6] In this story, a man is walking on the beach (men again). The beach is covered with pretty shells. The man takes one and carries it home. It is legitimately his, because he picked it up in the open, on no one's property, and no one else had yet claimed the shell. There were plenty of shells, so the shell is rightly his. If someone takes the shell from him without permission, that is wrongful, but if he sells the shell to someone voluntarily, then the ownership of the shell is rightly transferred. Obviously, Nozick is preoccupied with *property*, and so the original rightful act is used to explain where property came from, which in fact is every bit as "historically baseless" as the story liberals reject about Eve's chat with a perfidious snake and Rawls's story of collective amnesia. Yet these stories support the edifice of liberal humanism.

You can see how Rawls's fiction has several disembodied individuals collaborating on rules that cannot take any real (flesh and blood) person into account; and Nozick's fiction has just one disembodied being—a "rights-bearing individual" like Rawls's rights-bearing individual—who deals in either acquisition or "rational" exchange with other acquisitive individuals. Both are social contractarians. They simply have a disagreement about the basis of "rights" that attach to the cardboard characters in their respective stories. They have one more thing in common.

"The pictures of the state of nature" writes Pateman, "and the stories of the social contract found in the classic texts vary widely, but despite their differences on many important issues, the classic social contract theorists have a crucial feature in common. They all tell *patriarchal* stories."[7] With the notable exception of Thomas Hobbes, it turns out, the origins of political "rights" associated with social contractarianism, in the accounts given by the "fathers" of liberalism, *all* begin with the explicit claim that women are subordinate to men *by nature*, whereas men are legitimately subordinate to other men only *by contract*. The fathers of the Enlightenment divided nature and culture, with nature marked as female and subordinate to culture, which was marked as male.[8] In every account except Hobbes (and Hobbes

6. Feser, "Nozick, Robert."

7. Pateman, *Sexual Contract*, 41.

8. Duden, *Woman Beneath the Skin*, 20–21: "From the end of the eighteenth century on 'nature' was created as an organizing category of thought. It was placed in opposition to 'culture,' thus representing the 'wholly other' whose laws could be investigated. This dichotomous way of thinking in opposite categories of nature and culture is shot through with sexual references and metaphors in which woman is equated with nature."

will find his way back to the subjugation of women by declaring a *coerced* agreement a contract), men and men alone can be regarded as "free and equal 'individuals.'" Biology determines sex, and biology—making men the superior beings—thereby determines that men shall rule women, based on defining women into a nature that has been declared subordinate to men.

The modern struggle for women's social emancipation began with the recognition of contradictions in liberal theory, and in the wake of that struggle, liberal theory has dropped any reference to sex, even though the conception of this unsexed "individual" retains all its earlier masculine characteristics. Jessica Benjamin writes that "the idea of the individual in modern liberal thought is tacitly defined as masculine even when women are included. Identifying the gender content of what is considered to be gender-neutral can be as difficult as undoing the assumption of essential gender differences."[9] We will see as we go along that this difficulty is created by the gender-neutral language of liberalism (which is also class-neutral and race-neutral) concealing the gendered origins of various forms of social power and *normalizing* existing culture by virtue of our lifelong immersion in it.

We can easily see that the corporate boardroom lacks females except to take the minutes and serve the coffee; but we typically think of the corporation and its boardroom as the product of the history of male dominance. This blind spot is maintained by norm-alization and gender-neutral liberal speech. We are then seduced by the argument that something called "equality" can efface history by putting more women on the board (as "gender decoys"). Shuffling the board may lead to small changes in its practices, but the function of the board is imbricated within the larger context of society and law. A few women in the boardroom do nothing that improves the lot of women generally, nor will they force the institution to adapt standpoints shared mostly by women. On the contrary, women in power have consistently adapted to the existing masculinized culture, where they serve as *honorary* males. This is why we need to read between the lines of gender-neutral speech.

The characters in liberal origin myths are diverse. Hobbes boils reality down to energy-driven material. Rousseau insists on people's inevitable sociality (as *men*). Rawls holds the "individual" to be twofold—a menu of preferences alongside a menu of productive functions. Rousseau insists on the retention of some human agency in a social milieu, yet he, like the others, still disembeds his "individual" from particular relations.[10]

---

9. Benjamin, *Bonds of Love*, 184.
10. Pateman, *Sexual Contract*, 39–40.

Origin Myths

There is a contract operating prior to the "social" contract. This is men's entitlement to sexual access to women: "sex right." Paternal rights were transformed by the liberal revolution into fraternal rights, but still these were *male* rights. Paternal rights *assumed paternity*, and paternity *assumed* "conjugal right"—that a man had a right of sexual access to *his* woman. Given that paternal and fraternal male political rights began with the right of a husband to exercise control over his wife, political right originates from sex right. This right originated patriarchally, through the rule of the fathers. Fathers rule mothers and daughters, and when daughters are given away it is to provide younger men with children to make them fathers, and to serve and obey them.

The men who led the American and French Revolutions understood their struggle as one against patriarchal *succession*—not against *patriarchy* defined as the rule of men. They opposed the hereditary rule of aristocratic families, who were seen as repressive *fathers* in the social family. In a very real sense, the struggle was articulated in Oedipal terms, as a struggle between sons and fathers. The French proclaimed the slogan *liberté, égalité, fraternité*, the latter term meaning *brother*-hood. The republic, this new political form, was conceived of as a polity of brothers, adult men with political agency; and this brotherhood not only constituted a representative form of governance, but something called *civil society* that would underwrite the political process. As we will see, *civil society* means public, as opposed to private, affairs. Included in the spoils of the struggle, in the minds of republican men, was equal hypothetical sexual access to all adult women, *bypassing the father*. The *paternal* rule over women was theoretically supplanted by the *fraternal* rule over women.[11] Post-revolutionary men, in the establishment of their legal equality, were willing to grant post-revolutionary women equality to make a contract, but only for one thing: marriage. This contract was an exchange of protection from all men (who theoretically had access to her) by one man, in exchange for obedience and sexual availability to that one man. Once the contract was signed, the woman became a political nonentity, invisible except through her husband, and she could make no subsequent contracts.

> By marriage, the husband and wife are one person by law: that is, the very being, or legal existence of the woman is suspended during the marriage, or at least is incorporated and consolidated into that of the husband; under whose wing, protection

---

11. Which mapped nicely onto the twelfth-century Catholic decision to allow marriage by contract.

and cover, she performs everything; and is therefore called . . . a *femme-covert* . . . her husband [is] her baron, or lord.[12]

A covered-woman, invisible to the public realm. This is where the legal concept in early liberal marriage law of *couverture* originated. A woman's husband was her representative in the public sphere, while she resided exclusively in the private, which was the little kingdom of the husband.[13] Women in public, who did not have a husband, were *unprotected*. We can still see this idea in operation today, explicitly or not, in the number of men who feel entitled to make advances, even offensive ones, toward women who appear to be "unattached." These unprotected women are, in a telling turn of phrase, "fair game."

As liberal language was de-gendered, it changed expression, not meaning. The classic thinkers of modernity all saw women as inferior and subordinate to men, and as Pateman says, "Contemporary contract theorists implicitly follow their example, but this goes unnoticed because they subsume feminine beings under the apparently universal, sexually neutered category of the 'individual.'"[14] The masculine individual was still assumed, but in the language of liberalism, women-as-*women* are invisible.

Even Kant, who does not peddle an origin myth with his claim to have discovered a basis for universal consensus in determinations of right and wrong, still describes his purely reasoning individual in a way that is recognizable only as one of his bourgeois European *male* contemporaries. Kant calls the contract "merely an idea of reason," necessary, as we saw with the other philosophers, to support already existing social relations and political arrangements.

Kant said that anyone with reason is a *person*, who thereby has the capacity for moral determinations, and therefore the right to enter into public life via the contract. He described the marriage contract as essentially a sexual contract—but went on to say, contradictorily, that human beings are sexually differentiated and that *women did not have the capacity for public life*. Even though they could contract for marriage.[15] Women, according to Kant, knew "nothing of *ought*, nothing of *must*, nothing of *due*."[16] Kant, like Rawls and Nozick after him, was fitting his conclusions to the existing order of which he was a part.

12. Blackstone, *Laws of England*, 442.
13. One still hears the cliché "a man's home is his castle," which derived from this republican idea.
14. Pateman, *Sexual Contract*, 42.
15. Kant, "Observations," 168–69.
16. Ibid., 157.

Origin Myths

In order to make their natural being recognizable, social contract theorists smuggle social characteristics into the natural condition, or their readers supply what is missing. The form of the state or political association that a theorist wishes to justify also influences the "natural" chacteristics that he gives to individuals; as Rawls stated . . . the aim of arguing from an original position, Rawls' equivalent to the state of nature, "is to get the desired solution."[17]

Rawls *tells* us that his own theory "tries to draw solely upon basic intuitive ideas that are embedded in the political institutions of a constitutional democratic regime and the public traditions of their interpretations."[18] So, contract theory is an *apologetic* for liberal society, a point admitted in so many words by philosophers from Kant to Rawls, who take the superiority of their class, their nationality, and their gender as self-evident. The uprooted "individual" of contract theory existed to put a universalizing gloss on the lives of the writers themselves, including the naturalization of women's subordination.

Christians make sense of their world through a story, too. Some theologians call church a narrative community.[19] Modern agnostics and atheists consign our story to the category of "just" a story, and rely for guidance in their lives upon the masculine "objectivity" we interrogated through Bordo's analysis of Descartes. Theologian Stanley Hauerwas says that "America is the exemplification of what I call the project of modernity. That project is the attempt to produce a people that believes it should have no story except the story it chose when it had no story. That is what Americans mean by freedom."[20] One of the stories we are encouraged to "choose" is the "war story." We are storied creatures.

Unlike the liberal origin myths, for Christians, every human being is uniquely *embodied*; we are identical with our fleshy and situated selves, and we are called to respond to our neighbor by clothing, feeding, and healing actual bodies. The Word was made *flesh*. In a stable. In Bethlehem. From a *particular* woman. That body broke bread with sinners and was nailed, bleeding, to a cross.

17. Pateman, *Sexual Contract*, 40–42.
18. Rawls, *Collected Papers*, 390.
19. Black, *Christian Moral Realism*, 317–18.
20. Hauerwas, "End of American Protestantism," para. 18.

In our own period of crisis-wracked consumer capitalism, perhaps the best way to approach this "individual" who keeps reappearing in political philosophy and law—known by some as *Homo economicus*—is through an examination of another slippery character, the *self*. While Christian teaching through the ages has mentioned something called "dying to self," I've not found this actual phrase in Scripture. The concept is formed around a collection of passages that talk about dying, often on the cross with Jesus, but also in baptism prior to a kind of rebirth. Scripture warns us about the dangers of immoderate desire, avarice, pride, concupiscence, the lust for power, hard-heartedness. But the phrase "dying to self" originates in our tradition, not our Scriptures. The conception of self as we came to understand it, and as we understand it today—hermetically sealed within the skin and moving through a world of objects—did not exist when the Scriptures were written. Second Timothy refers to "lovers of self," and in Matthew Jesus tells us to love our neighbor as ourselves, and so forth. So we have the sense that what we now refer to as selfishness is *not* good and that self-sacrifice for others is good, and we know that the traditional idea of "dying to self" is an encapsulation of that notion as it applies to repentance and conversion, but we don't find anything that resembles the modern attention given to the term *self*.

We have all heard terms like self-taught, self-reliant, self-loathing, *Self* magazine, self-esteem, self-satisfaction, self-deprecation, self-appraisal, self-incrimination, self-actualization, self-effacement, self-assurance, self-confidence, self-immolation, self-serving, self-promotion, self-denial, self-referential, and self-obsession. These variable uses indicate different ways of understanding *self*, as opposed to self-understanding. There is some cultural agreement about what the "self" is in each context; and yet there seems to be little attention given to what constitutes a *self*. Perhaps we feel the term is too basic to examine.

The relation between that political-economic-ideological "self," the theoretically disembodied one we see in liberal philosophy, and the profound cultural self-absorption of our time is sustained externally by the relentless re-creation of desire. We seek after self-fulfillment, self-esteem, self-assertion, self-actualization; and we do so with apparently little thought about what comes after this constant inflow to self. We never actually find out, because we die still consuming to satisfy the *next* manufactured need, because we believe in the idea of the infinite expansion of new needs and new things to satisfy them. In economics, this is called *growth*. Some call it *progress*. Some call it *normal*, because endless desire, too, has been naturalized. It appears infinite, but it is an illusion into which one is, actually ... well, absorbed. The self is a consuming voyeur.

We accept that we are "secular," ostensibly scientific, grounded in materiality instead of narrative. Our faith in modern institutions and the modern claim that scientific means secular (read: valid) lead us to believe that they—them—that if *they* speak using the same neutralized discourse as scientists, then we can assume that their philosophies of society and of power are based on some modern and objective material foundation. Alas, such is not the case. Not in the case of "the social contract" that underwrites our customs, policies, and laws. Each of these origin stories is a fabrication, and a Euro-masculine one constructed as an apologetic for the power of its author and his contemporaries—Hobbes, Rousseau, Kant, Locke, Mill, even Marx. In each case, these ushers of progress start with an imaginary metaphysical tale—not one any more scientifically or historically valid than the Edenic first couple and their reptilian interlocutor.[21]

"We are the only people who think themselves risen from savages," writes Marshal Sahlins. He continues:

> Everyone else believes they descended from gods. . . . We make both a folklore and a science of the idea, sometimes with little to distinguish between them. The development from a Hobbesian state of nature is the origin myth of Western capitalism. But just as Hobbes did not conceive that the commonwealth abolished the nature of man as wolf to other men, but merely held that it permitted its expression in comparative safety, so we continue to believe in the savage within us—of which we are slightly ashamed.[22]

Hobbes was more direct and unapologetic than other contract philosophers. He even granted women an original equal status with men in his origin myth, though both man and woman in Hobbes's primeval story are the moral equivalent of vampires; and, of course, men subdue women shortly after Hobbes's story begins. His real and most embarrassing admission was that contract was an agreement, yes, but one that was secured through domination. Even babies "contracted" with mothers to submit so the mother wouldn't expose them. This didn't disturb Hobbes in the least, since it was perfectly consistent with his origin myth that humans, at some starting point, were real dog-eat-dog, egotistical opportunists, but that their self-love, in conjunction with calculation, sometimes leads them to cooperate to

---

21. At least Marx attempted a speculative material history, which proved to be wrong.

22. Sahlins, *Culture and Practical Reason*, 53.

mutual advantage, providing the basis for civilization.[23] In popular culture, this is not an unfamiliar image. We are all schooled that we are approaching some transcendent epitome now that signifies what utterly horrifying barbarians we were in some imaginary past. The real evidence suggests that perhaps the opposite is true. Rousseau, at least, told a story of a Noble Savage, in the spirit of his own Romantic era.

Robert Bellah writes of Locke,

> The origin myth of America in this broader perspective is origin itself. According to John Locke, "In the beginning all the world was America." America stood for the primordial state of the world and man and was indeed seen, by the first generations of Europeans to learn of it, to be the last remaining remnant of that earlier time. The newness which was so prominent an attribute of what was called the "new" world was taken not just as newness to its European discoverers and explorers but as newness in some pristine and absolute sense: newness from the hands of God. That sense of indelible newness, which has been a blessing and a curse throughout our history, has not evaporated even today. If it gives us a sense that we come from nowhere, that our past is inchoate and our tradition shallow, so that we begin to doubt our own identity and some of the sensitive among us flee to more ancient lands with more structured traditions, it also gives us our openness to the future, our sense of unbounded possibility, our willingness to start again in a new place, a new occupation, a new ideology. Santayana has spoken of "the moral emptiness of a settlement where men and even houses are easily moved about, and no one, almost, lives where he was born or believes what he has been taught." Yet other Europeans have envied our capacity to act without being immobilized by ancient institutions.[24]

Rawls says that implicitly male individuals are by nature "equal" based on his origin myth, even though he follows up by telling us that "his *task is to find a picture of an original position that will confirm 'our' intuitions about existing institutions.*"[25] We have a cultural memory now of these stories, which is why Rawls gets away with reasoning "to get the *right* solution." The assumptions of cultural superiority, the masculinity of the "individual," and the intentional confirmation of our "intuitions" are presupposed.

23. Duncan, "Thomas Hobbes."
24. Bellah, *Broken Covenant*, 5.
25. Pateman, *Sexual Contract*, 42.

Origin Myths

Although there are many arguments among many liberal philosophers to this day, what joins them all is the shared belief in a special kind of self. In addition to the hidden but still operational sexual contract that is concealed inside the more well-known "social contract," this contract depends on a peculiarly modern idea of the self as property—the self as *owner* of a transferable body. One would think that in a society that prides itself on being grounded in empiricism, we would question the idea that there is some entity, apart from one's embodied existence, that owns her or his body. Yet, the idea that one's body is *not* alienable is almost incomprehensible to us. We believe that each person has the *right* to dispose of her or his body as she or he sees fit . . . to a point, of course. Suicide is still against the law in most states, even though no one is left to prosecute for violation; and we are prohibited from legally consuming certain kinds of drugs, a bureaucratic legal limitation on freedom. But the commonsense belief among most of us is that we can do as we wish with ourselves. Herein is a paradox.

If you sign an employment contract, as an employee, you are signing away yourself for a period of time; you are promising to *obey*, in exchange for a sum of money. You may be compelled by an economy of scarcity. When one looks at many of the most thankless and low-paid jobs, one quickly realizes that one can contract to live little better than a slave, even if one is a slave who can go home at night. Yet, as we sign the contract, me the big boss and you the tomato picker, both signatories are recognized by the law *as equal*. So, in a real sense, there could theoretically be a "slave contract." In fact, a good case could be made that we have many slave contracts in operation right now, which does not differ in many respects from a marriage contract, exchanging obedience for protection. This system works because of another bit of post-Enlightenment creativity, the idea of a formal separation between two "domains"—public and private. Prior to the Enlightenment, no such separation was understood.

> In contemporary contractarianism . . . the boundaries that separate one individual from another are so tightly drawn that an individual is pictured as existing without any relationship with others. The individual's capacities and attributes owe nothing to any other individual or to any social relationship; they are his alone. . . . The individual owns his body and his capacities as pieces of property, just as he owns material property. According to this view, each individual can and must see the world and other individuals only from the perspective of his subjective

assessment of how best to protect his property, or, as it is often put, from the perspective of his self-interest.[26]

Contract establishes a "civil" society that exists exclusively in that public sphere. The public sphere is politically relevant; and the private is to one degree or another immunized against political intervention, and counted as irrelevant to public/political discourse. Prior to feminist intervention, the public was a sphere of activity where men ruled fraternally; and in the private sphere, men ruled individually. Feminists have produced many of the best analyses of this public-private dichotomy, because feminist critique focuses on domination that happens apart from the public, political gaze. The domination of *women*, who in the past, and to a great degree in the present, have been excluded from the public sphere except as consumers, happens most often in the intimate settings of the private sphere. This is what feminists meant when they said, "The personal is the political." The same thing can be paraphrased as "the *private* is the political," *political* referring to social power. In the contractarian origin myths, which are Euro-American *male* myths, there are no political subjects who are not adult white men. The private realm of the husband-headed nuclear family is where the women and children can be hidden from public view and politics. Rousseau admitted of prior social relations in his origin myth, highlighting the public-private split in an explicitly gendered way. "The education of women," he wrote, "should always be relative to that of men. To please, to be useful to us, to make us love and esteem them, to educate us when young, to take care of us when grown up, to advise, to console us, to render our lives easy and agreeable; these are the duties of women at all times, and what they should be taught in their infancy."[27]

The marriage contract is a good example of how the public-private dichotomy underwrites the alienable body. The woman is a "possessive individual," a theoretically disembodied *self* who owns her body, which she can then *exchange* as property. Her body is alienable. Its ownership can be transferred. In that moment, she is transferred from the public sphere, where her floating-ghost-self is recognized as a legal *equal*, and into the private sphere, where the legal gaze can no longer penetrate. Her existence in civil society is *covert, covered* by her husband.

While this account draws a good deal of attention to the exploitative nature of this exchange, the focus of this inquiry is how this concept operates in the world we routinely think of as *more* egalitarian. In particular, we now see "the right to privacy" as a kind of precious patrimony (it *is*,

26. Ibid., 55.
27. Rousseau, "Emile," 45.

in fact, passed down from men). When one begins to reflect on all the common dilemmas we already recognize around this separation of public and private—in family law, for example—we begin to appreciate how ideological this separation actually is, and how impossible it is to maintain in practical reality. The shell game between what is public and private serves to conceal the relations of power from the eyes of the law by constructing an ideological wall between them. This applies to the issue of marital rape, for example, once considered an oxymoron and only recently recognized in law; of freewheeling ("private") campaign contributions in public elections; and of "intellectual property." *Abstraction* in the social contract—the emancipation of an idea from its concrete instantiations—serves to simultaneously conceal and reproduce domination. The actual person must be abstracted for the law and custom to successfully embody the contractarian order. However many billions of us there are, the universalizing imperative that maintains the separation between public and private must find a way to account for them all equally. This is a problem, because equality, at least in the material sense, can never be anything except a fiction. Not only are actual individual people not equal, they are in many ways incomparable. Can we establish the basis for equality on strength, and if so, which kinds of strength? On mental capacity? What kind? On height, weight, language, age? It becomes discernible, once raising the question of what is the basis for equality, that the attributes of *actual* persons only have meaning in situated, concrete practices. Nonetheless, the self that stands before the public, before the law, cannot manifest any attribute that places her or him above or below or aside from any other person. One can be neither fat nor thin, neither old nor young, neither rich nor poor. S/He is—like the monstrosities of the Hobbesian origin myth—without either history or personal attachment. Feminists have shown how the subjugation of the woman in a *private* home is not counted as an instance of domination in the *public* sphere—the only sphere that liberalism affirms as politically relevant. Equality is served. So is fraternity. And this observation is applicable to other axes of power in the "private sector," where there has been an exchange of obedience for protection precisely at the dividing wall between public and private. The transferability of self, of the body, not only ensures that the legal ghost who owns the body has something akin to autonomy (the ideological account), it ensures that the same body can be transferred readily between the public sphere and the private based on a "right." We all have the *right* to sell ourselves.

Wage labor ("free labor") was the alternative to slavery during the American Civil War—free to work, but also free to starve in circumstances where lack of money means the inability to subsist. The idea of the alienable self was perfected in practice in conjunction with the state-sponsored construction of the self-regulating market described by Karl Polanyi.[28] Individuals could be shifted, using *want* as the impetus, from point to point in a meshwork of productive activity, where each contracted to exchange obedience for a prescribed time each day for protection from impoverishment in an ever more enclosed and *privatized* world.

We all have the (public) *right* to sell ourselves; but it's a buyer's (private) market.

The liberal schema transports alienability from the law into our lives. The self is adrift. Whether the self is seen as socially constructed or individually contained, it is uprooted—a ghost who puts on this or that role, like a garment. The self is that anxious presence of the existentialists, perfectly free but with no direction but will and no constraint except death, which always has the last word. In consumer society, the self is a ruthless master possessed of unlimited desire.

MacIntyre calls modern society "emotivist." Emotivism is the philosophical claim that all moral positions are equally valid or invalid, because all rational and moral convictions rest ultimately on some "subjective" emotional ground. This is a deeper claim than Descartes's about suspicious subjectivity, because it also denies God as an ultimate referent. And here is where we again encounter the question, raised at the end of the last chapter, about manipulation. In modern society, says MacIntyre, this emotivist stance has erased the difference between manipulative and nonmanipulative relations, leaving two dominant forces in tension with one another—uprooted individualism (I'll do what I want) and bureaucratic control (we have to maintain order). This tension defines and delimits the possibilities of modernity, and so he calls modern metropolitan society a system of "bureaucratic individualism."

> On the one side there appear the self-defined protagonists of individual liberty, on the other the self-defined protagonists of planning and regulation, of the goods that are available through bureaucratic organization. But in fact what is crucial is that on which the contending parties agree, namely that there are only two alternative modes of social life open to us, one in which the free and arbitrary choices of individuals are sovereign and one in which the bureaucracy is sovereign, precisely so that it may limit the free and arbitrary choices of individuals. Given this deep cultural agreement, it is unsurprising that the politics of

---

28. Polanyi, *Great Transformation*, 71–80.

modern societies oscillate between a freedom which is nothing but a lack of regulation of individual behavior and forms of collectivist control designed only to limit the anarchy of self-interest. The consequences of a victory by one side or the other are often of the highest importance; but . . . both ways of life are in the long run intolerable. Thus the society in which we live is one in which bureaucracy and individualism are partners as well as antagonists. And it is in the cultural climate of this bureaucratic individualism that the emotivist self is naturally at home.[29]

The therapist, a reference-point role in modernity, is the expert who can help get your "self" adjusted. The goal of much therapy is to be re-optimized, like having an emotional tune-up. We have all learned to *need to learn* how to be well-adjusted. Adjusted to what is a question that seldom gets raised, and adjusted *toward* what is asked still less frequently. The therapeutic profession—and this is not a reflection on all forms of therapy—once declared that women suffer from "hysteria," and now, via the Diagnostic and Statistical Manual V, calls the inability to read or do mathematics at a certain tested "level" a medical "disorder."[30] Self*hood*—which is not a political fiction like the disembodied contractarian self, but a real experience—is no longer conceivable in any integral way. The modern self is chopped up by the partitioning of our lives into discrete and unrelated activities, each compelling us to adopt a different and appropriate "role" (we have adapted the language of a theater performance for social psychology!) for each situation. The political fiction of the *individual* self is a causative agent in the fragmentation of the *experienced* self. It is difficult to hold together the idea of an autonomous self and the lived experience of interdependence. This contradiction invariably creates psychic conflict. Stripped of identity by ideology, in a society that routinely dis-embeds us and re-embeds us, we ourselves are easily *reduced* to consumers. We internalize that reduction. We attempt to live into it faithfully. People can pay now for "personality makeovers" in order to be more successful at job hunting. We are performing Hobbes. My autonomous self will *manipulate* your autonomous self in order to ensure that you do not interfere with my access to my self's autonomy.

MacIntyre says that we have lost the capacity to differentiate between manipulative and nonmanipulative relations. This reminds me of my own recent attempt to get a job. I researched the interview process online and found that the company directed its managers, when the job would *not* be offered, to tell the interviewee, "I have a few more interviews today, and

29. MacIntyre, *After Virtue*, 34–35.
30. "Recent Updates to the Proposed Revisions to the DSM-5."

we'll call you later." At the end of the interview, these exact words were used to dismiss me. And there was no call. There never is. It was a boilerplate lie that the manager was required to tell under these particular circumstances. It was a *manipulative* communication, but if you were to ask most people in this culture if it was morally reproachable, they would tell you that she was doing her job as directed and therefore had done nothing wrong. She obeyed the rules. There is no differentiation between manipulative and nonmanipulative actions, in large part because there can be no universal "standard of morality" independent of a tradition-based community.

The free-floating self is a self who is inoculated from responsibility for all that exceeds the reach of his arm. This is *Homo economicus*, "economic man," a wretched, lonesome creature beset by choices at every instant—and with no higher authority to tell her or him how to assess those choices, much less how to escape them. This is the "emotive" self. Economic man was initially constructed as an actual male. Only after social movements pointed to the hypocrisy of the gender-neutral language of liberalism did women seize from liberalism a share in this self-exploiting category, which might now be renamed "the economic (wo)man," women being an afterthought in the liberal tradition.

The abstracted person is an ideological device that makes a liberatory claim even as it serves continued domination. As Pateman shows, there is a powerful white man in the story who is normative. The actual domination is a private matter, a concern of the private *sector*.

This regime is enforced by the state, but the social power that is enforced operates prior to the state. The liberal state is an institution of power, not the sole source of power. It can send police to your door to arrest you if you violate its rules, and these police are legally entitled to use all necessary force to ensure your compliance. The state can dispatch armed forces to occupy another country, or order a bombing, or sign allegedly binding treaties with other states. The state can declare what money is valid for paying taxes, and it can make rules for commerce. It can recognize marriages and validate "ownership" of property. The state makes the laws that we are then bound to follow (or face the aforementioned force), and even has courts to interpret the laws—because, as we have seen, these laws can never anticipate the complexity of real life nor the kinds of social pressures that emerge during the constant evolution of society. This interpretive process in the courts is designed to ensure the stability of the state through its continued legitimation.

Prior to the action of the state, the boss exercises power *over* an employee, the parent exercises power *over* a child, many men exercise (social and economic) power *over* many women.³¹ The question of what the state is, and does, cannot be answered without assessing how the liberal state relates to these other forms of power.

The state is constituted by a government, the vast organization of people who administer and manage a state, which is overseen by members and representatives of the dominant class. In the United Sates, and most states today, this class is the business class. State government has an administrative staff, generally organized as a bureaucracy, and armed bodies designed to enforce laws and control populations internally and for response to "external threats," which include threats to the state's extra-territorial interests. The state has the power to make and interpret laws, and force its citizens and residents to comply with those laws, and the power to collect taxes in order to sustain itself as an organization.

A political *regime* is a set of agreed upon *principles, norms, rules and decision-making procedures*, which govern the actions of the state. The political regime includes both state and civil society; and it transcends governments. The Obama *government* replaced the Bush *government*, but the *regime* remained the same.

> Civil society should not be confused with the people. The people can be considered as all the citizens having equal rights; civil society is citizens organized and weighted according to the power of the groups and organizations they are a part of. The state formally exerts its power over civil society and over the people. Actually civil society is the real source of power for the state, as it establishes the limits and conditions for the exercise of state power.³²

Catharine MacKinnon developed a feminist critique of the state.³³ MacKinnon is a law professor who says, "Gender is a social system that divides power."³⁴ Gender is more than that, of course, and not reducible to that; but MacKinnon's focus is on the law, which is an exercise of *official* power. This is basic to understanding the law with regard to gender, because gender as a power division has the notion of *difference* at its core, with difference as the justification for domination.

---

31. I already anticipate the argument that women actually exercise power over men, but that is adaptive, defensive, and negotiated power that is *not* borne out by or reflected in any concrete indices of actual social, economic, or political power. It is remarkable how quickly many persons or groups who are in power and have that power challenged will portray themselves as subordinate, even as victims.

32. Bresser-Pereira, "State, Civil Society," para. 12.

33. MacKinnon, *Toward a Feminist Theory of the State*.

34. Ibid., 160.

In a few societies, the state still puts this gender difference-as-power at the center of its legal edifice, but in liberal states where the struggle by women for legal equality has gone on for some time, this question of difference has been challenged, not with absolute success, but with some significant changes. Women successfully achieved legal "equality" in some spheres. Women, then, are legally assumed to be the *same* as men, because the "individual" is legally without a biological sex and, more significantly, no longer recognized as a situated person in a culturally mediated gender regime. In this way, the law for the *abstractly equal* person does not recognize a pre-existing history of gendered social power or the existence of gender as cultural regime. Liberal law conceals (and often reproduces) concrete power *inequality* behind abstract political *equality*.

Anatole France famously said, "The law, in its majestic equality, forbids rich as well as poor from sleeping under bridges, begging in the streets, and stealing bread."[35]

Abstract legal equality refuses to see gender as an historically evolved social inequality that exists *prior to* the operation of the law. Most of the rules of behavior imposed on members of society are determined prior to and without state action. Women in the U.S. were regarded as extensions of men in the nineteenth century, denied control over personal decisions and property by marriage *coverture* into the twentieth century, denied the right to vote until after World War I. Many women and their male allies tried for ten hard years to get a simple equality amendment for women added to the Constitution, finally failing ratification in 1982. On average, women still make only three quarters of what men do in the U.S., and those numbers are dramatically more stratified when race is introduced into the calculations.

The social reality of perceived difference and material inequality is reflected inaccurately by the liberal state's legal assumption (in many instances) of sameness and equality. As in all forms of Jeffersonian liberalism, including libertarianism, it is intentionally ahistorical and intentionally blind to the "private sector." Both history and context embarrass abstraction, and liberal power inhabits abstraction.

The U.S. Constitution was written in such a way that it reflected existing conditions as natural and limited state intervention to the public sector—to civil affairs, leaving "nature" to itself. Male power was assumed. White power was assumed. Propertied power was assumed. Every incursion against those power systems by the state itself was propelled not from within the state, but from without, by social movements.

---

35. France, *Red Lily*, 95.

Origin Myths

MacKinnon calls ours the neutral or "negative" state. It has a preponderance of "Thou shall nots," the Bill of Rights being a good example. Since state power is erected *upon* prior-to-the-law social power, just as we can call the U.S. liberal state a "capitalist" state,[36] we can call it a male state. The "neutral" state professes neutrality, objectivity. The state claims to be a neutral arbiter of abstract equality, and thus sidesteps the issue of concrete inequality, pushing power inequality *into nature or privacy*, assuming itself out of any prerogative to intervene. The negative state is the liberal state that says what the state shall *not* do—no laws shall be made abridging this freedom or that freedom—which can then only meaningfully apply to those who already have the material means to exercise these freedoms. As A. J. Liebling quipped, "Freedom of the press is guaranteed only to those who own one."[37] The liberal state's legal episteme is neutral only in its refusal to consider *actual* inequality. This requires that we are all complicit in maintaining this fiction, which we generally do, because it has become common sense. Its fictional quality has been rendered invisible by ideology that is taught in civics classes in state-run, compulsory public schools.

> Unlike the ways in which men systematically enslave, violate, dehumanize, and exterminate other men, men's forms of dominance over women have been accomplished socially as well as economically prior to the operation of law, without express state acts, often in intimate contexts, as everyday life.[38]

If the liberal state is prohibited from intervening in affairs declared private (the basis for tacit state support for domestic abuse until well into the twentieth century—"a man's home is his castle"), and if the private or civil sphere is the sphere in which male power is most directly exercised, then the state simply forecloses a political solution to that system of unequal power. This is also the contradiction in the liberal state and the liberal conception of law that allows white men to sue for "reverse discrimination" and that equates corporate campaign spending during elections with "free speech." Power that exists prior to the operation of law is legally denied.

The disembodied self within this intractable system of power often *feels* vacant, because this self has *been* vacated in both epistemology and law. Consumption fills the void. Compulsive consumption becomes a displacement activity in the face of what can only appear as overwhelming inertia or chaos. The incoherence of modern culture appears orderly, because this

---

36. Nothing in law declares the United States to be "capitalist."

37. Liebling, "Freedom of the Press," quoted by Cohen, "Surviving without Newspapers," para. 3.

38. MacKinnon, *Toward a Feminist Theogy*, 161.

displacement activity of consumption is *ordering* our activity. Work. Spend. Sleep. Repeat. Gendered power has also been subsumed into the consumer order, one that is largely in the private domain. Men are measured by their big toys; women are measured by sex appeal (to men)—sex appeal equated with the demobilization of women (e.g., on spiked heels), the silencing of women, the infantilization of women (e.g., the pressure to rid women of body hair), the sexual availability of women, and the marginalization of women who are for whatever reason not perceived as sexually desirable.

This is liberation.

The production of desire is necessary to sustain this order's displacement behaviors and its myth of infinite growth. Economic (wo)man is a creature driven by desire. This ghost-robot alliance, alas, is *self*-referential in every way, entrained to be so by a lifetime of highly sophisticated, electronic propaganda, all aimed at producing a dual idea in each of us: desire is infinite, and happiness consists in the satisfaction of desires. Then you die.[39]

In contractarian society, I have a *right* to my desires, and an uninflected *right* to seek their satisfaction. I am a rights-bearing, history-free, abstract individual, and I can buy whatever I want. It's a free country. Whether my relations with others are manipulative or nonmanipulative makes no difference, because this is no longer a recognizable distinction. We are theorized into the condition of lab rats who have been overstimulated into a state of chronic aggression. Consumerism comes down to entitled selves. Desire that you have a right to quench becomes desire as the prison of manufactured obsession. My *self* has a legal right to get as much as I can for me, to do whatever feels good to me, to base my perceptions of the universe on me. I am now the perfect political being, the perfect strategic being, the singular redoubt of internality, surrounded by externalities, asserting my *self* against all those other selves. I am become the Hobbesian monstrosity. I am now living in a permanent war-episteme, in de Certeau's strategic fortress. My autonomous self will manipulate your autonomous self in order to ensure that you do not interfere with my access to my self's autonomy.

Of course, we are not that, even when we desperately try to behave as if we are. If humans need love and need to belong, and I believe they do, then a self-indulgent consumer society injures us, fragments us, alienates us. More than that, it enslaves us. Ivan Illich said, "In a consumer society there are inevitably two kinds of slaves: the prisoners of addiction and the

---

39. Here is the rub; and so we are encouraged to ignore and deny death, to pretend there is no such thing.

prisoners of envy."[40] In this, at least, liberalism has managed to achieve a kind of sexual equality.

What liberal civil society brings into being is a state that is prohibited from looking at any of its actual, embodied citizens, in the interest of preserving order among all its citizens through the application of laws written in the sterile language of the technocrat. There are the rules, such as they are, and each citizen will theoretically be measured against the rules themselves with no account of any difference between citizens. Power is safely concealed behind the privacy wall, for good or ill. We are habituated to this condition, so much so that it can seem strange to believe that things could be otherwise; and yet, as Christians, we are called to be strange in exactly that way.

Since there are multiple and influential ethical frameworks at work in modern metropolitan society, and since these frameworks are incommensurable, the solution is to refuse any public ethical stance at all (which, it turns out, is not possible). The social contract has given rise to the denial of any difference between manipulative and nonmanipulative relations. This is an entirely inadequate framework for Christians, whose prime directive is to love the neighbor, because love and manipulation—the reduction of the other to an object to serve one's own ends—are antithetical.

> Contemporary moral experience . . . has a paradoxical nature. For each of us is taught to see himself or herself as an autonomous moral agent; but each of us also becomes engaged by modes of practice, aesthetic or bureaucratic, which involve us in manipulative relationships with others. Seeking to protect the autonomy that we have learned to prize, we aspire ourselves *not* to be manipulated by others; seeking to incarnate our own principles and stand-point in the world of practice, we find no way open to us to do so except by directing toward others those very manipulative modes of relationship which each of us aspires to resist in our own case. The incoherence of our attitudes and our experience arises from the incoherent conceptual scheme which we have inherited.[41]

In a morally incoherent society, says MacIntyre, where there are multiple ethical frameworks operating that are not even comparable on their own terms, public debate devolves into assertion and counter-assertion, because there is no authoritative foundation of shared premises for the assessment of incommensurable truth claims. The assumption is that truth

40. Illich, *Tools for Conviviality*, 47.
41. MacIntyre, *After Virtue*, 68.

and ethical action *cannot be determined* in the public sphere, and that these are private preoccupations. The public sphere must, therefore, attempt to establish standards, policies, and laws that are impersonal, transcending the personal; yet there is only a reduction to the theoretical common denominator of moral behavior being in the eye of the beholder. This is unrealizable in actual society, and defaults to bureaucratic rule. Still, it retains its ideological force in both custom and law. This is the essence of "emotivism":

> Emotivism is the doctrine that all evaluative judgments and more specifically all moral judgments are nothing but expressions of preference, expressions of attitude or feeling, insofar as they are moral or evaluative in character.[42]

Domination shifts from the public to the private; the public sphere then goes blind.

> They came to Bethsaida, and some people brought a blind man and begged Jesus to touch him. He took the blind man by the hand and led him outside the village. When he had spit on the man's eyes and put his hands on him, Jesus asked, "Do you see anything?"
> He looked up and said, "I see people; they look like trees walking around."
> Once more Jesus put his hands on the man's eyes. Then his eyes were opened, his sight was restored, and he saw everything clearly. Jesus sent him home, saying, "Don't even go into the village." (Mark 8:22–26)

What happens to the idea and experience of self in a world where one is *obliged by custom and accepted practice* to objectify others and manipulate them? Skill at the manipulation of others is actually a handsomely rewarded profession now. What is the price we pay for this form of "autonomy"? This is surely a sinful condition, and just as surely a sinful idea—a betrayal of the very essence of *agape*. This spiritual impoverishment has come to *define* our social landscape.

It is the antithesis of the Beatitudes. Self versus selves.

The normative self now is what the broken or deficient self was in the past—the self-centeredness of the venal and the immature transformed into virtue—which is the satisfaction and constant re-creation of desire. *Ram tough! Pantene, because I'm worth it!*

42. Ibid., 11–12.

Welcome, Economic (Wo)Man, to liberal equality.

What is the price we pay for this equality, as men and as women? As dominators, as dominated? Read on.

21

Paradox of Domination

"Gender"... has challenged and in part overthrown the received wisdom in social, cultural, and political history. No longer can masculinity confidently be located in specifically "masculine" contexts of work, family, and homosocial networks. Its discursive traces are to be found in every area of culture and society...[1]

—John Tosh

Perhaps it is because this conception of the individual reflects a powerful experience... the experience of a paradox as painful, or even intolerable. Perhaps also, because of a continuing fear that dependency on the other is a threat to independence, that recognition of the other comprises the self. When the conflict between dependence and independence becomes too intense, the psyche gives up the paradox in favor of an opposition.[2]

—Jessica Benjamin

Mutuality exists in tension. The absence of tension is, finally, death.

1. Tosh, "Hegemonic Masculinity," 41.
2. Benjamin, *Bonds of Love*, 50.

War is violence organized for collective domination. The question is called in combat: who will prevail and who will be vanquished? In liberal society, this question is sublimated, where every conquest is not a matter of life or death, though imposing one's will is the goal of manipulative relations. Domination is central to our overall discussion of war, church, and masculinity. As contentious as psychological and psychoanalytic theories are, our discussion of domination requires some account of the psychology of domination.

In Dostoyevsky's *The Brothers Karamozov*, two brothers, Ivan and Alyosha, have a conversation. Alyosha is a monk, and Ivan is an atheist raising questions about God and church to challenge his brother. Ivan tells Alyosha a story about Jesus returning to earth in Seville during the Spanish Inquisition. In the story, Jesus performs miracles, arousing the love of the people, and just as happened in the Gospels, Jesus is arrested—this time by the church, by the inquisitors—and sentenced to be burned at the stake. The Grand Inquisitor interviews Jesus the night before the scheduled execution. The Inquisitor tells Jesus that he has disrupted the activity of the church, explaining to Jesus that he had made a mistake when he was being tempted in the wilderness (Matt 4:1–11). The three temptations of the evil one are to turn stones to bread, to survive being thrown off the temple wall, and to have all the kingdoms of earth bow before him. The Inquisitor says they are all the same temptation—the temptation to political domination. Feed the people and they will be still. Dazzle them with magic and they will be awestruck. Control them through force, and they can be redeemed whether they like it or not. The people are weak and stupid, explains the Grand Inquisitor to Jesus; he never really understood human nature. Ivan tells Alyosha that the Grand Inquisitor is actually an atheist, like Ivan, but that he has chosen for the good of humanity to raise up the church's power over this chaotic species. The devil was right, says the Inquisitor. The spirit of death and destruction—that is, domination and conquest—is necessary to control humankind.

"We are not with Thee, but with [the devil], and that is our secret! For centuries have we abandoned Thee to follow him."

At the end of Ivan's story, Christ kisses the Inquisitor on the mouth, and the Inquisitor releases Him.

When Ivan finishes his story, he asks if Alyosha is now done with him; will he renounce Ivan as his brother? Alyosha kisses his brother on the mouth. Ivan says, "That's plagiarism."[3]

The church meets Hobbes, but in Dostoevsky—even in Ivan the unbeliever—Hobbes has to stand before Christ.

We saw in the last chapter that some of the criticisms of liberalism raised by postliberal Christians are shared by feminists. The radical feminist tradition is a standpoint preoccupied with the intersection of gender and political domination. Politics is power. Power is politics.

Politics is more than mere power, however; it is collective action in the name of a community, including the rules and norms that govern collective action and give it direction, coherence, and stability. The term originates in *polis*, Greek for "city," and *polites*, "citizens of the city." A citizen is one who is entitled to participate in decision-making that affects the whole city. In that Greek city, free men were political agents, and women were excluded. And giving the radical feminists their due, violent domination is used to control the politics of all societies *beyond a certain scale*. If politics is about collective action in the name of a community, then those actions might originate in either "concordant or discordant dispositions."[4] If people achieve a level of consensus, or *concordance*, decisions taken together do not require one person or group to impose its will on others by force to achieve that collective action. If there is *discord* over what collective action needs to be taken or how it is to be accomplished, then one person or group must impose its will by force on the rest of the polity. In some cases, there can be mutual agreement that all will comply voluntarily with the will of a majority when there is an impasse in decision-making. A committee of ten might agree to such an arrangement, in which six people will agree on a solution, and the other four will see it done, even though they continue to disagree. This option forecloses force, or violence, as the means to achieve collective action—unless this process is to determine who will control the means of force, in which case the agreement to abide by a certain majority is a truce among decision-makers, leaving force in the hands of the hypothetical 51 percent to employ against those who refuse to go along. This is the model of representative democracy.

---

3. Dostoyevsky, *Brothers Karamozov*, ch. 5.
4. Howes, *Toward a Credible Pacifism*, 88.

Paradox of Domination

Carl Philipp Gottfried von Clausewitz (1780–1831) articulated "principles of war" that are still taught to military officers today. His principles were purely instrumental. They were formulated for winning battles and campaigns, full stop. The reasons for war were immaterial to him. He was a specialist. Determinations about the moral character of the war are outsourced to the state. As Alfred Lord Tennyson would write, "Theirs not to reason why, theirs but to do and die."[5]

Clausewitz:

> Each strives by physical force to compel the other to submit to his will: his first object is to throw his adversary, and thus to render him incapable of further resistance.
>
> *War therefore is an act of violence to compel our opponent to fulfill our will.*
>
> Violence arms itself with the inventions of Art and Science in order to contend against violence. Self-imposed restrictions, almost imperceptible and hardly worth mentioning, termed usages of International Law, accompany it without essentially impairing its power. Violence, that is to say physical force (for there is no moral force without the conception of states and law), is therefore the *means*; the compulsory submission of the enemy to our will is the ultimate *object*. In order to attain this object fully, the enemy must be disarmed; and this is, correctly speaking, the real aim of hostilities in theory. It takes the place of the final object, and puts it aside in a manner as something not properly belonging to war.[6]

Physical force, violence, is applied against the bodies of others to make them submit or to destroy them—the essence of domination, and its ultimate form. "There is no moral force without . . . states and law." I remember that old ad against drug abuse: "This is your mind; this is your mind on drugs." *This is your war; this is your war on Hobbes.*

The enemy is a key aspect of the *object*. When I was a soldier who made operational plans, every "mission" was stated with an "objective." In a world without distinction between manipulative and nonmanipulative relations, all others are potentially reduced to objects—means to an end. This is man-thought. Jessica Benjamin's psychoanalytic criticism unmasks the gendered "genesis of the psychic structure in which one person plays subject and the other must serve as object."[7]

---

5. Tennyson, "Charge of the Light Brigade," lines 14–15.
6. Clausewitz, *On War*, bk. I, ch. 1, pt. 2.
7. Benjamin, *Bonds of Love*, 7.

> The point of departure ... is ... that woman functions as man's primary other, his opposite—playing nature to his reason, immanence to his transcendence, primordial oneness to his individuated separateness, and object to his subject. ... Gender polarity underlies such familiar dualisms as autonomy and dependency, and thus establishes the coordinates for the position of master and slave.[8]

Earlier, I said that "violence works." While this is one of the reasons that violence is employed, it is equally important that violence sometimes does *not* work. Sometimes violence creates a result contrary to the intent of the one who initiates it *and* contrary to the intent of the defender. Still, we see people, especially men, use violence without any guarantee of its "working"; and we see war continue even when it does not "work," or succeed in its *objectives*.

The United States, with its overwhelming military technical superiority, has had an abysmal record of political success with war in recent years. Despite killing more than two million Vietnamese and destroying millions of acres of land, the United States was defeated in Vietnam. It was stalemated in Korea. It was defeated again in Iraq, and again now in Afghanistan. Bush attempted regime change in Iraq and inadvertently won the Iran-Iraq War (which everyone thought was past) ... on behalf of Iran.

Rawls, Nozick, Locke, Rousseau, and Hobbes all employed foundational myths to justify their views on economics and justice. There is also a foundational myth routinely used for war. The myth is that there is an aggressor against innocents or one's own people that must be stopped; therefore the war is just. Hitler employed this story; but so has every other belligerent in the wars of the twentieth and twenty-first centuries.[9] As we saw in chapter 19, lying for strategic or political deception is endemic to war. And while there is sometimes a grain of truth in the war lie, the actual motives for war are always more complex and less transcendent. Power and pragmatism generally trump justice.

There is a real element of gamesmanship in the predisposition of men in power to employ war as "politics by other means."[10] Given the sketchy record of success in war and its utter unpredictability, we have to return to the discomfiting possibility, stated earlier, that some men *love* war. Given the popularity of war games, it is safe to say that a lot of men love war, or at least the idea of war. Two of the most popular pastimes for metropolitan

---

8. Ibid.
9. Also during the Crusades.
10. Clausewitz, *On War*.

Paradox of Domination 235

men of all ages, when they find themselves alone with their computers, are war games and pornography. Both have become subjects for the study of addiction.

In following chapters, we will look at the development of liberal masculinity and war at the end of the nineteenth century and beginning of the twentieth. A watershed event in this period was the development of a new conceptual framework for inquiring into human motivations—psychoanalysis.

> It was Freud's achievement to discover that unmasking arbitrariness in others may always be a defence against uncovering it in ourselves. . . . Educated men and women had internalized what they aspired to reject. . . . But even more important was Freud's presentation of the inherited conscience as superego, as an irrational part of ourselves whose commands we need, for the sake of our psychic health, to be freed from.[11]

Sigmund Freud succeeded in introducing a new episteme into metropolitan Atlantic culture:[12] psychoanalysis. To this day, we use Freudian terminology in our everyday speech. We talk about "ego" and "Freudian slips" and the "subconscious" all the time. Above, I used the word *sublimated*.

While psychology has gained a few insights into the psychic life of the individual, it has also imposed new epistemes on the psyche and medicalized human actions.[13] One well-known example is the debate over something called Attention Deficit Hyperactivity Disorder (ADHD). More than 10 percent of American schoolchildren have been diagnosed with this "disorder," and most are using prescription drugs to "control" it.[14] The symptoms of this alleged disorder are inattentiveness and impulsivity. Most children diagnosed with ADHD see those "symptoms" ameliorated without drugs as they get older. Critics say that inattentiveness and impulsivity are characteristics of young people that are ameliorated in the process of maturation, that this is not a disorder at all, as most kids are to one degree or another inattentive and impulsive. Differences in degree are simply differences in individual children, part of our natural diversity. Inattentiveness and impulsivity are problematic because the children who are more inattentive and impulsive are more difficult to control in a classroom environment. In effect, say critics, we are drugging children to conform to an artificial en-

11. MacIntyre, *After Virtue*, 72.

12. This includes white Australia, for example, even though it is not, geographically, Atlantic. It is still a culture that resembles the Euro-North American culture in significant ways.

13. Medicalization is treating a previously nonmedical condition or problem as if it requires medical intervention by a credentialed monopoly of professionals.

14. Preidt, "ADHD."

vironment, a school, and calling *failure to conform* a medical issue requiring professional therapeutic intervention. Whether you agree with these critics or not, this is an example of *medicalization*.[15]

There is a danger in using "medicine," referring here to a credentialed professional monopoly, as a way of enforcing social norms by calling them health *disorders*. In the Soviet Union, psychiatric diagnoses were frequently used as pretexts for locking up people who were considered political threats, and there are questionable involuntary commitments to institutions in the West even today. Women, in the past, were committed to institutions for "hysteria," which often meant behaving in ways inconsistent with male rule. There is also a philosophical dilemma raised by medicalization used to assert a kind of biological determinism, which might be used either to evade responsibility for certain actions or to foreclose the possibility of personal change. Finally, there is the danger of opportunism in using more and more diagnoses as the pretext for peddling profitable new drugs.[16]

15. Duden, *Woman Beneath the Skin*, 18. Medicalization corresponds to the emergence of the "modern body," which Duden also calls the "industrial body." "The industrial body," she remarks, "stands as the focal point of a powerful and diverse service organization" (ibid., 7)—an organization of which the medical monopoly is a part. "A violent process began in the seventeenth century, one in which the body as the embodiment of localized social vitality was symbolically broken: in the witch trials the body of woman was demonized, de-atomized on the scaffold; by being displayed as an anatomical patchwork, it was deprived of its meaningful opacity. Before the body could be constituted as the object of descriptive observation, it first had to be devalued as a vehicle of symbolic meaning" (ibid., 10). She goes on to explain, "This body, the vague corporeality of popular culture, became offensive in the course of the eighteenth century—increasingly so as the new creation of a 'bourgeois body' progressed. . . . Labor was only very gradually discovered as an economic value, not merely as a precondition for the processing of goods, but as a scarce resource, a factor in the competition among nations. The subject body thus acquired economic value. . . . His life span and his physical ability to work became statistically measurable quantities of the national economy. . . . The rising class, the bourgeoisie, developed the embodiment of the individual. . . . New medical insights contributed only indirectly to this creation of a new physical-moral economy of the body, yet they did arise in a close interaction with the basic social patterns" (ibid., 13). "Medical policy was intended to protect the state from 'wasting an instrument of the body politic.' The 'catechization of health' became necessary to impart to the state and the burgher a new view of the body: 'Whoever neglects the precious treasure of health offends all of society'" (ibid., 18).

16. With those caveats, I am not saying that there is no place for medicine, that there are no diagnostic norms against which health can be measured, or that there are not sometimes organic reasons for problematic behavior. I take an opioid for an occasionally inflamed gall bladder, and the medication ameliorates the very real pain—a good thing. There is little doubt that certain cardiac arrhythmias are an indication that someone is in danger. Murder committed by someone who is severely schizophrenic—that is, someone who hallucinates and is organically incapable of rational thought—is morally distinguishable from someone who commits murder out of greed, revenge, or jealousy.

Ivan Illich describes institutional developments as having two watersheds: one in which the institution and its practice begins actually improving things, and another in which it begins to create as much mischief as it resolves.[17] At some point in the practice of medicine, doctors started saving more people than they killed. At another point, the paradigm of medicine extends itself into realms of existence where it creates mischief, like drugging children so they can attend a compulsory state institution. I want to emphasize this business of medicalization now, because we are about to look at the development of ideas about psychoanalysis, psychology, psychiatry, and psychotherapy that can exist anywhere between or beyond these two watersheds, that of improving understanding and intervention and that of becoming iatrogenic.[18]

There is an additional danger of *totalization* in studying people from a psychoanalytic standpoint, of beginning to believe that this is the ultimate standpoint of knowledge and that psychodynamic processes are universal, that is, that they operate apart from specific times, places, and cultures. Freud was not universal. He was a bourgeois European male.

> Freud conceptualized "libido" as a psychic energy, and he did so with concepts and terms adopted, in part verbatim, from Helmholtz.[19] He linked the body to the new mythology of energy, which was assuming a central place in the sciences in the wake of discoveries in physics. Just as "reproduction" had embedded the body of women into the context of labor force, and as earlier notions about the waste of bodily strength through ejaculation during intercourse had embedded it in a "spermatic economy," physics manifested itself within the body as "sexuality."[20]

Psychoanalysis began in Europe and became influential in Europe and the United States at the same time that these Atlantic states were becoming influential throughout the world. Psychoanalysis was ethnocentric, though with globalization under American auspices, the epistemes that had their origins in Europe and the United States are now becoming hegemonic

---

17. Illich, *Tools for Conviviality*, 1-5. Illich calls this the watershed of "counterproductivity."

18. Iatrogenesis generally refers to preventable harm caused by a medical treatment. One goes to the hospital to have her tonsils taken out, in one example, and gets a staph infection from someone or something in the hospital—or in another example, antibiotic resistance. Here I use it in these senses, but also as a broader analogy: sometimes the treatment is worse than what it cures.

19. Hermann Ludwig Ferdinand von Helmholtz (1821–94), a German physician and physicist.

20. Duden, *Woman Beneath the Skin*, 29.

elsewhere. The psychodynamics described are not *natural*, even if their terms of reference have achieved a dubious catholicity.

With those warnings in place, we can begin with Freud and with a criticism of Freud by feminist psychoanalyst Jessica Benjamin.

By the end of the nineteenth century, the philosophical primacy of the "individual" was widely accepted, especially as that individual was described in the Hobbesian origin myth, a predator in a war of all against all. The social contract had given rise to the Leviathan, the sovereign state, which secured a peace against human predispositions with the possibility of improvement, which was called *civilization*. The individual was a lone wolf who had to be domesticated for his own good. The thing within humans that required domestication—as it had been since the fathers of the Enlightenment said so—was called *nature*, now internalized as *human* nature. Nature, a dangerous and chaotic force that held greater sway in women and brown people, called for reason ruled by European male objectivity to subdue it. Freud interiorized this drama as a set of competing psychic phantoms: instinctual drive, ego, and superego. The instinctual drive was the wolf, the animal appetites. The ego was the I-ness, the enclosed sense of self, which bargained between the instinctual drives and the superego. The superego was the conscience, that interiorized cop, the *forum internum* that the church had invented for its members in the thirteenth century to make them fit citizens of the *societas perfecta*.[21]

Freud:

> Men are not gentle, friendly creatures wishing for love, who simply defend themselves if they are attacked, but that a powerful measure of desire for aggression has to be reckoned as part of their instinctual endowment. The result is that their neighbor is to them not only a possible helper or sexual object, but also a temptation to them to gratify their aggressiveness on him, to exploit his capacity for work without recompense, to use him sexually without his consent, to seize his possessions, to humiliate him, to cause him pain, to torture and to kill him. *Homo homini lupus*; who has the courage to dispute it in the face of all the evidence in his own life and in history? This aggressive cruelty usually lies in wait for some provocation, or else it steps into the service of some other purpose, the aim of which might as well have been achieved by milder measures. In circumstances that favor it, when those forces in the mind which ordinarily inhibit

---

21. Illich, *Rivers North of the Future*, 92–93.

it cease to operate, it also manifests itself spontaneously and reveals men as savage beasts to whom the thought of sparing their own kind is alien. Anyone who calls to mind the atrocities of the early migrations, of the invasion by the Huns or by the so-called Mongols under Jenghiz Khan and Tamurlane, of the sack of Jerusalem by the pious Crusaders, even indeed the horrors of the last world-war, will have to bow his head humbly before the truth of this view of man.[22]

MacIntyre said that Freud unmasked our unmasking as projections of ourselves. The context of his remark is the failure of modernity manifest in the *emotivist self* to establish any universally acceptable basis for moral decision-making, based on the incommensurable premises between contending rootless "individuals." Said differently, society had become a collection of "discordant dispositions," necessitating bureaucratic control. Freud's accomplishment, according to MacIntyre, was to explain why the unmasking of one position by the other is seemingly interminable. There was no *rational* basis any longer for asserting a moral position. Each of us is the captive of preconscious desires in conflict with irrational but necessary superegos. MacIntyre goes on to say that Freud was mistaken in his belief that he had made some moral discovery, rather than creating an insight about the ramifications of the emotive self.[23]

Benjamin's criticism of Freud is based on Freud's implicit acceptance of the *Homo economicus*—in Freud's more feral version above, *Homo homini lupus*, a wolf man[24]—a pure strategic being, trapped inside the boundaries of his redoubt, himself the subject and the world his object. Benjamin calls this approach to psychoanalysis *intrapsychic*, and against it she proposes a model of psychic life that is fundamentally social, between subjects, not between subject and objects. This approach is called *intersubjective*.

> The intersubjective view, as distinguished from the intrapsychic, refers to what happens in the field of self and other. Whereas the intrapsychic perspective conceives of the person as a discrete unit with a complex internal structure, intersubjective theory describes capacities that emerge in the interaction between self and others. Thus intersubjective theory, even when describing the self alone, sees its aloneness as a particular point in the

---

22. Freud, *Civilization and Its Discontents*, 58.
23. MacIntyre, *After Virtue*, 72.
24. Actual wolves are quite sociable and cooperative.

spectrum of relationships rather than as the original, "natural state" of the individual.[25]

The term *intersubjectivity* was coined by Jürgen Habermas.[26] Benjamin's thesis begins with the human need for *recognition*. Human beings have a need to belong. They need to be with other people, and they need to be recognized by them as well as granting recognition. Synonyms for *recognition* in common speech include *acceptance, affirmation, validation,* and *love*. Recognition is mutual. Both of us need to do it at once. For you to recognize me, I need to acknowledge you as a subject like myself, and vice versa. Research with mothers and infants shows that this *mutuality* begins very early. Unlike the object-relations approach of intrapsychic analysis, the child is not merely an appetite aimed at a breast or seeking warmth. The child and mother actually recognize one another. An infant in short order knows the sight, smell, and sound of his or her mother and takes pleasure in her presence beyond the mere satisfaction of appetites.[27]

In this mutuality, psychic boundaries are necessarily permeable; therefore there is an element of vulnerability. There is also an element of self-assertion. Self-assertion exists *in tension* with the desire for mutuality when we simultaneously recognize another and want something from him or her. When that tension, or balance, is broken by the *polarization* of self-assertion and vulnerability between two people, the love that is constituted in mutuality—in *fusion*, as Hartsock puts it—gives itself over to a dynamic of domination. Benjamin emphasizes this dynamic in her study of sadomasochistic relations, when "the inability to sustain paradox . . . convert[s] the exchange of recognition into domination and submission."[28]

The "fit" that Illich describes in the encounter between the Samaritan and the robbed and beaten Jew (Luke 10:25–37) is that mutuality, which in the parable transgresses social boundaries, renders them permeable with love. It is the paradox that you are mine and still you, and I am yours and still me. Beck talks about love as the permeability of boundaries in the context of disgust psychology, saying, "Love is on the *inside* of the symbolic self."[29] This intersubjective dynamic creates a situation in which "the other plays an active part in the struggle of the individual to creatively discover and accept reality."[30] Refusal to accept reality can disrupt intersubjectivity,

25. Benjamin, *Bonds of Love*, 20.
26. Habermas, *Time of Transitions*, 150–51.
27. Benjamin, *Bonds of Love*, 13.
28. Ibid., 12.
29. Beck, *Unclean*, 86.
30. Ibid., 45.

and failure of mutual recognition makes acceptance impossible. Referring to Hegel, Benjamin summarizes this paradox as the simultaneous need for the "independence and dependence of the self-conscious."[31] In Hegel, this is a struggle to the death that leads to a master-slave relation, because in Hegel, as in Freud and Hobbes, mutuality is foreclosed by a view of the person as a strategic being. Benjamin allows for a *tension* between independence and dependence in which mutuality is possible.

Part of this tension is the fact that the other person is *held in my mind* in a way that never completely accords with the other person's own experience of existence. This can produce expectations, the frustration of expectations, misunderstandings. In a sense, the other person must continually be destroyed *in my mind*, then observed to have survived that destruction in order for me to reassure myself of her existence, an existence that makes recognition possible. Her independence is necessary for her to recognize me, subject to subject. Yet the way I know she is independent is by challenging her independence through my own self-assertion.

We have all experienced this tension with our children, our friends, our lovers, our spouses, or our parents. When this dynamic involves a ready state of forgiveness, of starting over, power is negotiated and mutuality is retained. When one ego has to prevail and another submit, mutuality is lost and a domination-submission dynamic replaces it. The submissive then desires revenge. The dominator loses recognition, because his objectification of the other out of a desire for *omnipotence* (also the original sin) has erased the subjectivity necessary for mutual recognition.

If one asserts his will, destroying the other *in his mind*, and the other survives without becoming combative, without pitting the two egos against one another, then rapprochement is possible. Serial experiences of rapprochement lead to attunement, and the earliest experiences of attunement—usually between mother and child, but now a little more often including the father—are bound to the development and experience of the erotic, that psychosomatic sense of deep attachment.

The erotic here does not mean simply sexual feeling, but the experience of oneness, which presupposes the permeability of boundaries. Children who are raised in a zero-sum atmosphere of parental omnipotence form powerful defensive psychic boundaries early, which can lead to abject submission accompanied by feelings of vengefulness and resentment. They often have difficulty later in life forming relationships characterized by mutuality. On the other hand, children who experience attunement, which is a balance of self-assertion and recognition (*not* permissiveness),

---

31. Quoted in Benjamin, *Bonds of Love*, 32.

are habituated to the practices of mutuality. Erotic attachments later in life, which can include sexual attraction, are likely to reflect these early experiences of attachment; and some will tend toward attunement, while others will tend toward the domination-submission dynamic. While this is not a perfectly predictable pattern, the sons of men who abused the boys' mothers are more likely to abuse their partners, and the daughters of men who abused the girls' mothers are more likely to neglect or abuse their children.[32]

As we have seen already, masculinity constructed as domination eroticizes violence. A tragic paradox here is that women in a society where masculinity is constructed as domination are indoctrinated to find dominance in men sexually attractive, which makes Benjamin's study of the domination-submission dynamic, as opposed to simply domination, so important. In war, where domination masculinity is given its freest reign, there is also an extreme submission to authority, the fear and adoration of dominant figures. This might be anything from an admired infantry squad leader to the Führer. If we cannot understand the submission half of this dynamic, we cannot fully grasp the power of domination and its relation to the persistence of conquest-masculinity.

> Even the most sophisticated feminist thinkers frequently shy away from the analysis of submission, for fear that in admitting woman's participation in the relationship of domination, the onus of responsibility will appear to shift from men to women, and the moral victory from women to men. More generally, this has been a weakness of radical politics: to idealize the oppressed, as if their politics and culture were untouched by the system of domination, as if people did not participate in their own submission. To reduce domination to a simple relation of doer and done-to is to substitute moral outrage for analysis. Such a simplification, moreover, reproduces the structure of gender polarity under the guise of attacking it.[33]

While I agree with Benjamin as far as she goes here, I am also uncomfortable with the notion of participation in one's own submission—but because this analysis flirts with one of the dangers I listed above, that of privileging the analysis of the psychodynamic above an understanding of the social conditions that give rise to and reproduce them. Both the psychology and the sociology are important, and they are in practical reality inextricable from one another, divided and categorized only for the purpose

---

32. Rosenberg and Wilcox, "The Importance of Fathers."
33. Benjamin, *Bonds of Love*, 9–10.

of analysis.[34] Benjamin's point, well taken, is that there is more here than simply politics and power. The need for recognition, which is powerfully primal, projects us into domination-submission dynamics without our understanding why we act in the ways we do. There are two sides to this breakdown of mutuality. Both pay a price in the loss of mutuality.[35] This domination-submission dynamic pertains to men's attitudes toward women and to men's submission to authority in the practice of war, as well as the worship of authority in militaristic societies.

In gangster films and urban crime films, we often see violent men in search of something called "respect." This conceit is a clarified artistic version of the relationship between the desire for recognition and the desire for omnipotence coalesced into a domination dynamic. The "man of respect" in the gangster genre is actually a man who is feared. He is admired, too, but for his capacity to create fear. If you fail to recognize him, that is, give him his due respect, he might hurt you or kill you. The problem for this man is that he can never know mutuality. At the same time that he asserts himself through the desire for omnipotence, he forecloses the possibility that the other can *see* him in the same way that we described in the parable of the Good Samaritan or the relationship between close friends: I am yours and still mine, you are mine and still yours.

"Do you *see* this woman?" is a question that takes on special relevance in this light.

This domination-respect is an *anti*-erotic connection. One's sense of belonging does not entail contact, or *fusion*, presupposing the permeability of one's boundaries. There is not the vulnerability of love, but a world seen through a bulletproof one-way mirror.

Benjamin notes that in Freud, the origins of domination are understood as an Oedipal conflict, a primal conflict between son and father. This is not surprising, because Freud inherited a modern society that was only recently a result of republican conflicts that were regarded in exactly that way, as we saw in Pateman. In Freud's psychic origin myth, the son overthrows the father, but then his fear of the lawlessness of his own son compels

---

34. It is not for me to suggest how women will find their various ways out of this dilemma; but I will say that the way out may begin with women refusing to see themselves through men's eyes and refusing to see other women as the enemy. These are both tall orders in a male-dominant society, where our gender socialization begins at birth—and where being a good man is so often equated with dominance and being a good woman is so often equated with attractiveness and submission to a man.

35. These are not comparable prices, so we are not trying to measure one against the other, i.e., "men are as harmed by patriarchy as women." This is a false proposition on two counts. It minimizes the material harm to women, and it pretends that the whole issue revolves around its political implications.

him to replicate the repressions of the father. This was the basis, according to Freud (and of Hegel and Hobbes, without specific references to Oedipus), of civilization. Freud died in 1939, having fled Austria before the Nazi takeover, and as Benjamin says, "The historic problem that shaped the inquiry into domination most powerfully was . . . the appearance of fascist mass movements with their ecstatic submission to hypnotic leaders."[36] There was a vigorous debate among psychoanalysts of the time about this and related problems, using Freud and his categories, but in every discussion the only actors were men. Women, except as the spoils of struggle or as temptresses, were still essentially invisible.

Freud introduced the idea that early precognitive experience may exert a powerful influence on the rest of our lives. His specific account of that precognitive experience was European and male. In Freud's account of male and female development, both the male and female child begin as little men. Each then moves into an Oedipal phase, whereupon the boy has to detach from and dis-identify with his mother, and the girl realizes that, like her mother, she lacks a penis. The boy experiences a desire to possess his mother, a mimetic rivalry with his father. The girl experiences a desire for the father to regain the penis she suffers without. The boy's id desires Mom, but the boy's ego says, Dad is bigger than you and he sleeps with Mom, so get over it (the "reality principle"). The boy fears Dad will castrate him, and out of a sense of self-defense, he begins to identify with Dad (Stockholm syndrome before Stockholm syndrome). The girl also wants to possess the mother, because like the boy, the mother was the person with whom she originally developed an erotic attachment in infancy. But when she realizes she doesn't have a penis, the *instrument of possession*, she experiences an envy of Dad and Brother, or a least of their penises. She then resents Mom for having Dad and his penis. From this stage, Freud has the boy and girl go through a process of maturation, wherein both are finally *identified with the father*, and this results in a normative assertive male and a normative passive female. Freud considered separation and dis-identification with the mother to be critical for the male's *and* female's development. The boy would be *like* him, and the girl would be *for* him.

> Analyzing the oedipal model in Freud's original formulations and in the work of later psychoanalysts, we find this common thread: the idea of the father as the protector, or even savior, from a mother who would pull us back into the "limitless narcissism" of infancy. The privileging of the father's role . . . can be found in almost every version of the oedipal model. It also

---

36. Benjamin, *Bonds of Love*, 6.

underlies the current popular diagnosis of our social malaise: a rampant narcissism that stems from the loss of authority or the absence of the father.[37]

Yet a world divided between public and private, with the man having agency in the public world, is a world where *any* child will identify, as a part of his or her grasping for independence, with a parent who seems to flourish in that world. The intrapsychic approach had foreclosed any explanation of identification with the father, which was observable, that included extrapsychic social structures, the very cultural and economic structures that reproduce gender regimes, and within them gendered domination.

The result was not only the reproduction of the gender regime by a story fitted to the status quo, but the medicalization of problems that might actually have social bases. We drug children to go to school—and rarely question what actually goes on at school. So-called post-traumatic stress disorder (PTSD) can be treated with drugs and adaptive therapy, but this doesn't lead back to the question of war or rape, two major causes of PTSD, or to questioning a prevailing militarism or rape culture.

Psychotherapeutic specialties—using an intrapsychic or medicalized approach—cannot penetrate the cultural origins and social structures of masculinity constructed as domination or violence as long as they attend only to the symbolic world of the infant and child as if it was both universal and immunized from formative and variant cultural influences. Boys, who are indoctrinated into the idea that dependency is a threat to their selfhood as a male, will turn against the mother, and against all women, as a deleterious influence. They *will* close the border. "Why is the border closed between the genders? Feminist theory concludes that the derogation of the female side of the polarity leads to a hardening of the opposition between male and female individuality as they are now constructed."[38]

The search for recognition is transformed into a struggle for omnipotence—understood as a flight from dependency (*real* men are independent!)—not by an imbalance between id, ego, and superego, but by the cultural construction of masculinity and femininity. Because boys generally form their first and deepest attachment to their mothers, this is a painful process of separation that can contribute to deep confusion, as well as resentment *toward* and irrational desire for revenge *against* women: *You* made me dependent! *You* told me no! *You* threatened my boundaries with *feminine* vulnerability!

---

37. Ibid., 135.
38. Ibid., 113.

War demands men who are willing to commit violence. A society dedicated to war will promote a form of masculinity that includes the will to violence and the praise of violence. But as Benjamin shows, the predisposition for violence, or at least domination, begins as a struggle for autonomy that abandons mutuality, or *fusion*. Fusion is the I-am-yours-and-still-me-and-you-are-mine-and-still-you. Buber called this the I-Thou relation. Jesus and St. Paul called it love. Fusion presupposes permeable boundaries; and "the derogation of the female side of the polarity leads to a hardening of the opposition between male and female."

Masculinity is *culturally formed* in the practice of war; but masculinity is *learned* by the person, from infancy. It is irrevocably combined with the formation, as well as the perversion, of *eros*. "Power," says Nancy Hartsock, "irreducibly involves questions of *eros*."[39]

The association between eros, hostility, and domination, learned during a man's earliest formative years, is not incidental to domination in the other spheres of life. It is vital for the reproduction of conquest-masculinity; and the normalization of conquest-masculinity in culture reproduces that developmental model: "To the extent that either sexual relations or other relations are structured by a dynamic of domination/submission, the others as well will operate along these dimensions, and in consequence, the community as a whole will be structured by domination."[40]

Can the church stand *in* this kind of world and yet *apart* from it in a way that prefigures the kingdom of God? So far, we have largely accommodated the dominant culture. We are faced with an impasse. Domination, beginning as the desire for recognition and mutuality (love), reduces the dominated to an *object*, a nonperson *incapable of granting that recognition*. The boundary breached by the Samaritan is thrown open through vulnerability (even to death on a cross). The other is admitted inside the boundary that was sealed, armed by the will to power. If the love of God is our salvation, then domination forecloses our own ability to receive it.

Gender is a regime, an embedded set of norms that attach to human sexual dimorphism in known societies. *Sexuality* is a modern category, disembedded inasmuch as it is attributed to individuals almost as a possession or

---

39. Hartsock, *Money, Sex, and Power*, 155.
40. Ibid., 155.

Paradox of Domination

appendage. An individual (disembedded category) has (possessive) a certain *sexuality* (the category itself portable, or disembedded). The distinction that the modern category aims at is the *experience* of oneself sexually. Critical as I am of the disembodied individual behind this term for a decidedly bodily experience, I will use it here for an analysis.[41]

Sociologist Jeffry Weeks says that "sex is relational, is shaped in social interaction, and can only be understood in historical context."[42] Agreed. Human "sexuality" is not *natural*. Hartsock presumes as much when she uses the term *sexuality*. Let's summarize some of her thoughts.[43]

Psychoanalyst Robert Stoller (1924-91) made the uncontroversial assertion that threats to one's core "gender identity" (like a man's sense of masculinity) are experienced as threats to one's very being.[44] This is why you would not go into a bar, for example, and tell a strange man that he is a "pussy." He is likely to assault you. If you told the same strange man, "You are an electrician," he might tell you that you are confusing him with

---

41. Duden, *Woman Beneath the Skin*, 28–29: "Reproduction [the idea and term] emerged and was linked to the concept of production as that term moved into the center of political economy around 1850. During those decades more and more necessities of life were transformed into the need for goods, and all goods were seen as the result of a process that was perceived as culturally disembedded and labeled 'production.' Capital and work were productive factors; the uterus as well as domestic work were newly defined as factors whereby labor force reproduced itself. *Homo economicus* was equipped with a biological body that reflected this economic division of labor. Reproduction was inscribed upon a woman's body as her true 'destiny,' and the body she was given became living proof of the natural origin of economic concepts.... The emergence of 'sexuality' reflected on the level of the body a new view of the physical universe, very similar to the way in which reproduction reflected the new view of a society that was economic. Sexuality cannot be found [in the eighteenth century].... Our modern 'sexuality' took shape with and after the Marquis de Sade. With de Sade sexuality became visible, describable, dissectable. Only here did the history of attitudes toward lust reach the stage Foucault has called an epistemological faultline. With this transformation, sexuality became one of the many layers which together comprised the anatomized body as a multilayered text."

42. Weeks, *Sex, Politics, and Society*, 12.

43. One of my objections to the radical constructivists is that they assume the *disembedded* liberal individual and the *portability* of sexual identity. Sexual identity *is* culturally constructed; but that is not the same as saying that it is undetermined, that it is like a garment that the ghostlike "individual" can exchange at will. Sexual identity is not *natural*, but it is certainly and deeply embedded because the person who experiences it is embedded—in a specific time, place, culture, and family. The few people in any society who have the liberty to "escape" from sexual norms, or gender, are already possessed of enough privilege to "get away with" certain transgressions. Rich aesthetes can "play" with gender, for example, in ways that a poor woman or man cannot.

44. Stoller, *Perversion*, 12–14.

someone else, but he is far less likely to feel compelled to defend his identity by force.[45]

Stoller said that people also defend their sexual identities *in their sexual lives* through *perversion*.[46] By this he did not mean our colloquial meaning of deviance from the norm or sexual crime, but the transformation of the sex act into something different than *fusion* or *attunement* when that permeability of boundaries is experienced as a threat (for example, to male autonomy). In Latin, the term *pervertere* means "to turn away from." This can take the form of hostility, revenge, degradation, dehumanization, fetishization, or any number of strategies that create a bulwark against fusion, that permeability which is to be feared.

The academically lauded French philosopher-pornographer Georges Bataille equated coitus with killing, saying that each "is intentional like the act of a man who lays bare, desires and wants to penetrate his victim. The lover strips the beloved of her identity no less than the bloodstained priest his human or animal victim. The woman in the hands of the assailant is despoiled of her being. . . . [She] loses the firm barrier that once separated her from others . . . [and] is brusquely laid open to the violence of the sexual urges set loose in the organs of reproduction; she is laid open to the impersonal violence that overwhelms her from without."[47]

Lover equals (male) assailant; female equals victim.

Hartsock disclaims any suggestion that Stoller's analysis relieves men of moral agency and accountability for their actions[48] through the medicalization of the association of sex and hostility; it simply provides an insight into male formation during which *autonomy* and *omnipotence* are drilled into boys alongside a big helping of plain misogyny. The danger here is that hostility and violence are eroticized; and *the erotic life of men can become dependent on these perversions.* Men come to be sexually stimulated by hostility even when they know better.

Stoller himself was taken aback when he was forced to admit that most heterosexual unions contained some element of the perverse, that is, of hostility, dehumanization, and/or fetishization.[49] Yet that is exactly the point that many radical feminists have been making for some time, eliciting the accusation that they "hate men." They had been saying that in a gender regime characterized by domination, actual sexual relations between

---

45. I do not recommend this as a practical experiment.
46. Stoller, *Perversion*, 12–14.
47. Bataille, *Death and Sensuality*, 9.
48. Hartsock, *Money, Sex, and Power*, 161.
49. Stoller, *Perversion*, 97.

actual people are always inflected by power. This claim put them at odds with liberal feminists, who saw the only problem with sex as the denial of women's desire through archaic rules that limited sexual activity, that is, by a "double standard." Liberals then make disembedded claims like "sex is healthy" and "sex is good." There is even a strain of feminism that now calls itself sex-positive, which means pro-pornography, suggesting that those who refuse to understand sex apart from social power are somehow sex-*negative*—a straw man that evades the centrality of masculine sexual identity constructed as domination and submission.

As Benjamin and Hartsock explain, women in male-dominant society internalize male norms. Just as domination is eroticized, so is submission. An aspect of eros that Hartsock associates with gender and power is the denial of the body, and this too ramifies through masculinity and militarism.

In Hartsock's treatment as well as Benjamin's, each analyzes the sadomasochistic fantasy novel *Story of O*, by French author Anne Desclos, a.k.a. Pauline Réage.[50] The masochist in this fantasy, a woman named simply O (she is reduced to a symbolic orifice), revels in her loss of boundaries, in their repeated transgression by powerful others. The men are wearing full-body masks with only their penises exposed, directing her eyes to their penises so she will know that "there resides your master." Benjamin observes,

> O's physical humiliation and abuse represent a search for an elusive spiritual or psychological satisfaction. Her masochism is a search for recognition through an other who is powerful enough to bestow recognition. This other has the power for which the self longs, and through his recognition she gains it, though vicariously.[51]

O is repeatedly violated by one man, who, upon violating her in one way and destroying the very subjectivity that is necessary for her to recognize him, must find new and deeper forms of debasement and humiliation to demonstrate "respect." When no further debasement seems possible, he surrenders her to a more powerful male (an Oedipal exchange), and the more powerful male begins her sexual debasement anew, "giving" her to others for sex, even mutilating her by enlarging her anus. O, for her part, enjoys *the thought* of her tortures, hates going through them, and enjoys *having survived* them. Her need for recognition is inflamed with every instance of its denial, until the powerful man becomes like a god, and her debasement makes her feel like a martyr. The more distant he becomes, the more she increases her devotion. She becomes like an addict chasing a fix

---

50. Réage, *Story of O*.
51. Benjamin, *Bonds of Love*, 56.

who becomes addicted to the chase: "O is actually willing to risk complete annihilation of her person in order to continue to be the object of her lover's desire—to be recognized."[52]

The nondominant male in the story exhausts the capacity for recognition from his object through her serial submissions; then he gives her away to the more powerful man (the father) to gain his recognition from the father when it is no longer possible from the debased woman.

The woman is faced ultimately with her psychic annihilation.

Mutuality exists in tension. The absence of tension is, finally, death.

> He will swallow up death for all time,
> And the Lord GOD will wipe tears away from all faces,
> And He will remove the reproach of His people from all
>   the earth;
> For the LORD has spoken. (Isa 25:8)

---

52. Ibid., 60.

22

Disgust, Transgression, and Sex

Everything in life is part of it. Nothing is off in its own corner, isolated from the rest. While on the surface this may seem self-evident, the favorite conceit of male culture is that experience can be fractured, literally its bones split, and that one can examine the splinters as if they were not part of the bone, or the bone as if it were not part of the body. This conceit replicates in its values and methodology the sexual reductionism of the male and is derived from it.

—Andrea Dworkin[1]

Loathing for the body, in the sense that bodily needs and desires are humiliating, appears in another way in pornography in the form of the contrast between a man's self-control and the woman's frenzied abandon.

—Nancy C. M. Hartsock[2]

The body serves simultaneously as erotic object and the source of shame and disgust. Christian ruminations on the subject of sex have too often failed to account for the dynamic of domination-submission and its gendered bases, seldom attended to the psychology of sex, and focused instead

---

1. Dworkin, *Pornography*, 67.
2. Hartsock, *Money, Sex, and Power*, 173.

on reproducing shame about the body as a means of controlling sex. This has been an abysmal failure in theory and practice. To explain why, we need to augment our understanding of intersubjective psychology with a field called "disgust psychology."

One of the aspects of the Christian story that drew me to Christianity was that Jesus committed serial infractions of the purity codes—by touching dead people, street people, lepers, menstruating women, and by exercising table fellowship with the "unclean." In Richard Beck's *Unclean*, he says two things in the introduction, one psychological, one theological: "disgust is a boundary psychology," and (paraphrasing) that "sacrifice" inscribes boundaries, while mercy crosses them. For those who did not immediately get the reference, Beck is writing about Matt 9:13, and Jesus's confrontation with the Pharisees over "eating with sinners and tax collectors."[3]

"But go and learn what this means," says Jesus. "'I desire mercy, not sacrifice.' For I have not come to call the righteous, but sinners." A reference that the Pharisees knew came from Hos 6:6: "For I desire mercy, not sacrifice, and acknowledgment of God rather than burnt offerings." The significance of this distinction is not immediately apparent, nor is its relation to "disgust psychology," associated with psychologist Paul Rozin. Beck unpacked this relation through the synthesis of several lines of psychological research.

Beck's focus on disgust psychology aims at overcoming wrongs that pose as rights because they are *felt* as right based on learned feelings of disgust. His point could be made apart from theology—for example, in politics or personal relationships or just common sense: *feeling* that something is wrong (or right) does not necessarily make it so.

> The danger of refusing to reflect upon the psychological dynamics of faith and belief is that what we feel to be self-evidently true, for psychological reasons, might be, upon inspection, highly questionable, intellectually or morally. Too often, as we all know, the "feeling of rightness" trumps sober reflection and moral discernment.[4]

Beck is asking Christians to review their personal convictions with this fallacy in mind, beginning with a self-evaluation of what elicits the disgust reaction.[5]

---

3. Beck, *Unclean*, 2.
4. Ibid., 5.
5. I ask readers to hold in mind the disgust reactions associated with sex, which have been common among many devout Christians, and which we could see in some of the comments about women from the church fathers in the account of witch hunts.

Linda Kintz names the socialized emotional response that *precedes* our exercise of rational analysis as "resonance."[6] This sense of resonance is often confused with the sacred. If the resonance is *felt*, then that feeling is indicative of contact with the sacred, which effectively forecloses any deeper examination. That powerful emotional response is then understood as sacred (and sometimes as *natural*). This is true in part because we believe that transcendence is an experience associated with euphoria. Heroin addicts will tell you that their first dose was akin to "seeing God." The "feeling of rightness" can in turn undermine critical reflection.[7]

Beck explains one way in which "the world" supplants the Gospels through the mobilization of disgust. He describes disgust as a *promiscuous* emotion. While babies show no sign of disgust at anything, gladly putting everything into their mouths, by the time we are grown we have learned to be disgusted by a whole range of things. Beck names certain foods, bodily outputs, creatures, sexual behaviors, the dead, gore, deformity, poor hygiene, and moral offenses, as a few examples, to demonstrate disgust's *promiscuity*.

The "core disgust," the one that establishes the coordinates for other forms of disgust, is offense at certain *oral incorporations*—disgust at the fact or idea of certain things entering the body through the mouth. Evolutionary biologists would be quick to tell us that this capacity for disgust and its association with putting things in the mouth probably had an adaptive function. Promiscuous eating can threaten one's survival. Rozin developed a schema for disgust based on core disgust, in which core disgust is metaphorically extrapolated into "sociomoral disgust" and "animal-reminder disgust."

Beck explains with the "Dixie cup" thought experiment. Imagine spitting into a Dixie cup. Now imagine putting the saliva back in your mouth to swallow it. Objectively speaking, the substance in the cup is exactly what we swallow all day long with no reaction whatsoever. Psychologically speaking, that substance is radically transformed by crossing the *boundary* between the "inside" and the "outside."[8] The response you likely had while reading this thought experiment was a disgust response. You scrunched your nose and raised your upper lip, maybe stuck out your tongue, as if to expel something that tastes bad. If the stimulus for this expression is immediate and at hand, as opposed to simply conversational, then it is accompanied by bodily reactions—shielding, turning away, experiencing nausea (the physical urge to expel something from the inside to the outside).

6. Kintz, *Between Jesus and the Market*.

7. This is crucial to understanding how the hygiene/eugenics movement and Western imperialism at the beginning of the twentieth century worked together, which we will cover in greater detail in chapters 24 and 26.

8. Beck, *Unclean*, 1–2.

Mary Douglas's anthropology of purity[9] describes an associated notion of *contagion*. Contagion is that sense that merely coming into contact with certain people, places, and things will pollute you. That pollution is often irremediable, precisely because each time the point of pollution is recalled the disgust reaction is viscerally recalled with it. If the disgust reaction loses its visceral force, it can be transformed into a more distant reaction: *contempt*. The rich might be disgusted by the poor when they are in close proximity, or touching them in ways that suggest familiarity, but when proximity is necessary—using servants, for example—the poor can be held in the less visceral and more viscerally sustainable *contempt*. Disgust is a *boundary psychology*. Disgust stimulates the desire for withdrawal and avoidance in mild cases, and "rejection, expulsion, and elimination" in powerful cases. *Elimination* can be easily translated here to *extermination*.

Disgust is accompanied by *magical thinking*—ideas that are not consistent with logical or rational analysis. One of Beck's concerns, as a Christian *and* a psychologist, is that "when disgust regulates moral, social, or religious experience, irrational thinking is unwittingly imported into the life of the church."[10] He gives us four principles of *contagion*:

1. *Contact*: contamination is caused by contact or physical proximity.
2. *Dose insensitivity*: minimal amounts, even microamounts, of the pollutant confer harm.
3. *Permanence*: once contaminated, nothing can be done to rehabilitate the object.
4. *Negativity dominance*: when a pollutant and a pure object come into contact, the pollutant is "stronger" and ruins the pure object.[11]

The pure object, conversely, doesn't render the pollutant acceptable or palatable. These principles are learned early.

Contamination associated with disgust has been around since prehistory. In ancient history, Scripture provides examples of detailed purity codes, in Leviticus, that far predate any notion of "germs," for example. In the New Testament, those codes are still in force when Jesus is criticized for eating with the wrong people, not washing his hands before eating, and touching the "unclean." A dramatic reversal of contamination principles is that a touch from Jesus renders an "unclean" person clean—the opposite of "negativity dominance," wherein one speck of contamination ruins the whole. When the church feels "defiled" by the world, it is reproducing

9. Douglas, *Purity and Danger*.
10. Beck, *Unclean*, 27.
11. Ibid., 27–28.

negativity dominance, even though the New Testament describe an opposite process—the church redeeming the world, just as Jesus *cleansed* lepers with a forbidden touch. In Amy Laura Hall's history of the "progressive" church in the early twentieth-century United States,[12] she notes that *cleanliness* was equated with godliness, and there was a *racial* line drawn between pure and impure that gave rise to a powerful eugenics movement that required a Hitler, with his special earnestness in pursuit of "racial purity," to discredit it. Those missions that are most Jesus-like—that bring the church into contact with the sick and despised, that act on the assumption that crossing boundaries redeems (purifies) both those who are touched and those who touch—are those that put people into bodily contact with one another (Mother Teresa or Catherine of Siena tending the sick, for example). No practice freaks new Christians out more, in my brief experience, than foot-washing. In practice, it can be an overwhelming experience of grace.

Because purity metaphors *entail* a disgust reaction, it is easy for metaphors to steer theological reflection toward exclusion and boundary-inscription, toward the kind of othering that results in the declaration of enemies (and war), which is the opposite of the teachings of Jesus (though often enough compatible with the teachings of many churches). The metaphorical translation of *core* disgust, explains Beck, shapes *sociomoral* disgust—disgust at particular kinds of moral "failure," and even against whole peoples—and animal-reminder disgust—revulsion at reminders of our animal nature (reminders that trigger an existential dread at the inevitability of death). Here is where Beck meets Hartsock and Benjamin.

Unexamined premises, says Beck, are damaging to the church, to the body of Christ—that same Christ who was born in close proximity to farm animals, who ate with sinners, who put his hands on skin lesions, rubbed spit in people's eyes, allowed a street woman to kiss his feet and wash them with her hair, washed the feet of his own disciples, and sanctified the living, sweating, dying human body.

Disgust can be projected to overcome cognitive dissonance.[13] As combat veterans know, *prior to* entering a conflict, one may believe that foreign people are just people, but when the soldier's position *vis-à-vis* the foreigner compels him to control, abuse, or kill, he redefines the foreigner as less human. During the Stanford Prison Experiment, in which students were placed in the role of prisoners and prison guards, the "guards" quickly began

---

12. Hall, *Conceiving Parenthood*.

13. Cognitive dissonance, here, is a contradiction between what one believes and what one does.

abusing "prisoners" to fulfill the role of controlling guards.[14] The guards found the prisoners repulsive as a way of justifying the abuse demanded by their "role."

Beck says that love and disgust are reciprocal. This is similar to Benjamin's claim that domination is related to mutuality gone awry. About "self," on boundaries and incorporation, Beck says,

> As the self gets symbolically extended so does disgust psychology, the primal psychology that monitors the boundary of the body. Disgust accompanies the self as it reaches into the world, continuing to provide emotional markers denoting "inside" and "outside," the boundary points of the symbolic self.[15]

Beck describes love rendering boundaries permeable and how spatial metaphors describe this—being "close," having a "circle of friends," and so forth.

> Given that disgust monitors the boundaries of selfhood and intimacy it should come as no surprise then that love involves a suspension of disgust and contamination sensitivity. More strongly, disgust is a *prerequisite* of love. Love, to be love, requires a backdrop of disgust. For someone to move "inside" there must be a preexisting condition of having been "outside," being exterior and other. In short, disgust establishes boundaries of contact. Love enters as a secondary mechanism when those boundaries are transgressed or dismantled.[16]

In Hartsock, "loathing for the body" is entangled with the erotic and with "transgression." I believe there is a gap here in Beck's description of love with regard to power. To describe my discomfort with Beck's account of love and disgust,[17] I will begin with C. S. Lewis's definitions of love.[18] Lewis treats four kinds of love: *storge, phileo, agape,* and *eros. Storge* means affection, fondness through familiarity. *Philia* is friendship. *Agape* means unconditional love—in Christian terms, *caritas,* the love for others that reflects God's love. *Eros* refers to love with the element of sex, which Lewis differentiates from simply *wanting* sexually, which he called *Venus.*

In Beck's important account, we are missing what Stoller and Hartsock said about perversion and how this is *also* related to forms of *transgression.*

14. Zimbardo, *Stanford Prison Experiment.*
15. Beck, *Unclean,* 86.
16. Ibid., 86–87.
17. I like Beck's book very much and strongly recommend it.
18. Lewis, *The Four Loves.*

Regarding *agape*, *storge*, and *philia*, I support Beck's thesis that love entails overcoming boundaries, and that boundaries can be inscribed by disgust. In the realm of *eros*, however, I find it problematic. *Eros*—here meaning love with the component of sex—must be understood in the light of power. Sex and power are linked. That link reveals something different about boundaries and the unilateral ability to cross them. As Stoller and Hartsock suggest, sex understood as "nasty" can be paradoxically arousing.

> The dichotomy between spiritual love and "carnal knowledge" is recreated in the persistent fantasy of transforming the virgin into a whore. She begins pure, innocent, fresh, even in a sense disembodied, and is degraded and defiled in sometimes imaginative and bizarre ways.
>
> Transgression here is a marker of privilege, and the object of the transgression will often be degraded, humiliated, or destroyed.
>
> Transgression is important here: Forbidden practices are being engaged in. The violation of the boundaries of society breaks its taboos. Yet the act of violating a taboo, of seeing or doing something forbidden, does not do away with its forbidden status. Indeed, in the ways women's bodies are degraded and defiled in the transformation of virgin into whore, the boundaries between the forbidden and the permitted are simultaneously upheld and broken. Put another way, the obsessive transformation of virgin into whore simply crosses over and over again the boundary between them. Without the boundary, there could be no transformation. And without the boundary, the thrill of transgression would disappear.[19]

Hartsock summarizes the lure of pornography as the substitution of control for intimacy, attractive because it evades the danger of fusion, the losing of oneself in union with another that Beck describes as love: the breakdown of the boundary around the self. In much pornography, the misogyny is pronounced, and women are described, erotically for the male viewer, as objects of disgust who are humiliated by sexual contact. Ejaculation onto the body or the face of a woman, for example, is a common porn convention in which the substance that becomes *unclean* upon leaving the body contaminates or defiles the female (who is portrayed as desperately wanting it, as out of control with desire). This disgust, this hatred, is *eroticized* at the expense of women by virtue of women's collective subordination to men. The eroticized disgust/transgression boundary can be "crossed

---

19. Hartsock, *Money, Sex, and Power*, 172.

again and again." As we know from accounts of pornography addiction, the border-crossings can become routinized, leading to an escalation dynamic, wherein more and more degrading, edgy, and "extreme" acts are required to achieve the same goal, which is to psychologically aid masturbation.[20] Disgust actually *enhances* the thrill, which must lead us to the question of how boundaries function in relation to *privilege*. Just as the imperial trooper can cross a boundary into the forbidden zone to be temporarily released from the taboo on killing, and just as he can return, if he survives, back to his position of relative comfort and safety, men in a male-dominant society can cross boundaries with thrill-seeking in mind—and what they feel and do has nothing to do with love and everything to do with desire coded as control and objectification.

Beck writes that "the biological, animal function of sex isn't all there is to human sexuality. For humans, sex can be experienced as a deeply *spiritual* activity. Sex is often an experience of spiritual exultation and transcendence. Further, the deepest feelings of human love and union are often experienced within the sex act. . . . In short, sex is dual."[21] Sex is experienced dramatically differently by men and women, however, because there is a power differential that is invariably implicated in *all* sex. "Sexuality" cannot stand as a floating signifier. It is constructed from childhood as power. The disturbing news, as Stoller and Hartsock show, is that sexual excitement for most men *requires* elements of perversion, that is, objectification, dehumanization, and/or fetishization. The eroticization of the loathing for the body transforms sex, for many men, into a revenge fantasy that projects that loathing onto the bodies of women.[22]

Beck's own reference to animal-reminder disgust, particularly mortality-reminder disgust, is pertinent here, because *women* have served as signifiers for *men's* anxieties about body and mortality, and women have been men's targets of projection. It was St. John Chrysostom, writing in the third century, who said,

> It does not profit a man to marry. For what is a woman but an enemy of friendship, an inescapable punishment, a necessary evil, a natural temptation, a domestic danger, delectable mischief, a fault in nature, painted with beautiful colors?
> The whole of her body is nothing less than phlegm, blood, bile, rheum and the fluid of digested food. . . . If you consider what is stored up behind those lovely eyes, the angle of the nose,

---

20. Jaffe, "Internet Porn Addiction."
21. Beck, *Unclean*, 159.
22. See chapter 32, "Taboo."

the mouth and the cheeks you will agree that the well-proportioned body is only a whitened sepulcher.[23]

A sepulcher. A tomb. The body of a woman is a reminder of *mortality*, among other things, because her body is permeable. Life grows inside her. Her body produces milk for an infant. She menstruates. The "hard penetration" of women's bodies by men, in fact and in fantasy, is sometimes seemingly an act of vengeance for that reminder, and for male desire that is interpreted as the threat of dependency. This is particularly important because of what Beck *does* write about "the influence of disgust upon moral reasoning and the experience of sin within the life of the church." Disgust does not just erect and monitor boundaries. It is implicated in the erotic play of dominance and privilege, because the dominant one can cross the boundary for his transgressive buzz, which men can experience as almost overwhelming desire,[24] even *a condition for arousal*.

Masculine *fear of fusion* erects another kind of boundary in which disgust is conflated with desire and confused with love from a *normative* male perspective. Marshall Brown, the elite soldier and serial rapist, transgressed the boundary again and again, saying to each of his victims, "I am sorry, I have to do this."

When I was in the army, if an operation was planned, for example, to destroy a facility or rescue prisoners, crossing the boundary into enemy territory, a thrilling and threatening experience, was referred to as "insertion"; returning back across the line was called "extraction." Between insertion and extraction, something violent was accomplished, which included shooting and explosions during the *climax* of the operation.

Julia Kristeva, a Bulgarian-French psychoanalyst and social critic, elaborating on the Cartesian subject-object dichotomy, describes a realm called the *abject*. Abjection, being brought low in status or esteem, is Kristeva's term for those things that, in the post-Cartesian era, fall between subject and object and thereby disrupt both categories. Examples might include feces or menstrual discharge or a corpse. Disgust reactions to these things are associated with their challenge to the boundary between subject and object.

> It is . . . not lack of cleanliness or health that causes abjection but what disturbs identity, system, order. What does not respect

---

23. Quoted in Aquilina, "One Flesh of Purest Gold," para. 2.

24. I am thinking now about the sexual assaults committed by Mennonite peace theologian John Howard Yoder.

borders, positions, rules. The in-between, the ambiguous, the composite.[25]

Anything that violates the boundaries of the body, as Beck points out, becomes unclean when it passes beyond that boundary, but then something happens to it that makes it neither subject nor object, something that disturbs both categories because it violates our symbolic order. It has to be cast out of the dual order into a netherworld of abjection. This is the psychoanalytic key to disgust as mortality-reminder. The abject is what reminds us that we are indeed permeable, but more: we are going to die. By extension, the abject is anything that disturbs the social imaginary, anything that refuses to fit into the cultural consensus that *underwrites* order. The story of Pat Tillman's death by friendly fire not only breaks up the opportunistic fiction invented by the Army; it also upsets a larger narrative that includes the Special Operations mystique, the soldier-hero narrative about the troops involved, and the "America the Savior" story.

Abjection is about a kind of disaffiliation, and one of the ideas from which the abject is most disaffiliated is *respectability*. It was with the invention of "respectability" that sexual matters were generalized as "disgusting," St. John Chrysostom's aversions notwithstanding.

---

25. Kristeva, *Powers of Horror*, 4.

23

Respectability

"Separate spheres" was a formula that held that adult males should dominate a family's relationship to the outside or public world while adult women properly should take direction of the domestic world.

—Woodruff Smith[1]

When the Pharisees saw this, they asked his disciples, "Why does your teacher eat with tax collectors and sinners?"

—Matthew 9:11

Shame about the body as a means of controlling sex has been a failure in practice and theory for Christians. This shaming was not a general feature of Western culture prior to the nineteenth century. Squeamishness is associated with the Victorian period more than any other era, which was part of a *performance* called *respectability*. Throughout the post-Classical era, through early feudalism, into the High Middle Ages, and even into the republican era, sex was spoken of openly and frequently. If one reads Shakespeare or Chaucer, there are commonplace and direct references to images and language like "making the beast with two backs." *Haute culture* had

---

1. Smith, *Consumption*, 175.

always differentiated itself from the main culture, and in some cases put on airs of faux sensitivity about sex; but the vernacular cultures of Europe and even post-Puritan, colonial North American culture were ribald in thought and speech.

By the time Freud began projecting his own sexual insecurities onto the general population, however, sex and other matters of the body had become a kind of discursive taboo; and this taboo was an aspect of what some referred to as "bourgeois respectability," a reference to the mores of the now dominant urban business class, for whom the body could create a sense of abjection. Freud's sex-talk scandalized the very people who lived according to its unwritten standards, though Freud himself lived his life as a perfect model of this "respectability."[2]

Freud's intrapsychic mythology, similar to the philosophers of the Enlightenment and liberal theory, pretended to delve deep into something called the unconscious rather than a fictional past, but his conclusions, like theirs, were predetermined. At the end of the day, Freud was developing a new apologetic for "civilization," a conceit that dominated this period of imperial expansion and consolidation. The Atlantic states were bringing "civilization" to "savages."

Freud was also arguing that women, whom he had spent years interrogating for the "pathology" of "hysteria," were maladaptive to the prescribed roles of their day because of some sexually developmental defect (at least an implicit rebuke to the rising tide of eugenic theories in his day).[3] The roles Freud found normative for men and women were those he observed in late nineteenth-century Vienna, and they were integral to the metropolitan conception of respectability: "rational masculinity" and "domestic femininity."

Early modernity came dressed as a lamb, as emancipation from the ills of the past, and with good reason. The exhaustion with Christendom's centuries of bloodletting that gave rise to this experiment was real. But the blood did not cease to flow. Military actions became an export. A new form of empire was rising. In the European cores of this imperial venture, where wealth was accumulating, people began to *want* differently. Contrary to economic determinism, however, Woodruff Smith writes, "One should not

---

2. Webster, *Why Freud Was Wrong*, 249.
3. Brunner, *Freud and the Politics of Psychoanalysis*, 13–23.

... necessarily assume that economic effects always derived from economic causes."[4] There is always a psychological dimension to social changes.

In 1998, Randall Kennedy writes about the struggle for *respectability* in African America:

> A ... core intuition of the politics of respectability is that, for a stigmatized racial minority, successful efforts to move upward in society must be accompanied at every step by a keen attentiveness to the morality of means, the reputation of the group, and the need to be extra-careful in order to avoid the derogatory charges lying in wait in a hostile environment.[5]

This kind of grasping at respectability, especially among classes of people who are trying to "move up," for whatever group in whatever time, is not primarily motivated by economic concerns; money is a means to an end, but the goals are *status* and *acceptance*. This grasping for status, however, has powerful economic consequences. Respectability has fashion and consumption codes; but they materially demand the circulation and accumulation of money. Smith's *Consumption and the Making of Respectability, 1600–1800* examines the use of consumer goods in early modern Europe and America from the perspective of what they *mean*.

> A very large portion of the demand in Europe and the Americas for consumer goods in the nineteenth century arose from people's use of those goods to signal and maintain their respectability. It is not uncommon to connect Victorian behavior of all sorts, from sex to purchasing, with respectability, but few systematic attempts have been made either to analyze what "respectability" is or to trace its history. It is normally linked discursively to the "middle class" or to "bourgeois society," but the history of the linkage is seldom pursued. I decided to focus my attention on respectability. I discovered that the set of sociocultural phenomena to which the word *respectability* (and its cognates in other languages) came to be applied in the eighteenth century constituted a distinct and enormously significant cultural pattern that was central to the "modernity" of the Western and imperial worlds. Respectability gave meaning—moral and political as well as social and economic—to consumption, thereby permitting the construction of a host of connections between purchasing commodities and thinking and acting appropriately. In other words, by looking at the relationships between

---

4. Smith, *Consumption*, 12.
5. Kennedy, *Race, Crime, Law*, 20.

respectability and consumption, it is possible to place the latter in many of its historical contexts.[6]

Respectability is not just a status; it is a performance, for an audience. We are sending an actor's signals, a set of cultural meanings, to the audience, which in consumer society can mean anyone who I imagine might be observing me. These performances are ritualized in order for them to be correctly understood. We all have an idea, whether we concur with it or not, of what is meant by "acting like a lady," for example. Actions become performances that signify respectability. Respectability as performance requires props, however, which must be purchased on the market: consumer goods.

When Jesus calls people "hypocrites," he is using the Greek word for play-actor, someone who takes the stage to pretend. In Matt 23, Jesus rebuked the authorities who had lost touch with the spirit of the law, identifying them as "hypocrites," play-actors. What of our own churches, where the pretense of respectability is a deeply inscribed cultural norm?

In successive assimilations of subcultures, nations elaborate class structures. In the modernist project, a growing domestic middle class became an ever more essential part of the European and U.S. nation-states. This middle class did not conjure itself out of cabbage patches but emerged from poorer classes with aspirations to "move up." These aspirations are part of both a collective and subjective terrain. A feature of that subjective terrain is the desire for acceptance by those who are on the next rung up, which corresponds to a felt need for "respectability." Respectability is a ruthless idol, effective at enforcing conformity. A cognate of it was at work when Jesus was accused of gluttony and drunkenness and rebuked for eating with ne'er-do-wells or touching menstruating women and corpses. These were purity codes, akin to but not synonymous with modern respectability.

Smith traces respectability through the urban democratization of the availability and use of particular commodities—calico, silk, spices, tea, coffee, and sugar, which correspond to developments in "gentility" and fashion. Virtue was being realigned with ideas of personal optimization. "Rational masculinity" and "domestic femininity" were being articulated as the gendered norms of respectability.

Rapid industrialization resulted in crises of masculinity in some European and American social sectors. Factory work employed men, women, and children, for example, and put working-class men into direct competition with working-class women for jobs—a massive disruption of the

6. Smith, *Consumption*, 3.

preceding vernacular gender orders, where separate meant complementary and cooperative gender roles in household production. More women became visible in this public sector, creating insecurities among men about other men being in unsupervised contact with "our" women and about women's potential for infidelity. Artisans were being displaced by mass production, destabilizing their identities and forcing them into dependence on more powerful men. The problem of "unemployment" grew as vernacular economies disappeared and money became a necessity for survival. Men felt the loss or the threat of loss of their role as providers. Finally, lower-class men did not have access to the consumer goods that would accompany the development of "rational masculinity," and likewise lower-class women had difficulty *performing* "domestic femininity."[7]

Just as Gregory locates the takeoff of capitalist modernity in the Dutch Republic, so Smith also gives a privilege of place to the Dutch, as the commercial center that gave rise to the Dutch East India Company (1602). It began providing the necessary quantities of these new consumer goods to Europe to transform up-and-coming Europeans into consumers of Asian commodities. The English East India Company had been founded two years before the Dutch venture, but the greater sophistication of Dutch commercial institutions allowed the Dutch to outperform the British. The Dutch enterprise was more "closely connected to the primary business structures that supplied all of Europe with commercial capital and to the central nodes of the networks that distributed overseas imports in Europe."[8] The Dutch established the trade norms that would predominate between Europe and Asia, because during the seventeenth century, the Dutch Republic was the single largest business in the world.[9] Both the Dutch and the British would come to dominate Asian trade, though the Dutch pushed the British out of the spice trade, forcing the British to concentrate on a special Asian fabric: calico—printed or painted heavy cotton and silks.

Anyone today can understand or at least recognize the power of fashion, especially among urban dwellers. Originally used as tablecloths, calico

---

7. Moore, "Men in Crisis." As a result, one of the only venues that was still available for men of lower rank to demonstrate masculine virtue on a par with higher-ranking men was in military service.

The fear arose that the new, urbane, business-class masculinity would feminize men and weaken the nation, leading to the kinds of probative masculine practices we will describe in chapter 24, "Progress and the Fear of the Feminine." Working-class men, asserting their physicality in opposition to genteel masculinity, actually fuelled the movement among higher-ranking men to engage in various man-sports to prove their physical vigor and toughness.

8. Smith, *Consumption*, 48.

9. Ibid.

became a clothing craze in the mid-seventeenth century that spread from the salons of Paris, the fashion center of the day, throughout Europe rather like a contagion. The salons, presided over by French aristocratic women who had become the umpires of "taste," gave calicoes their initial impetus; but the surfeit of the material in Asia and the capacity of the British to import calicoes sustained the craze and resulted in falling prices, which enabled their use by greater numbers of people. In England, calico use expanded and gained in popularity for a century, even after rival textile makers had persuaded the English government to ban their import. The British simply shipped the calicoes to neighboring states, then depended on smugglers to finalize the distribution.[10]

The entrepreneurs of Britain found that the craze could be sustained indefinitely by changing the print designs as frequently as we see changes today in computer software. Everyone who *could* simply had to have the latest design; it had become a matter of status. The British had gone from *responding* to demand to *creating* it.[11]

Calicoes were popular because they functioned as what Smith names a "substitute status commodity" for silks. They allowed more people to participate in the "culture of gentility." It wasn't merely the "conspicuous consumption" named in Thorstein Veblen's sociology; these items had meaning *beyond* the mere display of wealth. Gentility meant being "in," and "in" meant "well-mannered." It was a complicated social hieroglyphic "through which the complex status hierarchy of Europe manifested itself in, among other things, fashionable consumption behavior."[12]

Another fashion that began to define genteel respectability was underwear. There was a rising premium placed on cleanliness, and underwear, which was not affordable for many poor people, was proof of one's hygienic suitability. Anyone who is offended today by young men's display of underwear beneath their trousers with the "prison sag" would likely be apoplectic if he or she were transported back to the early eighteenth century. Apparently, displays of one's undergarments went by the rule "more is better." People wanted to let others *know* that they were wearing underwear, and wanted to prove that it was silk or silk-and-linen underwear. They wanted others to *know* that it was expensive, clean, or new. Cleanliness itself was becoming more and more a display of status: "It showed that the wearer had servants to keep his or her underwear in order."[13]

10. Eacott, "Making an Imperial Compromise."

11. Smith, *Consumption*, 20–21: It also created the beginnings of mercantilist resistance, angering French textile traders and even evoking violence from London silk-weavers (ibid., 22).

12. Ibid., 23.

13. Ibid., 60.

Until the post-Reformation era, sensuality and luxury were considered by most European Christians to be moral hazards. With urban habituation to consumption and its powerful associations with gentility and respectability, Christians of several confessions found themselves rationalizing consumption; and the door to capitalist Europe and America opened wider. As Hobbes had said in a self-fulfilling prophecy, "The value of all things contracted for, is measured by the Appetite of the Contractors. . . . The *Value*, or WORTH of a man, is as of all things, his Price; that is to say, so much as would be given for the use of his Power."[14] People themselves, according to Hobbes, were commodities. "As in other things, so in men, not the seller, but the buyer determines the Price. For let a man (as most men do,) rate themselves at the highest Value they can; yet their true Value is no more than it is esteemed by others."[15] The mentality of the market society was coming into its own despite the objections of some Christians.

> Especially in northwestern Europe, other rulers and their subjects, Protestants and Catholics alike, heeded what was afoot in the United Provinces [Netherlands]. Led by Dutch precedent and before it was theorized, European Christians began more deliberately to create what would become a capitalist society out of late medieval capitalist practices midwifed by Reformation-era relgio-political disruptions born of disagreements about God's truth.[16]

The church's contradictory adoption of state power and war had after several centuries borne its peculiar political fruit—the market-*dominated* society.[17]

> Even more by the end of the Thirty Years War and the English civil wars, frustrated with failed goals and fed up with the catastrophic financial, military, and human costs of waging war for God, in religiously divided areas Christians across confessional boundaries increasingly drew the unsurprising conclusion that they would rather learn somehow to live alongside, if not in harmony with, those with whom they disagreed. In this way, early modern Christian rulers and their subjects paradoxically

14. Hobbes, *Leviathan*, ch. 15.
15. Ibid.
16. Gregory, *Unintended Reformation*, 278.
17. This description is not Marxian, but from Karl Polanyi, who unlike Marx did not find market actions to be a scratch that inevitably turns to gangrene. Polanyi described several kinds of economic activity that can coexist—market exchange being only one of them; but he criticized modern economies for having let market relations dominate all others, a domination that converts three things that ought not to be commodities into commodities: land, labor, and money.

became the agents of their self-colonization by capitalism and consumption. By their actions, they essentially turned their backs on biblical teachings about material things, teachings that had largely been shared across confessional lines.[18]

The urban European cores were rewarded by access to more stuff. Locally, at least, it appeared Mammon was the more peaceful God. In this process, Christian principles were not effaced *de jure*, but *de facto*; and these changes were rationalized to fit the new reality by privatizing religion. With the public-private dichotomy, there was a place to safely tuck away faith while people made money.[19]

The division of life into two spheres, public and private, the former in the polis and the latter in the home, gave rise to the gendered core of genteel respectability: "rational masculinity" and "domestic femininity." Religion, too, was being privatized, and the churches then subordinated to the market-dominated state. Imperial plunder abroad during the European states' relative balance of power guaranteed increasing flows of those goods required to sustain what Gregory calls "the goods life."[20]

Hegel would come to lament that the urban lifestyle of the business class was so genteel that men would lack a transcendent purpose, and that urbane life might become an *effeminate* "bog" in which nothing transcends individual interests;[21] and, of course, that transcendent purpose was the state itself—Hobbes's Leviathan. Military conscription became the practice that legally embodied a reorientation of the sacred from God to the state.[22] Imperial war and nation-worship complemented gentility and served as the antidote to its threats of feminization.

We can see in Kipling's literature how these two aspects of masculinity were fused into a single masculine ideology. A real man had to have good manners and be comfortable in a drawing room; but he needed occasionally to test his mettle against the brigands of the darker races and stand his watch on the borderline between civilization and barbarity. He was obliged by the code of "rational masculinity" to be a good head of household, hence the complementary development of "domestic femininity" as constitutive of respectability in the "private" realm.

This does not mean women had no agency; many women embraced domestic femininity as an improvement over their pasts and certainly

18. Gregory, *Unintended Reformation*, 278.
19. Ibid.
20. Ibid., 235–97.
21. Clarke, "Fetal Attraction," 166–68.
22. Krehbiel, "Conscription."

better than a factory floor. Let's not forget that this standard was exercised by women who already enjoyed a certain affluence. Urban men frequently showed women who were good at domestic femininity a special courtesy and ceded household matters to them, while the man did business and hung out in coffeehouses talking politics. As Illich points out in his distinction between "vernacular" gender and modern gender, in the countryside where subsistence farms still existed prior to enclosure, production was centered at home, and while tasks were split between men and women, there was no significance to the public-private dichotomy. Men and women were not potential competitors in a distinctly public sphere.[23]

Caffeinated beverages marked both realms within the public and private spheres: tea at home and coffee in the male coffeehouses, the gentleman's public square. Tea and coffee became in-demand imports, and their consumption became the addictive markers of respectability. Along with powdered wigs and underwear, caffeinated beverages were commodities that had *meaning* in the construction of respectability.[24] The custom of a Sunday suit and "dressing up" for church was part of this trend. One was under pressure to buy special clothes in a respectability performance for a church that began with an advocate for the poor.

One trope of respectability was the preoccupation with health, which was also seen as a respectability marker, one that—like today—enjoyed various fads and was promoted by self-described experts. Coffee, tea, tobacco, and sugar (which accompanied the beverages) were all described as healthful. What was new in all this was the notion that virtue equals respectability equals health, which translated into a preoccupation with optimizing one's "health" as a sign of one's virtue. Ben Franklin did not take a *moral* position on sex, for example, but recommended ejaculation inside a suitable woman at optimal intervals, "for health." Ejaculating too often was unhealthy, as was too infrequently, according to the popular beliefs of the day. Women, it was believed, also benefited from properly spaced episodes of sexual release.[25]

Sugar was lambasted by a few physicians who associated it with dental caries and obesity; but that did nothing to stem its use or the obligation to provide it at tea time or in the coffeehouses. Most physicians and sugar advocates lauded it as medicinal, likely a position supported by sugar importers.[26] A respectable household served tea to guests, with sugar, and in a rather ritualized fashion. Gentlemen's coffeehouses, likewise, provided

---

23. Illich, *Gender*, 67–89.
24. Another addictive stimulant made its way to the coffeehouses: tobacco.
25. Franklin, *Autobiography*, 78.
26. Whose industry was utterly dependent on the Atlantic slave trade.

the signature beverage with sugar, and were filled with tobacco smoke that swirled through the sounds of well-mannered, and self-importantly male, political discourse.

The term *respectability* first appeared, as far as historians can tell, in 1785,[27] yet by 1813, when Jane Austen published *Pride and Prejudice*, she used it in iterations too numerous to sensibly count. *Respectability* appeared alongside notions of genteel domestic femininity and rational, coffeehouse masculinity at about the same time that another new word appeared: *civilization*.

Smith researched the origins of the term *civilization* and found the first modern definition around the time of the American Revolution. Samuel Johnson objected to the word as a neologism, sticking with the term *civility*, which was "associated with gentility."[28] *Civilization* appeared alongside ideas like Manifest Destiny, "part of a historical process that supposedly leads humankind to general improvement: in other words, 'progress.'"[29]

By the nineteenth century, with the British Empire consolidated and American continental expansion complete, "respectability" would give rise to some gender anxieties for men, foreshadowed in Hegel's concerns about civilization's effeminizing potential.

The American man's republican masculinity, which saw itself conquering the aristocratic father as well as savages and the wilderness, had crashed into the cataclysm of the American Civil War, then crawled westward to complete the annihilation of indigenous societies.

Europe was stalemated in a balance of power that left its nation-states to direct their martial energies into ever harsher exploitation in Africa and Asia. Conquests complete, the triumphant business class on both sides of the Atlantic turned to its more aesthetic pursuits. The parlor and the coffeehouse were the sets for rational masculinity and domestic femininity, but they also reflected an image back to some men that put them in uncomfortable proximity to women. How was a culture that revolved around a piano in the parlor going to police the boundary between civilization and colony?

This question was raised in the mid-nineteenth century by the Protestant purveyors of a new idea: "muscular Christianity."

27. *Online Etymology Dictionary*, s.v. "Respectability."
28. Smith, *Consumption*, 179.
29. Ibid.

24

Progress and Fear of the Feminine

The man must be glad to do a man's work, to dare and to endure and to labor; to keep himself, and to keep those dependent upon him. The woman must be the housewife, the helpmeet of the homemaker, the wise and the fearless mother of many healthy children.... When men fear work or fear righteous war, when women fear motherhood, they tremble on the brink of doom; and well it is that they should vanish from the earth.

—Theodore Roosevelt[1]

If politics ... were reshaped in part by new norms of masculinity, war (to adapt Clausewitz's dictum) became masculinity by other means.

—John Horne[2]

When Sigmund Freud was publishing "The Psychical Mechanism of Forgetting" in 1898, a young lieutenant-colonel named Theodore Roosevelt, from a fabulously wealthy family of Manhattan land speculators, was leading a cavalry regiment in Cuba during the Spanish-American War. After the Civil War, the United States had maintained a very small standing military, and

---

1. Roosevelt, "Strenuous Life," para. 3.
2. Horne, "Age of Nation-States and World War," 31.

these cobbled-together outfits under the command of influential men with military fantasies were necessary to fill the gap when the opportunity to pounce on Spanish colonies presented itself.

Meanwhile, a dramatic change had occurred in the status of women. As taxed wage labor became the predominant means for making a living for men without land, women, who in farm families were part of the essential production process, were transformed into something called "housewives." We are not talking here about the businessman's wife in her piano parlor, but about the far larger number of women who were married to wage workers. The vernacular economy of the subsistence farm was being swept away by an industrial economy, and women in the home became "shadow workers"[3]—unwaged participants in the process of adding value to commodities in households that no longer produced, but only consumed.

> I designate as shadow work the time, toil, and effort that must be expended in order to add to any purchased commodity the value without which it is unfit for use. Therefore, shadow work names an activity in which people must engage to whatever degree they attempt to satisfy their needs by means of commodities.... When a modern housewife goes to the market, picks up eggs, then drives home in her car, takes the elevator to the seventh floor, turns on the stove, takes butter from the refrigerator, and fries the eggs, she adds value to the commodity with each one of these steps. This is not what her grandmother did. [Illich is writing in 1982.] The latter looked for eggs in the chicken coop, cut a piece from the lard she had rendered, lit some wood her kids had gathered on the commons, and added the salt she had bought.... The grandmother carries out woman's gender-specific tasks in creating subsistence; the new housewife must put up with the household burden of shadow work.[4]

In the late nineteenth and early twentieth century, a dreary working-class reflection of the coffeehouse and parlor—the shop floor and the consuming household—characterized the new model urban family: an economic point of consumption, the man bringing home some money and the woman using it to get those things to which her labor added enough value to make them fit for use. Man was being redefined as earner, woman as consumer, domestic servant, child care manager, and sex object/breeder.

---

3. Illich, *Gender*, 46–66. Illich coined the term "shadow work" for those kinds of work that do not appear in official calculations of economic activity, but that appear only alongside post-vernacular, monetized economies.

4. Ibid., 49.

Even today, if we watch daytime television—which is still oriented toward "housewives," even with many more women earning wages—we will see advertisements for value-addable family "needs": products to assist with domestic chores, products for childcare, and products that claim to increase a woman's sex appeal.

Maria Mies notes that before a new or refreshed process of domination can occur, the object of that domination must be exteriorized,[5] or separated. When this separation is characterized as progress, it usually means progress for one subject with reciprocal "retrogression" for the other. In the process of "housewifization,"[6] men became *more* public beings and women *more* private. For those in vernacular economies, where production and consumption were co-located, the work was gender divided, but the complementary tasks were not alienated in the sense of wage labor or household drudgery. Mies showed a correspondence between the practical and ideological exteriorization of women and the exteriorization of nature and colonies.

Powerful men are conquerors, and what they conquer is threefold: women, nature, and colonies. It is during this period that racialized social Darwinism gains ground, and many anthropological speculations (new origin myths) revolve around the myth of an ancient "man, the hunter." War is a central feature of this trifold conquest-episteme.

> The historical development of the division of labor in general, and the sexual division of labor in particular, was/is not an evolutionary and peaceful process, based on the ever-progressing development of productive forces (mainly technology) and specialization, but a violent one by which first certain categories of men, later certain peoples, were able mainly by virtue of arms and warfare to establish an exploitative relationship between themselves and women, and other peoples and classes.
>
> Within such a predatory mode of production, which is intrinsically patriarchal, warfare and conquest become the most "productive" modes of production. The quick accumulation of material wealth—not based on regular subsistence work in one's own community, but on looting and robbery—facilitates the faster development of technology in those societies which are based on conquest and warfare. This technological development, however, again is not oriented principally towards the satisfaction of subsistence needs of the community as a whole, but towards further warfare, conquest and accumulation.[7]

---

5. Mies here uses this term in a way that echoes Descartes's *res externa*.
6. Mies's neologism.
7. Mies, *Patriarchy and Accumulation*, 74.

Western "civilization" after the Enlightenment developed through the conquest of colonies. American expansion after the Civil War was driven by a war against indigenous people until the Spanish-American War, whereupon the United States began expanding its extra-continental colonies through inter-imperial war. The normative/ideal Western male was defined by his separateness, by boundaries separating him from women, from nature, and from the "unwashed masses" of conquered colonies. He was unlike any of these, and yet he was obliged to transgress those boundaries in order to subdue women, nature, and colonies. Women were *domesticated*. Nature was *tamed*. Colonies were *disciplined* for extraction.

By the Victorian period in the latter part of the nineteenth century, anxious and influential men like the founders of "muscular Christianity" began to describe a "crisis of masculinity" for "white" men based on a surfeit of gentility and migration to the "soft life" of the cities. One of the most vocal of these critics would become the president of the United States: Theodore Roosevelt.

Roosevelt was an emblematic leader when "a fear about the softness of American society raised doubts about the capacity of the United States to carry out its imperial destiny."[8] Continental expansion had ceased, and with it the basis of the national myth of frontier masculinity. There was a fear that the loss of masculinity constructed as conquest would lead to national impotence. Churches spread this fear as well, along with the fear that urban life would bring about a "moral softening." Immigration had increased, and this discourse included talk about "race suicide."[9]

Imperialism was embraced as Manifest Destiny, as the Christianization and civilization of the dark others and the means for the reclamation of white masculinity. Roosevelt rebuked American opposition to the bloody occupation of the Philippines:

> I have scant patience with those who fear to undertake the task of governing the Philippines . . . [who] shrink from it because of the expense and trouble; but I have even scanter patience with those who make a pretense of humanitarianism to hide and cover their timidity, and who cant about "liberty" and "the consent of the governed" in order to excuse themselves from their unwillingness to play the part of men. Their doctrine, if carried out, would make it incumbent upon us to leave the Apaches of Arizona to work out their own salvation, and to decline to interfere with a single Indian reservation. Their doctrines condemn

---

8. Perelman and Portillo, "Football, Eugenics, Imperial Destiny," para. 1.
9. Ibid.

your forefathers and mine for ever having settled in these United States.[10]

Racial superiority discourse was not new, but by the turn of the century it had taken on a distinctly Darwinian idiom.[11] Muscular Christianity explicitly embraced the narrative of white supremacy based on this amalgam of "science," Manifest Destiny, and martial masculinity, calling this amalgam "natural theology."[12] Just as American Protestantism had urged its communicants to financial success as a sign of God's providence, men felt compelled to *live into* an idea of *fit*-ness. Muscular Christianity was literally about muscles inasmuch as it promoted something then called "physical culture," the progenitor of bodybuilding and today's media-hyped Adonis complex among males.

Lampooned by social critics like Sinclair Lewis and H. L. Mencken, muscular Christianity achieved a foothold in American culture among the influential and contributed substantially to turn-of-the-century militarism.[13] Fashion and other commodity-promotion phenomena had introduced the manufactured preoccupations of women into the public sphere, that is, the marketplace, where women's "influence" was perceived as a threat, especially to impressionable urban boys.

In the novel *Tom Brown at Oxford* (1861), Thomas Hughes, one of the founding fathers of "muscular Christianity," wrote that it is "a good thing to have strong and well exercised bodies.... The least of the muscular Christians has hold of the old chivalrous and Christian belief, that a man's body is given him to be trained and *brought into subjection*, and then used for the protection of the weak, the advancement of all righteous causes, and the *subduing of the earth* which God has given to the children of men."[14] Theodore Roosevelt said that the book should be mandatory reading for Americans.

---

10. Roosevelt, "Strenuous Life," para. 15.

11. Not to be confused with evolutionary biology, which makes no reference to "survival of the *fittest*."

12. Kingsley, "Natural Theology."

13. Kimmel and Aronson, *Men and Masculinities*, 587–88. Muscular Christianity is enjoying a resurgence thanks to evangelical pastor Mark Driscoll and other celebrity preachers of Christian machismo. Then as now, it is a reaction to the insecurity experienced by dominant men during periods of gender instability.

14. Hughes, *Tom Brown at Oxford*, 129–30, my italics.

In 1910, W. W. Hastings, the dean of a physical education school in Battle Creek, Michigan, delivered a lecture titled "Racial Hygiene and Vigor,"[15] which combined the themes of hygiene, eugenics, racial superiority, and "physical culture" and which closely mirrored the thought of Roosevelt, who would go on to be the leading political light of the Progressive Movement.

Roosevelt was raised by a stern father who never forgave himself for mustering out of the Civil War and who indoctrinated the frail, asthmatic boy with frontier "conquer nature and the savages" masculinity.[16] By the time Theodore was grown, however, the frontier had been "tamed," and young Theodore had to direct his conquest imperative elsewhere. He became an avid hunter, "testing himself against nature" by shooting animals, and he joined the cavalry to participate in the Spanish-American War. The new frontier was *colonies*, where the American nation could emulate their British predecessors by building an exploitable periphery full of conquered and compliant natives. As to women? Theodore was raised in the domestic femininity tradition, but his eugenic concern with women was as breeders of "fit" children "numerous enough" to populate the nation. In his 1905 speech "On American Motherhood," he said,

> No piled-up wealth, no splendor of material growth, no brilliance of artistic development, will permanently avail any people unless its home life is healthy, unless the average man possesses honesty, courage, common sense, and decency, unless he works hard and is willing at need to fight hard; and unless the average woman is a good wife, a good mother, able and willing to perform the first and greatest duty of womanhood, able and willing to bear, and to bring up as they should be brought up, healthy children, sound in body, mind, and character, and numerous enough so that the race shall increase and not decrease.[17]

Like Jean Bodin—the great philosopher of early political liberalism, the lawyer and witch hunter—Roosevelt called birth control murder. In this, he differed from his fellow eugenics advocate Margaret Sanger. In a reply to Roosevelt's opposition to birth control in 1917, the Malthusian Sanger wrote,

> The trouble with nearly all writers who oppose birth control is that they consider only proximate instead of ultimate effects. They want large numbers of high quality citizens. Therefore, they contend, let the existing high quality citizens have more

---

15. Hastings, "Racial Hygiene and Vigor."
16. Streeter, "All in the Family."
17. Roosevelt, "On American Motherhood," para. 3.

children. They assume that families now living in comfortable circumstances will be able to maintain their standards, no matter how many additional children are born. In other words, they expect quality to take care of itself.

We advocates of birth control know that one cannot make quality by insisting on quantity. One cannot make better people simply by having more people.

Mr. Roosevelt says that in order to make a man into a better citizen, we must first have the man. The right environment in which to receive and develop the man is of great importance. Society, as at present constituted, does not provide the means of rearing unrestricted hordes of human beings into intelligent citizenship. Therefore, birth control has become necessary as a check upon the blind working of ignorance and poverty.[18]

And so began a debate between white liberal feminists and white male "conservatives" in which both sides were mutually committed to *an imperial vision of progress*. This debate continues today between, for example, a Hillary Clinton and a Rick Santorum. *White* feminism demanded both the franchise and reproductive control, the latter expressed in racial eugenic terms. Economic expansion required a drive for extra-national colonization.

In the March 2005 edition of *The Organization of American Historians Magazine*, Bruce Fehn published "Theodore Roosevelt and American Masculinity," in which he wrote, "With the help of cooperative news writers, who continually published stories of his physical exploits, Roosevelt became the 'most famous purveyor' of manly activity as an antidote to 'the fear of the feminization of American men.'"[19]

Two aspects of this highly publicized masculinity were notable: the triple conquest-objects—women, nature, and colonies—and defining masculinity *against* women, that is, being manly means precisely being *not* like a woman. The expectations of men, beginning in boyhood, in social situations was that they would learn the arts of domination—physical, romantic, political, and symbolic. This conditioned desire on the part of men to adopt the role and hold the status of dominator requires the objects of domination for its fulfillment.

What was central to Western *modernity*—as an economic accumulation regime—was the incorporation of *colonial expansion* into the material

---

18. Sanger, "Answer to Mr. Roosevelt," 66–67.
19. Fehn, "Theodore Roosevelt and American Masculinity," 52.

economy as well as the symbolic one. Mies writes not about the development of medieval Christianity or about the ancient Sumerians, but about the emergence and evolution of *Western modernity*. The domination of women had preceded the other two forms of domination—of nature and of colonies—albeit in different forms. The peculiar modern form of domination of nature, however, was explicitly associated with the Enlightenment and Merchant's "death of nature." Colonies corresponded to the domination of (unruly, chaotic, womanly) nature as an integral practice of empire, with its core-periphery dynamic.[20]

The state was the guarantor of profit, meaning (*a*) access to feedstocks, (*b*) a supply of workers, (*c*) the legal right to dispose of waste at low or no cost (called externalization), and (*d*) a market of consumers big enough to soak up the product. Because this was inherently expansionist, it required businessmen to reach beyond their borders for some or all of these "resources" as they became exhausted or unavailable in the cores. Expansion required the intervention of the state to claim distant lands and subdue restive or resistant peoples. Expansion also required a moral justification, because there was enough residual commitment, in a Christian society, to *caritas* to find the idea of bald-faced plunder offensive and irreconcilable with the faith. That justification became *progress*, associated in the national imagination with respectability and civilization. We weren't conquering or exploiting "those people"; we were enlightening them and civilizing them. Conquest was a form of charity.

In 1899, Rudyard Kipling published a poem in *McClure's*, a popular magazine of the time, titled "The White Man's Burden." The poem was written explicitly as an apology for colonialism; it claimed the "white man's burden" was to civilize the "darker races." Plunder was transformed into altruism, albeit an altruism that would have to be carried out with tough love, including war. The first stanza reads,

> Take up the White Man's burden—
> Send forth the best ye breed—
> Go, bind your sons to exile

---

20. Core-periphery dynamic is a concept from world-systems theory. In this approach, flows of materials that constitute wealth or serve as feedstocks for the manufacture of wealth are tracked, as well as the use of monetary and military power to ensure those flows. The destinations of wealth are cores, and the exploited regions from which extraction takes place are peripheries. The Atlantic slave trade transfers workers (slaves) from one periphery to another (the Caribbean), where sugar plantations are used to exploit the land after the Taino people have been exterminated, and the sugar is sold in Europe for a profit. Europe is the core. Africa and the Caribbean are the peripheries.

> To serve your captives' need;
> To wait, in heavy harness,
>
> On fluttered folk and wild—
> Your new-caught sullen peoples,
> Half devil and half child.²¹

Women have heretofore been described as the slaves of lust and symbols of demonic disorder, and they had *also* been described as children. In either case, the "half devil, half child" requires containment and tutelage ... from men, "real men." Mies says that colonies and women are conflated when women are "defined *into* nature."

Mies, citing Merchant's *Death of Nature*, writes,

> Carolyn Merchant has shown that the destruction of nature as a living organism—and the rise of modern science and technology, together with the rise of male scientists as the new high priests—has its close parallel in the violent attack on women during the witch hunt. . . . Merchant does not extend her analysis to the relation of the New Men to their colonies. Yet an understanding of this relation is absolutely necessary, because we cannot understand the modern developments, including our present problems, unless we include all those who were "defined into nature" . . . Mother Earth, Women, and Colonies.²²

The late Victorian, reactive masculinity complex was a hothouse for the aggressive militarism epitomized in the public persona of Theodore Roosevelt and the social movement with which he was most closely identified: Progressivism.

Militarism was not an epithet at the dawn of the twentieth century; it was celebrated. Indiana Senator Albert Beveridge, in an editorial for the *Los Angeles Times*, wrote, "Every generation of Americans has been soldiers. Militarism in America! Yes, indeed there is enough militarism in the blood of the free young men of this republic not only to defeat the world at arms, but to defeat every military uprising among ourselves that might seek to overthrow the republic. The future of the institutions of the republic is in the hands of the republic's young men, and in their hands those institutions are secure."²³ The reference to blood in this case is racial. The jurist and future

---

21. Kipling, "White Man's Burden," lines 1–8.
22. Mies, *Patriarchy and Accumulation*, 75.
23. Beveridge, "Our Peerless Flag Is There!"

secretary of state during Theodore Roosevelt's presidency, Elihu Root, who was a great proponent of building a modern military in the United States, referred in the same way to "the blood," meaning an inhering American (read: Anglo-Saxon) racial superiority—"the American race," he said.[24]

Several vehicles were employed for the militarization of the United States during the Progressive Era, among the most prominent being public schools, colleges, sports, Boy Scouting, and gun culture.

> The particular utopia American believers chose to bring to the schoolhouse was Prussian. The seed that became American schooling, twentieth-century style, was planted in 1806 when Napoleon's amateur soldiers bested the professional soldiers of Prussia at the battle of Jena. When your business is renting soldiers and employing diplomatic extortion under threat of your soldiery, losing a battle like that is pretty serious. Something had to be done.[25]

John Taylor Gatto's history of compulsory public schools begins with war. The German philosopher bridging Kant and Hegel was Johann Gottlieb Fichte (1762–1814). After the German defeat at Jena, Fichte delivered a speech titled "Address to the German Nation," in which he castigated Prussia's lack of devotion to the nation and prescribed a regimen of disciplined conditioning for citizenship. This was the beginning of the modern compulsory public school.[26] In 1819, Prussia launched the first national system of public education. Its goals were clear. Children were to be trained for one of several fates: obedient soldier, obedient worker, obedient clerk, or obedient civil servant.[27] All would be entrained to national values and "uniformity in thought, word, and deed."[28] The models for this training were military organization, horse training, and animal husbandry.

The most widely known and influential proponent of the Prussian system for the United States was Horace Mann (1796–1859). A Unitarian devotee of phrenology, Mann called for a national and compulsory free public school system with a regimented curriculum and standardized, centralized teacher training, which he had observed and admired among the

24. Possner, *Rise of Militarism*, 7.
25. Gatto, *Weapons of Mass Instruction*, 131.
26. Ibid.
27. Today, a similar system in the United States prevails, called "tracking."
28. Gatto, *Weapons of Mass Instruction*.

Prussians.[29] Mann believed that such a system would ameliorate poverty, a belief that persists today among American public-education advocates in spite of consistent evidence to the contrary over the last century.[30] Mann's proposals were only locally implemented when he died and the Civil War began.

The Prussian regimentation paid off in 1870 when Prussia again went to war with France and crushed them in less than a year. It was this victory that caught the attention of many aspiring social engineers in the United States, sending them back to Mann's theses, and they began proselytizing in earnest for a school system similar to the Germans'. With the Progressive Movement, they finally prevailed. What schools there had been in the United States were largely preparatory schooling for the elite or places to learn piety, good manners, and the rudiments of literacy and numeracy.

In 1970, when Ivan Illich wrote *Deschooling Society*, the Prussian model was apparent (it still is), albeit now as a product called "education," the ritualization of which has become part of the liturgy of progress.

> Many students, especially those who are poor, intuitively know what the schools do for them. They school them to confuse process and substance. Once these become blurred, a new logic is assumed: the more treatment there is, the better are the results; or, escalation leads to success. The pupil is thereby "schooled" to confuse teaching with learning, grade advancement with education, a diploma with competence, and fluency with the ability to say something new. His imagination is "schooled" to accept service in place of value. Medical treatment is mistaken for health care, social work for the improvement of community life, police protection for safety, military poise for national security, the rat race for productive work.[31]

To this day, the belief that something called "education" is essential persists with overwhelming force, and few question the goodness of education as a compulsory *product*. We do not say you need to undergo a regimented process of standardized teaching by certified "experts," aimed at the acquisition of a credential, even though that is exactly what happens; we say, "You need an education." To question the value of this *education* today is to seem a visitor from another planet. The supposed value of the product,

29. Sanders, "Horace Mann, Part II."

30. Average annual public-school spending in the United States at the time of this writing is more than a trillion dollars. The stratification between rich and poor in the U.S. has never been steeper, with 10 percent of the population controlling almost three-quarters of the wealth, and the bottom 40 percent controlling two-tenths of 1 percent.

31. Illich, *Deschooling Society*, 1.

education, has not always seemed so apparent. It only became common sense after the entire society had been indoctrinated in *progress*. The roots of this progress were capital accumulation, war, and nationalism.

Education was one of the key goals of the Progressive reformers. Introduction to the military arts for boys was a key part of most curricula, and military training in land grant colleges was the beginning of what would become the Reserve Officer Training Corps (ROTC). The United States military designated active duty officers to work in high schools and colleges, as well as the numerous new military-style private schools, to train young men in "military science."[32] Progressives were concerned about the feminization of men, the recent influx of non-English speaking immigrants, the temptations to vice of urban life for boys, and a general lack of discipline among the young. The compulsory public school, modeled on the Prussian military, was a ready-made "solution." Progressives equated "good citizenship" with respect for authority.[33] The marching and drilling we see today in schools—attend any football game—is purely military in its origins.

By the end of the nineteenth century, football, a new game promoted in the schools and military academies and modeled on war, was vigorously embraced by those who bewailed the crisis of masculinity in urban Western culture. Roosevelt was an avid supporter of football in universities; he and his contemporaries saw universities as training grounds for the master race. In a letter to a famous football coach, Walter Camp of Yale University, Roosevelt wrote,

> The man on the farm and in the workshop here, as in other countries, is apt to get enough physical work; but we were tending steadily in America to produce in our leisure and sedentary classes a type of man not much above the Bengalee baboo, and from this the athletic spirit has saved us. Of all games I personally like football best, and I would rather see my boys play it than see them play any other. I have no patience with the people who declaim against it because it necessitates rough play and occasional injuries. The rough play, if confined within manly and honorable limits, is an advantage.[34]

---

32. Possner, *Rise of Militarism*, 14–30.

33. Ibid.

34. Letter to Walter Camp, quoted in Perelman and Portillo, "Football, Eugenics, and Imperial Destiny."

Progress and Fear of the Feminine

In 1910, when black boxer Jack Johnson stunningly defeated the undefeated white champion, James Jeffries, Roosevelt wrote to the magazine *Outlook* that prizefighting should be banned.[35] This boxing victory did not fit the racial narrative of Roosevelt or of most white Americans at the time.

Football was a rendition of rugby, a British man-sport that imperial ideologues in the United States credited for the ability of the British to seize and hold an empire.[36] Football coaches were used as military advisors to develop physical training programs; and the Army-Navy game between West Point and Annapolis was promoted as a nationwide spectacle. While the first Army-Navy game was played on a roped-off field at West Point in 1890, by 1908 it was attended by thirty thousand at Philadelphia's Franklin Field and heavily hyped in the *New York Times*.[37]

The game, drenched in military metaphors, was also a business opportunity:

> Because football seemed to reflect the aspirations of modern business, which was the greatest beneficiary of imperial expansion, it supported the imperial destiny. In so far as the fostering of the expanding professional and administrative middle class was concerned, American football provided strict rules for the Ivy League players compared with the ill-defined organization of traditional rugby. In this way, the organization of football came to resemble the newly emerging vision of scientific management of business.[38]

The legacy of this military-sports-business model can be seen today in the crossover between books on management that cite military leadership and successful sports coaching.

Football resulted in an alarming number of injuries and deaths, conjuring the wrath of a few public women and fellow male critics of both sports and militarism; but Senator Henry Cabot Lodge, an ardent militarist, made his case before the graduating class of Harvard in 1896, saying, "Injuries incurred on the playing field are part of the price which the English-speaking race has paid for being world conquerors."[39]

35. Powell, "100 Years After."
36. Perelman and Portillo, "Football, Eugenics, and Imperial Destiny."
37. Possner, *Rise of Militarism*, 38–39.
38. Perelman and Portillo, "Football, Eugenics, and Imperial Destiny."
39 Dean, *Imperial Brotherhood*, 32.

The American Boy Scouts were founded in 1910, modeled on an English version of the same founded by General Robert Baden-Powell, as an antidote to urbanization's deleterious effect on boys' manliness, individualism, and patriotism. Many of the early scout leaders were former military men, and the male mythos they promoted was frontier masculinity, with figures like Daniel Boone as archetypes.[40] The closing of the frontier was considered by Progressive men and muscular Christians alike a dangerous loss for American masculinity. Scouting was seen as a corrective for potentially feminizing contamination in the school classroom, which, while it promoted a Prussian respect for authority, co-located girls with boys. Allen Warren writes that scouting was understood to promote the personality of a combination of "military scout, trapper, and colonial frontiersman." Baden-Powell, the guru of the scouting movement, believed that schools were remiss in their concentration on literacy and the classics, which, after all, might be mastered by girls as well as boys. He wanted to build men, and a particular kind of man at that. Baden-Powell even decried football, though not participation in it but the fact that urban male youth were hanging out around the matches, where they "slouched" and smoked cigarettes.[41] Roosevelt himself pointed out that industrial civilization had these downsides, and praised scouting as an activity that would build men who were "good soldiers and good citizens."[42]

Not everyone was overwhelmed with enthusiasm for Progressive masculinity, Roosevelt's male posturing, or scouting. The burgeoning socialist movement and the Industrial Workers of the World were quick to point out that there was an authoritarian edge to these developments that might be used against the labor movement. The Western Federation of Miners issued a statement that said scouting was designed for "an effective army of servile, dog-like automats . . . a trained body of flunkies, strikebreakers, and in case of need, policemen and soldiers."[43] In fact, the Boy Scouts were used on various occasions for strikebreaking, and some unions threatened to expel anyone who allowed their boys to join, saying the boys were being indoctrinated into "fealty to . . . employers" and that the purpose of scouting was "to capture the minds . . . of children for the military state."[44]

Churches now routinely support scouting as a character-building activity, with little thought about its origins, its goals, or its inhering militarism.

40. Possner, *Rise of Militarism*, 31–35
41. Warren, "Popular Manliness, 201.
42. Cited in Possner, *Rise of Militarism*, 33.
43. Ibid., 35.
44. Norwood, *Strikebreaking and Intimidation*, 11.

The Boy Scouts trained members in shooting, as well; and today there are still merit badges awarded for rifle and shotgun shooting.

In 1912, one scout shot another with a rifle, and there was a temporary discontinuation of the "marksmanship" badge, but lobbying from the National Rifle Association (NRA) got the merit badge reinstated in 1914.[45]

The NRA, established in 1871 by veteran Civil War officers, was conceived after former Union generals estimated that troops had fired one thousand rounds of ammunition for every Confederate soldier killed. Begun as a marksmanship improvement association, it soon became the go-to organization for men with a powerful interest in guns.[46]

Prior to the Civil War, personal gun ownership was marginal. Guns were handmade and expensive. After the mass production of guns for the Civil War, however, the leftover firearms were ubiquitous; and industrialized gun manufacture became a highly profitable postwar enterprise. During the war, Samuel Colt's Hartford factory produced guns that were sold to both Union and Confederate forces. Southern customers were even given a 10 percent incentive discount for mass direct factory orders.[47]

Race has always been mixed with American gun culture. Union soldiers occupied the South during Reconstruction, sometimes arming black men for self-defense; and Southern white men reacted by engaging in guerrilla-like actions against Union troops and outright terrorism against African Americans. Radical Republican masculinity, African American masculinity, and Southern white masculinity all came to identify themselves with repeating firearms.

> By 1876, the nation's centennial year, a reactionary tidal wave had swept away the remnants of Radical Reconstruction in the South. Paramilitary white supremacists in Louisiana, Mississippi, and South Carolina justified their armed assaults on Republican-led state and local offices by invoking their revolutionary forefathers' armed revolt against tyranny. Organizing gun and rifle clubs throughout the Deep South, these self-proclaimed "minutemen" set out to "redeem" the white race from the ignominy of defeat and emancipation. To them, black citizenship signaled the worst kind of corruption.[48]

45. Petterchak, *Lone Scout*, 69.
46. Emberton, "Real Origin of America's Gun Culture."
47. Ibid., para. 2.
48. Ibid., para. 5.

Listening today to the gun-culturist/conspiracy-theorist/radio talk show host Alex Jones, we can hear a direct echo of this Revolutionary War mythology:

> I'm here to tell you, 1776 will commence again if you try to take our firearms! It doesn't matter how many lemmings you get out there in the street begging for them to have their guns taken. We will not relinquish them. Do you understand?[49]

References to the Revolutionary War as proof that "God, Guts, and Guns Made America Free" are fictional. In truth, during the latter eighteenth century in the thirteen colonies, not one in a hundred men had a gun, and the guns they had were muskets, barely capable of hitting another man beyond twenty feet. A dozen colonials once ambushed Major Pitcairn of the British Army at ten yards, all firing, and neither Pitcairn nor his horse received a scratch. It took up to four minutes to reload a musket. A soldier could run a third to half a mile in that time, the reason bayonet charges followed infantry volleys. The single most effective combat weapon after artillery *was* the bayonet. The reason the Revolutionary War dragged on as long as it did was the extreme shortage of weapons.

Successful hunters employed traps, not guns, and Americans overwhelmingly consumed livestock for meat. Only white male Protestant property owners were allowed by law to have firearms, and many of them opted against it. A decent gun cost as much as a skilled laborer made in six months. The legends promoted by stories like *The Deerslayer* and films like *The Last of the Mohicans* and *The Patriot* are plain nonsense. The archetype of the great marksmen of the colonies as the basis for an effective citizen-soldier militia has zero basis in history.[50]

By the late nineteenth century, the popular myth was not the Revolutionary War but the "conquest of the frontier," meaning westward expansion, with its displacement or extermination of indigenous people. This was when the cowboy myth was created, and even promoted, through rambling circuses like Buffalo Bill's Wild West show (1872–1910), using aging and self-aggrandizing legends of the "Old West." In addition to promoting a particular version of masculinity, Western expansion legends were a kind of geographic cure for the divisions of the Civil War. American men could set aside the grievances of the Civil War by looking westward, renewing the basis for white male ideological unity in the discourse of "taming the West."

---

49. Interview with Piers Morgan, cited in ibid., para. 1.
50. Petersen, "Arming America."

William "Buffalo Bill" Cody (1846–1917) was himself a great admirer of William Sherman, who called for outright Indian extermination, and of George Custer, whom he saw as a white martyr. Cody's show, usually billed alongside military tournaments,[51] reenacted "battles" between white men and Indians that emphasized Indian savagery and white nobility.

Republican masculinity emphasized the somewhat Oedipal struggle for "liberty" against the aristocratic fathers; frontier masculinity was an artifact of expansion and empire building. Real men were those who, on civilization's behalf and as civilization's racial representatives, left the comforts of the core and ventured into the borderlands to establish new outposts against the disorder of nature and those peoples defined into nature—the savages, the natives. The gun, for frontier masculinity, had (and still has) a real, but also an imaginary and a symbolic existence. Guns were certainly used by soldiers during the Indian Wars, and at the end of the century for the war to gain Spain's colonies. But in the fantasies constructed by military reenactments and circuses like the Cody show, the idea was implanted—and it can still be seen in Westerns—that most men went armed all the time. This was not, in fact, the case. Armed men were generally soldiers, law enforcement, criminals, and semi-official thugs. Men who hunted with guns, as they do today, would dust off the rifle or shotgun that was stored in the house. Gun control laws in the "Old West," that is, legendary towns like Dodge City, Tombstone, and Deadwood, were actually far stricter than most gun control laws today. Municipal law enforcement generally required that any firearm inside city limits had to be stored at the local law enforcement office.[52]

The rise of gun culture among Progressives was closely associated with these fantasy histories of the Old West; and the gun became a phallic symbol representing the male forces of order against the feminine disorder of nature and natives. But the signature events that gave rise to twentieth-century gun culture were the Spanish-American and Philippine-American wars, where marksmanship failures were again blamed for battlefield deficiencies.

The NRA, which had become moribund by this time, was reconstituted in 1900, and began sponsoring rifle marksmanship competitions.[53] In 1902, at the NRA grand competition at Sea Girt, New Jersey, Roosevelt gave an opening address in which he proclaimed, "We have prided ourselves on being an army of marksmen,"[54] explicitly tying Progressive era men's newfound preoccupation with guns to imperial militarism. The rifle teams

51. Possner, *Rise of Militarism*, 42–44.
52. Winkler, "Wild West Gun Control."
53. Possner, *Rise of Militarism*, 85–86.
54. *New York Times*, "The President at Sea Girt Camp."

in early NRA competitions were comprised exclusively of men who were members of the armed forces, cementing a relationship between the NRA and the War Department, which persists to this day.

> The 1903 Sea Girt tournament Sunday opened with an open-air service. Conducted by the Rev. J. Madison Hare, chaplain of the Third Regiment of the New Jersey National Guard: "Responsive Bible readings and the singing of the hymns 'Adoration' and 'America' preceded the sermon. Chaplain Hare's theme was 'An Improved Score.'"[55]

Marksmanship was understood as a manifestation of white male superiority, demonstrating technological prowess, good health, and self-control. An article in the *Los Angeles Times* in 1909 declared in its headline, "Marksmen Are Born, Not Manufactured," lest it be assumed that the traits of a great marksman could be taught to just anyone.

> The rifle type of man is a muscular, lean, quiet fellow of nervous temperament, but whose nerves are under the complete control of the will.[56]

As we will see in the next chapter, however, World War I was brewing, and when it boiled over, the value of marksmanship would be trumped by machine guns and artillery. Masculinity would again be destabilized.

---

55. Possner, *Rise of Militarism*, 87.
56. *Los Angeles Times*, "Marksmen Are Born."

25

Shell Shock

I found him staring into the fire. He had not shaved, and his trousers were half open. I could get nothing out of him.... He did not appear to be ill. We agreed to let him rest, to let him stay in his billet till the battalion came out of the trenches, but the next day when everyone had gone up the line he blew his head off.

—Charles Watson, WWI veteran[1]

The government will ... go on in the highly democratic method of conscripting American manhood for European slaughter.

—Emma Goldman, 1917[2]

Jack Johnson's defeat of white boxing opponents wasn't the only thing in the first decade of the twentieth century to queer the Progressive narrative about white supremacy. In a war that had broken out between industrializing Japan and Russia over control of the Korean Peninsula, Japan defeated the Russians, who were seen as fellow Europeans. Naval power, now fueled by petroleum and projected with rifled cannon, was decisive in this defeat.

1. Cited in May, "Lord Moran's Memoir," 95.
2. Goldman, "Address to the Jury," 56.

This was the first big war of the twentieth century (February 1904–September 1905), and an East Asian power had defeated a European one.[3]

Anti-Asian prejudice was already powerful in the United States, especially on the West Coast. In 1905, sixty-seven labor unions had come together to form the Japanese and Korean Exclusion League at San Francisco. In 1907, over five hundred union men in Bellingham, Washington, rioted against South Asian immigrants. The League was renamed the Asiatic Exclusion League.[4]

A 1906 *Los Angeles Times* editorial hyperventilated, "The Japanese fleet could shell, sack, and burn every city on the whole coast line. . . . Any attack by land on the part of any power the United States can well discount, but the destruction possible by a hostile fleet of powerful modern warships of the coastal cities is an appalling contemplation."[5]

Japanophobia coincided with two industrial innovations in the United States: Fordism and Taylorism. Fordism was a new system of mass production pioneered for Ford Motors, and Taylorism a new system of "scientific management" theorized by Frederick Winslow Taylor. Together they had accelerated production rates, supported with massive research and development efforts by engineers. This transformation of industry was put to use in the development of armaments.[6]

The newest preoccupation of weapons developers had become coastal artillery. The race was on to shoot bigger payloads further, with greater accuracy, and from more hardened positions than could be achieved by the increasingly large and longer-range naval cannons.[7] The result was the development of highly lethal artillery munitions, fired with terrifying accuracy across the horizon. This technology was transferred to towed artillery for ground combat.

In 1861, Richard Jordan Gatling invented an automatic-loading, sequential-fire gun, the prototype of the machine gun. Its use was limited during the Civil War because the gun generated so much smoke from the burnt powder that the gunner's sight was blocked in short order, and his position became painfully obvious to enemy shooters. In the latter nineteenth century, smokeless powder was invented, and the Europeans used the sequence-fire guns to successfully kill large numbers of ill-armed Africans and Asians in colonial skirmishes and massacres. In 1884, Sir Hiram

3. Connaughton, *The War of the Rising Sun*.
4. Cahn, "The 1907 Bellingham Riots.
5. *Los Angeles Times*, "The Paths to Peace."
6. Possner, *Rise of Militarism*, 215.
7. Ibid., 217–19.

Maxim improved the design by using the recoil of the fired round to initiate the reloading cycle, replacing the hand crank. The Maxim Gun was the first modern machine gun, and it employed ammunition that was linked into belts. A gunner could simply hold the trigger down and achieve a very high cyclic rate of fire stabilized from a steel tripod. Several more models of machine gun were quickly developed using this basic design.

Military planners and theorists never anticipated how the dual development of long-range rifled artillery and the machine gun would change the calculations of a war between great powers.

Harry Stout has suggested that the American Civil War established the American civil religion, merging church and state into one.[8] World War I consolidated the merger, giving large numbers of Northern and Southern white men the opportunity to fight alongside each other under the same flag. Progressive churches flocked to the banner and cast the war for the first time as "self-sacrificial service to other nations," giving it an altruistic theme and cosigning its international character.[9]

These messianic themes concealed a more pecuniary motive. The war itself was undertaken during the Woodrow Wilson administration. Wilson had run on a peace platform; but the U.S. had bankrolled the Allies. When it looked as if New York's financial institutions might be facing the prospect of an Allied defeat, Wilson beat the drum and sent the troops to secure repayment of the debt.[10]

The war had begun with an inter-imperial rivalry between Great Britain and the up-and-coming Germany. No one anticipated the scale of the destruction or the horror of this war. Infantry charges met with the withering lethality of the new machine gun, turning the European war into a slaughterhouse of attrition fought from pestilent trenches. These static trenches were then subjected to screeching storms of across-the-horizon artillery. Poison gas was deployed—and those who did not drown on their own blistered lungs or go blind were forced to bear life in the trenches, where they could wait for random artillery death, their respirations echoing in the sweaty rubber-and-glass masks strapped to their faces, lice feasting on their bodies, their macerated feet peeling away inside wet, muddy boots. In the Somme offensive alone, there were more than a million casualties.

8. Stout, *Upon the Altar*.
9. Gamble, *War for Righteousness*, 187.
10. Hudson, *Super Imperialism*, 41–55.

Glory in battle gave way to the valorization of a kind of grim individual endurance.[11] The shock of the war's senseless destruction gave rise to Christian pacifist as well as humanist war opposition. Christian pacifists, socialists, women's groups, and a host of artists and intellectuals questioned the reasons for the war, and the reasons for *war* in general. By 1920, public opinion had tilted in support of Benjamin Joseph Salmon, a Catholic pacifist who had been sentenced to twenty-five years' hard labor for refusing induction. Said Salmon,

> Regardless of nationality, all men are brothers. God is "our Father who art in heaven." The commandment "Thou shalt not kill" is unconditional and inexorable. . . . The lowly Nazarene taught us the doctrine of non-resistance, and so convinced was he of the soundness of that doctrine that he sealed his belief with death on the cross. When human law conflicts with Divine law, my duty is clear. Conscience, my infallible guide, impels me to tell you that prison, death, or both, are infinitely preferable to joining any branch of the Army.[12]

After more than two years of beatings and forced-feeding in response to a hunger strike, he was released. While Salmon was incarcerated, he received no support from his church hierarchy. Cardinal John Farley of New York said, "I consider it little short of treason. . . . Every citizen of this nation, no matter what his private opinion or his political leanings, should support the President and his advisers to the limit of his ability."[13] Church and state were *again* one, and morality had *again* been outsourced to the state. The fact that the war was fought by Christians, who were engaged in killing other Christians, gave most Allied and Central Powers churches no pause. Each declared the other apostates and enemies of God. Nationalism had grotesquely triumphed over Christianity *and* Christendom.

Meanwhile, the imagination of war was being confronted by its new reality. Machine guns, artillery, and poison gas confronted the old symbols, and they began to lose their meanings. With the loss of meaning, men and masculinity were confronted with a new crisis, which Nietzsche had already named—the death of God. The God of the univocal metaphysic was, for many participants and observers, nowhere to be found in the trenches, and the name of God seemed to many a kind of obscenity on the lips of the war's apologists.

---

11. The selection processes for elite military units still test foremost for endurance—note chapter 2 on the Selection and Assessment Course for Delta Force.

12. Letter to Woodrow Wilson, cited in Finney, *Unsung Hero*, 118–19.

13. Cited in Parachin, *Eleven Modern Mystics*, 30.

Two decades later, Dalton Trumbo wrote *Johnny Got His Gun*, a novel in which a soldier gravely wounded by artillery finds himself in the hospital with no arms, no legs, no face, no eyes, and no tongue. He tries to suffocate himself, but cannot because he has a tracheotomy. He is a prisoner in his own war-maimed body. This image undermined the public imagination of the war as redemptive, and in place of a flag or two fingers held aloft in the symbol of victory, the reader was left facing this human stump, exchanging gases through a tube, thinking ever thinking without the capacity to act.

The sheer numbers of men being conscripted into the war to compensate for battlefield attrition combined with the industrial bases of the war to create labor shortages. Women were increasingly pulled into the workforce to replace men and to fill the ranks at munitions factories. Women filled the military ranks as nurses, too. In Russia, combat personnel shortages became so extreme that women were formed into fifteen battalions of all-female fighters, with names like the "Women's Battalion of Death." Many of these women would fight in female infantry units for the Bolsheviks during the Russian Civil War, which came on the heels of the Great War.[14] Just as industrial capitalism would eventually blur gender lines to increase the consumer base, industrial war began to blur the gender lines that were established in the age of respectability. Rational masculinity was faced with the irrational horror of the trenches; and domestic femininity was overcome to supply the slaughter. The probative masculinity of Roosevelt and the Progressives, which saw militarism as the antidote for urban effeminacy in men, was likewise challenged.

> The most important aspect of [the] construction of masculinity and the focus on courage as its core was that it made the masculine ideal unobtainable. A man's honor needed to be earned, and a man could not do this without showing courage in the face of some type of challenge to that honor. This could be achieved in the world of sports, but this was a poor substitute for the ultimate test of one's honor, which was combat.[15]

The intensity of the slaughter and the mechanical-industrial nature of warfare came head to head with masculinity as a probative practice. Being a "real man" requires constant proof in practice. Under the barrages of invisible artillery and in the face of machine guns and gas, men were learning firsthand that no man is without limits to his courage and resolve. Men saw and experienced this limit. Under the rain of artillery or facing clouds of gas with no means of self-defense, the most disciplined and courageous of them

---

14 Griese and Stites, "Russia: Revolution and War."
15. Moblo, "Failed Men."

would eventually succumb to a loss of control or an almost catatonic state of inaction characterized by something that would be called "the thousand-yard stare." A new word entered into the vocabulary of soldiers and medicine: *shell shock*.[16]

Men came home from the war crazed and crippled. They found women who were more public and more independent. Not only were many women reluctant to return to strictly domestic practices; many men found themselves unable to fit into a society that no longer made sense to them. Men would come home unconvinced of the rationality of what they had just undergone, but also with contradictory resentments against those who had caused the war—often understood as the rich—and those who had for whatever reasons been exempted from participation (also the rich).[17] Men who had spent a long time away worried about their wives' and girlfriends' infidelities. Men who had stayed behind were seen as potential sexual opportunists.[18] Women, for their part, were not only pulling double duty as childrearers and workers, but many of them lived in constant fear of the arrival of a telegram.

As physicians began to understand the patterns associated with shell shock, another gender division eroded. Shell shock had the same symptoms described by Freud and others as a female malady, *hysteria*,[19] a breakdown caused by the combination of fear and helplessness.[20] The treatments for shell shock were adapted from the treatments for "hysteria," and men were keenly aware that they were being treated "like women." Many men, in reaction to the disgust they felt in discovering "womanly" things in themselves, became increasingly hostile toward women, feeling compelled to engage in compensatory risky practices.

Hemingway's protagonist in the novel *The Sun Also Rises*, Jake Barnes, was castrated by a war wound, and after the war Hemingway has his character further emasculated by the lead female character, Lady Brett Ashley (note the masculine name Brett)—a projection of Hemingway's own dislike and fear of women.

Where in nonindustrial gender orders being a *man* was described in opposition to being a *boy*, increasingly being a man was understood as being not-like-a-woman. The paradox in this kind of binary opposition, as opposed to complementary gender in cooperative household production, is

16. Hochschild, *To End All Wars*, 242.
17. Moblo, "Failed Men."
18. Ibid.
19. From Latin *hystericus*, meaning "of the womb."
20. Showalter, *The Female Malady*.

that now being a man *required* a negative construction of woman in order to exist. Man was no longer defined as the complement of woman, but *over-against* woman.

In the recruiting propaganda for World War I, there was a nearly equal distribution of recruiting posters featuring Uncle Sam and his female counterparts, Lady Liberty and Lady Columbia. By the time World War II recruiting took off, the female characters disappeared entirely, and Uncle Sam was represented now as bigger, meaner, and more muscular.[21]

According to Amy Greenberg, prior to the war, notions of masculinity were being pulled in three directions at once.[22] Respectable Victorian masculinity was organized around technical or economic expertise. The primitive masculinity of social Darwinism was based on a notion of "man the hunter." And martial masculinity was predicated on tough aggressiveness that comported with the imperatives of territorial expansion. The ideal man, then, was one who could be genteel and restrained at home and work, unrestrained in the application of violence beyond the borders, and someone who hunts animals.

For men who were not independently wealthy, normative masculinity partaking of these conceits was an unattainable ideal. Only someone like a Theodore Roosevelt, unconstrained by the necessity to work in a factory, for example, could play at all three—urban gentleman, soldier, and hunter. For the rest, there was only one place to assert themselves—the military. When the call went up to join the ranks in World War I, before men were confronted with being shelled and huddling in a muddy trench, there was tremendous enthusiasm, an infectious sense of manly adventure. One diarist wrote, "War to us [recruits] was just a big game—then—but later, what disillusionment, how different to what we had imagined."[23]

Victorian ideals of self-reliance were blown up in the trenches. Men returned with no illusions about their physical vulnerability or their ability to go it alone. Moreover, they returned with a deep fatalism.[24] To protect their own psyches, veterans became callous.

To this day, the inculcation of callousness is part of basic military training. I spoke with an Iraq War veteran, a female MP, who had been ordered to drive extremely fast to avoid being ambushed. She accidentally ran over a child, and her vehicle commander, a sergeant, told her to keep going. "Shit

---

21. Jarvis, *Male Body at War*, 35–44.
22. Greenberg, *Manifest Manhood*, 8.
23. Meyer, *Men of War*, 137.
24. Ibid., 139.

happens," he said. She still doesn't know if she killed the child. She will never know; and this instant in time now haunts her days and dreams.

A philosophical consequence of the Great War was nihilism. If you want to draw the line that leads from Friedrich Nietzsche (1844–1900) to Karl Barth (1886–1968), that line runs through the trenches of the Somme. Nietzsche's devastating critique of genteel society, with its terrifying metaphysical implications, took on new meaning in the wake of the war, which for many confirmed Nietzsche's threat of meaninglessness.

> "Whither is God?" he cried. "I shall tell you. We have killed him—you and I. All of us are his murderers. But how have we done this? How were we able to drink up the sea? Who gave us the sponge to wipe away the entire horizon? What did we do when we unchained this earth from its sun? Whither is it moving now? Whither are we moving now? Away from all suns? Are we not plunging continually? Backward, sideward, forward, in all directions? Is there any up or down left? Are we not straying as through an infinite nothing? Do we not feel the breath of empty space? Has it not become colder? Is not night and more night coming on all the while? . . . God is dead. God remains dead. And we have killed him. How shall we, the murderers of all murderers, comfort ourselves? What was holiest and most powerful of all that the world has yet owned has bled to death under our knives.[25]

Karen Carr writes, "Barth's *Roemerbrief* becomes all the more important when one realizes that the emphasis on meaninglessness as the ground of the genuinely human life was not limited to the theological sphere."[26] It should not be surprising, given how masculinity itself had taken on a quasi-religious status during the Progressive era, that with the loss of faith in the wake of the war, masculinity would reconstitute itself in nihilism. Darwin had made us monkeys. Freud turned us into sock puppets for the subconscious. Industrialism turned us into the extensions of machines. Labor historian Stephen Meyer writes, "Removing the male traits of brawn and brain from workplace skills, Taylorism and Fordism redefined skill as the endurance of repetitious and monotonous tasks and their speedy and dexterous performance. For both craftsmen and laborers, their work be-

---

25. Nietzsche, *Gay Science*, sec. 125.
26. Carr, *Banalization of Nihilism*, 2.

came unmanly."[27] The Great War turned us into a pink spray in an artillery burst. Or not. It was out of our control. A crapshoot. Dumb luck.

After the war, not only did society become more pluralistic in an orgy of consumption, the forms of masculinity multiplied, provoking a renewed effort by state and civil society to promote a normative bi-pole of masculinity-femininity. Its critics among cultural leaders and veterans notwithstanding, American nationalism was reanimated by a new enemy: Bolshevism.

Because the history of the state-communist experience is now behind us, it is difficult to appreciate how terrifying the 1917 revolution in Russia was to Western capitalists. One year *before* the Great War concluded, Russian soldiers, disillusioned by the war, had joined with Russian social democrats, unionists, and peasants to overthrow the Romanov aristocracy in the name of socialism. During the civil war that followed, the United States, Great Britain, Japan, and eleven other nations sent a combined military force to invade Russia on behalf of the anticommunist White Army, where they remained for two years before the Red Army expelled them.

A subsequent crackdown in the United States on all political radicals came to be known as the Red Scare; it lasted from 1919 to 1921. There was enormous unrest among members of the labor movement and a strong current of anticapitalism; and the Red Scare was whipped up as a pretext to extinguish political dissidents. In 1918, with the war still going in Europe and the Middle East, the United States passed a draconian anti-dissent law called the Sedition Act. It would take two years after the war before it was proved in court that the law did not pass Constitutional muster.

The industrial economy in the United States, built up by war manufacturing, raced into production in the immediate postwar period, and stock speculation with it. The United States, untouched on its own shores by the war, found itself awash in money. This exuberance overshot and the economy nosedived in 1920–21, so the Federal Reserve opened the tap on credit. The economy then went on a speculative bacchanalia that was named the Roaring Twenties.

Mass production and new technologies made vastly more consumer goods available to a much larger portion of the population. Radio and films came into their own. The government funded massive road construction projects in support of the new automobile industry. Typewriters, telephones, and privately owned guns were accompanied by mass electrification. It was

---

27. Quoted in Jarvis, *Male Body at War*, 18.

party time at the dawn of mass consumer capitalism. The majority of the United States for the first time in history was urban-dwelling.

Gender was bent. There was greater toleration—at least among the aesthetes who were not overly preoccupied with making a living—for sexual experimentation, for homosexual encounters, for women's fashion imitating men's and men's reverting to the genteel, even camp. Women achieved the franchise. When the Sedition Act was repealed, social criticism flourished, from the likes of Sinclair Lewis on the left to Ezra Pound on the right.

It was party time, and parties love alcohol.

An experiment was launched in the United States, driven by the progressive churches, especially the Methodists, to legally ban alcohol. Prohibition lasted from 1920 to 1933, with strong support from the Ku Klux Klan. This gave rise to the popularity of lawbreaking in the form of "speakeasies," illegal bars and dance halls where liquor was served. Illegal alcohol created a highly lucrative organized crime industry. Gangsters became notorious and admired at the same time in this era in which nihilism and class struggle existed alongside one another.

Understandably, the forces of civil society and state were not comfortable with this anarchic pluralism, even if it was highly profitable. The scions of industry and of social control needed a new weapon in the struggle for the hearts and minds of the masses. They found that weapon in a new idea: public relations.

26

Nation, Race, and Hygiene

> Even Satan disguises himself as an angel of light.
>
> —2 CORINTHIANS 11:14

> Emotivism entails the obliteration of any genuine distinction between manipulative and non-manipulative social relations.
>
> —ALASDAIR MACINTYRE[1]

Emotivism is the metaphysical claim that every moral position rests ultimately upon a pre-rational prejudice, an attitude, or an emotion. It is a cornerstone of modern society, because it is the basis of our tolerance, as far as it is not constrained by bureaucratic prerogative, for pluralism. It is, however, no basis for discerning right Christian practice.

    We *ought* to differentiate between manipulative and nonmanipulative social relations. We *oughtn't*, as Christians, set out to deceive or obfuscate, to mobilize the emotions or prejudices of others for gain. The history and practice of public relations is important for Christians to understand, because we are living in a society that is shot through with the influence of this manipulative practice. In many cases, we are confronted with the seeming necessity of engaging in manipulation in the course of our jobs.

---

1. MacIntyre, *After Virtue*, 23.

At the end of World War I, the nephew of Sigmund Freud, Edward Bernays (1891–1995), was invited to the 1919 Paris Peace Conference by President Woodrow Wilson. Bernays was extremely impressed by the efficacy of certain kinds of war propaganda, and based on his uncle's research into subconscious motivation, he wondered how this kind of mass propaganda might be employed in peacetime for social control and commerce. An example of the propaganda that impressed Bernays was a World War I British recruiting poster, which went to the heart of martial masculinity. A silhouetted Boy Scout in his paramilitary uniform is looking up at his father, a silhouetted man in a business suit. Alongside the silhouettes was written:

WHAT WILL YOUR ANSWER BE

When your boy asks you

"Father, what did YOU do to help when our empire fought for freedom?"

ENLIST NOW[2]

Bernays unabashedly used the words "manipulate" and "manipulation" in his treatises on *propaganda*—a term he would transpose into the more benign "public relations." His worldview was decidedly mechanistic, and he believed that democracy contained a terrible potential to undermine progress and civilization.[3]

> The conscious and intelligent manipulation of the organized habits and opinions of the masses is an important element in democratic society. Those who manipulate the unseen mechanism of society constitute an invisible government which is the true ruling power. We are governed, our minds moulded, our tastes formed, our ideas suggested largely by men we have never heard of. This is a logical result of the way in which our democratic society is organized. Vast numbers of human beings must cooperate if they are to live together as a smoothly functioning society. In almost every act of our lives, whether in the sphere of politics or business, in our social conduct or our ethical thinking, we are dominated by the relatively small number of persons who understand the mental processes and social patterns of

---

2. From the Elizabeth Ball Collection of World War I posters.
3. Bernays, *Propaganda*, 75.

the masses. It is they who *pull the wires that control the public mind.*[4]

Bernays did not invent propaganda. It has been a feature of politics and war for millennia. With the dawn of mass commodity production, propaganda has been used to create demand where none existed. Bernays *systematized* it, and suggested—in concert with his time, with Fordism and Taylorism and the emphasis on specialization—that public relations ought to be a professional specialty. He incorporated his belief that human beings were not rationally motivated, and objectified the public. The public "mind" was the object of his manipulation, the people connected to wires, like marionettes. The responsibility of leadership is to learn how to pull them.

Bernays mounted a successful campaign to get more women to begin smoking as a demonstration of his method, and for a substantial fee from the tobacco industry.[5] By 1929, women marched in Easter Sunday Parades with lit cigarettes, which were touted as "torches of freedom," making cigarette smoking a symbol of social emancipation.[6]

Public relations was employed after the war to reorient masculinity from the war to building up the nation at home and to overcome the pluralism and gender destabilizations of the postwar years. In the new discourse of male and female, race, nation, and progress, the watchword was "hygiene." And so "social hygiene" became the first Bernaysian mass public relations campaign after the war, conducted in the name of *progress*.

The word *progress*, used in the sense of historical inevitability, didn't appear until around 1600, and then only occasionally. It was not an ideological term until the nineteenth century, and then mostly in the United States, especially around the time of the Civil War. The British long considered it to be an Americanism. By the turn of the twentieth century, the term became the root of a new American noun that was explicitly ideological: progressive.

The "scandal of particularity" with regard to progress is that it is not universal and axiomatic; it is a particular notional *construction* of a particular culture and epoch. Particularity forces us to turn to an embarrassing question about results. If this is just an idea, what is our idea of the goal of progress? What is the final *result* that progress aims at, or that it is being

---

4. Ibid., 37.
5. Brandt, "Recruiting Women Smokers."
6. Ibid.

pulled toward? How do we know when we have reached the goal? Honest natural science, ironically enough, has confronted us with some pretty scary answers about where our current *progressive* trajectory has aimed us. Ronald Wright writes that "material progress creates problems that are—or seem to be—soluble only by further progress . . . the devil here is *in the scale*: a good bang can be useful; a better bang can end the world."[7]

Progress constructed as economic "growth," the belief in ceaseless commodification, has thrust humanity into simultaneous and terrifying ecological and cultural impasses. Progress has given us the ability to wreck the biosphere and blow ourselves up, yet the very people who seem most interested at the moment in turning these trajectories around insist on calling themselves "progressives." This to some degree accounts for why our record at turning things around has been so dismal. We use the methods of progress to correct the problems of progress.[8]

Smith documented the emergence of cleanliness, respectability, and progress as part of the same constellation of meaning in affluent Western culture and showed how consumption was part of that movement, tangentially understood but materially essential to it. This constellation of respectability, progress, and cleanliness was inscribed on a worldview that drew a borderline between the civilized imperial cores and the barbaric (we now say "under-*developed*") peripheries.[9] Women were charged with upholding civilization through domestic respectability. They promoted progress via domestic femininity, including the provision of an appropriate environment for raising children. Roosevelt emphasized the role of women as breeders, *producing* vigorous citizens and soldiers. After the war, public relations amplified the notions of Anglo-Saxon superiority, a providential United States tutoring its colonies, and of *progress*, in order to conform the American public to the postwar buildup of a white industrialized nation.

The discourse was increasingly medicalized. The body, like the soldier's *inducted* body, was the *object* of a program of professional evaluation and optimization; and the body politic was likewise understood as one that had to be simultaneously optimized and protected from disease and disability. The female body became a site of social re-production. The womb became the means of production for new citizens.[10]

7. Wright, *Short History of Progress*, 7.
8. This is the cycle that Illich named "iatrogenesis."
9. Smith, *Consumption and the Making of Respectability*.
10. Duden, *Woman Beneath the Skin*, 17–18: "Birth, at one time primarily a social, semi-public event among women, now became ideally a private event that had to be attended to in accordance with the logic of a physiologic mechanism. This reduction of birth to a bodily mechanism went hand in hand with a shift in the meaning of birth:

Western Europeans and Americans, prior to the eighteenth century, did not bathe for hygienic reasons. The modern idea of *hygiene* did not yet exist. They bathed occasionally in baths that were reputed to contain health-inducing minerals and other qualities, the idea being that one could soak these qualities up through the skin.[11] The maternal side of my own family comes from Hot Springs, Arkansas, where geothermic activity heats fresh-water springs to which many people still attribute almost magical qualities, including the belief that drinking the water will increase male sexual vigor. People still pay well to bathe along the somewhat famous Bathhouse Row, even to take enemas with the stuff.[12]

Daily immersion or shower baths are a very recent custom, and only a few nations consider daily bathing necessary for health.[13] The natural odor of the body, washed or unwashed, was not considered offensive (it is a *learned* distaste) until it came to differentiate those who had to do physical labor from those who did not. Reducing the intensity of one's natural odor came first to be associated with gentility, not hygiene.[14] The hygienic aspect was introduced with the popularization of the idea of "germs" only in the nineteenth century. Inexpensive soap[15] was not generally available until after 1800, and soap manufacturers were, of course, quick to tout its more frequent consumption (which became a *weekly* bath). The separation between civilization and barbarism, especially during the Victorian era, came to be the separation between the "washed" and the "unwashed."[16]

Amy Laura Hall, a Methodist minister and ethics professor, collected old ads from the latter nineteenth to the mid-twentieth century pertaining to children, childbirth, motherhood, and family. She published them as part of her analysis in *Conceiving Parenthood*. She shows how hygiene was

---

what had been a 'passage,' a threshold experience with analogies between birth and death, became a productive process. Many of the factors involved in the creation of gynecological medicine, which scholarly literature has interpreted as the enforcement of male power over the female body, reveal equally clearly the means that were involved in creating a new kind of corporeality. The new 'body' was defined through the process of isolating the female organs from the traditional undefined body."

11. Ashenburg, "The Filthy, Stinking Truth."
12. Called "high colonic irrigation," or "colon hydrotherapy."
13. Ashenburg, "The Filthy, Stinking Truth."
14. Smith, *Consumption and the Making of Respectability*.
15. Made from palm oil, an African export shipped abroad by imperial plunderers, contributing to the core-periphery dynamic.
16. Smith, *Consumption and the Making of Respectability*.

conceptually tied to monetized consumption, to the experience of one's own body, to the boundaries between the civilized and uncivilized (clean and unclean), and to the apotheosis of the nation-state.

Figure 1.1 in *Conceiving Parenthood* is a poster published by the American Social Hygiene Association, circa 1922. On the poster is a plump, healthy, smiling, naked, white baby, sitting on a blanket. The poster title is "The Baby." White is generic, normative. The script beneath the baby photo reads,

> Human beings, too, are mammals, and fertilization and development take place within the mother. The period of development or pregnancy is nine months. At birth the muscles contract and push the baby through the birth canal (vagina) into the outer world. The human mother can bring more than the simple animal instincts to the aid of her new-born child. Real motherhood develops by the addition of knowledge and understanding to the mother's instinctive love.[17]

The story of this baby, this *hygienic* baby, is specifically a white American baby "of the proper sort." The story, however, begins with a vagina, or even more functionally, a "birth canal." In this narrative, the woman has been reduced to an incubator for a new citizen, her body providing a "birth canal" to facilitate production. This poster was part of a campaign for better hygiene. This hygiene extended from the microcosm inside the baby itself to the hazardous social macrocosm, where hygienic babies and unhygienic babies had to be kept separate to prevent cross-border contamination, the infection of the desirable infant. Hall writes,

> This poster is characteristic of a shift that unquestionably enabled notable gains in infant health through public-awareness campaigns for domestic hygiene. But the hygiene came at a cost, for the benefits were socially, economically, and racially encoded. "The baby" on which the domestic hygiene effort focused was too often a specific baby—a baby the logic of the day judged to be worth the effort. At the same time that social and medical scientists focused on "the baby," they established what were touted as objective, factual, indisputable tools for determining just which babies were worth the effort. The same language system by which the mothers, social workers, and physicians could measure gains lent scientific legitimacy to a calculus of human life. This calculus reflected a growing sense that the individual baby was a precious but fragile commodity to

---

17. Hall, *Conceiving Parenthood*, 22.

Nation, Race, and Hygiene

be quantifiably evaluated, carefully habituated, and hygienically safeguarded from those humans and households on the *other* side of a divide.[18]

The nationwide push for social hygiene was coupled with the rise of an aggressive eugenics movement. The same leaders, intellectuals, and advertisers who crafted and sustained the social hygiene movement and its emphasis on eugenics promoted a new vision of "the right" family—nuclear, white, affluent, patriotic, and obedient.

Capital accumulation was racialized from the moment that it began to require distant inputs. The world was divided between the civilized *us* and the barbaric *them*. By the early twentieth century, the U.S. government was actively involved in eugenics.

Mainline Protestant churches lent a justifying hand in the national campaign with the development of that unique theological amalgam called "natural theology," which appealed to "nature" instead of revelation. The colonization of Protestant theology by the desire for capital accumulation made social Darwinism[19] synonymous with "nature." Nature dictates natural selection, and since nature is of God, then capitalist modernity is the progressive fulfillment of the promise of the kingdom of God. The term *hygiene* described and policed the boundaries of this emerging and ordained future. This meant not only keeping "germs" out of your food; it meant keeping the elect separate from the *others*. Eugenics was central to this project.

With this new moral framework in hand, the U.S. state felt not only entitled but obliged to take up the task of building the eugenic paradise. It was in 1927 that Oliver Wendell Holmes spoke on behalf of the Supreme Court of the United States, reviewing *Buck v. Bell*, regarding involuntary sterilization of the "unfit."

> It is better for all the world, if instead of waiting to execute degenerate offspring for crime, or to let them starve for their imbecility, society can prevent those who are manifestly unfit from continuing their kind. The principle that sustains compulsory vaccination is broad enough to cover cutting the Fallopian tubes. Three generations of imbeciles are enough.[20]

The scientistic[21] frame of mind that led to the eugenics movement in the United States and elsewhere in the world was based on this very unscientific

---

18. Ibid., 23.
19. Not to be confused with Darwin's actual theses on natural selection.
20. *Buck v. Bell*, 274 U.S. 200 (1927).
21. A word Foucault coined to differentiate "scientific," a restricted and cautious *method*, from "scientistic," a pseudo-scientific *ideology* based on domination.

extrapolation of the ideas associated with, for example, boiling drinking water, to *disinfecting* the body politic.

"The irony," writes Hall, "involves my belief that the very Protestant tradition that should have emphasized a sense of divine gratuity, human contingency, sufficient abundance, and the radical giftedness of all life came in twentieth-century America instead to epitomize *justification through meticulously planned procreation.*"[22] Echoing Smith's dyad of rational masculinity and domestic femininity as constitutive of respectability, she calls the emergence of the hygiene/eugenics movement a "culture of carefully delineated, racially encoded domesticity."[23] These were perceptions fabricated by public relations people and applied to the progressive project. That project established a hygienic chain of being, with its microcosm in the mother's womb and macrocosm in a world divided between fit nations and unfit ones.

Historically speaking, hygiene and progress are fraternal twins, accounting for the Progressive Movement's embrace of eugenics as "social hygiene"; neither progressives nor mainline Protestants questioned it until Hitler gave us an example of eugenics-in-earnest.[24]

White liberal feminism has been forced to live with an embarrassment of history. Conservatives and other anti-feminists can cite blatantly eugenicist and racist positions taken by early, high-profile, American white feminists like Margaret Sanger. An ardent Malthusian, Sanger left her self-indictments etched on the annals of history:

> No woman shall have the legal right to bear a child . . . without a permit for parenthood.[25]

> Birth control must lead ultimately . . . to a cleaner race.[26]

> We should hire three or four colored ministers, preferably with social-service backgrounds, and with engaging personalities. The most successful educational approach to the Negro is through a religious appeal. We don't want the word to go out that we want to exterminate the Negro population, and the

---

22. Hall, *Conceiving Parenthood*, 9–10
23. Ibid., 10.
24. In the U.S., progressives, including many mainstream ecumenical churches, supported multiple involuntary sterilization campaigns.
25. Sanger, "America Needs a Code for Babies."
26. Sanger, "Morality and Birth Control."

minister is the man who can straighten out that idea if it ever occurs to any of their more rebellious members.²⁷

Eugenic sterilization is an urgent need. . . . We must prevent multiplication of this bad stock.²⁸

Eugenics is . . . the most adequate and thorough avenue to the solution of racial, political and social problems.²⁹

Birth control itself, often denounced as a violation of natural law, is nothing more or less than the facilitation of the process of weeding out the unfit, of preventing the birth of defectives or of those who will become defectives.³⁰

As an advocate of birth control I wish . . . to point out that the unbalance between the birth rate of the "unfit" and the "fit," admittedly the greatest present menace to civilization, can never be rectified by the inauguration of a cradle competition between these two classes. In this matter, the example of the inferior classes, the fertility of the feeble-minded, the mentally defective, the poverty-stricken classes, should not be held up for emulation. . . . On the contrary, the most urgent problem today is how to limit and discourage the over-fertility of the mentally and physically defective.³¹

The campaign for birth control is not merely of eugenic value, but is practically identical with the final aims of eugenics.³²

Our failure to segregate morons who are increasing and multiplying . . . demonstrates our foolhardy and extravagant sentimentalism. . . . [Philanthropists] encourage the healthier and more normal sections of the world to shoulder the burden of unthinking and indiscriminate fecundity of others; which brings with it, as I think the reader must agree, a dead weight of human waste. Instead of decreasing and aiming to eliminate the stocks that are most detrimental to the future of the race and the world, it tends to render them to a menacing degree dominant. . . . We are paying for, and even submitting to, the dictates of

---

27. Sanger, Letter to Dr. Clarence Gamble.
28. Sanger, Letter to *Birth Control Review*.
29. Sanger, "Eugenic Value of Birth Control Propaganda."
30. Ibid.
31. Ibid.
32. Ibid.

an ever-increasing, unceasingly spawning class of human beings who never should have been born at all.[33]

The undeniably feeble-minded should, indeed, not only be discouraged but prevented from propagating their kind.[34]

Give certain dysgenic groups in our population their choice of segregation or sterilization.[35]

Those who know me know that I am not anti-feminist. The bad leavening in this bread is not women's emancipation but *progress* understood as the marker for *civilization*, which included, and still includes, the delusion that we can "improve" our own species. This is God-playing, the poison pill we swallowed when we learned to do natural science, not science inherently and in-itself, but science in the saddle of (ironically) Euro-masculine arrogance and expansion-economics.

Lest anyone think that this vision has disappeared or was limited to early white feminists and Progressives, other famous eugenicists include Hermann J. Muller, John Maynard Keynes, Bertrand Russell, Theodosius Dobzhansky, Elmer Pendell, Jacques Cousteau, Glayde Whitney, Barbara Marx Hubbard, and Richard Dawkins—the latter coining the term "the selfish gene" to describe *his* ideological version of Darwinian evolution. In the 1920s and 1930s, scientists from either the political left or right would not have found the idea of designer babies particularly dangerous, though of course they would not have used that phrase. Today, I suspect that the idea is too dangerous for comfortable discussion, and Adolf Hitler is largely responsible for the change. "Nobody wants to be caught agreeing with that monster," writes Dawkins, "even in a single particular." And yet,

> The specter of Hitler has led some scientists to stray from "ought" to "is" and deny that breeding for human qualities is even possible. But if you can breed cattle for milk yield, horses for running speed, and dogs for herding skill, why on Earth should it be impossible to breed humans for mathematical, musical or athletic ability? Objections such as "these are not one-dimensional abilities" apply equally to cows, horses and dogs and never stopped anybody in practice.
>
> I wonder whether, some 60 years after Hitler's death, we might at least venture to ask what the moral difference is between breeding for musical ability and forcing a child to take

---

33. Sanger, "The Cruelty of Charity."
34. Sanger, "Dangers of Cradle Competition."
35. Sanger, "A Plan for Peace."

music lessons. Or why it is acceptable to train fast runners and high jumpers but not to breed them. I can think of some answers, and they are good ones, which would probably end up persuading me. But hasn't the time come when we should stop being frightened even to put the question?[36]

Hitler's progress set progress back decades, dammit!

The racialism of eugenics was always inside the seed named "progress." At one point, "progressive" Protestants actually talked about searching for a "cleanliness" gene![37] Hall notes in an interview how, while churches have rejected the "excesses" of early eugenics, their members still carefully "plan" their families and seem to have selected progress over the basic tenets of their own faith:

> While studying bioethics at Yale, I served at a merged, downtown church—African-American and white, working class and bourgeois-bohemian, professors and homeless folks—a church trying to know every child as part of the Body of Christ. In this context, I wanted to ask why so many mainline Christians are frightened to put our children in schools with children with disabilities or children who speak Spanish or children who live in impoverished neighborhoods? How is it that white Protestants, who worship a babe born in a manger, came to view a birth planned through in vitro fertilization as more legitimately a gift than a child conceived by an undocumented Latina teenager?[38]

Sanger, who is better remembered for her advocacy of birth control than of eugenics (in her mind, they were inseparable), is still seen by many as a kind of feminist founding mother. Her apologists can take some responsibility for the efficacy of right-wing abuse of her eugenics advocacy to tar feminism with the same brush as Hitler. The reason some of her apologists are partly responsible is that by downplaying or disappearing Sanger's ideas on eugenics to preserve her image now that eugenics (named as such) has gone out of style, they have opened themselves to the accusation of propagandizing through selective truth-telling, an example of *manipulative speech*.

In an article for the Methodist magazine *Together* (1957!), Sanger says, "History's greatest race is speeding to its climax: Population versus world food supplies. And the way it looks now, there may soon be *Too Many*

---

36. Dawkins, "Afterword," 300.
37. Hall, "Better Homes and Children."
38. Ibid., 177.

People."³⁹ The article is accompanied by a photograph of South Asian men in turbans. It exhorts Methodists to support birth control abroad.

"The World is exploding at the seams," Sanger warns. "From the Orient to South America, from Eastern Europe to the U.S., soaring birth rates are posing future problems potentially more dangerous than the H-bomb."⁴⁰

Sanger's language evokes visions of pest infestation with phrases such as "teeming Asia." She calls for a "new worldwide domestic order through the promotion of properly calibrated, usefully capable children."⁴¹ The United States, of course, is identified as the proper political vehicle for the export of this progress, an imperial rationalization hardly a step removed from Rudyard Kipling's exhortations to tutor those who are "half devil and half child."

Hall includes an eight-page subsection on the 1933–34 Century of Progress Exposition in Chicago, an event that had World Fair atmosphere and World Fair hype. The exposition featured baby-food leviathan Gerber, advertising itself as the bringer of "*progress* in infant feeding." The fair also featured a new invention: the baby incubator—with live white babies in them for demonstration purposes.

> The baby incubator with live babies offers a conceptual link between the exposition's "Forward, Ever Forward!" exhibits of science and industry and the Midway, at the center of the fair, with such attractions as Ripley's Believe It or Not Odditorium, a sampling of "freak shows," Darkest Africa, and the Old Plantation Show.⁴²

Echoing through this contrast between modern and premodern are Bodin and Bacon, advocating instrumental order in the face of a female nature's chaos and disorder, now projected onto primitive peoples and the "unfit." Nature itself must be conquered, and in this guise, we observe the eternal re-emergence of masculinity constructed as conquest. Even the female womb must be controlled, reduced to a "birth canal," and managed by men, by the physiological technocrats of the medical profession.

Most of the assumptions of progress, including the eugenics movement, thanks to the success of public relations, were in fact internalized by white America, and these assumptions are embodied today in the ever more anxious testing for genetic defects of adults as prospective parents and of

39. Sanger, "Too Many People," cited in Hall, *Conceiving Parenthood*, 16.
40. Ibid.
41. Hall, *Conceiving Parenthood*, 16.
42. Ibid., 158.

the unborn. They are embodied in the ideal of the nuclear family, which was forged by the eugenics movement (Grandma and Grandpa have some retrograde ideas about raising children!), and in the notion of "responsible" family planning. These hidden assumptions still operate in tandem with gender, race, and class preconceptions dating back to the latter nineteenth century. Chief among those ideas is the idea of women constructed as citizen-incubators, raising "productive citizens" who *will* "succeed," because lack of success is a marker of unfitness and a stain on the reputation of parents on the other side of the hygienic borderline. To prove that one's family belongs among the elect, then, we have learned to measure how many and what kind of kids to have, and how to enroll them at ever earlier ages in the child-success industry, lest they be suspected as one of the tainted.

Hygiene became a social metaphor. Beck refers to this metaphorical leap as "sociomoral disgust."[43]

> On the playground, "cooties" seems harmless (unless you've been on the other end of that game). But sociomoral disgust can quickly scale up in intensity and become the engine behind the very worst kind of human atrocities.... Sociomoral disgust is implicated in the creation of monsters and scapegoats, where outgroup members are demonized and selected for exclusion or elimination.[44]

The same logic of extermination can be observed from the manufactured compulsion to kill all the "germs" on every exposed surface, to spraying fields with poisons to eliminate "weeds," to giving the "dysgenic" a choice between sterilization or segregation (segregation ... how?), to the comparison of Jews with vermin in advance of building extermination camps. Hygiene comes to mean cleansing the body, the family, the social body of impurities, applying the roach spray or the broad-spectrum antibiotic to the threatened body politic. It is medicalized speech, but there is nothing scientific about it. It is an ideology that might best be called "exterminism."

Progress, however, was interrupted.

In 1929, the speculative financial orgy collapsed under its own weight, creating a new crisis of economy and with it a crisis of masculinity; and it would be answered in some quarters by a lethal combination of man-talk and eugenics.

43. Beck, *Unclean*, 34–50.
44. Ibid., 92.

In gender terms, fascism was a naked reassertion of male supremacy in societies that had been moving toward equality for women. To accomplish this, fascism promoted new images of hegemonic masculinity, glorifying irrationality (the "triumph of the will," thinking with "the blood") and the unrestrained violence of the frontline soldier.[45]

---

45. Connell, *Masculinities*, 193.

27

The Art of Depression

Never before had American men experienced such a massive and system-wide shock to their ability to prove manhood by providing for their families.

—MICHAEL KIMMEL, ON THE GREAT DEPRESSION[1]

No medium has contributed more greatly than the film to the maintenance of the national morale during a period featured [sic] by revolution, riot and political turmoil in other countries.

—WILL HAYS, PRESIDENT OF THE MOTION PICTURE PRODUCERS AND DISTRIBUTORS, 1934[2]

During the Roaring Twenties, while speculators gassed the economic bubble, U.S. bankers collected their war debts. European allies could not pay, but Wall Street would not forgive. Indebted Europe turned on defeated Germany to extract reparations to make good on Wall Street's markers. Germany was strangled into a baleful state of despair. The era was pregnant with a dual cataclysm: the Great Depression and the Second World War.

---

1. Kimmel, *Manhood in America*, 192.
2. Cited in Guimond, *American Photography*, 105.

In 1931, President Herbert Hoover declared, "What this country needs is a good big laugh.... If someone could get off a good joke every ten days, I think our troubles would be over."³ The following year he was trounced in the general election by Theodore Roosevelt's fifth cousin, Franklin Roosevelt, who had married Eleanor Roosevelt (her maiden name)—Theodore's niece and Franklin's own fifth cousin. Roosevelt received significant help from a new source in his campaign, an emerging Hollywood giant named Warner Brothers. The outlines of our own time appeared in the period between the two world wars.

The postwar era prior to the Great Depression was a period in which the Enlightenment certainties, the promises of progress, and the boosterism of the first two decades of the century had fallen under the shadow of the mechanized slaughter of the Great War and the threat of rising revolutionary feeling among industrial workers, whose interest was piqued by the events of 1917. Masculinities multiplied in response to manifold upheavals, measured against one another and all against women.

During the Roaring Twenties and Prohibition, the speakeasies had created a general social tolerance for breaking the law. That tolerance allowed very different kinds of people to share this scofflaw solidarity in a consumer space. The festive atmosphere of the clubs permitted various kinds of gender subversions, playfully enacted away from the rigors and worries of working-class and rural life. "Pansy clubs," the first gay bars, were patronized by men and women whether they were seeking same-sex liaisons or not. "Homosexuality" had only recently been invented by the profession of psychoanalysis, and it was not yet understood as an "identity" but as a performance (in both senses of the word).⁴ These clubs for same-sex liaisons were the first confirmed instance of something that would come to be called "gay subculture."⁵

In mass production work, employers were hiring more and more women, putting male and female into direct competition.⁶ One journalist renamed Detroit "She-Town":

> Because women can do the semi-skilled work of running punch presses and drills in the auto factories, men are being laid off to join the mob of unemployed workers. Women are being given

---

3. Ibid.
4. Paris, "The Invention of Homosexuality."
5. Halsall, "Homosexuality in the Middle Ages."
6. Meyer, "Men at Work?"

jobs because the prevailing wage for them is 20¢ to 30¢ an hour lower for the same work. Detroit is beginning to take on the aspects of a "she-town" in which the woman works out and the man looks after the kids.[7]

The white-collar masculinity that was hegemonic among the business class was counterposed to an ever more self-conscious working-class masculinity by the union movement and the growing movement for socialism. Southern white masculinity was challenged by the return of black war veterans.

Then the Great Depression hit. The nation was struggling through a financial collapse that summarily dropped five million people[8] into the category of "hard-core unemployed," and ramified into tens of millions losing jobs and being forced back into the job market with a substantially lowered wage floor.[9] The financial collapse was combined with an ecological catastrophe called the Dust Bowl. Deep-plow farming, encouraged after World War I by the government, unanchored the soil. A massive drought dried out the Plains States, and the topsoil was blown away in massive dust storms. One storm dropped 12 million pounds of dust onto Chicago in a single day. The skies across several states were blackened for days at a time with airborne topsoil.[10] Two and a half million people were displaced from the Great Plains.

Men, who in the postwar era were encouraged to see themselves as providers for their families, were either cast adrift on the job market or forced into working conditions they would not have heretofore accepted. Unemployed men found their wives less subject to them, especially when the wives were finding spot work unavailable to men. Children listened more to their mothers than their fathers. Drunkenness was accompanied far more frequently by men physically attacking their wives; and for many men the "pansy" became a target for their violent insecurities. Active homophobia came to the fore during the Great Depression.

In Europe, conditions were sometimes even more dire, especially in postwar Germany, where extracted war reparations left the country in a state of abject despair. The powerful and malignant reply to both 1917 and to the Great Depression in Germany was the emergence of a hypermasculine version of racial-national renewal that would come to be known as fascism. By the mid-1930s, the force of this particular version of masculinity

7. Ibid., para. 3.
8. The total U.S. population at the time was around 123 million.
9. Jensen, "Causes and Cures of Unemployment."
10. Ribas, "When the Dust Settled."

would make itself felt in both sympathetic and critical narratives across the Atlantic. Fascism combined its macho hypernationalism, the narratives of progress and eugenics, and a Teutonic mythical nostalgia.

What would emerge from this gender turmoil as hegemonic could not be clearly seen then, but in retrospect, because mass media and popular culture had become such powerful homogenizing forces, we can track the development of a pre-World War II hegemonic masculinity and the masculinities that revolved around mass media and literature through the male cultural archetypes of the postwar and Depression era.[11]

In the United States, Hollywood was mobilized as a palliative. Chirpy movies with happy endings became a major film entrée.[12] Westerns were most popular with men and boys. The Western hearkened to American mythical frontier masculinity, portrayed by "virile" men—heroic, autonomous characters who dominated women, land, animals, and savages,[13] a story of mastery and control as the antidote to the vagaries of the Great Depression.

"The hero's triumph over the wild things dramatizes the mastery of the patriarchy," writes Margery Hourihan.[14] Virility breaks down the resistance of all things passive—and we see in many films, as well as in bodice-ripper literature, how the female lead nearly swoons before the masculine mojo of the leading man.

> Significantly, the American adventure story has been generally addressed to men, who have used it to learn to run risks, fight, defeat and dominate others. In American culture and letters, adventure, masculinity and violence thus seem to remain three inseparable terms.[15]

Marvin Severson goes a step further, saying that the "violent American male is not simply a figure in American life, a figure of entertainment, but rather *the* figure around which American culture is oriented."[16] Richard Slotkin notes that mythic-frontier masculinity exists along the boundary between the civilized and the savage, as a kind of sentinel; this is the film convention of "men who know Indians."[17]

11. Severson, "Superior to All Men."
12. Guimond, *American Photography*, 105–6.
13. Severson, "Superior to All Men," 3.
14. Hourihan, *Deconstructing the Hero*, 107.
15. Armengol, "Gendering Men."
16. Severson, "Superior to All Men," 5.
17. Slotkin, *Gunfighter Nation*, 47.

The initial exchange involves purely tactical knowledge. The frontiersmen become "men who know Indians" and learn to fight savages according to "savage" rules that echo those of the Norman knight and Viking Berserker. But the Indians teach more than tactics. Their fanatical determination to maintain their lands and tribal integrity provides a model of nationalist patriotism that Whites will have to relearn: White patriotism has been undermined by the spirit of self-interestedness and materialism.[18]

James Fenimore Cooper meets Davy Crockett. These special mythical frontiersmen "mediated the categories of savage and civilized, embodying the violence of the frontier and the renewal of Eastern civilized life."[19] Conversely, we see the appearance of a gangster film genre featuring, like postwar literature, a male antihero. While violent, the antihero was a reflection not of the status quo, but of a deep suspicion and implicit critique of the establishment. The antihero was not upright. He was damaged, like the veterans of the Great War.

If we want to see the first intimations of *Man on Fire*, which we unpacked for its gendered film conventions in chapter 12, the postwar and Depression era marks the origin of both the "man who knows Indians" and the damaged antihero, now as a composite stock film convention. The rebellion in literature that gave rise to the antihero, and therefore to the character Creasy, has been co-opted and commodified, complete with Denzel Washington as a race decoy. But the successful and familiar *formulas* remain. The character Creasy is a "man who knows Indians," this time in Latin America (the Western convention). Creasy is a man broken by war, disillusioned (a post-World War I antihero convention), yet sent (by God!) back to "the frontier" to redeem himself through the one thing that still makes him a man—ruthless violence. He saves a little blonde girl from the bad Mexicans (including her bad Mexican father), so he never threatens the audience with an adult white damsel in distress and the possibility of mixed-race sexual tension.[20]

18. Ibid.
19. Severson, "Superior to All Men," 6.
20. The curious thing about this particular cliché is how blatantly untrue it has actually been. Imperial representatives, in particular occupying soldiers, are in most cases shockingly divorced from the realities of the culture where they ply their trades. In an interview in November 2013, Ann Jones, a reporter and humanitarian aid volunteer with extensive experience in Afghanistan, remarked, "I lived among Afghan civilians for so long, so when I went onto military bases I saw how remote [U.S. soldiers] were from any understanding of who Afghans are and how they live. And it was almost like going to a different planet. And you'd hear about their strategies and their plans and

Man on Fire's composite, commercial archetype contains a sanitized vestige of the literary rebellion *against* the pre-World War I and pre-Depression-era culture of relentless Progressive optimism; and the antihero archetypes that appear in Depression-era literature are broken parodies of the frontier masculinity.

Marvin Severson traces the development of this period's American literary masculine archetypes in reaction to the development of fascism with a study of the writers William Faulkner, Dashiell Hammett, Ernest Hemingway, John Steinbeck, and Richard Wright, each of whom wrote with the *fascist male* in view.

Hemingway presented men who hunted big game, caught big fish, and engaged in bullfights as proof of masculinity. His antiheroes were either literally or figuratively castrated and they were very ambivalent about nationalism. Like veterans returning from the trenches, they have been disfigured, crippled, and disillusioned. Even Hemingway's Robert Jordan, a character who volunteered to fight against Spanish fascism, is motivated not by patriotism but by his aversion to fascism as a form of supernationalism that he (and Hemingway) found offensive. The novel *For Whom the Bell Tolls* unreels around a plot with plenty of action, but the principal thematic preoccupation is with death, with mortality in a disenchanted world. The "good guys" and "bad guys" are often difficult to discern. Masculinity itself is no longer framed around the sacred or even around progress, but in the context of a restless existential doubt. A man must prove himself just to prove to himself he is a man, then he dies. His courage, unmoored from reason and justice, consists merely of facing this abyss gracefully.

Dashiell Hammett's post-WWI antihero detective doesn't even have a name. He is known by a pseudonym, "the Continental Op." The Op wades into the emerging *noir* genre, a violent man who finds nothing sacred and who from that stance can display an unabashed contempt as he uncovers the rot under the surface of "respectable" society. It is what Op sees as a corporate fixer and a thug that marks this hard-boiled genre of detective fiction as social criticism.

---

what they were doing and their theories about Afghans—and of course a lot of their theories about Afghanistan came from the war in Iraq, which was an entirely different war. So it was really remarkable to me how little there was to be learned from being with the military except the exposure of how little they knew about where they were and who they were dealing with. . . . The military understands the civilians much less well than the civilians understand the military" (Jones, "A Lot of Them Kill Their Wives").

> Whereas [cowboy] figures represent the power of violent masculinity to reinforce American identity through the exclusion or eradication of elements that counter civilization, elements whose criminal and racial identities undermine the tacit and spontaneous will of a free, liberal society, Hammett's anti-hero, the Continental Op, parodies such figures. He lacks the idealism and moral rectitude of the frontier hero. And unlike the British detective of Doyle or the Golden Age of detective fiction, the Op has little trust in reason or a civilized domestic order worth preserving against irrational crime and foreign threats. In fact, the Op does little in the way of Sherlock Holmes's deductive reasoning, instead steadily piecing together the likely story of a crime through intense legwork. And in the end, the Op does little to reestablish traditional order; his work does not purge civilization of its impurities, but rather reveals the pervasion of those impurities in all strata of society.[21]

The Op, as it turns out, is also a "man who knows Indians," only the Indians are transplanted from the frontier to the modern urban scene as criminals, often racially encoded, but in the end no worse than many of the rich and powerful white citizens who employ the Op. Hammett, it should be noted, would eventually join the American Communist Party, which was in the forefront of the movement for racial equality in the 1920s and 1930s.

What differentiates the Op from the violent heroes before him is his disillusionment, his general disenchantment. What differentiates him from fascists is his decidedly non-ideological nature. What makes these male literary characters all the same, and the same as Hemingway's emasculated and disillusioned characters, is the persistent identification of manhood with violence. Women aren't written as passive domestic appurtenances, but as inscrutable yet attractive threats. The *femme fatale* calls on ancient misogynistic notions of women *qua* danger. In noir, she also serves as a counter-archetype to domestic femininity, and respectable femininity is portrayed as bourgeois hypocrisy.

Severson traces the Continental Op into and through Hammett's later Sam Spade character, Raymond Chandler's Philip Marlowe, Kurosawa's *Yojimbo*, and finally Clint Eastwood's spaghetti western character, "The Man with No Name," where the implicit critique of the cowboy hero comes full circle and is transformed into its commodified revision in 1964, 1965, and 1966—another period of growing social destabilization around class, race, and gender.[22]

---

21. Severson, "Superior to All Men," 24.
22. Ibid., 31.

In *Sanctuary*, a hard-boiled novel Faulkner dubiously claims he wrote simply for money, Faulkner's violent male characters don't simply expose the seamy side of middle-class modernity but deploy a terrifying counter-narrative to the nineteenth-century notions of domestic tranquility, including "rational masculinity" and "domestic femininity."[23]

> *Family* and *home* were central terms in the discourse of respectability in the late eighteenth and nineteenth centuries. Home and family constituted not only the appropriate sphere of women's activity, but the fundamental structure on which much of the respectable world was supposed to rest.[24]

Where the sentimental fiction of the foregoing century made hearth and home a sanctuary from, as well as the *raison d'etre* for, the hustle of the public market, Faulkner uses the homes of the rich, occupied or abandoned, as sites of utter moral decay, places where the stench of a broken human nature is sealed off and hidden from public view. The market/home, public/private dichotomy are brought together in *Sanctuary* in a rural home, no longer the domain of a domestic female but a ruthlessly antisocial Memphis bootlegger's hideout. This formerly respectable domestic setting becomes the site of a brutal rape and murder.[25] The characters are bonded to one another by domination, lucre, and perverted lust. In the Gothic creepiness of the old house, the catastrophic cascade of criminality and death that envelopes the characters is, however, set in motion by the most staid and middle-class characters who are, to the public eye, the embodiment of respectability, which is exposed as simulation.

In Faulkner, as in Hemingway, men are castrated, figuratively by women and literally by a lynch mob.[26] Where Hammett's broken characters retain some semblance of agency through violence, in Faulkner, even violent men remain ineffectual, captives of a lurid and unpredictable fate.[27]

In Faulkner's *Light in August*, women again are the catalysts for chaos; men, again, are violent. In this novel, the racial narrative explicit, one character is clearly the fascist. Faulkner himself said in an interview, "If I recall [Percy Grimm] aright, he was the Fascist Galahad who saved the white race by murdering [Joe] Christmas [a light-skinned, biracial man who passes for

---

23. Ibid., 105.
24. Smith, *Consumption and the Making of Respectability*, 110.
25. Severson, "Superior to All Men," 101.
26. Ibid., 104.
27. Ibid., 105.

white]. I didn't realize until after Hitler got into the newspapers that I had created a Nazi before he did."[28]

Grimm was a National Guardsman, a military man, who hated Jews and African Americans. Joe Christmas is a mixed-race criminal who falls for a very androgynous woman named Joanna Burden, who lives—no surprise by now—in an old plantation manor house. Christmas and Burden are both, then, ambiguous—racially and sexually—and so pose a threat to the constitution of the community. They have an affair. She is killed. Christmas is suspected of murdering Burden (the novel never resolves this question). Grimm will eventually shoot Christmas to death, and then, yes, castrate him.

This summary does the story no justice, but it outlines Faulkner's critique of his own Southern culture and the American racial and gender narratives of his day. This was strong stuff back in 1932. Regardless of how Faulkner would dissimulate in later years about not realizing he had created a Nazi in Grimm, Hitler was prominently "in the newspapers" well before *Light in August* was published.

Fascism's masculinist response to the postwar era on both sides of the Atlantic was a reaction against the destabilization of masculinities brought about by the Great War, the October Revolution, and the Depression. American men of letters were not prepared to abandon the association of masculinity with violence; but they were equally unprepared to accept the violent authoritarianism of some national father figure or the premises of eugenics.

Sinclair Lewis, whose novels *Elmer Gantry*, *Main Street*, and *Babbitt* gutted profiteering preachers, middle-class respectability, and American materialism, confronted fascism head-on in his *It Can't Happen Here*. In this semi-satirical story of American fascism, the movement is led by a charismatic and populist politician modeled on Louisiana's Huey Long, then considering a run for the presidency. The antihero is not a violent man but a soft-handed, intellectual news editor named Dormeus Jessup. Jessup only becomes hardened by incarceration in a prison camp, becoming a fighter when he is released near the end of the novel. Lewis, himself a reserved intellectual man, does finally send his man to fight. His portrayal of an ineffectual, if moral, man is remarkable because it corresponds to Lewis's literary treatment of women, which was both realistic and respectful. It is more than a little interesting that the same writer who de-macho-fies his

---

28. Quoted in Brinkmeyer, "Faulkner and the Democratic Crisis," 92.

male protagonist is one of the few male writers who proved capable of treating women as enfleshed human beings instead of symbolic appendages or threats.[29]

Lewis's novel doesn't simplify fascism as mere hypermasculinism, however. The hothouse in which fascism grows and flourishes is the American middle class—trivial, superficial, uncritical, comfortable, complacent, and conformist: middle-aged white men like the ones we see in civic fraternal organizations are happy to host and applaud the silver-tongued demagogue—Chamber of Commerce types. Their utter disinterest in self-criticism and casual sense of entitlement constitutes the soil for the growth of creeping authoritarianism. The title, *It Can't Happen Here*, is a statement of this comfortable complacency. The relation between shallow mercantile men, a demagogic leader, and uniformed men with guns reflected the set of complementary masculinities that constituted fascism, an alliance between an authoritarian government and the business class.

If Lewis warned about the seeds of a future American fascism, John Steinbeck's *The Grapes of Wrath* showed that the sprouts were already apparent on the American scene: "Lewis's novel argues for the plausibility of fascism in an American milieu; Steinbeck posits that proto-fascist oppression is not merely plausible, but that it is common in contemporary America."[30]

The title is drawn from the lyrics of a Civil War-era Union marching song, one that portrays a vengeful God acting through the military: "Mine eyes have seen the glory of the coming of the Lord; / He is trampling out the vintage where the grapes of wrath are stored; / He hath loosed the fateful lightning of His terrible swift sword: / His truth is marching on."

The Grapes of Wrath is set in the early era of the New Deal.[31] The protagonists—Oklahoma farmers driven west by the Dust Bowl and phony promises of a Gold Coast—find themselves in work camps organized by local business tycoons, operated under miserable conditions, and overseen by an army of thugs—a fair representation of some West Coast labor camps.

---

29. It is also interesting that Lewis's notional fascist militia called itself the Minute Men—harkening back to both republican and frontier masculinity—and that today the Minuteman Project (MMP), founded in 2005, is a paramilitary organization of extreme xenophobes who unofficially "patrol" the U.S./Mexican border. Not only does this recall the male obsession with borders, MMP founder Jim Gilchrist, a Vietnam combat veteran and professed Christian, promotes military masculinity as necessary to prevent "the death of this nation." See Johnson, "At Columbia, Students Attack Minuteman Founder."

30. Severson, "Superior to All Men," 216.

31. A set of Keynesian social programs established in the 1930s by the Franklin Roosevelt administration to offset the economic devastation of the Great Depression and blunt the revolutionary political edge that developed in response to the crisis.

In the story, one federal camp is a refuge for a limited number of workers, serving as a base for union organizing. Unionization efforts are met with violence, mirroring what happened in Germany after the Nazis came to power—the right wing used by the business class as a mailed fist to break the left. In Steinbeck's novel, the poor Dust Bowl refugees are transformed into a pseudo-race of inferior others, called Oakies.

Steinbeck's narrative draws ironically on the westward expansion themes of the American frontier mythology, with its autonomous frontier masculine archetype—now, in Steinbeck's narrative, a cruel caricature.[32] One of the characters remarks, "Grampa . . . had to kill the Indians and drive them away," even as they themselves are now being "driven away."[33]

In the end, the story's main character, Tom Joad, redeems himself and his community, reclaiming his dignity as a man by killing. Masculinity is redefined again and again, but in the end, it seems, the essence of masculinity, even if it requires some form of justice to validate it, is to kill.

Masculinity constructed as violence is indelible. In the absence of any consensus about justice, masculinity is constructed purely as violence. Masculinity *is* violence. Violence *is* masculinity. Again, as Severson observes, the "violent American male is not simply a figure in American life, a figure of entertainment, but rather *the* figure around which American culture is oriented."[34] The violent man transcends political ideology.

Just as there are standpoints of women that differ in every circumstance from the standpoints of co-located men, in a racialized society, there are standpoints of the racialized other that invariably differ from the standpoints of the racially normative. Hemingway, Hammett, Faulkner, Lewis, Steinbeck—none could ever assume the standpoint of a black man in America. African American Richard Wright, however, could; and Severson analyzes Wright's novel *Native Son* for the racial counternarrative.

Wright's protagonist, Bigger Thomas, does not have the option of being a frontier man, nor its ironic reflection as the hard-boiled detective-type, nor the detached intellectual critic that is Lewis's character, nor the re-masculinized labor leader of *The Grapes of Wrath*. He is not white:

> He must be a brutal killer, a murderer, and this is precisely because, though he repeatedly shows the nascent class

---

32. Severson, "Superior to All Men," 217.
33. Ibid., 218.
34. Ibid., 5.

consciousness of a Tom Joad and the independence of a Doremus Jessup or even Hammett's detectives, in Jim Crow America he is allowed full access to neither American identity nor the narratives that support it. Thus, his narrative cannot make the heroic turn of those novels.[35]

Wright's novel is divided into three parts, titled "Fear," "Flight," and "Fate."

The novel begins with an ironic inversion of the masculine narrative. Men prove themselves in violent heroic actions against the threat of savage others—portrayed as pestilence or vermin, contaminators—imperiling civilization, or its symbolical embodiment as "our women." Bigger's first antagonist is literally vermin, a large rat that is in the room with Bigger and his family—his brother, sister, and mother. The rat "pulses with fear." Bigger chases the rat comically around the house, finally killing it with a frying pan—a woman's tool. His brother remarks that the rat is "a big bastard," telling the reader just what Bigger is bigger than—a rat. Bigger teases his sister with the rat carcass. She faints. Bigger is rebuked by his mother. Bigger nurses a loathing for his family, arising from his self-loathing for being unable to better provide for them. "Fear" in the title and in the rat mirrors the fear that Bigger and his poolroom acquaintances have of white society. He and his pals hatch fantasy crimes against white people to seize their wealth, then go to the movies instead.

Film and pop culture representations are where Bigger and his buddies see white models of masculinity, especially the hard-boiled characters, that are both out of reach and dangerously attractive. They do not have in their own lives the kind of control that movie characters do, so they affect tough-guy roles as compensation for their own social impotence. Their affectations are cover for their fear. This lack of a fixed standpoint, this "double-consciousness," in Wright's novel was described by the African American social critic W. E. B. Du Bois and by the Martiniquan social critic Frantz Fanon. It is the experience of having to see oneself at all times, from a lower position on the gradient of social power, from the standpoint of one's own experience, constantly attending to the perceptions of oneself by the more powerful.

Du Bois wrote, "One ever feels his twoness—an American, a Negro; two souls, two thoughts, two unreconciled strivings; two warring ideals in one dark body, whose dogged strength alone keeps it from being torn asunder."[36] Feminists were quick to recognize a similar double-conscious-

---

35. Ibid., 260–61.
36. Du Bois, *Souls of Black Folk*, ch. 1.

ness in the lives of women, and multiple-consciousness in the lives of women who were also racially "non-normative." Patricia Collins, an African American law professor, writes,

> Disempowered people can develop, in the words of W. E. B. Du Bois, a "double consciousness" concerning their placement in power relations. On the other hand, for reasons of survival, they must understand (but not necessarily believe) how the powerful see them, usually as less intelligent, less morally capable, less hard-working, less beautiful, or all of the above. Disempowered groups armed with this knowledge often mold their ideas and behaviors to the ideas and expectations of more powerful groups. For example, in a society where men have such power over women that they view women as sexual objects, women learn to anticipate male behavior—they adjust their style of dress to repel or attract men; they refuse to go out unaccompanied at night; or they fall silent when men talk, all in response to knowing how men view and treat women.[37]

Bigger's toughness is a (white) theater mask, appropriated from the movies, concealing his powerlessness. There is neither access to actual social power nor escape from it. Fanon's book *Black Skin, White Masks* explores this subject psychoanalytically with regard to language, sex, dependency, and recognition.[38] Writes Fanon,

> The Negro is comparison. There is the first truth. He is comparison: that is, he is constantly preoccupied with self-evaluation and with the ego-ideal. Whenever he comes into contact with someone else, the question of value, of merit, arises. . . . The question is always whether [the other Negro] is less intelligent than I, blacker than I, less respectable than I. Every position of one's own, every effort at security, is based on relations of dependence, with the diminution of the other. It is the wreckage of what surrounds me that provides the foundation for my virility.[39]

Virility! This is Fanon, Bigger Thomas, even Richard Wright himself. And still, in the mirror image of the dominant culture, the question is not

---

37. Collins, *Another Kind of Public Education*, 9.

38. In a note from my friend Kara Slade, an Episcopalian priest: "It's also interesting in *Black Skin, White Masks* that Fanon *really* doesn't know what to do with the figure of the black woman in his analysis. *Black Skin, White Masks* is definitely a work of Fanon's own search for masculinity—and it is noteworthy how the Western, European construction of 'MAN' is the figure he is ultimately both fighting against and trying to become."

39. Fanon, *Black Skin, White Masks*, 163–64.

of personhood, but of *man*hood—not of agency, but "virility." And again, in Wright, even the most broken and incoherent attempt to assert that manhood is through domination and violence. When Bigger intimidates his colleague Gus, he forces Gus to lick the blade of Bigger's knife in a demonstration of submission. One can almost hear *GI Jane*, as an honorary male, after beating her drill instructor, issuing the command, "Suck my dick!"

In *Native Son*, Bigger is emasculated like protagonists in earlier works. He is emasculated not just by white society, but by women. His mother nags him about not being a proper provider, the respectable male role according to white society. He is emasculated by a white woman, Mary Dalton, his "benefactress" who has him drive the car while she has sex with her boyfriend in the backseat. And it is Mary who Bigger will inadvertently kill in the first part of the book, suffocating her with a pillow and feeding her body into a furnace out of fear of discovery.

Joel Dinerstein says this urban black male pose signifies a break with shuffling, passive forms of black male accommodation to the dominant culture. The black tough guy—à la Bigger Thomas—is "the rebellious semiotics of hiding in plain sight, of bringing one's sullen hostility into public discourse," with something Dinerstein calls "the cool mask."[40]

Bigger's fear, alternating with his violent aggression, leads him to kill and kill again (women!) ... then flee (Fear, Flight, Fate) ... until fate catches up with him when he is sent to death row. Instead of the masculine fantasy he sees in gangster films—going down fighting—he is taken in after being captured using a fire hose, the way people break up dog fights.[41] When Bigger is tried, the cultural narrative that accompanies his trial is the "black male rapist" threatening white womanhood. The conduct of the trial, and the social conduct of the society that Bigger is born into, is not the nascent fascism of Faulkner's tales, or the notional fascism of Lewis', but a living fascism that is only visible to the invisible—and one that Bigger both fears and admires as a man. It leads to his own violent masculine authoritarianism, which paradoxically is trumped by the same.

In the modern world, especially in my own country, history has made it impossible to have a deep conversation about sex or war without a discussion of race. One of the difficulties of this intersectionality between race, sex, and war is, again, that the prerogative for violence and control has, to a great

---

40. Dinerstein, "'Uncle Tom is Dead!'"
41. Severson, "Superior to All Men," 291.

degree, been transhistorically and transculturally identified with males. Various forms of machismo have thrived *within* (and even nourished) "racial" and "ethnic" divisions. In the United States, one needn't look too closley in a white Protestant church, or a Latino Catholic church, or an African American Protestant church to find a pattern of patriarchs at the helm. Together they constitute Sunday as the most segregated day of the week; and they will differ, sometimes dramatically, on a range of social issues based on their various standpoints within the national socioeconomic structure. By the same token, it is not difficult to find a surprising degree of homogeneity of thought among a substantial number of these mostly male church leaders on two sexual issues. They collectively decry and shame women for perceptions of promiscuity, blaming women's promiscuity, real and imagined, for a host of social ills. They are hostile to people who are not "heterosexual." This correspondence of the identification of prerogative with men and the antipathy toward "homosexuals" and women who are perceived as promiscuous is not accidental. These are two aspects of the same transhistorical and transcultural male power. In the following chapter, I will explain why I put the terms "homosexual" and "heterosexual" inside these scare quotes.

28

Homos and Harlots

Persons habitually or occasionally engaged in homosexual or other perverse sexual practices are unsuitable for military service and should be excluded. Feminine bodily characteristics, effeminacy in dress or manner, or a patulous rectum are not consistently found in such persons, but where present should lead to careful psychiatric examination. If the individual admits or claims homosexuality or other sexual perversion, he should be referred to his local board for further psychiatric and social investigation. If an individual has a record as a pervert he should be rejected.

—Mobilization Regulations for Selective Service 1–9, Section XX, Paragraph (2)h, 1940

For what is a woman but an enemy of friendship, an inescapable punishment, a necessary evil, a natural temptation, a domestic danger, delectable mischief, a fault in nature, painted with beautiful colors?

—St. John Chrysostom, archbishop of Constantinople, 397 CE[1]

---

1. Quoted in Aquilina, "One Flesh of Purest Gold," para. 2.

Homos and Harlots

The Roosevelt administration's New Deal programs included projects like the Works Progress Administration Federal Art Project, the Treasury Relief Art Project, and the Public Works Art Project. Promoted as art democratization, the majority of the production from the arts projects was propaganda:[2] "Although it is impossible to characterize the New Deal art in terms of any one style or content matter, public art as a whole was intended to supply the American people with optimism, patriotism, and a sense of common heritage and purpose."[3]

Much of the art promoted other federal public works jobs programs, like the Works Progress Administration, the Civil Works Administration, and the Civilian Conservation Corps—projects whose main purpose was to employ unemployed men and simultaneously promote middle-class masculine virtues such as breadwinning, hygiene, and respect for authority. Men's bodies in this promotional art were vigorous, virile, and muscular. This image was conceived as an antidote to the imagery of local socialist, trade union, and Soviet propaganda that likewise appealed to muscular masculine archetypes (militant in *resisting* capitalist bosses).[4]

Men were portrayed with square-jawed, serious, and determined faces, often shirtless, and rippling with muscles. Art depicting married couples emphasized—against earlier ideals of private and companionate marriage—their combined role as the patriotic and determined heterosexual citizen-pair.[5]

The muscular male bodies were white.

President Roosevelt's own body, bent and withering with poliomyelitis, was selectively displayed to conceal his infirmity for an unprecedented four presidential terms, with the active cooperation of the American press. His wheelchair was never on public display.[6]

Of all the programs promoted by publicly funded art in the United States during the Great Depression, one stands out because it was the most paramilitary: the Civilian Conservation Corps (CCC). The CCC was signed into being in 1933 by executive order and would employ 2.9 million men between the ages of seventeen and twenty-five. These young men were physically inspected using medical/hygienic "induction standards," shaved, shorn, and put into uniforms. They were placed under the direction of military supervisors, directing them not only in work but in daily calisthenics

---

2. Jarvis, *Male Body at War*, 25.
3. Ibid.
4. Ibid., 25–27.
5. Ibid., 26.
6. Ibid., 30–31.

and inspections. Between 1933 and 1942, they planted more than two billion trees, laid down more than one hundred thousand miles of road, raised more than sixty thousand miles of firewall, constructed forty-five thousand bridges, built more than three hundred thousand small dams, and stocked more than one billion fish in ponds, lakes, and watercourses. They worked and lived in camps, and so were able to send home more than two-thirds of their wages ($30 a month).[7]

Historians can only speculate about when Roosevelt decided the United States would likely go to war. Roosevelt was concerned before he took office about the 1931 Japanese invasion of Manchuria, and he had early misgivings about mid-decade German rearmament. By 1937, the Japanese had sunk an American gunboat and invaded northern China. Germany had occupied the Rhineland and sent troops to support Franco in Spain. In 1938, Hitler began obvious war preparations for his eastern campaign.

Roosevelt himself was facing stiff opposition at home after a fresh recession hit in 1937. Most historians agree that somewhere between 1937 and 1939, Roosevelt believed that American entry into a second international war was almost inevitable. The CCC was not conceived as a preparation for war. When the specter of war was manifest, however, the CCC, administered along military lines using military-aged males, became the incubator for rebuilding the United States armed forces. The director of the Federal Service Administration, Paul McNutt, said the CCC was the central institutional effort "to build up the strength and vigor of society."[8] When the military *was* built back up in preparation for World War II, CCC veterans were prized by the military as noncommissioned officers, the first-line supervisors for soldiers, sailors, and airmen.[9]

In 1940, Hitler's armies conquered France, and the Roosevelt administration signed into law the Selective Training and Service Act of 1940—the draft. Roy Helton, in that same year, wrote for *Harper's* that "the feminine influence on Western life . . . has mounted into dominance over every era." Helton's discourse in the article was masculine and eugenic. He called for "resolution to raise up on this continent the strongest, ablest, hardiest, and most intelligent race of men and women that ever inhabited the world." That his rhetoric mirrors the racial diatribes of Germany, with whom the U.S. would be at war in a mere three months, seems to have embarrassed him not at all.[10] It was between programs like the CCC and the military draft that

7. Salmond, *Civilian Conservation Corps*.
8. Jarvis, *Male Body at War*, 22.
9. Ibid.
10. Quoted in Cuordileone, *Manhood*, 13.

a national masculine renewal was planned and executed by the state. For this renewal, women and "non-heterosexuals" served as signposts for what "real men" are not.

An important change in the symbolic imagination of sex during the Great Depression occurred around the subject of homosexuality. The gender destabilizations of the Depression and the consequent crises of masculinity redirected male insecurities into a special form of hatred and aggression against "homosexual" males, or "pansies."

I place the term "homosexual" in quotes because it is a very recent neologism. Homosexuality as either diagnostic category or "sexual identity" was not invented until the late nineteenth century, and it didn't come into popular use until the Great Depression when men were reaching desperately for normative masculine identities. Prior to the invention of homosexuality and heterosexuality (and now an extending list of *-sexualities), people's sexual acts were understood episodically for individuals and communally through a set of restrictions to prevent discord (incest, adultery, etc.). Sex was policed by family and community, and it had not become the object of "scientific" taxonomies. A man might be married and be known to occasionally engage in "buggery" of some sort, but he was never classified according to the anatomical objects of his transient or his sustained desires, as "having" (as a possessive "individual") an "orientation."

Interestingly, the emergence of sexual "deviance" using medical models corresponds in time and place to the emergence of eugenic theories. To explain how homosexuality developed, we again need to return to Sir Francis Bacon and the invention of the "fact":

> "Fact" is in modern culture a folk-concept with an aristocratic ancestry. When Lord Chancellor Bacon as part of the propaganda for his astonishing and idiosyncratic amalgam of past Platonism and future empiricism enjoined his followers to abjure speculation and collect facts, he was immediately understood ... to have identified facts as collector's items, to be gathered in with the same enthusiasm that at other times has informed the collection of Spode china or the numbers of railway engines.[11]

When Havelock Ellis (1859–1939) wrote the first medical treatise (1897) published on the topic of "homosexuality," a term he abhorred because it mixed Greek with Latin, the discipline of anthropology was busy

11. MacIntyre, *After Virtue*, 79.

adding a scientific cachet to imperial racism using phrenology—studying bumps in people's skulls for clues about intelligence, criminal proclivities, and sexual deviance. The attention to these "facts," hearkening back to Descartes, was a way to allegedly avoid subjectivity and produce sound scientific conclusions. This was about to become a major controversy, because psychoanalysis would base its findings on *subjectively* reported case studies to discover the secrets of sex, while anthropologists and physicians wanted to stick to the *facts* of direct observation. The migration of observation from physical objects to mental ones was a controversial shift. This controversy was heightened because the very same methods that confirmed imperial assertions about the inferiority of non-Aryans were those that claimed to be able to infer sexual deviance and/or underdevelopment from physical attributes. The merged politics of race and sex had infiltrated "science." Eugenics and sex were inseparable.

Ellis himself was a firm believer in white supremacy, as was his wife, Edith Lees, an early feminist who openly had affairs with other women. Both were very public supporters of the eugenics movement. Ellis argued for tolerance toward "homosexuals," not surprisingly because he tolerated his wife's own dalliances, even though he described same-sex attraction as deviant, medicalizing it as "sexual inversion." He placed himself squarely in the middle of the controversy between anthropology and psychoanalysis by borrowing concepts from each in his publications.[12]

In the "facts" camp was the unexamined belief that the body had *physically observable symbolic markers*. Those markers themselves were the "facts" that interested various scientists. In the latter nineteenth century, doctors and researchers were captivated by *anthropometry*, the incessant and detailed measurement of bodies.[13] The preoccupation with finding physical evidence for racial and gender beliefs is not surprising, given that in both cases what was at stake were power-inflected social boundaries, even if the methods strike some of us now as humorously silly.[14]

"The question of sex—with the racial questions that rest on it—stands before the coming generations as the chief problem for solution," wrote Ellis in *Sexual Inversion*.[15] Siobhan Somerville writes, "In its assumptions about

---

12. Somerville, "Scientific Racism," 245.

13. Ibid.

14. There are still advocates for biological determinism at work in the scientific community, but they have abandoned head bumps for "genes" in their quest.

15. Ellis, *Sexual Inversion*, xxx.

somatic differences . . . *Sexual Inversion* . . . drew upon and participated in history of the scientific investigation of race."[16]

The study of the somatic landscape for clues to sexual predisposition began with the study of the bodies—living and dead—of African women. Comparative anatomists claimed from the mid-nineteenth century until World War II that black women had differing sexual anatomies from white women—specifically, larger clitorises. This claim was used to support the idea that black women were naturally more lascivious than their white counterparts, who, it was also claimed, had tiny, well-hooded (modest?) clitorises. This symbolism mapped perfectly onto notions of a chaste "white womanhood" and the un-rape-ability of black women; but it was also transferred to the idea of *sexual inversion*—later called homosexuality—when the claim was made that same-sex attraction in females could be identified by the presence of a prominent clitoris. This claim was made in medical journals well into the twentieth century.[17]

This "prominence" was taken as a sign of underdevelopment: lesbians were underdeveloped (an idea that found favor with Freud, albeit without the anatomical element), and Africans were evolutionarily underdeveloped. The same "sexologists" who proposed these notions described same-sex attraction as deviant, yes, but also cross-racial attraction as deviant. Miscegenation was seen as extremely threatening. Theodore Roosevelt had termed it "race suicide" in an era when Jim Crow was being consolidated in the South and the North was seeing waves of immigration from southern Europe and Ireland.[18] Of particular concern, and of particular significance in the wave of postwar lynching in the South, was the belief that black men had a perverse and overwhelming attraction to white women—an idea that had long haunted the Southern white male imagination and translated into the bogeyman of the satyr-like black rapist.

Richard von Kraft-Ebing (1840–1902) published a treatise in 1886 titled *Psychopathia Sexualis*, in which he categorized sexual deviance as a "cerebral neurosis" in four categories: sexual desire at the wrong age, too much sexual desire, too little sexual desire, and misdirected sexual desire.[19] This was the work that sparked the first major controversy with the "fact" chasers, because Kraft-Ebing's research depended upon self-reporting. Case histories reported by "perverts," said the fact-physicians, were simply not

16. Somerville, "Scientific Racism," 245.
17. Ibid., 246–49.
18. Ibid., 239–50.
19. Kraft-Ebing, *Pyschopathia Sexualis*.

reliable—not good, *objective* science like that which relied on somatic markers such as clitoral prominence and skull topography.

"The 'speaking pervert,'" writes Somerville, "was a challenge to the 'truth' of medical examination and threatened to contradict the traditional source of medical evidence, the patient's mute physical body as interpreted by the physician."[20]

Ellis was actually trying to move away from the "guilty body" in his own "studies," which is why he combined comparative anatomy with the ideas of psychoanalysis, his position being that if a perversion was hurting no one, the "pervert" didn't deserve harsh punishment (his wife presumably included).

In this appearance of "homosexuality" and, later, "heterosexuality"— aside from an association with eugenics and race and its reinscription of power-inflected social boundaries—"identity" was now becoming associated with the abstraction of the object of one's sexual desire. One is now *defined*—placed into a category—not as a biological woman or man, or even a biologically ambiguous gender, nor understood by who specifically one shares a sexual attraction with, but by the abstracted sexual object. Bob is not attracted to Jim. Homosexuals are *men* who are attracted to *men*, even though no man is attracted to all other men, nor is any woman who experiences same-sex attraction attracted to all other women.[21] This question has become further muddied today by the politics of "sexual orientation," wherein biological determinism is now deployed *on behalf* of "sexual minorities" to advocate for legal equality. I was born this way; this is natural, so it shouldn't be held against me. In this legalistic account, there is no account for either social power or propaganda. Why did "heterosexual" men in the past find larger women desirable, for example, or what accounts for the sexual desirability of foot binding, or why are some women attracted to this or that kind of man, wearing this or that kind of clothes? This contention of congenital same-sex attraction has further confused the debate over "rights" because some anti-homosexual Christians have seized on the contradictions raised about congenital homosexuality and research showing the "invention of homosexuality" to buttress *their* position. Contradiction

---

20. Somerville, "Scientific Racism," 251. As a Special Forces medic working under the supervision of army doctors, I had more than one male physician tell me, "All women are liars until proven otherwise."

21. In my own considerable experience of sixty-three years, I have known a fair number of people who are identified, and even self-identified, as heterosexual or homosexual yet who have deviated—pun intended—from their "orientations" at certain points, and even some who have "switched" midlife, though always in response to a particular partner.

piles onto contradiction in much the same way it did during the debate between physicalists and psychologists during Ellis's time; and in the same way, both sides of the debate have failed to question their own assumptions.

The point here is that *homosexual* and *heterosexual* are recent categorical inventions that specifically imbricate themselves with other disembedded modern notions including the medicalization of personality, and with particular historical periods, especially the Depression. The function of these categories was not only similar to the categories of race-talk, but race-talk and sex-talk informed one another as epistemes in the struggle to maintain and reinscribe the boundaries of power. The construction and reconstruction of masculinity is inextricable from this dynamic; and as we will see, the discovery of the guilty homosexual body was part of the preparation for the ultimate political solution to the Great Depression—another world war.

Johann Gottlieb Fichte (1762–1814) was a "father" of German nationalism and German idealism. One of his central contentions about the state was "the more female the woman and the more male the man . . . the healthier the society and the state."[22] Each of the European states and the United States across the Atlantic subscribed to some version of this belief; and every state played an active role in trying to reconstruct a normative masculinity in the wake of World War I. State involvement in the construction of a normative masculinity was best embodied in Theodore Roosevelt before the war; but that is not to say the state abandoned this project after the war. In fact, in response to the destabilizations of masculinity in Europe and the United States, states doubled down in their efforts. Germany, in particular, saw the resurgence of nationalism in a guise that was explicitly martial and assertive of a normative masculinity that was martial.

In 1932, German elections catapulted the National Socialists (Nazis) into a parliamentary majority in the Reichstag. Party chief Adolph Hitler's public rants about German *emasculation* after the Versailles Treaty and his appeal to a Teutonic racial nationalism and martial masculinity galvanized many of the impoverished and suffering Germans, as Nazi paramilitaries engaged in thuggish violence across the country. In 1933, Hitler was appointed chancellor of Germany, and the Nazi-dominated Reichstag, faced with a near majority of communists, dispensed with the office of the president after Hindenburg's term. A brutal suppression of the communists

---

22. Cited in Mosse, *Image of Man*, 55.

followed. When President Hindenburg died in 1934, Hitler was already effectively the ruler of Germany. He immediately began a national economic revival program based on the remilitarization of Germany and the rejection of Versailles.

Hitler was a great admirer of the United States, and his racial policies were in many respects based on past U.S. policies. He was particularly inspired by Indian removal and extermination campaigns, modeling his camp policies to a large extent on the Bosque Redondo internment camp in New Mexico (1863–68), where thirty-five hundred Navajos and Mescalero Apaches were imprisoned and starved.[23] Hitler followed the American eugenics movement very closely, on one occasion writing to a fellow Nazi, "Now that we know the laws of heredity, it is possible to a large extent to prevent unhealthy and severely handicapped beings from coming into the world. I have studied with interest the laws of several American states concerning prevention of reproduction by people whose progeny would, in all probability, be of no value or be injurious to the racial stock."[24] Hitler's own eugenics policies received accolades from many American eugenicists in return, including the San Diego–based Human Betterment Foundation.[25]

The preoccupation with eugenics inevitably created a concern with sex, given sex's role in generation, and the construction of a science around eugenics led to a similar "scientific" construction of sexual practices, now understood medically as "sexuality," homo- or hetero-. As we have shown above, there was a close correspondence between the physicalist accounts of "homosexuality" and racial eugenics.

Havelock Ellis, who was for a time one of Margaret Sanger's lovers,[26] resigned as a Fellow with the Eugenics Society in 1931, over a dispute with them about legal sterilization. Ellis apparently thought that bringing legislation into the question would slow down sterilization efforts.[27] This was the same year in which Adolph Hitler made the cover of *Time* magazine. This was also the year in which *People* magazine published an article titled "Wanted: Better Babies: How Shall We Get Them?":

> Any scheme for obtaining a more favorably balanced birth rate by economic means must be judged by at least two main criteria. First, how far does it exercise the right kind of selection and thereby satisfy the requirements of eugenics? Second, how

23. Mandelbaum, "Hitler's Inspiration and Guide."
24. Black, "Hitler's Debt to America."
25. Ibid.
26. Katz et al., *Margaret Sanger Papers*.
27. Wyndham, *Norman Haire and the Study of Sex*, 242–43.

fully does it satisfy the economic requirement of insuring the selected families against the decline in the standard of living which is often the penalty of having children? For our present purpose, and in the present nebulous state of knowledge, the right kind of selection means one that increases the number of children in families where both parents rise well above the average in intelligence, strength of character, and general value as members of society. Insurance against a decline in the standard of living means more than relief of the sudden financial strain which often accompanies the birth of a child. It means also that as the number of children increases up to reasonable limits, the family is not obligated to economize to a degree that it is painful or humiliating, but can live essentially as before. Some sacrifice on the part of parents for the sake of the children is doubtless desirable, but it is obviously too much to ask ordinary human beings to step down to a lower economic level and build a new set of social relationships because they have three or four children. It has been suggested that some kind of insurance might solve the economic phase of the problem of the dangerously low birth rate among the finest of our middle classes. Such insurance might provide for the payment of specific sums whenever a child is born, or for the education of the child after it leaves the public schools.[28]

By 1935, psychiatrist George Henry and his Committee for the Study of Sex Variants were busily scrutinizing "homosexual bodies" for signs of the disorder. Henry and his colleagues believed that "sexuality" existed on a continuum from fully normal to fully "inverted," which was discernible through anatomical examination.[29] Some examinations might have been problematic with live subjects, like measuring the size of the hypothalamus, but there were outward signs as well. Distribution of body hair, for example, could suggest that the subject was nearer or further from the norm or nearer or further from "inversion."[30] You could be very heterosexual or a little homosexual or severely homosexual, depending on where you fell along the continuum.

By the time the male body was being examined and managed for conscription into military service in 1940, physicians knew exactly what they were looking for. In addition to "patulous rectums," doctors examined potential inductees for pubic hair patterns, fat deposition patterns,

28. Huntington et al., "Wanted: Better Babies."
29. Terry, *American Obsession*, 179.
30. Ibid.

"homosexual" gestures, gait, as well as facial and verbal responses to questions like "Do you prefer the company of girls or fellows?"[31]

The management of the male body for civil service and war was accompanied by a recoding of the female body as a source of danger. Sexually transmitted disease was treated like a living enemy, and women were a disease vector.

> In addition to its ardent interest in studying homosexuality ... the military was also vigilant in its management of venereal infections. Through various venereal disease control and prevention management programs, the military monitored not only the bodies and sex lives of servicemen but also the bodies of civilian women with whom they had sexual relations. According to official military rhetoric, these surveillance and management programs were aimed at protecting the health and productiveness of servicemen as well as the well-being and morality of the nation as a whole. While the servicemen themselves often viewed venereal disease prevention films and programs as "something between ludicrous and dreadful," the military, in conjunction with government and private agencies, poured a tremendous amount of resources into stamping out these "enemies within."[32]

There was a controversy about this. Some military leaders subscribed to the belief that real men wanted and partook of sex, and if they didn't they were suspect. Without prostitutes and "loose women" for sexual "outlets" (this is the steam-boiler theory of sex, where failure to "let off steam" can cause leaks or explosions), men might turn into homosexuals. A number of flag officers went on record with their belief that "if they don't fuck, they won't fight."[33] The official position, however, was that "loose women" were an enemy as formidable as foreigners under arms.

Manhood itself was at stake. "Manhood—Sex" begins a 1940 War Department pamphlet on venereal disease, "is what makes a man a strong two-fisted fellow. No little undeveloped boy can grow to splendid manhood without sex organs. They make a boy grow up with a vigorous body, and they give him grit and strength." The pamphlet explains that "male cells" account for virtues like courage, but that these cells and organs can be damaged by "a loose woman, whether she takes money or not."[34]

31. Jarvis, *Male Body at War*, 74–75.
32. Ibid., 77.
33. Bailey and Farber, "Hotel Street."
34. Pamphlet RG-215, "Sex Hygiene and Venereal Disease," quoted in Jarvis, *Male Body at War*, 81.

Prostitutes were not described as women who were exploited for sex by men, but *as the victimizers of men*. "While on duty," states one article in the *American Journal of Public Health*, "the Navy man is surrounded with and protected by every known means of safeguarding his health, the cost of which represents a considerable investment, while conversely, when he leaves his ship or station on liberty he all too frequently is *victimized* by a depraved or sordid group of *exploiters*, who care nothing for his health."[35]

Soldiers and sailors were warned to avoid loose women just as they would an enemy "booby trap." One brochure showed a "loose woman" seductively attired on the street, with the words printed across her image: *Booby Trap*. Another pamphlet claimed, "For every man the enemy puts out of action—she puts out three."[36]

> Artists designing posters for the army and navy likewise used military rhetoric and images to characterize prostitutes, V-girls, and other "loose women" as wartime enemies. Often juxtaposing images of supposedly promiscuous women with pictures of Axis leaders, the posters labeled the women as "another enemy to national defense.[37]

One wartime poster showed a Japanese soldier with his arm over a voluptuous white woman, saying, "You're a pal, babe. Keep up the good work."[38]

And so I will refer the reader back to the words of St. John Chrysostom at the beginning of the chapter. Men have a long history of projecting their own sexual failings and indiscipline onto women (John 8:7).[39]

Suitably armored against the threats of homos and harlots, men were prepared for their next adventure. To war!

---

35. Lang, "What the Navy Is Doing."
36. Jarvis, *Male Body at War*, 79.
37. Ibid., 80.
38. Ibid.
39. "When they kept on questioning him, he straightened up and said to them, 'Let any one of you who is without sin be the first to throw a stone at her.'"

29

Second World War

C-for-Charlie, as one man, was curious to see: to see a man die. Curious with a hushed, breathless awe. They could not help but be; fresh blood was so very red, and gaping holes in bared flesh were such curious, strange sights. It was all obscene somehow. Something which they all felt should not be looked at, somehow, but which they were compelled to look at, to cluster closer and study.

—James Jones[1]

Jesus actually descends right into [the] zone of death, the fallenness of the creature. His death witnessed to a mode of life, and his resurrection was an affirmation of that mode of life; a distinct way of being human was complete and full and utterly accomplished in him. His mode of life, the way he lived, was fugitive from the order of things. He cared for the poor, fed the hungry, hung out with menaces to society, refused to judge according to our measure of judgment (indeed, his judgment was against all judgment); he worked on the Sabbath, doing good and healing the sick even and especially on that day. This was his mode of life, his way of being human. And it was a threat.[2]

—J. Kameron Carter

---

1. Jones, *Thin Red Line*, 333.
2. Carter and Kline, "Race, Theology, Abjection."

At the end of chapter 22, "Disgust, Transgression, and Sex," we touched on Julia Kristeva's ideas about *abjection*—about those phenomena that threaten the distinction between subject and object, and thereby threaten the symbolic order that underwrites stability and power. In the quote above from James Jones's World War II novel *The Thin Red Line*, we see a group of men gathered around a corpse that simultaneously repels and fascinates them. The corpse, in a sense, is the ultimate abjection—a thing that tells us in stark terms that "as you are, I once was; as I am, you shall be." You, the subject, will inevitably become this decaying object.

This was the terrible image that accompanied the two fugitives on the road to Emmaus, too. The one they expected to triumph, the New David, had been cut down from a cross, reduced to a bloody corpse, a feast for flies. The fugitives were *abjectly* demoralized (Luke 24:13–24).

During World War II, the American government closely controlled all information about the war, and the media was strictly overseen and censored. One forbidden image was genital wounds. Written accounts of genital wounds were rewritten as "abdominal wounds" by government censors.[3] A man's gonads being blown off constituted an unacceptable and gendered form of abjection that could disrupt narratives about the masculine nation, because the vulnerability of the male body in war, especially in this most direct sense, could create a demoralizing and dislocative shock to both soldiers and the public. War was so intensely identified with masculinity that the idea of men being literally emasculated by war was incompatible with the carefully constructed social imaginary of the war itself.

Our cultural memory of World War II in the United States has been constructed by film as much as any other medium. Whether battle hagiographies like *A Bridge Too Far* and *The Sands of Iwo Jima*, or biographies like *Patton*, or "band of brothers" films like *The Big Red One* and *Saving Private Ryan*, or war-critical naturalism like *Das Boot* and *The Thin Red Line*, or Nazi-milieu accounts like *The Pianist* and *Schindler's List*, World War II films rarely show the ways in which the war was publicized and promoted in the United States as a white man's war. The Good War narrative that invariably overwrites accounts of World War II—based on the horrors of the Hitler regime—is embarrassed by the actual degree to which white racism (and its attendant white masculinity) was incorporated into both practice and ideology in the preparation for and prosecution of the war. The

3. Roeder, *Censored War*.

actual race-gender narratives of the war have now become an abjection that threatens a national masculine myth.

Tom Brokaw, in his popular book of the same name, called the Americans who fought during World War II "the Greatest Generation."[4] His account of that generation is closely reflected in Steven Spielberg's award-winning film *Saving Private Ryan*, featuring Tom Hanks as the protagonist detachment's leader, Captain Miller.

> Miller's characterization [is] as benevolent father figure to his subordinates, whose respect he commands with gentle authoritativeness. Miller and his men must find and protect the titular Ryan (Matt Damon), who is to be sent home following the deaths of his brothers in combat. Upon locating Ryan, Miller enacts paternal protectiveness *in extremis*, using himself as a human shield, and sacrifices himself to martyr his ideal configuration of wartime masculinity.[5]

"Greater love has no one than this," as the Gospel says (John 15:13). This is a story of sacrifice and honor, inflected with Christian-esque martyrdom.

Vin Diesel's character, Caparzo, the first of the band to be killed, is vaguely "ethnic" in appearance and speech, and has a Jewish pal, Private Mellish, whose bout of weeping when he is given a Nazi youth knife reminds us that the purpose of the war is to stop the Nazi anti-Semites. A Southern white boy is the detachment sniper, fighting alongside New Yorkers and the Midwestern schoolteacher who commands them. As close as Spielberg can get, without reminding us that black soldiers were in strictly segregated units, he constructs a pluralist microcosm in the detachment.

The reality in the United States when it went to war with the Axis Powers was Jim Crow in the South, deep structural racism in the North, widespread white hatred of Asians, and Jewish social exclusion. When the United Nations Monetary and Financial Conference was held in 1944, as the end of the war came into view, it had to select a site in New Hampshire, because earlier choices for conference sites would not do: they were hotels that did not allow Jewish guests, and several of Roosevelt's Treasury staff, including Secretary of the Treasury Henry Morgenthau, were Jewish.[6]

In 1943, between May and August, there were five racial riots in the United States. In May, while German U-boats were being scattered by the United States in the Atlantic, five black Mobile, Alabama, shipyard workers, involved in war production, were promoted to welding positions. White

---

4. Brokaw, *Greatest Generation*.
5. Hamad, *Postfeminism and Paternity*, 38.
6. De Vries, "Bretton Woods Conference."

workers organized a four-thousand-strong mob that was allowed onto the work sites by management, which proceeded to attack black workers with bricks and tools, leading to a mass exodus of black workers following the riot.[7]

In early to mid-June, while Allied bombers hit Naples and Sicily, Los Angeles-based white Navy men had become involved in a series of altercations with Mexican-American and African-American youths, who had established a local subculture that included wearing baggy suits called "zoot suits." Beginning on June 3rd, the Navy men organized themselves into phalanxes, rode in taxicabs to places where the "zoot-suiters" were known to hang out, and moved through the streets with clubs, beating hundreds of young men—many as young as thirteen and fourteen—and every person who tried to defend them. The Navy men stripped their victims in the street, then urinated on their suits before burning them. This went on for almost two weeks before the Navy Shore Patrol stopped it, declaring the Navy perpetrators innocent and claiming they had acted in self-defense.[8]

In mid-June, as the U.S. was winning a decisive battle at Guadalcanal, a riot broke out in Beaumont, Texas, another war production center. Based on two separate accusations from white women that they had been sexually assaulted by black men, white workers led by members of the Ku Klux Klan organized a mob of, again, around four thousand, which marched into the African American section of town, injuring more than fifty people and killing three, destroying local black businesses, and ransacking more than a hundred black homes.[9]

In late June, while the Allies prepared to bomb the Ruhr industrial valley in Germany, in another stronghold of the Ku Klux Klan, Detroit, a fight between a black worker and a white Navy man ignited a racial tinderbox, and a three-day street melee erupted between blacks and whites that resulted in more than eighteen hundred arrests, six hundred injuries, and thirty-four dead, twenty-five of them black—and seventeen of *those* killed by police.[10]

On August 1st, while the Germans gassed 2,897 Roma and U.S. bombers hit German-controlled refineries in Romania, a New York City policeman struck an African American woman, and a black soldier named Robert Bandy tried to intervene. The policeman shot Bandy, wounding

---

7. See http://www.pbs.org/thewar/the_witnesses_towns_mobile.htm.

8. For more on the L.A. zoot suit riots, see http://www.laalmanac.com/history/hi07t.htm.

9. See http://www.blackpast.org/aaw/beaumont-race-riot-1943.

10. For more, see http://www.pbs.org/wgbh/americanexperience/features/general-article/eleanor-riots/.

him. Bystanders who were outraged began spreading the word. The rumor circulated that Bandy was dead. A riot ensued, fueled by years of resentment against white law enforcement in Harlem, and the violence resulted in six dead, more than four hundred injured, and more than five hundred arrests.[11]

The industrial war forced the state to mobilize as many resources as possible. Black men were hired into war production with white men, and women entered wage labor in unprecedented numbers. Depression-era unemployment and the sudden explosion of war jobs launched waves of migration, shuffling the American demographic deck.

The United States found itself denouncing Nazi racism even as it actively pursued a racist ideological attack on the Japanese and maintained a racial caste system inside its own borders. The white masculinity that buttressed the war would be thrown into crisis by early setbacks against the Japanese that challenged "white superiority." After the war, the eventual discovery of the scope and brutality of Nazi atrocities would expose the exterminist seed lodged within the category "white."

There was an ideological reformation during the war, and the category white had to be expanded to mobilize more support for what was still constructed as a "white man's war." By the end of the war, the Office of War Information (OWI) found itself selling the idea of a racially pluralist and democratic America, and once that fiction was before the public, as the nation would discover in the years after the war, it would be impossible to take back.

Germany was inundated with visual propaganda under Hitler—paintings, posters, and statues. Masculinity, as it had been since the eugenics movement began in the West, was closely associated with "physical culture"—bodybuilding. The male form was represented in Nazi art as lean and heavily muscled, modeling its bodily archetypes on Greek and Roman art, with facial features that emphasized "Aryan" beauty. Figures of men were often nude and hairless, emphasizing the idea of a clean, self-contained, impermeable boundary at the skin. The torsos of the Nazi male archetype were modeled on breastplate armor to reinforce the idea of impermeability and lack of vulnerability. Feet were planted firmly apart, hands often doubled into fists, and visages sternly aimed at the horizon.[12]

---

11. See http://thehistorybox.com/ny_city/riots/SectionIII/printerfriendly/nycity_riots_article7a.htm.

12. Jarvis, *Male Body at War*, 44–47.

American war propaganda also emphasized men's bodies as hardened, using the terms "steely," "like iron," and "hard as nails" to describe them. And while Nazi images did the same, they were often hyper-idealized and standing naked to merge a Classical aesthetic with a racial purity ideal. American images had well-muscled men who were dirty, hairy-chested, at least partly clothed, and almost always in contact with big guns or big rounds of artillery ammunition displayed in decidedly phallic ways. The underlying narrative was that of the citizen-solider, the industrial worker cum soldier, of men fused with their machines, with a look of determined anger on their faces. A "now you've pissed us off" look.[13]

Christine Jarvis concludes that the transformation of working man into fighting hero mapped onto a popular American art genre, the comic book superhero:

> The aesthetics of American figures . . . were based on the bodily ideals evinced in comic books. . . . Superheroes could, with the aid of a magic word or swirling costume change, transform themselves . . . into superhumans with abilities and bodily characteristics that exceeded the realm of mortal powers.[14]

The fight against Germany was understood as a fight between men, whose associations are always either social or competitive (*never* intimate!). When that sociality broke down, it was time for a competition; and with that martial competition came a competition of ideas, of democracy versus dictatorship (in two different white nations). This was Athens versus Sparta.

Disney produced war propaganda films that caricatured Hitler as a lunatic, even as it included what would now be considered deeply offensive stereotypes of American Indians, Jews, Asians, and African Americans.[15] In the case of the Japanese, however, American propaganda was deeply and intentionally racialized.

Anti-Japanese sentiment had prevailed in the United States for decades, anti-Asian racism for a century.[16] The stereotype of the Asian man before the war had been highly feminized; Asian males were portrayed as nearly hairless men with "small bones" who did laundry or cooked. The one-sided and brutal American war against Filipino resisters had been portrayed at times as probative masculinity through big-game hunting.[17]

13. Ibid., 48–50
14. Ibid., 52.
15. Joseph, "9 Most Racist Disney Characters."
16. Jarvis, *Male Body at War*, 121–22.
17. Brewer, "Selling Empire."

This portrayal became a crisis for white American political masculinity when the Japanese military devastated the United States Navy at Pearl Harbor, then delivered another series of humiliating military defeats of Allied forces in the Pacific Theater over the following year and a half. If the Japanese were "effeminate" men, why were they trouncing American and British forces? Bill Stevens, a World War II veteran, remarked, "The white hang up about the infinite superiority of the white man to any man of color did not prepare the American white for the Japanese."[18]

"In the months following Pearl Harbor," writes Jarvis, "the government, military, and media . . . endeavored to recharacterize its Asian opponent." Japan had to be re-masculinized in the eyes of Americans to rehabilitate white American political and martial masculinity. The signifiers of manhood and race, as applied to the Japanese, were transformed. From being known and effeminized, the Japanese became inscrutable. The reason the white nations were taken off guard was that Japan was misunderstood, being as it was, otherly-other.[19]

The Japanese soldier was newly represented as physically tough and a good shot, though he was simultaneously portrayed as ugly, with "splayed toes," and as having no appreciation for human life—a kind of supervillain.[20] *Time* magazine and the OWI repeatedly published materials about Japanese ugliness, treachery, cruelty, and unbridled lust. One propaganda poster showed a snarling Japanese solider holding a knife to the throat of a terrified white woman, with text that read, "Keep this HORROR from your home . . . Invest 10% in War Bonds"[21]—a tithe to the state and the war to protect white womanhood. Slotkin traces these images to earlier racial stereotypes:

> Poster images of the Japanese as ape-like monsters raping and murdering White women draw more heavily on the iconography of Black stereotypes (from films like *Birth of a Nation*) than from the images of Western-movie Indians.[22]

So pervasive was the white American hatred of the Japanese that hardly a voice was raised in objection as President Franklin Delano Roosevelt signed Executive Orders 9066 and 9102—ordering the dispossession of property and incarceration in prison camps of 110,000 people in the United

---

18. Quoted in Jarvis, *Male Body at War*, 124.
19. Ibid., 125.
20. Ibid., 126.
21. Ibid., 126–27.
22. Slotkin, *Gunfighter Nation*, 319.

States who had Japanese ancestry, more than 60 percent of whom were American citizens.[23] Even the American Communist Party, which had been at the forefront in the fight against racism in the South through the 1920s and 1930s, supported Roosevelt's racist order and delisted its Japanese-American members.[24]

By 1942, Hollywood had begun a campaign called "Slap the Jap," in which the entertainment industry produced magazines, films, radio programs, and cartoons that portrayed the "yellow peril" as pestilence and disease—the same strategy being used in Germany against Jews. The Japanese were compared to rats, snakes, roaches, and lice—an implicit call for extermination that paved the way for acceptance of what would come to Nagasaki and Hiroshima in 1945.[25] The Japanese were unclean; they were like dangerous germs, and the disinfectant was the bomb.

A new archetype of white warrior came into being—the jungle fighter, a man "who learned to *match* savagery with savagery to achieve victory."[26] This is a man who has learned to "know Indians" of a new sort, a man who has learned to accept the grime of jungle combat and with it the grime of moral ambiguity. He knows he has to get dirty, physically and morally, if he is to win against the savages—the tough, treacherous, and ruthless monkeys.[27] This, God help us, was the archetype into which we were indoctrinated for Vietnam. Historian Samuel Eliot Morison writes,

> This may shock you reader: but it is exactly how we felt. We were fighting no civilized, knightly war. . . . We were back in the primitive days of fighting against Indians on the American frontier; no holds barred and no quarter. The Japs wanted it that way, thought they could thus terrify an "effete democracy"; and that is what they got, with the additional horrors of war that modern science can produce.[28]

Since the Chinese became critical to the Allied war effort in Asia and the Pacific, war propagandists had to develop differentiations between good East Asians and bad East Asians for a white public that had learned very well how to hate East Asians. Both *Time* and *Life* published articles explaining to white people how to differentiate between Japanese and Chinese, in what seems to us today a bizarre exercise in racial physical anthropology.

23. Jarvis, *Male Body at War*, 123.
24. Iiyama, "Recalling U.S. Detention."
25. Dick, *Star-Spangled Screen*, 230.
26. Slotkin, *Gunfighter Nation*, 321.
27. Ibid., 323–24.
28. Morison, *Struggle for Guadalcanal*, 187.

Americans had begun attacking Asians almost immediately after the Pearl Harbor raid, and the articles purported to explain the difference between the two "races" to help Americans tell the good Asians from "the enemy alien Japs."[29]

As the OWI, the media, and Hollywood staggered back and forth between the meanings of fighting Germans and Italians, the shifting signifiers for fighting the "perilous yellow" Japanese, the reality of race riots in cities all over the country, and a system of legal apartheid in the South, the definition of "whiteness" opened a crack to admit a few other ex-others. Americanization programs had been started to assimilate Eastern and Southern Europeans in the 1920s. One well-known Americanization booster was E. P. Cubberly, who explained, "Our task is to break up their groups or settlements, to assimilate and amalgamate these people as part of our American race, to implant in their children the Anglo-Saxon conception of righteousness, law and order, and popular government."[30]

Setting aside his Lamarckian description of "race," his faith in the superiority of the white Anglo-Saxon Protestant man was typical of his fellow WASPs, even "progressive." The Ku Klux Klan, then an immensely powerful political organization in the North and South, opposed this idea outright, and engaged in violence against African Americans and political candidates who were Catholic and Jewish.[31]

After the contradictions of the war began to surface, especially as men of various ethnicities in the armed forces proved their manhood alongside "white" men, Americanization began to take on a new significance. The scope of the mobilization, military and civilian, forced American society and war propagandists to reorganize representations of the American body politic. Diversity began to be celebrated in OWI posters. One even showed John Henry and Paul Bunyan, black and white mythical strong men, shirtless, muscular, standing together astride the world, glaring down as a terrified Hitler and his staff, barely knee high before the two giants, cringing in fear. "Let's go to work, brother!!" says the poster.[32]

The reality in the military, however, remained one where a single "ethnicity," African American, was systematically segregated from the rest of the armed forces into all-black units, commanded by twice as many officers per capita, and with white officers placed over black.

---

29. Jarvis, *Male Body at War*, 131–32.
30. Ibid., 137.
31. Ibid.
32. Ibid., 52–53.

"White" is constructed. The category came into being in Europe with the beginning of the slave trade. It was reconstructed by law in the Virginia Colony to exclude slaves, indentured servants, and indigenous peoples. It was further refined in its codified definition during the nineteenth and twentieth centuries by immigration policy. It was expanded during the same period by virtue of land ownership, wealth, and political power. And it was consolidated in the first half of the twentieth century by urban and suburban segregation.[33]

Military service during the Second World War opened the door to normativity, to what "whiteness" had signified, to every group except one: people of African descent. That is not to say that the doors were flung wide and none of the other outgroups suffered from discrimination after the war. They did, and some still do. But the official recognition of their full citizenship came through proof of masculinity for men in military service. What would come to define normative across those lines, in addition to constructions of masculinity, was the *countertype* represented by African Americans.

Even as recently as my own tenure with special operations in the military, where I worked alongside Latinos and Pacific Islanders in substantial numbers within mostly "white" units (true of Special Forces, Rangers, SEALs, and the more secretive counterterrorism outfits), negrophobia exerted a cohesive effect between nonblack ethnicities and "whites." Expressions of dislike or disdain for African Americans were common among these nonblack members, and validated the nonblack nonwhites as normative, as honorary white men.

Generals during World War II almost unanimously opposed the integration of black soldiers with other units that had otherwise been integrated out of fear that the common belief in white society that black soldiers were intellectually and morally inferior might be true; and they claimed, as opponents of female and gay integration in combat arms do today, that war was too serious a business to take risks for utopian social experiments. Such experiments threatened both "morale" and "readiness."[34]

The paradox of negrophobia in the World War II military was that while it was based on the lower valuation of black lives by the dominant culture, blacks were, where possible, systematically excluded, even to a large degree among the few black infantry units, from participation in combat. Most black soldiers were concentrated in labor and service specialties.

33. Helfland, "Constructing Whiteness."
34. Canaday, "U.S. Military Integration."

Generals tried as much as possible to keep black combat arms units away from combat. This suggests that what was at stake in terms of hegemonic masculinity was important enough to put more white troops in harm's way to maintain the exclusion of black troops from combat experience.

The draft signed into law in 1940 was closely watched by black male leaders around the United States. As with some advocates for black male legal and social equality since the Civil War, there was a prevailing belief that warfare had a special status among practices associated with manhood, and that black men's participation in the military would move them closer to acceptance by the dominant culture. Robert Vann, Charles Houston, William Hastie, and the leadership of the NAACP all pushed for an amendment to the 1937 Mobilization Act, upon which Selective Service was based, that would prohibit racial discrimination in the armed forces.

Senator Robert Wagner (NY) and Representative Hamilton Fish (NY) sponsored the amendment, and it was passed by politicians who were concerned with increasing levels of black activism.[35] Roosevelt had even appointed the nation's first black general in 1940, Benjamin O. Davis. The amendment was revealed over time as political window dressing by a clause within it giving military leaders summary authority to determine *how* it would be implemented, with no legal recourse for anyone who was dismissed by those military leaders along the way, nor any recourse with regard to systematic combat exclusion.[36]

Standardized tests were developed to sort recruits. The tests were culturally biased, *designed with black troops in mind for the purpose of excluding them* from certain specialties. Years later, Secretary of War Henry Stimson would write in his diary that "the Army had adopted rigid requirements for literacy mainly to keep down the number of colored troops"[37] (levels of overall black literacy were low in the country).

Regardless of the actions taken by the military and political hierarchy to keep black men out of combat, some black soldiers did see combat and performed as well as white units; and toward the end of the war, manpower shortages forced the integration of a few infantry units in northern Europe.[38] These exclusions became a sore point with the African American press, and it would be no exaggeration to say that the agitations that would culminate in the African American mass movements of the late 1950s, 1960s, and 1970s can be traced to this period. It was in 1948, just three years after the

---

35. U.S. Statutes at Large, 1940, vol. 54, 885.
36. Flynn, "Selective Service and American Blacks."
37. Quoted in McGuire, *Taps for a Jim Crow Army*, xxviii.
38. Lee, *Employment of Negro Troops*, 405–21.

war ended, that racial segregation in the military was banned by executive order.³⁹

In some respects, World War II decisively consolidated secular rule. World War I had been as traumatic for churches as it had been for combatants and European civilians caught in the war's crossfire. Gerald Lawson Sittser wrote of American churches,

> Church leaders became disillusioned after the First World War. With few exceptions they recoiled from the memory of the war and its outcome. Many Christians had witnessed the carnage firsthand. The senseless butchering of humanity horrified them. Poison gas, barbed wire, machine guns, airplanes, tanks—technological "advances" over the last war which Americans had fought—exposed the ugly nature of modern warfare. Clergy in particular wanted nothing more to do with war. The death of several millions only exacerbated the sense of revulsion to war that many Christians felt.⁴⁰

Christian pacifism enjoyed a surge in the interwar years, but it was still in the minority and still embedded in a culture that celebrated a powerful, although now less-than-totalizing, patriotism and militarism.⁴¹ The rise of fascism, however, and its aggressive militarism began to erode the post-World War I aversion to war. The deep ambivalence about war among American churches was not decisively overcome until Pearl Harbor galvanized the nation for war and swept away "anti-patriotic" voices in a way that is familiar to any of us who remember September 11, 2001.⁴²

Once the United States was fully engaged in the war, churches began to fall into line. No one was more influential in adapting Protestant thought to the needs of the American state than Reinhold Niebuhr, who is seen by many as the father of something called Christian Realism. Christian Realism first displaced the Social Gospel movement in American Protestantism that had begun with the progressives, then aligned itself with many of the initiatives of the New Deal. Niebuhr was a New Deal Democrat who supported government initiatives to "correct social problems." He eventually lost faith in some of the social engineering schemes supported by Social

---

39. Executive Order 9981, President Harry S. Truman, July 26, 1948.
40. Sittser, *Cautious Patriotism*, 16–17.
41. Ibid., 16–20.
42. Ibid., 21.

Gospel advocates and began criticizing them for their utopianism. While this seemed a turn away from the progressive vision of making history come out right, Niebuhr did not abandon either the centrality of the nation-state, the centrality of the United States, or the belief in the necessity for making war.[43] In fact, World War II was responsible for making Niebuhr as influential as he was because he articulated support for the war not just against liberal ambivalence but against the pacifists. Niebuhr wrote in 1941, "Protestant Christians . . . stand confronted with the ultimate crisis of the whole civilization of which we are a part and whose existence has made possible the survival of our type of faith and our type of church. . . . The inconceivable has happened. We are witnessing the first effective revolution against Christian civilization since the days of Constantine."[44] Niebuhr was not actually saying anything that had not been said before. He was identifying "civilization" with Christendom and the United States with civilization. It is no accident that most U.S. presidents and elected officials since World War II have described their Christianity, regardless of confession, in terms consistent with Christian Realism. It is an apologetic for state and war using a theological idiom.

Christian Realism has flourished since World War II *because* of World War II and its mythic status as "the good war." And of all the justifications for calling this the good war, which included dictatorship, expansionism, and racial purity doctrines, none survive critical scrutiny in light of U.S. support for various and sundry dictatorships, U.S. expansionism and interventionism, and U.S. racial history—the exception being the scale and the nightmarish character of Nazi Germany's extermination of Jews, against which the United States and its allies intervened far too late.

The role of the church in the development of European anti-Semitism is undeniable; therefore, there is no way to erase the line through history that leads from St. John Chrysostom, to anti-Jewish massacres carried out by the Crusaders, to Luther's virulent hatred of Jews, to Catholic complicity with Nazis (even as other Catholics opposed them). Hitler was baptized a Roman Catholic. In 386 CE, Chrysostom wrote the first of eight homilies titled "Against the Jews," in which he told his followers,

> God's presence makes a place frightening because he has power over life and death. In our churches we hear countless homilies

---

43. Hauerwas, "On Keeping Theological Ethics Theological."
44. Niebuhr, "Christianity and Crisis."

on eternal punishments, on rivers of fire, on the venomous worm, on bonds that cannot be burst, or exterior darkness. But the Jews neither know nor dream of these things. They live for their bellies, they gape for the things of this world, their condition is not better than that of pigs or goats because of their wanton ways and excessive gluttony. They know but one thing: to fill their bellies and be drunk, to get all cut and bruised, to be hurt and wounded while fighting for their favorite charioteers.[45]

In 1543, Luther wrote an anti-Semitic screed titled *Concerning the Jews and Their Lies*. Luther's words sound in retrospect as though they could have been spoken on *Kristallnacht*: "Let the magistrates burn their synagogues," he exhorted, "and let whatever escapes be covered with sand and mud. Let them be forced to work, and if this avails nothing, we will be compelled to expel them like dogs." Hitler, who frequently cited Luther's tirades against the Jews, told Roman Catholic Bishop Wilhelm Berning of Osnabrück in 1933,

I have been attacked because of my handling of the Jewish question. The Catholic Church considered the Jews pestilent for fifteen hundred years, put them in ghettos, etc., because it recognized the Jews for what they were. In the epoch of liberalism the danger was no longer recognized. I am moving back toward the time in which a fifteen-hundred-year-long tradition was implemented. I do not set race over religion, but I recognize the representatives of this race as pestilent for the state and for the Church, and perhaps I am thereby doing Christianity a great service by pushing them out of schools and public functions.

The record of this meeting shows that Berning made no response.[46]

The Catholic priest Charles Coughlin, a powerful supporter of Roosevelt's early New Deal and a popular radio show host, was such a venomous anti-Semite that he was silenced during the war by the American Catholic hierarchy.[47] Neither the Roman Catholic nor the Protestant confession can evade its culpability for participation in the conditions that led to war, for the outbreak of the war itself, or for the conduct of the war. In every single case, every major confession lined up behind its own national leadership, demonstrating conclusively that nation trumped church, that war trumped the Gospels, and that martial masculinity trumped the exemplary and vulnerable nonviolence of Jesus.

45. Chrysostom, *Adv. Iud.* I.2.6.
46. Quoted in Rhonheimer, "The Holocaust."
47. Tentley, "Vox Populi?"

Weapons are masculine threat displays:

> The relationship between "masculine" men and weapons is such a prevailing cliché that one finds it everywhere, from advertising to left-wing revolutionary posters, fascist imagery to the novels of Hemingway, war memorials to homoerotic art, from the porn industry to feminist critiques of male militarism. Weapons systems are designed mostly by men, marketed mostly for men and used mostly by men—and in many parts of the world, they are the primary source of death for men. Boys are given guns and swords to play with or they make them for themselves. Adolescent male warriors and middle-aged male hunters pose for cameras brandishing their weapons. . . . War memorials depict muscular men clutching their guns or hurling grenades with flexed, oversized pectoral muscles bulging out of the opened shirts of their uniforms.[48]

When, in 1945, the outcome of the Second World War after Stalingrad was a mathematical certainty, the United States was already turning its eyes toward the Soviet Union. When the Manhattan Project successfully detonated an atomic bomb, President Truman made his decision to use this weapon against Japan, twice, with several factors in mind—none by itself sufficient to justify vaporizing two cities, but together enough for Truman. Though the Japanese were already suing for peace terms, one idea was that the bomb would summarily end the war and force the Japanese to surrender without conditions. Another reason was to satisfy the American need for revenge after Pearl Harbor. Mass bombing of civilians had already been established as a precedent with Dresden and the firebombing of Japan; one bombing run over Tokyo alone had killed more than one hundred thousand people in 1944. Another justification was the enormous expense of the Manhattan Project. Finally, and this reason was perhaps the most strategically "defensible" one (on strategic and amoral terms), the bomb would send a message to the Soviet Union about how things were going to be after the war.[49]

The bomb was used for "demonstration effect."

William Laurence, a journalist who was invited by the government to witness the bombing of Nagasaki, writing about the immediate aftermath of detonation, said, "Then, just as it appeared as though the thing had settled down into a state of permanence, there came shooting out of the top a giant

---

48. Myrttinen, "Disarming Masculinities," 37.
49. Donohoe, "Understanding the Decision to Drop the Bomb."

mushroom that increased the size of the pillar to a total of 45,000 feet. The mushroom top was even more alive than the pillar, seething and boiling in a white fury of creamy foam..."[50]

Two bombs had killed more than 105,000 men, women, and children, and injured more than 94,000.[51] Within four months, another 105,000-plus would die of radiation aftereffects.[52] With the end of the war, a new and frightful age of martial masculinity had been inaugurated.

50. Quoted in Cohn, "Sex and Death in the Rational World," 694–95.
51. National Science Digital Library, "The Atomic Bombing."
52. Radiation Effects Research Foundation.

30

Bombs, Babies, and 'Burbs

Now I am become death, destroyer of worlds.

—Robert Oppenheimer,
upon witnessing the first atomic bomb test

Progress is our most important product.

—General Electric tag line, 1954,
delivered on television by Ronald Reagan[1]

In 1984, Carol Cohn—now the director of the Consortium on Gender, Security and Human Rights in Boston—was invited along with forty-seven other college teachers to attend a summer workshop on "nuclear doctrine," featuring a host of "defense intellectuals." (After the war, in 1949, the War Department had changed its name to the Department of Defense, suggesting that every military action taken by the United States is defensive in nature.) Cohn was one of ten women who attended.[2] She writes that the gathering threw her into a state of disequilibrium. The "defense intellectuals" were affable, likeable men, who discussed "scenarios" that anticipated the deaths of millions of people, in a language that was simultaneously sexual and techni-

---

1. *General Electric Reports*, "The Reagan Centennial."
2. Cohn, "Sex and Death in the Rational World," 687.

cal, never mentioning that human beings would be killed in these scenarios. She became so fascinated by this dissonance that she continued working with these "defense intellectuals" for a year to better understand them and her reaction to them.[3]

After a time, listening to lectures and panels and engaging in debates, she was surprised to find that her original sense of shock at the "extraordinary abstraction and removal from what I knew as reality" was not increased during her year with these men, but that she found herself becoming comfortable with the language and concepts they used:

> As I learned their language, as I became more and more engaged with their information and their arguments, I found that my own thinking was changing. Soon, I could no longer cling to the comfort of studying an external and objectified "them." I had to confront a new question: How can *I* think this way?[4]

She termed their language "technostrategic." It is characterized by bloodless terms like "throw weights," "counterforce exchanges," and "deterrent postures." Bombs are called "clean" if they leave behind less radiation hazard. These defense intellectuals coined the term *collateral damage*. There are no bodies, no wounds; there is no agony or grief. One nuclear missile is actually named "The Peacekeeper."[5] Technostrategic language can also be, paradoxically, very sexual. Missiles and "payloads" are constructed with "penetration aids." Missiles stand by in "silos" (evoking the family farm), which are alternatively referred to as "holes." There was a discussion about why a good missile requires a "nice hole." One official talked about releasing "80 percent of our megatonnage in one orgasmic whump." The introduction of a successful nuclear test means a country (like India) has "lost its nuclear virginity."[6]

Male "defense intellectuals" also appropriate motherhood for themselves in what Cohn calls "male birth" tropes. This is a time-honored patriarchal tradition dating to prehistory, when we think about women "carrying" a man's baby—this transfer of the power of generation from women to men. At Los Alamos, the first atomic bomb was referred to as "Oppenheimer's baby." The first hydrogen bomb was called "Edward Teller's baby," though others disputed this, claiming that Teller was just the mother and the true father was Stanislaw Ulam, who had "inseminated" Teller with

---

3. Ibid., 687–88.
4. Ibid., 688.
5. Ibid., 692.
6. Ibid., 696.

the idea. During the first nuclear tests, scientists said they hoped for a "boy" (a successful explosion) and not a "girl" (a dud). The first successful test of the hydrogen bomb at Enewetak Atoll was announced with the message to Los Alamos, "It's a boy."[7]

Nuclear technostrategic talk also has a theological/ecclesial idiom. Oppenheimer's reference to the Hindu god Krishna's boast "I am become death" was just the first claim to godhood when the first bomb exploded. Nuclear scientists and policymakers still refer to themselves unabashedly as "the nuclear priesthood." The first bomb test was referred to as "Trinity"—a reference, as understood by the scientists, to "the unity of the male [sic] forces of Creation."[8]

Cohn admitted that she learned to *enjoy* using technostrategic language. Its terms were "racy, sexy, snappy." Upon reflection she realized that she enjoyed "the thrill of being able to manipulate an arcane language, the power of entering the secret kingdom, being someone in the know."[9] Cohn said that using the language made her feel in control and that her mastery of it made her feel that the "whole thing" of nuclear weapons and nuclear war is therefore "under control":

> The more conversations I participated in using this language, the less frightened I was of nuclear war. . . . Structurally, speaking technostrategic language removes [us] from the position of victim, and puts [us] in the position of the planner, the user, the actor.[10]

Peace, notes Cohn, is replaced in this man-jargon by the term *strategic stability*. We can begin to see, then, using Cohn's testimony to her own experience, the capacity of language to simultaneously reproduce and conceal power. Cohn was not the victim of coercion, but seduction. Technostrategic language, a highly refined and targeted form of abstraction, becomes intellectual Rohypnol, a conceptual "roofie." She concludes that "as the pleasures [of talking this man-talk] deepen, so do the dangers. The activity of trying to out-reason nuclear strategists in their own games gets you thinking inside their rules, tacitly accepting all the unspoken assumptions of their paradigms. You become subject to the tyranny of concepts. The language shapes your categories of thought and defines the boundaries of imagination."[11]

---

7. Ibid., 699–700.

8. Ibid., 702.

9. I've seen this same delight on the faces of war-reporting newscasters when they throw around their military lingo.

10. Cohn, "Sex and Death in the Rational World," 704.

11. Ibid., 704.

The Cold War, the "baby boom," and the invention of the American car-suburb comprised the context of my birth.

On August 29, 1949, less than fifteen months before I was born, the Soviet Union conducted its first successful atomic bomb test, shocking President Harry Truman, who had ordered the annihilation of two cities just four years earlier as a warning to Stalin. The warning had "worked," but not in the way Truman had anticipated. Upon learning of this successful test, Truman ordered a nuclear and conventional military buildup. The arms race and the Cold War had begun.[12]

According to the U.S. Census Bureau, I was born five years into the post-World War II baby boom, which lasted from 1946 until 1964.[13] Between 1947 and 1951, William Levitt & Sons built a mass-produced community of three "neighborhoods"—that is, the houses were mass produced and modular—and it was named Levittown, in Long Island, New York. By most reckoning, this was the first tract-house suburb. Levitt had learned mass production using interchangeable parts while he served in the Navy during the war. Levittown was designed to cash in on a postwar economic boom that was buttressed by housing loans made available to all veterans as part of the GI Bill. Levittown did not allow black residents.

From the time of my birth until I was four, I lived in a city house; and between the ages of twelve and seventeen, I lived in suburban tract housing. In the interim, I lived on the edge of a town of less than three thousand people in an old poured-concrete house on five acres, where we were allowed to hunt rabbits and squirrels across the gravel street near miles of grape farms.

In the United States, the period between the end of the Second World War (1945) and the year I went to Vietnam (1970) was marked by the Cold War, but also by tremendous domestic social struggles around the issues of culture, economics, race, and gender. The nation was sick of war, even as it revered those who had fought the war. In 1952, the year after I was born, the former supreme commander of the Allied Forces, Republican Dwight Eisenhower, was elected president of the United States, ending twenty consecutive years of Democratic control in the White House. Keynesian demand-side economics, combined with the tremendous postwar industrial

---

12. Long, "First Soviet Atomic Test."
13. U.S. Securities and Exchange Commission, "Oldest Baby Boomers Turn 60!"

infrastructure and the lack of significant domestic damage from the war, left the United States at the head of the postwar global economy, with low unemployment at home. The education benefits of the GI Bill created a boom in college enrollment and led within four years to a highly educated workforce. In the 1950s, the American economy "grew" by 37 percent, and household disposable income rose by 30 percent. Female employment rose 18 percent. The number of televisions owned by Americans in 1950 increased tenfold in 1951. The bomb, which for some people had created a profound sense of foreboding, was transformed by public relations into a source of technological optimism. We were entering "the atomic age," a recoding of the progress narrative, but now with a chirpy enthusiasm for "the future."

In 1955 Eisenhower's special assistant on disarmament, Harold Stassen, wrote an article for *Ladies' Home Journal* titled "Atoms for Peace":

> Imagine a world in which there is no disease . . . where hunger is unknown . . . where food never rots and crops never spoil . . . Where "dirt" is an old-fashioned word, and routine household tasks are just a matter of pressing a few buttons. . . . A world where no one ever stokes a furnace or curses the smog, where the air everywhere is as fresh as on a mountaintop and the breeze from a factory as sweet as from a rose. . . . Imagine the world of the future. . . . The world that nuclear energy can create for all of us.[14]

Rational masculinity was back, finished with its masculine excursion into the war for civilization; and the men of science were about to lead us all into a new future.

"The 'Atomic Age' was to provide limitless sources of power," writes Amy Laura Hall in response to the Stassen article, "fueling shiny new refrigerators and other gadgets to perform routine household tasks in a jiffy."[15] But the same article warned readers against obstructionists: "Try living in a primitive society without doctors, sewers, medicines and machinery of any but the most basic sort for about six weeks—and then see if they can still work up an argument against it."[16]

One of the most effective vehicles for the public relations of American futurism was the Walt Disney Company, which had prospered during the war by making propaganda and military training films for the United States.

---

14. Stassen, "Atoms for Peace," 48.
15. Hall, *Conceiving Parenthood*, 345.
16. Hall, "Better Homes and Children," para. 10.

Bombs, Babies, and 'Burbs

The Disney empire was quick to recognize the value of television and had already signed contracts for regular television programming by 1950.[17]

"Disney was the ideal venue for the government's propaganda effort," writes Mark Langer. "Not only did Disney have a long-standing track record of creating government propaganda, but, as *Time* magazine reported in 1954, almost one billion people worldwide had seen at least one Disney film. After all, Disney was a leader not only in the film industry, but in publishing, television and the amusement park business."[18]

In 1957, Disney produced the animated "Our Friend the Atom" in partnership with the Navy and General Dynamics (which was contracted for the first nuclear submarines—one of the "peaceful" applications of nuclear technology). The animated feature was aired during the "Tomorrowland" segment of Disney's weekly television program, which promoted "futurism." Says the narrator, "The story of the atom is like [the genie in the bottle fable], come true through science. For centuries we have been casting our nets into the sea of the great unknown in search of knowledge. Finally, we found a vessel and, like the one in the fable, it contains the genie."[19] The Gospel (casting the net) meets scientific knowledge meets the magic wish-granter (the genie). The bomb was going to lead us into a future of unlimited energy—which translated into an age of electrically powered slave-machines that would support us in lives of leisure, safety, and hygiene. The safety and hygiene emphases, if the reader will recall, were built into the progressive vision—that one marked by rational men, domestic women, and "better babies."[20] As early as 1921, this vision was being expounded by Christine Frederick, a home economist and women's magazine editor who was a devotee of Frederick Taylor's scientific management principles and an early proponent of planned obsolescence to increase industry profits.

> Electrically operated equipment, such as vacuum cleaner, washer and dishwasher, will replace a large share of the work usually done by a permanent servant. Indeed, it may be said that "the one way out" of the servant problem in the future is the much wider use of power machinery in the home.[21]

Davin Heckman, in *A Small World: Smart Houses and the Dream of a Perfect Day*, describes how the postwar boom, the television, the suburban

---

17. Langer, "Disney's Atomic Fleet."
18. Ibid., para. 9.
19. Ibid.
20. Hall, *Conceiving Parenthood*, 11.
21. Frederick, *Household Engineering*, 393.

tract house, and the radical technological optimism of the day combined to transform baby boomers and their parents into a *spectator society*, plugged into a Foucauldian disciplinary grid—home as a kind of technological conformity machine.[22] The mass-produced home, available to veterans with VHA or civilians with FHA loans, was not only inexpensive, it was offered with a 1934 New Deal financial innovation—the thirty-year mortgage.[23] One of the big innovations of the mass-produced, suburban house was space. Compared to city dwellings, these homes were very spacious, and unlike farm homes, they were not built to the specifications of one landowning family.

> The practical concerns of the mass-produced house, along with advancements in building techniques, ensured that the open-space plan would become the norm. It offered an easy way to skirt the problem of customization by transforming the interior of the home into dynamic, multifunctional, customizable space.[24]

This space was designed to do two things at once: increase the space available for family intimacy and decisively separate the interior space from the surrounding community. So contact with family—now normatively understood as father, mother, children—was *increased*, and contact with neighbors was *decreased*. The increased intimacy envisioned by designers, of course, could translate into something less benign if there were "problems" within the now enclosed family, like abuse or just a plain emotional pressure cooker.

"The result," says Heckman, "was a reorientation of notions of privacy and community."[25]

The houses were wired for electricity, and industry was already making "labor-saving" appliances that were marketed to "housewives." The introduction of television, however, transformed the intimate living space into something new: a place where new experiences could be created for the viewer. This not only answered the problem of boredom that might accompany greater isolation from the outside, it offered a diversion from boredom or worse within the private space of the home. The actual outside world had been further cut off, but a new conduit to a simulated "outside" was placed inside. The person living in the house could experience life outside, but now (safely) as a spectator. The new modular home with the television created

22. Heckman, *Small World*.
23. National Housing Act of 1934, Public Law 84–345, 48 Statute 847.
24. Heckman, *Small World*, 39.
25. Ibid., 40.

the conditions for something undreamed of in the service of social control. "The house, filled with television," writes Heckman, "had become a powerful site for the production of meaning."[26]

For a young boy like me, television was nothing short of magic. By the time I started "getting into trouble" as a teenager, I had spent countless hours in front of this audiovisual datastream soaking up what I was, what I wanted to be, what I was supposed to be, and how to be a man. And I spent less time watching television than most of the people I knew. When I became addicted to tobacco, I would stay out of the house so I could smoke. When I discovered alcohol, I stayed out even more. When I discovered drugs, still more.[27] And yet . . . I was formed by television—by productions with clever men behind them who taught me how to walk, talk, think, and desire, who told me what was sad, what was funny, what was acceptable, what was unacceptable. No child has an adequate defense against public relations experts.

In all that apparent diversity of programming, with all its narratives, its tropes, its archetypes, its signifiers, the programs were the products of design. They were designed to capture my attention, to hold that attention with a story, to allow me to participate in the stories without any real threat (I was just a boy sitting cross-legged on the floor with the cathode rays flickering across my face), and to sell me (via my parents) the things that were advertised during the breaks. In all that diversity of programming, there were no deviations from the norms of respectability, progress, male supremacy, or American exceptionalism, except when embodied in a "bad guy," whereupon these deviations were punished. Delivered in thirty- or sixty-minute bite-sized chunks, these programs reached inside the living rooms of millions of people at once and conformed a generation of adults and children to its narratives, its tropes, its archetypes, and its signifiers. Television even explained to us how a "wholesome" family was supposed to act in the modular, superficially customized spectator home, with *Ozzie and Harriet*, *Dennis the Menace*, *Father Knows Best*, and *Leave It to Beaver*. From these, we learned that our *actual* families were deviant or inadequate.

Contact with the "outside world" was more and more with a simulated "outside world" that could not be matched by the quotidian real one. In fact, the banal reality outside the door, after the war, in the lap of technological affluence, was built on monotonous, alienated work in a thoroughly

---

26. Ibid., 41.

27. Intoxicants and television have a common payoff, like effortless, instantaneous gratification and an escape from reality. The difference, which makes television potentially more dangerous, is that television transmits ideas and values that persist after the television is turned off. Some people combine the two—for example, by smoking a joint and watching *Sponge Bob*.

Taylorized society and sustained by household commodities turned into use-values by other household commodities. There were no signposts of meaning. That was *all* provided through the media.

All the old markers of place and identity were shifting and disappearing. My own father, born in 1906, before the invention of the car, had grown up on a Michigan farm, was raised in the Seventh-Day Adventist Church, and ran traplines on the way to school—a school that he quit attending at an early age, living more or less outdoors with his brothers. By the time I was born in San Diego, in 1951, he was living in a house in El Cajon (Spanish for "the box") because it was conveniently located near his place of work, an assembly line in an aircraft factory, while my mother did the housework and shopping. For a time, my maternal grandmother lived with us before she died. By the time I was walking and talking, my mother took advantage of a new device to assist her with the child care (my sister was born when I was eighteen months old, my brother when I was three): the television.

Life had become partitioned. Work was where you went to be a cog for eight hours a day to receive a paycheck. It had nothing to do with home, which was in a "residential" urban or suburban neighborhood. With television, the fatigued worker and the fatigued mom/housewife could settle down in a safe place, at little cost, and check out of reality for a while as they were alternately "informed," entertained, and inveigled to buy alongside their bored kids. No one then said much about being indoctrinated. But there was no meaning to be found in driving the same rivets into the same part of the same fuselage day in and day out, nor was there much meaning in throwing diapers into the washing machine and pushing a carpet sweeper, then opening some cans to make dinner. These were activities that had become meaning-neutral. The real action was vicarious and neatly packaged and designed not to offend or provoke much thought. Work was balanced with fun, which was a television, a movie, or a trip to a theme park (we lived very near Disneyland).

It didn't take long before the only thing I wanted to do was watch television. "Lifestyle" technologies—the TV, the theme park, and the film—became, as Michael Sobel puts it, "a solution to the existential problems of boredom, meaninglessness, and lack of control, problems created by the confluence of affluence and the destruction of the traditional centers of meaning, religion, work, family, and community."[28] Heckman remarks, "Lifestyle is a technology by which subjects are able to tell a story about themselves through consumption."[29] Sobel and Heckman bring us forward

---

28. Sobel, *Lifestyle and Social Structure*, 171.
29. Heckman, *Small World*, 86.

in time from 1951, describing developments *after* the advent of television and suburbia; but the seeds were visible—looking back now to El Cajon, back to the box. By the time we actually did live in a suburb, in 1963, when both my parents were working in yet another aircraft factory (building fighter-bombers for the Air Force), I turned twelve years old in a state of perpetual boredom; and the TV was like my maintenance dose of heroin. I also hung on my father's stories about when he ran away from home, when he hunted moose, when he caught lake trout through the ice, when he went to jail for transporting bootleg liquor during Prohibition. Outside my front door there were houses that looked alike, with little lawns that looked alike, where we boarded a yellow bus five days a week to listen to teachers who all sounded alike in rooms that all looked alike; and what we had to look forward to was finishing school so we could work—doing the same things over and over to make enough money to survive, and having fun through consumption when we had time off.

At school, from time to time, we were required to do a drill called "Duck and Cover." (Nothing to do with waterfowl.) This was a drill on how to survive a nuclear attack by the Russians. We would survive nuclear warheads by ducking—getting down low so the window glass didn't rip through our bodies—then covering—getting under something face down to protect ourselves from falling debris. The signal to "duck and cover" was seeing a flash that was "brighter than the sun." We never discussed the possibility that one might not be able to see well enough after looking at this flash to find cover. We were shown an animated duck-and-cover instruction film, produced by the Federal Civil Defense Administration, featuring Bert the Turtle. To really appreciate the dissonance of the period, one needs to watch an episode of *Father Knows Best*, with its phony reassurances of domestic normalcy, then watch *Duck and Cover*.

I was an early reader, doing the basics at three, and I consumed books. By the time I was six, I knew the name of every dinosaur that was then known. When I was ten, I found a book at the James Memorial Public Library in St. James, Missouri, titled *On the Beach*, by Nevil Shute. When I put the book down, I had lost a form of innocence. It is a story about World War III, in which a series of nuclear "exchanges" (there's that bloodless language!) blanket the world in radioactive fallout that kills every human being on the planet. The story features suicide pills. Shute's novel was published in 1957, the same year in which *Leave It to Beaver*, *The Pat Boone Chevy Showroom*, and *Maverick* debuted, and one year after the Montgomery Bus Boycott. It was two years after the *Ladies' Home Journal* had printed Director of Foreign Operations Harold Stassen's article that told us to "imagine a world in which there is no disease . . . where hunger is unknown . . . where food never rots and crops never spoil . . . where 'dirt' is an old-fashioned word, and routine household tasks are just a matter of pressing a few buttons. . . . A world where no one ever stokes a furnace or curses the smog, where the air everywhere is as fresh as on a mountaintop and the breeze from a factory as sweet as from a rose. . . . Imagine the world of the future. . . . The world that nuclear energy can create for all of us."[30]

These competing narratives—one of technocratic bliss and domesticated consumer tranquility, and the other of threat from a nuclear-armed World Communist Conspiracy (which would become commingled with "agitators" in the homeland, especially the black freedom movement)—could not be sustained indefinitely; and this contradiction would reach critical mass in the 1960s and 1970s.

There were other competing narratives, too. The Eisenhower years combined a head-scratching war in Korea, New Deal Keynesianism, and corporate boosterism, a composite that one writer called "half-Republican and half-Socialist."[31] The economic expansion that this period produced stood down political ideology, and many Americans now understood themselves to be distinctly nonideological on domestic politics—even as they were coming to see the world as divided between the democratic Us and the communist Them.

After World War II, the leaders of the nation, civic and political, wanted to leave the war behind and begin the process of consolidating the power they had inherited in the wake of European destruction and the unraveling of European empires. American men themselves were keen to settle back down, get jobs, and raise families. Their collective masculinity had been proven abroad in combat, and their political masculinity was proven by the bomb. The nation required a new mythic narrative, now that "democracy had triumphed over dictatorship" and military action would become a sideline (in Korea?) while the nation's efforts were directed toward the postwar surge in capital accumulation driven by technological innovation and consumer demand. Not only the nation, but the re-establishment of a hegemonic masculinity required a revised mythic narrative. One cultural manifestation of this shift was the renewed popularity of the Western. Richard Slotkin writes,

---

30. Stassen, "Atoms for Peace."
31. Charles Willeford, quoted in McCann, *Gumshoe America*, 200.

In the midst of this ideological turmoil, the Western and its informing mythology offered a language and a set of conceptual structures rich in devices for defining the differences between competing races, classes, cultures, social orders, and moral codes. It incorporated these definitions in pseudo-historical narratives which suggested that human [male] heroism could shape the course of future events. Moreover, the preoccupation with violence that characterizes the Western and the Myth of the Frontier made its formulations particularly useful during a period of continual conflict between the claims of democratic procedure and Cold War policies that required the use of armed force.[32]

As we will see, this contradiction between "democratic" and conformist *Father Knows Best* masculinity and the Western hero cum secret warrior masculinity was being resolved by making these two forms complementary, with the former supportive of the latter, but supportive in a passive and vicarious way. The good suburban husband and father would virtuously consume and work, and his participation in the bloodletting of the warrior would be as a spectator. The cowboy-hero became the *symbol* for political masculinity.

In the two elections in which George W. Bush ran for president, we saw this transfer of cowboy-hero symbolism to the individual candidate/officeholder; it was politically effective even though Bush himself was born in 1946 to a wealthy Eastern patrician family and was a frat boy and cheerleader at Yale University. Simulation and symbol trumped reality.

In 1947, Hollywood produced fourteen Westerns; the following year the number jumped to thirty-one. In 1952, it produced forty Westerns, and in 1956 a total of forty-six. After 1956, there was a dip in production caused by competition in the genre from television. From 1955 to 1970, Westerns were consistently among the highest-rated television series, pulling on average about a third of all viewers.[33]

The interplay between film, fiction, television, popular norms, and power is complex. Cultural productions do not generate a certain politics, nor does a certain political practice play a direct causative role in the production of cultural myths and archetypes. Politics and public discourse about it create clusters of public concern—these are the things that are "important." Yet if those public concerns have no connection with the real, material concerns of most people's lives, they are likely to be ignored.

---

32. Slotkin, *Gunfighter Nation*, 350.
33. Ibid., 347–48.

Pre-existing patterns within culture interact with these concerns, and there is a dialectical give-and-take between "art" and "reality." Art itself, when it is a commodity, has to take into account its salability, its likelihood of being accepted. Does it connect to popular concerns or the way people live their lives in a particular period, even if that connection is controversial? Controversy can be salable! Symbols that are not recognizable, however, will not provoke a response; and there are already numerous mythic landscapes with which a particular "public" may be familiar.

Art has a special ability to create emotional resonance that is not the case with many forms of "rational" public discourse. That's why art is always part of any social change movement; it can mobilize emotions as well as new conversations. In combination, art, power, and mass communication have established a form of power unthinkable to local despots and transient emperors of the past, a means for rendering the governed incapable of imagining anything *except* how they are governed. In a nation of hundreds of millions of people, a largely conformist population is a prerequisite to effective bureaucratic administration combined with autonomy of the state to exercise its military and security apparatuses.

> An analytics of government . . . views practices of government in their complex and variable relations to the different ways in which "truth" is produced in social, cultural, and political practices. On the one hand, we govern others and ourselves according to what we take to be true about who we are, what aspects of our existence should be worked upon, how, with what means, and to what ends. We thus govern others and ourselves according to various truths about our existence and nature as human beings. On the other hand, the ways in which we govern and conduct ourselves give rise to different ways of producing truth.[34]

Just as Carol Cohn, after speaking technostrategic for a time, found that "the more conversations I participated in using this language, the less frightened I was of nuclear war," the power of mass media, if it uses the same idiom as power, can establish the actuality of that power as given, as common sense.

The postwar Western movie had several archetypical storylines, which Slotkin has named and described: the town-tamer, the cavalry and the Indians, the revised outlaw, the gunfighter, the High Noon showdown, and the good man with a gun. The Western genre gave each of these narratives

---

34. Dean, *Governmentality*, 27.

a wide "mythic space" in which to tell these differing stories.[35] Cold War Westerns all had some defining *borderline*, whether it was a river, a fort's palisade, a street, a fence, or the (fragile) boundary between civilization and wilderness, or savagery. A hero or protagonist had to cross those borderlines and by transgressing them "reveal the meaning of the frontier line" as he entered the dark side to protect the good side. Sometimes, after we were schooled in the psychoanalytic wolf-man, as the protagonist dealt with the "darkness" across the border, he also dealt with the darkness within himself. It is always a *he*. In the Western, the audience was to understand the boundary that separates their past from the viewing present, and therein they understood this to be a tale of *progress*. Last but certainly not least, there was a resolution, a "regeneration" accomplished by male violence.[36]

This was, by the way, exactly how I imagined Vietnam before I actually went there. Now, forty-five years later, I have begun to understand why.

"A cowboy will not submit tamely to an insult," said Theodore Roosevelt, "and is ever ready to avenge his own wrongs; nor has he an overwrought fear of shedding blood. He possesses, in fact, few of the emasculated, milk-and-water moralities admired by the pseudo-philanthropists; but he does possess, to a very high degree, the stern, manly qualities that are invaluable to a nation."[37]

Women in the Cold War Western were portrayed as either markers of civilization and domesticity or threats to manhood—sometimes both at the same time. "While the essential qualities of womanhood that tie women to domesticity are nostalgically honored in Westerns," writes Edward Buscombe, "femininity as a social force is represented as a threat to masculine independence and as the negative against which individual masculinities are tested."[38]

While the Western film may seem a long way from *Father Knows Best*, it is actually its gender ideology mirror. Humorous skits were based on the modern husband and father being clueless around the home and children, and his dissociation at home was met with the amused tolerance of the "little lady," who knows this is her domain, while the public world is his. Outside the home, the man is confident, a provider, and part of the male network of social protection. The Western in *Fort Apache* or *High Noon* is the historical myth that *leads to* the myth of the modern family represented in *Father*

---

35. Slotkin, *Gunfighter Nation*, 351.
36. Ibid., 352.
37. Roosevelt and Remington, *Ranch Life*, 55.
38. Buscombe, *BFI Companion*, 181.

Knows Best or *Leave It to Beaver*. Together, they are a *progress narrative*—a before-and-after photo display.[39]

Westerns supported the peculiar military adventure in Korea in as much as they inscribed racialized and militarized boundaries between civilization and threat. The popular Marine Colonel Lewis "Chesty" Puller—a good friend of Western film director John Ford (*Fort Apache*, *Rio Grande*, et al.)—gave a speech to his troops in Korea, exhorting them to write to their families about getting "harder" for America:

> Tell 'em there's no secret weapon for our country but to get hard, to get in there and fight. I want you to make 'em understand. Our country won't go on forever, if we stay soft as we are now. There won't be an America—because some foreign soldiers will invade us and take our women and breed a hardier race.[40]

And so we are back to protecting white womanhood, a basic Klan theme. By being hard . . . not soft.

Even in the supposedly countercultural, non-Western James Dean classic *Rebel Without a Cause* (1955), the protagonist, Jim Stark, is portrayed as a young man who needs to prove himself through high-risk actions. His family is portrayed as nonnormative—his father weak-willed, his mother domineering—and this is one source of his alienation. But alienated males then prove their masculinity by fighting with knives and playing automotive "chicken." As countercultural as this purports to be, his home is dysfunctional because of a usurped male authority; and the characters, just as in any Cold War Western, are driven by their internalization of violent "male codes." The film is, gender-wise, every bit as conservative as a Shakespeare tragedy.

If Westerns simultaneously defined women into the domestic sphere and defined men as not-like-women, another popular art form of the period, the crime novel, displayed a more direct and violent misogyny. The genre of crime writing was, as we saw in chapter 27, a form of social criticism during the Great Depression. In the Cold War era, it was transformed into a highly racialized transfer of martial masculinity from the war abroad to defense against dark others and wicked women at home.

Raymond Chandler, Ross MacDonald, and Mickey Spillane were among the most well-known and successful crime fiction writers of the

---

39. For a boy who grew up watching *Father Knows Best* and who chose to live into *Fort Apache*, there was still a way to learn frontier masculinity: join the military.

40. Quoted in Slotkin, *Gunfighter Nation*, 363.

early Cold War era; and even though their styles, characters, and politics were distinct from one another, they can be taken together as emblematic of the period's sensibilities, at least American white men's sensibilities, about the association of violence and masculinity after the war.

Chandler came into his own before the war as a hard-boiled fiction writer and a contemporary of Dashiell Hammett. His work bridged the Great Depression, the Second World War and the postwar 1940s and 1950s. His most famous character was private detective Philip Marlowe, who begins his career with the publication of *The Big Sleep* in 1939 and endures until *Playback* in 1958, the year before Chandler died. Marlowe is a single, hard-drinking, hard-fighting, pistol-packing urban tough guy—a cowboy transplanted from the frontier to the big city, where the borderline between civilization and danger runs through racially divided streets and through human hearts. Chandler wrote of a hardened male fraternity facing the corruptions of modernity. For Chandler, the corruptions of modernity were *all* manifestations of effeminacy: women, genteel intellectuals, and bureaucrats. "Chandler returned time and again" says Sean McCann, "to a vision of male fellowship and showed the way it was undermined by the various evils of the modern world."[41] While Hammett had held his nose to write for pulp crime fiction magazines, Chandler saw it as both manly and populist:

> Though unsophisticated, the magazines were "honest and forthright," he argued. Against "the pseudo-literate pretentiousness" of middlebrow journalism and the shallow withdrawal of "literary life"—each of which seemed to Chandler reprehensibly "feminine"—they remained a masculine world of vital competition.[42]

Chandler, as narrator and through his protagonist, referred to blacks as "niggers," described Jews using blatant anti-Semitic stereotypes, attributed to Mexicans an innate criminality, and despised homosexuals. But no prejudice marred his writing with as much force as his hatred of women: "Even when he turned in the later 1940s from the class-oriented populism of the New Deal to a racialized idea of national consciousness, Chandler's virulent anti-feminism would remain consistent," writes McCann.

His protagonist Marlowe is constantly approached by seductive *femmes fatales*, but as a real man in control, he not only resists them but kills them when necessary. He makes objectifying comments about every female he encounters; and if a female becomes "hysterical," he slaps her. And with Chandler, the women *enjoy* being slapped by Marlowe. Chandler's wide

41. McCann, *Gumshoe America*, 140–41.
42. Ibid., 147.

acceptance shows that he was not, as he would be considered today, out of the mainstream with regard to his racism, homophobia, and misogyny, but that he was squarely within the white male mainstream. It would be decades before he was critiqued for his various chauvinisms.

"His novels made common cause with the complaints of the most prominent intellectuals of the day," McCann explains, "sometimes eliciting the qualified approval of those critics—and distanced his work from a booming popular culture that celebrated . . . suburbanization, mass consumerism, middlebrow culture, a bureaucratic state, and the mediation of ethnic and racial division."[43]

He was, in effect, espousing a republican masculinity not unlike that celebrated in *Birth of a Nation*, D. W. Griffith's extremely popular 1915 silent film, which portrayed the Ku Klux Klan as populist heroes and defenders of national honor. In that sense, as evidenced by his disdain for the narratives of respectable futurism that were boosted in this period, he *was* countercultural. The common denominators that remained, albeit coded differently, between boosters of the technocratic future and hard-boiled crime fiction protagonists were American nationalism, white supremacy, and male supremacy.

Chandler's position as a bridge between the Great Depression/New Deal and the Eisenhower years reflected a shift in urban noir literature. Chandler's social critique, like Hammett's, emphasized class division both in its stories and in its populist aesthetic assertions. Hammett and Chandler wrote for the "pulps," crime-story magazines that disappeared after the war, displaced by a new publishing industry—trade paperback novels.

Chandler got in on the paperback boom, but his sun was setting as two other noir fiction authors' were rising: Ross MacDonald and Mickey Spillane. The differences and similarities between MacDonald and Spillane are both revealing, and in key respects mirror the differences and similarities between liberal philosophers John Rawls and Robert Nozick, whom we examined in chapter 20. Spillane was comparable to Nozick as a conservative-liberal, and MacDonald similar to Rawls as a liberal-liberal.

Mickey Spillane's character was a hypermacho WWII veteran, private detective Mike Hammer (no phallic symbolism *there*). MacDonald's character was Lew Archer (an arrow instead of a hammer), a more genteel (but still tough) private detective who was likewise a veteran of the war. Hammer was a Marine noncommissioned officer. Archer was a captain in Army Military Intelligence. Hammer operates on the gritty streets of New York. Archer does his thing in outer Los Angeles, often in the wealthy suburbs. Hammer is mostly motivated by anger. Archer is mostly motivated by compassion.

---

43. Ibid., 193.

Hammer represents Everyman. Archer represents the postwar, GI Bill intellectual—a kind of "talented tenth" among white people.[44]

Spillane wrote women as evil, morally crippled creatures or as straight-up submissive sex objects. The antagonist in his first novel was an emasculating female psychologist. MacDonald wrote more complex female characters (which gave him his staying power in the market after Spillane faded); but MacDonald constructed his women as victim/perpetrators using the analytical categories of Freud. (MacDonald told Newsweek, in 1971, "Freud was one of the . . . greatest influences on me. He made myth into psychiatry, and I've been trying to turn it back into myth again."[45]) Both authors' protagonists cast objectifying gazes on women as proof of virility.

Mike Hammer enjoys violence. Lew Archer sees it as a necessary evil. Both employ it—and it is always redemptive.

One can see the outlines of MacIntyre's archetypical Nozickians and Rawlsians—the working-class stiff who knows what is his (dammit!) and is suspicious of intellectuals, and the liberal petit bourgeois who shows a paternalistic concern for the unfortunate. Yet both construct justice from the assumption that the postwar American order is normative; both agree that violence is a male prerogative (that it becomes perverse in females); and both resolve conflict with killing. That both protagonists are former military men should not be surprising.

My intent here is not to take a back alley through cultural criticism of the early Cold War era but to point out that these were significant elements in the cultural atmosphere during my formative years. This was where "my head was at" when the 1960s blew right past me. When Martin Luther King Jr. was speaking at Riverside Church one year before he was assassinated, and telling us that a bomb dropped in Vietnam exploded over Harlem, I was inoculated against the momentous changes in the United States, because I lived at 76 Ruth Drive in St. Charles, Missouri; and when my boring-ass, stamped-out neighborhood got to me, I could watch a Western, read a tough-guy book, waste some oxygen reading Ayn Rand,[46] or sniff

---

44. "Talented tenth" refers to a talented 10 percent of a group that will lift the fortunes of the other 90 percent. Originally used by white liberal philanthropists in the early twentieth century for talented African Americans, it was appropriated by the young W. E. B. Du Bois to describe a kind of black vanguard in the racial equality struggle.

45. Quoted in Jones, "Passion for Mercy," para. 8.

46. The author of *The Fountainhead*, a novel in which a rape is described as an erotic experience for the female lead, and another novel, *Atlas Shrugged*, a Bible-length book that uses vulgar Nietzscheism in a dystopian apologetic for a mythical system called "laissez faire capitalism." One speech by her lead character consumes sixty-four pages, which is a summation of her "philosophy."

airplane glue. That other stuff was just background noise. In 1967, I was a high school sophomore; and my biggest thrills were drinking and trying to cajole local girls into having sex with me. Given that I had no real character except what had been formed in a period of enforced superficiality, simple-minded politics, and lots and lots of television, it's a wonder I didn't turn out worse. Heck, I thought reading Ayn Rand made me an intellectual and an iconoclast. I was indefinitely suspended from school in my junior year over a refusal to cut my hair (this was how I manifested my masculine independence) but managed to catch up in an adjacent county's school, using a phony address, so I had the requisite credits to finish on time (1969) when I was readmitted the following year. When I got that diploma, I wasn't even thinking about the army. It was while I was bumming around that summer that a guy I knew returned and showed us pictures of Vietnam—and I made note of how much his status had improved—that I first got the idea, whereupon I went to see a movie that had been out for a year called *The Green Berets*, starring John Wayne.

The Green Berets was, by any standard, a really crappy film. But I wasn't into cinematic aesthetics when I was seventeen; I watched movies and television programs that projected male fantasies of control, domination, and worshipful women who adored controlling, dominating men. The film was a bald piece of propaganda that fitted nicely with the dangerous crackpot ideas I was absorbing from my favorite author, Ayn Rand. *The Green Berets*, like *Zero Dark Thirty* and *Black Hawk Down* (the latter two arguably had better production values), was produced with the active participation of the United States Department of Defense and the blessing of the executive branch, precisely *because* it was propaganda that supported the official line from Washington.[47] *The Green Berets* supported every official lie about the war, in addition to deploying every frontier masculinity trope in the book. The poor, *good* South Vietnamese, including innocent and charming women and children, are being victimized by the *bad* North Vietnamese, who are obeying their masters from China and the Soviet Union (no account here of the intense hostility between these two countries at the time). Colonel Kirby (Wayne) and his team (colonels do not command Special Forces teams) are Indian fighters (who "know Indians," and have some good and obsequiously loyal Indian/Vietnamese scouts), accompanied by a liberal, war-skeptical reporter (David Janssen), who is converted when the Viet Cong rape a little girl to death and kill a little orphan boy's dog, in a place code-named... "Dodge City." Get it?[48] Moreover, does the reader "get"

---

47. Slotkin, *Gunfighter Nation*, 520–21.
48. Ibid., 522.

the similarities to *Man on Fire*? In the end of the film, Colonel Kirby and the orphan boy, Hamchuk, are holding hands on the beach as the sun sets behind the water. In addition to its saccharine, sentimental manipulation, the film has the sun setting in the East, since the eastern edge of Vietnam actually faces the South China Sea. The west, where the sun generally sets, is bordered by Cambodia and Laos.

But between Ayn Rand and John Wayne and the J. Edgar Hoover book my Dad had lying around the house—not to mention seventeen years of living at the height of the Cold War (duck and cover!), and seventeen years of being indoctrinated in manhood as redemptive violence, and because the suburbs were a deadly alienating bore—I became convinced that the war in Vietnam, which I did not see as an invasion and occupation, was a monumental struggle between Good and Evil in which I could become a real man. My girlfriend broke up with me (because I was also a job-hopping drunk who stayed up all night by eating diet pills?) in December 1969, and the next month—I'll show her!—I made a visit to my local army recruiter. Maybe, when I came back as a war-hardened hero, I could be a tough private detective. I had teenage acne and could barely grow a moustache.

31

The Herd

Saul replied, "Say to David, 'The king wants no other price for the bride than a hundred Philistine foreskins, to take revenge on his enemies.'"

—1 Samuel 18:25

We are the unwilling, sent by the unqualified, to do the unnecessary for the ungrateful.

—Helmet graffiti, Vietnam

"It don't mean nuthin."

I learned that phrase in Vietnam. We said it when someone was killed. We said it when the mail didn't come out on the resupply bird. We said it when we got busted. We said it when we were shriveled up with four days of ceaseless rain. We said it when we watched the ARVNs beating the shit out of a prisoner. We said it when we got jungle rot. We said it while the house burned after we set the roof thatch on fire. We said it when we smoked opium in a whorehouse. We said it if we killed a child. We said it when we were just tired and it was a long way to our DEROS date.

"Fuck it. Don't mean nuthin."

Postmodern philosophy in the boonies.

The Herd

I entered the army with a head full of Ayn Rand's smug, circular logic and a flaccid, indolent, adolescent body. I had rationalized the army and internalized the culture's masculine ideal . . . minus football. I never liked football. I enlisted intent on becoming a Green Beret.

In basic training, I was summarily reduced to a slobbering, fainthearted fool by a plague of sadistic drill sergeants. How I recoiled from the reality of hard work when my skinny limbs and tar-speckled lungs encountered real, deep-down fatigue! Within one day, I wanted nothing more than to retreat to my hometown, where I could fritter away the hours bargaining with girls for sex, drinking beer, and trying to one-up my acquaintances in debates on topics about which none of us knew a damn thing. With time, however, my body hardened, my bluster returned, I became accustomed to being named Dickhead (we were all named Dickhead), and I came to recognize the ever clean, ever starched drill sergeants as the embodiment of power. Stockholm at Fort Leonard Wood.

We sang "Yellow Bird" when we marched:

> *A yellow bird*
> *With a yellow bill*
> *Was perched upon*
> *My windowsill.*
> *I lured him in*
> *With bits of bread*
> *And then I smashed*
> *His fucking head.*

. . . two, three, four, *hut*, two, three, four . . .

When terrorism researchers described the Stockholm syndrome, they patted themselves on the back for discovering that captives will eventually identify with their captors. Abusive husbands and drill sergeants have known this for a long time. So have battered wives and basic trainees. We even came to admire our drill sergeants, each day identifying with them more and more.

A big shift for me, a kid from the 'burbs, was being in the army with a lot of African Americans. About half of my drill instructors were black, too. My attitude on race at that time was white-privilege neutral. Like many white people, I equated racism with active, personal hatred based on color. If I didn't *hate* anyone for *being* black, then I was not a racist. Simple as that. "Prejudiced" we called it then. My limited intellectual constructions at the time were so roped to the individualist dogma of Ayn Rand that I had no capacity to understand structural racism, or social structures at all. Every door in my mind had been safely closed. Since black was half the time the color of power in my new world, I adapted to that with little friction.

In fact, my favorite drill was a sergeant named Smith, a black man who was arguably the most soft-spoken of our cadre. He almost whispered when he was chewing your ass. He was immaculately pressed, tall, slender, with chiseled features. His head was made for the campaign hat, which he wore with the brim fore and aft tipped up almost imperceptibly. On his right shoulder, he wore his combat patch, the patch for the unit he'd belonged to in Vietnam: a blue background, with a white wing carrying a red bayonet. Arched over the patch was a blue and white AIRBORNE tab. The brilliant colors of that patch pierced the predawn halftones ahead of anything else— this bit of brilliance, as Smith's silhouette strode before the morning formation. That patch defeated the darkness.

The patch represented a unit that was created for, deployed to, and stood down in Vietnam. It was the 173rd Airborne Brigade. Trainees seized onto bits and pieces of combat lore. The 173rd, nicknamed "The Herd," had a kind of mythic status in the infantry. It was known for hard fighting, long stays in the field without rest, clannishness, and ferocity. You could almost see it like an aura around Smith; it was there—in the opacity of his eyes.

I coveted that patch. Smith had something unnamable that I wanted. It wasn't confidence, and it wasn't contempt, and it wasn't sorrow, though there was an element of each in Smith's deportment. It was something Sisyphean that attracted us, especially the youngest of us. We all agreed that Smith was somehow . . . cool. I knew I could be like him if I got that patch. I got my wish.

I went to Vietnam.

I managed to get through Infantry Advanced Individual Training (AIT) in Fort Polk, Louisiana, then Airborne (Parachuting) School in Fort Benning, Georgia; but I let go of the Special Forces idea. It took an extra year or more, and I was afraid I would miss Vietnam. They sent me to the Non-Commissioned Officers Academy before "jump school," and I quit (giving up the chance to be promoted to sergeant upon completion) because I didn't want to miss the war. On my nineteenth birthday in 1970, I lost four hours out of

The Herd

the day by crossing east to west over the International Date Line en route to the Republic of Vietnam. I was about to get my patch.

The turnover rate in the 173rd Airborne Brigade was so high that every single one of the more than two hundred men in my graduating class at Airborne School was sent to "The Herd." At Camrahn Bay, I was in-processed by a phalanx of faceless staff workers and introduced to high-quality marijuana by an acquaintance from AIT. At Charang Valley, we received our brigade's weeklong indoctrination before being forwarded to our units. I was taught how to stir human shit in the burnout latrines, and we watched the cadre, for their entertainment and ours, shoot CS gas canisters at the civilians who were picking through the adjacent garbage dump.

That was my first glimpse of how the rules had changed. You could launch 40mm gas grenades into the middle of groups of women and children as casually and thoughtlessly as you could skip a stone. The risk that a grenade body might hit and kill someone was not even taken into account. Hell, that was part of the fun. (Chuckle, chuckle . . . "fuckin' gooks!") In the United States, livestock was given more deference.

Even through the haze of the opium-impregnated Laotian marijuana that we could buy cheap at the compound gate, I could see that there was something going on here that was not like John Wayne holding that Vietnamese orphan's hand on the beach at sunset. Our side was shooting gas canisters at orphans to kill time until they could get "back to the world." "The world" was a euphemism for the U.S. Vietnam was outside "the world," a place where the old meanings and rules were suspended. "Don't mean nuthin'." Apart from the TV, back in the 'burbs, there wasn't much meaning to start with, truth be told. Beaver-fucking-Cleaver hadn't been to Vietnam.

Some of the NCOs would show us their photo collections—pictures of dead Vietnamese with heads hollowed out and bodies mutilated by high-powered ammunition. They were proud of the pictures, their hunting trophies, and they enjoyed watching us react to them, or trying to show no reaction. The abjection of the corpse that hasn't been prettied up by undertakers was no longer a stumbling block to some of these men, some of them very young; it was the gateway into a realm that was almost spiritual in its untouchability. A place where you could look back and down on respectable folk almost with a kind of pity from the demonic freedom of living in the netherworld of the abject. We heard rumors of men who collected ears using mosquito repellent as a preservative. Human ears. Before I left, I saw this . . . became this.

At Tam Quan District, when I joined my platoon, I offered a piece of C-ration gum to a teenage girl. We were on my first walking patrol, and she seemed frightened, reluctant to take it. Butler, a hard-assed little black dude from DC, turned to our squad leader, Sergeant Hamby—white guy, red hair, maybe twenty years old—and pointed at me. They both laughed, the kind of laugh that people laugh in the abject-zone; and Butler spat at me, "Fuckin' missionary!" Butler called me a do-gooder, told me you don't "treat gooks like that" or you'll get killed ("ripped off" was the term), asked me if I wanted "to marry that dink bitch." I was now in the company of men. Real men. They scared me.

Less than two weeks after I joined Second Platoon, Company A, 4th Battalion, 503rd Infantry (Airborne), 173rd Airborne Brigade, I single-handedly repelled a night attack. While on guard along the bunkered perimeter, on a pitch-black night, a magnesium trip flare ignited not twenty meters to my front; and my heart tried to jackhammer out of my chest. Someone had tripped the flare in the concertina wire directly in front of me. Someone alive and moving toward *me*, intent on killing *me*, and now I was completely blinded by the intense light of the flare, spots swimming across my field of vision. A night or two before, I can't remember now, we had watched an attack down in the valley (we were perched atop a big hill overlooking it) against one of the Stag Team outposts, a sudden outburst of automatic weapons on both sides, with tracer rounds streaming and bouncing all over the place. From a distance, the gunshots made the sound of woodpeckers drilling a tree back home. Then it had been over. Now I was trying to remember, as the flare kept burning and smoking, what I was supposed to do. The claymore! I had the claymore mine detonation device (a "clacker"). I heard people on the other guard posts shuffling, rifles clattering as we went on alert, movement in the sleeping bunkers. I picked up the clacker, pushed the safety clip aside, hunkered down in the bunker, calling out, "Fire in the hole!" and gave the clacker a snap. The explosion to my front was deafening, and when I looked up the mine had scattered bits of burning magnesium from the trip flare, now sparkling like little smoking stars scattered down the rocky, orange hillside.

We stayed at 100 percent alert all night—everyone awake and in fighting positions. When daylight came, we went forward to see what had tripped the flare. There wasn't much to find, but what there was proved that I had repelled a stray dog brought up the hill by the smell of our ration trash. My nickname then became Dog-Boy, soon shortened to Dog.

We all had nicknames. One night in the big bunker, we were smoking "Bongson bombers," me lying in a box-bunk called "the coffin," when Ski (a murderer at nineteen) looked around and started laughing. "We got Hawk,

Rat, Mac, Slick, Ski, and Goff the Dog in the coffin." Shit like that was funny when you smoked o-jays.

Our hill was steep. These were fixed positions out of which we patrolled the valley during a phase called "pacification." The hill had been scraped clean of topsoil and vegetation by bulldozers called Roan plows. We could see the ville below us, the South China Sea in the eastern distance, and in the west, at night, the lights of the city of Bongson. Our company headquarters was a couple of kilometers north, and our battalion headquarters in Landing Zone (LZ) North English was eight to ten kilometers away, between us and Bongson. Most of the valley was checkerboarded in cultivated plots and the wet shiny parts were rice paddies. South of us were the mountains—towering, thick, and deep green.

The subsoil that remained on our hill after the plows was orange, and we were constantly covered in a layer of orange dust. You could smack your pantlegs and the stuff would billow off of them. The heat caused us to sweat all day long, and the orange dust would get wet and gather in the creases of our skin. You could roll strings of grime off your skin most of the day and never be done with it. When you bathed out of a bucket, if the wind was blowing (and it was almost always blowing in the day), the dust would start to stick to you before you dried off, and your towel would show it.

Not long after my dog defense night, while I was outside the wire at the entrance to our perimeter buying candy and soda from the "Coke girls"—young Vietnamese women who peddled to us—a sniper took a shot at me. A loud crack like it was right next to my ears, followed by a hollow thump from down in the valley. The coke girls dropped to the ground, then bundled their wares in a second and ran down the side of the hill. I was stoned and I just stood there, watching them run. Someone shouted at me from a bunker, and when I looked back, another round cracked just as close. Then I realized what was happening. Someone in the ville was trying to kill me. I scooted back inside the perimeter, safely behind the berm.

A day or two afterwards, our medic—an agitated guy with thick strawberry hair and glasses—came up to me out of the blue and confided in me that the next patrol out was "gonna kill a dink." I wondered, *how could they know that*? But I was stoned again, and my mind went elsewhere as Doc chattered on with the excited manner of someone in possession of a special secret.

I did not go out with that patrol. My squad leader did, but with a put-together detachment—a seasoned radio guy, and several old-timers from the three squads. The platoon was half African American, including our platoon sergeant, but on this patrol the only black guy was Austin, nicknamed Hawk. If I recall correctly, the whole patrol was six men, average age about twenty. Within minutes of the patrol disappearing into the ville, there was an unbelievable eruption of automatic weapons fire, punctuated by a bursting grenade—whump! Cowboy, our platoon senior communicator, came running out of the communications bunker and yelled "Contact!" He went back in, then reemerged seconds later, calling out, "No friendly KIA, no friendly WIA, one enemy KIA!"[1]

I was on guard in the overwatch bunker when the patrol came struggling up the hill. From around two hundred meters away, they dragged what appeared to be a long, heavy sack. First two guys would drag. Then two others would spell them. Then two more.

When they approached the wire I finally made out the form of an old woman, lifeless, covered like a doughnut with fine, orange dust, being towed up the hill by her blouse, which was tied around her ankles to make a handle. Her head, dragging behind her, bounced loosely over the potholes and stones. In different places on her body, spots of blood were leaking out through the coating of dust. The dust was in her mouth, stuck to her teeth. Her fixed, half-open eyes were muddy with dust as well. Her hair was long and, having come undone, was wildly tangled in an anarchy of dry dust, twigs, and gravel.

After catching his breath—that was a steep hill; it always made us suck air when we came back, but now there was this weight, too—Hamby told the platoon leader that the old woman had thrown a grenade at them. Then he uttered a short laugh, still out of breath. The platoon leader accepted the story without question, instructing them to get the body outside the perimeter as he turned to go back to the command hooch (where he stayed most of every day, segregated from the rest of us) at the center of the hilltop.

The corpse was placed on a flat LZ outside the wire where we received helicopters. A rope was tied to her feet, then fed back to the bunker that overwatched the LZ. They told me we took this precaution because the Viet Cong sometimes stole back the bodies of their dead after dark.

She had thrown a grenade. You had to do it, I told the patrol members (and myself). Everything was on the up and up. She was VC, and she threw a grenade. Hamby just gave me a blank look. Ski, who was scheduled to go back stateside soon, started laughing at me. Hawk fixed a sad, stony stare on me for a moment, then went to his bunker. Doc's eyes shifted back and forth, with a kind of mad half-smile. His hands were still shaking and covered in blood. He'd stuck his fingers into the holes in her chest and head before declaring her dead. Rat, my mentor ("cherry dad," we called them), changed the subject and asked if I still had the shits (I had gone overboard on C-ration chocolate when the pot I smoked made me hungry, and my

---

1. KIA, killed in action; WIA, wounded in action.

bowels rebelled). Mac, a buck sergeant like Hamby, looked angry, then stalked away, disappearing into a bunker. Suddenly, I had no easy answers. A boundless emptiness came into me, and it would never go away. This was what it meant to be a jungle fighter, a man "who learned to match savagery with savagery to achieve victory."[2]

The next day the body had begun to bloat and draw a cloud of flies. We had to drag it away from the center of the LZ so the battalion commander could land in his helicopter. He was rotating out of his command—his ticket punched, as we said—and he smiled at us benignly like a gentle father. He told us how proud he was to have worked with us. He congratulated us on our kill. I stood there without sound or motion, enraged that no one had prepared me for this—not Mom, not Dad, not Walt Disney, not Ayn-fucking-Rand. Everyone had been in on it except me, the short kid who read books and ate chocolate bars until his bowels turned to Jell-O.

Two days after the kill, some guys from LZ English flew in with a distraught young South Vietnamese lieutenant. They showed the lieutenant the body, which by now had been wrapped in a poncho because of the smell and the flies. The young lieutenant flipped open the poncho and studied the remains for a moment. He saw something he recognized, then he collapsed right there on the ground next to the body, wailing and crying and beating the ground with his hands. Then he glared at us through his tears, the whole watching platoon, and screamed something at us. They must have told him the story about the grenade. The guys from LZ English led him off and coaxed him back onto the chopper so they could fly away.

The dead woman was his mother.

With the progression of hours and days, as is the case with young men, the discussions became more emboldened. Each retelling was another blow to my shattered innocence. A booby trap had killed JoJo last month. As repayment, it was okay to kill an old woman hoeing a vegetable patch. To "kill a dink for JoJo." This was Vietnam, my truest and most tangible introduction to the possibilities of human action.

I was in the company of my peers. I needed their acceptance. They looked like me. They liked the same music. We got high together. We became misty-eyed with each other over letters from home. Many claimed that after the army they wanted to become hippies (for the drugs, music, and allegedly easy women). In the extremity of our circumstance, in my

---

2. Slotkin, *Gunfighter Nation*, 321.

platoon, the lines between black and white were erased and replaced by the line between GIs and "gooks." It was a brotherhood of youth, engaged voluntarily or not in a race war. I think that's what Hawk was thinking—the one black man with the kill patrol—not long after the kill, when he gave me that long, sad look. He would become a heroin addict after that. I don't know if he ever really came home. Sometimes, I'm not sure I did, or can . . . or should be allowed to.

The first time I tossed a burning heat tab onto the thatched roof of a barn, it was like pledging a fraternity. I was accepted more thoroughly than I ever had been in my life—accepted into a fraternity that was untouchable by anything but death. You don't just set the building on fire. You giggle when the weeping, wailing family tries to put it out. Then you have become crazy enough to be safe. Mimesis.

Months later, I was a relative old-timer. We'd left our "pacification" installations after Christmas and gone back "on swing," patrolling through the mountains, bedding down in shallow scrapes or between rocks wherever we found ourselves at the end of the day, unprotected from the weather. I was accustomed now to the steep, slippery trails that we hacked out a yard at a time with machetes. My M60 machine gun was no more bother than carrying a briefcase. I had a human skull mounted on top of my rucksack, tied on with an embroidered headband through two bullet holes in the occipital area (a gunship had killed him, or her, from above). The mandible was secured to the cranium with medical adhesive tape that had turned gray. My ear was pierced. I'd done it with a pencil, a sewing needle and a bar of soap at a whorehouse in Lodu Beach. My boots were scuffed down to a tan, the second pair. I looked crazy, walked crazy, was high any time I had anything to get high with. I didn't even use the tablets to treat my water anymore. Drank it straight from the streams. I could sleep in a mud hole. I could put one foot in front of the other indefinitely. I was angry all the time, even when I smiled and laughed, even when I lay in the frame of the rucksack, letting the wind blow the sweat off of me, smoking and talking about what I might want to do when I got back to "the world." I fantasized about killing officers.

On swing, we stayed in the "free fire" zones for the most part—areas where we were cleared to kill any human being that wasn't wearing our OG-107 fatigue uniforms. We'd stay out for forty-five to sixty days in between three- to five-day stand-downs, rest periods inside fixed installations. We walked up. We walked down. Days in, days out. Sun or rain. During the monsoon season, it was rain or harder rain. We would see no one but ourselves, unless it was to shoot them, or call in Napalm or Phugas or artillery to kill them from afar. Walking, left toe then right toe, chipping mindlessly forward into the crushed vegetation. "Humping the boonies."

Only rarely did we venture near a road or a ville, and this was when we'd stop some enterprising Vietnamese to secure more drugs. We bought pot by the sandbag full; pure heroin the size of a sugar cube for five bucks. And Obisetol, an over-the-counter speed to help us stay awake. They recognized us, the guys who had drugs for sale, and we recognized them. The rest, they were just more dinks.

One day, we were beside a road. A young Vietnamese man pedaled past me with a bicycle that had two saddle baskets full of sugarcane. He smiled at me as he approached.

"Keep movin', you fuckin' gook." That was me. I said that.

He stopped. I leapt to my feet at his impertinence.

He seemed utterly unafraid, just sad. He spoke English.

"This my home," he told me. "I am Vietnamese. You and me, why can't we be friend?"

He was very direct. My intimidation did not work at all, and I was paralyzed. I couldn't shoot him right there on the road . . . and honestly I didn't want to. His question was simple, and I had no answer. He snapped off a length of sugarcane and handed it to me. Reluctantly, I took it. I was trying to maintain my hateful look, but it was hard. I'd spent months cultivating it. Now I felt foolish because he was not afraid. Then he rode away. I'd never eaten sugarcane before, never known that explosion of liquid, melon-like sweetness. A guy from Puerto Rico showed me how to peel it using a bayonet.

For the rest of the day, I fought hard to stop the hole the man on the bike had driven into my dam with his simple act of courage and hospitality. That night the dam ruptured in the darkness. I cried quietly through a whole guard shift, wanting more than anything just to go home.

I was suddenly stunned at how effortless my transformation had become.

I know plenty about racism.

Looking back—I can't be sure—but one day, in the spring of 1971, I may have met Jesus on a bicycle.

32

Taboo

In 1993, I was part of the ill-fated adventure in Somalia called Task Force Ranger. We were charged with the mission of capturing the most powerful warlord in that shattered nation, Mohammed Farah Aidid. I was expelled over a conflict that had developed between myself and a captain who, I suspect, had been hit in the head one too many times playing college football. So I was not there for the tactical defeat at Bakara marketplace in South Mogadishu that was eventually made into the book and film, *Black Hawk Down*. I was thrown out just days before it, and I wonder to this day if it was Providence.

I was, however, involved in a firefight just before my expulsion; and that was also the first time I had been in armed combat alongside a female. Sue (not her real name) was with the Central Intelligence Agency. If the military part of the mission was ill-considered, the CIA part was ludicrous. White agents were circulating around Mogadishu trying to gather intelligence, as unobtrusive as maggots in a dish of caviar. Intelligence agents and military special operators, contrary to idealized and magnified versions of them portrayed in the entertainment media, are not all warrior-philosophers who can leap tall buildings in a single bound. They are regular human beings in most respects, frequently alcoholics, and not infrequently made dull-witted by their own arrogance. I speak from experience.

Sue was in and out of the tactical operations center, always with a couple of men. She was no more than thirty years old, so I inferred that she was a junior member of the team. She had that "I want to be considered one of the boys" air about her, and the dull edges of unacknowledged humiliation over the institutional reality that she would never be fully accepted. She was probably an overachiever in every technical and academic endeavor, and scrupulously silent about anything political. She was trying to make it in a man's world. I'd seen it elsewhere before, and it's the rack.

She reminded me of some of the women I had known in the military and at West Point, driven into the whole milieu by both a desire for self-actualization and even a notion of breaking new ground for other women. She was swimming now in a sea of armed testosterone—Rangers, Delta Force, the CIA, all thrown together in a busted-up African airport, charged up with the energy of planning a colonial military adventure. The "boys" would glance at her sidearm dismissively, which tells you something about the "boys."

For reasons I'll never know, but probably to identify potential captives, she was assigned to the same vehicle I was for a raid we conducted near the K-4 traffic circle not far from the airport. It was a night mission, and our vehicle was part of a strongpoint security position near a large stadium. To make a long story short, we were hit with machine gun fire at close range, and we responded to it with crazy force, killing as it turns out not only our small band of assailants but also a lot of civilians who were encamped in the stadium. I had seen the civilians in their makeshift tents two days before during a day patrol, mostly skinny women and children, including many sickly infants, packed together without plans or hopes.

As chance would have it, Sue was directly to my right, armed with an M-16 for this excursion. Sue was within arm's reach of me when the Somali machine gun engaged us. I was the first person on the strongpoint to return fire, and I killed one, maybe two, of our assailants. The muzzle flash from the machine gun was directly across the street from me, no more than fifty feet away. My primary magazine was loaded with tracer ammunition, bullets that contain phosphorous so they leave a light streak along their trajectory. These are used to mark targets so others who have not yet oriented on their target will know where to fire, and so the shooter can know where his or her rounds are going.

When the rest of the strongpoint—three Hummers with an impressive array of firepower—began firing in the direction of my tracers, Sue shouted a question through the din: "Where is it?" (It being "the enemy.") "Straight in front of you," I told her, whereupon she shouldered her weapon and opened up on full automatic. Part of her burst strayed dangerously close to a detachment we had pushed out across the street, so I told her to switch to semiautomatic. She did, and continued to fire until the ceasefire was called by the senior officer on the point, a lieutenant colonel.

That was my one and only experience of combat with a woman. On a technical basis, she did very well. She did not freeze or become shocky and uncommunicative, which is the real acid test for combat troops. And she fired her weapon. The most common manifestation of combat panic is the inability to fire at all. Green troops have the idea when they are under fire sometimes that "if I don't do anything to upset them, they will quit trying to kill me." Sue followed instructions, which indicated she could still solve problems and behave with conscious intent. Women can "perform" in combat. That's not what this story is about.

The real story began when we got back to the aircraft hangar. Everyone cleaned weapons and equipment; we put a couple of slightly wounded soldiers in the field hospital there, and we went to sleep. The next day, as the story began to circulate that CIA Sue had participated in the firefight, there commenced a strange whispered outrage. Men demanded that she be prohibited from ever going on another combat mission. It was strange because no one seemed to question the rationale for this. She was not military, so it wasn't a question of her working outside her occupational specialty, as if that mattered in a firefight. She had not been an endangering impediment, and in fact had performed remarkably well for her first encounter with armed combat—better than the young Ranger who had fired a stray .50 caliber round into the door of the Humvee that was about six feet off my right shoulder. But the murmured demand was not to allow it again. The young Rangers in particular were upset by it, perhaps because a woman now had as much combat experience as they did. But there was something deeper and more visceral about the reaction—something akin to a primitive weapons taboo. They could no longer pass her by in the compound with that air of dismissive masculine prerogative that said, *I* am the man here, the gunfighter. Guns are men's tools.

After the Somalia mission, after the debacle at Bakara where Task Force Ranger was defeated in a ten-hour firefight by the Somali National Alliance, the whole mission was scrapped, and the beaten and wounded Rangers were returned to Fort Benning.

One of the Rangers I knew from the mission later told me about a party the Rangers organized, where two prostituted women were "hired" for the evening, and the wounded men, some still encumbered by medical casts and braces, took turns having public sex with them as they were cheered on by their mates.

As previously noted, Stoller and Hartsock observe that sexual excitement for most men requires elements of perversion—that is, objectification, dehumanization, and fetishization. The eroticization of the loathing for the body transforms sex, for many men, into a revenge fantasy that projects that loathing onto the bodies of women.

Make of it what you will.

33

Consent

Gonaives, Haiti, September 1994

The guys bagged out hard. Their bellies were full. They had been baked all day by the grueling Gonaives heat. We had chased and been eluded, chased and captured, assisted with the food riots. So they slept powerfully. Except me. I have never been a deep or sound sleeper.

By four in the afternoon, I was bored and antsy. I knew what it was, but that didn't ameliorate the way it felt. I was going through adrenaline withdrawal again.

By five o'clock in the afternoon, Ali and Kyle had stirred. Two fellow junkies. "Wanna take a walk around town?" I asked. "Sure," they said. The guys had followed me to this point, and we had had more than our share of excitement. I was a good bet.

We slung on our webgear, grabbed our guns, and strolled on out into the street.

"There goes five-four," one of the guys out front said, "looking for trouble."

"Just takin' a stroll," I lied.

We walked left, past the site of the first day's confrontation, toward the ocean. Less than a mile from the ocean, toward the center of town, we encountered on foot what we had seen several times on vehicle patrol: the fallen iron Jesus. We stopped and examined it.

Iron Jesus was not an emaciated, tortured figure, all sagging abdomen and skinny limbs like the ones I had seen in Latin America. This Jesus was chalk white, with jet black hair and beard and *a body out of Gold's Gym. This was a thick, muscular Jesus with perfectly drilled holes in his hands and feet, who had fallen from the great white cross. The locals had propped him up by the bottom of the cross, a place generally reserved for the skull of Adam waiting to be reprieved from the dust and original sin. The giant bolts that had formerly suspended the savior had bent toward the ground, fracturing the reinforced concrete of the cross around the anchor points. This messiah was fifteen feet tall and made of solid iron. He must have weighed a ton. We wondered how the people had propped him up again, frail and slender as most of them were. Kyle said he would come by later and assess the feasibility of rehanging Christ on his cross.*

We walked further toward the sea. We encountered water in a small harbor, with three rusting ships and trash throbbing on the surface. We shifted along the waterfront, chatting with people through Ali as we went. We would talk a while, until a crowd began to smother us, then move along. Eventually we veered away from the water and into another warren of kai-pais (tiny houses made of batten and mud, the most common architecture in Haiti). The neighborhood, we would learn, was called Raboteau.

There are, in places like Raboteau, more pigs in the street than in other neighborhoods. The dogs are even mangier, skinnier, and more skittish. The hair of the dusty children with the roundworm bellies is redder (a sign of malnutrition). More teeth are missing from the mouths of the adults. The bones of limbs are more prominent. The eyes are wider with hunger, dying hope, and fear. The hair is more unkempt and nappy. The flies seem more in charge.

We traversed the neighborhood, and the fear was tangible. There had been a massacre here months before by the police. And we were carrying guns. Then we began greeting them: Bon swa. Good afternoon, with a wave and smile.

It was as if we were one moment in a scene from Night of the Living Dead, *and the next moment something breathed life into them. People broke into wide, teary-eyed smiles, waving frantically, laughing, adults and elderly as childlike in their relief as the children. The kids called out "Way! Way!"—look at me! As we proceeded, we created a procession, children at first, then everyone, until we had again formed a singing, chanting, laughing street demonstration.*

Ali told them to stay back, that we were performing security patrols. The older, stronger, and more responsible would then police the younger and more impulsive, holding them back, anxious to assist in their own security, the first they had even known.

> *At the outer edge of Raboteau, and as it was, the edge of town, there was an extensive plain, a mud flat really, that stretched for miles to a point where it blended with a distant cove in the ocean, between two smoke-blue mountains. South, along the flat, were farms, green and wet in the distance, a counterpoint to the dry, hot dustiness of Gonaives.*
>
> *The sun was setting, brilliant as usual—over Raboteau, the mud plain, the wandering pigs, the naked children, the hungry homes, the fallen Jesus. Haiti seemed in that moment of exhaustion and perplexity the most insoluble problem in the world. I did not say how I felt to my companions. I felt small, like one does when the distance between the stars pushes itself into your understanding, or when the inevitability of death leaps in front of you in the middle of the night.*
>
> *We returned through the darkened streets. My silence was washed away as we approached the garrison by the lingering street demonstrations in the front.*
>
> *In the end, we determined that we could not put iron Jesus back on his cross. He was just too damn heavy and we didn't have the right equipment.*[1]

I got into some trouble in Haiti in 1994 when I was Team Sergeant for a Special Forces A-Detachment—official trouble that got me fired. The accusation made against me in Vietnam, that I was being a "fuckin' missionary," came up again, this time articulated as "becoming too pro-Haitian." It was a troubling time for me and for my family, because for a while there was a chance I would go to prison. It was my last mission with the army; and fortunately, I didn't go to prison. I retired not long afterward. I've been trying to figure out why I was in the army ever since, and what the army did to me and to others. It's been two decades since that last mission—sometimes it seems no more than a moment—and this book is as close as I can get.

War is implicated in masculinity. Masculinity is implicated in war. Masculinity is implicated in the contempt for and domination of women. Together, these are implicated in the greatest sins of the church.

On August 11, 2012, in Steubenville, Ohio, a female high school student, a very young woman, got drunk at a party. Parties organized by young men are remarkably similar; and I have to imagine there was a whooping boisterousness at this party not unlike the party where the wounded Rangers

---

1. Goff, *Hideous Dream*, 173–75.

performed sex acts with prostituted women. Any of us who have been young men or who know young men know about what I'm describing. Midnight passed, and in the early morning hours of August 12, this sixteen-year-old student from nearby West Virginia was quite drunk.

Two popular high school football players (football again!), Trent Mays and Ma'lik Richmond, transported her to another party and then to the home of a friend whose parents were not home. She had vomited once. Then she passed out. She was stripped, violated with their fingers, had one man's penis placed in her mouth, and was photographed naked. Insertion of the fingers into her vagina constitutes rape under Ohio law. They also urinated and ejaculated on her. This went on for several hours. The young men then returned to the party, where they shared the photographs of their serial violations of her with their friends. They and their friends distributed the images via social media, proudly referring to the perpetrators as "the rape crew."

The social media provided the evidence. Rape charges were filed. The two young men were taken to trial. The perpetrators and the town's high school football coach were popular in Steubenville, an economically distressed former steel town, and there was a shocking amount of public support *for the rapists*. The victim became—in some sense here thankfully—invisible, until all three major cable news networks callously and opportunistically published the victim's name. Their subsequent retraction of her name did little to undo the damage, which was compounded in the coming days by highly sympathetic reporting of *the convicted perpetrators*, who were portrayed as boys who had tragically and suddenly lost promising futures.

The mainstream news media's empathy for the plight of the convicted young men was shameful in exactly the measure that this empathy was left unqualified by sensitivity for the young woman who was repeatedly violated—and is still being violated. That is one narrative, one with which I am overwhelmingly sympathetic.

There is another that is tougher and that Christians might attend to. These boys should be forgiven if they sincerely repent. That takes nothing away from the outrage that is due on behalf of the young woman who was raped. If Amish families can forgive a mass murderer who killed their children, the bar for other Christians who are called to forgive is pretty high.

This gets even more complicated.

One article by an African American woman noted that incarceration, such as it actually is in the U.S., will probably make greater predators out of inmates than when they go in. So punitive justice is done, and desert is factored into this aspect of justice, but we haven't seen past the desire for vengeance and into an actually existing system where machismo is valorized in sports, in fraternities, in the military, in business, and on hyperdrive *in prison*. I don't have an easy answer for this one, except to change how we do prison. The reality is, men who go to prison are not *less* likely to rape when they come out.

Many people in our culture celebrate the idea of prison rape as part of a just punishment—and for rape itself, this is an even greater temptation. In doing so, we reiterate the association of sex with hostility, aggression, and conquest—precisely the association in the mind of any rapist whom we are ostensibly punishing. In men's prison, there are "male" and "female" roles. We all know from chapter 12, "Torture and Redemption," what it means to be "a prison bitch," a notion that boldfaces the association between domination, aggression, and sex.

So much to think about . . . more for those of us who raised boys, who have grandsons, and who still associate with men. But let's return to women, because women are overwhelmingly the victims of rape; and men are overwhelmingly the perpetrators. The issue on my mind is one that is being discussed by the very people who are thinking beyond justice for the victim—and I am glad she got some semblance of justice. The verdict of guilty was right. They were guilty. I am thinking, as many people are, about what people can do to ensure that boys will become men who are less likely to rape in a culture that associates sex with hostility, control, aggression, and vengeance—a rape culture.

An article I read described a meeting of women who were raising boys. The women were asked what qualities they would like to see in their sons when their sons matured. The answers ranged from humor, to athleticism, to strength, to courage. When one woman said "kindness," the others were taken aback. Well, of course, yes, kindness, too . . . an afterthought, almost an obligation. And so masculinity and femininity as a hierarchy of power were reinscribed unthinkingly. The author then added, in her own editorial voice, that she wanted boys to become men who would understand what "consent" means.

A warning light started blinking in my mind. Feminists who have focused their analyses on sexually structured social power had wired that warning light in my head. It is attached to the term *consent*. Consent is easy to define out of context, but very slippery in real space and time. If a man and woman go on a date, and they are drinking, can her "consent" to sex after two drinks be considered meaningful "consent"? After four drinks?

Eight? If she would not have consented when she was sober, but she does consent when she gets tipsy, is consent qualifiable along some continuum, or is it a cut-and-dried affair with some observable line of demarcation? If a woman works with a man who offers her money for sex, and she has sex for money, is that meaningful consent? How about if she is a sole parent who is in trouble financially? How about if she needs the money because one of her children is ill and she can't afford a doctor? How about if she doesn't work *with* the man, but *for* the man, and she fears for her job? Is there a point in any of these scenarios where we call it "rape"? Not according to law, because the law says she "consents" if she is awake and does not say no. How about a married woman who has no desire for sex, or who finds sex with her husband, for any one of many reasons, unwanted or unpleasant; and her husband threatens her with separation or divorce? Is she consenting or being coerced? Is the situation more starkly apparent if the woman will be reduced to poverty by a divorce? If her children will suffer? How about a woman who lives in a society where her chances of flourishing are curtailed simply because she is a woman, and having a man as a "breadwinner" is understood as a kind of long-term necessity? Or how about a woman who lives in a society where she fears all men, based on her past experience with some or many men, and she feels it necessary to cleave to one man as protection against all other men? Are these the "choices" of any women you know?

Choice, in the real world, is never reducible to an instant. If one is honest, one can begin to see how this business of consent is not intelligible by law, which in liberal society is forced to reduce consent to a decontextualized episode—something with a beginning, a middle, and an end broken off from history, divorced from anticipated consequences. That's why rape is defined by law as a particular kind of force and a particular kind of sex (yes, rape *is* sex!), and determined in a voyeuristic, after-the-fact, and detailed re-living of the episode that forces the victim of a rape to revisit the pain, fear, and humiliation several times over.

This consent question exposes a danger with my entire thesis about war as formative of masculinity—the danger of accepting this account as totalizing, as *the* analytical framework for understanding male power. I need to own up to this right now, before we go a step further. Here is the greatest weakness of my account, even if the association here *between war and sex* is still part of the corrective. Several well-known men who are emblematic of peacemaking and opposition to war have displayed in word and deed their own inattention to and apparent denial of the power that men hold over women in the arena of sexual relations.

It seems that Gandhi, even and especially after taking his vows of chastity, slept naked with and bathed with a number of young women, as a kind of "testing" of his will, one that would occasionally result in "involuntary discharges."[2] Some were even the wives of his male disciples, whom he had directed not to have sex with their own wives as part of their pursuit of higher knowledge.

Dr. Martin Luther King, the great Christian leader of the nonviolent struggle against legal apartheid in the American South, did not preach the "formal" chastity of Gandhi as spiritual quest; he stepped out on his wife—that is, he committed adultery with women he encountered while he was on the road. He even told *Ebony* magazine that a man's infidelity was indicative of some fault in his wife; he gave "nagging" as one example.

John Howard Yoder, whose Christology is central for many Christian pacifists, myself included, sexually assaulted and abused dozens of women during his tenures as a professor of theology at two Mennonite seminaries—assaults he tried to justify as nonsexual because the incidents did not involve penile-vaginal intercourse. In some ways, his bullying of several victims involved a rationale similar to Gandhi's—that he was taking relations between men and women to some higher plane. His victims—whom we ought to *see*, whose *standpoints* should be valued as much as Yoder's—felt otherwise. They felt exploited, attacked, abused, and humiliated.

There is a tendency among people who admire these figures for some of the things they did—and they were extremely important things—to write this off as instances of *human* fallibility. Writing it off as *human* obscures the fact that all are men. That these are cases of *men* and sex is signficant, a signficance that disappears with the term *human* fallibility. Calling this human fallibility erases a power relation called gender.

We know that all forms of domination are not directly violent. We know about domination that can be exercised structurally, without direct violence. We submit to employers and do unpleasant jobs out of fear of want. Women's generalized dependency on men is in some ways the same. These forms of domination are built into the existing self-organization of particular societies in particular ways and are woven into the whole fabric of our social relations.

This pattern of men who oppose the kind of domination that is associated with war, and often as not the kind of structural domination that is associated with work (economic exploitation in workplaces), is perplexing *because* these same men seem so reluctant to recognize the ways in which women in male-dominated society are left with fewer reasonable choices in the face of structural male power. We fail to recognize that women are born into a system of *scarcity* by male supremacy that leads them to see

---

2. See Adams, "The Thrill of the Chaste."

other women as antagonists—as competition for men as sexual partners or husbands, yes, but also for the approval of men who are in control of workplaces, governments, and even social movements.

Men are seldom in the right position to judge when and how real women make their accommodations, but we shouldn't be free to discount the power that creates this circumstance. This failure of recognition underwrites men's ability to rationalize the ways in which we can take advantage of our own structural power as men vis-à-vis women. Male power has been so continuous and all-inclusive that it is self-naturalizing. It *appears* ontological, even when it is clearly cultural. For me, as a male, that is a very comfortable and comforting ontology.

One of the things Catherine MacKinnon wrote in her critique of the same problem with male radicals who participated in the social upheavals of the 1960s and 1970s actually sums the issue up very well: "Sexuality is to feminism what work is to marxism: that which is most one's own, yet most taken away." Note that she did not say that people ought not to work or have sex. She said that domination, direct or structural, in either relation alienates the person from *his* work or *her* "sexuality."[3] Carole Pateman showed how women are pushed into a sexual contract that exchanges protection for obedience. Implicit in this "contract," as we saw, is "sex-right," which is associated with the idea that men are *entitled* to have sex. The refusal of some Christian men—especially Christian men committed to nonviolence—to recognize that *there is no such thing as an entitlement to sex* is a spectacular form of hypocrisy. We cannot claim to oppose domination at the same time we attempt to exploit, control, deceive, and victimize our sisters.

I say this not as a righteous man, but as a lifelong sinner.

---

3. The critique of the term *sexuality* stands, even as we acknowledge that MacKinnon has a point. While I disagree in some respects with MacKinnon, in large part because of her consistent appropriation of a Marxist idiom with its emphasis on enemies, production, and "reproduction," her point that we live our lives as sexed bodies within some form of a gender-regime is well taken.

34

Clarifications

> The violent American male is not simply a figure in American life ... but rather the figure around which American culture is oriented.
>
> —Marvin Severson[1]

> Love never fails. But where there are prophecies, they will cease; where there are tongues, they will be stilled; where there is knowledge, it will pass away.
>
> —1 Corinthians 13:8

FALL AND REDEMPTION

From the standpoint of a Christian, I submit that the legal debates about consent may concern us, but those debates can only scratch the surface of our responsibility to discern the meanings of sexual consent. We are called to compassion, and I use that word, again, citing Walter Breuggemann:

> Jesus in his solidarity with the marginal ones is *moved to compassion*. Compassion constitutes a radical form of criticism, for it announces that the hurt is to be taken seriously, that the hurt

---

1. Severson, "Superior to All Men," 5.

is not to be accepted as normal and natural but is an abnormal and unacceptable condition for humanness. In the arrangement of "lawfulness" in Jesus' time, as in the ancient empire of Pharaoh, the one unpermitted quality of relation was compassion. Empires are never built or maintained on the basis of compassion. The norms of law (social control) are never accommodated to persons, but persons are accommodated to norms. Otherwise the norms will collapse and with them the whole power arrangement. Thus the compassion of Jesus is to be understood not simply as a personal emotional reaction but as a public criticism in which he dares to act upon his concern against the entire numbness of his social context.[2]

Do you *see* this woman?

The structural power of men over women that complicates the notion of consent must be subjected to a radical critique *by Christians*. Men, in a very real sense, constitute an empire that has women as its colonies. And men are implicated simply by virtue of being men. That is a shocking statement that runs against liberal sensibilities, but in a male-dominant society we men cannot escape from the social power that we inherit with our biological sex, any more than white people can escape from the social power they inherit in a white supremacist society. No one is saying it is our fault. What is being said is that we cannot escape our responsibility to *consciously* abdicate that power when and where we can, to name that power in the public square, and to model a different way of being together in our own communities. I fail to see how, as Christians called to compassion, we can escape an attitude of constant *contrition* in sexual matters. Not contrition as a hair shirt, but as sorrow at the brokenness of the world of which we are a part, as repentance (turning around), and as vigilance (stay awake!). Without contrition—*accepted as a gift*—and without vigilance, we cannot fully acknowledge the hurt, take the hurt seriously, and demonstrate that the hurt can no longer be accepted as the norm. We—*men*—must stay awake and not fall prey to somnambulance, to the anesthesia of power.

The hurt does not begin at the moment of "consent," but with the history that is excluded by the law, with the long-standing structural power of men-as-men over women-as-women. That doesn't mean we strip women of agency. Women are certainly agents, including sexual agents. But men's agency ought to be directed at not being stumbling blocks to our sisters. Men who take this question seriously, as Christians, can work to abdicate power as an ongoing practice, especially in sexual matters. We can take

---

2. Brueggemann, *Prophetic Imagination*, 88.

nothing for granted. We can avoid the twilight and not just the darkness. We can ask, and ask again, again, then listen, listen, and listen again. We can never, ever take *consent* for granted. This is a much bigger order than understanding the *legal* definition of consent. We have to see women, and see women in the fullness of history, "because you are not under the law, but under grace" (Rom 6:14).

We are not called to be legal. We're called to be holy.

We've spent a good deal of time looking at masculinity, at how masculinity tends toward war and vice versa, and how both tend to give women the choice between being invisible or becoming an enemy. We've paid much attention to the faces of masculinity, of war, and the hatred of women. This book has aimed to unmask the bodyguard of lies around all three. These are aspects not of creation but of the fall. Be not afraid. There is good news. This is not the end of the story.

In our accentuation of these attitudes, we have given relatively little space to Christian revelation. I hope it's come up often enough to remind us of why this sometimes painful sojourn is necessary. Yes, the point has been to show how our attachment to one or another construction of masculinity has secured our attachment to war and our animosity toward women; but the more crucial point, and I do mean *crucial*, is how our attachment to one or another construction of masculinity is a stumbling block between us and our neighbors—including women—and therefore between us and Christ. We cannot serve both Mammon and God, and this has been a scandal in the church. Neither can we serve both War and God, or Masculinity and God. An idol is an idol is an idol. We are not called to be *powerful*. We are not called to be *respectable*. We are not called to be *patriotic*. We are not called to be *masculine*. We are called to be holy.

Perhaps all I've done here is ceaselessly reiterate the meanings of boundaries, and of "transgression" as a policed portal across those boundaries. We have seen boundaries as integral to the strategic mindset. We have seen boundary transgression as a function of privilege. While Mary Douglas makes a case that boundaries are necessary to know who we are, and even to protect ourselves—as I write this, the walls of my house are protecting me from freezing temperatures and harsh winds—we have also seen what happens when we close and bar the gates. They become impediments to hospitality or love. They become the battlements of war.

How different would our *transgressions* be if church men were intentionally *not* successful, *not* autonomous, *not* "ready for sex," *not* ready to

Bibliography

Adams, Jad. "The Thrill of the Chaste: The Truth about Gandhi's Sex Life." The Independent, April 7, 2010. http://www.independent.co.uk/arts-entertainment/books/features/thrill-of-the-chaste-the-truth-about-gandhis-sex-life-1937411.html.
Adler, Alfred. *Understanding Human Nature—The Psychology of Personality*. Center City, MN: Hazelden Foundation, 1927.
Amnesty International. "Private Military and Security Companies—The Cost of Outsourcing War" (2013). http://www.amnestyusa.org/our-work/issues/business-and-human-rights/private-military-and-security-companies.
Andrade, Gabriel. "René Girard." *Internet Encyclopedia of Philosophy*. http://www.iep.utm.edu/girard/.
Aquilina, Mike. "One Flesh of Purest Gold: John Chrysostom's Discovery of the Blessings & Mysteries of Marriage." *Touchstone* 21.1 (2008). http://www.touchstonemag.com/archives/article.php?id=21-01-022-f.
Armengol, Josep M. "Gendering Men: Re-Visions of Violence as a Test of Manhood in American Literature." *Atlantis* 29 (2007) 75–92.
Armistead, Leigh, ed. *Information Operations: Warfare and the Hard Reality of Soft Power*. Washington, DC: Brassey's, 2004.
Arraf, Jane, et al. "Seven U.S. Troops Die in Baghdad Fighting." *CNN.com*, April 4, 2004. http://www.cnn.com/2004/WORLD/meast/04/04/iraq.main/index.html?iref=mpstoryview.
Ashenburg, Katherine. "The Filthy, Stinking Truth." Interview by Katharine Mieszkowski. *Salon*, November 30, 2007. http://www.salon.com/2007/11/30/dirt_on_clean/.
Associated Press. "Iraq Puts Captive Troops on TV." March 24, 2003. http://usatoday30.usatoday.com/news/world/iraq/2003-03-23-pows-iraq-usat_x.htm.
Bailey, Beth, and David Farber. "Hotel Street: Prostitution and the Politics of War." *Radical History Review* 52 (1992) 54–77.
Bamford, James. "The Man Who Sold the War." *Rolling Stone*, November 18, 2005. http://www.rollingstone.com/music/pictures/rolling-stones-biggest-scoops-exposes-and-controversies-2-aa-624/the-man-who-sold-the-war-by-james-bamford-3323040.
Barron, Robert. *The Priority of Christ: Toward a Postliberal Catholicism*. Grand Rapids: Brazos, 2007.
Basler, Roy. *Abraham Lincoln: His Speeches and Writings*. Cleveland: Da Capo, 2001.

Bataille, Georges. *Death and Sensuality*. New York: Arno, 1977.

BBC. "In an Ethical War, Whom Can You Fight?" *Ethics Guide*. http://www.bbc.co.uk/ethics/war/just/whom_1.shtml.

Beck, Richard. *Unclean: Meditations on Purity, Hospitality, and Morality*. Eugene, OR: Cascade, 2011.

Bellah, Robert. *The Broken Covenant: American Civil Religion in Time of Trial*. Chicago: University of Chicago Press, 1975.

Benjamin, Jessica. *The Bonds of Love: Psychoanalysis, Feminism, and the Problem of Domination*. Toronto: Random House, 1998.

Berkman, John, and Michael Cartwright, eds. *The Hauerwas Reader*. Durham: Duke University Press, 2001.

Bernays, Edward. *Propaganda*. New York: H. Liveright, 1928. http://www.whale.to/b/bernays.pdf.

Beveridge, Albert. "March of the Flag." Speech given September 16, 1898. http://voicesofdemocracy.umd.edu/beveridge-march-of-the-flag-speech-text/.

———. "Our Peerless Flag Is There! The Last Stage of the Great Contest." *Los Angeles Times*, November 4, 1900.

Black, Edwin. "Hitler's Debt to America." *The Guardian*, February 5, 2004. http://www.theguardian.com/uk/2004/feb/06/race.usa.

Black, Rufus. *Christian Moral Realism: Natural Law, Narrative, Virtue, and the Gospel*. New York: Oxford University Press, 2000.

Blackstone, William. *Commentaries on the Laws of England*. 2 vols. Chicago: Callaghan, 1899.

Bordo, Susan. *The Flight to Objectivity: Essays on Cartesianism and Culture*. Albany: State University of New York Press, 1987.

Bosco, David. "Moral Principle vs. Military Necessity." *The American Scholar* (Winter 2008). http://theamericanscholar.org/moral-principle-vs-military-necessity/.

Bourne, E. G., ed. *The Voyages of Columbus and of John Cabot*. In *The Northmen, Columbus and Cabot, 985–1503*. New York: Scribner's, 1906.

Brandt, Allen M. "Recruiting Women Smokers: The Engineering of Consent." *Journal of the American Medical Women's Association* 51 (1996) 63–66.

Bresser-Pereira, Luiz Carlos. "State, Civil Society and Democratic Legitimacy." *Lua Nova—Revista de Cultura y Politica* 36 (1995) 85–104.

Brewer, Susan. "Selling Empire: American Propaganda and War in the Philippines." *The 4th Media*, October 22, 2013. http://www.4thmedia.org/2013/10/22/selling-empire-american-propaganda-and-war-in-the-philippines/.

Brinkmeyer, Robert H., Jr. "Faulkner and the Democratic Crisis." In *Faulkner and Ideology*, edited by Donald M. Kartiganer and Ann J. Abadie, 70–94. Jackson: University of Mississippi Press, 1995.

Broadbent, Lucy. "Rape in the US Military: America's Dirty Little Secret." *The Guardian*, December 9, 2011. http://www.theguardian.com/society/2011/dec/09/rape-us-military.

Broedel, Hans Peter. *The Malleus Maleficarum and the Construction of Witchcraft*. Manchester: Manchester University Press, 2003.

Brokaw, Tom. *The Greatest Generation*. New York: Random House, 2001.

Browning, Don. "Rethinking Homosexuality." *Christian Century*, October 11, 1989, 911–16.

Broyles, William, Jr. "Why Men Love War." *Esquire*, November 1984, 55–65.

Brueggemann, Walter. 2nd ed. Minneapolis: Fortress, 2001.
Brunner, José. *Freud and the Politics of Psychoanalysis*. New Brunswick, NJ: Transaction, 2001.
Brym, Robert J. *New Society*. Toronto: Nelson Education, 2008.
Bufe, Charles Q. *The Heretic's Handbook of Quotations*. Tucson: See Sharp, 2001.
Bulliet, Richard, et al. *The Earth and Its Peoples: A Global History*. Vol. 1, *To 1550*. Stamford, CT: Cenage Learning, 2010.
Buscombe, Edward. *The BFI Companion to the Western*. New York: Macmillan, 1988.
Bushnell, Horace. "The Doctrine of Loyalty." *New Englander and Yale Review* 22 (1863) 560–81.
Butler, Chris. "The Rise of the Dutch Republic in the 1600s." *The Flow of History* (2007). http://www.flowofhistory.com/units/west/14/FC93.
Cahn, David. "The 1907 Bellingham Riots in Historical Context." *Seattle Civil Rights and Labor History Project* (2008). http://depts.washington.edu/civilr/bham_history.htm.
Canaday, Margot. "U.S. Military Integration of Religious, Ethnic, and Racial Minorities in the Twentieth Century." Palm Center White Paper, May 1, 2001. http://www.palmcenter.org/publications/dadt/u_s_military_integration_of_religious_ethnic_and_racial_minorities_in_the_twentieth_century.
Carnahan, Burrus M. *Lincoln on Trial: Southern Civilians and the Law of War*. Lexington: University of Kentucky Press, 2010.
Carr, Karen Leslie. *The Banalization of Nihilism: Twentieth-Century Responses to Meaninglessness*. Albany: State University of New York Press, 1992.
Carroll, Dillon Jackson. "Confederate Soldiers in the Civil War: Masculinity, War Experience, and Religion." PhD diss., California State University-Chico, 2009.
Carter, J. Kameron. "Race, Theology, and the Politics of Abjection: An Interview with J. Kameron Carter." Interview by David Kline. *The Other Journal*, March 26, 2012. http://theotherjournal.com/2012/03/26/race-theology-and-the-politics-of-abjection-an-interview-with-j-kameron-carter-part-i/.
Cavanaugh, William. "At Odds with the Pope: Legitimate Authority and Just Wars." *Commonweal*, May 23, 2003, 11–13.
———. "Faith Fires Back—a Conversation with Stanley Hauerwas." *Duke Magazine* 88 (2002) 10–13.
———. "A Fire Strong Enough to Consume the House: The Wars of Religion and the State." *Modern Theology* 11 (1995) 397–420.
———. *Migrations of the Holy: God, State and the Political Meaning of the Church*. Grand Rapids: Eerdmans, 2011.
Certeau, Michel de. *The Practice of Everyday Life*. Translated by Steven Randall. Berkeley: University of California Press, 1984.
Chamberlain, N. H. *The Assassination of President Lincoln*. New York: G. W. Carleton, 1865.
Chisholm, Hugh. "Gregory VII." In *Encyclopedia Britannica* 11:526. New York: University Press, 1911.
Clarke, Eric O. "Fetal Attraction: Hegel's An-aestheics of Gender." In *Feminist Interpretations of G. W. F. Hegel*, edited by Patricia Jagentowicz Mills, 149–75. University Park: Pennsylvania State University Press, 1996.
Clausewitz, Carl von. *On War*. Translated by J. J. Graham. London: N. Trübner, 1873. http://www.clausewitz.com/readings/OnWar1873/BK1ch01.html.

Clement of Alexandria. *Paedagogus*. Translated by Alexander Roberts and James Donaldson. http://www.ellopos.net/elpenor/greek-texts/fathers/clement-alexandria/instructor.asp.

Clines, David J. A. *Interested Parties: The Ideology of Writers and Readers of the Hebrew Bible*. Sheffield: Sheffield Academic, 1995.

Coakley, Sarah. *Powers and Submissions: Spirituality, Philosophy and Gender*. Malden, MA: Blackwell, 2006.

Coen, Noam. "Surviving without Newspapers." *New York Times*, June 6, 2009. http://www.nytimes.com/2009/06/07/weekinreview/07cohen.html?_r=1&.

Cohn, Carol. "Sex and Death in the Rational World of Defense Intellectuals." *Signs* 12 (1987) 687–718.

Collins, Patricia Hill. *Another Kind of Public Education: Race, Schools, the Media, and Democratic Possibilities*. Boston: Beacon, 2009.

Collins, Tony. *Sport in Capitalist Society: A Short History*. New York: Routledge, 2013.

Connaughton, R. M. *The War of the Rising Sun and the Tumbling Bear: A Military History of the Russo-Japanese War, 1904–5*. New York: Routledge, 1992.

Connell, R. W. *Masculinities*. Berkeley: University of California Press, 1995.

Cooper, Richard. "General Casts War in Religious Terms." *Los Angeles Times*, October 16, 2003. http://articles.latimes.com/2003/oct/16/nation/na-general16.

Corbin, David Alan. *Life, Work, and Rebellion in the Coal Fields: The Southern West Virginia Miners, 1880–1922*. Urbana: University of Illinois Press, 1981.

Covolo, Enrique del. "The Historical Origin of Indulgences." *Catholic Culture*, May 19, 1999. http://www.catholicculture.org/culture/library/view.cfm?id=1054&CFID=13690226&CFTOKEN=11202176.

Cowardin, James A., and John D. Hammersley. "War and Peace." *Richmond Times Dispatch*, June 26, 1862. http://www.perseus.tufts.edu/hopper/text?doc=Perseus%3Atext%3A2006.05.0511%3Aarticle%3Dpos%3D31.

Crenshaw, Kimberle. "Demarginalizing the Intersection of Race and Sex." *University of Chicago Legal Forum* (1989) 139–67. http://web.calstatela.edu/faculty/tbettch/Crenshaw%20Demarginalizing%20Intersection%20Race%20Sex.pdf.

Cuordileone, Kyle A. *Manhood and American Political Culture in the Cold War*. New York: Routledge, 2005.

Curran, Charles E. *Catholic Social Teaching, 1891–Present: Historical, Theological, and Ethical Analysis*. Washington, DC: Georgetown University Press, 2007.

Dales, Douglas, et al. *Glory Descending: Michael Ramsey and His Writings*. Grand Rapids: Eerdmans, 2005.

Davis, Mike. "The Perfect Fire." *Tom Dispatch*, October 27, 2003. http://www.tomdispatch.com/post/1032/.

Dawkins, Richard. "Afterword." In *What Is Your Dangerous Idea?*, edited by John Brockman, 297–305. New York: Harper Perennial, 2007.

Dean, Mitchell. *Governmentality: Power and Rule in Modern Society*. London: Sage, 2010.

Dean, Robert D. *Imperial Brotherhood: Gender and the Making of Cold War Foreign Policy*. Amherst: University of Massachusetts Press, 2001.

Descartes, Rene. *Discourse on Method and Meditations of First Philosophy*. Digireads, Stilwell, 2005.

De Vries, Margaret Gerritsen. "The Bretton Woods Conference and the Birth of the International Monetary Fund." *Studien von Zeitfragen* 35 (2001). http://www.jahrbuch2001.studien-von-zeitfragen.net/Weltfinanz/GERRIT_1/gerrit_1.HTM.

Dick, Bernard F. *The Star-Spangled Screen: The American World War II in Film*. Lexington: University of Kentucky Press, 1985.

Dilorenzo, Thomas J. "Indian Genocide and Republican Power." *Consortium News*, October 7, 2010. http://www.consortiumnews.com/2010/100610b.html.

Dinerstein, Joel. "'Uncle Tom Is Dead!': Wright, Himes, and Ellison Lay a Mask to Rest." *African American Review* 43 (2009) 83–99.

Donaldson, Stephen. "Who's Your Daddy?" *This American Life*, January 8, 1999. http://www.thisamericanlife.org/radio-archives/episode/119/lockup?act=3.

Donohoe, Nathan. "Understanding the Decision to Drop the Bomb on Hiroshima and Nagasaki." *CSIS.org*, August 10, 2012. https://csis.org/blog/understanding-decision-drop-bomb-hiroshima-and-nagasaki.

Dostoyevsky, Fyodor. *The Brothers Karamozov* (1880). Translated by Constance Garnett. http://www.online-literature.com/dostoevsky/brothers_karamazov/.

Douglas, Mary. *Purity and Danger: An Analysis of the Concepts of Pollution and Taboo*. New York: Routledge, 1996.

Douglass, Frederick. *Narrative of the Life of Frederick Douglass, Written by Himself*. 1845. Reprint, Mexico City: JPM, 2010.

Du Bois, W. E. B. *The Souls of Black Folk: Essays and Sketches*. Chicago: A. C. McClurg, 1903. http://www.bartleby.com/114/.

Duden, Barbara. *Disembodying Women: Perspectives on Pregnancy and the Unborn*. Cambridge: Harvard University Press, 1993.

———. *The Woman Beneath the Skin*. Cambridge: Harvard University Press, 1991.

Dudink, Stefan. "Masculinity, Effeminacy, Time: Conceptual Change in the Dutch Age of Democratic Revolutions." In *Masculinities in Politics and War: Gendering Modern History*, edited by Stefan Dudink et al., 77–95. Manchester: Manchester University Press, 2004.

Duncan, Stewart. "Thomas Hobbes." *Stanford Encyclopedia of Philosophy* (Summer 2013). http://plato.stanford.edu/archives/sum2013/entries/hobbes/.

Dworkin, Andrea. *Pornography: Men Possessing Women*. London: Women's Press, 1981.

Dyer, Christopher. *Making a Living in the Middle Ages: The People of Britain, 850–1520*. New Haven: Yale University Press, 2009.

Eacott, Jonathan P. "Making an Imperial Compromise: The Calico Acts, the Atlantic Colonies, and the Structure of the British Empire." *William and Mary Quarterly* 69 (2012) 731–63.

Eisenstein, Sergei. "A Dialectic Approach to Film Form." In *Film Form: Essays in Film Theory*, edited and translated by Jay Leyda, 53–55. New York: Harcourt, Brace, 1949.

Eisenstein, Zillah. "Disciplining Female Bodies for Khaki." Keynote address for the North American Society for the Sociology of Sport (NASSS), Montreal, Canada, October 2003. http://www.ithaca.edu/zillah/womenandsport.pdf.

Ellis, Havelock. *Sexual Inversion*. London: Wilson and McMillan, 1897.

Emberton, Carole. "The Real Origin of America's Gun Culture." *History News Network*, January 14, 2013. http://hnn.us/article/150088.

"Ex-NFL Star Tillman Makes 'Ultimate Sacrifice.'" *NBCNews.com*, April 26, 2004. http://www.nbcnews.com/id/4815441/ns/world_news/t/ex-nfl-star-tillman-makes-ultimate-sacrifice/#.VFpv7YvF9OE.

Fanon, Frantz. *Black Skin, White Masks*. Translated by Richard Philcox. New York: Grove, 2008.

Faucette, Michael Brian. "Warner Brothers Forgotten Men: Representations of Shifting Masculinities in 1930s Hollywood." PhD diss., University of Kansas, 2010.

Fehn, Bruce. "Theodore Roosevelt and American Masculinity." *OAH Magazine of History* 19 (2005) 52–60.

Feser, Edward. "Nozick, Robert." *Internet Encyclopedia of Philosophy* (2005). http://www.iep.utm.edu/nozick/.

Finke, David. "Fact Checking Pinker on the World's Bloodiest Atrocity." *Patheos*, November 10, 2011. http://www.patheos.com/blogs/camelswithhammers/2011/11/fact-checking-pinker-on-worlds-bloodiest-atrocity/.

Finney, Torin. *Unsung Hero of the Great War: The Life and Witness of Ben Salmon*. Mahwah, NJ: Paulist, 1989.

Flynn, George Q. "Selective Service and American Blacks during World War II." *The Journal of Negro History* 69 (1984) 14–25.

Ford, Glen, and Nellie Baile. "Tea Party White Nationalism." *Black Agenda Report*, January 11, 2011. http://blackagendareport.com/category/us-politics/tea-party-white-nationalism.

Fortescue, Adrian. "The Eastern Schism." In vol. 13 of *The Catholic Encyclopedia*. New York: Appleton, 1912. http://www.newadvent.org/cathen/13535a.htm.

Foster, Brad D. "Constructing Heroic Identities: Masculinity and the Western Film." PhD diss., Oregon State University, 2007.

France, Anatole. *The Red Lily*. 1894. Reprint, Gloucester: Dodo, 2007.

Franklin, Benjamin. *The Autobiography of Benjamin Franklin*. Edited by Charles W. Eliot. Electronic Classic Series, Pennsylvania State University-Hazelton. http://www2.hn.psu.edu/faculty/jmanis/franklin/a_b_benf.pdf.

Frederick, Christine. *Household Engineering: Scientific Management in the Home*. Chicago: American School of Home Economics, 1921.

Freeman, Samuel. "Original Position." *The Stanford Encyclopedia of Philosophy* (Spring 2012). http://plato.stanford.edu/cgi-bin/encyclopedia/archinfo.cgi?entry=original-position.

Freud, Sigmund. *Civilization and Its Discontents*. Translated by Joan Riviere. London: Hogarth, 1963.

Friefeld, Jacob. "Oh the Confusion of It All: Misadventures in Masculine Communication during the Secession Crisis." *The History Roll*, January 7, 2011. http://historyroll.com/?p=260.

Gamble, Richard M. *The War for Righteousness: Progressive Christianity, the Great War, and the Rise of the Messianic Nation*. Wilmington, DE: ISI, 2003.

Gatto, John Taylor. *Weapons of Mass Instruction—a Schoolteacher's Journey through the Dark World of Compulsory Instruction*. Gabriola Island, BC: New Society, 2009.

Geauvreau, Dave. "A Brief Word Study on 'Witch/Witchcraft/Witchcrafts.'" *Logos Resource Pages*. http://logosresourcepages.org/Occult/witch_define.htm.

Gibbons, Jenny. "Recent Developments in the Study of the Great European Witch Hunt." *Pomegranate: The International Journal of Pagan Studies* 5 (1998). http://www.kersplebedeb.com/mystuff/feminist/gibbons_witch.html.

Gibbs, Nancy. "At Home: The Private Jessica Lynch." *Time*, November 17, 2003. http://content.time.com/time/magazine/article/0,9171,1006147,00.html.

Glaber, Rodulfi. *Historarum Libri Quinque*. Oxford: Oxford University Press, 1989.

Goff, Stan. "The Fog of Fame—Three-Part Series on the Death of Pat Tillman." *Counterpunch*, August 9, 2007. http://www.counterpunch.org/2007/08/09/the-fog-of-fame/.

———. *Hideous Dream: A Soldier's Memoir of the US Invasion of Haiti*. New York: Soft Skull, 2000.

———. "Jessica Lynch, Plural." *Counterpunch*, December 13–15, 2003. http://www.counterpunch.org/2003/12/13/jessica-lynch-plural/.

Goldman, Emma. "Address to the Jury." In *Anarchism on Trial: Speeches of Alexander Berkman and Emma Goldman before the United States District Court in the City of New York, July, 1917*, 56–66. New York: Mother Earth, 1917.

Grant, Gary, et al. "Black Farmers United: The Struggle against Powers and Principalities." *Journal of Pan-African Studies* 5 (2012) 3–22.

Greenberg, Amy S. *Manifest Manhood and the Antebellum American Empire*. Cambridge: Cambridge University Press, 2005.

Gregory, Brad S. *Salvation at Stake: Christian Martyrdom in Early Modern Europe*. Cambridge: Harvard University Press, 2001.

———. *The Unintended Reformation: How a Religious Revolution Secularized Society*. Cambridge: Belknap Press of Harvard University Press, 2012.

Griese, Ann Eliot, and Richard Stites. "Russia: Revolution and War." In *Female Soldiers: Combatants or Noncombatants? Historical and Contemporary Perspectives*, edited by Nancy Goldman Loring, 61–84. Westport, CT: Greenwood, 1982.

Guardini, Romano. "The Church and the Catholic" (1935). http://www.ewtn.com/library/CHRIST/CHUCAT.TXT.

Guimond, James. *American Photography and the American Dream*. Chapel Hill: University of North Carolina Press, 1991.

Habermas, Jürgen. *Time of Transitions*. Edited and translated by Ciaran Cronin and Max Pensky. Cambridge: Polity, 2006.

Haldon, J. F. *Byzantium in the Seventeenth Century*. Cambridge: Cambridge University Press, 2003.

Hall, Allan. "The 'Kindly' Auschwitz Commander Who Sent Youngsters to Gas Chambers then Went Home to Play Hide and Seek with His Children." *MailOnline*, February 1, 2013. http://www.dailymail.co.uk/news/article-2271863/The-kindly-Auschwitz-commander-beat-prisoners-death-went-home-make-dinner-beloved-children.html.

Hall, Amy Laura. "Better Homes and Children: The Brave New World of Meticulously Planned Parenthood." *Books and Culture*, November/December 2005. http://www.booksandculture.com/articles/2005/novdec/9.18.html?start=2.

———. "A Christian Vagina Monologue." *The Other Journal*, February 24, 2014. http://theotherjournal.com/2014/02/24/a-christian-vagina-monologue/.

———. *Conceiving Parenthood: American Protestantism and the Spirit of Reproduction*. Grand Rapids: Eerdmans, 2008.

Halsall, Paul. "The Experience of Homosexuality in the Middle Ages." Term paper, Fordham University, 1988. http://www.fordham.edu/halsall/pwh/gaymidages.asp.

Hamad, Hannah. *Postfeminism and Paternity in Contemporary US Film: Framing Fatherhood*. New York: Routledge, 2013.

Haney, Eric. *Inside Delta Force: The Story of America's Elite Counterterrorist Unit*. New York: Delacorte, 2006.

Hartsock, Nancy C. M. *Money, Sex, and Power: Toward a Feminist Historical Materialism*. New York: Longman, 1998.

Hastings, W. W. "Racial Hygiene and Vigor." *American Physical Education Review* 15 (1910) 81–92.

Hauerwas, Stanley. "Christian Soldiers." *Charlotte Observer*, May 31, 1993. Reprinted in *The Hauerwas Reader*, edited by John Berkman and Michael Cartwright, 519–21. Durham: Duke University Press, 2001.

———. "The End of American Protestantism." *ABC Religion and Ethics*, July 2, 2013. http://www.abc.net.au/religion/articles/2013/07/02/3794561.htm.

———. "Going On: Why a Theologian Can Never Retire." *ABC Religion and Ethics*, September 17, 2013. http://www.abc.net.au/religion/articles/2013/09/17/3850299.htm.

———. "How Real Is America's Faith?" *The Guardian*, October 15, 2010. http://www.theguardian.com/commentisfree/belief/2010/oct/16/faith-america-secular-britain.

———. "Just How Realistic Is Just War Theory? The Case for Christian Realism." *ABC Religion and Ethics*, September 2, 2003. http://www.abc.net.au/religion/articles/2013/09/02/3839028.htm.

———. "On Keeping Theological Ethics Theological." In *The Hauerwas Reader*, edited by John Berkman and Michael Cartwright, 51–74. Durham: Duke University Press, 2001.

———. *War and the American Difference: Theological Reflections on Violence and National Identity*. Grand Rapids: Baker Academic, 2011.

Haynes, Deborah. "Footage Exposes Abuse in 'Britain's Abu Ghraib.'" *Times Online*, November 5, 2010. http://www.thetimes.co.uk/tto/news/uk/defence/article2796813.ece.

Heckman, Davin. *A Small World: Smart Houses and the Dream of a Perfect Day*. Durham: Duke University Press, 2008.

Helfland, Judy. "Constructing Whiteness." http://racism.org/index.php?option=com_content&view=article&id=378:white11a2&catid=66:white-european-american&Itemid=237.

Helton, Roy. "The Inner Threat: Our Own Softness." *Harpers*, September 1940, 337–44.

Hennessy, Rosemary. *Profit and Pleasure: Sexual Identities in Late Capitalism*. New York: Routledge, 2000.

Hersh, Seymour. "Torture at Abu Ghraib." *New Yorker*, May 10, 2004. http://www.newyorker.com/archive/2004/05/10/040510fa_fact.

Hobbes, Thomas. "Of Man, Being the First Part of Leviathan." New York: Collier, 1909. http://www.bartleby.com/34/5/15.html.

Hochschild, Adam. *To End All Wars: A Story of Loyalty and Rebellion, 1914–1918*. Boston: Mariner, 2011.

hooks, bell. *Outlaw Culture: Resisting Representations*. New York: Routledge, 1994.

———. "Seduced by Violence No More." In *Debating Sexual Correctness: Pornography, Sexual Harassment, Date Rape and the Politics of Sexual Equality*, edited by Adele Stan, 229–44. New York: Delta, 1995.

fight, and *not* afraid to be compared to women? If we *refused* to dominate, humiliate, or retaliate? How different is the transgression of the well-off sexual aesthete or the man among women in male-dominant society from the kind of transgression that students committed at great peril during the Freedom Rides, or the transgressions of Jesus that got him nailed up in a Jerusalem killing ground.

The world is fallen; but the world has also been redeemed. That's why we can "get away" with being *not* successful, *not* autonomous, *not* "ready for sex," *not* ready to fight, and *not* afraid to be compared to women. God has our back.

BAD BARGAIN

Before we could have an honest conversation about war, we needed to have an honest look at actual war without all the polemical maneuvers and without resort to a hypothetical world. We reached back, way back, to the second century, and worked forward—with enough detail along the way to evoke the truth about war, about the powers, and about masculinity and the devaluation of women. There was no pretty time, when the masculine powers were as they ought to be, which were then corrupted by the misapplication of principles, any more than there was a Rawlsian or Nozickian or Hobbesian origin.

This critique is not a substitute account of the fall. Modernity is not unique in its fallen-ness; it is not, as we have shown, even separable from Christendom. It is Christendom's perverse offspring. That same God-dispensing pride evident in our origin story has operated through each of these epochs. War is transhistorical. So is pride. Christendom had institutionally outsourced the morality of war long before that outsourcing went to the state, long before Hobbes and Locke. And women were early on described as threats to men, even by the church fathers. First Timothy is the first time the Eve-evil trope was trotted out in the canon, trading the Gospel story of Jesus's gender subversions for the "respectable" reassertion of male control over women, in what Amy Laura Hall calls "a bad bargain."[3] "The silencing of women in First Timothy," she writes, "has to do with how Christian women are to understand their bodies, their sexuality, and their place in the Greco-Roman world." And there we have it: church versus the world—church follows world. The bad bargain was "to trade salvation in Jesus Christ for the

---

3. Though Paul is traditionally claimed as the author, most scholars now agree that the epistle was written well after Paul was martyred (62–67 CE), probably around the beginning of the second century, as a polemic against Gnosticism.

measured technicality of gender conformity in the Greco-Roman Empire."[4] We adapted to the pagans. We are still adapting to them.

What happens when we try to discern—as Christians—where is *Jesus*? And who is Jesus? Who and whose are we? When I was in 2nd Ranger Battalion back in 1979, the battalion that Pat and Kevin Tillman joined more than two decades later, we had many members who openly admired fascism. A fellow NCO said to me in a moment of clarity, "Rangers shouldn't worship Jesus. He's, like, a passive little loser. We should be worshipping Woden or something."

Yet another fellow Ranger remarked about women, "How can you trust anything that can bleed five days a month and doesn't die?"

Same people; same culture. War, women, and masculinity.

God help me. God help them. God help us.

SEX IN CHURCH

In attending so closely to sex and war, I've overlooked an enormous number of topics about sex that have been on the mind of the church—of churches from every confession—including homosexuality, birth control, abortion, and marriage.

I touched on homosexuality enough to historicize it and connect the contempt for homosexuals with the desire to police gender lines; but I intentionally did not get tangled up in the debates about who can rub what with whom. Most people who are living their lives as "heterosexuals" have a long way to go at removing the logs from their own eyes before they can begin to pass judgment on the relationships of others based on how they make love. Instead of this fixation, I wonder if we could take a while—say, a century or two—to stand down on these questions and focus instead on whether the sexual relationships *we*, as Christias, enter into with others are characterized by love, mutuality, respect, and care—that is, whether our actions toward one another are guided not by a rulebook but by the Holy Spirit. I have no problem with heterosexual unions that are conjugal, exclusive, and generative. I have done this myself. I'm married now. But I have seen so many, so very many, heterosexual marriages that are conducted like truce negotiations, that are carried out in the spirit of mutual self-interest, that are entered into because of physical attraction that fades, and carried on to ugly divorces when people find out they don't really like each other. So very many marriages today are so very different behind closed doors than the public face both partners agree upon before they go back to their

---

4. Hall, "Christian Vagina Monologue," para. 28.

secret wars and mutual deceptions. And I've known of homosexual unions that are just as dreadful. And some that are good and caring, just as I have seen heterosexual unions that are good and caring. Children raised in good and caring homes will learn to be good and caring; and children raised in homes where two adults pursue their own interests will learn to be selfish. I have seen this. For reasons I've not discerned, children raised in same-sex couples' homes do not seem any more or less likely to seek out homosexual partners or heterosexual ones when they become sexually mature. One member of my family who is gay and who had the same partner for many years raised three daughters, all of whom are now in monogamous heterosexual relationships. These things are not within my remit. These are two good women. They are good to each other. I believe God smiles on their relationship because of that goodness. As a Christian, no matter who stands before me, the first thing I ought to be thinking about, and I don't always, is washing his or her feet. No one feels invited before a judge. With all the difficulties in this day and age of getting past a lifetime of indoctrination to mine-more-now, if two people can find love—love that is caring and mutual and respectful—I will not judge them. So I'm taking a century or two off from sexual rulebooks to wash feet.

Birth control and abortion—they are not the same thing, but they bring up some of the same issues. Again, I hope men will have the humility and good sense to cede these questions to women for their reflection for a while, then listen, listen, listen; because women have the most at stake. I oppose abortion, on principle, but I am equally opposed to criminalizing it. If every woman who has had an abortion was sent to prison today, I would see many of my loved ones and friends disappear. Criminalizing abortion, in my opinion, is an exercise of Constantinianism. We again are trying to criminalize sin, to *enforce* the Gospels using the powers; and we can see where that has gotten us in the past.

I have no personal objection to people having sex without the possibility of procreation. When it is not power-tripping or exploitation, I believe good sex is a marvelous gift from God. I do, however, have some concerns—as should be obvious in my repeated references to Amy Laura Hall's work—about the way birth control techniques, and occasionally abortion, have been used as a privatized form of eugenics. Techniques and the intents are not synonymous.

These are separate questions for the world and for the church. We need not follow the world (though that is what we have done too often), but neither should we seek to run the world. What do we do in our church that is exemplary? Do we cast before us the image of the peaceable kingdom of God?

Speaking of the church in the (post)modern world, I have to say something about the sex trade, which many progressives today defend as consensual, as falling into the category of "work," like a job: sex-work, they call it. Christians could have something important to say about this conflation of prostitution and other forms of "work," because we have a narrative that goes deeper by far than the disembedded language of progress and liberality. But Christians can only fully demonstrate our understanding of this when we stop thinking of women in the sex trade as sinners and begin to understand them as what they predominantly are: abused, enslaved, and exploited. Christians shouldn't be the judges of women in prostitution and its latest highly profitable (for men) instantiation—mass-produced pornography for electronic distribution. We should be the experts. We should be the ones explaining to others that the average age of entry into prostitution is thirteen years old. We ought to be the ones who teach the public that the majority of these women were victims of childhood incest, that most of them "work" under the threat of violence, that more than 80 percent have been raped, most far more than once, and many regularly. Three quarters of them have been beaten, often repeatedly, and three quarters have at one time or another been homeless. The average prostitute has unprotected sex around three hundred times a year. Many have been internationally trafficked. Worldwide, many exist as slaves. These would be the points we could make when someone tells us that prostitution is consensual, that it is a contract. We cannot do that and judge them; and we cannot do that and fail to name the system of male power within which these women and children, male and female, are captives.

THE F-WORD

In speaking about masculinity and war, and masculinity and misogyny, I hope it is clear that that my reliance on feminists for many insights has nothing to do with "the reactive valorization of femininity," as Jessica Benjamin once called the new-age affinity for notions like The Divine Feminine, and which reinscribe notions of some free-floating feminine *essence*. I've thumped the drum about social construction enough. Likewise, those proponents of reclaiming masculinity "mythopoetcially," by finding their "inner wild men," strike me as not just misguided but often plain silly.

Feminism is a term that has been multiply appropriated by its proponents and mightily abused by its opponents. It is impossible to speak of it in one voice. Calling Camille Paglia a feminist, for example, has the same effect on me as calling China socialist.

Feminists did the heavy lifting—too much of it. Men ought not to be exempt from keeping gendered power front and center in their analyses, and we *have* exempted ourselves too often in thinking of gendered power as a "women's issue." Men themselves need to contribute to our understanding of how and why we do the things we do, as men. Ignoring gender is a function of our privilege.

This book owes its existence to feminism, "not the fun kind," as the late Andrea Dworkin said. These reflections rest on *many* shoulders, the gifts of many minds. My coverage of philosophy, of psychology, of history, and of social criticism, feminist and otherwise, has been unjust to everyone cited in the bibliography. My representations have been scant and spotty, incomplete and oversimplified. I've taken terrible liberties in using bits of the best as spotlights to illuminate these theses, and I owe many people an apology for that: philosophers and students of philosophy who have forgotten more than I'll ever know about philosophy; psychologists and students of psychology in whose deep waters I only skimmed on the surface; women and men who have spent whole lives committed to social criticism, while I was stalking around in a uniform. More than anything, I have been presumptuous with regard to theology, because I spent five decades denying it, and in the short time since my baptism, I have discovered every day that these are the deepest waters of all. I could study for the rest of my days and never even approach the depth of understanding of so many others. These are just my limitations, never mind my brokenness. Because of those limitations and that brokenness, and because every reader will be different, I cannot know if I chose the right places to be teacherly, the right places to tell a story, or the right places to back away and leave some room for the reader to participate in thinking through this business away from my textual chatter. Every reader is a teacher. Every reader has his or her own stories.

If there is one unavoidable flaw in my historicizing masculinity, misogyny, war, and church, it is that history has been recorded without so many of the vernacular voices—without the experiences of those who "got by" apart from the Sturm und Drang of the powerful. In relying on history as it has been given, as a record of power, I have surely reproduced to a substantial degree all the distortions that were already in that bias. About the lives of many people in all these places and periods there is much that we will never know. I apologize to all of them, my brothers and sisters who have gone before us, who have been forgotten by all but God.

Speaking of the past, I also need to acknowledge the injustice and the danger of retrojecting today's "values" onto people in the past. That is especially true of the church fathers and others whom, I admit, I have stood before the dock with the worst they had to offer. They were the captives of their societies as much as we are, and in many respects, they knew not what they were doing. (By the same token, women *did* know what was done to them even when they accepted it; how could they not?) My purpose was not to discredit the church fathers, because they still taught much from which we have learned, ought to learn, and will keep learning. My aim in bringing their remarks about gender to the fore was historical. I was documenting attitudes, and yes, those attitudes will likely be judged anachronistically.

That said, everything we have learned in our own period has not been wrong; and our own epoch produced the conditions in which women were able to assert their standpoints in the public sphere and remove our excuses. Women have told us that it hurts, the way they have been treated; and we men are obliged now to acknowledge the hurt by listening. When someone tells a Christian man that he is hurting her, it seems that he—that I—should stop, listen, take that hurt seriously, and repent (turn around). Whatever excuses we might make for those who came before, we cannot carry them forward without trying to silence women, and that is exactly what anti-feminists are attempting to do. Sometimes, that is what doctrine intends to do.

GENDER AND SEX

I have quoted Ivan Illich extensively, and he has been a tremendous influence on my life and my conversion, first to Christianity, then to Catholicism. In several places in this book, I have quoted passages of his from a book called simply *Gender*. It was a controversial book, and it was roundly attacked, especially by a number of feminists. Unfortunately, in my opinion, many of those attacks were aimed at a straw man, because they clearly misrepresented what he was saying. Being unfamiliar with his Christian episteme, they superimposed modern categories on his work in ways that were inappropriate. It is unfortunate, for one reason, because there was—and I say this with my hat in my hand before this great mind—one monumental error in the book, in which he claimed that *gender*, as I have appropriated his definition of it more than once here—differences between the tools, clothing, practices, spaces, preoccupations, and even the language of men and women that divides communities into complementary spheres—has gone by the wayside, bulldozed by "sex." He was wrong.

Illich pointed out, correctly, that there were substantial differences between gender in vernacular (subsistence) communities and modern ones. His claim that *gender* had gone by the wayside in modernity, that it has been disappeared by "sex," by which he means something akin to how I have used "sexuality," a disembedded category that is hypothetically and legally appended to an abstracted "individual," does not conform to what I see around me. And I think his distinction is valid. But his claim that "sex," as such, has *displaced* gender is simply not supportable. Sex, used in this sense, has simply recoded gender in the way Pateman describes—women who were under a paternal regime have been placed under a fraternal regime.

Anyone who pays attention today can see that men and women still overwhelmingly have different tools, clothing, practices, spaces, preoccupations, and language, even if they can more readily move between the two spheres. What has happened, instead of displacement, has been the increased *sexualization* of the gender regime, and this has been most apparent in the sexualized backlash against feminism. Gender divides the tools, clothing, practices, spaces, preoccupations, and language of men and women into complementary spheres, but—as MacKinnon points out—gender also still divides power.

Certainly in recent years we have seen cross-infiltration and homogenization in several of these areas, especially tools, given the advancement of deskilling technology. The computer has become a highly androgynous tool, for example, even if the use of its applications still reflects division of both emphasis and power. When we attend to what people write in virtual spaces, it is seldom difficult to determine whether a man or a woman is writing; and when these spaces turn to argument and debate, we see that men can readily push women out of those spaces with verbal bullying. The dangers that many men pose to women, and which preoccupy women more than most men know, are reflected in these virtual spaces, where women can be made to feel unsafe and abused even in virtual anonymity.

Even as the androgynization of tools has progressed in workspaces, the implements used by men and women apart from unisex workspaces have continued to be gender-divided. One particular type of tool or implement that is still seen as masculine is the weapon, especially the gun. Even with the portrayal of more and more women in entertainment media using guns, in the actual world, men are still overwhelmingly those who own, use, and show an unhealthy interest in guns. This accounts in some ways for the overreaction of the young Rangers in Somalia, who have chosen the gun as the tool of their trade as an alternative to the unisex workspaces of civilian life.

As women and men have infiltrated further across the old boundaries in work—ever more specialized and deskilled—and work has been further separated from local production, residence, kinship, and community, there has been an intensification of gender division in the sexual arena, especially since the so-called sexual revolution, which rather than critique the promiscuity of men has asserted the right of women to be equally promiscuous, a trend that is celebrated and promoted by many men, as it gives them greater access to women's bodies. This has not been a good thing for women, whose objectification has intensified.

Men and women alike are now encouraged by mass media and advertising to "market" themselves as sexual commodities; but this has not created anything that could be interpreted as equality of social power.

Instead, gender constructed by the hoary norms of male power expressed as sexual desire has been concentrated in product lines to make men appear bigger, more confident, and more muscular, and women more silent, demobilized, infantilized, and sexually receptive. I note as one example that in recent years there has been increasing pressure on women not just to eliminate the naturally occurring hair on their legs and armpits, but now to get rid of the hair on their *mons pubis*—which makes them appear (to sexual partners) more like prepubescent girls than women. Much of the sexual pressure on women now, both in appearance and sexual performance, is being driven by the explosion of Internet pornography, which more men are demanding that their female partners imitate.

Most of the women I know play an asexual, nonviolent game called Candy Crush on their computers; they play it, and they socialize online about it. Most men I have known well enough to know what they do in front of their computers watch porn or play war games.

Sex and war.

It is not vernacular; those days are gone. But it *is* (ever more *sexualized*) gender.

IT IS FINISHED.

In John 19:29-30, Jesus swallows a mouthful of vinegar, then dies on the cross. "It is finished," he says, and his heart stops beating.

When he had called the first disciples, he did not tell them to memorize the Scriptures, become celibate, take up arms, or set themselves up as judges. He said, "Follow me." Men and women alike did just that. They followed him through Galilee, through town and country, through homes and synagogues, through Tyre and Sidon, up Mount Tabor, into Judea, through Perea, and into Jerusalem. Men and women, they followed him on Palm Sunday, to the temple for the cleansing, and back to the Mount of Olives. But on that last day, the men peeled away, and only the women went the rest of the way to the final destination—the execution ground and body dump at Golgotha. The men were afraid.

We know this is not the end of the story. So what is it that is finished? The Gospel hasn't yet finished its story. We, the church, *still* haven't reached the end of the story either. We are somewhere *between* Pentecost and Parousia. The story continues; and now you and I are part of the story.

This book has dealt a great deal with the sins of the church (and with my own). When I participate in the Mass, just before we pass the peace and just after we say the *Pater Noster*, our priest says, "Look not upon our sins, but on the faith of your church." The theological debate that comes to mind in the context of this prayer—look not on our *sins* but on our *faith*—is the *pistis Christou* controversy. Does this mean "faith *in* Christ" or "the faith(fullness) *of* Christ"? The latter makes sense of this prayer to me. Do not look on our failings but on our faithfulness, that same faithfulness that Jesus exercised even until he said, with the taste of vinegar in his mouth, "It is finished."

People ask people like me—those who are aggressive in naming the sins of the church but who choose to stick with her—"Why would you associate yourself with an institution that has so much bad history?" (For decades, I asked the same question.) This question can apply to the issue of war and the church as well as women and the church; and I hope I've made enough of a case for the relation between the two to at least stimulate some reflection and discussion, especially among my fellow Christian men. It is to us that I repeat Jesus's question, "Do you see this woman?" But why do I stick with the church?

When Illich remarked, with great reluctance because of its association with Darbyism,[5] on the notion of "the Anti-Christ" as something that appears *inside* the church, as the *mysterium iniquitatis*, he said that this evil "belongs to those things which only the initiated Christian can know."[6] Illich remained a devoted member of the church to his death. There can be no Anti-Christ without Christ. Michael Ramsey, archbishop of Canterbury, wrote,

> [Jesus'] Church on earth is ... scandalous, with question marks set against it by bewildered men and women, and with the question mark of Calvary at the centre of its teaching. Yet precisely *there* is the power of God to be found, if only Christians know

---

5. Darbyism, sometimes called "dispensationalism," is a Protestant tendency named after John Nelson Darby (1800–82). Darby and his followers had a very literal interpretation of the book of Revelation as a specific set of predictions, and that interpretation gave rise to what is sometimes called "rapture" theology. The Anti-Christ figured heavily into their interpretations, and various figures over the years have been (mis)identified as this figure.

6. Illich, *Rivers North of the Future*, 60.

> whence they come and whither they go. They are sent to be the place where the Passion of Jesus is known, and where witness is borne to the resurrection from the dead. Hence the philanthropist, the reformer, the broad-minded modern person can never understand, in terms of their own ideals, what the Church is or what it means. Of course it is scandalous, of course it is formed of sinners whose sinfulness is exposed by the light of the Cross, of course there is an awful question mark at its centre. These things must needs be, if it is indeed the Body of Christ crucified and risen from the dead.[7]

The church is called the Body of Christ. It is a crucified body, resurrected once alone, and to rise again with us sinners. "It is not those who are healthy who need a physician, but those who are sick; I did not come to call the righteous, but sinners" (Mark 2:17). If we are a church of sinners, then I *belong* in church.

> "Father, forgive them; for they do not know what they are doing." And they cast lots, dividing up His garments among themselves. (Luke 23:34)

It is we who continue to crucify Jesus. It is also we who are his eyes and ears, hands and feet, his vulnerable heart. The church is animated by the Holy Spirit, and by human beings. We are already. We are not yet.

Romano Guardini wrote, "Christ lives on in the Church, but Christ Crucified." Dorothy Day liked to paraphrase Guardini's remark thus: "The church is the cross on which Christ is crucified."[8] Just as Jesus loves us as we are, we must love the church as she is, while being courageously honest in pointing to her faults, and more courageously looking beyond her faults to the faith that animates her, the *pistis Christou*, faithfulness even unto a cross and motivated by a deathless love.

> We must be convinced of her indestructibility and at the same time resolved to do everything that lies within our power, each in his [sic] own way and to the extent of his responsibility, to bring her closer to her ideal.[9]

What, then, is *finished*?

I am a Catholic, and what I will say about Catholic Social Teaching here may not apply to other confessions, but I'll wager that for most

---

7. Ramsey, *Gospel and the Catholic Church*, 4, cited in Dales et al., *Glory Descending*, 100.

8. Guardini, "Church and the Catholic," Part 3.

9. Ibid.

Christian confessions, especially in the nation-state under whose jurisdiction I reside—the United States—the following understanding of the state is shared. According to *Gaudium et spes* (1965),

> Human beings' social nature makes it evident that the progress of the human person and advance of society hinge on one another. . . . This social life is not something added on to the human being. . . . Among those social ties which the human being needs for one's own development, some, like the family and political community, relate with greater immediacy to one's innermost nature. . . .
>
> It is therefore obvious that the political community and public authority are based on human nature and hence belong to an order of things divinely foreordained.[10]

Progress. Advance. Development. Foreordained.

Charles Curran interprets it thus:

> In the Catholic understanding, the state is a natural society that is based on the social nature that the Creator has given to human beings.[11]

Yet, as we have already seen, the premises—progress, development, etc.—are not natural, nor is the state form that Curran extrapolates from it. Social organization existed apart from any notion of progress and prior to the invention of the modern state, ergo prior to the state's constitution of the generalized social order that justified itself through the notion of progress. Both *Gaudium et spes* and Curran have adopted the naturalization fallacy that perpetuates the reproduction of the present political order. They have ignored the very contingent nature of the modern state, and of all political orders that appear as both cause and consequence of war. William Cavanaugh, a Catholic theologian, has been particularly astute at pointing out how ahistorical this notion is:

> The state does not arise as the establishment of a uniform system of common good and justice on behalf of a society of people; rather, a society is brought into being by the centralization of royal power.
>
> The agent of this change is war.[12]

---

10. *Gaudium et spes*, nos. 25, 74.
11. Curran, *Catholic Social Teaching*, 138.
12. Cavanaugh, *Migrations of the Holy*, 14.

Cavanaugh's book *Migrations of the Holy* effectively demolishes the fallacious reasoning of *Gaudium et spes* and of the assumptions that Curran draws from it. I hope this book has added a dram or two of weight to that rebuttal. This thesis about state and war has not been my main point, however, but the basis upon which to build a case that there is yet another source of fallacious reasoning that is also antithetical to the Gospels, and that this accounts for our predisposition to war. That is the deep-seated and fundamentally fearful need that men experience to achieve a male-ness that is defined at the end of the day by violence and the domination or destruction of others. There is an idol inside the idol of the state, inside the idol of the king and the *imperium*, inside the idol of war; and that is the idol of the conquering male.

The nationalism that emerged full flower in the nineteenth century—that we saw bloom over the corpses at Gettysburg, Chickamauga, and Spotsylvania—was not solely a political phenomenon. It was a manifestation of masculinity, and a Davidic masculinity at that. The confrontation of fear on the battlefield, whether actual, imagined, or symbolic, is for men the symptom of a deeper fear, and that is the fear that they will be seen in the way that they see women, or rather the way they *do not see* women.

Even at the risk of injury or death from within, we cannot muster the courage to dismantle the boundaries, to stand down the defensive perimeters, to surrender the esteem of equally frightened and equally aggressive men, to be as vulnerable as a man being scourged before he is tied and nailed to a convict's cross.

This vulnerability is even more terrifying in an age when we have been isolated—reduced to a Hobbesian individual, or a Sartrean one—left adrift in a sea of dissolved communities with our *rights*, and the amorphous, Kafkaesque, lawyer-land of *the state* as the sole guarantor of these inscrutable, gelatinous reconditions. Little wonder that, after all these years, we are suffering from a collective Stockholm syndrome, the deep identification with our captors that translates into a bumper sticker stating, without irony, "I will fight for freedom."

In one sense, we ought to be afraid. All we men need to do is look one step "below" us and see that there are people who breathe the same air we do who have accepted the real prisoner's dilemma, that of the convict who may have to choose his jocker as protection from the other convicts. Women are raised with this choice, and step away from it at great risk. All we men need to do is fear a walk in the park alone, to be judged by how young, how thin, how hairless, how symmetrically featured we are, to be raped and disbelieved, to feel compelled to look in our backseats before entering our parked cars. To be excluded from a calling. To be a metaphor for weakness and cowardice. To be used as a receptacle for masturbation because we feel we have no place else to go. To be beaten by someone who will tell us later how he loves us. To be the scapegoat for a man's desire, or his lack of it. To stand in the presence of others without recognition. To be silenced, immobilized, masked, and reinterpreted. To hear "old woman," "little girl," "cunt," and "bitch" used as epithets to put *men* down. To be defined by those who can never know what it is like to live in our skins. To be invisible except when we can make ourselves into a more effective sexual object, and still to be invisible.

Do you see this woman?

We men have a hell of a lot to be afraid of, and we know it. We observe it every day, right across that borderline, just over that force field that stands between two radically different standpoints that are sharing the same air. When a man like Mark Driscoll lashes out, he is lashing out at his own profound sexual terror. He is terrified that he might be treated like a woman, or worse, confused with a *woman*, like that diminished and reviled *woman* who Jesus invites into the house of Simon the Pharisee, and that *woman* who had had seven demons[13] to whom the Christ revealed himself risen from the tomb.

The first time we were called "fag" or "sissy" in a schoolyard or were cuffed by a father because we ran away from a fight, we learned what it was like to be diminished and reviled, and we didn't like it. Some of us learned how to belong by internalizing the bully, the cruel father, the tough guy. But our first lesson was brought with fear, and our accommodations were made out of that fear, even the fear of appearing afraid.

I jumped out of an airplane more than four hundred times when I was in the army, to prove I wasn't afraid; and the truth was I was terrified every single time—doubly terrified, terrified of the act and more terrified that I would succumb to my fear in front of other men. That was how powerful the fear of losing the esteem of other men was for me, more powerful than the fear of death—and still it was fear. That's what probative masculinity is all about.

I believe that we will be in full communion only when we are in full communion—and that would mean *with* our sisters. Before we can be in full communion, we shall have to make a genuine effort to *listen* to our sisters, to refrain from *telling* them what their lives are like, to study what the world is like across that borderline, to recognize and renounce the power we hold at the expense of our sisters. This is vastly more difficult than "equality." Our

---

13. In the numeral idiom of the time, "seven" signified "all." She had been afflicted by all the demons.

collective subjugation of women and our affinity for war is a *skandalon*, a stumbling block to that full communion. These two aspects of violence and the power of the potential for violence have a common source in *fear*.

Male violence and the male desire to control women is driven by fear, the same fear that the male disciples displayed on the last day. This fear at the core of male life—real, imagined, and symbolic—is hurtful to men, hurting us in the absolutely most important way we can be hurt as Christians. It is preventing us from fully participating in the history of our salvation as it is embodied in Christ.

The vulnerability we attribute to women with disdain, that breakdown of boundaries, that ability to suffer and nurture in the same movement, is a gift. It is *the* gift. And we reject it, along with the women whom we reduce to the symbols of this fearful vulnerability, and yet this is precisely what Christ has offered us men, too.

In Christ, the Davidic warrior is supplanted by the nonviolent martyr. The pinnacle of virtue in man's *kosmos* was found in combat, where women were excluded. Martyrdom, but also servanthood, is open to all—male and female; but it requires the faithfulness of Christ, and it demands vulnerability.

> Augustine calls the martyrs the means by which the false religion of the earthly city is exposed and the true religion is made known. The effects of sin are apparent in martyrdom, but the martyr confronts death as if it has lost its sting, as if it no longer ultimately matters. Because the kingdom is already present, Christ's victory over death is the only reality. The *already* and *not yet* are not balanced in martyrdom; rather, the violence of the *not yet* is exposed as belonging to a type of rule that is passing away. In their imitation of Christ, the martyrs and not the violent become the key to reading and performing history eschatologically.[14]

We have been saved "from the tragedy of inevitable violence."[15] The drama of crucifixion and resurrection is the centerpiece of history; and it releases us from the necessity of fear through this most vulnerable of loves. Christ is Lord!

It is finished.

---

14. Cavanaugh, *Migrations of the Holy*, 62–63. The Augustine reference is to *City of God* VIII.27.

15. Ibid., 64.

Peace I leave with you; my peace I give you. I do not give to you as the world gives. Do not let your hearts be troubled, and do not be afraid. (John 14:27)

Horn, Dan. "To What Extent Was the Protestant Reformation Responsible for the Witch-Hunts in the Years 1520–1650?" http://thomas-hardye.dorset.sch.uk/documents/news_12/dan_horn.pdf.

Hornborg, Alf. "Knowledge of Persons, Knowledge of Things: Animism, Fetishism, and Objectivism as Strategies for Knowing (or Not Knowing) the World." *Ethnos* 71 (2006) 21–32.

———. *The Power of the Machine: Global Inequalities of Technology, Economy, and the Environment*. Walnut Creek, CA: AltaMira, 2001.

Horne, John. "The Age of Nation-States and World War." In *Masculinities in Politics and War: Gendering Modern History*, edited by Stefan Dudink et al., 22–40. Manchester: Manchester University Press, 2004.

Hourihan, Margery. *Deconstructing the Hero: Literary Theory and Children's Literature*. New York: Routledge, 1997.

Howes, Dustin Ells. *Toward a Credible Pacifism: Violence and the Possibility of Politics*. Albany: State University of New York Press, 2009.

Hudson, Michael. *Super Imperialism: The Origins and Fundamentals of World Dominance*. London: Pluto, 2003.

Hughes, Thomas. *Tom Brown at Oxford*. New York: John W. Lovell, 1861.

Huntington, Ellsworth, et al. "Wanted: Better Babies; How Shall We Get Them?" *People*, April 1931, 2–3.

Iiyama, Patti. "Recalling U.S. Detention of Japanese Americans." *The Militant*, January 17, 2001. http://www.themilitant.com/2011/7502/750258.html.

Illich, Ivan. *Deschooling Society*. New York: Harper & Row, 1970. http://www.preservenet.com/theory/Illich/Deschooling/intro.html.

———. "The Educational Enterprise in the Light of the Gospel." Lecture given in Chicago, Illinois, November 13, 1988. http://ournature.org/~novembre/illich/1988_Educational.html.

———. *Gender*. 1st ed. New York: Pantheon, 1982.

———. *The Rivers North of the Future: The Testament of Ivan Illich*. As told to David Cayley. Toronto: House of Anansi, 2005.

———. *Tools for Conviviality*. 1973. Reprint, London: Marion Boyars, 2001.

Jaffe, Adi. "Internet Porn Addiction." *Psychology Today*, November 11, 2011. http://www.psychologytoday.com/blog/all-about-addiction/201111/internet-porn-addiction-why-is-free-porn-so-irresistible.

Jarvis, Christine S. *The Male Body at War: American Masculinity during World War II*. DeKalb: Northern Illinois University Press, 2004.

Jeffords, Susan. "Telling the War Story." In *It's Our Military, Too! Women and the US Military*, edited by Judith Hicks Steihm, 220–32. Philadelphia: Temple University Press, 2002.

Jenks, Gregory C. "The Quest for the Historical Nazareth." http://www.academia.edu/3988852/The_Quest_for_the_Historical_Nazareth.

Jensen, Richard T. "The Causes and Cures of Unemployment in the Great Depression." *Journal of Interdisciplinary History* 19 (1989) 553–83.

Jensen, Robert. "Rape Is Normal." *Counterpunch*, September 4, 2002. http://www.counterpunch.org/2002/09/04/rape-is-normal/.

Johari, J. C. *Contemporary Political Theory: New Dimensions, Basic Concepts and Major Trends*. New Delhi: Sterling, 2006.

John Paul II, Pope. "Address to the Women Religious of Turin." September 4, 1988. http://www.catholicculture.org/culture/library/view.cfm?recnum=5548.
Johnson, Eliana. "At Columbia, Students Attack Minuteman Founder." *New York Sun*, October 5, 2006. http://www.nysun.com/new-york/at-columbia-students-attack-minuteman-founder/41020/.
Jolly, Karen, et al. *Witchcraft and Magic in Europe: The Middle Ages*. London: Athlone, 2002.
Jones, Adam. "Case Study: The European Witch-Hunts, c. 1450–1750." Gendercide.org. http://www.gendercide.org/case_witchhunts.html.
Jones, Ann. "A Lot of Them Kill Their Wives." Interview by Josh Eidelson. *Salon*, November 12, 2013. http://www.salon.com/2013/11/12/%E2%80%9Ca_lot_of_them_kill_their_wives%E2%80%9D_journalist_warns_of_post_deployment_crime_waves/.
Jones, James. *The Thin Red Line*. 1962. Excerpted in *The Norton Book of Modern War*, edited by Paul Fussel, 325–35. New York: Norton, 1991.
Jones, Tobias. "A Passion for Mercy." *The Guardian*, July 31, 2009. http://www.theguardian.com/books/2009/aug/01/ross-macdonald-crime-novels.
Jordan, Sandra. "Who Killed Private First Class LaVena L. Johnson?" *New Pittsburgh Courier*, June 17, 2008. http://archive.is/qAGGv.
Jordanes. *The Origins and Deeds of the Goths*. Translated by Charles C. Mierow. http://people.ucalgary.ca/~vandersp/Courses/texts/jordgeti.html.
Joseph, Ben. "The 9 Most Racist Disney Characters." *Cracked*, January 21, 2008. http://www.cracked.com/article_15677_the-9-most-racist-disney-characters.html.
Juvin, Hervé. *The Coming of the Body*. New York: Verso, 2010.
Kamen, Henry. *The Spanish Inquisition: A Historical Revision*. New Haven: Yale University Press, 1998.
Kampfner, John. "The Truth about Jessica." *The Guardian*, May 15, 2003. http://www.theguardian.com/world/2003/may/15/iraq.usa2.
Kant, Immanuel. "Observations on the Feeling of the Beautiful and Sublime." In *Woman in Western Thought*, edited by M. L. Osborne, 154–95. New York: Random House, 1979.
Katz, Esther, et al. *The Margaret Sanger Papers: Margaret Sanger and The Woman Rebel, 1914–1916*. Electronic ed. Columbia, SC: Model Editions Partnership, University of South Carolina, 1999.
Katz, Steven T. *The Holocaust in Historical Context*. Vol. 1. Oxford: Oxford University Press, 1994.
Kellner, Douglas. "Jean Baudrillard." *Stanford Encyclopedia of Philosophy*, March 7, 2007. http://plato.stanford.edu/entries/baudrillard/.
Kennedy, Randall. *Race, Crime, and the Law*. New York: Vintage, 1998.
Kibbey, Ann. "The Current Political Climate: Gender and the American Ideology of War." *Genders* 37 (2003). http://www.genders.org/g37/g37_editorial.html.
Kimmel, Michael. "Consuming Manhood: The Feminization of American Culture and the Re-creation of the Male Body." In *The Male Body: Features, Destinies, Exposures*, edited by Laurence Goldstein, 12–14. Ann Arbor: University of Michigan Press.
———. *Manhood in America: A Cultural History*. Oxford: Oxford University Press, 2011.
Kimmel, Michael, and Amy Aronson. *Men and Masculinities*. Santa Barbara, CA: ABC-CLIO, 2004.

King, Karen. "Women in Ancient Christianity: The New Discoveries." *PBS Frontline*, April 1998. http://www.pbs.org/wgbh/pages/frontline/shows/religion/first/women.html.

Kingsley, Charles. "The Natural Theology of the Future." Address to Sion College, January 10, 1871. http://www.online-literature.com/charles-kingsley/scientific/7/.

Kintz, Linda. *Between Jesus and the Market: The Emotions That Matter in Right-Wing America*. Durham: Duke University Press, 1997.

Kipling, Rudyard. "The White Man's Burden." *McClure's*, February 1899. http://www.unz.org/Pub/McClures-1899feb-00290.

Knight, Margaret. *Honest to Man: Christian Ethics Reexamined*. Amherst, MA: Prometheus, 1974.

Kors, Alan C., and Edward Peters, eds. *Witchcraft in Europe, 1100–1700: A Documentary History*. Philadelphia: University of Pennsylvania Press, 1972.

Krafft-Ebing, Richard von. *Pyschopathia Sexualis*. 1886. Reprint, Burbank, CA: Bloat, 1999.

Krehbiel, Nicholas A. "Conscription." *Oxford Bibliographies* (2013). http://www.oxfordbibliographies.com/view/document/obo-9780199791279/obo-9780199791279-0120.xml.

Kristeva, Julia. *Powers of Horror: An Essay on Abjection*. Translated by Leon S. Roudiez. New York: Columbia University Press, 1992.

Kroeger, Catherine. "The Neglected History of Women in the Early Church." *Christian History Institute* 17 (1988). https://www.christianhistoryinstitute.org/magazine/issue/women-in-the-early-church/.

Lang, F. R. "What the Navy Is Doing to Protect Its Personnel from Venereal Disease." *American Journal of Public Health* 31 (1941) 1032–39.

Langan, John. "The Elements of St. Augustine's Just War Theory." *The Journal of Religious Ethics* 12 (1984) 19–38.

Langer, Mark. "Disney's Atomic Fleet." *Animation World Magazine* 3.1 (April 1998). http://www.awn.com/mag/issue3.1/3.1pages/3.1langerdisney.html.

Lee, Ulysses Grant. *The Employment of Negro Troops*. Washington, DC: Office of the Chief of Military History, U.S. Army. 1966.

Leitenberg, Milton. "Deaths in Wars and Conflicts in the Twentieth Century." Cornell University, Peace Studies Program, Occasional Paper 29. 3rd ed. (2006). http://www.cissm.umd.edu/papers/files/deathswarsconflictsjune52006.pdf.

Leung, Janice Y. "A Critique of Marx's View of the Taiping Rebellion and Its Origins." *Armstrong Undergraduate Journal of History* 3.2 (April 2013). http://www.armstrong.edu/Initiatives/history_journal/history_journal_a_critique_of_marxs_view_of_the_taiping_rebellion_and_its_o.

Lewis, C. S. *The Four Loves*. New York: Harcourt, Brace, 1960. http://online.santarosa.edu/homepage/jaharonian/TheFourLoves.pdf.

Lincoln, Abraham. "Second Inaugural Address." Delivered March 4, 1865. http://www.bartleby.com/124/pres32.html.

Long, Tony. "August 29, 1949: First Soviet Atomic Test Stuns West." *Wired*, August 29, 2007. http://www.wired.com/science/discoveries/news/2007/08/dayintech_0829.

Los Angeles Times. "Marksmen Are Born, Not Manufactured." February 14, 1909, V17.

———. "The Paths to Peace." March 7, 1906, I4.

Loughlin, James. "Pope Alexander VI." In vol. 1 of *The Catholic Encyclopedia*. New York: Robert Appleton, 1907. http://www.newadvent.org/cathen/01289a.htm.

MacCulloch, Diarmaid. "The Holy Beach-Towel Hypothesis." *The Guardian*, April 2, 2004. http://www.theguardian.com/books/2004/apr/03/historybooks.highereducation.

———. *Reformation: Europe's House Divided, 1490–1700*. New York: Penguin, 2003.

MacIntyre, Alasdair. *After Virtue*. Notre Dame: University of Notre Dame Press, 1984.

———. *God, Philosophy, Universities: A Selective History of the Catholic Philosophical Traditions*. Lanham, MD: Rowman and Littlefield, 2009.

MacKinnon, Catharine. *Toward a Feminist Theory of the State*. Cambridge: Harvard University Press, 1989.

Mandelbaum, Lia. "Hitler's Inspiration and Guide: The Native American Holocaust." *Jewish Journal*, June 18, 2013. http://www.jewishjournal.com/sacredintentions/item/hitlers_inspiration_and_guide_the_native_american_holocaust.

Mangan, J. A., and James Walvin. *Manliness and Morality: Middle-Class Masculinity in Britain and America, 1800–1940*. Hampshire: Palgrave Macmillan, 1987.

Mann, Horace K. *The Lives of the Popes in the Early Middle Ages*. Vol. 4, *The Popes in the Days of Feudal Anarchy*. London: Kegan, Paul, Trench, Trubner, 1903.

Mansur, Ahmed, and Larigh Mushtaq. "Al Jazeera Reporters Give Bloody Firsthand Account of April '04 U.S. Siege of Fallujah." *Democracy Now/AlJazeera*, February 22, 2006. http://www.democracynow.org/2006/2/22/exclusive_al_jazeera_reporters_give_bloody.

Mattox, J. Mark. "Augustine: Political and Social Philosophy." In *Internet Encyclopedia of Philosophy*. Online: http://www.iep.utm.edu/aug-poso/#SH3c.

Mark, Joshua J. "War." *Ancient History Encyclopedia*. http://www.ancient.eu.com/war/.

Marvin, Carolyn, and David W. Ingle. *Blood Sacrifice and the Nation: Totem Rituals and the American Flag*. New York: Cambridge University Press, 1999.

May, Carl. "Lord Moran's Memoir: Shell Shock and the Pathology of Fear." *Journal of the Royal Society of Medicine* 91 (1998) 95–100.

McCafferty, Hugo. "The Strega and the History of Witchcraft in Italy, Part III." *Swide*, October 28, 2012. http://www.swide.com/art-culture/exhibition/legends-of-italy-the-strega-and-the-history-of-witchcraft-for-halloween-2012/2012/10/28.

McCann, Sean. *Gumshoe America: Hard-Boiled Fiction and the Rise and Fall of New Deal Liberalism*. Durham: Duke University Press, 2000.

McDermott, Terry. "'Zero Dark Thirty': Why the Fabrication?" *Los Angeles Times*, December 23, 2012. http://articles.latimes.com/2012/dec/23/opinion/la-oe-1223-mcdermott-torture-bigelow-zero-dark-20121223.

McGuire, Phillip, ed. *Taps for a Jim Crow Army: Letters from Black Soldiers in World War II*. Lexington: University Press of Kentucky, 1993.

McKittterick, Rosamond. *The Early Middle Ages*. Oxford: Oxford University Press, 2001.

McQuaid, John. "Mining the Mountains." *Smithsonian*, January 2009. http://www.smithsonianmag.com/ecocenter-energy/mining-the-mountains-130454620/?no-ist.

Merchant, Carolyn. *The Death of Nature: Women, Ecology, and the Scientific Revolution*. New York: HarperCollins, 1983.

———. "The Violence of Impediments: Francis Bacon and the Origins of Experimentation." *Isis* 99 (2008) 731–60. http://leopold.asu.edu/sustainability/sites/default/files/Warren,%20Violence%20of%20Impediments,%20Merchant_2.pdf.

Meyer, Jessica. *Men of War: Masculinity and the First World War in Britain*. New York: Palgrave Macmillan, 2009.
Meyer, Stephen. "Men at Work? Masculinity and Mass Production in the 1920s and 1930s." *Automobile in American Life and Society* (2004). http://www.autolife.umd.umich.edu/Labor/L_Overview/L_Overview5.htm.
Mies, Maria. *Patriarchy and Accumulation on a World Scale: Women in the International Division of Labor*. London: Zed, 1999.
Miller, Robert J. *Native America, Discovered and Conquered: Thomas Jefferson, Lewis and Clark, and Manifest Destiny*. Westport, CT: Greenwood, 2006.
Mills, Charles. *The Racial Contract*. Ithaca: Cornell University Press, 1999.
Moblo, Brandon. "Failed Men: The Postwar Crisis of Masculinity in France, 1918–1930." Grad. paper, Grand Valley State University, 2008. http://scholarworks.gvsu.edu/cgi/viewcontent.cgi?article=1006&context=sss.
Monter, William. "Witch Trials in Continental Europe." In *Witchcraft and Magic in Europe: The Period of the Witch Trials*, edited by Bengt Ankarloo et al., 1–5. Philadelphia: University of Pennsylvania Press, 2002.
Moore, Keith. "Men in Crisis: British, French, and American Masculinity" (2012). http://www.academia.edu/4279601/Men_in_Crisis_British_French_and_American_Masculinity-A_Historiography.
Morison, Samuel Eliot. *The Struggle for Guadalcanal, August 1942–February 1943*. History of United States Naval Operations in World War II 5. Boston: Little, Brown, 1949.
Mosse, George Lachmann. *The Image of Man: The Creation of Modern Masculinity*. Oxford: Oxford University Press, 1996.
Muscio, Inga. *Cunt: A Declaration of Independence*. Seattle: Seal, 2002.
Myers, Ched. *Binding the Strong Man: A Political Reading of Mark's Story of Jesus*. Maryknoll, NY: Orbis, 1994.
Myrttinen, Henri. "Disarming Masculinities." *Disarmament Forum* 4 (2003) 37–46.
New York Times. "The President at Sea Girt Camp." July 25, 1902. http://query.nytimes.com/gst/abstract.html?res=990CE3DF1030E733A25756C2A9619C946397D6CF.
Niebuhr, Reinhold. "Christianity and Crisis." *New York Times*, February 10, 1941, E10.
Nietzsche, Friedrich Wilhelm. *The Gay Science*. 1882. http://markandrewholmes.com/godisdead.html.
Norwood, Stephen Harlan. *Strikebreaking and Intimidation: Mercenaries and Masculinity in the Twentieth Century*. Chapel Hill: University of North Carolina Press, 2002.
O'Brien, Joseph V. "World War II: Combatants and Casualties (1937–45)." *Obee's History* (2007). http://www.asdk12.org/staff/miller_roger/pages/US_History/WWII/World%20War%20II%20casualities.pdf.
Offen, Lee G. "The Eighty Years War (1568–1648)." *History Reconsidered* (2010). http://historyreconsidered.net/eighty_Years_War_1568_1648.html.
Oldenbourg, Zoe. *Massacre at Montségur: A History of the Albiginsian Crusade*. New Haven: Phoenix, 2001.
Olson, Marie-Louise. "Not ONE Word of Official Account of Raid That Killed Bin Laden Is True, Claims Award-Winning Journalist Seymour Hersh." *Daily Mail UK*, September 28, 2013. http://www.dailymail.co.uk/news/article-2436610/

Pathetic-Award-winning-Journalist-Seymour-Hersh-slams-American-press-challenging-US-governments-LIES-Bin-Laden-raid.html.

Orr, James. "Witch; Witchcraft." *International Standard Bible Encyclopedia—Bible History Online* (1915). http://www.bible-history.com/isbe/W/WITCH%3B+WITCHCRAFT/.

O'Sullivan, John. "The Great Nation of Futurity." *The United States Democratic Review* 6.23 (1839) 426–30. https://www.mtholyoke.edu/acad/intrel/osulliva.htm.

Parachin, Victor M. *Eleven Modern Mystics and the Secrets of a Happy, Holy Life*. Carol Stream, IL: Hope, 2011.

Paris, Jenell, and Veritas Riff. "The Invention of Homosexuality . . . and Heterosexuality." *Patheos*, October 3, 2011. http://www.patheos.com/Resources/Additional-Resources/Invention-of-Homosexuality-and-Heterosexuality-Jenell-Paris-Veritas-Riff-10-03-2011.html.

Pateman, Carole. *The Sexual Contract*. Stanford: Stanford University Press, 1988.

Perelman, Michael, and Vincent Portillo. "Football, Eugenics, and Imperial Destiny—The Brutal Legacy of Muscular Christianity." *CounterPunch*, August 9–11, 2013. http://www.counterpunch.org/2013/08/09/the-brutal-legacy-of-the-muscular-christian-movement/.

Peters, Edward. *The First Crusade: The Chronicle of Fulcher of Chartres and Other Source Materials*. Philadelphia: University of Pennsylvania Press, 1971.

Petersen, James R. "Arming America: When Did We Become a Gun Culture?" *Playboy*, January 2001, 69. http://www.guncite.com/gun_control_bellesiles_plby.html.

Petterchak, Janice A. *Lone Scout: W. D. Boyce and American Boy Scouting*. Ann Arbor: Legacy, 2003.

Pew Research Center. "Public Attitudes Toward the War in Iraq 2003–2008." March 19, 2008. http://www.pewresearch.org/2008/03/19/public-attitudes-toward-the-war-in-iraq-20032008/.

Phelips, Vivian. *The Churches and Modern Thought*. London: Watts, 1906.

Phillips, Kyra. "Rush Transcript: 3 Navy Seals Charged with Death of Iraq Detainee." *CNN*, September 24, 2004. http://www.cnn.com/2004/LAW/09/24/detainee.death.seals/.

Piore, Adam. "Why I Risked My Life." *Newsweek*, October 29, 2003. http://archive.is/TXJYS.

Placher, William C. *A History of Christian Theology: An Introduction*. Philadelphia: Westminster, 1983.

Polanyi, Karl. *The Great Transformation: The Political and Economic Origins of Our Time*. Boston: Beacon, 1944.

Possner, Roger. *The Rise of Militarism in the Progressive Era, 1900–1914*. Jefferson, NC: McFarland, 2009.

Potter, Mitch. "The Real 'Saving Private Lynch.'" *Toronto Star*, May 5, 2003. http://www.counterglow.com/forum/archive/index.php/t-12965.html.

Powell, Jeff. "100 Years after His Greatest Triumph, Jack Johnson's Final Fight Is in the Hands of Barack Obama." *UK Mail*, July 7, 2010. http://www.dailymail.co.uk/sport/othersports/article-1292193/JEFF-POWELL-Jack-Johnsons-final-fight-hands-Barack-Obama.html.

Preidt, Robert. "One in 10 US Kids Diagnosed with ADHD." *HealthDay*, April 1, 2013. http://www.webmd.com/add-adhd/childhood-adhd/news/20130401/one-in-10-us-kids-diagnosed-with-adhd-report.

Bibliography 431

Putney, C. "Muscular Christianity." *The Encyclopedia of Informal Education* (2003). www.infed.org/christianeducation/muscular_christianity.htm.

Rawls, John. *Collected Papers*. Edited by Samuel Freeman. Cambridge: Harvard University Press, 1999.

Réage, Pauline. *Story of O*. Translated by Sabine d'Estrée. New York: Ballantine, 1981.

Reiff, Phillip. *The Triumph of the Therapeutic: Uses of Faith after Freud*. Chicago: University of Chicago Press, 1987.

Rhea, Gordon. *The Battles for Spotsylvania Courthouse and the Road to Yellow Tavern, May 7–12, 1864*. Baton Rouge: Louisiana State University Press, 1997.

Rhonheimer, Martin. "The Holocaust: What Was Not Said." *First Things*, November 2003. http://www.firstthings.com/article/2007/01/the-holocaust-what-was-not-said.

Ribas, Jorge. "When the Dust Settled." *The Nature Conservancy*, November 19, 2012. http://www.nature.org/ourinitiatives/regions/northamerica/when-the-dust-settled.xml.

Rich, Adrienne. "Compulsory Heterosexuality." In *The Lesbian and Gay Studies Reader*, edited by Henry Abelove et al., 227–54. New York: Routledge, 1993.

Roeder, George, Jr. *The Censored War: American Visual Experience during World War II*. New Haven: Yale University Press, 1993.

Roosevelt, Theodore. "On American Motherhood." Speech before the National Congress of Mothers, Washington, DC, March 13, 1905. http://www.nationalcenter.org/TRooseveltMotherhood.html.

———. "The Strenuous Life." Speech before the Hamilton Club, Chicago, Illinois, April 10, 1899. http://www.bartleby.com/58/1.html.

Roosevelt, Theodore, and Frederick Remington. *Ranch Life and the Hunting Trail*. New York: Century, 1899.

Rosenberg, Howard L. "Real Story of Jessica Lynch's Convoy." *ABC News*, June 17, 2003. http://abcnews.go.com/Nightline/story?id=128387.

Rosenberg, Jeffrey, and W. Bradford Wilcox. "The Importance of Fathers in the Healthy Development of Children." Office on Child Abuse and Neglect, U.S. Children's Bureau. 2006. https://www.childwelfare.gov/pubs/usermanuals/fatherhood/.

Rossi, Melissa. *What Every American Should Know about the Middle East*. New York: Penguin, 2008.

Rousseau, Jean Jacques. "Emile." In *Women, the Family, and Freedom: The Debate in Documents*, edited by Susan Groag Bell and Karen M. Offen, 1:42–95. Stanford: Stanford University Press, 1983.

Runciman, Steven. *A History of the Crusades*. 3 vols. Cambridge: Cambridge University Press, 1951–54.

Russell, Jesse, and Ronald Cohn. *Malleus Maleficarum*. Key Biscayne, FL: Bookvika, 2012.

Sahlins, Marshall. *Culture and Practical Reason*. Chicago: University of Chicago Press, 1976.

Salmond, John. *The Civilian Conservation Corps, 1933–1942: A New Deal Case Study*. Durham: Duke University Press, 1967.

Sanders, Laura D. "Horace Mann, Part II: Prussia Comes to America." *Orthodoxy Today*, July 22, 2010. http://www.orthodoxytoday.org/view/sanders-horace-mann-part-ii-prussia-comes-to-america.

Sanger, Margaret. "America Needs a Code for Babies." *American Weekly*, March 27, 1934. https://www.nyu.edu/projects/sanger/webedition/app/documents/show.php?sangerDoc=101807.xml.
———. "An Answer to Mr. Roosevelt." *The Metropolitan Magazine*, December 1917. https://www.nyu.edu/projects/sanger/webedition/app/documents/show.php?sangerDoc=320325.xml.
———. "The Cruelty of Charity." In *The Pivot of Civilization*, 105–23. Swarthmore College Library Edition, 1922.
———. "The Dangers of Cradle Competition." In *The Pivot of Civilization*, 170–89. Swarthmore College Library Edition, 1922.
———. "The Eugenic Value of Birth Control Propaganda." *Birth Control Review*, October 1921, 5. http://www.nyu.edu/projects/sanger/webedition/app/documents/show.php?sangerDoc=238946.xml.
———. Letter to *Birth Control Review*. April 1933. http://gerardnadal.com/2009/12/30/margaret-sanger-in-her-own-words/.
———. Letter to Dr. Clarence Gamble. 1939. http://gerardnadal.com/2009/12/30/margaret-sanger-in-her-own-words/.
———. "Morality and Birth Control." *Birth Control Review*, February-March 1918, 11. http://www.nyu.edu/projects/sanger/webedition/app/documents/show.php?sangerDoc=213391.xml.
———. "A Plan for Peace." *Birth Control Review*, April 1932, 107–8.
Sapolsky, Robert, and Lisa Share. "Emergence of a Peaceful Culture in Wild Baboons." *PLOS Biology* 2.4 (2004). http://www.plosbiology.org/article/info%3Adoi%2F10.1371%2Fjournal.pbio.0020124.
Saraiva, António José. *The Marrano Factory: The Portuguese Inquisition and Its New Christians, 1536–1765*. Translated, revised, and augmented by H. P. Salomon and I. S. D. Sassoon. Leiden: Brill, 2001.
Saunders, John Jospeh. *The History of the Mongol Conquests*. London: Routledge and Kegan Paul, 1971.
Scaruffi, Piero. "Wars and Casualties of the 20th and 21st Centuries." *Politics-Massacre* (2009). http://www.scaruffi.com/politics/massacre.html.
Schmidt, Susan, and Vernon Loeb. "She Was Fighting to the Death." *Washington Post*, April 3, 2003. http://old.post-gazette.com/nation/20030403rescuenatp3.asp.
Sears, Steven W., ed. *The Civil War Papers of George B. McClellan*. New York: Da Capo, 1989.
Segrest, Mab. *Born to Belonging: Writings on Spirit and Justice*. New Brunswick: Rutgers University Press, 2002.
Severson, Marvin J. "'Superior to All Men': Violent Masculinity, Fascism, and American Identity in Depression-Era American Literature." PhD diss., Tulane University, 2013.
Showalter, Elaine. *The Female Malady: Women, Madness and English Culture, 1830–1980*. New York: Penguin, 1987.
Sittser, Gerald Lawson. *A Cautious Patriotism: American Churches in the Second World War*. Chapel Hill: University of North Carolina Press, 1997.
Slotkin, Richard. *Gunfighter Nation: The Myth of the Frontier in Twentieth Century America*. Norman: University of Oklahoma Press, 1998.
Smith, William. "The Heart of a Cardinal . . ." *First in the Nation*, April 28, 2004. http://firstinthenation.us/2004/04/28/the_heart_of_a_cardinal/.

Smith, Woodruff. *Consumption and the Making of Respectability*. New York: Routledge, 2002.
Smith-Rosenberg, Carroll. "The Republican Gentleman: The Race to Rhetorical Stability in the New United States." In *Masculinities in Politics and War: Gendering Modern History*, edited by Stefan Dudink et al., 61–76. Manchester: Manchester University Press, 2004.
Sobel, Michael E. *Lifestyle and Social Structure: Concepts, Definitions, Analysis*. New York: Academic Press, 1981.
Somerville, Siobhan. "Scientific Racism and the Emergence of the Homosexual Body." *Journal of the History of Sexuality* 5 (1994) 243–66.
Sommer, Doris. *Foundational Fictions: The National Romance of Latin America*. Berkeley: University of California Press, 1991.
Stassen, Harold. "Atoms for Peace." *Ladies' Home Journal*, August 1955, 48–49.
Stauber, John, and Sheldon Rampton. "How PR Sold the War in the Persian Gulf." *Center for Media and Democracy's PR Watch*, December 2005. http://www.prwatch.org/books/tsigfy10.html.
Stephens, Scott. "'This Is My Body, Given for You': At the Foot of the Cross with Thomas Hirschhorn." *ABC Religion and Ethics*, December 20, 2013. http://www.abc.net.au/religion/articles/2013/12/20/3915769.htm.
Stern, Karl. "Descartes and Gender." In *Feminist Interpretations of René Descartes*, edited by Susan Bordo, 29–47. University Park: Pennsylvania State University Press, 1999.
———. *The Flight from Woman*. New York: Farrar, Straus and Giroux, 1965.
Stoller, Robert. *Perversion*. New York, Pantheon, 1975.
Stout, Harry S. *Upon the Altar of the Nation: A Moral History of the Civil War*. New York: Penguin, 2006.
Stout, Harry S., and Christopher Grasso. "Civil War, Religion, and Communications: The Case of Richmond." In *Religion and the American Civil War*, edited by Randall M. Miller et al., 313–58. New York: Oxford University Press, 1998.
Streeter, Stephen M. "All in the Family: The Roosevelts' Obsession with War." Review of *The Lion's Pride: Theodore Roosevelt and His Family in Peace and War*, by Edward J. Renehan Jr. *H-Net Online*, April 2000. http://www.h-net.org/reviews/showrev.php?id=4023.
Strong, James. *Strong's Exhaustive Concordance of the Bible*. Peabody, MA: Hendrickson, 2007.
Swanson, R. N. *Indulgences in Late Medieval England: Passports to Paradise?* Cambridge: Cambridge University Press, 2007.
Taleb, Nassim Nicholas. *The Black Swan: The Impact of the Highly Improbable*. New York: Random House, 2007.
Tarico, Valerie. "Christian Leaders Have Always Been Misogynists." *Salon*, July 2, 2013. http://www.salon.com/2013/07/02/christians_have_always_been_misogynists_partner/.
Taylor, Charles. *Modern Social Imaginaries*. Durham: Duke University Press, 2004.
———. *A Secular Age*. Cambridge: Belknap Press of Harvard University Press, 2007.
Tentley, Leslie Woodcock. "Vox Populi? Revisiting the Career of Father Charles Coughlin." *H-Net Online*, April 1997. http://www.h-net.org/reviews/showrev.php?id=961.

Terry, Jennifer. *An American Obsession: Science, Medicine, and Homosexuality in Modern Society*. Chicago: University of Chicago Press, 1999.

Thurston, Herbert. "Witchcraft." In vol. 15 of *The Catholic Encyclopedia*. New York: Appleton, 1912. http://www.newadvent.org/cathen/15674a.htm.

Tillman, Mary, with Narda Zacchino. *Boots on the Ground by Dusk: My Tribute to Pat Tillman*. New York: Modern Times, 2008.

Tosh, John. "Hegemonic Masculinity and the History of Gender." In *Masculinities in Politics and War: Gendering Modern History*, edited by Stefan Dudink et al., 41–56. Manchester: Manchester University Press, 2004.

Trulock, Alice Rains. *In the Hands of Providence: Joshua L. Chamberlain and the American Civil War*. Chapel Hill: University of North Carolina Press, 1992.

Tyerman, Christopher. *God's War: A New History of the Crusades*. Cambridge: Harvard University Press, 2006.

"Ulysses S. Grant." *WhiteHouse. gov*. http://www.whitehouse.gov/about/presidents/ulyssessgrant.

U.S. Securities and Exchange Commission. "Oldest Baby Boomers Turn 60!" http://www.sec.gov/spotlight/seniors/oldestboomers2007.htm.

Verhey, Allen. *Nature and Altering It*. Grand Rapids: Eerdmans, 2010.

Wallace-Murphy, Tim, and Marilyn Hopkins. *Custodians of Truth: The Continuance of Rex Deus*. San Francisco: Red Wheel/Weiser, 2005.

Walton, Melissa. "The Scandalous Reputation of Pope Alexander VI." *CLIO Journal*. http://cliojournal.wikispaces.com/The+Scandalous+Reputation+of+Pope+Alexander+VI.

Waugh, John C. "Mexican War: Proving Ground for Future American Civil War Generals." *HistoryNet.com*, April 12, 1996. http://www.historynet.com/mexican-war-the-proving-ground-for-future-american-civil-war-generals.htm.

Weber, Max. "Science as a Vocation." Speech delivered at Munich University, 1918. http://www.wisdom.weizmann.ac.il/~oded/X/WeberScienceVocation.pdf.

Webster, Richard. *Why Freud Was Wrong: Sin, Science, and Psychoanalysis*. New York: Basic Books, 1995.

Weeks, Jeffrey. *Sex, Politics, and Society*. Essex: Longman, 1981.

Wink, Walter. "The Myth of Redemptive Violence." Edited extract from *The Powers That Be*. *The Bible in Transmission* (Spring 1999) 7–9. http://www2.goshen.edu/~joannab/women/wink99.pdf.

Winkler, Adam. "Did the Wild West Have More Gun Control than We Do Today?" *HuffingtonPost.com*, September 9, 2011. http://www.huffingtonpost.com/adam-winkler/did-the-wild-west-have-mo_b_956035.html.

Wolfram, Stephen. *A New Kind of Science*. Champaigne, IL: Wolfram Media, 2002.

Wolin, Sheldon. *Politics and Vision: Continuity and Innovation in Western Political Thought*. Princeton: Princeton University Press, 2004.

Woodward, C. Vann. *Mary Chestnut's Civil War*. New Haven: Yale University Press, 1993.

Wright, Ronald. *A Short History of Progress*. Cambridge: Da Capo, 2005.

Wulf, Christoph. "Mimetic Learning." *Designs for Learning* 1.1 (March 2008). http://www.designsforlearning.nu/08/no1/no1_08_wulf.pdf.

Wyeth, Will. "Justinian I." *Ancient History Encyclopedia* (2012). http://www.ancient.eu.com/Justinian_I/.

Wyndham, Diana. *Norman Haire and the Study of Sex*. Sydney: Sydney University Press, 2012.

Zimbardo, Phillip G. *The Stanford Prison Experiment: A Study of the Psychology of Imprisonment Conducted at Stanford University* (1999–2014). http://www.prisonexp.org/.

Žižek, Slavoj. "Connections of the Freudian Field to Philosophy and Popular Culture." *Zizlacan* (1997). http://www.lacan.com/zizlacan3.htm.

Index of Names

Abizaid, General John, 197
Abu Ghraib, 23, 93, 98, 99, 189, 197, 203
Achard of Monmerle, 101
Adams, Jad, 396
Agrippa, 143
Aidid, Mohammed Farah, 386
Albertus Magnus, Saint, 66
Alexander, Jacqui, 116
Alexios I Komnenos, Emperor, 105–6
Ambrose, Saint, 42
Andrade, Gabriel, 81
Aquilina, Mike, 47, 259, 328
Aristotle, 69, 79, 84, 145
Armengol, Josep M., 316
Aronson, Amy, 275
Arraff, Jane, 188
Armistead, Leigh, 185
Arnaud Aimery, Abbot, 107
Ashenburg, Katherine, 303
Augustine of Hippo, Saint, 44, 63, 65, 105, 160, 167–68
Austen, Jane, 270

Bacon, Sir Francis, 113, 133, 135–37, 143–45, 310, 331
Baden-Powell, General Robert, 283
Bailey, Beth, 338
Baker, Staff Sergeant Greg, 196–99, 199
Bamford, James, 185
Bandy, Robert, 343–44
Bar-Lev, Amir, 193
Barron, Robert, 140
Barth, Karl, 5, 32, 296

Bas, General Khial, 198–99
Basler, Roy, 163
Bataille, Georges, 248
Baudrillard, Jean, 69, 156
Beck, Richard, 15, 110, 135, 240, 252–59, 311
Beevers, Lieutenant Colonel Matthew, 198
Bellah, Robert, 216
Benjamin, Jessica, 16, 210, 230, 234, 237, 239–45, 249, 256, 255
Bentham, Jeremy, 60
Berkman, John, 101
Bernays, Edward, 155, 300–301
Berning, Bishop Wilhelm, 353
Berry, Wendell, 70
Beveridge, Senator Albert, 280
Bigelow, Katherine, 202
Black, Edwin, 336
Black, Rufus, 213
Blackstone, Sir William, 212
Bodin, Jean, 55–56, 162, 276, 310
Bonaparte, Napoleon/Napoleon/Napoleonic, 97, 280
Boone, Daniel, 284
Bordo, Susan, 127–37, 213
Borgia, Rodrigo de (also see Pope Alexander VI), 48, 55, 162
Bosco, David, 168
Bourne, E. G., 137
Boykin, General William (Jerry), 18–19
Bragg, General Braxton, 153
Brandt, Allen M., 301
Bresser-Pereira, Luiz Carlos, 224

Brewer, Susan, 345
Brinkmeyer, Robert H. Jr., 321
Broadbent, Lucy, 203
Broedel, Hans Peter, 58
Brokaw, Tom, 341
Brown, Marshall, 16–27, 86, 116–17, 259
Broyles, William Jr., 73–74
Brueggemann, Walter, xxi, 399
Brunner, José, 263
Bufe, Charles Q., 33
Bulliet, Richard, 45
Burnside, Ambrose, 153
Buscombe, Edward, 369
Bush, President George W., xviii, 115–16, 184, 197–99, 223, 234, 367
Bushnell, Horace, 171
Butler, Chris, 122

Cahn, David, 291
Calvinism/Calvin, Jean, 49, 124
Camus, Albert, 19
Canaday, Margot, 349
Carnahan, Burrus M., 164
Carr, Karen Leslie, 296
Carroll, Dillon Jackson, 155
Carter, J. Kameron, 341
Cartwright, Michael, 102
Catherine of Siena, 255
Cavanaugh, William, 51, 69, 92, 101, 108–9, 166, 172–73, 411–14
Certeau, Michel de, 86–89, 226
Chalabi, Ahmad, 180, 184
Chamberlain, General Joshua, 169
Chamberlain, N. H., 171
Chandler, Raymond, 319, 370–72
Charlemagne, 43, 103
Charles I, King of England, 123
Charles V, Emperor, 49, 121
Chisholm, Hugh, 105
Chomsky, Noam, 201
Christ (see Jesus)
Chrysostom, St. John, 47, 258, 260, 328, 339, 352–53
Churchill, Winston, 201
Clarke, D. A. (De), xxv, 24, 187
Clarke, Eric O., 268

Clausewitz, Carl von, 75, 148, 154, 233–34, 271
Clement of Alexandria, Bishop, 65–66
Clines, David J. A., 37–40
Clinton, President Bill, 184
Clinton, Senator/Secretary of State Hillary, 277
Coakley, Sarah, 114
Cody, William "Buffalo Bill," 287
Cohn, Carole, 357n10, 355–58, 368
Cohn, Ronald, 59
Collins, Patricia Hill, 324
Collins, Tony, 160
Colon, Cristobal (Christopher Columbus), 48, 137
Colt, Samuel, 285
Columbus, Christopher. *See* Colon, Cristobal.
Connaughton, R. M., 290
Connell, R. W., 8, 22, 27, 312
Constantine, Emperor, 65, 352
Cooper, James Fenimore, 317
Cooper, Richard, 19
Corbett, Tommy, 16
Corbin, David Alan, 178
Coughlin, Father Charles, 353
Cousteau, Jacques, 308
Cowardin, James A., 160
Crenshaw, Kimberly, 26
Crockett, Davy, 317
Cubberly, E. P., 348
Cuordileone, Kyle A., 331
Curran, Charles E., 411
Custer, General George Armstrong, 287

Dales, Douglas, 410
Dalton, Mary, 326
Damon, Matt, 342
Darby, John Nelson/Darbyism, 409
Darwin, Charles/Darwin/ism/social Darwinism, 40, 273, 275, 295–96, 305, 308
David, King, 33–41, 341, 376, 412, 414
Davis, General Benjamin O., 350
Davis, Jefferson, 153
Davis, Mike, 99
Dawkins, Richard, 308–9

Index of Names

Day, Dorothy, 6, 134, 410
Dean, James, 370
Dean, Mitchell, 368
Dean, Robert D., 284
Descartes, René, 122, 127–37, 144, 206, 213, 220, 273
Desclos, Anne, a.k.a. Pauline Réage, 249
DeVries, Margaret Gerritsen, 342
Dick, Bernard F., 347
Diesel, Vin, 342
Dilorenzo, Thomas J., 165
Dinerstein, Joel, 326
Distasi, Larry, 96
Dobzhansky, Theodosius, 308,
Donaldson, Stephen, 95–96
Donohoe, Nathan, 355
Dostoyevsky, Fyodor, 231–32
Douglas, Mary, 128, 131, 253, 400
Douglass, Frederick, 111
Dowdy, First Sergeant Robert, 180, 182
Doyle, Arthur Conan, 319
Driscoll, Mark, 276, 413
Du Bois, W. E. B., 324, 373
Duden, Barbara, 142–42, 209, 236–37, 247, 302
Duncan, Stewart, 216
Dworkin, Andrea, 25, 251, 405
Dyer, Christopher, 49

Eacott, Jonathan P., 267
Eastwood, Clint, 319
Eisenhower, General/President Dwight D., xiii, 359–60, 366, 372
Eisenstein, Sergei, 116
Eisenstein, Zillah, 187
Élan Kesilman née Mackall Goff, xxiv, 12
Ellis, Havelock, 331–36
Emberton, Carole, 285

Fanon, Frantz, 117, 324–25
Farber, David, 339
Farley, Cardinal John, 292
Faulkner, William, 318–21, 323, 326
Fehn, Bruce, 277
Feser, Edward, 209

Fichte, Johann Gottlieb, 280, 335
Finney, Torin, 293
Fish, Representative Hamilton, 350
Flynn, George Q., 351
Forrest, Nathan Bedford, 169
Ford, John, 370
Fortescue, Adrian, 52
Foucault, Michel, xxv, 34, 247, 305
France, Anatole, 224
Franco, Francisco, 99, 330
Franklin, Benjamin, 199, 269
Frederick, Christine, 361
Freeman, Samuel, 209
Frei, Hans, 69
Freud, Sigmund, 81, 235–40, 243–44, 261–62, 271, 294, 296, 299, 333, 373
Friefeld, Jacob, 157–59, 424

Galileo, 128, 130
Gamble, Clarence, 307
Gamble, Richard M., 291
Gandhi, Mohandas, 396–97
Gatling, Richard Jordan, 290
Gatto, John Taylor, 280
Geauvreau, Dave, 44
Gibbs, Nancy, 178
Gibbons, Jenny, 53
Gilchrist, Jim, 322
Gilden, Terry, 15
Girard, René, 81–82
Glaber, Rodulfi, 105
Goldman, Emma, 289
Grant, Gary, 83
Grant, Ulysses S., 73, 153, 161, 163, 168
Grasso, Christopher, 171
Gratian, 44
Greenberg, Amy S., 295
Gregory, Brad, 48, 51–52, 57, 100, 119–27, 147, 265, 267–68
Gregory of Nazianzus, Saint, 32
Griese, Ann Eliot, 294
Gross, Taylor, 198
Guardini, Romano, 410
Guimond, James, 314, 316

Habermas, Jurgen, 240

Haldon, J. S., 51
Hall, Allan, 79
Hall, Amy Laura, ix–xiii, xxiv, xxv, 70, 254, 303–11, 360–61, 401–3
Halsall, Paul, 315
Hamad, Hannah, 343
Hammersley, John D., 159
Hammett, Dashiell, 318–24, 371–72
Haney, Eric, 16
Hanks, Tom, 342
Hare, Reverend J. Madison, 288
Hartsock, Nancy C. M., 15–16, 21, 23, 90, 111–12, 135, 240, 246–49, 251, 255–58, 389
Hastie, William, 350
Hastings, W. W., 278, 426
Hauerwas, Stanley, ix, xi, xii, xv, xix, xxv, 5, 50, 70, 77, 78, 83, 101, 102, 126–27, 165–66, 213, 352
Haynes, Deborah, 94
Heckman, Davin, xxv, 361–64
Helfland, Judy, 350
Hegel, Georg W. F., 56, 241, 243, 268, 270, 280
Heisenberg, Werner, 177
Helton, Roy, 332, 426
Hemingway, Ernest, 294, 318–19, 320, 323, 354
Hennessy, Rosemary, 95
Henry IV, King, 104–6
Henry, Dr. George, 337
Heon, Frederick, 20
Hersh, Seymour, 188
Himmler, Heinrich, 73
Hindenburg, Paul von, 335–36
Hitler, Adolph, 99, 164, 174, 234, 255, 306, 308–9, 321, 330, 335–36, 341, 344–45, 348, 352–53
Hobbes, Thomas, 56, 58, 61, 122–23, 128, 205, 209–10, 215–16, 219, 221, 226, 231–34, 238, 240, 243–44, 267–68, 401, 412
Hochschild, Adam, 295
Hodne, Major David, 191–92, 197, 199
Holmes, Oliver Wendell, 305
hooks, bell, 21, 23
Hoover, President Herbert, 313
Hoover, J. Edgar, xvii, 375

Hopkins, Marilyn, 54
Horn, Dan, 49
Hornborg, Alf, 126, 137
Horne, John, 119, 271
Hourihan, Margery, 316
Houssona, Dr. Harith, 183
Houston, Charles, 350
Houston, Sam, 152
Howes, Dustin Ells, 232
Hubbard, Barbara Marx, 308
Hudson, Michael, 292
Hughes, Thomas, 40, 275
Hunter, James, xi
Huntington, Ellsworth, 337
Hussein, Saddam, 185

Iiyama, Patti, 348
Illich, Ivan, xxv, 25–26, 46, 51, 54–55, 59, 61, 69, 97, 124, 127, 129–30, 139–40, 141–42, 144, 226–27, 236, 238, 240, 268, 272, 281, 302, 406, 409
Ingle, David W., 171

Jackson, Andrew, 157
Jackson, Thomas "Stonewall," 153, 160–61
Jaffe, Adi, 258
James I, King of England, 144
Janssen, David, 374
Jarvis, Christine S., 296–97, 329–39, 344–48
Jefferson, Thomas, 157, 224
Jeffords, Susan, 176–77, 186, 201, 203
Jeffries, James, 283
Jenks, Gregory C., 65
Jensen, Richard T., 315
Jensen, Robert, 22
Jerome, Saint, 65
Jesus (the Christ/of Nazareth), vi, x, xi, xii, xix, xx, xxi, 2, 3, 7, 30, 32, 35–42, 49–50, 57, 65, 68, 72, 80, 85, 87, 95, 100, 111, 118, 122–24, 148–49, 155, 160, 169, 214, 228, 231, 252–55, 264, 340, 353, 385, 390–92, 398–401, 408–10, 413
Johari, J. C., 72
Johnson, Eliana, 322

Index of Names

Johnson, Jack, 283, 289
Johnson, Dr. John, 202
Johnson, LaVena, 202–3
Johnson, Linda, 202
Johnson, Samuel, 270
Jolly, Karen, 45
Jones, Adam 46
Jones, Alex, 286
Jones, Ann, 317–18
Jones, James, 340–41
Jones, Tobias, 373
Jordan, Sandra, 203
Jordanes, 44
Joseph, Ben, 345
Justinian I, Emperor, 50, 52
Juvin, Hervé, 114, 177

Kampfner, John, 183–86
Kant, Immanuel, 212–13, 215, 280
Katz, Esther, 336
Katz, Stephen, 64–65
Kellner, Douglas, 156
Kennedy, Randall, 263
Kensinger, General Philip R. Jr., 200
Kerr, Clark, 146
Keynes, John Maynard, 308, 322, 359, 366
Khafazi, Dr. Mahdi, 183
Khazaal, Sabah, 183
Kibbey, Ann, 116
Kimmel, Michael, 275, 313
King, Karen, 49
King, Captain Troy, 180–81
Kingsley, Charles, 40, 275
Kintz, Linda, 79–81, 95, 253
Kipling, Rudyard, 268, 278–79, 310
Knight, Captain James, 14–15
Knight, Margaret, 65
Kors, Alan, 42–45, 52–53, 55
Kraft-Ebing, Richard von, 333
Kramer, Heinrich (aka Institorius), 57–58
Krehbiel, Nicholas A., 268
Kristeva, Julia, 259–60, 341
Kroeger, Catherine, 50, 65
Kurosawa, Akira, 310

Laden, Osama bin, 116, 202

Lang, F. R., 339
Langer, Mark, 361
Laurence, William, 354
Law, General Evander, 159
Lawton, General Alexander, 160
Lee, Robert E., 153, 168
Lee, Ulysses Grant, 350
Lees, Edith, 332
Leitenberg, Milton, 72
Leung, Janice Y., 72
Levitt, William & Sons, 359
Lewis, C. S., 256
Lewis, Sinclair, 275, 298, 321–23, 326
Lieber, Francis, 167–68
Liebling, A.J., 225
Lincoln, Abraham, 153, 161–71
Lindbeck, George, 69
Locke, John, 205, 215–16, 234, 401
Lodge, Senator Henry Cabot, 283
Loeb, Vernon, 176, 186
Long, Huey, 321
Long, Tony, 359
Loughlin, James, 48
Luther, Martin, 48, 61, 352–53
Lynch, Jessica, 176–203

MacCulloch, Diarmaid, 58, 100,102
MacDonald, Ross, 370, 372–73
Machiavelli, Niccolò, 123
MacIntyre, Alisdair, xi, 69, 84, 102, 133, 140, 142, 145–46, 206–7, 220–21, 227, 235, 239, 299, 331, 373
MacKinnon, Catherine, 21–22, 24–25, 223, 225, 397, 407
Malthus, Thomas, 276, 306
Mandelbaum, Lia, 336
Mann, Horace K., 280
Mansur, Ahmed, 188
Maritain, Jacques, 119
Marvin, Carolyn, 171
Marx, Karl, 69, 215, 267, 397
Mathison, Carrie, x
Maxim, Sir Hiram, 291
May, Carl, 290
Mays, Trent, 393
McCafferty, Hugo, 43
McCain, Senator John, 198

Index of Names

McCann, Sean, 366, 371–72
McChrystal, General Stanley, 197, 199
McClellan, General George, 153, 161–62
McDermott, Terry, 203
McGuire, Phillip, 351
McNutt, Paul, 330
McQuaid, John, 178
Mencken, H. L., 275
Merchant, Carolyn, 134–36, 142–44, 278–79
Meyer, Jessica, 295
Meyer, Stephen, 296–97, 314
Mies, Maria, 25, 56–57, 61, 69, 134, 137, 273, 278–79
Mill, John Stuart, 215
Miller, Robert J., 152
Moblo, Brandon, 294–95
Monter, William, 46
Moore, Demi, 75
Moore, Keith, 265
Morgan, Piers, 286
Morgenthau, Secretary of the Treasury Henry, 342
Morison, Samuel Eliot, 347
Mosse, George Lachmann, 97, 335
Mother Teresa, 255
Muller, Herrmann J., 308
Muscio, Inga, 24, 25
Mushtaq, Larigh, 188
Mussolini, Benito, xxii, 71, 99
Myers, Ched, 87
Myrttinen, Henri, 354

Niebuhr, Reinhold, 251–52
Nietzsche, Friedrich Wilhelm, 292, 296, 373
Norwood, Stephen Harlan, 284
Nozick, Robert, 206–12, 234, 372–73, 401

O'Brien, Archbishop Edwin, 172
O'Brien, Joseph, 72
Oldenbourg, Zoe, 53
Olson, Marie-Louise, 202
O'Neal, Private First Class Bryan, 195–96
Oppenheimer, Robert, 356–57

O'Reilly, Bill, 173
Origen, 65
Orr, James, 43
Otto I, Emperor, 104
Oto de Lagery (Urban II), 104–5

Paglia, Camille, 404
Parachin, Victor M., 293
Paris, Jenell, 314
Pascal, Blaise, 132
Pateman, Carole, 59, 208–22, 243, 397, 406
Patton, General George, ix, 341
Pendell, Elmer, 308
Perelman, Michael, 274, 282–83
Peter the Hermit, 106–7
Peters, Edward, 103
Petterchak, Janice A., 285
Phelips, Vivian, 42, 66–67
Philip II, Emperor, 121
Phillips, Kyra, 94
Pickstock, Catherine, 70
Pietsewa, Lori, 180, 182, 187
Piore, Adam, 184
Polanyi, Karl, 142, 149–51, 219, 267
Pope(s); Alexander IV, 52; Alexander VI, 48, 55; Clement III, 104; Gregory VII, 45, 101. 105–7; Innocent VIII, 58; John XII, 104; John XXII, 52; John Paul II, 68, 173; Leo III, 104; Sixtus IV, 48; Urban II, 101, 104, 106–9, 172; Victor III, 104
Pope, General John, 162–63
Portillo, Vincent, 275, 283–83
Possner, Roger, 280–90
Potter, Mitch, 184
Pound, Ezra, 298
Powell, General/Secretary of State Colin, 116
Powell, Jeff, 284
Preidt, Robert, 235
Puller, Colonel Lewis "Chesty," 370
Putney, Clifford, 40

Rampton, Sheldon, 106
Ramsey, Archbishop of Canterbury Michael, 409–10

Index of Names

Rand, Ayn, xix, 373–75, 377, 378
Rawls, John, 206–13, 216, 234, 372–73, 401
Reagan, Ronald, 356
Rehaief, Mohammed al, 184
Rhea, Gordon, 165
Rhonheimer, Martin, 353
Ribas, Jorge, 315
Rich, Adrienne, 97
Richmond, Ma'lik, 393
Riff, Veritas, 314
Roeder, George Jr., 341
Rondstadt, Linda, 94
Roosevelt, Eleanor, 314
Roosevelt, Franklin, 314, 322, 328–30, 342, 346–47, 350
Roosevelt, Theodore, 271, 274–77, 280, 282–84, 287, 293, 295, 302, 314, 333, 335, 369
Root, Secretary of State Elihu, 279
Rosenberg, Howard L., 179
Rosenberg, Jeffrey, 242
Rossi, Melissa, 185
Rousseau, Jean Jacques, 210, 215, 216, 218, 234
Rozin, Paul, 252–53
Rumsfeld, Donald, 180, 190–91, 197
Runciman, Steven, 107
Russell, Bertrand, 308
Russell, Jesse, 58

Sade, Marquis de, 247
Sahlins, Marshal, 215
Salmon, Benjamin Joseph, 292
Salmond, John, 330
Sanders, Laura D., 281
Sanger, Margaret, 276–77, 306–10, 336
Santayana, George, 216
Santorum, Senator Rick, 277
Sapolsky, Robert, 28–30
Saraiva, António José, 51
Sartre, Jean Paul, 19, 412
Saunders, John Joseph, 72
Scaruffi, Piero, 73
Schenk, N. H., 171
Schmidt, Susan, 176, 186
Scott, Ridley, 201
Sears, Steven W., 161

Sedgwick, General John, 164
Segrest, Mab, 15, 117
Severson, Marvin J., 316–26, 398
Shakespeare, William, 129, 370
Share, Lisa, 28–31
Sherman, General William T., 153, 160–61, 163–64, 166, 168–69, 287
Showalter, Elaine, 294
Shute, Nevil, 365
Shwail, Dr. Jamal Kadhim, 183
Simon the Pharisee, vi, xx, xxi, 41, 413
Sittser, Gerald Lawson, 351
Slade, Kara, xii, xxiv, 325
Slotkin, Richard, 316, 346–47, 366–68, 369–70, 374, 383
Smith, William, 189
Smith, Woodruff, 261–70, 302–3, 306, 320
Sobel, Michael E., 364
Somerville, Siobhan, 332–34
Sommer, Doris, 71
Spielberg, Stephen, 342
Spillane, Mickey, 370–73
Springer, Jacob, 57
Stassen, Harold, 360, 365–66
Stauber, John, 106
Stebbins, James T., 170
Steinbeck, John, 318, 322–23
Stephens, Scott, 115–16, 435
Stern, Karl, 134–35
Stites, Richard, 293
Stimson, Secretary of War Henry, 350
Stoller, Robert, 247–48, 256–58, 388
Stout, Harry S., 150–71, 291
Stowell, Myron E., 170
Streeter, Stephen M., 276
Swanson, R. N., 48

Tamarlane/Tamurlane, 72, 239
Tanner, Kathryn, 3, 69
Tarico, Valerie, 28
Taylor, Charles, 91, 92, 139
Taylor, Frederick Winslow, 290, 296, 301, 361, 364
Teller, Edward, 357
Tennyson, Alfred Lord, 233
Tentley, Leslie Woodcock, 353

Terry, Jennifer, 337
Tertullian, 28, 30, 65
Thani, 195–96, 200
Theodosius, 49, 50, 58
Thurston, Herbert, 45
Tillman, Kevin, 188–91, 193, 196, 402
Tillman, Mary ("Dannie"), 192, 200
Tillman, Pat, 183, 188–202, 203, 260, 401
Tillman, Richard, 189
Tosh, John, 38, 230
Trulock, Alice Rains, 169
Truman, President Harry S., 351, 354, 359
Trumbo, Dalton, 293
Tyerman, Christopher, 51, 101–7

Uthlaut, First Lieutenant David, 191–97

Vann, Robert, 350
Veblen, Thorstein, 266
Verhey, Allen, 137

Wagner, Senator Robert, 350
Walken, Christopher, 93
Wallace-Murphy, Tim, 53
Walton, Melissa, 48
Warren, Allen, 284
Washington, Denzel, 93–99
Watson, Charles, 289

Waugh, John C., 153
Wayne, John, 374–75, 379
Weber, Max, 124–25, 142, 145
Webster, Richard, 262
Weeks, Jeffry, 247
Weeks, Staff Sergeant Matthew, 195–96
Westmoreland, General William, 191
Whitman, Charles, 19
Whitney, Glayde, 308
Wilcox, W. Bradford, 242
William of Orange, 121
Williams, William R., 167
Wilson, President Woodrow, 159, 291–92, 0
Wink, Walter, 8, 92
Winkler, Adam, 287
Wirzba, Norman, 69
Woodward, C. Vann, 160
Wright, Richard, 318, 323–25
Wright, Ronald, 302
Wulf, Christoph, 77, 79–82
Wyeth, Will, 50
Wyndham, Diana, 336

Yoder, John Howard, 5, 259, 396
Young, Lissa, 26

Zimbardo, Philip, 256
Žižek, Slavoj, 81
Zwingli, Huldrych, 49

Index of Biblical References

EXODUS

22:18	43

1 SAMUEL

6:14	38
6:18	38
18:25	376

2 SAMUEL

11	38
13:23–29	39

ISAIAH

2:4	xi
25:8	250

PSALMS

50:9–12	143

HOSEA

6:6	252

HAGGAI

2:8	143

MATTHEW

4:1–11	41, 231
4:8–10	100, 149
5	148
5:33–37	59
5:39	149
5:44	41
9:11	261
9:13	252
10:16	91
10:35–39	41
13:33	63
18:22	149
19:1–12	41
19:24	149
23	264

MARK

1:12–13	41, 124
2:17	410
2:27	85, 149
5:6–9	111
8:22–26	228
9:40	155
12:13	125
13:37	118

LUKE

4:1–13	41
6:27	149
7:36–50	xx
7:43–44	vi
9:46–48	41
10:25–37	xx, 61, 149, 240
22:19–20	86
23:34	410
24:13–24	341

JOHN

6:15	41
8:7	339
14:27	415
15:13	342
19:29–30	408

ACTS

1:6	41

1 CORINTHIANS

13:8	398

GALATIANS

5:18	62

EPHESIANS

4:25	177

PHILIPPIANS

2:5–8	xx

1 TIMOTHY

	66, 401

2 TIMOTHY

2:15	176

www.ingramcontent.com/pod-product-compliance
Lightning Source LLC
Chambersburg PA
CBHW021231300426
44111CB00007B/501